EUROPEAN UNION CORPORATE TAX LAW

SECOND EDITION

How does EU law affect Member State corporate tax systems and the cross-border activities of companies? This book traces the historical development of EU corporate tax law and provides an in-depth analysis of a number of issues affecting companies, groups of companies, and permanent establishments. Christiana HJI Panayi examines existing legislation, soft law, and the case law of the Court of Justice, as well as the Commission's burgeoning external tax policy initiatives. The book not only explores the tax issues pertaining to direct investment, but also analyzes the taxation of passive investment income, corporate reorganisations, exit taxes, and the treatment of anti-abuse regimes. Through this analysis, the book highlights the convergences and divergences arising from the interplay between EU corporate tax law and international tax law, especially the OECD Model Tax Convention. This second edition also reviews developments in the context of the State aid prohibition and high-profile investigations on Member State tax rulings.

Christiana HJI Panayi is a Professor in Tax Law in the Centre for Commercial Law Studies at Queen Mary University of London. She has served as an expert member in the European Commission's Joint Transfer Pricing Forum, the Platform for Tax Good Governance and the UK's Institute for Fiscal Studies. She has previously held positions at NYU and Sorbonne University. She is a (non-practicing) solicitor of England & Wales and an advocate of the Cyprus Supreme Court.

CAMBRIDGE TAX LAW

Tax law is a growing area of interest. It is included as a subdivision in many areas of study and is a key consideration in business needs throughout the world. Books in this series expose the theoretical underpinning behind the law to shed light on taxation systems, so that the questions to be asked when addressing an issue become clear. These academic books, written by leading scholars, are a central port of call for information on tax law, with content illustrated by case law and legislation. The books will be of interest to those studying law, business, economics, accounting and finance courses.

Series Editor
Professor Peter Harris
Law Faculty, University of Cambridge, Director of the Centre for Tax Law.

Professor Harris brings a wealth of experience to the series. He has taught and presented tax courses at more than a dozen different universities in as many countries and has acted as an external tax consultant for the International Monetary Fund for over twenty years.

European Union Corporate Tax Law

Second Edition

CHRISTIANA HJI PANAYI

Queen Mary University of London

CAMBRIDGE
UNIVERSITY PRESS

University Printing House, Cambridge CB2 8BS, United Kingdom

One Liberty Plaza, 20th Floor, New York, NY 10006, USA

477 Williamstown Road, Port Melbourne, VIC 3207, Australia

314–321, 3rd Floor, Plot 3, Splendor Forum, Jasola District Centre, New Delhi – 110025, India

79 Anson Road, #06–04/06, Singapore 079906

Cambridge University Press is part of the University of Cambridge.

It furthers the University's mission by disseminating knowledge in the pursuit of education, learning, and research at the highest international levels of excellence.

www.cambridge.org
Information on this title: www.cambridge.org/9781108839020
DOI: 10.1017/9781108979528

© Christiana HJI Panayi 2013, 2021

This publication is in copyright. Subject to statutory exception and to the provisions of relevant collective licensing agreements, no reproduction of any part may take place without the written permission of Cambridge University Press.

First published 2013

Second Edition 2021

A catalogue record for this publication is available from the British Library.

Library of Congress Cataloging-in-Publication Data
NAMES: HJI Panayi, Christiana, author.
TITLE: European Union corporate tax law / Christiana HJI Panayi, Queen Mary University of London.
DESCRIPTION: Second edition. | Cambridge, UK ; New York, NY : Cambridge University Press, 2021. | Series: Cambridge tax law series | Includes bibliographical references and index.
IDENTIFIERS: LCCN 2021008904 | ISBN 9781108839020 (hardback) | ISBN 9781108979528 (ebook)
SUBJECTS: LCSH: Corporations – Taxation – Law and legislation – European Union countries.
CLASSIFICATION: LCC KJE7198 .P36 2021 | DDC 343.2406/7–dc23
LC record available at https://lccn.loc.gov/2021008904

ISBN 978-1-108-83902-0 Hardback

Cambridge University Press has no responsibility for the persistence or accuracy of URLs for external or third-party internet websites referred to in this publication and does not guarantee that any content on such websites is, or will remain, accurate or appropriate.

To my children – Maria, Nikos and George

Contents

Foreword to the First Edition by Malcolm Gammie QC		page xi
Foreword to the First Edition by Michael Lang		xv
Foreword to the Second Edition by Philip Baker		xvii
Preface to the First Edition		xix
Preface to the Second Edition		xxi

1 **A Historical Trajectory of EU Corporate Tax Law**   1
    1.1 Introduction   1
    1.2 The Historical Background   6
       1.2.1 The Neumark Report   6
       1.2.2 The Segrè Report   8
       1.2.3 The Programme for the Harmonisation of Direct Taxation   9
       1.2.4 The Van den Tempel Report   10
       1.2.5 The Commission's 1975 Proposal and Its Aftermath   11
       1.2.6 The Ruding Report   14
    1.3 Harmful Tax Competition and the Tax Package   15
    1.4 The 2001 Company Tax Study   17
    1.5 The Aftermath to the 2001 Company Tax Study   19
    1.6 The BEPS and Post-BEPS era: The Rise of Tax Good Governance and Fair Taxation   21
       1.6.1 Good Governance in Tax Matters and the Development of the EU's External Fiscal Policy   22
       1.6.2 EU List of Non-Cooperative Jurisdictions   27
       1.6.3 Tax Good Governance and Fair Taxation as a Prelude to Comprehensive Tax Reform   29
       1.6.4 The Brexit Saga   31
    1.7 The Future of EU Corporate Tax Law   34

2	EU Corporate Tax Legislation		35
	2.1 The Parent-Subsidiary Directive		35
		2.1.1 Profit Distribution	37
		2.1.2 Eligibility Requirements	38
		2.1.3 Taxing the Profit Distribution	43
		2.1.4 What Is a Withholding Tax?	47
		2.1.5 Tax Avoidance and the Parent-Subsidiary Directive	52
	2.2 The Merger Directive		62
	2.3 The Interest and Royalties Directive		62
		2.3.1 Eligible Companies, Permanent Establishments and Beneficial Ownership	64
		2.3.2 Interest, Royalties and Excluded Payments	67
		2.3.3 The Taxation of the Payer/Debtor	69
	2.4 The Arbitration Convention		71
	2.5 The Tax Dispute Resolution Mechanisms Directive		73
	2.6 The Anti-Tax Avoidance Directive		75
	2.7 Directives on Mutual Assistance and Tax Transparency		78
	2.8 Pending Legislative Proposals		81
		2.8.1 The CCTB/CCCTB	82
		2.8.2 The Financial Transaction Tax	88
		2.8.3 Proposals for Taxation of the Digital Economy	91
3	The Court of Justice and the Development of EU Corporate Tax Law		94
	3.1 Tax Litigation in the Court of Justice		94
	3.2 Fundamental Freedoms and Direct Taxation		99
		3.2.1 Free Movement of Goods	99
		3.2.2 Free Movement of Persons	100
		3.2.3 Freedom to Provide Services	103
		3.2.4 Free Movement of Capital	106
	3.3 Methodology of the Court of Justice		112
		3.3.1 Finding the Relevant Freedom	112
		3.3.2 Discrimination and Restriction Approach	115
		3.3.3 Tax Treaties and Double Taxation	121
		3.3.4 Overall or Per-Country Approach?	127
	3.4 Conclusion		132
4	Tax Obstacles to the Cross-Border Movement of Companies: Direct Investment		134
	4.1 Company Residence		134
	4.2 Issues with the Taxation of Corporate Groups		137
		4.2.1 Expenses in Foreign Holdings	139
		4.2.2 Cross-Border Loss Relief	142
		4.2.3 Controlled Foreign Companies	161

4.3		Issues with the Taxation of Permanent Establishments	162
	4.3.1	Defining Permanent Establishments	162
	4.3.2	The Different Treatment of Permanent Establishments and Companies	163
	4.3.3	Rules for the Attribution of Profits and Expenses	170
	4.3.4	Notional Payments and Expenses	174
	4.3.5	Cross-Border Loss Relief	177

5 Tax Obstacles to Cross-Border Portfolio Investment — 193

5.1		Double Taxation Relief Mechanisms	193
5.2		The Taxation of Inbound Dividends	197
	5.2.1	The Early Cases: Individual Shareholders	198
	5.2.2	Later Cases: Corporate Shareholders	200
	5.2.3	Economic and Juridical Double Taxation – The Home State Perspective	213
5.3		The Taxation of Outbound Dividends	216
	5.3.1	The Early Cases	216
	5.3.2	Later Cases – Consolidation of the Court's Principles	220
	5.3.3	The Relevance of Tax Treaties – Neutralisation of Host State Taxes?	232
	5.3.4	Economic and Juridical Double Taxation – The Host State Perspective?	236
	5.3.5	Taxation on Gross Basis or Net Basis and Other Deductions	238
	5.3.6	Other Developments	243
5.4		The Taxation of Interest and Royalties	245

6 Reorganisations under EU Tax Law — 249

6.1		Corporate Reorganisations and the Merger Directive	250
	6.1.1	The Scope of the Merger Directive	250
	6.1.2	Reliefs under the Merger Directive	253
	6.1.3	Case Law on the Merger Directive	256
6.2		Corporate Migration and Exit Taxes	269
	6.2.1	Exit Taxes	269
	6.2.2	The Early Exit Tax Cases on Individuals	272
	6.2.3	The National Grid Indus Case and Its Aftermath	275
	6.2.4	The Exit Tax Provision of the Anti-Tax Avoidance Directive	286
6.3		Transfer of Assets Within the Same Company	288

7 Tax Avoidance and EU Law — 291

7.1		An EU Principle of Abuse of Tax Law?	291
7.2		Controlled Foreign Companies	297
	7.2.1	CFCs in EU Tax Case Law	298

		7.2.2	CFCs and the Anti-Tax Avoidance Directive	306
	7.3	\multicolumn{2}{l	}{Interest Deductibility Restrictions}	310

	7.2.2	CFCs and the Anti-Tax Avoidance Directive	306
7.3		Interest Deductibility Restrictions	310
	7.3.1	Thin Capitalisation in EU Tax Case Law	311
	7.3.2	Interest Deductibility Limitation Rule and the Anti-Tax Avoidance Directive	320
7.4		Transfer Pricing	322
7.5		Other Anti-Abuse Provisions	328

8 State Aid and Taxation 331

8.1		Introduction	331
8.2		The Role of the Commission and Member States	336
8.3		The Role of National Courts	337
8.4		State Aid and Taxes	339
8.5		Tax Rulings, Advance Pricing Agreements and State Aid	346
	8.5.1	The Belgian Excess Profits Regime	348
	8.5.2	The Starbucks and Fiat Investigations	350
	8.5.3	The Apple Investigation	353
	8.5.4	The McDonald's Investigation	357
	8.5.5	Other Investigations	359

9 EU Corporate Tax Law: More Interim Conclusions and Thoughts 361

Foreword to the First Edition by Malcolm Gammie QC

For more than fifty years the European Project, currently incarnated as the European Union, has struggled with the issues of corporate taxation.[1] At an early stage the European Commission recognised that, in an ideal world, Member States should address these issues. So long as two or more states are engaged in a project to create a single market, national taxation of corporate profits is likely to present an obstacle to that project. The production of a single market system for taxing corporate profits raises a number of significant difficulties, however. The corporate tax is in effect a compromise: a surrogate, or an essential backstop, for the national system of taxing personal income. As a result, the corporate tax is likely to be tailored to the policies and priorities of national taxes on income. Nowhere is this more apparent than in the choices that states make for taxing company dividends. Dividend taxation systems link the corporate and personal tax systems and are the mechanism through which states integrate the two. They can be designed to reduce the distortion in financing via debt and equity by matching the deductibility of interest in computing profits with a credit for the corporate tax paid on profits, or by conferring a partial or complete dividend deduction or exemption.

At the same time, the jurisdictional limits of national taxation demand as a practical matter that states draw a line between what is national or domestic and what is international or cross-border. The international corporate tax system is founded on concepts of residence, of arm's length transfer pricing and of crediting foreign tax or exempting foreign income. At the same time cross-border taxation of dividends works on a classical basis, under which the residence country taxes profit distributions without regard to the source country's taxation of the profits. The economic and juridical taxation that results, and the distortion that these taxes produce in comparison to debt finance, are likely to be significant barriers to cross-border investment and the single market. None of these are ordinarily found as features of a true single market, where 'residence' in a particular place in the market is irrelevant and where sub-national taxing jurisdictions more likely operate on

---

[1] I include dividend taxation as part of corporate taxation.

a territorial basis, with formulary apportionment as necessary, and do not assert any right to tax dividends. The publication by the European Commission in 1975 of a Draft Directive for the harmonisation of dividend taxation on an 'imputation' model attracted the attention of those in the United Kingdom with an interest in these matters. The UK had adopted a partial imputation system in 1973, abandoning its 1965 classical system and reverting more closely to its pre-1965 model. In the context of the UK's recent entry to the European Economic Community, it seemed as though the UK had made the correct choice and had charted a course compatible with the future development of an EEC corporate tax system.

As with other Commission initiatives, the 1975 Draft Directive came to naught and was finally withdrawn in April 1990. Indeed, the core problem from the outset with any Commission initiative was the failure of governments to truly engage in whatever debate then ensued. It would be many years before this changed. The pressures of the developing single market on corporate and dividend tax systems were not, however, going to abate and work by the Institute for Fiscal Studies drew attention to the importance of addressing the distortions created for cross-border investment by dividend withholding taxes.[2] It was against that backdrop and the preparations for the 'completion' of the single market from 1993 that the Member States adopted the French package of measures in Dublin on 11 June 1990. In 1990 the Commission also appointed the Ruding Committee to consider the fundamental issues that corporate tax systems raised for the single market. This represented the high-water mark at the time and, for some, offered renewed optimism for future progress; an optimism that was soon dashed by Member States' reaction to the Ruding Committee Report in 1992. It would take until the early 2000s before the Commission, led by Commissioner Mario Monti, would pursue with any real vigour the possibility of radical corporate tax measures.

The real development that was emerging in the mid-1990s, however, was the jurisprudence of the European Court of Justice. In 2012 it is easy to forget how irrelevant Community law was to daily corporate tax practice until well into the 1990s. From early beginnings in the 1986 *Avoir Fiscal* case,[3] concerning dividend imputation, references from national courts gathered pace throughout the 1990s and into the new millennium. This enabled the Court, with the benefit of the judicial activism of judges such as Michel Wathelet of Belgium and David Edwards of the UK, to assert the priority of the treaty freedoms over national tax systems that discriminated as a matter of course between the national and domestic and the international and cross-border. The extension of a restriction-based analysis to the tax sphere guaranteed the need for governments to take note of the impact of these developments on their tax systems and to reassess fundamentally their approach to

---

[2] M. P. Devereux and Marie Pearson, *Corporate Tax Harmonisation and Economic Efficiency*, IFS Report Series No. 35, October 1989.

[3] Case 270/83, Commission v. French Republic, EC Court of Justice, 28 January 1986.

and their engagement with the debate on corporate tax systems within the single market.

It is against this backdrop that Christiana HJI Panayi has reviewed the efforts of more than fifty years to achieve some rational progress in the corporate tax field and considers the limited corporate tax measures that have been adopted or are under discussion. A significant part of her book, however, is taken up with an analysis of the current case law and its implications for corporate taxation. The basic parameters set by the case law within which Member States can legislate in the corporate tax field are now relatively clear. There nevertheless remains substantial scope for analysis by commentators such as the current author to elucidate and cast light on the significant number of cases that now exist. Without political agreement on the role and direction for corporate taxes within Europe, Member States are left to strike the right balance between those matters within their competence and those that lie within the sphere and competence of the European Union. There is an ongoing need for expert criticism and commentary on their efforts. Progress in the corporate tax sphere may no longer be 'glacial',[4] but it may yet be some years before the current author can limit her task in a future edit scribing and analysing a single European corporate tax system.

Malcolm Gammie QC

---

[4] John Isaac (Deputy Chairman, Inland Revenue), 'Corporate Tax Harmonisation', in Malcolm Gammie and Bill Robinson (eds), *Beyond 1992: A European Tax System*, Proceedings of the Fourth IFS Residential Conference, IFS Commentary No. 13, 989.

Foreword to the First Edition by Michael Lang

Tax law is still within the competence of the Member States. However, European Union law has become quite important. The Court of Justice of the European Union has become an important player. Before 1986 probably only a few experts had foreseen which limits the Court of Justice would put on the legislation of the Member States. In the meantime the Court has rendered hundreds of decisions. Today it is fair to say that the Court has developed common rules that serve as a framework for Member States. Judges who are interpreting their domestic law in the various Member States have no choice other than to take European Union law into account when rendering their decisions.

Since the Court of Justice of the European Union can only act as a 'negative legislator', the European Commission has tried to propose 'positive legislation'. In the meantime the European legislator has introduced some directives in the area of direct taxation that are part of European secondary law. Those directives do not have a broad scope yet and the Commission has started to propose new initiatives. In the area of corporate tax law the proposal for a CCCTB has become very important.

Christiana HJI Panayi has made the effort to not only collect all the rules and decisions that are relevant in the area of corporate taxation, but has also tried to bring all of the rules into a system and to describe that system in an understandable way. This task has been very successful and Christiana has written an extremely interesting book. She discusses European primary law as well as European secondary law. What is fascinating is the fact that it is much easier to see the full picture having read the whole book. At the same time she points to the open issues that cannot Court of Justice of the European Union alone, but which need the action of the European legislator.

Therefore, I hope that not only will students and practitioners study the book, but that policy-makers all over Europe will make use of her research and will draw the conclusion that greater harmonisation is needed in the area of corporate tax law.

Michael Lang

Foreword to the Second Edition by Philip Baker

I am delighted to have been asked to write the foreword to this second edition of Christiana HJI Panayi's extremely readable book on European Union Corporate Tax Law. It is a great pleasure to be able to recommend this book. It is interesting to note at the outset that in the mid-1980s there was just about enough material to discuss on European Community tax law to merit a half course in the London LLM degree: now the topic of EU corporate direct taxation merits a book all of its own (and a second edition at that).

This is the second edition of the book that first appeared in 2013. The new edition updates materials to the end of August 2020. This includes the most recent cases from the Court of Justice of the European Union, including the decisions on state aid in FIAT, Starbucks and Apple, the last of which appeared in mid-July 2020. Other recent material added to the book includes a brief discussion of Brexit, the Tax Dispute Resolution Mechanism Directive, the Anti-Tax Avoidance Directive and the judgments in the Danish beneficial ownership cases.

The update of the contents to the end of August 2020 is particularly helpful to those in the United Kingdom: as a consequence of the ending of the Implementation Period for Brexit in the United Kingdom, effectively a 'snapshot' is to be taken of EU law as at the end of 2020. This snapshot of the law will continue as 'retained EU law' until displaced by legislation or by new, UK case law. In that context, this book – not quite stating matters as at the end of 2020, but very close – will prove to be particularly useful and may have a particularly long shelf life. We will be referring to it for some time to see where EU direct, corporate taxes had reached by late 2020.

Earlier books on EU tax law have tended to structure the material around each of the basic freedoms. This book follows the more recent approach, which is to order the material around particular topical issues. After an initial chapter on the historical background to EU corporate tax law, the second chapter focuses on the limited amount of corporate tax legislation, including some of the pending legislative proposals for a CCTB/CCCTB, a financial transaction tax, and the proposal for taxation of the digital economy. Chapter 3 then focuses on the role of the Court of Justice in the development of EU corporate tax law and explains how cases reach the Court. The next two chapters then look at cross-border transactions of companies from the point of view first of direct investment (including cross-border loss relief, controlled foreign companies, and issues related to permanent establishments) and then cross-border portfolio investment, particularly focused on inbound and outbound dividends. A chapter on reorganisations under EU tax law includes both cross-border mergers and a detailed examination of the exit tax case law. Quite novel in this area is a chapter on tax avoidance and EU law, including discussion of controlled foreign companies and transfer pricing. Finally, in terms of substantive chapters, there is a discussion of state aid and taxation. This is, of course, the biggest growth area in the field of EU law and taxation over the last 20 years, and the book includes the latest decisions.

As the author explains, the limited competence of the European Union in the field of direct taxation has meant that much of the development has taken place by way of negative harmonisation through decisions of the Court of Justice, and through the development of soft law instruments. On the case law, the book is particularly rich, with references to all the leading cases, and will prove a particularly useful guide, particularly, as explained, on the position of case law as at the latter part of 2020. Much of this case law and soft law is set in the context of the general principles of international taxation: how those principles provide a backdrop to the EU rules, and how those EU rules depart from international tax rules as they apply between countries that are not members of the European Union.

It has been seven years since the previous edition of the book (during which the arrival of three children no doubt diverted the author's attention away from a new edition). Given the speed of development of EU tax law, particularly with regard to corporations, there is every reason to expect that this book will continue to appear in new editions on a regular basis in future years. The author of this foreword anticipates that it will probably be less than five years before developments in case law and legislation prompt the author to produce a third edition (assuming no more children come along to divert her attention!).

There is one point to note for future editions. It is reasonable to project that the next edition will include a separate chapter on the protection of taxpayers' rights, with particular reference to the growing case law of the Court of Justice on the application of the Charter of Fundamental Rights, including its application to corporate taxpayers.

This is a readable and enjoyable book, which has no doubt benefited tremendously from the author's lecturing on EU tax law. I am delighted to welcome this book into the growing collection of excellent texts – books and articles – written by the author.

Philip Baker QC
Field Court Tax Chambers
Gray's Inn

Preface to the First Edition

I decided to write this book after many years of teaching international tax law and EU tax law at Queen Mary, University of London and many years of research in this field. I assumed it would be easy to write a book that combines the two topics in examining the corporate angle to the tax developments in the European Union. I also assumed it would be easy to write this book while on maternity leave, after having my first child. Both of these assumptions proved wrong.

There was an enormous amount of material to be covered and the case law of the Court of Justice, especially the more recent one, was very challenging. The interplay with the OECD Model and general international tax law was always a source of potential conflict, generating interesting developments. The changes were fast-paced and often unpredictable. Trying to discern the past, present and future of EU corporate tax law was certainly not an easy task.

In writing the various chapters, I often found myself rereading old cases and gaining a different perspective from the one I had initially. I also developed a better understanding of endogenous changes in the case law in various areas. Some of the judgments were, however, completely perplexing – an indication of what I thought was the uneasiness of the Court of Justice in dealing with certain issues. Nevertheless, my admiration for the Court of Justice and its work in this area grew. The fact that today we have a developing body of principles that form what could be considered as the corporate tax law of the European Union is mostly attributable to the Court of Justice, as well as the Commission and national courts that trigger the European judicial process. The book depicts these themes and discusses the existing principles of EU corporate tax law.

This book would not have been written had it not been for my family. I would like to thank my husband Zak Palexas for his continuous inspiration, support and encouragement. I would also like to thank my parents for their help and the endless hours of babysitting they had to endure in order for me to be able to complete the book on time. Most of all I would like to thank my daughter Maria for her patience in becoming so heavily involved in the tax world at such a young age. The number of times she shook her head in disbelief, deleted paragraphs from the draft and tore up papers lying around is perhaps an indication that the current state of the law is in need of some improvement. It is hoped that future editions of this book will reflect that.

Preface to the Second Edition

The first edition to this book was met with enthusiasm and positive comments. I had been postponing the second edition to this book for some time. There was always so much going on in the EU, so my natural inclination was to let the dust settle before writing a second edition.

However, when there is a constant hurricane of developments, the dust never settles. Therefore, I eventually started working on the second edition to this book in February 2020, after the UK's exit from the EU. In some regards, my timing could not have been worse, as due to the global pandemic, I soon found myself in lockdown with three energetic small children with very little appetite for home schooling. However, from another perspective, my timing could not have been better, as it became obvious that in this historical point in time the EU had come to a crossroad – its overall existence and raison d'être were being debated and had to be justified. I felt it was crucial to capture this moment in the context of EU corporate tax law and offer my thoughts.

Special thanks to Joy Svasti-Salee, Philip Baker, Katerina Perrou and Dimitrios Kyriazis for the insightful comments on earlier versions of this manuscript. All errors are of the author, of course.

The contents of this book are based on materials available up to 1 August 2020.

1

A Historical Trajectory of EU Corporate Tax Law

1.1 INTRODUCTION

Member State corporate tax regimes are heavily influenced by European Union law. What is notable, however, is the absence of comprehensive harmonising legislation. This is attributed to a number of factors.

Arguably, the most important factor is the lack of Union competence in direct tax matters. Under the principle of attribution of powers,[1] a cornerstone of the European legal structure, the Union[2] and its institutions only enjoy competence in the areas of law assigned or conferred to them under the Treaties. This principle of attribution of powers must be respected both internally and in the Union's external sphere of affairs. Therefore, every act must be based on a general or specific Treaty provision (the legal basis) empowering the Union, expressly or impliedly, to act.

It is widely acknowledged that Member States have retained competence in direct tax matters. Successive European Treaties have been silent on direct tax and more generally on EU taxes. While the Treaties dealt with indirect taxes to some extent,[3] there were never any references to direct taxes. As a corollary, there has never been an explicit legislative base for the harmonisation of direct taxes.[4] General legislative bases under Articles 115 and 352 of the Treaty on the Functioning of the European Union (TFEU) have been used for direct tax legislation. These legislative bases focus on the attainment of the Internal Market and their use is strictly policed by the Court of Justice.[5]

---

[1] Art 5 Treaty on European Union (TEU).
[2] Following the Lisbon Treaty, the TEU was amended and the Treaty establishing the European Community (EC Treaty) was amended and renamed as the Treaty on the Functioning of the European Union (TFEU). Thereafter, the name 'European Union' replaced and succeeded the 'European Community'.
[3] See Art 28 TFEU, which provides for a Union based upon a customs union. See Arts 30 and 110 TFEU, which led to the harmonisation of excise duties.
[4] By contrast, there is an explicit tax base for harmonisation of indirect taxes under Art 113 TFEU.
[5] There have been a number of cases where the EU legislation was challenged on the basis of misuse of one of these general Treaty bases. See Annette Schrauwen, 'Sources of EU Law for Integration in

Article 115 TFEU authorises the Council to issue directives for the approximation of laws, regulations or administrative provisions of Member States directly affecting the establishment and functioning of the Internal Market. Directives can only be adopted under Article 115 on the basis of unanimity. In addition, Article 352 TFEU authorises the Council, on a proposal from the Commission and after obtaining the consent of the European Parliament,[6] to adopt appropriate measures when Union action is necessary to attain one of the objectives of the Treaties. Again, the Council (i.e. all Member States in Council) has to act unanimously. There is another general legal basis for harmonisation under Article 116 TFEU, which could be used for legislative action when differences in Member State laws are distorting the conditions of competition in the Internal Market. Although this legislative base does not require unanimity and does not exclude direct tax measures,[7] it has never been used for tax harmonisation purposes.

Overall, the fiscal veto, that is the power of even one Member State to object to a harmonising measure in direct tax law, is a fiercely guarded prerogative that has survived successive Treaty amendments and previous attempts to move to qualified majority voting.[8] In general, the Commission has always tried to base its proposals on one of the general legislative provisions that require unanimity – Articles 115 or 352 TFEU.[9] Therefore, lack of explicit competence combined with the fiscal veto under 'proxy' bases meant that the regulation of direct taxes was left within the competence of the Member States. Although the fiscal veto was reiterated (by default) with the ratification of the Treaty of Lisbon, recently, there have been attempts to overcome the limitations of the unanimity requirement, which at the time of writing have not reached fruition.[10]

Another contributing factor to the scarce legislation is that international (direct) taxation was historically not as regulated as other areas such as trade or investment. In principle, every country has jurisdiction to tax however it pleases. Whilst there are model tax treaties, such as the OECD Model Tax Convention[11] or the UN Model

---

Taxation', ch 1 in Dennis Weber (ed), *Traditional and Alternative Routes to European Tax Integration* (Amsterdam: IBFD, 2010).

[6] Under ex-Art 308 EC there was only a duty to consult the European Parliament.

[7] Contrast with Art 114 TFEU, where it is expressly stated that it cannot be used for direct taxes.

[8] See, for example, the draft Treaty establishing a Constitution for Europe (Constitutional Treaty), which provided for qualified majority voting for measures on company taxation when the Council unanimously found that these measures related to administrative cooperation or combated tax fraud and tax evasion. See Art III-63. The Constitutional Treaty was never ratified by all Member States and the Treaty of Lisbon was drafted to replace it.

[9] The same approach was followed with ex-Art 293 EC, which provided that Member States must as far as possible enter into negotiations to secure, inter alia, the abolition of double taxation. This provision has been interpreted as not having direct effect. See Case C-336/96 Gilly [1998] ECR I-2793, para 16. Therefore, ex-Art 293 EC could not be used as a legal basis for direct tax legislation. In any case, this provision has now been abolished from the TFEU. See analysis in 3.3.3.

[10] See Commission Communication, *Towards a More Efficient and Democratic Decision Making in EU Tax Policy*, COM(2019) 8 final (15.01.2019); Commission Communication, *An action plan for fair and simple taxation supporting the recovery strategy*, COM(2020) 312 final (15.07.2020), p 2, discussed at 1.6.

[11] OECD Model Tax Convention on Income and on Capital, last updated 2017.

Tax Convention (UN Model)[12] that recommend ways of allocating tax jurisdiction between the country of source and the country of residence, these models are not binding on countries[13] and are regularly updated. It is, therefore, quite understandable why, when the EEC was created in the mid-1950s, the regulation of direct taxes was not seen as a priority; nor as an option for that matter. The main priority was the removal of the distortions caused by trade barriers – hence the concentration on the harmonisation of indirect taxes.

However, it has long been recognised that there are tax obstacles that create serious impediments to the integration of the market – tax obstacles for which the international tax community and the OECD Model Tax Convention do not offer solutions, or not very good ones. As far as corporate taxes are concerned, many of the problems arise from the interaction of different systems of taxation of Member States, who have different approaches to the integration of shareholder and corporate taxes. For example, under the classical system profits are taxed independently in the hands of the company and its shareholders. This leads to the phenomenon of economic double taxation – that is where there is more than one tax imposed in respect of the *same income*, even if the taxes are paid by different persons, and which affects domestic and foreign shareholders the same way. By contrast, under an imputation (or tax credit) system, part of the corporation tax on distributed profits is credited against income tax, so relief to mitigate economic double taxation on dividends is given at shareholder level. Under a split-rate system, relief for economic double taxation on dividends is given at company level, as a lower rate of corporation tax applies for distributed than for retained profits. To the extent that the tax credit or the lower tax rate for distributed dividends is reserved for resident shareholders, then non-resident shareholders would incur economic double taxation. As shown in this book, the OECD Model Tax Convention does not offer any solutions on economic double taxation, deferring to states' discretion in dealing with it.

Cross-border investments lead to further problems. The same person may be taxed twice by two different states over the same income. This is juridical double taxation. In the Introduction to the OECD Model Tax Convention this is defined 'as the imposition of comparable taxes in two (or more) States on the same taxpayer in respect of the same subject matter and for identical periods'.[14] For example, if a company is taxed on a worldwide basis, then foreign profits may be taxed in the state in which they accrue (source state or, in this book, host state). The same profits may also be taxed in the state of residence of the company (residence state or, in this book, home state) leading to juridical double taxation. Similarly, cross-border passive investment income such as dividends may be taxed both in the state of the

---

[12] United Nations Model Double Taxation Convention between Developed and Developing Countries (2017).
[13] Some countries, such as the USA, have their own models. The US Model was last updated in 2016.
[14] Introduction to the OECD Model Tax Convention, para 1.

distributing company (the host state) and the state of residence of the shareholder (the home state). As will be shown in later chapters of this book, usually in such situations either the host state does not tax or does not fully tax the income, or the home state *exempts* foreign profits or gives a *credit* for the foreign (withholding) tax paid. The exemption method and the credit method are important double taxation relief mechanisms.[15]

The reliefs can be provided either on a unilateral basis or a bilateral basis (through tax treaties) or on a multilateral basis (through multilateral tax agreements). Some of these reliefs are contained in the OECD Model Tax Convention, whose avowed purpose is to eliminate or mitigate juridical double taxation but not economic double taxation.

From an EU perspective, whilst both types of double taxation are problematic as the increased tax burden creates economic distortions and inefficiencies,[16] in the absence of EU legislation to remove the distortions, action cannot be taken unless the general Treaty provisions are breached. As shown in later chapters, the major point of conflict that has empowered the Union (indirectly) to act is derived from a different stance on non-discrimination and the comparability of residents and non-residents. Under established international tax law and the OECD Model Tax Convention, residents and non-residents are not in a comparable situation. Under EU law, this cannot be assumed and has to be proved in each case.

As shown throughout this book, this deceptively simple issue of the (non–) comparability of residents and non-residents has had a huge impact on how juridical double taxation and economic double taxation are dealt with in the European Union and the ability of Member States to choose between classical systems and imputation systems of taxation. The non-discrimination principle, on its own and through the medium of specific fundamental freedoms, as interpreted by the Court of Justice, has also led to further developments, circumscribing Member States' overall powers to structure their corporate tax systems. For example, a host state may not be able to tax branches of foreign companies more heavily than resident companies. In addition, a home state may not be able to limit the availability of loss relief to resident group companies or domestic branches only – it may have to extend it to non-resident companies or branches. Similar restrictions may arise in the taxation of inbound and outbound passive investment income. A host state may no longer be able to impose withholding taxes on outbound dividends when domestic dividends are exempt. Or a home state may have to extend the imputation credit to

---

[15] See also analysis in 5.1.
[16] See, for example, the OECD Commentary on the harmful effects of juridical double taxation in Introduction to the OECD Model Tax Convention, para 1. See also American Law Institute, *Integration of the Individual and Corporate Income Taxes* (Philadelphia: Federal Income Tax Project, 1993); Treasury Department, *Report on Integration of the Individual and Corporate Tax Systems: Taxing Business Income Once* (Washington Government Printing Office, 1992); Christiana HJI Panayi, *Double Taxation, Tax Treaties, Treaty Shopping and the European Community*, EUCOTAX Series (Alphen aan den Rijn: Kluwer Law International, 2007), ch 1.

shareholders receiving foreign dividends as well. Furthermore, reliefs and deferrals granted for domestic reorganisations may have to be extended to cross-border ones. Finally, although Member State tax avoidance regimes have to be drafted in a specific way so as to be EU-compatible and proportional, there is also new legislation which forces Member States to adopt some *de minimis* anti-abuse rules. Apart from discriminatory tax burdens assessed on the basis of fundamental freedoms and/or the relevant directives, the book also considers what is, to an extent, the reverse situation: tax reliefs given to selected undertakings contrary to the state aid prohibition. All these issues are examined in Chapters 3 to 8.

This book strives to show how EU law has become of prime importance as far as the cross-border movement of companies and the cross-border investment in such companies is concerned. Topics such as the harmonisation of the corporate tax base, the taxation of subsidiaries and branches, the taxation of passive investment income, economic and juridical double taxation, corporate reorganisations, anti-abuse rules and the impact of the state aid rules are considered in detail. What becomes evident is that, notwithstanding the lack of competence in direct tax matters, this has become an area densely regulated as a result of both positive and negative integration. It is shown in Chapter 2 that the Union has legislated in a number of areas, including corporate tax law, where it was deemed expedient for the proper functioning of the internal market. Therefore, integration through proper legislative routes, that is positive integration, *does* exist, but it is scarce compared to the growing volume of case law. Topics discussed in this book illustrate how the legislative vacuum was addressed by the Court of Justice by interpreting and applying several general provisions of successive EU Treaties in the direct tax context. This is also called negative integration. In the analysis, the pivotal role of the Commission in some of the legislative and judicial developments also becomes obvious. This EU institution has long been vocal on the detrimental effect of tax obstacles to the completion of the Single Market and later on the Internal Market.[17]

Notwithstanding these developments, it will be shown that the limitations of international tax law in these areas have not been addressed under EU law. This is understandable given that the main generator of developments until recently – the Court of Justice – can only respond to specific questions referred to it. It cannot act as a substitute legislator and construct a comprehensive tax system. As a result, there are still many tax obstacles that impede the completion of the Internal Market. This book considers some of these obstacles from a corporate angle. The book also considers new developments, in the aftermath of the BEPS project, which seem to go some way in strengthening the rights of Member States to protect their tax bases, rather than force them to remove tax obstacles to cross-border movement, as was traditionally the case.

[17] Although technically the two terms (as well as 'common market') are not synonymous, they tend to be used interchangeably. Broadly, these terms reflect steps towards the EU's economic integration, the common market being first, leading to the Single Market, which ultimately led to the Internal Market.

In order to understand the current situation, an overview of the historical background to some of the legislative proposals is apt. It is shown that efforts to put in place a comprehensive system for corporate taxation have long been debated, though so far not many materialised, at least not the ones that were focused on corporate tax harmonisation. By contrast, piecemeal legislative solutions (e.g. directives, conventions) and soft law have always been more feasible.[18] In fact, the use of soft law has more recently intensified in the context of developing a common external tax policy and beyond.[19]

1.2 THE HISTORICAL BACKGROUND

The main concern of the Community, now called the Union, as far as corporate tax law was concerned, has always been the degree of harmonisation needed. Proposals for the harmonisation of corporate taxes have a long history. Whilst initial proposals recommended the unification of Member States' corporate tax systems with a single tax rate and a uniform tax on distributed profits, subsequent proposals moved away from harmonisation to coordination and ad hoc legislative solutions.[20] What is evident early on is that the Community oscillated between the classical system and the imputation system, with its main focus being harmonisation rather than coordination. This is reflected in the recommendations of the various reports produced in the last fifty years.

1.2.1 *The Neumark Report*

In 1960 the Commission set up a committee of taxation and financial experts, under the chairmanship of Professor Fritz Neumark, to investigate all aspects of taxation in relation to the common market. The Neumark Report,[21] published in 1962, broadly recommended harmonisation of income tax, capital gains tax, corporation tax and indirect taxes, though the committee insisted that the aim was not uniformity.[22]

According to the Neumark Committee, harmonisation was not a synonym for unification to the committee and the latter should have been avoided.[23] Complete

---

[18] See Franco Roccatagliata, 'The European Commission's Soft-Law Approach and Its Possible Impact on EC Tax Law Interpretation', in Pasquale Pistone (ed), *Legal Remedies in European Tax Law* (Amsterdam: IBFD, 2009). See also Chapter 2 of this book.
[19] See 1.6.1.
[20] See Christiana HJI Panayi, 'The Early Proposals for a European Corporate Tax Policy', in *Studies in the History of Tax Law* (Hart Publishing, 2019) 365–89.
[21] 'Report of the Fiscal and Financial Committee' in *The EEC Reports on Tax Harmonisation* (Amsterdam: IBFD, 1963) *(Neumark Report)*. For general commentary see Alex Easson, 'Harmonisation of direct taxation in the European Community: from Neumark to Ruding' (1992) 40 *Canadian Tax Journal*, 600–38, 604.
[22] *Neumark Report*, p 102.
[23] See also analysis in Adolfo Martin Jimenez, *Towards Corporate Tax Harmonization in the European Community: An Institutional and Procedural Analysis*, Series on International Taxation (London: Kluwer Law International, 1999), p 108.

unification of the tax systems of the Member States was not considered to be 'as necessary from the aspect of integration policy, since experience proves that on many grounds moderate differences limited to the nature (structure) and to the rate of taxes do not hinder the free play of competition'.[24]

Adopting a clearly centralist approach, the Neumark Committee considered it desirable to levy the same type of single tax on income in all Member States, with the same structure of scales, even if the rates were different.[25] As far as company taxation was concerned, the committee recommended a special tax on companies. Under this proposal, retained profits would be taxed at 50 per cent,[26] whereas distributed profits would be taxed, in the form of withholding tax at source, at a recommended rate of 25 per cent and not less than 15 per cent.[27]

For distributed profits, a relatively low rate of 10–20 per cent was to be applied to EEC-resident recipient persons, who owned either registered or bearer shares. A higher rate of at least 25 per cent would apply to all other persons.[28] The Neumark Committee further suggested that, if dividend recipients provided information of their identity, then the withholding tax should be reimbursed to the state in which the shareholders were domiciled.[29] It would seem that incentives for information exchange were considered very early on.

Dividends distributed from subsidiaries to parent companies would be exempt from withholding tax, unless the parent company was established outside of the EC, or there was uncertainty whether the beneficiary of the dividends was a company or an individual. Under certain circumstances[30] dividends received by parent companies from their subsidiaries would also be exempt, to the extent that the parent company intended to distribute the dividends received to its shareholders.

The Neumark Committee recognised the importance of double tax treaties and the OECD Model Tax Convention in resolving double taxation.[31] However, the OECD rules had to be amended and supplemented 'in such a way that they respond more adequately to the specific needs of the Common Market'.[32] It was further recommended that a multilateral tax convention should replace the network of bilateral conventions.[33]

---

[24] *Neumark Report*, p 102.
[25] Ibid, p 119.
[26] That would have been a split-rate system as existing at the time in Germany. See *Neumark Report*, pp 122–3, 139. See also Appendix F: Harmonization of the Taxes on Companies and on Dividends, written by Prof Bernard Schendstok, who discussed in greater detail how specific elements of the proposed system could be applied.
[27] *Neumark Report*, p 139.
[28] Ibid, pp 139–40.
[29] Ibid.
[30] There had to be a participation of at least 15–20 per cent of the capital of the distributing company, held at least one or two years before distribution of the dividend. See generally ibid, pp 140–1.
[31] Ibid, p 143.
[32] Ibid.
[33] Ibid, pp 143–4.

Tax harmonisation was seen as a dynamic process, divided into stages over time and put into effect in successive steps.[34] The Neumark Committee set out a timetable for tax harmonisation measures. Three phases were identified. The first phase would entail the reform of turnover taxes. There would also be preparatory work on company tax reform and the conclusion of a multilateral convention. The second phase would entail the harmonisation of company taxes and personal income taxes, as well as the conclusion of a multilateral convention. Wealth taxes and death duties would also be considered. In the third phase all proposed reforms would be put into application. A common information service as well as a specialist tax court for appeals at European level would be explored.[35]

The Community never went past the first phase. This is not surprising given the hostility of Member States to rules that seek to harmonise corporate tax rates – not just back then but throughout the Community's existence. Notwithstanding this well-known fact, subsequent reports also recommended the imposition of uniform corporate tax rates. Unsurprisingly, again none of these proposals were ever adopted.

1.2.2 The Segrè Report

The Segrè Report was produced by a committee of experts, under the chairmanship of Professor Claudio Segrè. The committee was asked to examine the general measures that should be taken to develop a European capital market and its implications for Member States.[36] Chapter 14 of this report examined the tax obstacles to the development of 'a capital market of truly European dimensions'[37] and made suggestions as to how to eliminate them.

The Segrè Committee identified as a general aim the attainment of a 'degree of fiscal neutrality that will allow capital movements to take place within the Community in conditions similar to those on a domestic market'.[38] For this aim to be achieved, the tax system had to be neutral as to the location of the investment, the type of investment (direct investment or through an intermediary) and methods of financing. There were three major obstacles to this; namely, double taxation,[39] preferential treatment of investments made in the country of residence[40] and different treatment (from Member State to Member State) of income paid to non-residents.[41] To date these obstacles still plague the Internal Market.

---

[34] Ibid, p 152.
[35] Ibid, pp 154–5.
[36] EEC Commission, *The Development of a European Capital Market* (Brussels: EEC Commission, 1966) (Segrè Report), p 11.
[37] Segrè Report, p 293.
[38] Ibid, p 293.
[39] This included international double taxation and double taxation of investments made through a financial intermediary. See *Segrè Report*, pp 294–6.
[40] Ibid, pp 296–7.
[41] Ibid, pp 297–8.

Similar to the conclusions of the Neumark Report, here the Segrè Committee found that the ideal way of eliminating double taxation was through the conclusion of a multilateral convention. As this could take some time, it was deemed appropriate in the interim to look for temporary solutions such as unilateral or bilateral measures.[42]

As regards dividends paid to non-residents, host states could impose a withholding tax, provided that this tax was wholly allowable for the purposes of the shareholders' tax liability in their country of residence and any excess was refundable.[43] 'To the shareholder, the withholding tax would then always be simply an advance payment of tax, and hence would hardly influence his choice of country of investment whatever the rate of the tax.'[44] It was preferable that the rate be the same in all countries and identical with that of the withholding taxes levied on resident shareholders.[45]

As regards inbound dividends, rather than exemption, which was the recommendation of the Neumark Report, this committee recommended the extension of the tax credit to foreign dividends, otherwise there would be discrimination 'between income from "national" shares and income from foreign shares, and between residents and non-residents'.[46] An even better solution was to give non-residents a refund of corporation tax equivalent to the tax credit.[47] Although at the time the extension of a tax credit to non-resident shareholders may have appeared to be a very drastic recommendation, it will be shown in later chapters that the case law of the Court of Justice has led to very similar, if not more drastic, results.

1.2.3 The Programme for the Harmonisation of Direct Taxation

In 1969, under its Programme for the Harmonisation of Direct Taxation,[48] the Commission looked at direct taxes in the context of, inter alia, the movement of capital, company restructurings and inter-corporate payments. Again, as the title of the Programme suggests, the emphasis was on harmonisation. The Programme proposed a number of harmonisation measures such as the harmonisation of withholding taxes on dividends and interest, elimination of discriminatory tax

---

[42] Ibid, p 296.
[43] Ibid, p 300.
[44] Ibid.
[45] Ibid. There was a similar suggestion in the conclusions in that Member States in their capacity as host states or home states should either tax income in one country only or divide revenue between the two by imposing a withholding tax in the host state and systematically allow it for tax purposes in the beneficiary's home state. Ibid, p 311.
[46] Ibid, p 301.
[47] Ibid, p 301.
[48] 'Programme d'harmonisation des impots directs', Commission Communication of 26 June 1967, Bulletin Supplement No. 8. This was a follow-up to the more general 'Program on Tax Harmonisation' (Commission Communication of 8 February 1967, Bulletin Supplement No. 8). See Jiménez, *Towards Corporate Tax Harmonization in the European Community*, pp 109–11.

rules against non-residents, removal of tax obstacles to cross-border mergers, elimination of double taxation in parent-subsidiary relationships and use of tax incentives.[49]

This Programme led to proposals for a directive on cross-border corporate restructurings and a directive on the taxation arrangements applicable to parent companies and subsidiaries – the precursors to the Merger Directive[50] and the Parent-Subsidiary Directive[51] enacted twenty years later.

1.2.4 The Van den Tempel Report

This report[52] was produced by Professor A. J. van den Tempel at the request of the Commission. Similar to the previous reports, this report approached the issues from a tax harmonisation perspective. However, contrary to the Segrè Report, here the classical system of corporation tax was recommended as the best solution.

The report considered the structures of corporation tax in the Community and the taxation of undistributed and distributed corporate profits. Three[53] systems were considered: the classical system, the imputation system and the split-rate system. As discussed above, under the classical system, which was called the 'classic' system in this report, profits were taxed independently in the hands of the company and its shareholders.[54] Under the imputation (or tax credit) system part of the corporation tax on distributed profits was credited against the income tax charge on the shareholder.[55] Under the split-rate system a lower rate of corporation tax applied for distributed than for retained profits.[56]

In the Van den Tempel Report it was argued that the imputation and split-rate systems were in certain respects preferable to the classical system. As noted in the report, they were more neutral as far as the choice of the legal form of the enterprise was concerned and the choice of debt or equity financing.[57] However, they were

---

[49] Jiménez, *Towards Corporate Tax Harmonization in the European Community*, p 110.
[50] See Chapter 6.
[51] See Chapter 2.
[52] A. J. van den Tempel, *Corporation Tax and Individual Income Tax in the European Communities*, Competition: Approximation of Legislation Series (Brussels: 1970) (*Van den Tempel Report*).
[53] Three other systems diverging from the above were also summarily discussed. These were the system of complete avoidance of economic double taxation on dividends, either by not imposing the corporation tax on the distributed profit or by fully crediting the corporation tax on the distributed profit (ibid, pp 32–3), the system of fiscal transparency whereby all corporate profits are treated as if accruing to shareholders (ibid, pp 33–4) and the system of deduction from corporate profit of a primary dividend corresponding to the return on debt financing (pp 34–6). All three were rejected as unworkable.
[54] This system applied, at the time, in the Netherlands, Luxembourg and the UK and formerly, to the Federal German Republic and in France. See ibid, p 7.
[55] This system applied in France and Belgium. Ibid, p 7.
[56] This system applied at the time in Western Germany.
[57] *Van den Tempel Report*, p 40.

burdened with administrative complexity. The report concluded that the classical system was 'the most suitable to be adopted as a harmonised system in the European Communities',[58] offering the possibility of attaining capital export and capital import neutrality.[59]

This proposal was not followed up.

1.2.5 The Commission's 1975 Proposal and Its Aftermath

Contrary to the recommendations of the Van den Tempel Report, this proposal[60] recommended a common partial imputation system of company tax whereby Community shareholders would receive a (reimbursable) tax credit. A narrow band of rates was set both for the tax and the credit.

The Commission argued in the explanatory memorandum to this proposal that the classical system did not relieve economic double taxation of dividends and made distributions more expensive.[61] Moreover, the imputation system offered neutrality as regards the legal form of the undertakings.[62] It also prevented tax avoidance by persons subject to high personal tax rates through sheltering profits in a company.[63] In addition, the Commission invoked fairness reasons. Under the classical system, shareholders subject to low personal taxes were disadvantaged compared to those subject to higher personal taxes, as dividends were taxed in the same way and no tax credit was given to reduce the excessive tax burden.[64]

As it made distributions more expensive, this created a bias in favour of the self-financing of firms rather than financing from outside sources. It also created another bias in favour of major shareholders as opposed to small shareholders who preferred distributions.[65]

Broadly, under the Commission proposal Member States would apply a rate of corporation tax within the range of 45–55 per cent to both distributed and undistributed profits,[66] with the possibility of derogations in certain cases.[67] Dividends distributed would be subject to 25 per cent withholding tax 'no matter who is the

---

[58] Ibid, p 41.
[59] Farmer and Lyal, EC Tax Law, p 21.
[60] Proposal for a Council Directive concerning the harmonization of systems of company taxation and of withholding taxes on dividends. Transmitted to the Council by the Commission on 1 August 1975. COM(75) 392 final, 23 July 1975. Bulletin of the European Communities, Supplement 10/75.
[61] Ibid, p 7, para 5.
[62] As reasoned in the report, individuals and partnerships were usually subject to high tax rates compared to the corporate tax rate. The difference under the imputation system was smaller. Ibid, pp 7–8, para 8.
[63] Ibid, p 8, para 10.
[64] Ibid, p 8, para 9.
[65] Ibid.
[66] Art 3(1). There were also provisions for a compensatory tax to be levied in situations where the corporation tax had not been charged at the rate normally applicable in the Member State. See Art 9.
[67] Art 3(2).

recipient of those dividends'.[68] No withholding tax would apply to dividends distributed to a parent company.

As regards the tax credit rate on distributed dividends, this would be fixed by the Member State of the recipient but remain within the range of 45–55 per cent.[69] The tax credit would be set off against the final tax liability of the dividend recipient.[70] When withholding taxes collected by a Member State were set off or refunded in another Member State, the Member State that collected the withholding taxes had to refund them to the other Member State.[71] Member States could share the amount of withholding tax under bilateral agreements.[72]

Initially, the Commission's proposal was endorsed by both the Committee on Economic and Monetary Affairs and the Committee on Budgets of the European Parliament, subject to certain reservations.[73] However, the proposal was eventually rejected by the European Parliament. Following this, the Commission began to study the possibility of greater cross-border cooperation, since harmonisation of taxes would be ineffective if there continued to be differences in the level of collection and, as a corollary, the effective tax burden. This led to a Council resolution in 1975 on the measures to be taken by the Community to combat international tax evasion and avoidance[74] and to the Mutual Assistance Directives in 1977.[75]

In a report to the Council on the scope for convergence of tax systems,[76] the Commission raised the difficulties of framing a common tax policy similar to that applied by Member States, unless substantial progress was made towards integration. Tax harmonisation was not intended 'to serve the purpose of instituting a Community tax policy' but rather 'formed part of the means and powers granted to the Community to carry out its responsibilities'.[77] The Commission recognised that aligning Member States' tax policies was not as straightforward due to their tax sovereignty and the different economic and social underpinnings of their tax systems.[78] The harmonisation of tax rates was especially difficult and could only occur at a much more advanced stage of economic integration.[79] 'Then, however, it

---

[68] Art 14(1). This would be subject to different provisions under tax treaties between Member States and a third country.
[69] Arts 4 and 8.
[70] Art 16.
[71] Art 17(1).
[72] Art 17(3).
[73] See analysis in European Parliament Working Documents 1979–1980, *Interim Report drawn up on behalf of the Committee on Economic and Monetary Affairs on the harmonization of company taxation and of withholding taxes on dividends*. Rapporteur: Mr K. Nyborg (2 May 1979, Doc 104/79).
[74] Council Resolution of 10 February 1975 on the measures to be taken by the Community in order to combat international tax evasion and avoidance ([1975] OJ C35/1–2).
[75] See Chapter 2.
[76] Report from the Commission to the Council on the Scope for Convergence of Tax Systems in the Community, Brussels, 23 April 1980, COM(80)139 final 2.
[77] Ibid, pp 5–6, para 3.
[78] Ibid, pp 6–7, para 5.
[79] Ibid, p 8, para 7.

will be absolutely necessary, since the harmonisation of structures and bases of assessment will no longer be sufficient.'[80]

As far as company taxation was concerned, the Commission recommended the adoption of its 1975 proposal on company taxation and withholding taxes on dividends. It also identified the need for some coordination of investment incentives granted by Member States in connection with the basis of assessment for taxes on profits.[81] Overall, as far as legislative proposals were concerned, this report was imbued with a sense of pragmatism.

The 1975 proposal was eventually withdrawn. Draft proposals for the harmonisation of loss relief rules presented in 1984–5[82] and 1990[83] were also subsequently withdrawn. Furthermore, a draft proposal of 1988 for the harmonisation of the tax base of enterprises was never even tabled, due to the reluctance of most Member States.[84]

The 1990 Guidelines for Company Taxation[85] followed a *de minimis* legislative approach. Priority was given to existing proposals for the Merger Directive, the Parent-Subsidiary Directive and the Arbitration Convention,[86] which were

---

[80] Ibid.

[81] Ibid, p 14, para 19. See also conclusions, in paras 101–10, pp 64–5.

[82] Proposal for a Council Directive on the harmonization of the laws of the Member States relating to tax arrangements for the carry-over of losses of undertakings, [1984] OJ C253/5. This proposal was amended in 1985. See Amendment to the Proposal for a Council Directive on the harmonization of the laws of the Member States relating to tax arrangements for the carry-over of losses of undertakings, [1985] OJ C170/3. This proposal was intended to harmonise *domestic* loss relief regimes, by providing for unlimited carry-forward and a three-year carry-back of losses. The initial proposal suggested a two-year carry-back, but this was extended under the amended proposal in 1985. Cross-border loss relief was not addressed. It was up to the Member States to include losses of foreign permanent establishments and subsidiaries within the losses that were to be carried back or carried forward. The Commission withdrew the proposal in 1996: [1997] OJ C2/6. As argued in the Commission Staff Working Paper 'Company Taxation in the Internal Market' in 2001 (SEC(2001) 1681, p 340), domestic loss relief arrangements fell under the institutional sphere of competence of Member States and ought not to be interfered with.

[83] Proposal for a Council Directive concerning arrangements for the taking into account by enterprises of the losses of their permanent establishments and subsidiaries situated in other Member States, COM(90) 595 final. The proposal was later on withdrawn. In its 2001 Communication, the Commission identified the need for a new round of technical preparatory meetings before any action could be launched. The Commission recognised that the discussions would have to take into account the fact that loss compensation and group consolidation were intimately linked to more comprehensive solutions such as a consolidated corporate tax base. Communication from the Commission to the Council, the European Parliament and the Economic and Social Committee, *Towards an Internal Market without Tax Obstacles. A Strategy for Providing Companies with a Consolidated Corporate Tax Base for their EU-wide Activities*, COM(2001) 582 final, pp 13, 15–17.

[84] A preliminary draft was produced by the Commission in 1988. See preliminary draft proposal for a Directive on the harmonisation of rules for determining the taxable profits of undertakings, XV/27/88-EN. See also Han Kogels, 'Unity Divided' (2012) 21(3) *EC Tax Review* 117–23, 120–1.

[85] Commission Communication to Parliament and the Council, *Guidelines on Company Taxation*, Brussels 20 April 1990, SEC(90) 601 final.

[86] The Commission mentioned two future proposals: one for cross-border loss relief and another for the abolition of withholding taxes on interest and royalty payments between group companies. Ibid, pp 7–8.

eventually adopted. In the same year the Commission published a proposal for a directive on the taxation of interest and royalty payments between group companies.[87] This was later revised[88] but still rejected in Council. It was not until this proposal was included in the Monti tax package in 1997 that effective negotiations began.[89]

1.2.6 The Ruding Report

In 1990 a committee of independent experts was appointed by the Commission under the chairmanship of Mr Onno Ruding (a former finance minister of the Netherlands) to study the impact of taxation on the location of investments and the allocation of profits between businesses in different Member States, and to propose remedial action.[90] After a number of meetings, the committee produced a report to the Commission on 18 March 1992 – the Ruding Report.[91]

The Ruding Committee found that some national rules, such as withholding taxes on inter-corporate payments, differences in corporation tax rates and the tax base, and methods of eliminating double taxation were biased against both inward and outward investment. This led to differences in the cost of capital and, as a corollary, a distortion of capital flows and of competition, especially in the financial sector. Market forces were not enough to eliminate these distortions.

Three main priorities were set for remedial action, namely: the elimination of corporation tax obstacles to cross-border investment,[92] the establishment of minimum corporation tax rates and a minimum common tax base[93] and the transparency of tax incentives. The Ruding Committee set out a detailed schedule of three phases[94] for the implementation of these proposals.

Very importantly, during the first phase Member States applying imputation taxes on the distribution of profits earned in another Member State would be obliged to

---

[87] COM(90) 571.
[88] COM(93) 196.
[89] See 2.3.
[90] Farmer and Lyal, *EC Tax Law*, pp 296–9; Jíménez, *Towards Corporate Tax Harmonization in the European Community*, pp 131–5.
[91] See Report of the Committee of Independent Experts on Company Taxation, March 1992.
[92] This entailed the abolition of withholding taxes, the cross-border relief of foreign losses, completion of the network of tax treaties, extending the scope of the Parent-Subsidiary Directive to all taxable businesses and reducing the participation threshold, the adoption of the proposed Interest and Royalties Directive, the ratification of the Arbitration Convention by all Member States, etc.
[93] The experts looked at components of the tax base and especially the depreciation of assets, the harmonisation of dates for the payment of taxes, etc. It is noteworthy that there were dissenting views as to the form of the common corporation tax system. See Professor Radler's proposals in Annex 10A of the Report and the dissenting view of K. Messere in Annex 10B.
[94] The first phase was to run until 1994. The second phase was to run concurrently with the second phase of economic and monetary union. This was due to commence on 1 January 1994, according to the Treaty on Economic and Monetary Union. The third phase was to coincide with full economic and monetary union. See Farmer and Lyal, *EC Tax Law*, p 298.

allow such tax to be reduced by the corporation tax paid by the subsidiary or permanent establishment in the other Member State. Relief for domestic dividends received would be extended to inbound dividends. Moreover, rather controversially, a minimum corporation tax of 30 per cent would apply on both retained and distributed income, followed by a maximum rate of 40 per cent in the second phase.

The Commission's response to the Ruding Report was cautious.[95] Whilst it agreed with the committee's recommendations on elimination of double taxation (e.g. the extension of the Parent-Subsidiary Directive, the Merger Directive and further work on transfer pricing and thin capitalisation),[96] the Commission was much more reserved towards recommendations on harmonisation of corporate taxes. The recommendations were found to be too far-reaching and required further study.[97] This response evinced the Commission's clear move away from harmonisation proposals and its endorsement of piecemeal and ad hoc solutions.

The Council agreed with the Commission's conclusions.[98] It raised the issue of subsidiarity and rejected the Ruding Committee's proposal for a minimum rate of corporation tax of 30 per cent. Although the Council recognised the importance of eliminating double taxation on cross-border income flows, it also emphasised the importance of ensuring adequate and effective taxation at least once.

At this point it became obvious that the rhetoric against unfair competition and double non-taxation had begun to emerge. The Commission's efforts to tackle harmful tax competition moved in parallel with those of the OECD's,[99] whose harmful tax competition project marked the beginning of a new era in international tax law.

1.3 HARMFUL TAX COMPETITION AND THE TAX PACKAGE

The distortionary effects of harmful tax competition in the EU were first officially raised by the then Commissioner for the Internal Market, Mario Monti, in his first Memorandum.[100] It was thought that the effectiveness of the Internal Market could

---

[95] Commission Communication to the Council and the European Parliament indicating the guidelines on company taxation linked to the further development of the internal market, SEC(92) 118 final.

[96] It was proposed to replace the 'list' approach with a 'residency' and 'subject-to-tax' criterion. Following a positive opinion from the European Parliament ([1994] OJ C128), negotiations started in Council, but were eventually suspended due to the priority given to the 1997 tax package, discussed in 1.3. See also Chapter 2.

[97] Frans Vanistendael, 'Comments on the Ruding Committee Report' (1992) 1 *EC Tax Review*, 3–13; Malcolm Gammie, *The Ruding Committee Report: An Initial Response* (London: Institute for Fiscal Studies, 1992); Donal de Buitleir, 'The Ruding Committee Report and the EC Commission's Response' (1993) 33(1) *European Taxation*, 15–21. See also IFA, vol 18a, 'Harmonization of Corporate Taxes in the EC', Proceedings of a Seminar held in Florence, Italy, in 1993 during the 47th Congress of the International Fiscal Association (Deventer: Kluwer, 1994).

[98] See conclusions of the ECOFIN Council of 23 November 1992.

[99] See OECD, *Harmful Tax Competition: An Emerging Global Issue* (1998) and subsequent reports.

[100] Commission of the European Communities, Discussion Paper for the Informal Meeting of ECOFIN Ministers, SEC(96) 487 final.

be endangered by the presence of tax rules appearing as legitimate state aid[101] but falling within the scope of harmful tax competition.

Following the Monti Memorandum, a tax package to tackle harmful tax competition was launched.[102] The tax package was meant to address three areas of concern, namely corporate taxation, savings taxation and interest and royalty payments. All three areas had to move in parallel. Lack of agreement in one area stopped progress in other areas.

The Commission proposed the following specific measures:

(a) a Code of Conduct on business taxation;
(b) a common system of taxation of interest paid to individuals; and
(c) a directive, similar to the Parent-Subsidiary Directive, to eliminate withholding taxes on interest and royalty payments between companies in different Member States.

On 1 December 1997 the finance ministers of all the Member States unanimously agreed to adopt the tax package.[103] This included the Code of Conduct[104] and a more rigorous application of the rules on state aid in the field of business taxation. The finance ministers also asked the Commission to submit proposals for directives on the taxation of savings, and on interest and royalty payments between companies.

In so far as savings taxation was concerned, there were two recommendations – imposing either a withholding tax at source or an obligation to exchange information on interest income from savings. The result was the Savings Directive:[105] an agreement between Member States for automatic exchange of information on individuals who earn savings income, in the form of interest payments, in one EU Member State but who reside in another Member State. The paying agent (i.e. the financial institution paying the interest income) would collect the tax or the information. Three Member States (Austria, Belgium and Luxembourg) had opted to apply alternative arrangements during a transitional period.

The Interest and Royalties Directive[106] was meant to address similar concerns. It was the least controversial proposal of the package. In fact, agreement on a draft was reached from the outset, but as progress was linked to the Savings Directive, delays on its implementation were inevitable.

---

[101] For an analysis of the state aid prohibition in the context of direct tax law, see Chapter 8.
[102] Toward Tax Co-ordination in the European Union, A Package to Tackle Harmful Tax Competition, Doc COM(97) 495 final (1 October 1997).
[103] See [1998] OJ C 2/1.
[104] Conclusions of the ECOFIN Council Meeting on 1 December 1997 concerning taxation policy – Resolution of the Council and the Representatives of the Governments of the Member States, meeting within the Council of 1 December 1997 on a code of conduct for business taxation – Taxation of saving [1998] OJ C 2/1–6.
[105] Council Directive 2003/48/EC of 3 June 2003 on taxation of savings income in the form of interest payments. This directive is no longer in force.
[106] See 2.3.

On 1 December 1998 the ECOFIN Council in Vienna approved the first progress report of the Code of Conduct group, which had been created to assess compliance with the Code of Conduct. The ECOFIN Council also asked the Commission for an analytical study on company taxation in the European Community. An official mandate was subsequently issued, which in 2001 led to the Commission's Company Tax Study, examined next.

1.4 THE 2001 COMPANY TAX STUDY

In this study,[107] the Commission sought to identify the main tax provisions that may hamper cross-border economic activity in the Single Market. It was noted that since the Ruding Report the globalisation process had significantly changed the international economic landscape, creating new challenges for national company tax systems and at the same time requiring more integration of international markets. Furthermore, the increase in international mergers and acquisitions had an impact on the way in which companies and tax administrations confronted the taxation of such transactions.[108] Overall, the introduction of the Internal Market in 1993 significantly changed the scenery for the company tax systems of Member States.[109]

Another major development was the introduction of the Economic and Monetary Union. Now that monetary and exchange rate restrictions were no longer nationally available policy tools, the question of tax competition became more prevalent. Whilst the Economic and Monetary Union increased the integration achieved by the Internal Market, it also highlighted numerous tax problems hindering the completion of an integrated EU capital market,[110] such as discriminatory dividend taxation, unavailability of cross-border loss relief, unavailability of reliefs and deferrals in case of cross-border reorganisations, transfer pricing, double taxation as a result of conflicting taxing rights and so on.[111] There was no attempt to provide an exhaustive list or detailed classification of any of the obstacles that were presented.

The Commission identified two approaches that could be used to tackle these obstacles. Targeted solutions could be used to remedy specific obstacles, for example, amendments to the relevant directives and coordinating measures. The possibility of adopting a comprehensive solution was examined as an alternative. It was reiterated numerous times in the Company Tax Study[112] that the existence of the fifteen (at the time) tax systems was the source of the majority of the obstacles. All the suggested comprehensive measures were predicated on a single tax base and, according to the

---

[107] 'Company Taxation in the Internal Market', SEC(2001) 1681 (Company Tax Study).
[108] Ibid, p 20.
[109] Ibid, pp 22–3.
[110] Ibid, p 24.
[111] The Company Tax Study also looked at tax-related labour costs and issues pertaining to small and medium-sized enterprises and partnerships. See Pt III of the Company Tax Study.
[112] Ibid, pp 2, 8, 14, 372.

Commission, had the potential of reducing compliance costs for European businesses.[113] Four suggestions of a long-term nature were made.

Firstly, Home State Taxation was discussed. Under this method, all or a group of Member States agree to allow certain enterprises with operations in numerous Member States to compute their taxable base according to the tax rules of a single Member State – the home state.[114] Only the method of calculating the base would change, as each Member State would continue to set the tax rate on its share of the group's profits. As the foreign subsidiaries would be treated as domestic ones subject to the existing local rules of the home state, cross-border loss relief would be attained and transfer pricing between participating Member States would be eliminated.

Secondly, a Common (Consolidated) Tax Base was considered. Here, instead of extending the application of each of the existing national tax systems across the EU, the Commission suggested an additional but optional new tax base that would be adopted across the EU.[115] Following the 2001 Company Tax Study, the Commission concentrated its efforts on this suggestion, which eventually led to a proposal for a Common Consolidated Corporate Tax Base.[116]

An additional variation on the 'common base' theme was also suggested – the European Union Company Income Tax (EUCIT). This entailed not only a new single tax base but also a uniform tax rate. The revenues raised would be used to fund the EU institutions and activities with any excess allocated between Member States according to an agreed formula. The EUCIT could be administered by individual Member States, with each Member State applying its own tax rate to its allocated share of the tax base. It was acknowledged in the Company Tax Study that this method would be politically contentious, as it would be perceived as leading to the establishment of a federal EU Tax.[117]

Finally, a compulsory harmonised tax base in the EU could be enacted. Apart from the new tax base, which would replace all Member State bases, there would also be consolidation and formulary apportionment.[118]

The Commission concluded that fundamental benefits could flow from any of the comprehensive approaches, expressing its preference for the Common (Consolidated) Base.[119] However, it was conceded that implementation of Home State Taxation was potentially a quicker process, since it relied on existing systems.

With hindsight, the Commission's 2001 Company Tax Study set the parameters for future developments in the area of corporate tax law. Most of the targeted

---

[113] Ibid, p 372.
[114] Ibid, p 373. It was acknowledged that the idea of Home State Taxation had originally been developed in academic research – see Sven-Olof Lodin and Malcolm Gammie, *Home State Taxation* (Amsterdam: IBFD, 2001).
[115] Company Tax Study, p 375.
[116] See 2.8.1.
[117] Company Tax Study, p 377.
[118] Ibid, p 378.
[119] Ibid, p 380.

measures were implemented either voluntarily or as a result of the Court of Justice's judgments. As far as the comprehensive measures were concerned, a debate on the harmonisation of tax bases (re-)started, which led to some developments. Since the 2001 Company Tax Study, Home State Taxation has been advanced as an initiative of tax simplification for small and medium-sized enterprises.[120] Most progress was achieved vis-à-vis the second comprehensive proposal. There have since been two proposals for a Common Consolidated Corporate Tax Base (CCCTB) that are yet to be approved in Council.[121]

Arguably, the ingenuity of the Company Tax Study lay in the fact that the necessity of targeted measures that could be implemented swiftly and on an ad hoc basis was decoupled from the necessity of comprehensive proposals, which were more politically controversial and required a longer 'gestation' period. Perhaps this is why most previous proposals failed.

1.5 THE AFTERMATH TO THE 2001 COMPANY TAX STUDY

Since the Company Tax Study was published, the Commission began intensive follow-up work both on the various targeted measures and the long-term proposals for a common tax base. In 2003 the Commission released a Communication[122] in which it emphasised the continuing need to adapt company taxation in the EU. It confirmed the commitment made in the Company Tax Study and the two-track strategy for dealing with existing tax problems. The Commission reviewed the progress on the targeted measures and reiterated the belief that the common consolidated corporate tax base was the *only* means by which EU companies could overcome the aforementioned tax obstacles in a systematic way.[123] It presented ideas of a pilot scheme for the application of Home State Taxation to small and medium-sized enterprises.[124] A similar approach was followed in a Commission Communication in which the contribution of taxation and customs policies to the Lisbon strategy was highlighted.[125] In 2006 the Commission reported on the progress to date, with emphasis on the CCCTB.[126]

[120] See Communication from the Commission to the Council, the European Parliament and the European Economic and Social Committee, *Tackling the Corporation Tax Obstacles of Small and Medium-sized Enterprises in the Internal Market – Outline of a Possible Home State Taxation Pilot Scheme* (COM/2005/702/Final) and Impact Assessment SEC/05/1785.
[121] See 2.8.1.
[122] Communication from the Commission to the Council, the European Parliament and the European Economic and Social Committee, *An Internal Market without Company Tax Obstacles Achievements, Ongoing Initiatives and Remaining Challenges*, COM(2003) 726.
[123] Ibid, p 14.
[124] Ibid, p 13.
[125] Communication from the Commission to the Council, the European Parliament and the European Economic and Social Committee, *The Contribution of Taxation and Customs Policies to the Lisbon Strategy*, COM(2005) 532.
[126] Report from the Commission to the Council, the European Parliament and the European Economic and Social Committee, *Implementing the Community Lisbon Programme: Progress to Date and Next Steps towards a Common Consolidated Corporate Tax Base (CCCTB)*, COM(2006) 157.

Apart from these general policy statements, the Commission also published a number of Communications dealing with specific tax obstacles such as cross-border loss relief,[127] exit taxation[128] and anti-abuse measures[129] as well as a more general Communication on the coordination of Member State tax systems in the Internal Market.[130] Later on, the Commission's Communications focused on problems such as double taxation,[131] double non-taxation of companies and aggressive tax planning[132] and cross-border dividends.[133] The increasing reliance on soft law to improve its performance and legitimacy showed a shift in Commission tactics,[134] away from its overdependence on hard law.

There were also some important legislative developments. The Interest and Royalties Directive and the Savings Directive were enacted and existing direct tax directives were amended.[135]

Since the 2001 Company Tax Study, the Commission had also been working on a proposal for a CCCTB. The Commission was initially expected to make a legislative proposal on the CCCTB by the end of 2008, though this was postponed following the rejection of the Lisbon Treaty by the Irish people. Following the subsequent ratification of the Lisbon Treaty, in March 2011 the Commission published its proposal for the CCCTB and a detailed impact assessment.[136] Although the proposal was not immediately struck down on the basis of subsidiarity and enjoyed the support of the European Parliament, which in fact advocated the

---

[127] Communication from the Commission to the Council, the European Parliament and the European Economic and Social Committee, *Tax Treatment of Losses in Cross-Border Situations*, COM (2006) 824.
[128] Communication from the Commission to the Council, the European Parliament and the European Economic and Social Committee, *Exit Taxation and the Need for Co-ordination of Member States' Tax Policies*, COM(2006) 825.
[129] Communication from the Commission to the Council, the European Parliament and the European Economic and Social Committee, *Direct Taxation: Communication on the Application of Anti-abuse Measures – within the EU and in Relation to Third Countries*, COM(2007) 725.
[130] Communication from the Commission to the Council, the European Parliament and the European Economic and Social Committee, *Co-ordinating Member States' Direct Tax Systems in the Internal Market*, COM(2006) 823.
[131] See Communication from the Commission to the European Parliament, the Council and the European Economic and Social Committee, *Double Taxation in the Single Market*, COM(2011) 712 final.
[132] See Press Release IP/12/201.
[133] Public Consultation Paper, *Taxation Problems that Arise when Dividends are Distributed Across Borders to Portfolio and Individual Investors And Possible Solutions* (Commission, 2011). See also previously, Communication from the Commission to the Council, the European Parliament and the European Economic and Social Committee, *Dividend Taxation of Individuals in the Internal Market*, COM(2003) 810 final.
[134] See analysis in Hans Gribnau, 'The Code of Conduct for Business Taxation: An Evaluation of an EU Soft-Law Instrument', in Dennis Weber (ed), *Traditional and Alternative Routes to European Tax Integration* (Amsterdam: IBFD, 2010).
[135] For example, Parent-Subsidiary Directive, Merger Directive, etc. See analysis in Chapter 2.
[136] The 2011 version of the proposed CCCTB Directive was analysed in detail in the first edition of this book, in Chapter 3. This edition reviews the latest proposal in Chapter 2.

mandatory application of the CCCTB,[137] it was never brought for a vote in Council, as unanimity was unlikely to be attained.

There had already been suggestions to allow a few Member States to adopt the CCCTB under the enhanced cooperation procedure, even before the Commission postponed its work on it in 2008. As explained in Chapter 2, eventually the proposal was replaced with a new bifurcated proposal, in an attempt to try and get a common tax base approved first and subsequently consolidation.

1.6 THE BEPS AND POST-BEPS ERA: THE RISE OF TAX GOOD GOVERNANCE AND FAIR TAXATION

Following publication of the first edition of this book, an immensely important development took place in the international tax community, which also affected the development of EU corporate tax law. This was the BEPS project. BEPS is an acronym for Base Erosion and Profit Shifting and refers to tax avoidance strategies that exploit gaps and mismatches in tax rules to artificially shift profits to low or no-tax locations. With the backing of both G8 and G20 member countries, in 2013, the OECD published 15 Action items to address the main areas where it was felt that companies had been most aggressively accomplishing base erosion and profit shifting. This was the BEPS Action Plan.[138] Following an intensive two-year period in which the OECD produced drafts for all the action items, consulted various stakeholders and revised drafts, the Final Reports were published in October 2015.[139] These Final Reports contained several non-binding recommendations for each Action item considered. The OECD and G20 member countries made a political commitment to adopt the so-called four minimum standards derived from some of the Action items.[140]

As shown in later chapters, the Commission seized on the political momentum generated by the BEPS project and pushed through several amendments to existing tax legislation (e.g. the Parent-Subsidiary Directive, the Directive on Administrative Cooperation) as well as completely new legislation (e.g. the Anti-Tax Avoidance Directive and the Tax Dispute Resolution Mechanisms Directive). The Commission also relaunched a new CCCTB proposal, as well as several bold

---

[137] See Press Release published in Tax Analysts (2012 WTD 57–24).
[138] See OECD, *Action Plan on Base Erosion and Profit Shifting* (OECD 2013), www.oecd.org/ctp/BEPSActionPlan.pdf (BEPS Action Plan).
[139] See www.oecd.org/tax/beps-2d015-final-reports.htm.
[140] The BEPS minimum standards were the following: (1) the prevention of harmful tax practices, in particular, in relation to intellectual property and through the automatic exchange of information on tax rulings (Action 5); (2) countering treaty shopping to reduce the use of conduit companies in channelling investments (Action 6); (3) country-by-country reporting to provide tax administrations with an overall perspective of the operations of MNEs (Action 13); and (4) improving dispute resolution to ensure that the measures to counter double non-taxation does not result in double taxation (Action 14).

legislative proposals which are still pending. The legislative developments will be examined in more detail in Chapter 2.

Emboldened by recent developments, the Commission has also attempted to remove the veto power that Member States have in tax matters,[141] to overcome the often unavoidable stagnation in legislative developments. In January 2019, the Commission published its proposal[142] to move away from unanimity to qualified majority voting in the tax area and a suggested roadmap. Although this proposal never went very far, as shown in 1.6.3, there are now attempts to revive it.

In the remainder of this chapter, the soft law initiatives that emanated from the momentum generated from the BEPS project will be examined, as they seem to be laying the ground for the development of a common external fiscal policy, even in the absence of a common internal fiscal policy.

1.6.1 Good Governance in Tax Matters and the Development of the EU's External Fiscal Policy

Up until the EU's work in this area, the application of principles of good governance in an international fiscal setting focused heavily on domestic resource mobilisation and capacity building vis-à-vis developing countries, and, to a lesser extent, exchange of information and tax cooperation.[143] There were also efforts to build a code of best practices for tax authorities in their dealings with taxpayers, but mostly for large taxpayers and businesses.[144]

The EU's approach on good tax governance, early on, was more comprehensive and sought to address issues both in the context of developed and developing countries. At an ECOFIN meeting in 2008, one of the conclusions of the Council was to promote the principles of good governance in the tax area. These principles were described as 'the principles of transparency, exchange of information and fair tax competition, as subscribed to by Member States at Community level'.[145] Good governance in the tax area was identified as an essential means of combating cross-border tax fraud and evasion and strengthening the fight against money laundering, corruption, and the financing of

---

[141] Commission Communication, *Towards a More Efficient and Democratic Decision Making in EU Tax Policy*, COM(2019) 8 final (15.01.2019).
[142] Ibid. Indicatively, in this Communication it was noted that '[f]or the Commission, the question is no longer whether there is a need to move away from unanimity in taxation, but rather how and when to do it' (ibid, p 11).
[143] See, for example, OECD, *Citizen-State Relations: Improving Governance through Tax Reform* (Paris, 2010). For an overview of the initiatives internationally, see Pt II in Christiana HJI Panayi, 'The Europeanisation of Good Tax Governance', 36 (2018) 1 *Yearbook of European Law* 442–95.
[144] Ibid. Also see OECD *Study into the Role of Tax Intermediaries* (OECD, 2008).
[145] Press Release, 2866th Council Meeting, Economic and Financial Affairs (8850/08 (Presse 113), Brussels, 14 May 2008) p 22.

1.6 The BEPS and Post-BEPS Era

terrorism. This task, already buttressed by other initiatives,[146] was to be taken on by the Commission.

By inserting the component of fair tax competition, much vagueness and subjectivity has been introduced in this area. In any case, the Commission followed this definition and in 2009 it produced a Communication for the promotion of good governance in tax matters.[147] In this Communication, good governance in the tax area was assimilated to 'the need for international tax cooperation and common standards'[148] and the definition given by the ECOFIN Council in 2008 was repeated.[149] Measures were suggested to strengthen this principle within the EU and internationally. Several existing internal initiatives were identified, such as proposals to improve the Mutual Assistance Directives and the (now obsolete) Savings Directive. The Commission urged the Council to give the issue of good governance in the tax area appropriate political priority and to include provisions to that effect in general agreements with third countries.[150] Moreover, it was urged that EU-level arrangements with third countries should 'where appropriate, also include provisions similar to those applicable within the EU under State aid rules'.[151]

Following this Communication, the European Parliament adopted a resolution promoting good governance in the area of taxation,[152] reiterating the need for an EU policy of good tax governance.[153] It was obvious that a uniform policy on this matter would be easier to apply and enforce against third countries, than the policies of each Member State separately. As a first step, at a subsequent ECOFIN meeting, the Commission was given a mandate to initiate dialogue with Switzerland and Liechtenstein, to extend the Code of Conduct on Business Taxation beyond the Union for the first time.[154] This would facilitate the promotion of the adoption of the principles of the Code of Conduct in third countries.[155]

---

[146] Communications on Preventing and Combating Corporate and Financial Malpractice (COM (2006) 611), on Caribbean countries (COM (2006) 86), on Pacific countries (COM (2006) 248), on Hong Kong and Macao (COM (2006) 648), on Governance and Development (COM (2006) 421) and on EU competitiveness (COM (2006) 567).

[147] Communication from the Commission to the Council, the European Parliament and the European Economic and Social Committee, *Promoting Good Governance in Tax Matters*, COM(2009) 201 final, dated 28 April 2009 (Good Governance Communication). See Timothy Lyons, 'Promoting Good Governance in Tax Matters' [2009] *British Tax Review* 361; Gemma Martinez Barbara, Alicja Brodzka, Sebastiano Garufi and Wolfang Schön, 'Tax and Corporate Governance: A legal Approach', in Wolfgang Schön and others (eds), *Tax and Corporate Governance* (Berlin Heidelberg: Springer-Verlag, 2008).

[148] Good Governance Communication, p 4.

[149] Ibid, p 5.

[150] Ibid, p 10.

[151] Ibid, p 11.

[152] See European Parliament resolution of 10 February 2010 on promoting good governance in tax matters (2009/2174(INI)), para 1.

[153] Ibid, para 17.

[154] 3020th Council meeting Economic and Financial Affairs, Luxembourg, 8 June 2010, PRESSE 162, 10689/10.

[155] Ibid, p 20.

Shortly thereafter, in its 2010 Communication on Tax and Development,[156] the Commission set out domestic resource mobilisation as the policy basis for EU assistance to developing countries. The Communication focused on the synergies between tax and development policies.[157] Although it did not elaborate on the standards of good tax governance as it did in previous communications, it seemed to take it for granted that *its* view of good governance in the tax area was widely shared. This set the tone for what was to follow.

In 2012, in furtherance to the Commission's Action Plan to strengthen the fight against tax fraud and evasion,[158] the Commission published two recommendations. One dealt with aggressive tax planning.[159] The other recommendation dealt with good governance and measures to encourage third countries to apply minimum standards of good governance in tax matters.[160] To the Commission, these were two sides of the same coin. Member States should tackle aggressive tax planning but at the same time, they should also ensure that they, as well as any third countries they interact with, apply principles of good tax governance. By linking the EU's principles of good tax governance with the fight against aggressive tax planning, the Commission further legitimised its stance, facilitating the exporting of the EU standards.

In the Recommendation on Aggressive Tax Planning, all Member States were encouraged to take the same general approach towards aggressive tax planning, such as introducing subject-to-tax requirements unilaterally as well as in their treaty network, introducing general anti-abuse rules in their national legislation etc.[161] The Commission emphasised the importance of an EU-wide response to the problem of aggressive tax planning. The Commission undertook to monitor the implementation of these recommendations and to put pressure on countries whose progress was slow.

In the Recommendation on Good Tax Governance, the Commission sought to provide Member States a set of criteria to identify third countries that did not meet what it called 'minimum standards of good governance in tax matters' – effectively *its* minimum standards. According to the Commission, a third country only complied with minimum standards of good governance in tax matters where it had adopted legal, regulatory and administrative measures intended to comply with the standards

---

[156] Communication from the Commission to the European Parliament, the Council and the European Economic and Social Committee, *Tax and Development Cooperating with Developing Countries on Promoting Good Governance in Tax Matters*, COM/2010/0163 final.

[157] Ibid, p 2.

[158] Communication from the Commission to the European Parliament and the Council, *An Action Plan to Strengthen the Fight against Tax Fraud and Tax Evasion*, COM/2012/0722 final.

[159] Commission Recommendation of 6.12.2012 on Aggressive Tax Planning (C (2012) 8806 final) – henceforth, Recommendation on Aggressive Tax Planning.

[160] Commission Recommendation of 6.12.2012 regarding measures intended to encourage third countries to apply minimum standards of good governance in tax matters (C (2012) 8805 final) – henceforth, the Recommendation on Good Tax Governance.

[161] Recommendation on Aggressive Tax Planning, pp 4–5.

of transparency and exchange of information,[162] where it effectively applied those measures and did not operate harmful tax measures in the area of business taxation.[163] Tax measures which provided for a significantly lower effective level of taxation, including zero taxation, were to be regarded as potentially harmful.[164]

The Commission proposed a number of measures to be taken vis-à-vis third countries, with a view to encouraging them to comply with these standards. It was recommended that Member States should publish blacklists of third countries not complying with the minimum standards set out above.[165] Furthermore, Member States were encouraged to renegotiate, suspend or terminate tax treaties with non-compliant third countries, as well as initiate bilateral negotiations for tax treaties with compliant third countries. Member States were asked to consider offering closer cooperation and assistance to third countries, especially developing ones, which were committed to complying with the minimum standards. Such closer cooperation would assist those third countries in their fight against tax evasion and aggressive tax planning.[166]

The Recommendation on Good Tax Governance, together with the one on Aggressive Tax Planning and the Commission's Action Plan to strengthen the fight against tax fraud and evasion paved the way for the beginning of a new era. Thereafter it became obvious that the main focus of the Commission – and to an extent, the other EU institutions – was not only the elimination of tax obstacles to cross-border movement but also the protection of national tax bases and the prevention of tax avoidance. Furthermore, this Recommendation, although at the time seen as soft law, set the wheels in motion for the development of a more uniform external fiscal policy.

Following the Commission's External Strategy Communication in 2016, the EU's stance as regards third countries and their compliance with what the Commission considers as good tax governance has solidified but also expanded, in an effort to export this policy to third countries. The first step towards developing a uniform approach to good tax governance was taken in the context of the Commission's Action Plan for a Fair and Efficient Corporate Tax System in June 2015.[167] Very importantly, in the context of this Action Plan, the Commission published a first pan-EU online map of third-country non-cooperative tax jurisdictions. This was a map of non-EU tax jurisdictions which Member States had considered uncooperative under *their* own regimes. In other words, the Commission used the Member

---

[162] These were set out in the Annex of the Recommendation on Good Tax Governance, p 8.
[163] Ibid, pp 4–5.
[164] In assessing whether measures were harmful, the Recommendation urged Member States to take account of the conclusions reached by the Code of Conduct Group on Business Taxation on this issue. Ibid, p 5.
[165] Ibid.
[166] Ibid, p 6.
[167] Communication from the Commission to the European Parliament and the Council, *A Fair and Efficient Corporate Tax System in the European Union: 5 Key Areas for Action*, COM(2015) 302 final (17.06.2015).

States' benchmarks for non-compliance and not its own. There were about 30 non-EU tax jurisdictions in the first version of the map.[168] The map was to be updated periodically and used to develop a common EU strategy to deal with non-cooperative tax jurisdictions, including via coordinated counter-measures.[169]

As the diversity in Member States' approaches sent mixed messages to international partners, the Commission argued that a coordinated EU external strategy on tax good governance was essential to boost Member States' collective success in tackling tax avoidance and to ensure effective taxation.[170] The External Strategy Communication proposed a framework for a new EU external strategy, based on a revised tax good governance clause. The Commission identified the key measures which could help the EU to promote tax good governance globally but also allow it to better integrate tax good governance 'into the EU's wider external relation policies and support its international commitments, particularly in the area of development'.[171]

In this Communication, the EU standards for tax good governance were re-examined in light of fundamental changes in the global tax environment. The Commission recommended that a revised EU tax good governance clause should be negotiated and included in agreements with third countries. As regards transparency, this standard would be based on the two internationally agreed OECD standards: namely, exchange of information on request and automatic exchange of information.[172] As regards fair tax competition, the Commission made a dubious[173] claim that as a result of the BEPS project, fair tax competition had become central to the international agenda. In describing fair tax competition in Annex 1, the Commission linked this concept with that of harmful tax competition, as it did in the 2012 Recommendation on Good Tax Governance.

In the External Strategy Communication, the Commission had considered ways to enhance tax good governance through agreements with third countries. Bilateral and regional agreements with third countries were recommended as particularly useful legal instruments.[174] In fact, tax good governance clauses were already included in some trade agreements between the EU and third countries or regions, admittedly with mixed success so far. Whilst it was acknowledged that due to the

---

[168] Obviously, the first version was replaced by later versions. This is now replaced by the EU list of non-cooperative tax jurisdictions, examined in 1.6.2. See: https://ec.europa.eu/taxation_customs/business/company-tax/tax-good-governance/tax-good-governance-world-seen-eu-countries_en.
[169] Ibid, pp 12 and 13.
[170] Ibid, p 2.
[171] Ibid, p 3.
[172] See Annex 1, pp 2–3.
[173] Arguably, this was an exaggeration, as it was not *the* objective – nor even *an* objective – of the BEPS Action Plan to produce measures promoting *fair* tax competition. In fact, the BEPS Action Plan only mentioned the word 'fair' once, in stating that '[f]air competition is harmed by the distortions induced by BEPS' (BEPS Action Plan, p 9). 'Fairness' was also mentioned twice but in a generic way (see pp 8, 15 of BEPS Action Plan).
[174] Ibid, p 5.

diversity of the EU's international partners a one-size-fits-all approach was not practical, it was argued that an element of uniformity as regards tax good governance clauses was essential.

Without really explaining where the competence was derived from, the Commission took it upon itself, together with the Code of Conduct Group, to monitor non-EU countries' compliance with the tax good governance clause.[175] As part of this monitoring exercise, the Commission also announced its intention to develop a stand-alone screening process to assess and list third countries on the basis of their adherence to the EU standards of tax good governance. This was thought to be crucial to the development of a common EU approach.

Interestingly, the European Parliament had made similar general recommendations in the past, in the context of its TAXE 1 Special Committee resolution on tax rulings,[176] a study commissioned by the European Parliament,[177] and other reports.[178] The alignment of the Commission's and the European Parliament's objectives in this area (and the proposed means to achieve these objectives) was significantly buttressed by the international tax community's global mobilisation in the context of the BEPS project. This led to what the author has called elsewhere the Europeanisation of good tax governance standards.[179]

1.6.2 EU List of Non-Cooperative Jurisdictions

Following the recommendations in the Commission's External Strategy Communication, on 5 December 2017, the ECOFIN Council approved the first EU list of non-cooperative jurisdictions, colloquially also known as the EU Blacklist. Seventeen countries were identified as failing to meet the agreed tax good governance standards, and forty-seven countries committed to addressing deficiencies in their tax systems and to meet the required criteria. The Commission encouraged Member States to agree on coordinated sanctions to apply at national level against the listed jurisdictions.

---

[175] Ibid, p 6.
[176] See European Parliament resolution of 25 November 2015 on tax rulings and other measures similar in nature or effect (2015/2066(INI)), www.europarl.europa.eu/sides/getDoc.do?pubRef=-//EP//TEXT+TA+P8-TA-2015-0408+0+DOC+XML+V0//EN&language=EN#BKMD-8 and more specifically, para 152. Also see European Parliament, Special Committee on Tax Rulings and Other Measures Similar in Nature or Effect, *Report on tax rulings and other measures similar in nature or effect*.
[177] See European Parliament, *Promoting Good Tax-Governance in Third-Countries: The Role of The EU*, www.europarl.europa.eu/RegData/etudes/IDAN/2015/569976/IPOL_IDA(2015)569976_EN.pdf.
[178] See European Parliament, *Report with recommendations to the Commission on bringing transparency, coordination and convergence to Corporate Tax policies in the Union* (2015/2010(INL)), dated 2 December 2015, www.europarl.europa.eu/sides/getDoc.do?pubRef=-//EP//NONSGML+REPORT+A8-2015-0349+0+DOC+PDF+V0//EN.
[179] See Christiana HJI Panayi, 'The Europeanisation of Good Tax Governance', 36 (2018) 1 *Yearbook of European Law* 442–95, Pt III.B.

Interestingly, in the memo accompanying the press release for the EU list,[180] the criterion of fair tax competition was used *interchangeably* with that of fair taxation, generating even more confusion as to what this criterion actually encompasses.[181] These rather vague criteria were also subject to change. The Commission openly acknowledged the possibility that these criteria might change or become more stringent in the future,[182] a point it has repeated in its latest Communication on Tax Good Governance,[183] examined below.

Subsequently, the Commission published guidelines on the use of EU funds in order to ensure that EU funds were not channelled or transited through entities that are resident in blacklisted tax jurisdictions.[184] Standardised wording referring to the adoption of the EU list had already been inserted into various EU legal acts.[185] The Council also published guidance on foreign source income exemption regimes, which would serve as a further benchmark for the continued screening of third countries.[186] Furthermore, at the ECOFIN meeting on 5 December 2019, it was agreed that Member States should apply at least one of the following defensive legislative measures against non-cooperative jurisdictions: non-deductibility of costs,[187] controlled foreign company rules in accordance with the Anti-Tax Avoidance Directive, withholding tax measures,[188] limitation of participation exemption on profit distributions[189]

---

[180] See European Commission, Fact Sheet – Questions and Answers on the EU list of non-cooperative tax jurisdictions, Brussels, 5 December 2017. MEMO 17/5122

[181] For criticism, see Christiana HJI Panayi, 'The Europeanisation of Good Tax Governance', 484 et seq.

[182] Memo, p 4.

[183] Communication from the Commission to European Parliament and the Council on Tax Good Governance in the EU and beyond, COM(2020) 313 final (15.07.2020).

[184] See the German version of the guidance, https://ec.europa.eu/info/sites/info/files/economy-finance/c_2018_1756.pdf.

[185] For example, Regulation 2017/1601 establishing the European Fund for Sustainable Development and Regulation 2015/1017 establishing the European Fund for Strategic Investments.

[186] According to the guidance, an overtly broad definition of tax exempt income, notably foreign-sourced passive income without any conditions and/or a nexus not complying with the permanent establishment definition contained in the OECD Model Tax Convention would be considered harmful practices aimed at facilitating double non-taxation. See General Secretariat of the Council, *Guidance on foreign source income exemption regimes*, FISC 386, ECOFIN 877 (15 October 2019), https://data.consilium.europa.eu/doc/document/ST-13075-2019-INIT/en/pdf.

[187] It was recommended that Member States which opt for this measure should deny a deduction of costs and payments that otherwise would be deductible for the taxpayer when these costs and payments were directed to entities or persons in listed jurisdictions. The measure could target interest, royalties and other concessions on intellectual property assets and service fees.

[188] It was recommended that Member States that opt for this measure should apply withholding taxes at a higher rate for example on payments such as interest, royalties, service fees or remuneration, when these payments are treated as received in listed jurisdictions. Alternatively, or in combination with this measure, Member States could consider applying specific targeted withholding taxes to such payments.

[189] Member States that have rules that permit the exclusion or deduction of dividends or other profits received from foreign subsidiaries could deny or limit these participation exemptions if the dividends or other profits are treated as received from a listed jurisdiction.

and other administrative measures.[190] This guidance, which is not binding on Member States, also suggests that Member States could apply a reversal of the burden of proof and special documentation requirements to reinforce the effect of any of the defensive measures.

Since its publication, several countries have been removed or added (or removed and added back) to this list.[191] Overall, the whole process has been criticised for the perceived absence of transparency as regards the criteria for including and removing countries from the list and the fact that EU Member States are not subject to the same scrutiny. Although during the 2019 Austrian Presidency, there were suggestions that Member States should also be subject to the review process conducted by the Code of Conduct Group for the purposes of the list,[192] no concrete steps were taken to that effect. A similar recommendation was made in the TAXE 3 European Parliament committee report, where it was found that some Member States functioned as corporate tax havens.[193]

Overall, the EU list of non-cooperative tax jurisdictions and the guidance on sanctions are very important developments. The establishment of fair tax competition as a screening criterion, to be used interchangeably with fair taxation, an even more subjective concept, and the punitive effects of being listed as an uncooperative jurisdiction shows how the EU listing process has become a very powerful weapon in the Commission's efforts to steer a common external fiscal strategy. Recent initiatives also suggest that the building of consensus around these concepts is helping the Commission introduce proposals for more comprehensive tax reform within the EU as well.

1.6.3 Tax Good Governance and Fair Taxation as a Prelude to Comprehensive Tax Reform

On 15 July 2020, the Commission delivered another ambitious tax package aimed at supporting the EU's economic recovery and long-term growth. The package comprised of an Action Plan for Fair and Simple Taxation supporting the Recovery Strategy,[194] a Communication on Tax Good Governance in the EU

---

[190] Member States should apply at least one of the following administrative measures: (a) reinforced monitoring of certain transactions; (b) increased audit risks for taxpayers; (c) increased audit risks for taxpayers.

[191] See updated list available at www.consilium.europa.eu/en/policies/eu-list-of-non-cooperative-jurisdictions/.

[192] See report by Reuters, dated 10 October 2018, www.reuters.com/article/eu-tax-avoidance/eu-weighs-screening-member-states-over-tax-avoidance-official-idUSL8N1WQ4VB.

[193] See para 330, Report on financial crimes, tax evasion and tax avoidance European Parliament resolution of 26 March 2019 on financial crimes, tax evasion and tax avoidance (2018/2121(INI)), P8_TA-PROV(2019)0240, www.europarl.europa.eu/cmsdata/162244/P8_TA-PROV(2019)0240.pdf.

[194] Communication from the Commission to European Parliament and the Council – An action plan for fair and simple taxation supporting the recovery strategy, COM(2020) 312 final (15.07.2020).

and beyond[195] and a legislative proposal to amend the Directive on Administrative Cooperation.[196]

This Action Plan and the overall tax package were seen as part of a comprehensive tax agenda for a 'deep reform of the corporate tax system to fit our modern and increasingly digitalized economy'.[197] Although it did not cover issues relating to the setting of a minimum level of effective taxation of business profits, the Commission noted that it was actively supporting global discussions on this point, warning that it stood ready to act if no global agreement was reached.[198] It was stated that before the end of the year, a roadmap for business taxation in the EU would be published. Furthermore, in order to fully deliver on the EU's fair tax agenda, it was emphasised that all existing policy levers had to be activated, including the use of ordinary legislative procedure under Art 116 TFEU.[199] With this, the Commission once again openly threatened the treasured (by most Member States) fiscal veto.

The Annex[200] to the Action Plan Communication included 25 tax initiatives in both indirect tax and direct tax areas to be implemented until 2024. These initiatives centred around two pillars: the fight against tax evasion and tax simplification. Some of the initiatives focused on reduction of tax obstacles and unnecessary administrative burdens for businesses, assisting Member States in securing reliable tax revenues, helping tax authorities to better exploit existing data and share new data more efficiently, enhancing cooperative compliance and improving dispute resolution, promoting taxpayers' rights and others.

The Communication on Tax Good Governance continued with the theme developed so far of promoting fair taxation and addressing unfair tax competition in the EU and internationally. It was stated that reform of the Code of Conduct on Business Taxation and improvements to the EU list of non-cooperative jurisdictions were crucial to achieve these objectives.

In this Communication, the Commission made several bold statements. For example, in discussing the timing of the reform of the Code of Conduct for maximum effect, it was stated that 'if minimum effective taxation becomes a global standard, there will be a new floor on how low countries can go in using their tax rates to attract foreign businesses and investment'.[201] Even if there was no consensus on minimum taxation at global level, the Commission argued that this concept had to be introduced in the Code of Conduct 'as an EU standard, to

---

[195] Communication from the Commission to European Parliament and the Council on Tax Good Governance in the EU and beyond, COM(2020) 313 final (15.07.2020).
[196] Proposal for a Council Directive amending Directive 2011/16/EU on administrative cooperation in the field of taxation, COM(2020) 314 final (15.07.2020).
[197] An action plan for fair and simple taxation supporting the recovery strategy, p 2.
[198] Ibid.
[199] Ibid.
[200] Communication from the Commission to European Parliament and the Council – An action plan for fair and simple taxation supporting the recovery strategy – Annex, COM(2020) 312 final (15.07.2020).
[201] Ibid, pp 3–4.

modernize and clarify the concept of harmful tax competition and to ensure that all businesses pay their fair amount of tax when they generate profits in the Single Market'.[202] Undoubtedly, the introduction of a freestanding (EU) concept of minimum taxation in an amended Code of Conduct is a very controversial proposal.

The Commission also argued that it was necessary to review the scope and criteria of the Code of Conduct 'to cover all measures which pose a risk to fair tax competition',[203] so as to enable the scrutiny of general features of a Member State's corporate tax regime which are deemed harmful (e.g. tax residency rules which can lead to double non-taxation, citizenship schemes etc). In addition, the Commission recommended improving the governance of the Code of Conduct Group, among other things, by introducing qualified majority voting to speed up decision-making.[204]

A review of the EU listing process was also announced. More specifically, the Commission stated that it would review the geographical scope of the list and very importantly, the listing criteria, to ensure that 'they are up-to-date and adequately ambitious'.[205] It was obvious that the Commission's endgame was for the EU list to eventually prevail over any national lists.[206] Alignment and coordination of EU and Member State approaches was also recommended as far as funding policies were concerned, as well as the enhancement of defensive measures.[207] Rather arbitrarily, the Commission announced that it would expand the dialogue on tax good governance with third countries to encompass environmental taxes.[208]

A final area of action was to support partner countries in enhancing tax good governance, in line also with OECD, UN, IMF and other international initiatives.[209] The Communication also outlined the EU's approach to assisting developing countries in the area of taxation, in line with the UN's 2030 Sustainable Development agenda.

1.6.4 The Brexit Saga

Brexit is undeniably a development of historical significance. It is the first time a Member State has left the EU. Up until now, European countries were vying to enter the EU club, sacrificing a great deal of their sovereignty to become fully fledged members. Therefore, the UK's decision to leave the EU (after a marginal win of the Leave campaigners at the UK referendum of 23 June 2016) came as a shock for many. A few months later, Article 50 of TEU was triggered by the British

---

[202] Ibid, p 4.
[203] Ibid.
[204] Ibid.
[205] Ibid, p 7.
[206] Ibid, p 8.
[207] Ibid, pp 9–12.
[208] Ibid, pp 8–9.
[209] Ibid, pp 12–15.

Prime Minister. In the two-year period following the triggering of this provision, the British political establishment was engulfed with the question of what form of relationship the UK could realistically have with the EU. Even though this two-year period and a number of extensions lapsed, and the UK eventually left the EU, it does not seem that we are any wiser as to the answer to that initial question. At the time of finalising this book, the UK is still in the midst of a transition period and as such bound by all EU laws, without any involvement in the governance of the EU. During this period, the Court of Justice also continues to have jurisdiction during this period. This period is due to end on 31 December 2020.

Even in the absence of a global pandemic such as Covid-19, an eleven-month transition period to organise Britain's trade relationship with the EU and the rest of the world seems very optimistic. In any case, the UK government has indicated that it will not ask for an extension and has even legislated against an extension.[210] Therefore, unless there is a last-minute compromise by either or both parties (not unheard of in EU political affairs), there might not be a trade agreement between the EU and the UK.

Technically, as Member States have retained exclusive competence in the area of direct taxation and especially corporate taxation, leaving the EU is not expected to have much impact as in other harmonised areas (e.g. customs and excise). In fact, a great amount of the Brexit negotiations dealt with the latter. Member States can still set their tax bases, their tax rates and to a large extent can still design their fiscal policies. As shown in this book, under general EU law, there is an overall obligation not to discriminate against non-nationals, not to fall foul of the fundamental freedoms and the state aid prohibition, but there is no harmonisation. This is notwithstanding harmonisation proposals and initiatives throughout the years – the most important of which were considered in this chapter.

The UK's relationship with the EU is, for the time being, governed by two instruments: the Withdrawal Agreement[211] and the Political Declaration.[212] The Withdrawal Agreement provides detailed rules in specific areas for the orderly withdrawal of the UK from the EU. The Political Declaration sets out the framework for the future relationship between the EU and the UK and the structure of treaty negotiations on this relationship. The final version of the Political Declaration

---

[210] European Union Withdrawal Act 2018, s 15A, as amended by the European Union (Withdrawal Agreement) Act 2020, s 33.

[211] Agreement on the withdrawal of the United Kingdom of Great Britain and Northern Ireland from the European Union and the European Atomic Energy Community (2019/C 384 I/01). For the previous version of this agreement which was rejected several times by the UK Parliament, see Draft Agreement on the withdrawal of the United Kingdom of Great Britain and Northern Ireland from the European Union and the European Atomic Energy Community, as agreed at negotiators' level on 14 November 2018.

[212] See Political declaration setting out the framework for the future relationship between the European Union and the United Kingdom (2019/C 384 I/02).

signalled that the future relationship would be a looser form of economic and regulatory integration.[213]

It is beyond the scope of this book to examine these instruments and their impact on UK tax law. It is important to note, however, that a controversial aspect of the Political Declaration was the various commitments to level playing field arrangements, including in the area of taxation.[214] This provision requires both the UK and the EU to uphold the common high standards relating (inter alia) to tax matters and in particular to commit to the principles of good governance in the area of taxation and to the curbing of harmful tax practices.[215] Compared to the previous level playing field commitments included in the initial version of the Withdrawal Agreement, the current provision is broader but less prescriptive.[216]

It is obvious that the EU is concerned that the UK will engage in aggressive tax competition after Brexit by introducing a highly competitive regime, in order to attract capital and investments. This is at a time that the Commission is drawing plans to curb such practices within the EU, as shown in 1.6.3. The insertion of a tax good governance clause, which the EU is likely to insist upon in its future trade relationship with the UK, is nevertheless a very bold move. This shows the impact of the soft law initiatives discussed in the previous sections, but also the determination

---

[213] See Chalmers D, Davies G and Monti G, 'Updated Chapter 10: Brexit' (2020) *European Union Law: Text and Materials*, 4th edn (Cambridge University Press, 2019 Online Student Resources), p 6, www.cambridge.org/files/4915/9160/3600/9781108463591_c10_online.pdf.

[214] See para 77 of the 2019 Political Declaration, which reads as follows: 'Given the Union and the United Kingdom's geographic proximity and economic interdependence, the future relationship must ensure open and fair competition, encompassing robust commitments to ensure a level playing field. The precise nature of commitments should be commensurate with the scope and depth of the future relationship and the economic connectedness of the Parties. These commitments should prevent distortions of trade and unfair competitive advantages. To that end, the Parties should uphold the common high standards applicable in the Union and the United Kingdom at the end of the transition period in the areas of state aid, competition, social and employment standards, environment, climate change, and relevant tax matters. The Parties should in particular maintain a robust and comprehensive framework for competition and state aid control that prevents undue distortion of trade and competition; commit to the principles of good governance in the area of taxation and to the curbing of harmful tax practices; and maintain environmental, social and employment standards at the current high levels provided by the existing common standards. In so doing, they should rely on appropriate and relevant Union and international standards, and include appropriate mechanisms to ensure effective implementation domestically, enforcement and dispute settlement. The future relationship should also promote adherence to and effective implementation of relevant internationally agreed principles and rules in these domains, including the Paris Agreement.'

[215] Ibid.

[216] In the 2018 Withdrawal Agreement, the UK had committed to good governance in the tax area, which included the global standards on transparency and exchange of information, fair taxation, the BEPS standards and the Code of Conduct on Business Taxation. Also, it had committed to continue to apply the Directive on Administrative Cooperation (Directive 2011/16) and the Anti-Tax Avoidance Directive (Directive 2016/1164). The preceding Political Declaration contained similar provisions. See Art 79 (in Pt II, XIV 'Level playing field for open and fair competition') of Political declaration setting out the framework for the future relationship between the European Union and the United Kingdom (22 November 2018). These instruments were not ratified by the UK Parliament.

of the Commission (and the Union) to commit third countries to its vision of tax good governance.

Whether or not the UK will ultimately uphold these high standards would, arguably, depend on whether a (favourable) trade agreement is reached. At the time of writing, there is still, unfortunately, great uncertainty over the future relationship between the EU and the UK.

1.7 THE FUTURE OF EU CORPORATE TAX LAW

It is no secret that the Commission prefers (and has always preferred) EU-wide corporate harmonisation to promote the competitiveness of the Internal Market and the efficient allocation of capital. In the early years its approach was over-ambitious, the focus being on harmonisation as evinced in the various reports. However, in subsequent years it became apparent that ad hoc, targeted measures against specific tax obstacles had a better chance of success than harmonisation proposals that challenged fundamental aspects of Member States' tax systems. This approach was buttressed and to an extent became a necessity, following the erosive effect of the judgments of the Court of Justice. At the same time the Commission has not abandoned some of its more ambitious plans for reform, which tend to resurface when there is some momentum due to international tax reforms.

Indeed, the BEPS project has provided this much needed momentum for further EU harmonising legislation, even though most of this legislation focuses on the protection of Member State tax bases rather than the elimination of tax obstacles to cross-border movement, as was the leitmotif for the development of EU corporate tax law up until recently. These legislative developments are examined in detail in the next chapter. What was considered in this chapter from section 1.5 onwards were the soft law developments, which have helped shape the EU's external fiscal policy mostly as it relates to corporate matters. This is a remarkable achievement, considering how difficult it has proved historically for Member States to agree to *any* internal common fiscal rules. It would seem from the latest Action Plan that the various soft law initiatives have also given impetus to proposals and initiatives pursuing a more comprehensive tax agenda within the EU.

It is undeniable that since the first publication of this book, the power dynamics have changed in this area; so have the priorities of the Commission and of the remaining Member States. This is understandable given political developments the impact of which has not yet been fully absorbed in the fiscal setting. These issues will be further explored in Chapter 9.

The contents of this book are based on materials available up to 1 August 2020.

2

EU Corporate Tax Legislation

The strategic efforts of the Commission to promote further integration of Member State tax systems were explored in the previous chapter. It was explained how, in the past, institutional limitations played a crucial role in delaying integration, giving rise to ad hoc and targeted measures. There are currently eight instruments on direct[1] taxes which are mostly relevant to corporate taxation: seven Directives and one Convention. The Directives are the Parent-Subsidiary Directive, the Merger Directive, the Interest and Royalties Directive, the Anti-Tax Avoidance Directive, the Mutual Assistance Directive for the Recovery of Taxes, the Directive on Administrative Cooperation and the Tax Dispute Resolution Mechanisms Directive. There is also the Arbitration Convention, which aims to eliminate double taxation arising from transfer pricing adjustments and settle disputes between Member State competent authorities.

This chapter examines the above instruments and relevant case law of the Court of Justice[2] though the Merger Directive and the Anti-Tax Avoidance Directive are discussed in more detail in Chapter 6 and Chapter 7. This chapter also examines pending legislative initiatives, focusing on recent proposals and the Commission's work in progress.

2.1 THE PARENT-SUBSIDIARY DIRECTIVE

When dividends are paid cross-border, there can be both economic and juridical double taxation. There would be economic double taxation if the dividends have been taxed as corporate profits of the distributing company and then as dividends. There would also be juridical double taxation if the dividends were taxed upon

---

[1] For a long time, the only legislative instrument was the Capital Duties Directive enacted in 1969 (Council Directive 69/335/EEC), which dealt with indirect taxes on the raising of capital. Other than this Directive, all other legislative initiatives had failed or been postponed until the 1990s. See analysis in Chapter 1.

[2] Unless stated otherwise, case references throughout this book relate to the judgments of the Court of Justice.

distribution by the host state and in the hands of the recipient shareholder by the home state. The first tax would be a dividend/withholding type of tax; the latter would be an income tax. Countries that operate classical systems are often faced with this problem – the imposition of economic double taxation on corporate profits. Similar issues arise with interest and royalties, but as these tend to be deductible from corporate profits, the problem is one of juridical double taxation rather than economic double taxation.

The Dividends Article of the OECD Model Tax Convention gives a prima facie but non-exclusive right to tax to the state of residence of the recipient (i.e. the home state).[3] The state of the company paying the dividends (i.e. the host state) has an additional right to tax those dividends, but this is subject to limitations. The limitations vary according to whether the recipient beneficial owner, who must be a resident of the other contracting state, has a certain amount of shareholding in the distributing company's capital. If the beneficial owner is a company that holds directly at least 25 per cent of the capital of the company paying the dividends, then the host state tax cannot exceed 5 per cent of the gross amount of the dividends. Otherwise, the tax rate is limited to 15 per cent of the gross amount of the dividends.[4] The lower rate for higher shareholdings in the capital of the distributing company is attributable to the fact that the host state can already tax the company's profits.[5] The logic is that such payments of profits 'should be taxed less heavily to avoid recurrent taxation and to facilitate international investment'.[6]

It should be emphasised that, under the OECD Model Tax Convention, neither the home state nor the host state has exclusive taxing rights and this point is expressly made in the Commentary.[7] However, any host state withholding taxes can be limited according to the nature of the investment. Therefore, under the OECD Model Tax Convention, there is only an attempt to mitigate, rather than eliminate, economic and juridical double taxation.

By contrast, the starting point under the Parent-Subsidiary Directive[8] is that both juridical and economic double taxation should be eliminated as regards profit

---

[3] The first paragraph of Art 10 of the OECD Model Tax Convention provides that '[d]ividends paid by a company which is a resident of a Contracting State to a resident of the other Contracting State may be taxed in that other State'.

[4] There is an additional factor in that if the beneficiary of dividends paid by a distributing company in the host state has a permanent establishment in that state, then Art 10(1) and (2) of the OECD Model Tax Convention does not apply. See Art 10(4) of the OECD Model Tax Convention.

[5] OECD Commentary on Art 10, para 9.

[6] Ibid, para 10. It may also depend on whether the home state of the recipient taxes those profits.

[7] OECD Commentary on Art 10, para 4. As pointed out, exclusive taxing rights to either home states or host states would not have been acceptable, nor feasible. Ibid, paras 5–6.

[8] Council Directive 2011/96/EU of 30 November 2011 on the common system of taxation applicable in the case of parent companies and subsidiaries of different Member States (Parent-Subsidiary Directive). This has codified previous versions of the Directive: Council Directive 90/435/EEC of 23 July 1990 on the Common System of Taxation Applicable in the Case of Parent Companies and Subsidiaries in the Different Member States, amended by Council Directive 2003/123/EC of 22 December 2003.

distributions between parent companies and subsidiaries in different Member States, as well as through their permanent establishments.[9] To this end, under certain circumstances discussed below, the Directive prevents the host state – here the Member State in which a subsidiary company is resident – from imposing a withholding tax on profits distributed to its parent company. Furthermore, the Directive prevents the home state – here the Member State in which the parent company is resident – from taxing such distributed profits. If the Member State of the parent company does tax such profits, it has to allow the parent company to deduct from the amount of tax due to that fraction of the corporation tax paid by the subsidiary related to those profits. As stated in the Preamble to this Directive, the aim is to encourage the grouping together of companies from different Member States 'in order to create within the Union conditions analogous to those of an internal market and in order thus to ensure the effective functioning of such an internal market'.[10] In the context of the BEPS project, the Parent-Subsidiary Directive was amended to include stronger anti-abuse provisions, which are examined below.[11]

2.1.1 Profit Distribution

The term 'profit distribution' is not defined in the Parent-Subsidiary Directive, but it is meant to be more extensive than the term dividend. It is broadly thought that the term covers disguised or hidden dividend distributions,[12] but not capital gains from the sale or other alienation of the shares,[13] or liquidation distributions.[14] It is uncertain whether the term 'profit distribution' has to be interpreted according to the relevant Member State's law or whether it has an autonomous meaning. As recent case law suggests,[15] some concepts in the Directive are gradually gaining an autonomous meaning and interpretation, though domestic law may still be relevant. Guidance may also be sought from the OECD Model Tax Convention, especially if the Member State seeking to interpret the term is an OECD member country as well.

---

[9] Parent-Subsidiary Directive, Art 1. It should be noted that throughout the book, the terms 'branch' and 'permanent establishment' are used interchangeably. This is because while the OECD Model Tax Convention and the EU direct tax directives use the term 'permanent establishment', in case law references are more often made to a 'branch'.
[10] See Recital 4 of the Preamble.
[11] See 2.1.2. and 7.1.
[12] See Marjaana Helminen, 'Taxation of Passive Income', in Christiana HJI Panayi, Werner Halsehner, Edoardo Traversa (eds), *Research Handbook in European Union Taxation Law* (Elgar Publishing, 2020) ch 11; Marjaana Helminen, *The Dividend Concept in International Tax Law – Dividend Concepts between Corporate Entities* (The Hague: Kluwer Law, 1999).
[13] There is nothing preventing Member States from including capital gains in the definition of profit distributions.
[14] See Parent-Subsidiary Directive, Art 4(1).
[15] See, for example, the case law discussed in 2.1.5.

While a straightforward dividend might be recognised as a profit distribution for the purposes of the Directive by most Member States in their capacity as host states, problems may arise with more 'exotic' types of dividends.[16] In the first edition of this book, it was noted how it was uncertain at the time whether constructive dividends (e.g. interest payments recharacterised as dividends) would enjoy the protection of the Parent-Subsidiary Directive. As shown in 2.1.2, if there is no shareholding relationship (or the requisite shareholding relationship) between the payer of the recharacterised dividends and the recipient, then the Directive does not apply. Furthermore, if the issue is one of different characterisation between the Member State of the payer and the payee, then the 2014 amendment to the Parent-Subsidiary Directive[17] which tackles hybrid loans and mismatches would be relevant, as it provides that the parent company is only obliged to 'refrain from taxing such profits to the extent that such profits are not deductible by the subsidiary, and tax such profits to the extent that such profits are deductible by the subsidiary'.[18] The purpose of this amendment was to avoid situations of double non-taxation deriving from mismatches in the tax treatment of profit distributions between the Member States.[19] The situation could also fall under domestic anti-abuse rules or even the Directive's new general anti-abuse rule in Art 1(2), which is analysed in more detail below and in 2.1.5.

2.1.2 Eligibility Requirements

The Directive covers both the making and the receipt of profit distribution between a parent company and a subsidiary.[20] This is set out in Article 1 of the Directive, which also contains anti-abuse provisions. Domestic or agreement-based provisions required for the prevention of fraud or abuse are not prohibited.[21] Furthermore, the Parent-Subsidiary Directive was amended in 2015 to include a new general anti-abuse rule, which allows the Member States not to grant the benefits of the Directive to 'an arrangement or a series of arrangements that, having been put into place for the main purpose or one of the main purposes of obtaining a tax advantage which defeats the object or purpose of this Directive, are not genuine having regard to all relevant facts and circumstances'.[22] This provision is discussed further in section 2.1.5.

---

[16] Art 10(3) of the OECD Model Tax Convention.
[17] See Council Directive 2014/86/EU of 8 July 2014 amending Directive 2011/96/EU on the common system of taxation applicable in the case of parent companies and subsidiaries of different Member States. For this amendment's background, see Christiana HJI Panayi, *Advanced Issues in International and European Tax Law* (Hart Publishing, 2015), ch 5.
[18] See new Art 4(1)(a).
[19] See para 3, preamble to Council Directive 2014/86/EU of 8 July 2014.
[20] The Directive applies to distributions of profits received by parent companies from their subsidiaries in another Member State and vice versa Art 1(1).
[21] Parent-Subsidiary Directive, Art 1(4).
[22] See amended Art 1(2) introduced by Council Directive (EU) 2015/121 of 27 January 2015 amending Directive 2011/96/EU on the common system of taxation applicable in the case of parent companies

2.1 The Parent-Subsidiary Directive

In order to qualify as a company of a Member State, a company must:

(a) take one of the forms listed in the Annex of the Directive;[23]
(b) be considered to be resident in a Member State for tax purposes according to the laws of that Member State while not being considered, under the terms of a double taxation agreement concluded with a third state, to be resident for tax purposes outside the Union; and[24]
(c) be subject to one of the taxes listed in the Annex to the Directive, without the possibility of an option or of being exempt, or to any other tax which may be substituted for any of those taxes.[25]

With effect from 1 January 2005, the Directive applies to profit distributions from a subsidiary to a permanent establishment of a company in another Member State, but only if the subsidiary is situated in a Member State other than the Member State of the permanent establishment.[26] The Directive also applies to profit distributions made by companies of a Member State to permanent establishments situated in another Member State of companies of the same Member State as the distributing company.

The term 'permanent establishment' is described as a fixed place of business situated in a Member State through which the business of a company of another Member State is wholly or partly carried on in so far as the profits of that place of business are subject to tax in the Member State in which it is situated by virtue of the relevant tax treaty or, in the absence of such tax treaty, by national law.[27] This definition is very similar to the basic definition of the term under the OECD Model Tax Convention,[28] but not identical. While it is uncertain whether the concept of permanent establishment is to be interpreted in light of the OECD Model

---

and subsidiaries of different Member States. For this amendment's background, see Christiana HJI Panayi, *Advanced Issues in International and European Tax Law*, ch 5.

[23] Parent-Subsidiary Directive, Art 2(a)(i).
[24] Ibid, Art 2(a)(ii).
[25] Ibid, Art 2(a)(iii).
[26] This is similar to Art 10(4) of the OECD Model Tax Convention whereby when the beneficial owner of dividends in the home state carries on business in the state of the distributing company (i.e. the host state) through a permanent establishment, and the dividends are effectively connected with such host state permanent establishment, then Art 7 applies. As a result, dividends would be taxed fully without the limitations of Art 10, but expenses would have to be deducted. Art 10(4) does not apply just because the beneficiary of dividends paid by the distributing company in the source state has a permanent establishment in that state. The dividends must be paid in respect of holdings forming part of the assets of the permanent establishment or otherwise effectively connected with that establishment. This requires more than merely recording the shareholding in the books of the permanent establishment for accounting purposes. The 'economic' ownership of the holding must be allocated to that permanent establishment under the principles developed in the Committee's report entitled Attribution of Profits to Permanent Establishments. See paras 31–32.1 of the Commentary to Art 10. Art 10(4) of the OECD Model Tax Convention appears to be more nuanced than the provision of the Directive.
[27] Parent-Subsidiary Directive, Art 2(b).
[28] See Art 5(1) of the OECD Model Tax Convention.

Commentary and its post-BEPS amendments, arguably, to the extent that the Parent-Subsidiary Directive does not provide a more comprehensive definition, taxpayers (and tax authorities) can fall back on domestic or treaty-based definitions which might well be influenced by the OECD Model Commentary.[29]

Contrary to the Interest and Royalties Directive, the Parent-Subsidiary Directive does not contain any rules on determining when profits are considered to be paid by a company or a permanent establishment. A company is considered a parent company for the purposes of the Parent-Subsidiary Directive if it has a holding of at least 10 per cent of the capital in another company.[30] The threshold test of 10 per cent is a minimum standard, and the Member States may impose even lower thresholds. Member States also have the option to replace, by means of a bilateral agreement, the criterion of minimum holding in the capital with that of minimum holding of voting rights.[31]

It is not just the form of company which is prescribed or the type of tax which it should be subject to for the Directive to apply. The company must actually be liable to pay some tax and not be effectively exempt. In the Belgische Staat case,[32] the Court of Justice was asked to examine the applicability of the Parent-Subsidiary Directive on dividends paid by a Belgian subsidiary to its parent companies, which were Dutch investment funds.[27] As these funds were subject to corporate income tax but effectively *not* taxed in their country of residence, they did not qualify as a 'company of a Member State' for the purposes of the Parent-Subsidiary Directive. The Court of Justice emphasised that Article 2(c) of the Directive laid down a positive criterion (being subject to the tax in question) and a negative criterion (not being exempt from that tax and not having the possibility of an option to be exempt) for qualifying as a company.[33] Accordingly, just because the Dutch collective investment funds were 'subject to' a corporate income tax (albeit 0 per cent) on the distributions was not sufficient to fall within the scope of the Directive – they had to actually be liable to pay (*some*) corporate income tax. The same conclusion was reached in the Danish tax cases, where it was held that even if the Luxembourg investment fund was formally subject to corporate income tax in Luxembourg, it could not benefit from the Directive if the interest income was in fact exempt.[34]

---

[29] For example, the Parent-Subsidiary Directive does not contain provisions for an agency permanent establishment and a service permanent establishment. As explained in the first edition to this book, it is questionable whether a dividend paid to an agency permanent establishment or a service permanent establishment of a qualifying subsidiary can be entitled to the exemption under the Parent-Subsidiary Directive. Certainly, freedom of establishment and the freedom to provide services may be triggered.

[30] Parent-Subsidiary Directive, Art 3(1).

[31] Ibid, Art 3(2)(a). See also Georg Kofler, *The Relationship between the Fundamental Freedoms and Directives in the Area of Direct Taxation*, Dirritoe Pratica Tributaria Internazionale 2/2009.

[32] Case C-448/15 Belgische Staat v. Comm VA Wereldhave Belgium, ECLI:EU:C:2017:180.

[33] Ibid, para 31.

[34] Joined Cases C-115/16, C-118/16, C-119/16 and C-299/16 N Luxembourg 1, X Denmark A/S, C Danmark I, Z Denmark ApS, ECLI:EU:C:2019:134 and Joined Cases C-116/16 and C-117/16 T Danmark, Y Denmark Aps, ECLI:EU:C:2019:135 (the Danish tax cases). See analysis in 2.1.5.

Member States are allowed to refuse to apply the benefits of the Directive to companies that do not maintain the relevant holding for a certain period, not exceeding two years.[35] In Denkavit,[36] the Court of Justice found that this provision did not require the holding period to have elapsed on the date the dividend was paid in order for the parent company to be entitled to the benefit of the exemption. However, Member States were free to determine, in light of the requirements of their domestic legal systems, the detailed arrangements for ensuring that this period was observed.[37] As the Court of Justice noted, the Directive did not require a Member State to grant the exemption from the beginning of this period without being certain if it will be able to obtain payment of the tax later, if the parent company failed to observe the minimum holding period. Since the Directive was silent on the matter, it was not for the Court of Justice to impose a particular arrangement on the Member States. Therefore, the Member States were entitled to put in place mechanisms that ensured that the minimum holding period was observed before granting the benefit. To the extent that it was observed, however, the benefit had to be granted.

Whether or not a company is a parent company for the purposes of the Directive has been examined in a number of cases.

In Les Vergers du Vieux Tauves,[38] a Belgian court asked whether a company that owns a right of usufruct over shares in another company may or must be regarded as a parent company within the meaning of the Parent-Subsidiary Directive. The Court of Justice, disagreeing with its Advocate General, found that the right of a usufructuary was not covered by the Directive. For the parent company's status to be attributed to a company, Article 3 of the Directive required the company to have a holding in the capital of another company. This referred back to the legal relationship between the parent company and the subsidiary. Therefore, when the parent company transferred to a third party, in this case to a usufructuary, a legal relationship with the subsidiary, this did not make the usufructuary a parent company for the purposes of the Directive.[39] It was important for the parent company to receive distributed profits by virtue of its association with its subsidiary. In this case, however, the usufructuary received profits under its right of usufruct, rather than as a result of the association with its subsidiary.[40] The Court of Justice concluded that for the purposes of the Parent-Subsidiary Directive, the Community legislature regarded the 'parent company' as being one single company.[41] Nevertheless, the Court of Justice thought that there could be a breach of fundamental freedoms.

[35] Parent-Subsidiary Directive, Art 4(2).
[36] Joined Cases C-283/94, C-291/94 and C-292/94 Denkavit International BV, VITIC Amsterdam BV and Voormeer BV v. Bundesamt für Finanzen [1996] ECR I-5063.
[37] Ibid, para 34.
[38] Case C-48/07 Les Vergers du Vieux Tauves [2008] ECR I-10627.
[39] Ibid, paras 38–9.
[40] Ibid, para 41.
[41] Ibid, para 43.

The fact that under the Parent-Subsidiary Directive, the parent company's association with its subsidiary was in this case crucial for the purposes of conferring the exemption may have implications as far as recharacterised interest payments are concerned. If the existence of a shareholding relationship is a precondition for the application of the Parent-Subsidiary Directive, interest recharacterised as equity under thin capitalisation rules[42] may be completely excluded from the Directive's scope, as the underlying relationship would be a contractual one. Arguably, this situation could also be caught by the new amendment to the Directive aimed at excluding double non-taxation,[43] if the issue is one of different characterisation by the Member State of the payer and the Member State of the payee company.

In Gaz de France,[44] Advocate General Mazák and the Court of Justice followed a similarly restrictive interpretation of the Parent-Subsidiary Directive in finding that the term 'company of a Member State' under the Directive could only encompass one of the companies expressly listed in the relevant Annex. Here Gaz de France – Berliner Investissement SA was a company established in France, which had the legal form of a *société par actions simplifiée*.[45] When profits were distributed from its German wholly-owned subsidiary, the tax was withheld at source. It was disputed whether this French company could be a parent company for the purposes of the Directive. If not, the referring court asked whether there was, in any case, a breach of the freedom of establishment or the free movement of capital.

The Court of Justice held that under Article 2(a) and point (f) of the Annex, a French *société par actions simplifiée* was not a company of a Member State for the purposes of the Directive before it was amended in 2003. The Directive did not seek to introduce a common system for all companies of the Member States or all types of holdings.[46] In addition, the fundamental principle of legal certainty precluded the list of companies in the Annex to the Directive from being interpreted as merely an indicative list.[47] The extension of the scope of the Directive by analogy to other forms of comparable companies was not, therefore, admissible.[48] The Court of Justice also found that the restriction of the scope of the Directive, as a result of the list approach, was not enough to create a restriction on the freedom of establishment or the free movement of capital.[49] Given that all the direct tax Directives contain lists of the types of companies that can benefit from their provisions, the judgment of the Court of Justice in Gaz de France is understandable.

---

[42] For an overview of thin capitalisation regimes, see 7.3.
[43] Art 4(1)(a) of the Parent-Subsidiary Directive, analysed in 2.1.3.
[44] Case C-247/08 Gaz de France – Berliner Investissement SA v. Bundeszentralamt für Steuern [2009] ECR I-09225.
[45] After 2002, it had become a 'société anonyme'.
[46] Case C-247/08 Gaz de France, para 36.
[47] Ibid, para 38.
[48] Ibid, para 43.
[49] Ibid, paras 61–2.

Recently,⁵⁰ in the GVC Services case, the Court of Justice found that the Parent-Subsidiary Directive did not apply to companies incorporated in Gibraltar. It was noted that the Annex required that companies were incorporated under UK rules (or another Member State's rules). Following earlier case law, it was reiterated that for reasons of legal certainty, it was not possible to extend the scope of the Directive by analogy to companies other than those companies listed in the Annex. This was because the material scope of the Directive had been defined by means of an exhaustive list.

2.1.3 Taxing the Profit Distribution

It was shown above that, similarly to the OECD Model Tax Convention, the tax treatment under the Parent-Subsidiary Directive depends on whether the underlying association is a portfolio one or not – albeit with a divergent benchmark of 10 per cent rather than 25 per cent. However, once that benchmark is met, and the other relevant conditions are fulfilled, under the Directive, there is a prohibition for any home state or host state tax on the profit distributions. There is no beneficial ownership requirement as in Article 10 of the OECD Model Tax Convention and under the Interest and Royalties Directive. The implications of this were highlighted in the Danish tax cases, discussed in more detail in 2.1.5. Arguably, the new general anti-abuse provision of the Parent-Subsidiary Directive could be used by tax authorities to deal with situations where beneficial ownership might be lacking for these purposes.⁵¹ Furthermore, the general anti-abuse rule of the Anti-Tax Avoidance Directive could also be used in this way.⁵²

The Directive bases its analysis of inbound and outbound situations on subsidiaries paying dividends to parent companies. However, the reverse could also apply – that is, there could be profit distributions from parent companies to subsidiaries.⁵³ Arguably, in such cases, the wording of the Directive should be reversed so that 'parent company' reads as 'subsidiary company'. It would have been better if the terms 'distributing' and 'recipient' companies were used. The analysis here follows the wording of the Directive.

As far as the taxation of inbound payments is concerned, Article 4 is the focal point that caters for both exemption and credit countries.⁵⁴ Where a parent company or its permanent establishment, by virtue of the association of the parent company

---

⁵⁰ See Case C-458/18 GVC Services (Bulgaria) EOOD v. Direktor na Direktsia Obzhalvane I danacha asigurieina praktika –Sofia, ECLI:EU:C:2020:266.
⁵¹ See 2.1.5.
⁵² See 2.6 and 7.1.
⁵³ Parent-Subsidiary Directive, Art 1(1).
⁵⁴ See Uwe Ilhi, Kerstin Maimer, Peter Schonewille and IvarTuominen, 'Dividend Taxation in the European Union' (EU Report), *Trends in Company Shareholder Taxation: Single or Double Taxation?*, Cahiers de droit fiscal international, Vol 88a (The Hague: Kluwer Law International, 2003), p 77.

with its subsidiary, receives distributed profits, the home state (i.e. the Member State in which the parent company is resident or the permanent establishment is situated) must refrain from taxing the profits.[55] As mentioned in 2.1.1, in order to avoid double non-taxation, the 2014 amendment to this Directive has now qualified this obligation to exempt the profits received, to the extent that these profits were not deductible by the subsidiary.[56] This amendment also provides that if such profits were deductible by the subsidiary, then they should be taxed.[57] While this makes sense in jurisdictions which would otherwise have taxed parent companies on their inbound profits in the absence of the Parent-Subsidiary Directive, it is not clear how this provision is to be interpreted in cases where the jurisdiction under general law does not tax inbound distributions of profits at all.

The next subparagraph of Article 4(1) has remained the same and deals with credit countries. If the home state taxes the profit distributions, then it must allow the parent company and the permanent establishment to deduct from the amount of tax due the fraction of the underlying corporation tax related to those profits and paid by the subsidiary and any lower-tier subsidiaries.[58] These provisions do not apply where the company is in liquidation.[59] The credit does not need to exceed the tax due in the home state – it is an ordinary credit, not a full credit.[60] Furthermore, there is nothing (in the Directive) to stop the home state from applying the credit method to foreign-sourced dividends and the exemption method to domestic dividends, though in certain circumstances this may fall foul of freedom of establishment or the free movement of capital, as shown in Chapter 5.

There is also a prohibition for inbound withholding taxes. Under Article 6, the Member State of a parent company may not charge withholding taxes on the profits that such a company receives from its subsidiary. This was a special provision inserted for Belgium, which at the time imposed such taxes.

Member States have the option to provide that any charges relating to the holding and losses resulting from the distribution of the profits of the subsidiary may not be deducted from the taxable profits of the parent company.[61] This is because such costs

---

[55] Parent-Subsidiary Directive, Art 4(1)(a).
[56] Ibid, Art 4(1)(a).
[57] Ibid.
[58] This is subject to the condition that at each tier a company and its lower-tier subsidiary fall within the definitions laid down in Art 2 and meet the requirements provided for in Art 3, up to the limit of the corresponding tax amount due. See Art 4(1)(b).
[59] Parent-Subsidiary Directive, Art 4. See Case C-371/11 Punch Graphix Prepress Belgium NV v. Belgium, ECLI:EU:C:2012:647, where it was held that the dissolution of a company in a merger by acquisition could not be considered as liquidation for the purposes of Art 4(1) of the Parent-Subsidiary Directive.
[60] There is an exception for fiscally transparent companies. In such cases, the Member State of the parent company may tax it on its share of the profits of its (fiscally transparent) subsidiary as and when those profits arise. However, that Member State must not tax the distributed profits of the subsidiary: see Art 4(2).
[61] Parent-Subsidiary Directive, Art 4(3).

relate to exempt income. However, as held in the Bosal case,[62] this option must be exercised in compliance with general EU law. In this case, the Court of Justice found that freedom of establishment prohibited the Dutch legislation that made the deductibility of costs connected with a company's shareholding in a subsidiary in another Member State conditional on those costs being indirectly instrumental in making profits that were taxable in the Member State of the parent company. This was notwithstanding the fact that the option to deny the parent company's holding costs was allowed under the Parent-Subsidiary Directive.

Member States are further circumscribed in the exercise of this option in that, under Article 4(2) of the Directive, where the management costs relating to the holding are fixed at a flat rate, the fixed amount cannot exceed 5 per cent of the profits distributed by the subsidiary. In the Banque Fédérative du Crédit Mutual case,[63] the Court of Justice followed the opinion of Advocate General Sharpston that, in calculating the 5 per cent, it was not contrary to the Directive to take account of the gross amount of distributed profits.[64] Tax credits could be included in the fixed amount of the management costs relating to the parent company's holding in the subsidiary.[65] Therefore, it was the total amount of profits distributed, within the meaning of that provision, that was received by the parent company to which the rate of 5 per cent was to be applied.[66]

As mentioned, if the recipient's Member State chooses to tax the distribution, then it must give a credit for the underlying tax and any withholding tax. While this is an ordinary credit, the Court of Justice has held that it must still be given irrespective of whether or not the recipient company is loss-making.

In Cobelfret,[67] the Court of Justice found the Belgian dividend deduction regime incompatible with the Parent-Subsidiary Directive. Under this regime, inbound dividends were always included in a Belgian company's tax base, but the dividends[68] were only deducted in so far as the parent company had taxable profits in the relevant tax period. No deduction was made in a year when no profits were earned. Unused deductions could not be carried forward. This provision was applicable regardless of the origin of the received dividends. The Court of Justice found that the Belgian system did not provide for the systematic exemption of dividends, contrary to Article 4(1) of the Parent-Subsidiary Directive.[69] The fact that the same

---

[62] Case C-168/01 Bosal Holding BV v. Staatsecretaris van Financiën [2003] ECR I-9409. See analysis in 4.2.1.
[63] Case C-27/07 Banque Fédérative du Crédit Mutual [2008] ECR I-2067.
[64] Banque Federative du Crédit Mutual had argued that for the purposes of Art 4(2), 'profits distributed by the subsidiary' referred to profits net of withholding tax at source.
[65] Ibid, para 46.
[66] Ibid, para 47.
[67] Case C-138/07 Cobelfret [2009] ECR I-00731.
[68] The regime provided for the deduction of 95 per cent of the dividends.
[69] Case C-138/07 Cobelfret, para 35.

regime applied to dividends received from Belgian companies did not justify the wrongful transposition of the Directive into domestic law.[70]

Furthermore, the fact that the OECD Model Tax Convention contained no precise rules governing the arrangements under which the exemption system was to be implemented again did not mean that Belgium could establish its own rules contrary to the Parent-Subsidiary Directive.[71] Therefore, while a refund of the excess credit was not required under the Directive, Article 4(1) was interpreted as requiring the carry-forward of such credit.

In joined cases, KBC Bank and Beheer,[72] the Court of Justice followed Cobelfret and extended the scope of the decision to internal situations and potentially to dividends from third countries.

In a recent case, the Brussels Securities case,[73] the Court of Justice examined the compatibility of the combined application of the Belgian dividend received deduction with the imputation of other tax deductions; more specifically, the notional interest deduction. Under Belgian rules, dividends received by a parent company were first added to its taxable income, and afterwards, an amount corresponding to 95 per cent of those dividends was deducted. When the dividends received exceeded the taxable income, any surplus could be carried forward with no time limits and deducted against the taxable income of subsequent years. However, this surplus had to be deducted before other deductible items, in particular, the deduction for risk capital which could be carried forward for a maximum of seven years.

Both the Advocate General and the Court of Justice found the Belgian legislation in breach of Article 4 of the Parent-Subsidiary Directive. The fact that the surplus was to be carried forward in subsequent tax years indefinitely, with that deduction having priority over another tax deduction which could only be carried forward for a limited time, led to the loss of a tax advantage for the parent company and as a corollary, an increase of the effective corporate tax rate in subsequent years. This would not have happened if the dividends were excluded from the parent company's tax base. Therefore, Belgian rules were not fiscally neutral as regards the tax treatment of dividends received from foreign subsidiaries, in breach of Article 4 of the Parent-Subsidiary Directive. Arguably, this judgment has important implications in this area, as any restrictions that potentially result in the loss of a tax deduction could be construed as indirect taxation of dividends in breach of the Directive.

---

[70] Ibid, Belgium has since amended its legislation in accordance with the Court's decision. See also, a reference to the Court of Justice, which dealt with the same issues as in Cobelfret, Case C-514/08 Atenor Group SA v. Belgian State which was removed from the Court's register. See [2009] OJ C 141/36.
[71] Case C-138/07 Cobelfret, para 54.
[72] Joined Cases C-439/07 and 499/07 KBC Bank and Beleggen, Risicokapitaal, Beheer [2009] ECR I-4409, Order of the Court 4 June 2009.
[73] Case C-389/18 Brussels Securities SA v. État Belge, ECLI:EU:C:2019:1132.

The Parent-Subsidiary Directive also contains an important prohibition for outbound withholding taxes. Under Article 5(1), the Member State in which the subsidiary resides must not impose a withholding tax on a distribution by a subsidiary to a parent company.[74] Therefore, the Directive seeks to eliminate all taxation on the distribution, as it has already been taxed as corporate profits. Both juridical and economic double taxation are avoided when the Directive applies.

2.1.4 What Is a Withholding Tax?

Again, the term 'withholding tax' is not defined. Article 7 describes what the term does not cover,[75] but not what it does cover. The case law of the Court of Justice is useful in this respect.

In Epson,[76] the Court of Justice had to decide if the Portuguese succession and donation tax on transfers (without consideration) of shares in companies was a withholding tax. This tax was levied, at a flat rate of 5 per cent, on dividends paid by companies that had their seat in Portugal.[77] Portugal had argued that the succession and donation tax was not a withholding tax because it was not levied on income but on the value of the security. The Court of Justice disagreed. This was a withholding tax because the chargeable event was the payment of the dividend, the taxable amount was the income from the shares, and the taxable person was the holder of the shares. The Court of Justice emphasised that the actual name of the tax was immaterial. The objective of the Directive was to encourage cooperation between companies in several Member States. This objective would be undermined 'if the Member States were permitted deliberately to deprive companies in other Member States of the benefit of the Directive by subjecting them to taxes having the same effect as a tax on income, even if the name given to the latter places them in the category of tax assets'.[78]

---

[74] There used to be exceptions to the general rule for Greece, Germany and Portugal. See deleted Art 5 (2), (3) and (4) from the original version of the Directive. Where withholding taxes were levied in accordance with these exceptions, the Member State of the parent company had to give credit for such taxes. These derogations have now expired.

[75] See Art 7(1) of the Directive, which stipulates that the term does not cover an advance payment or prepayment *(précompte)* of corporation tax to the Member State of the subsidiary that is made in connection with a distribution of profits to its parent company. It is also clarified in Art 7(2) that the Directive does 'not affect the application of domestic or agreement-based provisions designed to eliminate or lessen economic double taxation of dividends, in particular provisions relating to the payment of tax credits to the recipients of dividends'.

[76] Case C-375/98 Ministério Público, Fazenda Pública v. Epson Europe BV [2000] ECR I-4243.

[77] Portugal was allowed, under ex Art 5(4) of the Directive, to levy a withholding tax on profits distributed to parent companies in the other Member States. The permitted rate of withholding tax was initially 15 per cent, falling to 10 per cent. The question was whether the 5 per cent succession and donation tax counted towards this 15 or 10 per cent limit, or whether that limit applied only to Portuguese corporate income tax.

[78] Case C-375/98 Ministério Público, Fazenda Público v. Epson Europe BV [2000] ECR I-4243, para 24.

In Athinaiki Zythopoiia,[79] the Court of Justice followed the same approach. Here, under Greek laws, when a company whose gross income included non-taxable income or income subject to special (reduced) taxation made a distribution of profits, those profits were deemed to arise proportionally from the non-taxable income or the income subject to special taxation. The grossed-up amounts of this income became fully taxable so far as they were deemed distributed. Those two categories of income would not have been taxable had they remained with the subsidiary and not been distributed to the parent company.

The referring court asked the Court of Justice whether this arrangement amounted to a withholding tax for the purposes of the Parent-Subsidiary Directive. The Court of Justice held that it did. The chargeable event for the taxation at issue was the payment of dividends. The amount of tax was directly related to the size of the distribution. This tax could not be treated as an advance payment or prepayment of corporation tax to the Member State of the subsidiary that was made in connection with a distribution of profits to its parent company, within the meaning of Article 7(1) of the Directive. The charge was on income and levied only in the event of a distribution of dividends and up to the limit of the dividends paid. This was shown by the fact, inter alia, that the increase in the basic taxable amount resulting from the distribution of profits could not be offset against losses carried forward from previous tax years. The Court of Justice stated that 'the nature of a tax, duty or charge must be determined by the court, under Community law, according to the objective characteristics by which it is levied, irrespective of its classification under national law'.[80]

In Océ van der Grinten v. IRC,[81] the Court of Justice looked at the distinction between a withholding tax on the repayment of tax credit and a withholding tax on distributed profits. Here a UK subsidiary distributed dividends to its Dutch parent company and paid advance corporation tax (ACT) to the Inland Revenue in respect of those dividends. Under English law, UK shareholders receiving dividends from UK companies on which the ACT had already been paid were entitled to a tax credit, but foreign shareholders were not. Under the United Kingdom–Netherlands double tax treaty, Dutch shareholders were entitled to one half of the credit. However, both the dividend and the tax credit were subject to 5 per cent tax in the UK.

The Court of Justice held that, in so far as the 5 per cent charge was imposed on the dividends (as opposed to the tax credit), this was a withholding tax prohibited by Article 5(1) of the Parent-Subsidiary Directive. This withholding tax was, however, allowed under Article 7(2), being an agreement-based provision relating to the payment of tax credits to the recipients of dividends and designed to mitigate double taxation.[82]

---

[79] Case C-294/99 Athinaiki Zythopoiia AE v. Greece [2001] ECR I-6797.
[80] Ibid, para 27.
[81] Case C-58/01 Océ van der Grinten v. IRC [2003] ECR I-9809.
[82] Ibid, para 84.

As for the 5 per cent charge on the tax credit, this was not a withholding tax, as it was imposed on the amount of the tax credit and not on the distributed profits. This charge bore some similarity to a withholding tax: the payment of the dividend triggered it, the shareholder was taxed on it, and the tax credit was proportional to the amount of the distribution. However, this charge was not the same as a withholding tax. Rather, it was a fiscal instrument designed to avoid economic double taxation first in the hands of the subsidiary and then in the hands of the parent company. It did not, however, constitute income from shares.[83] Therefore, according to the Court of Justice, there was no need to examine whether this charge fell within the ambit of Art. 7(2) of the Directive.

The above principles should be read in light of the Court's decision in Burda.[84] Here the Court of Justice had to decide whether a tax uplift calculated on the dividends paid by a German company to its Dutch parent was a withholding tax contrary to the Parent-Subsidiary Directive and the freedom of establishment. In 1998, Burda paid dividends to its Dutch parent company. After a tax audit, the German tax authorities reduced Burda's taxed equity basket[85] retroactively. As a result, the dividends paid in 1998 were deemed to have been paid out of the untaxed equity basket and were subject to the tax uplift. Burda argued that this was a withholding tax contrary to the Parent-Subsidiary Directive and the freedom of establishment. On a reference by the German Supreme Court, the Court of Justice found the German rule to be compatible with the Directive and the freedom of establishment. The tax uplift was not a withholding tax, because it was a tax burden of the subsidiary rather than the parent company. Therefore, the taxable person was not the holder of the shares.[86]

The Commission had argued that the economic effect of taxing the subsidiary corresponded to taxing the parent company in as much as the tax was withheld by the company distributing the profits and paid directly to the tax authorities.[87] The Court of Justice disagreed with this argument. There could be no economic assessment of the corporate tax uplift mechanism. Economic considerations, if at all relevant, formed a basis for the application of Article 5(1) of the Directive only if the conditions laid down in the case law were fulfilled.[88] This was not the situation here. Furthermore, there was no breach of freedom of establishment

---

[83] Ibid, para 56.
[84] Case C-284/06 Burda [2008] ECR I-4571.
[85] Under Germany's former imputation system, the distributable equity of German resident companies was divided into taxed and untaxed equity baskets. Depending on which basket was used, the distributing company's corporate tax was reduced or increased to 30 per cent. If a distribution was made out of the taxed basket, the corporation tax was reduced. If it was made out of the untaxed basket, corporation tax increased to 30 per cent. In addition, if a distribution was made out of the taxed basket, a shareholder was granted an imputation credit. Only resident shareholders were entitled to this tax credit.
[86] Case C-284/06 Burda, para 54.
[87] Ibid, para 59.
[88] Ibid, para 62.

because the tax uplift did not depend on the shareholder's place of residence.[89]

In Ferrero,[90] the Court of Justice examined another corrective mechanism in order to determine whether the withholding tax imposed was compatible with the Parent-Subsidiary Directive. Here an adjustment surtax was introduced by the Italian legislature to avoid a situation in which a company receiving a dividend distribution obtained, at the time of that distribution, a tax credit[91] for a tax that, for whatever reason, had not been previously paid by the distributing company or when minimal tax had been paid. The tax treaty between Italy and the Netherlands enabled Dutch parent companies to request a refund of the adjustment surtax paid on dividends distributed by their Italian subsidiaries.[92] However, this refund was subject to a 5 per cent withholding tax. The Italian courts questioned whether this withholding tax was compatible with the Parent-Subsidiary Directive,[93] and the issue was referred to the Court of Justice. The Court found this to be a corrective mechanism, compatible with the Directive.

The salient question was whether the refund of the adjustment surtax that gave rise to the 5 per cent tax could be regarded as a distribution of profits. The fact that the underlying tax treaty specifically categorised the refund of the adjustment surtax as 'dividends' was not decisive.[94] Citing Burda,[95] the Court of Justice found that the adjustment surtax was a corrective mechanism intended to prevent a tax credit from being granted for a tax that had not been paid.[96] The mechanism also applied regardless of whether the parent company was resident in the same Member State or another Member State.[97] The withholding tax on the refund of the adjustment surtax itself could not be regarded as a withholding tax prohibited under Article 5(1) of the Directive, since the taxable person was not the holder of the shares but the company making the distribution.[98] In essence, the refund of the adjustment surtax was considered by the Court of Justice to be equivalent to the transfer of tax revenue

---

[89] Ibid, paras 80–4.
[90] Joined Cases C-338/08 and C-339/08 P Ferrero e C SpA v. Agenzia delle Entrate – Ufficio di Alba and General Beverage Europe BV v. Agenzia delle Entrate – Ufficio di Torino 1 [2010] ECR I-05743.
[91] Under Italian law, an Italian company that received dividends was entitled to a tax credit equal to 9/16ths of the dividends distributed. As the Italian corporate tax rate was 36 per cent, the recipient effectively obtained a tax credit equivalent to the amount of tax charged by the company distributing the dividend.
[92] Art 10(3) of the Italy–Netherlands tax treaty. The Italian company could then deduct that amount in the first tax return it filed after the payment.
[93] Joined Cases C-338/08 and C-339/08, para 20. A withholding tax was also imposed on the dividends paid by the Italian companies to their Dutch parent companies. No questions were asked regarding the compatibility of this withholding tax, nor regarding the compatibility of the tax scheme applied to those dividends. See para 21.
[94] Ibid.
[95] Case C-284/06 Burda. See analysis above.
[96] Ibid, para 30.
[97] Joined Cases C-338/08 and C-339/08, para 33.
[98] Ibid, para 34.

from the Italian authorities to a Dutch company and could not be considered to be income from shares.[99] As a result, this was not a withholding tax contrary to the Parent-Subsidiary Directive.[100]

Later cases dealt with more complex issues relating to the Directive. In the Belgian Fairness Tax case,[14] the Court of Justice was asked to determine whether a Belgian tax was compatible with freedom of establishment and the provisions of the Parent-Subsidiary Directive. The Fairness Tax was a separate assessment of 5.15 per cent levied in case a Belgian company or foreign company with a permanent establishment in Belgium distributed a dividend during a taxable period in which the company's taxable profits were offset against notional interest deductions and/or carried forward tax losses. Shortly after this assessment was introduced, a Belgian corporate taxpayer filed an action before the Belgian Constitutional Court seeking the annulment of this tax. The case was referred to the Court of Justice.

Advocate General Kokott found that the Belgian legislation was compatible with freedom of establishment but was in breach of the Parent-Subsidiary Directive. By applying the Fairness Tax, if a resident corporate taxpayer redistributed dividends (in a taxable period after the taxable period in which it received those dividends), the dividends would be subject to a higher tax burden contrary to the Parent-Subsidiary Directive. This was because the dividends received were, upon redistribution, included (once again) in the tax base because of the Fairness Tax.

The Court of Justice broadly confirmed the Advocate General's opinion. As the taxable person, in this case, was not the holder of the shares but the distributing company, it was found that the Fairness Tax did not qualify as a withholding tax within the meaning of Article 5 of the Directive.[101] However, there was a breach of Article 4 of the Directive because, in the typical case of an intermediary holding company, the application of the Fairness Tax led to the taxation of more than 5 per cent of qualifying dividends received and redistributed by the intermediary. As regards compatibility with the freedom of establishment, it was for the referring court to ascertain whether the method of determining the taxable amount under the Fairness Tax put a non-resident company in a less advantageous position than a resident company.

Another similar case, the AFEP case,[102] was decided on the same day. Here, a French tax rule provided for an additional contribution to corporate income tax (a 3 per cent additional contribution) in respect of profits distributed by a resident company. The Court of Justice found this to be incompatible with the Parent-Subsidiary Directive. Reiterating its conclusion in the Belgian Fairness Tax case, the Court of Justice found that as regards Article 4 of the Directive,

---

[99] Ibid, para 40.
[100] Ibid, para 41.
[101] Ibid, para 67.
[102] Case C-365/16 Association française des entreprises privées (AFEP) and Others v. Ministre des finances et des comptes publics, ECLI:EU:C:2017:378.

there was no distinction between a tax due by the parent company when it received the distributed profits or when it subsequently redistributed those profits. The Court of Justice dismissed the argument put forward by the French government that this provision was applicable only at the stage of collection of profits and not of redistribution.[103] It was irrelevant whether the disputed tax was called a corporate income tax or a withholding tax since the exemption for the parent company under the Directive was not conditional on a certain type of tax. Rather, it applied to all taxes levied by the Member State of residence of the parent company on profits it received from an EU subsidiary.[104] As such, there was no need to answer the second question whether the contribution had the characteristics of a withholding tax.

2.1.5 Tax Avoidance and the Parent-Subsidiary Directive

As mentioned in 2.1.2, the Directive now contains two anti-abuse provisions. Initially, the only anti-abuse provision was listed in Article 1(2), which allowed domestic or agreement-based provisions required for the prevention of fraud or abuse. This has now been shifted to paragraph 4 of Article 1. Furthermore, following an amendment in 2015, the Parent-Subsidiary Directive now has a general anti-abuse provision, which allows the Member States not to grant the benefits of the Directive to 'an arrangement or a series of arrangements that, having been put into place for the main purpose or one of the main purposes of obtaining a tax advantage which defeats the object or purpose of this Directive, are not genuine having regard to all relevant facts and circumstances'.[105] An arrangement could comprise more than one step or part – that is, it could be a series of arrangements. An arrangement or a series of arrangements is to be regarded as not being genuine to the extent that it was not put into place for valid commercial reasons that reflect economic reality.[106] Arguably, the introduction of this general anti-abuse rule ensures fewer limits to the powers of tax authorities to challenge some structures.

As shown in the previous sections, the early cases on the Parent-Subsidiary Directive mostly dealt with the interpretation of provisions offering reliefs and exemptions. More recent case law focuses on the anti-abuse provision of the Directive (mostly ex-Article 1(2) now Article 1(4)), the extent to which the reliefs under the Directive could be held back by tax authorities and if so, under which circumstances.

---

[103] Ibid, para 29.
[104] Ibid, para 33.
[105] See amended Art 1(2) introduced by Council Directive (EU) 2015/121 of 27 January 2015 amending Directive 2011/96/EU on the common system of taxation applicable in the case of parent companies and subsidiaries of different Member States.
[106] See new Art 1(3).

2.1 The Parent-Subsidiary Directive

In the Eqiom and Enka case,[107] the Court of Justice examined the French tax authorities' refusal to exempt the withholding tax on dividend distributions on the basis of preventing tax evasion or abuse under ex-Article 1(2) of the Parent-Subsidiary Directive. The French company (Eqiom) made the dividend distributions to its Luxembourg parent company (Enka), which was controlled by a Cypriot company, which was itself controlled by a Swiss company. Although national laws in areas subject to exhaustive EU harmonisation were invariably assessed in light of the harmonising measure only (i.e. the Directive), the Court of Justice found that this was not the case here as regards ex-Article 1(2) of the Directive.[108] This provision reflected the general principle of EU law that no one may benefit from rights stemming from the EU legal system for abusive or fraudulent ends. As this provision allowed a derogation from the rules of the Directive, it had to be interpreted strictly,[109] and any Member State powers exercised under this provision could not go beyond the actual terms of that provision.[110]

The Court of Justice noted that ex-Article 1(2) of the Parent-Subsidiary Directive allowed domestic or agreement-based provisions which were 'required' for that purpose (i.e. for preventing tax evasion and abuse). It was questioned whether indeed the national tax legislation satisfied this necessity requirement.[111] In order for national legislation to be regarded as seeking to prevent tax evasion and abuse, its specific objective had to be to prevent conduct involving the creation of wholly artificial arrangements that did not reflect economic reality, the purpose of which was unduly to obtain a tax advantage.[112] Tax measures based on general presumptions or that automatically excluded certain categories of taxpayers from the tax advantage of the Directive went beyond what was necessary to prevent fraud and abuse.[113]

According to the Court of Justice, the mere fact that an EU resident company was directly or indirectly controlled by residents of third states did not, in itself, indicate the existence of a purely artificial arrangement.[114] By subjecting the exemption from withholding tax to the condition that the parent company must establish that the principal purpose or one of the principal purposes of the chain of interests was not to take advantage of the exemption, without the tax authorities being required to provide even prima facie evidence of fraud and abuse, the French tax legislation introduced a general presumption of fraud and abuse. This undermined the objective pursued by the Parent-Subsidiary Directive, namely the prevention of

---

[107] Case C-6/16 Eqiom SAS, formerly Holcim France SAS and Enka SA v. Ministre des Finances et des Comptes publics, ECLI:EU:C:2017:641.
[108] Ibid, paras 17–18.
[109] Ibid, para 26.
[110] Ibid, para 27.
[111] Ibid, paras 28–9.
[112] Ibid, para 30.
[113] Ibid, para 33.
[114] Ibid, para 34.

double taxation of profits distributed by a subsidiary to its parent company.[115] It was also emphasised that it did not follow from any provision of the Directive that the origin of the shareholders of companies resident in the European Union affected the right of those companies to rely on tax advantages provided for by that Directive.[116] While this was an indisputable confirmation at least in the context of the Parent-Subsidiary Directive, it would seem that later cases – namely the Danish tax cases discussed below – have refined this point, allowing the qualification of the rights under the Directive on the basis of an abstract concept of beneficial ownership.

The Court of Justice ruled that the French rules were contrary to ex-Article 1(2). It was also found that, by adopting an initial presumption of abuse where an EU parent company was controlled by shareholders in third states, while the withholding tax exemption was granted automatically to a French parent company even though shareholders in third states controlled it, the French rules restricted the freedom of establishment.[117] The Court of Justice noted that the objective of combating fraud and tax evasion – referring to the practice known as treaty shopping[118] – could potentially justify such a restriction. It was emphasised that the objective of combating fraud and tax evasion, whether under ex-Article 1(2) of the Parent-Subsidiary Directive or as justification to a restriction, had the same scope.[119] It was concluded that the French rules were contrary to ex-Article 1(2) of the Parent-Subsidiary Directive and to the freedom of establishment.

In a later case, the Argenta Spaarbank case,[120] the Court of Justice had to consider the Belgian rules which prevented deductions of costs that did not relate to exempt holdings. In this case, the Belgian tax authority disallowed a deduction of interest paid by a Belgian-based credit institution on the grounds that in the same tax year, this institution had also received exempt dividends from holdings that it had held for less than a full year at the time of distribution. The question referred to the Court of Justice was whether the Belgian rules were compatible with Article 4(2) and ex-Article 1(2) of the Directive.

As regards Article 4(2), the Court of Justice reiterated that this provision had to be interpreted strictly and must not go beyond its actual wording. The specific objective of this provision was to (allow Member States to) prevent a parent company from benefitting from a tax advantage (double deduction). Allowing Member States to deny parent companies the right to deduct interest that was *not* linked to the acquisition of holdings from which exempt dividends had been paid out would

---

[115] Ibid, para 36.
[116] Ibid, para 37.
[117] Ibid, paras 55–6. It was clarified earlier at para 42 that freedom of establishment was the relevant freedom as the legislation applied to companies holding at least 20 per cent of their subsidiaries' capital.
[118] Ibid, para 62.
[119] Ibid, para 64.
[120] Case C-39/16 Argenta Spaarbank v. Belgische Staat, ECLI:EU:C:2017:813.

manifestly go beyond what was necessary to achieve such an objective. As the interest did not relate to the financing of such holdings, the Belgian rules did not fall within the scope of Article 4(2) of the Parent-Subsidiary Directive. A similar conclusion was reached as regards to ex-Article 1(2). To the extent that the Belgian provision went beyond what was necessary for the prevention of fraud and abuse, it could not be relied upon.

In another important case, the Deister and Juhler case,[121] the Court of Justice assessed the compatibility of the former version of the German anti-treaty shopping rules with the Parent-Subsidiary Directive and freedom of establishment. Under German law, dividends distributed by a German subsidiary to a non-resident parent company were either exempt from income tax (on application by the taxable person) or subject to withholding tax. On application by the taxable person, this withholding tax could be refunded. However, the entitlement to exemption/refund was refused where, first, the non-resident parent company's shareholders would not have been entitled to this treatment if they had received those dividends directly, and, secondly, one of the following three conditions was satisfied: (a) the parent company's interposition was not justified by economic or other substantial reasons; (b) it did not earn more than 10 per cent of its gross income from its own economic activities; and (c) it did not take part in general economic commerce with a business establishment suitably equipped for its business purpose.[122]

In determining whether the non-resident parent company had its own economic activity, the German legislation only took account of the circumstances of the non-resident parent company. The organisational, economic or other substantial features of undertakings affiliated with that company were not considered. The structure and strategy of the group to which such a company belonged were not taken into account either. Consequently, when holdings were permanently spun off into a non-resident parent holding company, even if this was a genuine strategy of the group, the provisions of the German legislation were triggered and, as such, the exemption or refund was refused. By contrast, in the case of a resident parent holding company, the existence of a permanent involvement was sufficient for such a company to be granted an exemption or refund, even though its activities might have been marginal.[123] Another interesting feature of the German legislation was that in addition to the purely passive management of assets, the active management of a leasing, letting, investment, financing or holding company, in the case of a non-resident parent company, was not regarded as amounting to own economic activity within the meaning of the German legislation.[124]

[121] Joined Cases C-504/16 and C-613/16 Deister Holding AG and Juhler Holding A/S v. Bundeszentralamt für Steuern, ECLI:EU:C:2017:1009.
[122] Ibid, para 26.
[123] Ibid, paras 27–8.
[124] Ibid, para 29.

Following a request for a preliminary reference, the Court of Justice found that the German legislation was incompatible with the Parent-Subsidiary Directive and the freedom of establishment. It was emphasised that the Member States could not unilaterally introduce restrictive measures and subject the right to exemption from withholding tax under Article 5(1) of the Parent-Subsidiary Directive to various conditions.[125] Under ex-Article 1(2) of the Directive, Member States were only allowed to derogate from the provisions of the Directive in order to prevent tax evasion and abuse. Citing the Eqiom and Enka case,[126] the Court of Justice reiterated that in order for national legislation to be regarded as seeking to prevent tax evasion and abuse, its specific objective had to be to prevent conduct involving the creation of wholly artificial arrangements which did not reflect economic reality, the purpose of which was unduly to obtain a tax advantage.[127] A general presumption of fraud and abuse could not justify a fiscal measure that compromised a Directive's objective or the enjoyment of a fundamental freedom.[128] In order to determine whether an operation pursued the objective of fraud and abuse, national authorities should not confine themselves to applying general predetermined criteria but had to carry out an individual examination of the whole operation. Furthermore, it was found that the imposition of a general tax measure automatically excluding certain categories of taxable persons from the tax advantage, without the tax authorities being required to provide even prima facie evidence of fraud and abuse, went further than was necessary for preventing fraud and abuse.[129]

It was obvious that the German rules *ab initio* excluded a special group of taxpayers from the application of the Directive and created a general and irrefutable presumption of abuse.[130] The Court of Justice emphasised that a group's specific shareholding structure did not in itself satisfy ex-Article 1(2): the existence of a wholly artificial arrangement which did not reflect economic reality and whose purpose was unduly to obtain a tax advantage was not proved. Therefore, the German legislation was in breach of the Parent-Subsidiary Directive.

The German legislation was also found to be in breach of the freedom of establishment. The withholding tax exemption was subject to more onerous conditions only where a resident subsidiary distributed profits to a non-resident parent company. This difference in treatment was liable to deter a non-resident parent company from exercising an economic activity in Germany and, therefore, constituted a restriction to the freedom of establishment, which could not be justified. Interestingly, the Court of Justice noted that the fact that the economic activity of a non-resident parent company consisted in the management of its subsidiaries' assets

---

[125] Ibid, para 52.
[126] Ibid, para 30.
[127] Ibid, para 60.
[128] Ibid, para 61.
[129] Ibid, para 62.
[130] Ibid, para 63.

2.1 The Parent-Subsidiary Directive

or that the income of that company resulted only from such management was not enough to show the existence of a wholly artificial arrangement that did not reflect economic reality. Also, the fact that the management of assets was not considered to constitute an economic activity for the purposes of value-added tax was irrelevant, since the tax at issue in these proceedings and value-added tax were governed by distinct legal regimes, each pursuing different objectives.[131]

The judgment in Diester and Juhler, as well as in Eqiom and Enka is reminiscent of older judgments of the Court of Justice, where restrictions to fundamental freedoms and to the reliefs under Directives, as well as justifications based on preventing abuse or avoidance were interpreted strictly. Of course, these judgments should now be read in light of the new general anti-abuse rule of the Parent-Subsidiary Directive (and, arguably, the general anti-abuse rule of the Anti-Tax Avoidance Directive).[132] This rule explicitly requires from Member States not to allow the benefits of the Parent-Subsidiary Directive to apply to arrangements whose main purpose or one of its main purposes is to obtain an advantage contrary to the objectives of the Directive and without valid commercial reasons reflecting economic reality.[16]

These judgments should also be read in light of the guidance provided by the Court of Justice in the Danish tax cases,[133] which dealt with the interpretation of the Interest and Royalties Directive and the Parent-Subsidiary Directive and most specifically the interpretation of the beneficial ownership requirement.

The Z Denmark case (Case C-299/16) and three joined cases N Luxembourg 1 (Case C-115/16), X Denmark (Case C-118/16) and C Danmark 1 (Case C-119/16) all involved back-to-back financing transactions, under which a Danish resident subsidiary was financed by its non-resident parent company via a series of loans granted to intermediary holding companies resident in other Member States. Two joined cases, T Danmark (Case C-116/16) and Y Denmark (Case C-117/16), both concerned dividend distributions made by a Danish resident company to an intermediary holding company resident in the EU. In all these cases – which in this book are referred to as the Danish tax cases – the Danish companies requested an exemption of the Danish withholding tax levied on the payments made to the EU company, on the basis of the Interest and Royalties Directive and the Parent-Subsidiary Directive. The Danish tax authorities denied the exemption, arguing that this was a conduit structure and the company receiving the income was not the

---

[131] Ibid, para 73.
[132] See 2.6.
[133] See Joined Cases C-115/16, C-118/16, C-119/16 and C-299/16 N Luxembourg 1, X Denmark A/S, C Danmark I, Z Denmark ApS, ECLI:EU:C:2019:134 and Joined Cases C-116/16 and C-117/16 T Danmark, Y Denmark Aps, ECLI:EU:C:2019:135 (the Danish tax cases). For an excellent analysis, see Susi Baerentzen, 'Danish Cases on the Use of Holding Companies for Cross-Border Dividends and Interest – A New Test to Disentangle Abuse from Real Economic Activity?', 12 [2020] *World Tax Journal* 3–52. Also, see Enrique Sánchez de Castro Martín-Luengo, 'The ECJ's Danish Cases and the Spanish Withholding Tax Exemption in Respect of Interest Payments to EU Lenders: Some Reflections and Practical Implications' 60 [2020] 1 *European Taxation* 8–16.

beneficial owner of the payment. Following a reference to the Court of Justice, a very succinct judgment was produced that provided important guidance in a number of areas, in places deviating from earlier case law and the opinion of the Advocate General.

The Court of Justice first examined whether Denmark could rely on domestic or treaty-based anti-abuse provisions to tackle abuse of the Parent-Subsidiary Directive if it had not transposed ex-Article 1(2) into national law. On this point, it was noted that EU law prohibits abusive practices as a general principle. As such, Member States were obliged to deny the benefits of the Directives if these benefits had been claimed abusively. This conclusion applied irrespective of whether the Member States implemented domestic or agreement-based anti-abuse provisions in their domestic tax systems.[134] On this point, as explained in Chapter 7, the Court of Justice seems to have deviated from the Kofoed case.[135] Furthermore, it did not follow the opinion of its Advocate General who argued that the principle of legal certainty precluded the direct application of Directives – here, reliance by the tax authorities on ex-Article 1(2) of the Directive – when this provision had not been transposed into national law.

The Court of Justice also clarified that the benefits of the Directives should be denied if the tax advantage was the essential aim[136] of the transactions carried out by the taxpayer. Although it was for the referring courts to assess whether the arrangements under review were, in fact, abusive, the Court of Justice provided some guidance as to the constitutive elements of an abuse of rights under EU law. On the basis of previous case law, the Court of Justice confirmed that the notion of abuse relied on two elements: 'first, a combination of objective circumstances in which, despite formal observance of the conditions laid down by the EU rules, the purpose of those rules has not been achieved and, second, a subjective element consisting in the intention to obtain an advantage from the EU rules by artificially creating the conditions laid down for obtaining it'.[137]

A group of companies could be regarded as being an artificial arrangement where it was not set up for reasons that reflect economic reality, its structure was purely one of form, and its principal objective or one of its principal objectives was to obtain a tax advantage contrary to the aim or purpose of the applicable tax law.[138] The Court of Justice elaborated on indicia which the national court had to take into account in assessing whether an arrangement was 'intended to obtain improper entitlement to the exemption',[139] in particular whether the immediate recipient only played a conduit role and was obliged to pass the income on to entities established in

---

[134] Joint Cases C-115/16 et al. See analysis from para 95 et seq.
[135] Case C-321/05 Hans Markus Kofoed v. Skatteministeriet [2007] ECR I-05795. See analysis in 7.1.
[136] Joint Cases C-115/16 et al, para 107.
[137] Ibid, para 124.
[138] Ibid, para 127.
[139] Ibid, para 128.

third countries, 'with the consequence that it makes only an insignificant taxable profit when it acts as a conduit company in order to enable the flow of funds from the debtor company to the entity which is the beneficial owner of the sums paid'.[140] Such obligation did not necessarily arise only from a formal contractual or legal obligation but also by the fact that 'in substance', that company did not have the right to use and enjoy those sums.[141]

Another indication that a company acted as a conduit company would be where the sole activity of this company was the receipt of interest and its transmission to the beneficial owner or other conduit companies. The absence of actual economic activity had to be inferred from an analysis of all the relevant factors relating, 'in particular, to the management of the company, to its balance sheet, to the structure of its costs and to expenditure actually incurred, to the staff that it employs and to the premises and equipment that it has'.[142]

A further indication was whether the group structure was put in place simultaneously or close in time after the introduction of changes in the law that would have otherwise created an additional tax burden if the group had not changed its structure.[143] The Court of Justice noted that even if Denmark had concluded a tax treaty with the state of residence of the alleged ultimate beneficiary of the income, this could not in itself rule out the existence of 'an abuse of rights'.[144] Again, contrary to the Advocate General's opinion, it was held that if the national court found that there was abuse, the Member State was not required to identify the person it regarded as being the beneficial owner of the income, as it may be impossible for the national authorities to provide this information.[145]

The questions relating to the interest cases were also answered. The first question was whether the recipient of the interest was the beneficial owner, and thereby could enjoy the withholding tax exemption on the basis of the Interest and Royalties Directive. The Court of Justice confirmed that 'the concept of 'beneficial owner of the interest', which appears in Article 1(1) of Directive 2003/49, cannot refer to concepts of national law that vary in scope'.[146] The concept of 'beneficial owner of the interest' was to be interpreted as designating an entity that benefits from the interest that is paid to it.[147] From a brief review of the various linguistic versions of this term in the Directive, it was concluded that the term 'beneficial owner' concerned not a formally identified recipient but rather the entity which benefits economically from the interest received and as such has the power freely to determine its use. The Court of Justice emphasised that only an entity established in the

---

[140] Ibid, para 130.
[141] Ibid, para 132.
[142] Ibid, para 131.
[143] Ibid, para 133.
[144] Ibid, para 134–6.
[145] Ibid, para 143–5.
[146] Joined Cases C-116/16, para 84.
[147] Ibid, para 88.

EU could be a beneficial owner of the interest, capable of being entitled to the exemption.[148] The Court of Justice also noted that the mere fact that the company which received the interest in a Member State was not its 'beneficial owner' did not necessarily mean that the exemption provided for under the Directive was not applicable.[149]

Undeniably, the interpretation of beneficial ownership given by the Court of Justice is very similar to the interpretation of the concept in the OECD Model Commentaries.[150] In fact, it was affirmed by the Court of Justice that the successive amendments to the OECD Model Tax Convention and related commentaries were relevant in interpreting the concept of beneficial ownership under the Interest and Royalties Directive, as the original directive's proposal was based on the OECD work in this area.[151] Again, on this point, the Court of Justice went contrary to the opinion of the Advocate General who argued that the OECD Model Tax Convention and its related Commentary could not have a direct effect on the interpretation of an EU directive, even if the terms used were identical.

As for the burden of proof (in establishing the existence of abuse), the Court of Justice found that this lies primarily with the authorities of the Member State that challenged the application of the Directive. Contrary to the opinion of the Advocate General, the Court of Justice found that such authorities are not required to identify the beneficial owner of the income, but can just provide evidence indicating that the foreign recipient is a conduit company through which an abuse of rights has been committed.[152]

The Court of Justice also addressed several questions on the general interpretation of the Interest and Royalties Directive. Examining the case of the Luxembourg SICAR investment fund in the X Denmark case, the Court of Justice concluded that even if the SICAR was formally subject to corporate income tax in Luxembourg, it could not be considered a beneficial owner of the interest and benefit from the Directive if the interest income was exempt. This was for the referring court to decide.[153]

It was also questioned whether there would have been a breach of the fundamental freedoms if the Interest and Royalties Directive was inapplicable. The Court of Justice distinguished the situation whereby the inapplicability of the Directive arose because of fraud or abuse, and where the inapplicability arose in a non-abusive situation that did not meet the other requirements of the Directive.[154] In the first situation, the freedoms could not be relied upon because of the abuse. In the second situation, the freedoms could be relied upon, and compatibility with them could

---

[148] Ibid, para 89.
[149] Ibid, para 94.
[150] See Commentary to Art 10, para 12.3.
[151] Joint Cases C-115/16 et al, para 91.
[152] Ibid, para 143–4. Also see Joined Cases C-116/16, paras 115–20.
[153] Joint Cases C-115/16 et al, para 153.
[154] Ibid, paras 155–6.

be questioned. As such, following settled case law, the Court of Justice concluded that in non-abusive cases, the Danish withholding tax on interest paid to non-residents was in breach of the free movement of capital, insofar as resident taxpayers receiving Danish-sourced interest benefitted from a tax payment deferral,[155] or enjoyed lower late payment interest rates,[156] or could take into account any business expenses directly related to the interest income received when assessing their taxable income.[157]

While there are some important differences between the opinion of the Advocate General and the Court of Justice (e.g. whether the OECD material should be relevant in interpreting provisions of the Interest and Royalties Directive, whether in cases of abuse national tax authorities should be required to identify the beneficial owner of the income), nevertheless, the decision of the Court of Justice provides much-needed guidance in this area, and it is welcomed. This judgment has so far been followed by national courts in France,[158] Italy,[159] Spain[160] and the Netherlands,[161] as well as Switzerland.[162]

Overall, the Parent-Subsidiary Directive offers a workable solution to one of the most detrimental problems in international tax law – economic and juridical double taxation – only to the extent that its strict eligibility conditions are satisfied. Even with the participation threshold being lowered from 25 per cent to 10 per cent, the Directive still does not offer protection to companies not listed in the relevant Annex and for portfolio holdings[163] of less than 10 per cent. As shown in Chapter 5, the Court of Justice has addressed some of the limitations of the Parent-Subsidiary Directive through its judgments. However, the open-ended nature of the Directive's newly introduced general anti-abuse rule, which is aligned with the general anti-abuse rule of the Anti-Tax Avoidance Directive, as well as the provision preventing hybrid arrangements, suggests that the focus of the Directive is no longer just the alleviation of double taxation, but also the prevention of double non-taxation.

[155] Ibid, para 167.
[156] Ibid, para 172.
[157] Ibid, para 179.
[158] Conseil d'État decisions no 423809 et al of 5 June 2020.
[159] Corte di cassazione decision no 14756 of 10 July 2020.
[160] Hoge Raad decision no 18/00219 of 10 January 2020.
[161] Tribunal Económico-Administrativo Central, rec 185/2017 and rec 2188/2017, 8 October 2019.
[162] See Swiss Supreme Court, decision 2C-354/2018 of 20 April 2020. This was an outbound dividend case involving Art 15(1) of the Swiss-EU Savings Agreement which provided an exemption comparable to Art 5 of the Parent-Subsidiary Directive. For commentary, see Robert Danon, *Swiss Supreme Court Refers to the CJEU 'Danish cases' in Outbound Dividend Case Involving the Swiss-EU Savings Agreement*, in Kluwer International Tax Blog, available at: http://kluwertaxblog.com/2020/07/23/swiss-supreme-court-refers-to-the-cjeu-danish-cases-in-outbound-dividend-case-involving-the-swiss-eu-savings-agreement/?doing_wp_cron=1595584791.0748729705810546875000#_edn6.
[163] See also Wolfgang Schön, 'International tax coordination for a second-best world (Part II)' (2010) 2(1) *World Tax Journal*, 65–94 on how the distinction between portfolio and direct investment is nowadays obliterated and the continuing reliance on it is unsatisfactory.

2.2 THE MERGER DIRECTIVE

Cross-border mergers and divisions can be problematic from a tax perspective. For instance, a cross-border merger may require the winding-up of one of the companies to be merged, thus triggering the taxation of unrealised capital gains and fiscal reserves. Furthermore, previous year losses may not be carried over to the newly merged entity. In so far as domestic mergers are concerned, national laws usually provide for tax deferral on qualifying assets and stock or the carry-over of losses for the benefit of the acquiring company or shareholder. Such treatment is rarely extended to cross-border mergers, thus leading to a disadvantageous treatment compared to domestic mergers.

The objective of the Merger Directive[164] was to introduce tax rules to ensure that cross-border operations would not be at a disadvantage compared to similar domestic operations.[165] Broadly, the Directive applies to mergers, divisions, partial divisions, transfers of assets and exchanges of shares in which companies from two or more Member States are involved.[166] This Directive is analysed in greater detail in Chapter 6 in the context of reorganisations.

2.3 THE INTEREST AND ROYALTIES DIRECTIVE

After the Parent-Subsidiary Directive was enacted to deal with the double taxation of profit distributions, interest and royalty payments also had to be considered. This seemed to be less urgent because, unlike profit distributions, interest and royalties tend to be deductible from the taxable profits of the paying company. Therefore, the double taxation burden in this context is of a juridical nature and not of an economic nature, unless the deductibility of interest or royalty is disallowed under interest deductibility limitation rules.[167]

Tax treaties usually reduce or waive withholding taxes on such payments. The Interest Article of the OECD Model Tax Convention, Article 11, largely follows the Dividends Article. Article 11(1) provides that the home state may tax a resident on interest paid to it that arises in the host state. However, under Article 11(2) such interest may also be taxed in the host state in which it arises, but this right to tax is limited if the beneficial owner of the interest is a resident of the home state. The host state tax cannot exceed 10 per cent of the gross amount of the interest.[168] It is

---

[164] Council Directive 2009/133/EC of 19 October 2009 on the common system of taxation applicable to mergers, divisions, partial divisions, transfers of assets and exchanges of shares concerning companies of different Member States and to the transfer of the registered office of an SE or SCE between Member States (codified version) [2009] OJ L310/34 (Merger Directive).
[165] Merger Directive, Preamble, Recitals 4 and 5.
[166] Ibid, Art 1.
[167] See further 7.3.
[168] Similar to Art 10(4), under Art 11(4) of the OECD Model Tax Convention, the limitation to source state taxation does not apply if the beneficial owner of the interest carries on business in the host state in which interest arises through a permanent establishment and the debt-claim relating to that

2.3 The Interest and Royalties Directive

noteworthy that withholding taxes on interest tend to be much lower than on dividends even though dividends are paid out of taxed profits and are subject to a much higher overall tax burden in the host state. Arguably, this can be attributed to the fact that debt is considered to be more easily transferable than equity.[169]

Even more restrictive for host state withholding taxes, the Royalties Article of the OECD Model Tax Convention, Article 12, confers exclusive taxing rights to the home state.[170] Article 12(1) provides that royalties arising in a state and beneficially owned by a resident of the other state will be taxable only in that other state. Not all tax treaties follow this provision. By contrast, Article 12 of the UN Model Convention also provides for host State taxation of royalties.

Nevertheless, it has not always been the case that national tax provisions, combined with bilateral or multilateral agreements, can ensure the elimination of double taxation. Furthermore, their application often entails burdensome administrative formalities and cash-flow problems for the companies concerned.[171] Therefore, when the 1997 tax package was being discussed, there was still a need to establish a consistent way of preventing interest and royalties from being taxed twice. Some of these problems were meant to be addressed by the Interest and Royalties Directive.[172] As explained in the Recital to this Directive, the aim of this instrument was to prevent payments between companies situated in different Member States being subject to less favourable tax conditions than those applicable to the same transactions carried out between companies situated in the same Member State.[173]

Broadly, interest or royalty payments arising in a Member State are exempt from tax in that state, provided that the beneficial owner of the interest or royalties is a company of another Member State or a permanent establishment of a company of

---

interest is effectively connected with the permanent establishment. Here Art 7 applies and interest will be taxed on a net basis (i.e. after deduction of expenses). The Royalties Article contains the same provision. See Art 12(3). Both Articles preserve source state taxation on the non-arm's length amount of interest paid between parties in unique relationships. See Arts 11(6) and 12(4), respectively.

[169] See Schön, 'International tax coordination for a second-best world (Part II)', 85 and Wolfgang Schön, 'The distinct equity of the debt-equity distinction' (2012) 66 (9) *Bulletin for International Taxation*, 490–502.

[170] This is subject to the provisos in Art 12(3) and (4) of the OECD Model Tax Convention, as mentioned above.

[171] Council Directive 2003/49/EC of 3 June 2003 on a common system of taxation applicable to interest and royalty payments made between associated companies of different Member States, amended by Council Directive 2004/66/EC of 26 April 2004, Council Directive 2004/76/EC of 29 April 2004 and Council Directive 2006/98/EC of 20 November 2006 (Interest and Royalties Directive), Recital, para 2.

[172] The initial proposal for such a directive preceded the 1997 tax package. See Proposal for a Council Directive on a common system of taxation applicable to interest and royalty payments made between parent companies and subsidiaries in the different Member States, COM(1990) 571 final of 24 January 1991. The proposal was subsequently amended in 1993 (COM(1993) 196 final of 10 June 1993) and withdrawn in 1994. See Commission press release IP/94/1023 of 8 November 1994. In 1998, within the context of the tax package, the Commission adopted a second proposal (COM(1998) 67 final of 4 March 1998). This proposal eventually led to the Interest and Royalties Directive.

[173] Interest and Royalties Directive, Recital, para 1.

a Member State situated in another Member State.[174] By taxing the beneficial owner in the Member State of residence, 'it is guaranteed that such income is taxed in the same jurisdiction where the related expenditure is deductible (i.e. the cost of raising capital in the case of interest income, and research and development expenditure in the case of royalties)'.[175] The host state (i.e. the state of the payer/debtor company) may require attestation certifying that the requirements of the Directive have been fulfilled at the time of payment of the interest or royalties.[176] There were transitional periods for a number of the Member States, which have now expired.[177]

2.3.1 Eligible Companies, Permanent Establishments and Beneficial Ownership

As with the Parent-Subsidiary Directive, there are certain shareholding requirements for the exemption to apply. The exemption applies only if the company that is the payer, or the company whose permanent establishment is treated as the payer of interest or royalties is an 'associated company' of the company that is the beneficial owner, or whose permanent establishment is treated as the beneficial owner of the interest or royalties.[178]

An eligible company must be of a legal form listed in the Annex.[179] This Annex is narrower than the one in the Parent-Subsidiary Directive,[180] leading to situations where some economic operators wishing to benefit from both Directives eschew legal forms included in the Annex of only one of the Directives. An eligible company must be tax resident in a Member State and not in a third country under a tax treaty.[181] It must also be subject to corporate income tax, without being exempt, or to a tax that is identical or substantially similar and that is imposed after the Directive enters into force.[182] There does not seem to be a requirement for these conditions to be met in the same Member State. It should be noted that in the Danish tax cases, it

---

[174] Ibid, Art 1(1).
[175] Report from the Commission to the Council in accordance with Article 8 of the Council Directive 2003/49/EC on a common system of taxation applicable to interest and royalty payments made between associated companies of different Member States, COM(2009) 179 final, para 3.1.
[176] The host state may also make it a condition for exemption under the Directive that it has issued a decision granting the exemption following such an attestation. A decision on exemption must be given within three months at most after the attestation. Interest and Royalties Directive, Art 1(11)–(13).
[177] Ibid, Art 6.
[178] Ibid, Art 1(7).
[179] Ibid, Art 3(a)(i).
[180] For example, the European Company (Societas Europaea) and the European Cooperative Society (Societas Cooperative Europaea) are excluded from the Annex to the Interest and Royalties Directive, but there have been suggestions to include them. See Proposal for a Council Directive on a common system of taxation applicable to interest and royalty payments made between associated companies of different Member States, COM(2011) 714 final and accompanying impact assessment, SEC(2011)1332 final.
[181] Interest and Royalties Directive, Art 3(a)(ii).
[182] See Art 3(a)(iii), which also contains a list of the relevant taxes for each Member State.

2.3 The Interest and Royalties Directive

was reiterated that being formally subject to corporate income tax in Luxembourg was not enough to benefit from the Directive if the interest income was in fact exempt.[183]

A company is an 'associated company' of a second company if the first company has at least a direct minimum holding of 25 per cent in the capital of the second company, or the second company has a direct minimum holding of 25 per cent in the capital of the first company, or a third company has a direct minimum holding of 25 per cent in both the capital of the first company and second company.[184] Member States are allowed to replace the criterion of a minimum holding in the capital with that of a minimum holding of voting rights.[185] Contrary to the Parent-Subsidiary Directive, the Interest and Royalties Directive is currently limited to direct holdings.[186] Although there have been calls to change this and expand the scope of the Directive and include indirect holdings, as well as reduce the minimum holding association requirement to align it with that of the Parent-Subsidiary Directive,[187] the Interest and Royalties Directive has not been amended.

As under the Parent-Subsidiary Directive,[188] a permanent establishment is defined as a fixed place of business situated in a Member State through which the business of a company of another Member State is wholly or partly carried on.[189] This Directive deviates from the OECD Model's definition of a permanent establishment in the same way as does the Parent-Subsidiary Directive. It does not distinguish between preparatory or auxiliary activities and core business activities, nor does it provide for an agency permanent establishment or a service permanent establishment. The Directive does not apply if interest or royalties are paid by or to a permanent establishment in a third state and the business of the company is wholly or partly carried on through that permanent establishment.[190] Only EU permanent establishments can benefit from the exemption. It should be noted that while there is no tax-deductibility requirement under the Directive for companies acting as payers of interest or royalties, there is such a requirement for permanent establishments.[191]

---

[183] Joint Cases C-115/16 et al, para 153.
[184] Interest and Royalties Directive, Art 3(b).
[185] Ibid.
[186] Indirect holdings were included in all earlier drafts of the proposal. In the final version of the proposal, the Directive was restricted to direct holdings. See Dimitar Hristov, 'The Interest and Royalty Directive', in Michael Lang, Pasquale Pistone, Josef Schuch and Claus Staringer (eds), *Introduction to European Tax Law: Direct Taxation* (London: Spiramus Press, 2010, 2nd edn).
[187] See Report from the Commission to the Council in accordance with Article 8 of the Council Directive 2003/49/EC on a common system of taxation applicable to interest and royalty payments made between associated companies of different Member States, COM(2009) 179 final, para 3.4.2. This suggestion also features in the Commission's 2011 proposal to amend the Interest and Royalties Directive. COM(2011) 714 final, cited above.
[188] Parent-Subsidiary Directive, Art 2(2), examined above in 2.1.2.
[189] Interest and Royalties Directive, Art 3(c).
[190] Ibid, Art 1(8).
[191] See Art 1(3). It should be noted that as far as tax deductibility is concerned, it is unclear whether the payments should actually be deductible or whether the mere allocation of the expense to the

Contrary to the Parent-Subsidiary Directive, but similar to the Interest Article of the OECD Model Tax Convention, a beneficial ownership requirement has been inserted in the Interest and Royalties Directive to limit the possibilities of abuse by ineligible recipients who use conduit entities or other artificial arrangements. Under Article 1(4) of the Interest and Royalties Directive, a company is treated as the beneficial owner of interest or royalties only if it receives those payments for its own benefit and not as an intermediary, such as an agent, trustee or authorised signatory, for some other person.[192]

In the Interest and Royalties Directive, there is no subject-to-tax requirement for companies receiving the interest or royalties.[193] There is, however, such a requirement for permanent establishments receiving interest or royalties.[194] This creates discrepancies. It should be noted that in the Danish tax cases, discussed in detail in 2.1.5., it was emphasised that a recipient of interest could not be considered the beneficial owner of the interest for the purposes of the Directive if the interest income was in fact exempt. This statement goes some way in aligning the legal position of companies receiving interest or royalties with permanent establishments. The only remaining arbitrary difference would seem to be in the context of payers of interest and royalties: the payment must be tax deductible for the purposes of the permanent establishment but not so for the purposes of the company. However, the disadvantageous position of a permanent establishment vis-à-vis a company, if in a comparable situation, could be challenged on the basis of the freedom of establishment.[195]

As noted above in 2.1.5., in the Danish tax cases, the Court of Justice provided some very useful guidance on the interpretation of the requirement of beneficial ownership. It was found that the concept of the beneficial owner of the interest under the Interest and Royalties Directive could not refer to concepts of national law that vary in scope.[196] Instead, it was to be interpreted as designating an entity that actually benefitted from the interest paid to it – the entity that benefitted economically from the interest received and as such had the power freely to determine the use

---

permanent establishment suffices. Contrast the requirement under Art 11(5) of the OECD Model Tax Convention for the interest to be borne by a permanent establishment in order for this to be considered as the payer of the interest. Deductibility is not relevant. This provision is refined in the proposal to amend the Interest and Royalties Directive. See 2.3.4.

[192] A trustee does not appear to be excluded from the concept of beneficial owner under the OECD Model Tax Convention, which refers to 'agent or nominee'. See OECD Commentary on Arts 10(2), 11(2) and 12(1).

[193] Interest and Royalties Directive, Art 1(3). A subject-to-tax requirement could be deduced from the Preamble, where it is stated that it is 'necessary to ensure that interest and royalty payments are subject to tax once in a Member State'. Interest and Royalties Directive, Preamble, para 3. Also, see analysis in 2.3.2.

[194] Ibid, Art 1(5), also discussed immediately below.

[195] For discrimination and the different tax treatment of permanent establishments and companies, see Chapter 4.

[196] Joint Cases C-115/16 et al, para 84.

2.3 The Interest and Royalties Directive

to which it was put.[197] The OECD Model Tax Convention and related commentaries were relevant in interpreting this concept.[198]

2.3.2 Interest, Royalties and Excluded Payments

Interest is defined as:

> income from debt-claims of every kind, whether or not secured by mortgage and whether or not carrying a right to participate in the debtor's profits, and in particular, income from securities and income from bonds and debentures, including premiums and prizes attaching to such securities, bonds or debentures; penalty charges for late payment shall not be regarded as interest.[199]

Royalties are defined as:

> payments of any kind received as a consideration for the use of, or the right to use, any copyright of literary, artistic or scientific work, including cinematograph films and software, any patent, trade mark, design or model, plan, secret formula or process, or for information concerning industrial, commercial or scientific experience; payments for the use of, or the right to use, industrial, commercial or scientific equipment shall be regarded as royalties.[200]

These definitions are very similar to those under the OECD Model Tax Convention, but there are some differences. For example, the definition of interest under the OECD Model Tax Convention[201] does not cover income from government securities.[202] In addition, the definition of royalties under the OECD Model Tax Convention[203] seems narrower, as it does not include software payments, nor does it include payments for the use of, or the right to use industrial, commercial or scientific equipment. The author argued in the first edition of this book that the reason for this divergence of approach may be attributed to the fact that the Directive and the OECD Model Tax Convention have different objectives. The former seeks to abolish source taxation for certain types of income and, therefore, the aim is to include as much as possible within the definitions of qualifying payments – to the extent relevant

---

[197] Ibid, paras 88–9.
[198] Ibid, para 91.
[199] Interest and Royalties Directive, Art 2(a).
[200] Ibid, Art 2(b).
[201] See Art 11(3) of the OECD Model Tax Convention. The Commentary states that the term 'interest' covers income from debt-claims of every kind, whether or not secured by a mortgage and whether or not carrying a right to participate in profits. OECD Commentary to Art 11, para 18.
[202] As explained in Sandra Martinho Fernandes, Roberto Bernales, Suat Goeydeniz, Bob Michel, Oana Popa and Emanuela Santoro, 'A comprehensive analysis of proposals to amend the Interest and Royalties Directive – Part 2' (2011) 51(11) *European Taxation*, 445–64, at p 452, the reason government securities are not included in the definition of interest in the Directive is that the objective of the Directive is to eliminate double taxation on payments between associated companies and not from state institutions.
[203] See Art 12(2) of the OECD Model Tax Convention.

for associated companies. On the other hand, the OECD Model Tax Convention provides a blueprint for the allocation of taxing rights between contracting states, favouring residence-based taxation. Therefore, the aim is to have a limited definition of interest and royalties so that more items fall within the scope of business profits. The author also argued that overreliance on the OECD Model Tax Convention and its Commentaries might not be appropriate, given their non-binding and ambulatory nature. However, later case law suggests otherwise, and as shown above reliance on the OECD Model Tax Convention and Commentaries may actually be encouraged for the interpretation of certain terms of the Directive.

Being part of the 1997 tax package, prevention of tax evasion was just as important a goal of this Directive as eliminating withholding taxes on interest and royalty payments. The Preamble to the Interest and Royalties Directive, in fact, reiterates that it is 'necessary to ensure that interest and royalty payments are subject to tax once in a Member State'.[204] As with the Parent-Subsidiary and Merger Directives, Member States are, therefore, allowed to take measures to counter fraud and abuse.[205] Arguably, this provision is likely to be interpreted in a similar way to the anti-abuse provisions of the Parent-Subsidiary Directive.

Again, similar to the Parent-Subsidiary Directive, the Interest and Royalties Directive confers on the Member States the option not to apply its provisions to a company of another EU Member State or a permanent establishment of a company of another EU Member State if the required shareholding has not been maintained for an uninterrupted period of at least two years.[206] Therefore, non-compliance with the minimum holding period requirement may exclude some payments from the benefit of the Directive. It is likely that this provision is to be interpreted in the same way as it was interpreted in Denkavit,[207] in the context of the Parent-Subsidiary Directive. This may mean that a payment could benefit from the provisions of the Directive during the initial two-year period of ownership, provided the ownership has, in fact, been maintained for at least two years.[208]

Article 4(1) of the Interest and Royalties Directive contains a list of excluded payments for which the host state is not required to give an exemption. A distribution of profits or repayment of capital under domestic law may be excluded from the concept of interest or royalties,[209] as may payments from debt claims that carry a right to participate in the debtor's profits,[210] or entitle creditors to exchange their right to interest for a right to participate in the debtor's profits,[211] or contain no

[204] Interest and Royalties Directive, Preamble, para 3.
[205] Ibid, Art 5.
[206] Interest and Royalties Directive, Art 1(10).
[207] Joined Cases C-283/94, C-291/94 and C-292/94 Denkavit International BV, VITIC Amsterdam BV and Voormeer BV v. Bundesamt für Finanzen [1996] ECR I-5063. See analysis in 2.1.2.
[208] This was also the position taken in the Explanatory Memorandum to the 1998 version of the Directive.
[209] Interest and Royalties Directive, Art 4(1)(a).
[210] Ibid, Art 4(1)(b).
[211] Ibid, Art 4(1)(c).

2.3 The Interest and Royalties Directive

provision for repayment of the principal or if the repayment is due more than fifty years after the date of issue.[212]

Furthermore, non-arm's length transactions fall outside the scope of the Directive's protection. Under Article 4(2) of the Interest and Royalties Directive, where by reason of a special relationship between the payer and the beneficial owner of the interest or royalties or between one of them and some other person, the amount of the interest or royalties exceeds the amount that would have been agreed in the absence of such relationship, the Directive will only apply to the latter amount. To the extent that the payment of interest or royalties complies with the arm's length standard, then the Directive applies. Whether Member States will have to adapt this standard to an EU definition of the arm's length principle developed in the context of the state aid litigation[213] remains to be seen. Similarly, whether the increased reliance on the OECD materials following the Danish tax cases will have a spill-over effect on the OECD Transfer Pricing Guidelines remains to be seen.

The Directive does not specify how the excess payment will be treated. This has implications for the reclassification and the taxation of it. As the treatment of an excess amount appears to be a matter of domestic tax laws, then it is up to each Member State to allow its reclassification as a profit distribution. Furthermore, a reclassified distribution may not be covered by the Parent-Subsidiary Directive even if all the other conditions of the Directive are met and as such a withholding tax may be levied on it. Neither the Parent-Subsidiary Directive nor the Interest and Royalties Directive oblige the host State to exempt reclassified profit distributions from withholding taxes.[214] As already mentioned in 2.1.2, a payment reclassified as a profit distribution is not automatically considered to be a profit distribution for the purposes of the Parent-Subsidiary Directive. It depends on the (host) Member State's interpretation of the term 'dividend' or 'profit distribution'. Furthermore, following Les Vergers du Vieux Tauves,[215] anything short of a shareholding relationship between the distributing company and the receiving company is insufficient for the purposes of the Parent-Subsidiary Directive and may give the Member States the discretion not to apply the exemption of the latter Directive.

2.3.3 The Taxation of the Payer/Debtor

One issue that has arisen is whether the exemption under the Interest and Royalties Directive[216] only covers host state taxes levied on the payee (creditor) or whether it also covers host state taxes levied on the payer (debtor). This could have important

---

[212] Ibid, Art 4(1)(d).
[213] See Chapter 8.
[214] The 1998 version of the Interest and Royalties Directive provided for the reclassified payments to be covered under the Parent-Subsidiary Directive. This was also recommended in the Commission's 2009 report (COM(2009) 179 final).
[215] See Case C-48/07 Les Vergers du Vieux Tauves and analysis in 2.1.2.
[216] Interest and Royalties Directive, Art 1(1).

implications as, if the latter approach is chosen, then the host state may be prohibited from imposing taxes on the payer, for example, disallowing the deduction of interest or royalty payments. Pursuant to this latter interpretation, the Directive would provide for the elimination of both juridical and economic double taxation.

This interpretation, however, was not accepted in the Scheuten Solar case.[217] Here, the Court of Justice was asked to assess the compatibility of the German trade tax with the Interest and Royalties Directive. More specifically, it was was asked to determine whether Article 1(1) of the Directive precluded provisions of the German legislation under which loan interest paid by a company of one Member State to an associated company of another Member State was added to the basis of assessment to trade tax for the first company. The Court of Justice was also asked whether Article 1 (10) of the Directive was to be interpreted as meaning that a Member State had the option not to apply the Directive even where the conditions set out in Article 3(b) in relation to the existence of an associated company had not yet been maintained for an uninterrupted period of at least two years at the time of payment of the interest.

The Court of Justice, agreeing with the opinion of Advocate General Sharpston, found that there was no breach of the Interest and Royalties Directive. The aim of Article 1(1) of the Directive, read in light of Recitals 2 to 4 of the Preamble, was to avoid double taxation of cross-border payments of interest, but this provision concerned solely the tax position of the interest *creditor*.[218] The German legislation did not reduce the creditor's income and did not subject the interest paid to any taxation in the hands of the beneficial owner of the interest. It only related to the determination of the basis of assessment of the business tax to be paid in this case by the debtor of the interest.[219] The method of calculating the basis of the assessment of the payer of interest and the elements to be taken into account for that purpose (e.g. taking certain expenditure into consideration when performing that calculation) was not the subject of Article 1(1) of the Directive.[220] Given this finding, the Court of Justice did not consider it necessary to address the second question.[221]

---

[217] Case C-397/09 Scheuten Solar Technology GmbH v. Finanzamt Gelsenkirchen-Süd [2011] ECR I-06455.
[218] Ibid, para 28.
[219] Ibid, para 30. This point was reiterated in para 35. In considering the possible relevance of the Parent-Subsidiary Directive, the Court of Justice agreed with the Advocate General that there was nothing to suggest that the judgments in Case C-294/99 Athinaiki Zythopoiia [2001] ECR I-6797 and Case C-284/06 Burda [2008] ECR I-4571 could be of assistance in the interpretation of Art 1(1) of the Interest and Royalties Directive in relation to national legislation in this case. In those cases, it was the distribution of profits by a subsidiary to its parent company that was the event that gave rise to the tax in question. By contrast, the payments of interest at issue here did not constitute chargeable events for tax. The issue was the deductibility of such payments as expenditure to calculate the basis of an assessment of business tax.
[220] Case C-397/09 Scheuten Solar, para 31.
[221] Ibid, para 37.

It could be argued that the Court of Justice, in this case, did not deal with thin capitalisation rules but rather the rules on the assessment of the tax base of the debtor for trade tax purposes.[222] However, it is difficult to see how this interpretation could open up the way for thin capitalisation provisions (or other interest deductibility restrictions) to be covered by the Directive. It was evident in the Court's analysis that the focus was on whether national legislation led to a reduction of the creditor's income. In fact, in express terms, the Court of Justice stated that 'in the absence of a provision governing the rules for calculating the basis of assessment of the payer of interest, the scope of Article 1(1) of Directive 2003/49 cannot extend beyond the exemption it lays down'.[223]

Nevertheless, the fact remains that contrary to the stance of Advocate General Sharpston,[224] the Court of Justice refrained from stating whether double taxation under the Directive could, in addition to juridical double taxation, ever encompass economic double taxation. With the current focus on avoiding double non-taxation and aggressive tax planning, it is unlikely that addressing this point is now a priority.

2.4 THE ARBITRATION CONVENTION

The Arbitration Convention[225] seeks to establish an arbitration procedure that eliminates double taxation in the course of transfer pricing disputes between Member States. Unlike a Directive or Regulation, it is merely an agreement under public international law and, as such, is subject to the jurisdiction of national courts and not the Court of Justice. In the past, various Codes of Conduct[226] were produced with the

---

[222] See, for example, Fernandes et al, 'A comprehensive analysis of proposals to amend the Interest and Royalties Directive – Part 2', 458.
[223] Case C-397/09 Scheuten Solar, para 34.
[224] The Advocate General stated in unambiguous terms that 'double taxation' under this Directive only covered juridical double taxation (para 64) and only referred to the taxation of income received by the beneficial owner of interest (para 67).
[225] Convention 90/436/EEC of 23 July 1990 on the Elimination of Double Taxation in Connection with the Adjustment of Profits of Associated Enterprises (Arbitration Convention).
[226] See, for example, the Code of Conduct for the effective implementation of the EU Arbitration Convention. This Code of Conduct sought to ensure a more effective and uniform application of the Arbitration Convention by all Member States. See also the Revised Code of Conduct (2009/C 322/01). This Code of Conduct established common procedures concerning: (a) the starting point of the three-year period which is the deadline for a company suffering double taxation to present its case to the tax administration of the relevant Member State; (b) the starting point of the two-year period during which Member States' tax administrations must attempt to reach an agreement that eliminates the double taxation that is the subject of the complaint; (c) the arrangements during this mutual agreement procedure (the practical operation of the procedure, transparency and taxpayer participation); and (d) the practical arrangements for the second phase of the dispute resolution procedure (the establishment and functioning of the Advisory Commission that must then arbitrate in the case). This Code of Conduct also contained a recommendation to the Member States to suspend the collection of taxes during the dispute resolution procedure.

help of the EU Joint Transfer Pricing Forum to improve the functioning of the Arbitration Convention.

The Arbitration Convention entered into force on 1 January 1995 after ratification by all national parliaments. When Austria, Finland and Sweden joined the EU, a specific Treaty of Accession was concluded in 1995 to enable these countries to benefit from the Arbitration Convention. The original five-year duration of the Arbitration Convention was extended through a Protocol on 25 May 1999. Now the duration of the Arbitration Convention is extended automatically every five years unless Member States object to such extension. After the various waves of enlargement, a separate Accession Convention was necessary for the Arbitration Convention to apply to the new Member States.

The Arbitration Convention adopts the arm's length principle, enshrined in Article 9 of the OECD Model Tax Convention and elaborated in the OECD Transfer Pricing Guidelines for Multinational Enterprises and Tax Administrations.[227] The Arbitration Convention applies when profits of an enterprise of a Member State are included (or likely to be included) in the profits of an enterprise in another Member State.[228] It applies to all taxes on income and in particular to taxes listed in Article 2(2).

The objective of the Arbitration Convention, as set out in Article 4, is to establish a procedure to eliminate double taxation arising from profit adjustments made by the relevant Member States because of a violation of the arm's length principle between associated enterprises or the attribution of profits to a permanent establishment that is not equivalent to what it might be expected to derive if it were a distinct and separate enterprise engaged in the same or similar activities under the same or similar conditions and dealing on an arm's length basis. The terms 'enterprise' and 'permanent establishment' are not defined. Therefore, recourse is to be had to the domestic or tax treaty meaning of these terms.

The Arbitration Convention sets out a three-stage procedure for eliminating double taxation.

Firstly, the Member State has to notify the affected enterprise of its intention to make a tax adjustment and to hear of any objections. It must give the enterprise time to let the relevant associated party inform the other Member State, but the first Member State is not prevented from making the proposed adjustment.[229] Secondly, if the enterprise disagrees with the proposed adjustment, there is a three-year limit for it to present its case to its competent authorities, requesting a mutual agreement. This is irrespective of any remedies provided under the domestic law of the Member States.[230] Thirdly, if the competent authorities of the two relevant Member States fail to reach a mutual agreement within two years, they have to establish an Advisory

---

[227] The latest edition was published by the OECD in 2017.
[228] Arbitration Convention, Art 1.
[229] Ibid, Art 5.
[230] Ibid, Art 6.

Commission.[231] The composition of the Advisory Commission is set out in Article 9 of the Arbitration Convention. An appeal in national courts delays proceedings.

The Advisory Commission has to deliver its opinion within six months.[232] Following that, the competent authorities must make a decision that eliminates double taxation – which may deviate from the opinion of the Advisory Commission – within the next six months.[233] If they fail to do so, the opinion of the Advisory Commission becomes binding. Double taxation is regarded as eliminated if either the profits are included in the computation of taxable profits in one Member State only, or the tax chargeable on those profits in one Member State is reduced by an amount equal to the tax chargeable on them in the other.[234] This three-stage procedure is expected to be completed within six years.

There are certain escape routes for the competent authorities of the relevant Member States. If the complaint does not appear to be well-founded, then the competent authorities of the Member State of the complainant are not obliged to proceed to the mutual agreement stage.[235] Nor is there an obligation to proceed to the Advisory Commission stage, where the domestic law does not permit competent authorities to derogate from the decisions of their judicial bodies unless the (complainant) associated enterprise has allowed the time provided for appeal to expire, or has withdrawn any such appeal before a decision has been delivered.[236] Furthermore, the competent authorities of a Member State are not obliged to initiate the mutual agreement procedure or to set up the Advisory Commission where legal or administrative proceedings have resulted in a final ruling that, because of the transactions that gave rise to the adjustment, one of the enterprises concerned is liable for a serious administrative or criminal penalty.[237]

In the 2001 Company Tax Study,[238] it was suggested that the Arbitration Convention should be replaced by a Directive so that the Court of Justice has jurisdiction over its interpretation. It took almost two decades for this suggestion to be materialised through the adoption of the Tax Dispute Resolution Mechanisms Directive.[239] This is examined next.

2.5 THE TAX DISPUTE RESOLUTION MECHANISMS DIRECTIVE

The new Directive is aimed at facilitating and streamlining the resolution of tax disputes between the Member States. The Directive broadens the scope of the EU

[231] Ibid, Art 7.
[232] Ibid, Art 9.
[233] Ibid, Art 10.
[234] Ibid, Art 14.
[235] Ibid, Art 6(2).
[236] Ibid, Art 7(3).
[237] Ibid, Art 8(1), (2).
[238] See ch 1, analysis at 1.4.
[239] Council Directive (EU) 2017/1852 of 10 October 2017 on tax dispute resolution mechanisms in the European Union, [2017] OJ L 265/1.

rules on dispute resolution, which hitherto were limited to the Arbitration Convention and its focus on transfer pricing disputes. It should be pointed out that the Tax Dispute Resolution Mechanisms Directive does not officially replace the Arbitration Convention but provides an additional and, arguably, more efficient route for taxpayers to take in resolving their tax disputes with competent authorities.

The Tax Dispute Resolution Mechanisms Directive applies, inter alia, to disputes arising from the interpretation and application of tax treaties leading to double taxation. Article 1 of the Directive lays down 'rules on a mechanism to resolve disputes between the Member States when those disputes arise from the interpretation and application of agreements and conventions that provide for the elimination of double taxation of income and, where applicable, capital'. A combined reading of the provisions of this Directive suggests that double taxation may not even need to have occurred for the Directive to be applicable. Although the Directive stipulates that a Member State may – on a case-by-case basis – deny access to the dispute resolution procedure where the dispute does not involve double taxation,[240] the starting point is that even disputes not involving double taxation are within the scope of the Directive. This is also buttressed by the Preamble to this Directive.[241] Therefore, the Directive covers disputes on double taxation, as well as disputes arising from the wrongful application of any procedural or administrative rules (e.g. provisions on the exchange of information, or assistance in the collection of taxes).

Under the Tax Dispute Resolution Mechanisms Directive, any person who is a tax resident of a Member State according to the applicable tax treaty and whose taxation is directly affected by a matter giving rise to a dispute, may simultaneously submit a complaint to each of the concerned EU competent authorities.[242] Within six months of having received all the necessary documents, any concerned competent authorities may decide to resolve the dispute on a unilateral basis. If that does not happen, then the relevant competent authorities of the Member States involved must endeavour to solve the dispute by means of a mutual agreement procedure within a period of two years.[243] Any agreement reached under the mutual agreement procedure is binding on the competent authorities and enforceable by the taxpayer.[244]

If no agreement is reached, then upon a request by the taxpayer to the competent authorities of the Member States concerned, an Advisory Commission is set up.[245] The Tax Dispute Resolution Mechanisms Directive provides for mandatory

---

[240] Ibid, Art 17(6).
[241] See Preamble, para 6, which sets out that the resolution of disputes envisaged under this Directive, 'should apply to different interpretation and application of bilateral tax treaties and of the Union Arbitration Convention – in particular to different interpretation and application leading to double taxation'.
[242] This right must be exercised within three years from the receipt of the first notification of the action resulting in, or that will result in the dispute. See Art 3.
[243] Ibid, Art 4(1).
[244] Ibid, Art 4(2).
[245] Ibid, Art 6. The relevant competent authorities must also inform the taxpayer of the reasons that no agreement was reached. See Art 4(3).

resolution of double taxation disputes. Alternatively, Member States can request an Alternative Dispute Resolution Commission instead of the Advisory Commission, which will again have to deal with the dispute in a binding manner.[246] Taxpayers have several appeal possibilities to ensure that the competent authorities will apply the provisions of the Directive.

The Directive sets out when access to national courts should be granted for clarifying whether there is an obligation to eliminate double taxation and, if so, provides the national court with the power to take action.[247] Furthermore, the Directive allows the Member States to choose the methods for solving their double taxation disputes provided that double taxation is eliminated within the timelines laid down in the Directive. The Commission can also assist the Member States in the proceedings. Moreover, the Commission is required to develop a central repository which will archive the opinions of the Advisory Commission and the Alternative Dispute Resolution Commission (either the final decisions or the abstracts) and make them available online.[248]

The Member States had until 30 June 2019 to transpose the Directive into national laws and regulations. The Directive applies to complaints submitted after that date on questions relating to the tax year starting on or after 1 January 2018. In that respect, the Directive has some retrospective effect. Member States may even apply the Directive to complaints related to earlier tax years.

2.6 THE ANTI-TAX AVOIDANCE DIRECTIVE

The first version of the Anti-Tax Avoidance Directive (commonly abbreviated and known as the ATAD)[249] was part of the Commission's Anti-Tax Avoidance Package published in January 2016.[250] The Anti-Tax Avoidance Directive and the Package as a whole emanated from the Commission's ambitious agenda for a fairer, simpler and more effective corporate tax system in the EU,[251] which gained political support as a result of the momentum generated by the OECD/G20's BEPS project.

In the initial proposal,[252] the Commission proposed action in three areas covered by the BEPS Action Plan; namely, hybrid mismatches,[253] interest

---

[246] Ibid, Art 10.
[247] Ibid, Art 16.
[248] See Art 19.
[249] Proposal for a Council Directive Laying Down Rules against Tax Avoidance Practices that Directly Affect the Functioning of the Internal Market, COM(2016) 26 final (28 January 2016).
[250] See: https://ec.europa.eu/taxation_customs/business/company-tax/anti-tax-avoidance-package_en. Also, see analysis in Christiana HJI Panayi, 'The Europeanisation of Good Tax Governance', 36 (2018) 1 *Yearbook of European Law* 442–95, Pt III (C).
[251] Communication from the Commission to the European Parliament and the Council *A Fair and Efficient Corporate Tax System in the European Union: 5 Key Areas for Action*, COM(2015) 302 final (17 June 2015).
[252] Proposal for a Council Directive Laying Down Rules against Tax Avoidance Practices that Directly Affect the Functioning of the Internal Market, COM(2016) 26 final (28 January 2016).
[253] Action 2 of the BEPS Action Plan.

deductibility restrictions,[254] and controlled foreign company (CFC) rules.[255] The Commission also proposed action in three areas not covered by the BEPS Action Plan, namely: a general anti-abuse rule, a switch-over clause and rules to tackle exit taxation. Although there were concerns at the time, that the Union did not have the competence to enact rules in this area, these concerns were largely ignored. Only the switch-over clause was deleted in the final version of this Directive.[256]

Pursuant to the Anti-Tax Avoidance Directive, all taxpayers that are subject to corporate tax in a Member State, including subsidiaries of companies based in third countries will – from the date the provisions of the Directive become effective[257] – be scrutinised based on the five anti-abuse rules.[258] The Directive now provides for uniform (but de minimis) interest limitation rules to prevent multinational groups from artificially shifting their debt to jurisdictions with more generous deductibility rules; exit taxation rules to ensure that where a taxpayer moves assets or its tax residence out of the tax jurisdiction of a state, that state taxes the economic value of any capital gain created in its territory even though that gain has not yet been realised at the time of the exit; a general anti-abuse rule to cover gaps that may exist in Member State's specific anti-abuse rules; CFC rules to prevent the shifting of large amounts of profits towards controlled subsidiaries in low-tax jurisdictions; and rules on hybrid mismatches to prevent corporate taxpayers from taking advantage of disparities between national tax systems in order to reduce their overall tax liability. The provisions of this Directive are analysed in more detail in later chapters.[259]

The scope of the hybrid mismatch provision was further broadened to include provisions against hybrid mismatch arrangements with third countries. This proposal[260] was made in the context of the Corporate Tax Reform Package presented in October 2016.[261] Under this proposal, the hybrid provisions would not only apply to mismatch arrangements within the EU but also mismatches arising in relation to third countries. The hybrid provisions would also deal with mismatches involving permanent establishments, imported mismatches, hybrid transfers and dual resident

---

[254] Ibid, Action 4.
[255] Ibid, Action 3.
[256] Council Directive 2016/1164 of 12 July 2016 Laying Down Rules against Tax Avoidance Practices that Directly Affect the Functioning of the Internal Market, [2016] OJ L 193.
[257] Technically, Member States had until 31 December 2018 to transpose the Anti-Tax Avoidance Directive into their national laws and regulations, except for the exit taxation rules, for which they had until 31 December 2019. Member States that have targeted rules that are equally effective to the interest limitation rules may apply them until the OECD reaches an agreement on a minimum standard or until 1 January 2024 at the latest.
[258] Anti-Tax Avoidance Directive, Art 1.
[259] For the exit tax provision (Art 5), see analysis in 6.2.4. For the other provisions, see Chapter 7.
[260] See Proposal for a Council Directive amending Directive (EU) 2016/1164 as regards hybrid mismatches with third countries, COM(2016)687 final.
[261] See Commission Communication, *Building a fair, competitive and stable corporate tax system for the EU*, COM(2016) 682 final.

2.6 The Anti-Tax Avoidance Directive

mismatches. The rationale of the proposals was for the Member State to align its tax treatment with that of the third country unless the third country had already eliminated the mismatch. The proposal was formally approved in May 2017,[262] and the Member States had until 31 December 2019 to implement these rules, with the exception of rules on reverse hybrid mismatches, which could be transposed into domestic law by 31 December 2021.[263]

Harmonising the exception to the rules (i.e. the anti-abuse provisions) without harmonising the actual rules (i.e. the corporate tax base) is very problematic. These rules would have been perfectly acceptable in a framework where there was a common tax base, but not when the Member States have kept their competences to design their tax systems in a way that is compatible with the fundamental freedoms (and state aid). That is why some of these provisions, at least for some Member States, may seem out of place. For example, while there are no harmonised rules as to what gains should be taxable in a Member State and what the tax rate should be, there is a provision to ensure that in certain circumstances exit tax gains are taxable in the Member State of origin of the taxpayer, but deferment should be allowed (under conditions). Similarly, while there is no EU requirement for a minimum corporate tax rate and traditionally many Member States did not have any anti-deferral rules,[264] there are now provisions which effectively penalise a company from owning and controlling subsidiaries in low-tax jurisdictions. Finally, while there are no common corporate tax rules other than those set out in the Directives discussed above, nevertheless benefitting from mismatches in the national tax legislations of the Member States leading to double non-taxation is now against EU law.

Overall, the different Member State legal context in which these rules were supplanted has been largely ignored, with the EU assuming an overarching need for a minimum level of protection. As a result, there is some duplication of rules (e.g. when a Member State has its own general anti-abuse rule) and potentially a negative impact on the competitiveness of Member States. For smaller Member States, there is also an increased administrative burden imposed as a result of the rules. It should not be forgotten that the EU is a

---

[262] See Council Directive (EU) 2017/952 of 29 May 2017 amending Directive (EU) 2016/1164 as regards hybrid mismatches with third countries, [2017] OJ L 144 – often called ATAD II.

[263] In line with the compromise agreement, the amended Directive includes a carve-out option through to 31 December 2022, for hybrid regulatory capital in the banking sector, and a carve-out for financial traders involving hybrid transfers made in the ordinary course of business.

[264] See, for example, the study on aggressive tax planning, produced in the context of the Anti-Tax Avoidance Package which recognised that many Member States have no CFC rules or have ineffective CFC rules. Also, *Commission Communication on the Anti-Tax Avoidance Package: Next steps towards delivering effective taxation and greater tax transparency in the EU*, COM/2016/023 final. Also, see analysis in sec 7.2.2 of this book.

mixture of Member States of different sizes, economies, social policy needs and very importantly, of different philosophies of public finances.

2.7 DIRECTIVES ON MUTUAL ASSISTANCE AND TAX TRANSPARENCY

There has long existed EU secondary legislation that provided mutual assistance between tax authorities,[265] notwithstanding the lack of a central EU tax administration to oversee matters. This legislation has now been revised and updated in the form of the Directive on Mutual Assistance for the Recovery of Taxes[266] and the Directive on Administrative Cooperation.[267] These Directives have a wide scope of application. The previous version of these Directives was primarily used to deal with emigrating individuals who left outstanding tax bills, though the updated Directives are now unequivocally applicable to companies.[268]

The Directive on Administrative Cooperation (the 2011 version) introduced an important provision for *automatic* exchange of information. Heavily influenced by the US Foreign Account Tax Compliance Act (FATCA)[269] and the success of the

---

[265] See Council Directive 76/308/EEC of 15 March 1976 on Mutual Assistance for the Recovery of Claims Resulting from Operations Forming Part of the System of Financing the European Agricultural Guidance and Guarantee Fund and of Agricultural Levies and Customs Duties and in Respect of Value Added Tax and Certain Excise Duties, and Council Directive 77/799/EEC of 19 December 1977 Concerning Mutual Assistance by the Competent Authorities of the Member States in the Field of Direct Taxation and Taxation of Insurance Premiums.

[266] Council Directive 2010/24/EU of 16 March 2010 Concerning Mutual Assistance for the Recovery of Claims Relating to Taxes, Duties and Other Measures, repealing Council Directive 76/308/EEC of 15 March 1976 on Mutual Assistance for the Recovery of Claims Resulting from Operations Forming Part of the System of Financing the European Agricultural Guidance and Guarantee Fund and of Agricultural Levies and Customs Duties and in Respect of Value Added Tax and Certain Excise Duties.

[267] Council Directive 2011/16/EU of 15 February 2011 on administrative cooperation in the field of taxation, repealing Council Directive 77/799/EEC of 19 December 1977 Concerning Mutual Assistance by the Competent Authorities of the Member States in the Field of Direct Taxation and Taxation of Insurance Premiums. See also implementing Regulation (EU) No 1189/2011 for Council Directive 2010/24/EU on strengthening mutual assistance between the Member States in the recovery of taxes. The Commission has recently published a proposal for the codification of the Directive. The codification will not modify the content of the acts but will merely consolidate them. See Proposal for a Council Directive on administrative cooperation in the field of taxation (codification), COM/2020/49 final.

[268] For example, the new Mutual Assistance Directive 2010/24/EU applies to claims relating, inter alia, to all taxes and duties of any kind levied by or on behalf of a Member State. See Art 1(a). It is evident that companies are included in the concept of a debtor/addressee for the purposes of a claim. See paras 5 and 12 of the Preamble; Art 3(c)(ii) where companies are expressly included in the definition of 'persons'; Art 6; Art 11(2)(a); Art 20 on costs, etc. Also, under the Directive on Administrative Cooperation 2011/16/EU, it is made explicit that exchange of information can relate to natural and legal persons, to associations of persons and any other legal arrangement.

[269] FATCA was enacted as Title V of the Hiring Incentives to Restore Employment Act, Pub L. No 111-147, §§ 501–62, 124 Stat 71.

2.7 Directives on Mutual Assistance and Tax Transparency

now obsolete EU's Savings Directive,[270] it was stipulated that from January 2015, there would be automatic exchange of information for five types of income: namely, income from employment, director's fees, life insurance products not covered by other Directives, pensions, ownership of and income from immovable property.[271] While this and other provisions[272] of the new Directive were hailed as groundbreaking, by the time they became effective, more amendments began to be introduced for more extensive automatic exchange of information.

The first major amendment to the Directive on Administrative Cooperation was agreed in 2014,[273] in the midst of the OECD/G20's BEPS project. This amendment introduced automatic exchange of financial account information, similar to the OECD's Common Reporting Standard.[274] This allowed Member States to apply the widest possible scope of automatic exchange of information within the EU, covering most categories of income and capital held by private individuals and certain entities.[275]

The second amendment was agreed in 2015, partly as a response to the (impending) recommendations of the OECD/G20 under Action 5 of the BEPS Action Plan and partly as a response to the Luxembourg Leaks[276] and the Commission's state aid investigations into transfer pricing rulings given to multinationals.[277] This amendment introduced a provision for automatic exchange of information on tax rulings and advance pricing agreements,[278] under certain conditions.

A third amendment to the Directive was agreed in 2016, again as a response to the BEPS project and most specifically Action 13. This amendment introduced automatic exchange of country-by-country reports.[279] There were also calls for

---

[270] Council Directive 2003/48/EC of 3 June 2003 on taxation of savings income in the form of interest payments. Also, see Council Directive (EU) 2015/2060 on repeal.
[271] See Directive on Administrative Cooperation, Art 8.
[272] See, for example, the requirement for the transmission of third country information received by one Member State to another when this is useful under Art 16(3); the requirement for any wider cooperation provided by a Member State to a third country to be extended to other Member States (the most-favoured-national clause) under Art 19. Also, under specific circumstances, information by a Member State from a third country could be transmitted to the other Member States – see Art 24.
[273] Council Directive 2014/107/EU of 9 December 2014 amending Directive 2011/16/EU as regards the mandatory automatic exchange of information in the field of taxation, [2014] OJ L 359.
[274] See (OECD 2014) *Standard for Automatic Exchange of Financial Account Information in Tax Matters*, OECD Publishing, available at: https://doi.org/10.1787/9789264216525-en. There is now a revised edition: OECD (2017), *Standard for Automatic Exchange of Financial Account Information in Tax Matters, Second Edition*, OECD Publishing, available at: https://doi.org/10.1787/9789264267992-en.
[275] Austria was to be given an additional year to apply the new rules.
[276] On the Luxembourg Leaks, see www.icij.org/project/luxembourg-leaks.
[277] See Christiana HJI Panayi, *Advanced Issues in International and European Tax Law* (Hart Publishing, 2015), ch 7.
[278] Council Directive (EU) 2015/2376 of 8 December 2015 amending Directive 2011/16/EU as regards the mandatory automatic exchange of information in the field of taxation, [2015] OJ L 332.
[279] Council Directive (EU) 2016/881 of 25 May 2016 amending Directive 2011/16/EU as regards the mandatory automatic exchange of information in the field of taxation, [2016] OJ L 146.

information exchanges to be made public, though this Commission proposal[280] was never approved.

The latest amendment[281] was agreed in 2018. This amendment introduced automatic exchange of reportable cross-border arrangements in order to disclose potentially aggressive tax planning arrangements.[282] Again, this was heavily influenced by Action 12 of the BEPS Action Plan, which, however, did not result in a minimum standard being recommended.

Following the Commission's recent Action Plan for fair and simple taxation supporting the recovery strategy due to the Covid-19 pandemic,[283] there is now a proposal to amend this Directive again, in order to extend the scope of the automatic exchange of information rules to digital platforms.[284] This new proposal will ensure that Member States automatically exchange information on the revenues generated by sellers of goods and providers of services using online platforms. The proposal places an obligation on digital platform operators to provide information on such sellers of goods and providers of services. Clarificatory changes are also proposed on rules relating to the existing provisions on exchange of information on request and more specifically, on the standard of foreseeable relevance and group requests.

Overall, the amendments to the Directive on Administrative Cooperation have significantly enhanced and simplified cooperation between Member States by

---

[280] This initiative took the form of a proposal to amend the Accounting Directive requiring disclosure of financial accounts (2013/34/EU). As such, it only required a qualified majority and not unanimity. See Proposed amendment to Accounting Directive (2013/34/EU) regarding disclosure of income tax information (COM(2016) 198/2). Under this proposal, MNEs (EU/non-EU) with a consolidated turnover of EUR 750 million would be required to publish annually a report disclosing the profit and the tax accrued and paid in each Member State on a country-by-country basis for the EU Member States, and in the aggregate for all non-EU countries. The information, which would be less detailed than under the existing country-by-country reporting rules, would be made available in a stand-alone report on the company's website and be accessible to the public for at least five years. Companies would also have to file the report with a business register in the EU. See analysis in HJI Panayi, 'The Europeanisation of Good Tax Governance', Pt IV(A).

[281] A previous amendment agreed in 2016, introduced provisions providing for access to anti-money laundering information by tax authorities. See Council Directive (EU) 2016/2258 of 6 December 2016 amending Directive 2011/16/EU as regards access to anti-money-laundering information by tax authorities, [2016] OJ L 342.

[282] Council Directive (EU) 2018/822 of 25 May 2018 amending Directive 2011/16/EU as regards the mandatory automatic exchange of information in the field of taxation in relation to reportable cross-border arrangements, [2018] OJ L 139. Also see recently enacted Implementing Regulation (EU) 2019/532 amending Implementing Regulation (EU) 2015/2378 as regards the standard forms, including linguistic arrangements, for the mandatory automatic exchange of information on reportable cross-border arrangements. For commentary, see Franklin Cachia, 'Tax Transparency for Intermediaries: The Mandatory Disclosure Rules and Its EU Impact' (2018) 4 *EC Tax Review* 206–17; Roman Seer and Sascha Kargitta, 'Exchange of Information and Cooperation in Direct Taxation', in Christiana HJI Panayi, Werner Halsehner, Edoardo Traversa (eds), *Research Handbook in European Union Taxation Law* (Elgar Publishing, 2020) ch 22.

[283] Communication from the Commission to European Parliament and the Council, *An action plan for fair and simple taxation supporting the recovery strategy*, COM(2020) 312 final (15 July 2020).

[284] Proposal for a Council Directive amending Directive 2011/16/EU on administrative cooperation in the field of taxation, COM(2020) 314 final (15 July 2020).

making the automatic exchange of information more mainstream – arguably, the default position for important categories of information. This takes away the need for a prior request from one Member State to another – with all its associated delays and the potential legal obstacles that could arise in fulfilling that request. While there can still be requests for exchange of information in the traditional way, nevertheless, for important categories of information, the procedure for exchange has largely been taken outside the scope of the administrative powers of Member States. The increased availability of automatic exchange of information has also fast-tracked other forms of supranational cooperation, such as money-laundering rules.[285]

One cannot help but acknowledge the increasingly important role of the Commission in this area. Notably, under some of the amendments mentioned above, automatically exchanged information on tax rulings and advanced pricing agreements and automatically exchanged information on reportable cross-border arrangements will be stored in a central directory which is to be developed by the Commission.[286] Although there is not much information as to how these central directories will be run, what safeguards will be developed to avoid conflict of interests and how taxpayers' rights will be protected, this arrangement may empower the Commission to have a more strategic involvement in supra-national cooperation and the oversight of it. This role is likely to be further enhanced if the CCTB/CCCTB proposals are ever approved.

2.8 PENDING LEGISLATIVE PROPOSALS

The remainder of this chapter will deal with important legislative proposals which are still pending.

---

[285] See analysis in Christiana HJI Panayi, 'The Peripatetic Nature of EU Corporate Tax Law', 24 (2019) *Deakin Law Review* 1, 41–2.

[286] Under the provisions of the Directive introducing automatic exchange of information on rulings and advance pricing agreements (Directive 2015/2376/EU), the central directory will be 'accessible to all Member States and the Commission, to which Member States would upload and store information, instead of exchanging that information by secured email'. See para 19 of the Preamble. The practical arrangements necessary for the establishment of such a directory are to be adopted by the Commission in accordance with the procedure referred to in Art 26(2) of Directive 2011/16/EU. See amendments to paras 3 and 5 of Art 21. Similarly, under the provisions of the Directive introducing automatic exchange of information for reportable cross-border arrangements (Directive 2018/822/EU), the Commission must develop and provide technical and logistical support and a secure Member State central directory. See Art 21(5). Also, implementing powers are conferred on the Commission to adopt the necessary practical arrangements for upgrading the central directory. See para 16 of the Preamble. No central directory seems to be foreseen for the automatic exchange of country-by-country information. Such information will be exchanged electronically through the Common Communication Network (CCN). However, under the newly added para 6 of Art 21, '[t]he Commission shall, by means of implementing acts, adopt the necessary practical arrangements for the upgrading of the CCN network'.

2.8.1 *The CCTB/CCCTB*

Ever since the publication of the 2001 Company Tax Study, the Commission had been working on a project for a Common Consolidated Corporate Tax Base (CCCTB). On 16 March 2011, the Commission published the eagerly awaited first official proposal for the CCCTB.[287] Broadly, the 2011 CCCTB proposal provided companies with establishments in at least two Member States with detailed *optional* rules to compute their group taxable income according to one set of rules, those of the newly consolidated tax base, rather than according to the national tax bases of each Member State. The overall aim of the CCCTB was to reduce the costs of complying with different Member State tax regimes, to minimise tax arbitrage and simplify restructurings. It also aimed to provide a comprehensive consolidation of profits and losses on an EU basis.[288] In other words, the CCCTB was essentially proposed as an additional system – an alternative to Member States' existing corporate tax systems. The Commission extolled the proposal, in that it would offer companies a 'one-stop-shop' system for filing their tax returns, as well as provide for consolidation, leading to savings in compliance time and costs.[289] It was also claimed that the new system would bring tangible benefits for companies wishing to expand into the other Member States.[290]

Although the proposal was not immediately curbed on the basis of subsidiarity and enjoyed the support of the European Parliament, which in fact advocated for its mandatory application,[291] not much happened thereafter. After years of technical discussions in Council, it was clear that some of the provisions of the original CCCTB proposal and especially consolidation were too ambitious to be adopted. Several Member States and, in particular, the UK were opposed to this proposal, as they would lose much of their powers to determine their corporate tax policy. Smaller Member States were also concerned that formulary apportionment under this proposal would have the overall effect of shifting tax revenues to larger countries with larger markets such as France and Germany.[292]

It was widely thought that discussions on the more controversial aspects of the proposal – notably, consolidation and formulary apportionment – held back progress

---

[287] Proposal for a Council Directive on a Common Consolidated Corporate Tax Base (CCCTB) COM (2011), 121/4 2011/0058.
[288] See Commission press release, IP/11/319, dated 16 March 2011.
[289] The Commission estimated that the CCCTB would save businesses across the EU €700 million in reduced compliance costs, €1 billion in reduced costs to expand cross-border and €1.3 billion through consolidation. It was also estimated that businesses looking to expand cross-border would benefit from up to €1 billion in savings. See press release IP/11/319, dated 16 March 2011. Also see MEMO/11/171, dated 16 March 2011, p 2.
[290] Ibid, p 5.
[291] See Press Release published in Tax Analysts, 2012 WTD 57-24.
[292] See *Study on the economic and budgetary impact of the introduction of a common consolidated corporate tax base in the European Union*, commissioned by the Irish Department of Finance from EY in 2011. Also see Michael Devereux and Simon Loretz, *The Effects of EU Formula Apportionment on Corporate Tax Revenues*, Oxford University Centre for Business Taxation, WP 7/06.

2.8 Pending Legislative Proposals

on other less controversial but still important areas, which could be agreed more quickly. Furthermore, the 2011 CCCTB proposal was very much overshadowed by the high profile OECD/G20 BEPS project and the EU's eager response to this initiative.[293] Arguably, the 2011 CCCTB proposal had to be adjusted to be perceived as truly effective in tackling aggressive tax planning and not just to reduce compliance costs for multinationals.

Interest in the CCCTB was reinvigorated with the appointment of Jean-Claude Juncker as President of the European Commission in 2014. In October 2015, a consultation on the relaunch of the CCCTB was published[294] and in the 2015 Commission Action Plan for a Fair and Efficient Corporate Tax System,[295] the Commission announced that it would relaunch the CCCTB the following year. This was to be done through a two-step approach: Member States would first agree on rules for a common tax base, after which agreement would be reached on the consolidation element. Neither the original proposal published in 2011,[296] nor the later 2016 proposals involved changes to Member States' corporate tax rates.

Indeed, the proposals relaunched in October 2016 consisted of two separate Directives, one for a Common Corporate Tax Base (the CCTB Directive)[297] and the other, again, for a Common Consolidated Corporate Tax Base (the CCCTB Directive).[298] The difference between the CCTB and the CCCTB Directives was the cross-border consolidation of profits and losses, and the elimination of intra-group transactions. What is notable was that under the new proposals, the focus of attention had shifted from the objective of facilitating corporate groupings and simplifying compliance, to countering tax avoidance. In fact, the draft CCTB Directive contained provisions similar to those already adopted under the Anti-Tax Avoidance Directive, as far as the anti-abuse provisions were concerned.[299]

The first important feature of the original and the subsequent proposals is the common tax base. There are uniform rules for calculating the tax base of group members that fall under the scope of the proposals. The second significant feature of the proposals is consolidation, that is, the automatic set-off of profits and losses and

---

[293] HJI Panayi, *Advanced Issues in International and European Tax Law*, chapters 5–6.
[294] See Public consultation on the Re-launch of the Common Consolidated Corporate Tax Base (CCCTB), available at: http://ec.europa.eu/taxation_customs/common/consultations/tax/relaunch_ccctb_en.htm.
[295] Communication from the Commission to the European Parliament and the Council, *A Fair and Efficient Corporate Tax System in the European Union: 5 Key Areas for Action* COM(2015) 302 final, 17 June 2015.
[296] Proposal for a Council Directive on a Common Consolidated Corporate Tax Base (CCCTB) COM (2011), 121/4 2011/0058 (CNS). Also see Christiana HJI Panayi, *The Common Consolidated Corporate Tax Base and the UK* (Institute for Fiscal Studies, 2011).
[297] Proposal for a Council Directive on a Common Corporate Tax Base, COM(2016) 685 final (CCTB Directive).
[298] Proposal for a Council Directive on a Common Consolidated Corporate Tax Base, COM(2016) 683 final (CCCTB Directive).
[299] See Arts 13, 58–61a of CCTB Directive.

the elimination of intra-group transactions for group members. One central difference between the 2011 and the 2016 proposals is that the provisions for consolidation have now been moved to a different Directive in order to at least progress with the common tax base. Another important difference between the 2016 proposals and the 2011 proposal is that the new rules (i.e. the common tax base and subsequently consolidation) are *mandatory* for large corporate groups – defined as groups with a consolidated turnover exceeding €750 m.[300] It is no longer an option for eligible groups to choose between the new tax base or existing Member State rules, as it was in the 2011 proposal. However, companies falling outside the scope of the proposed Directive may opt to apply its rules under certain conditions (voluntary opt-in).[301] Therefore, if enacted, the CCTB/CCCTB proposals would replace Member States' corporate tax bases for eligible taxpayers rather than provide an additional optional tax base from which to choose.

Furthermore, the proposed rules are limited to EU resident companies (the qualifying subsidiaries)[302] and EU permanent establishments. Contrary to the 2011 CCCTB proposal, the revised permanent establishment definition refers only to permanent establishments situated in the European Union and belonging to a taxpayer resident for tax purposes in the European Union. The EU permanent establishments of third-country companies are not covered – their position is to be dealt with in bilateral tax treaties and national law.

As in the initial 2011 proposal, there is deliberately no formal link between the new tax base and international accounting standards such as IAS/IFRS. The methodology for adjusting financial accounts to arrive at the tax base (the 'bridge') is not defined and as such, companies are expected to continue to prepare their financial accounts based on their national accounting standards. Furthermore, under the new common tax base, as set out in the 2011 and the 2016 proposals, the profit and loss method is preferred over the tax balance sheet method.[303] The tax year is any 12-month period.[304] The tax base is designed broadly. It is stipulated in the Preamble that all revenues will be taxable unless expressly exempt.[305] The basic formulation of the tax base is the following: revenues less exempt revenues, deductible expenses and other deductible items.[306] All these concepts are defined in the proposals. There is also a list of non-deductible expenses.[307] The 2016 CCTB Directive (as the original 2011 proposal) also contains detailed rules on depreciation.[308] For the purposes of

---

[300] Ibid, Art 2(1)(c).
[301] Ibid, Art 2(3).
[302] A 'qualifying subsidiary' is defined as every immediate and lower-tier subsidiary in which the parent company has a right to exercise more than 50 per cent of the voting rights and has an ownership right amounting to more than 75 per cent of the subsidiary's capital or profit. See Art 5(1) of the CCTB Directive.
[303] See Art 6 (General Principles) of the CCTB Directive.
[304] See Art 6(4) of CCTB Directive.
[305] Preamble, p 9, CCTB Directive.
[306] Ibid, Art 7.
[307] Ibid, Art 12.
[308] See Ch IV, Art 30 et seq of CCTB Directive.

2.8 Pending Legislative Proposals

calculating the tax base, transactions are measured by reference, inter alia, to monetary consideration and market value.[309]

What is novel in the 2016 CCTB proposal is the very generous provision for deduction: the super-deduction for R&D costs. It is provided that on top of the amounts already deductible for R&D costs, a deduction of an extra 50 per cent of R&D costs each tax year will be granted for costs up to €20 m and 25 per cent for expenditure above this level. An enhanced 100 per cent extra deduction will be available to start-ups for R&D expenditure up to €20 m.[310] The CCTB Directive does not provide for a patent or innovation box, but this is thought to be a good alternative to entice the Member States to agree to the proposal and abandon their own patent boxes. It may also help attract high-value R&D activities to the EU.

Another addition to the CCTB proposal is the allowance for growth and investment (AGI), inserted to neutralise the current asymmetry between debt and equity financing.[311] The AGI is defined as the difference between the equity of a taxpayer and the tax value of its participation in the capital of associated enterprises.[312] Pursuant to this rule, taxpayers will be given a deduction in respect of a notional yield on defined increases in their equity (the AGI equity base).[313] This will be deductible from their taxable base subject to certain conditions to prevent tax avoidance. If an AGI equity base decreases, an amount equal to the notional yield of the AGI equity decrease shall become taxable. 'The outcome is a definitive advantage in favour of financing through debt as opposed to equity.'[314]

The CCCTB proposal sets out the conditions for the formation of a consolidated tax group, the mechanism for formulary apportionment and the allocation of the consolidated tax base to the relevant Member States. In addition, there are rules for entering and leaving a group, the treatment of losses, business reorganisations and the intra-group transfer of assets. Under the CCCTB proposal, consolidation would be mandatory to all groups that fall within the scope of the CCTB proposal. So effectively, consolidation would be mandatory for large groups (with a consolidated group revenue exceeding €750 m) and limited to EU companies and EU permanent establishments. Groups that do not meet the size threshold could opt in to benefit from consolidation.[315]

The formula for apportionment is identical to the one proposed in the 2011 CCCTB proposal and is based on three equally weighted factors: labour, assets and sales.[316] As in the 2011 proposal, intangible assets are excluded from the base of

---

[309] Ibid, Art 20.
[310] Ibid, Art 9(3).
[311] Ibid, Art 11.
[312] Ibid, Art 11(1).
[313] Ibid, Art 11(3).
[314] See explanatory memorandum of CCTB Directive, p 10.
[315] Art 2(3) of CCCTB Directive.
[316] See Ch VIII of CCCTB Directive.

the asset factor, and the sales factor is sales by destination.[317] The 2016 CCCTB Directive also contains sector-specific formulae for financial institutions,[318] insurance,[319] oil and gas,[320] shipping and air transport.[321]

As in the original proposal, there are detailed administrative provisions for consolidated groups. The CCCTB is meant to offer qualifying groups a one-stop-shop approach – the group would deal with one Member State tax administration in the EU, usually, the Member State where the group's parent company is tax resident. It should be pointed out that most of the proposed administrative functions under the CCCTB depend on Member State tax administrations and cooperation between them. The Commission only has an ad hoc role.

For example, the principal taxpayer must give notice to the principal tax authority for the creation of the group.[322] Also, the principal taxpayer must file the consolidated tax return with the principal tax authority,[323] even though the return is considered as an assessment of the tax liability of each group member.[324] There are rules prescribing the contents of the tax return,[325] the notification of errors in the tax return[326] and rules on electronic filing, tax returns and supporting documentation.[327] Where the principal taxpayer failed to file a consolidated tax return, the principal tax authority would issue an assessment within three months based on an estimate, taking into account all available information.[328] This could be appealed by the principal taxpayer.[329]

An essential feature of the proposed system is the sharing of information between competent authorities. The principal taxpayer's consolidated tax return and supporting documents are to be stored on a central database to which *all* the competent authorities will have access.[330] The advance ruling mechanism of the draft CCCTB Directive provides for some decentralisation of functions. A taxpayer can request an opinion from the competent authority of the Member State in which it is resident or has a permanent establishment.[331] Provided that all relevant information concerning the planned transaction or series of transactions are

---

[317] See Arts 37–8 of CCCTB Directive.
[318] Ibid, Art 40.
[319] Ibid, Art 41.
[320] Ibid, Art 42.
[321] Ibid, Art 43.
[322] Ibid, Art 46. For the terms of the notice and the information to be included, see Art 47.
[323] Ibid, Art 51.
[324] Ibid, Art 51(2).
[325] Ibid, Art 52.
[326] Ibid, Art 53.
[327] Ibid, Art 55.
[328] Ibid, Art 54.
[329] Ibid.
[330] Ibid, Art 57. All information communicated between competent authorities on matters relating to the CCCTB Directive is expected to be provided by electronic means using the common communication network/common system interface (CCN/CSI). Art 62.
[331] Art 61 of CCCTB Directive.

2.8 Pending Legislative Proposals

disclosed, the opinion issued by the competent authority will be binding on it. The competent authorities of more than one Member States can agree on a common opinion, where two or more group members in different Member States are directly involved in a specific transaction or a series of transactions, or where the request concerns the proposed composition of a group.[332]

Decentralisation of functions and Member State cooperation is also prevalent as regards audits[333] and appeals.[334] Audits may be initiated and coordinated by the principal tax authority, but the authorities of any Member State in which a group member is subject to tax may request the initiation of an audit.[335] The principal tax authority and the other competent authorities will *jointly* determine the audit and the group members to be audited.[336] The audit is conducted according to the legislation of the Member State in which it is carried out, subject to the required adjustments under the draft CCCTB Directive. The principal tax authority will compile the results of the audits. Therefore, the audit is centralised, and no time limits are set out.

The competent authority of the Member State in which a group member is resident or established may challenge a decision of the principal tax authority concerning the notice to opt or an amended assessment before the courts of the Member State of the principal tax authority within three months, having the same procedural rights as a taxpayer of that Member State in proceedings against a decision of the principal tax authority.[337] A principal taxpayer may appeal against a number of acts such as a decision rejecting a notice to opt, a notice requesting the disclosure of documents or information, an assessment on the failure to file a consolidated tax return etc.[338] Such appeal will not have any suspensory effect on the tax liability of a taxpayer.

Appeals are to be heard by competent administrative bodies in the Member State of the principal tax authority,[339] and if there are none, then the taxpayer may directly lodge a judicial appeal.[340] Again, a judicial appeal against a decision of the principal tax authority will be governed by the law of the Member State of that principal tax authority.[341] However, in making submissions to the national court, the principal tax authority will act in consultation with the other competent authorities.[342] The national court may order further

---

[332] Ibid.
[333] Ibid, Art 64.
[334] Ibid, Art 66.
[335] Ibid, Art 64.
[336] Ibid.
[337] Ibid, Art 65.
[338] Ibid, Art 66.
[339] Ibid, Art 67.
[340] Ibid.
[341] Ibid, Art 68.
[342] Ibid, Art 68(2).

evidence from the principal taxpayer and the principal tax authority, assisted by other competent authorities.[343]

Incidentally, when the 2011 CCCTB Directive was first released, it was thought that it provided a far too extensive mechanism for the sharing of information which went beyond the existing legislation at the time (i.e. tax treaties and Directive 77/799). However, as shown in 2.7, subsequent amendments to the Directive on Administrative Cooperation have gone much further than the proposals under the 2011 CCCTB Directive, which were broadly replicated in the 2016 CCCTB Directive.

Even though the draft CCTB/CCCTB Directives have still not been adopted at the time of writing, they remain high in the agenda of the Commission, with several compromise texts appearing since the 2016 relaunch.[344] The European Parliament has been very supportive of the proposed Directives and both the new Commission President, Ursula von der Leyen, and the new Commissioner dealing with taxation, Paolo Gentiloni, have indicated that the adoption of the CCTB/CCCTB would be a priority for them.[345]

2.8.2 *The Financial Transaction Tax*

The proposal for a Financial Transaction Tax has an interesting history. The Commission first proposed a common system of Financial Transaction Tax (FTT) on 28 September 2011.[346] The FTT was promoted as a levy, which would ensure that the financial sector contributed to the covering of the costs of the financial crisis, as well as discourage excessively risky activities by financial institutions. The FTT was not meant to affect citizens and businesses. The Commission estimated revenues of approximately €57 billion annually, with the possibility that some would be allocated to the EU Budget, thus reducing the contributions of Member States.

---

[343] Ibid, Art 68(3).
[344] See, for example, the Austrian Presidency compromise text published in December 2018: Proposal for a Council Directive on a Common Corporate Tax Base (CCTB), COM(2016) 685 final, 5 December 2018, available at: https://data.consilium.europa.eu/doc/document/ST-13024-2018-INIT/en/pdf. Also see the Romanian Presidency compromise text of the Proposal for a Council Directive on a Common Corporate Tax Base (CCTB) published by the Council of the European Union in June 2019: Proposal for a Council Directive on a Common Corporate Tax Base (CCTB), COM (2016) 685 final, 6 June 2019, available at: https://data.consilium.europa.eu/doc/document/ST-9676-2019-INIT/en/pdf.
[345] See the mission statement that Commissioner-designate Paolo Gentiloni received from President-elect Ursula von der Leyen on 10 September 2019, available at: https://ec.europa.eu/commission/sites/beta-political/files/mission-letter-paolo-gentiloni_en.pdf.
[346] Proposal for a Council Directive on a common system of financial transaction tax and amending Directive 2008/7/EC, COM(2011) 594 final, Brussels, 28 September 2011. Also, see the accompanying impact assessment: Commission Staff Working Paper, Impact Assessment accompanying the document Proposal for a Council Directive on a common system of financial transaction tax and amending Directive 2008/7/EC (28 September 2011), SEC(2011) 1102 final.

2.8 Pending Legislative Proposals

The FTT would only apply if one of the two parties is a financial institution and if one of the two parties – whether the financial institution or the non-financial institution – is established in a Member State. A tax of 0.1 per cent for most financial transactions other than derivatives and 0.01 per cent for derivative contracts was envisaged. These were minimum rates, and the participating Member States were entitled to apply higher rates.

Under the FTT, the term 'financial transactions'[347] was defined broadly to include the sale or purchase of financial instruments, money-market instruments, units or shares in collective investment undertakings, transfers of financial instruments between group entities and the conclusion or modification of derivatives. Transactions on the primary market were exempt. Some other transactions were not included, such as spot currency transactions, consumer transactions (e.g. concluding insurance contracts, mortgage lending), the issuing of government bonds and transactions with certain bodies (e.g. central banks of Member States).

'Financial institutions' were very broadly defined and comprised of all financial institutions and special purpose vehicles, as well as certain non-financial companies where a significant part of their overall activities was financial.[348] Some institutions such as the European Financial Stability Facility and national central banks were excluded from the definition. Very importantly, a financial institution and a person that is not a financial institution would be deemed to be established in a Member State under a number of criteria.[349] Therefore, under certain circumstances, non-EU financial institutions would be deemed EU-established. There was an escape clause in that no FTT would be levied where there was no link between the economic substance of the transaction and the territory of any Member State.[350] Each financial institution that was a party to the financial transaction would pay FTT, and there would be joint and several liability.[351]

This version of the Directive was never approved as there were strong objections from some Member States. By June 2012 at the ECOFIN meeting, it became clear that the Commission's proposal had not gathered the necessary support to be adopted by the Member States and could only be adopted through the enhanced cooperation procedure set out under the EU Treaties.[352] In the January 2013 ECOFIN Council, the adoption of the FTT through enhanced cooperation was

---

[347] See Art 2(1)(1) of the draft 2011 FTT Directive.
[348] Ibid, Art 2(7).
[349] Where the financial institution has been authorised to act as a financial institution, in respect of transactions covered by authorisation (Art 3(1)(a)); where it has its registered seat (Art 3(1)(b)); where it has its permanent address or usual residence (Art 3(1)(c)); where it has a branch, in respect of transactions carried out by the branch (Art 3(1)(d)); where it is a party to a financial transaction with a party established in the EU, or it is acting as an intermediary for a party of a financial transaction where one of the parties is established in the EU (Art 3(1)(e)). This list was hierarchical, so if more than one of the conditions were met, the first had priority. See Art 3(2) of the draft 2011 FTT Directive.
[350] See Art 3(3) of the draft 2011 FTT Directive.
[351] Ibid, Art 9.
[352] Article 20 TEU and Arts 326–34 TFEU.

approved by qualified majority. The UK, Luxembourg, Malta and the Czech Republic raised concerns that the Commission had not provided any analysis of the impacts that an FTT through enhanced cooperation would have on the individual Member States. The dissenting Member States abstained from voting.

On 14 February 2013, the Commission adopted a proposal for a Council Directive implementing enhanced cooperation in FTT.[353] The revenue estimate was adjusted to €30–35 billion per year. Part of this would be added to the EU Budget directly as an own resource, reducing the contributions of participating Member States accordingly. This proposal had to be unanimously approved by the participating Member States to be adopted by them. Compared to the 2011 FTT proposal, the most important change was introducing the issuance principle, whereby financial instruments issued in the participating Member States would be taxed when traded, even if the parties trading them were not established in the FTT Member States. This principle was thought to be very contentious, as in certain circumstances it could have extraterritorial effects.[354] A general anti-abuse rule was also inserted.

The Commission's revised proposal met with strong disagreement from the UK government which eventually referred to the Court of Justice the authorising decision to adopt the FTT through enhanced cooperation.[355] It was argued that the use of enhanced cooperation to introduce the FTT would have extraterritorial effect and would result in the non-participating Member States incurring implementation and collection costs.[356] The Court of Justice rejected the UK's challenge on a rather technical point: the UK's arguments were based on the draft Directive, which was not part of the decision to authorise the use of enhanced cooperation. The review of the Court of Justice was limited to whether that decision was valid in light of Art 20 TEU and Arts 326–334 TFEU, which defined the substantive and procedural conditions relating to the granting of such authorisation. Overall, the Court of Justice found the challenge to be premature. The overtone of the decision was that if, and when, an FTT was adopted under enhanced cooperation, it would be possible for the UK to challenge the measures at that point. Therefore, a subsequent challenge could be admissible, depending on the form and scope of any FTT.

Even though the Commission had the requisite minimum number of Member States to pursue the revised proposal through enhanced cooperation, not much has

[353] Proposal for a Council Directive implementing enhanced cooperation in the area of financial transaction tax, COM(2011) 71 final. Also, see accompanying Commission Staff Working Document, 'Impact Assessment accompanying the document Proposal for a Council Directive implementing enhanced cooperation in the area of financial transaction tax: analysis of policy options and impacts', SWD(2013) 28 final of 14 February 2013.
[354] See Christiana HJI Panayi, 'The EU's Financial Transaction Tax, Enhanced Cooperation and the UK's challenge' [2013] 8 *European Taxation* pp 358–67.
[355] Case C-209/13 UK v. Council, ECLI:EU:C:2014:283.
[356] The potential extraterritoriality of the amended proposal was also raised in an internal legal opinion prepared by the EU Council Legal Service. See David D Stewart and Stephanie Soong Johnston, 'EU Council Opinion Casts Doubt on Legality of Financial Transaction Tax', 2013 WTD 176-1.

happened since the publication of this proposal. While throughout the years most interested Member States reiterated their commitment to implementing the FTT at ECOFIN meetings, behind the scenes, there has been disagreement as to the central components of the proposal and a lukewarm approach by some of the participating Member States. Nevertheless, this proposal still features on the agenda of the Commission and some Member States.

2.8.3 *Proposals for Taxation of the Digital Economy*

The proper taxation of the digital economy has been a major theme of the OECD/G20's BEPS project and its aftermath. The Commission has also tried to tackle the issue through some interesting proposals. In September 2017, the Commission published the Communication on a fair and efficient tax system for the digital market in the EU.[357] In this Communication, the Commission outlined the problems policymakers face in ensuring that the digital economy is taxed fairly. The Commission set out the two main challenges that had to be addressed: *where* to tax (the nexus issue) and *what* to tax (the value creation issue). In addressing these challenges, the Commission reviewed potential long-term and short-term solutions.[358]

In March 2018, the Commission published a proposal for a Directive on the introduction of a digital permanent establishment concept based on significant digital presence[359] and a proposal for a Directive on a Digital Services Tax.[360] These proposals were accompanied by a Recommendation to the Member States to amend their tax treaties with third countries so that the same rules apply to EU and non-EU companies.[361] The Commission offered to assist the Member States with exploratory talks on implementing these proposals at an international level. The Commission also released a Communication on the tax challenges raised by the digital economy,[362] in which it analysed its long-term and short-term legislative measures for ensuring the fair taxation of profits within the EU.

---

[357] Communication from the Commission to the European Parliament and the Council, A *Fair and Efficient Tax System in the European Union for the Digital Single Market*, COM(2017) 547 final, Brussels, 21 September 2017.

[358] For example, a long-term solution was to incorporate provisions in the CCTB/CCCTB Directives, and short-term solutions were an equalisation tax on turnover of digitalised companies or a levy on revenues generated from the provision of digital services or advertising activity. See suggestions in p 10 of the Communication.

[359] Proposal for a Council Directive laying down rules relating to the corporate taxation of a significant digital presence, COM(2018) 147 final.

[360] Proposal for a Council Directive on the common system of a digital services tax on revenues resulting from the provision of certain digital services, COM(2018) 148 final.

[361] Commission Recommendation of 21 March 2018 relating to the corporate taxation of a significant digital presence, C(2018) 1650 final.

[362] Communication from the Commission to the European Parliament and the Council, *Time to establish a modern, fair and efficient taxation standard for the digital economy*, COM(2018) 146 final.

The first legislative proposal for a digital permanent establishment represented a long-term measure for taxing the digital economy. The proposal would enable the taxation of profits from digital activities, insofar as such profits were attributable to a significant digital presence maintained by entities (EU or non-EU) in a Member State. The requirement of a significant digital presence was deemed to be met if the business carried on in the relevant Member State consisted wholly or partly of the supply of digital services through a digital interface and at least one of the following conditions was met at group level:

(1) revenues resulting from the supply of digital services to users located in a Member State exceeds €7 million;
(2) the number of users of one or more of those digital services located in a Member State exceeds 100,000;
(3) the number of business contracts for the supply of digital services concluded by users located in a Member State exceeds 3,000.

There were rules to determine the profits attributable to significant digital presence, based on functional analysis and the economically significant activities relevant to the development, enhancement, maintenance, protection and exploitation of the enterprise's intangible assets. Very importantly, in determining the profits attributable to the significant digital presence, the taxpayer was to use the profit split method unless an alternative method was more appropriate.

This Directive would apply to all taxpayers subject to corporation tax in one or more Member States and entities resident for tax purposes in a third country, in respect of their significant digital presence in a Member State. It would not apply if an entity was tax resident in a third country, unless there was a tax treaty in force with the Member State in which there was a significant digital presence, which included similar provisions on significant digital presence and attribution of profits as in the draft Directive.

The second legislative proposal was a short-term measure: imposing a tax on the revenues resulting from the provision of certain digital services. The digital services tax would apply at the rate of 3 per cent on gross revenues created from activities where users play a major role in value creation, including revenues from the following activities: selling of online advertising space, making available to users of a multi-sided digital interface, the transmission of data collected about users and generated from users' activities on digital interfaces.

Only entities with total annual worldwide revenues of €750 million and EU taxable revenues of €50 million would be subject to this tax, irrespective of whether they were established in a Member State or third country. There were rules as regards the place of taxation – the location of the users of the taxable service. This approach followed the logic that the users' involvement in the digital activities of a company generated the value for that company, which may not necessarily entail payment from the users' side, or which may involve payment from some users only.[363] The Commission estimated that €5 billion could be generated in revenue per year for the Member States if the tax was applied at a rate of 3 per cent.[364]

In its Recommendation, the Commission argued that the Member States should amend existing tax treaties between the Member States and third countries to introduce the concept of significant digital presence and the rules for attributing profits to such a significant digital presence.

Luxembourg and Ireland have vehemently opposed the digital services tax, calling for discussions on a global approach at the OECD level. The other Member States have also followed suit. One recurrent argument is that this shift in taxing rights based on the location of the digital user in value creation is a major deviation from internationally recognised taxation principles and should be agreed at an international level and not by the EU unilaterally. Even the European Parliament has proposed[365] a sunset clause, under which a digital services tax would be a temporary levy until an agreement has been reached internationally. It was also recommended that the Member States most adversely affected by the introduction of the tax could be allocated a greater part of the revenue from this tax.[366]

Whether or not a watered-down version of the Commission's digital tax proposals will be eventually approved remains to be seen. Nevertheless, fair rules on digital taxation remain a priority for the Commission. It should be noted that the EU proposals are quite different from the OECD's ongoing work over a unified approach to deal with taxation of the digital economy.[367] Given that support for the OECD's unified approach seems to be unravelling with the OECD Secretariat unable to reach consensus and the US recently pulling out of the project (or seeking to 'pause' it),[368] there is a strong possibility that at least some of the Commission's digital tax proposals will be enacted. Interestingly, in the Commission's Covid-19 recovery plan, one of the options listed to help finance the recovery funding is a digital tax based on the OECD's work or the EU's own action if the OECD fails.[369]

---

[363] Proposal for a Council Directive on the common system of a digital services tax on revenues resulting from the provision of certain digital services, COM(2018) 148 final, p 11.

[364] See Questions and Answers on a Fair and Efficient Tax System in the EU for the Digital Single Market, Factsheet, available at http://europa.eu/rapid/press-release_MEMO-18-2141_en.htm.

[365] See Draft Report on the proposal for a Council directive on the common system of a digital services tax on revenues resulting from the provision of certain digital services (COM(2018)0148 – C8-0137/2018 – 2018/0073(CNS)).

[366] Ibid. Other proposed amendments included a rate increase from 3 to 5 per cent and broadening the scope to cover the supply of digital content and online sales.

[367] See OECD Public consultation document, Secretariat Proposal for a 'Unified Approach' under Pillar One (OECD 2019), available at: www.oecd.org/tax/beps/public-consultation-document-secretariat-proposal-unified-approach-pillar-one.pdf.

[368] In a letter dated 12 June 2020 to the finance ministers of France, Italy, Spain and the United Kingdom, US Treasury Secretary Steven T. Mnuchin asked for discussions to be paused to resume later in the year. The letter can be found at: https://assets.kpmg/content/dam/kpmg/us/pdf/2020/06/tnf-mnuchin-oecd-jun19-2020.PDF.

[369] See Commission Communication, *Europe's Moment: Repair and Prepare for the Next Generation*, COM(2020) 456 final (27 May 2020).

3

The Court of Justice and the Development of EU Corporate Tax Law

The reasons for the rather limited legislative action in the field of direct taxation at least initially were considered in Chapter 1. This chapter looks at how this legislative vacuum was addressed by the Court of Justice, which has been instrumental in interpreting and applying several general provisions of successive EU Treaties in the direct tax context.

3.1 TAX LITIGATION IN THE COURT OF JUSTICE

There are mainly two ways in which direct tax cases get to the Court of Justice: through infringement proceedings against Member States and as a result of preliminary references from national courts.

An infringement proceeding[1] is usually initiated following a complaint or a parliamentary question or petition to the European Parliament. Frequently, as far as direct tax disputes are concerned, infringement proceedings are commenced ex officio. The use of the infringement procedure is a very important weapon in the arsenal of the Commission.

When the Commission decides to open an infringement procedure, it addresses a 'letter of formal notice' to the Member State concerned, which has to submit its observations by a specified date.[2] In light of the reply or absence of a reply from the relevant Member State, the Commission may decide to address a 'reasoned opinion' to the Member State, clearly setting out the reasons why it considers there to be an infringement of EU law and how the Member State should comply within a specified period.[3] Following the reasoned opinion and the Member State's

---

[1] See Arts 258–60 TFEU. For state aid, the infringement procedure is governed by the state aid articles. See Chapter 8.
[2] The deadline for response is at the discretion of the Commission. It is normally two months but may be one week or less.
[3] Again, the deadline for the response is at the discretion of the Commission – it is normally two months but may be one week or less.

response to it,[4] the Commission may decide to bring an action before the Court of Justice.

At any stage the Commission may decide not to proceed with the infringement procedure, especially where the Member State provides credible assurances as to its intention to remove the infringement. The Commission has an overall discretion on whether and when to introduce cases before the Court of Justice. The Court of Justice will not normally question the manner in which such discretion is exercised. If a case is referred to it, the Court of Justice can only determine whether the relevant Member State has failed to fulfil its obligations.

The judgments of the Court of Justice in infringement proceedings are of a declaratory nature. Technically, there can only be a finding of violation[5] or no violation. Although the Court of Justice has no power to annul a measure or order a Member State to take specific action to remedy or remove a violation, its finding obliges the Member State to take all necessary measures to comply. If a Member State does not comply with this duty, there are financial sanctions.[6]

The Commission often uses infringement proceedings as a means of encouraging and stimulating a progressive evolution of EU laws and policies.[7] This is particularly obvious in the area of direct tax law, as shown throughout this book. However, not all possible instances of incompatibility come to the attention of the Commission, nor is the Commission able to pursue all cases. This unsystematic approach is exacerbated by the fact that the other means by which a case ends up in the Court of Justice, the preliminary reference mechanism, is even more random.[8]

Under the preliminary reference mechanism[9] a national court (or tribunal) may request a ruling from the Court of Justice on the interpretation of the Treaties or the validity and interpretation of acts of the institutions, bodies, offices or agencies of the Union, when such ruling is necessary to enable the national court to decide a case. A national court against whose decisions there is no judicial remedy under national law (i.e. a final court without a right of appeal) is obliged to make a reference.

Several important principles of EU law have been established by preliminary rulings, sometimes as a result of referrals by national courts at first instance.

---

[4] A Member State's unforeseen difficulties in implementing the Commission's letter of notice or reasoned opinion may be submitted for consideration to the Commission. However, the complexity of EU legislation to be transposed, the large number of implementing measures required or the brevity of the time limits for transposition cannot be used as a defence. See Luca Prete and Ben Smulders, 'The coming of age of infringement proceedings' (2010) 47(1) *Common Market Law Review*, 9–61, 38ff.
[5] The violation is established with effects ex tunc, though there is a possibility of limiting the retroactive effects of the reasoning.
[6] See Art 260(2) TFEU.
[7] Prete and Smulders, 'The coming of age of infringement proceedings', 14.
[8] Tracey A. Kaye, 'Direct taxation in the European Union: from Maastricht to Lisbon' (2012) 35(5) *Fordham International Law Journal*, 1231–59, 1235.
[9] See Art 267 TFEU. See Alan Zalasinki, 'Law and Facts and the Interpretative Jurisdiction of the ECJ in Preliminary Rulings in Direct Tax Matters', in Pasquale Pistone (ed), *Legal Remedies in European Tax Law* (Amsterdam: IBFD, 2009).

Therefore, this Treaty provision is very empowering, both for national courts and for litigants, in the case of final courts. In addition, the preliminary ruling mechanism furthers cooperation between the Court of Justice and national courts. It tries to ensure the effective and uniform application of EU laws by minimising the possibility of divergent interpretations by national courts. However, it is not an appeal procedure. The Court of Justice does not entertain challenges to the jurisdiction of the referring court based on national law. Moreover, sometimes the Court does not specifically reply to the questions posed by the national court, or leaves a lot of discretion to the referring court, thus, perhaps, not offering the level of legal protection requested by the litigant taxpayers.[10]

The Court of Justice's ruling takes the form of a judgment or reasoned order, in which the questions referred are answered in a general way. The referring court is bound by the interpretation of EU law given in the ruling and must give full effect to it. The referring court may have to refuse to apply conflicting provisions of national law, even if adopted subsequently.

In principle, other national courts are bound by the ruling of the Court of Justice when the same problem arises. However, in the absence of another referral to the Court of Justice or infringement proceedings, there is no guarantee that national courts of one Member State would follow a ruling relating to tax laws of another Member State. This is a general problem also as regards the reception of judgments following infringement proceedings against one Member State in another Member State. Both types of judicial actions depend heavily on national courts for the accurate and effective implementation of EU law. The fact that some Member State national courts have a better understanding of EU law and/or are more proactive in referring than other national courts that are more likely to find resort to the doctrine of acte éclairé or acte clair,[11] increases rather than reduces the possibility of divergent interpretation and application of EU law.

There are some safeguards, though again these depend on judicial activity. For instance, the Commission could bring an infringement proceeding for non-application of EU law against the Member State in which the previous legal action arose. Alternatively, following Köbler,[12] an affected taxpayer may bring a claim

---

[10] See Ana Paula Dourado, 'The Legal Protection of Taxpayers in the Framework of Preliminary Questions', in Pasquale Pistone (ed), *Legal Remedies in European Tax Law* (Amsterdam: IBFD, 2009).

[11] For the application of these doctrines by national courts in the tax field see, inter alios, Servaas van Thiel, 'Justifications in Community law for income tax restrictions on free movement: acte clair rules that can be readily applied by national courts – Part 1' (2008) 48(6) *European Taxation*, 279–90; Servaas van Thiel, 'Justifications in Community law for income tax restrictions on free movement: acte clair rules that can be readily applied by national courts – Part 2' (2008) 48(7) *European Taxation*, 339–50.

[12] Case C-224/01 Köbler v. Republic of Austria [2003] ECR I-10239. For commentary, see inter alios, James E. Pfander, 'Köbler v. Austria: expositional supremacy and member state liability' (2006) 17(2) *European Business Law Review*, 275–97; Peter Wattel, 'Köbler, CILFIT and Welthgrove: we can't go

against the Member State for damages[13] if the national court[14] had failed to refer when it was manifestly apparent that it should have referred to the Court of Justice. However, there are limitations to these safeguards. Both courses of action are against Member States for failure to act in some way that deprived their nationals of their Union rights. They do not reverse the decision of the national court *not* to refer. In fact, they have no actual impact on that decision.[15] In addition, since state liability is enforced through national courts, national procedures would again determine how the claim is to be adjudicated.

More recently, it has been held that the Commission could refer a Member State to the Court of Justice for failure to refer. In the Commission v. France case,[16] it was found that a Member State would be in breach of its obligations under Article 267 TFEU if its final court refused to refer the matter to the Court of Justice. It was held that in the absence of established acte clair in this area and in order to prevent incorrect interpretation of EU law, the French Conseil d'État (in this case) was legally required under EU law to submit a preliminary reference to the Court of Justice,[17] as no judicial remedy was available under national law. Since it had not done so, France was found to be in breach of EU law. This is a helpful precedent which puts pressure on Member State final courts to be extra cautious in applying the acte clair doctrine. However, it relies on the proactiveness of the Commission and its ability (and resources) to constantly monitor the case law at Member State level.

The problems are exacerbated when the legislative response (if any) to the judgment of the Court of Justice is unsatisfactory. Some Member States, especially if they have not been directly targeted by an infringement proceeding or a preliminary reference, may postpone necessary reforms and not set aside incompatible legislation. If amendments are made, these may not be sufficient to meet the concerns of EU law. Nor may they have retroactive effect to cure the breach. In addition, they may not be

---

on meeting like this' (2004) 41(1) *Common Market Law Review*, 177–90. See also an analogous decision of the European Court of Human Rights in Dulaurans v. France 34553/97 [2000] ECHR 108.

[13] This would be pursuant to the Francovich principle of state liability: Joined Cases C-6/90 and C-9/90 Andrea Francovich and Others v. Italian Republic [1991] ECR I-05357.

[14] The decision focused on a court adjudicating at last instance, as this was the last judicial body before which individuals may assert their rights conferred on them by EU law. As the Court of Justice noted, it followed from 'the requirements inherent in the protection of the rights of individuals relying on Community law that they must have the possibility of obtaining redress in the national courts for the damage caused by the infringement of those rights owing to a decision of a court adjudicating at last instance'. Case C-224/01 Köbler, para 36.

[15] As emphasised, '[t]he applicant in an action to establish the liability of the State will, if successful, secure an order against it for reparation of the damage incurred but not necessarily a declaration invalidating the status of *res judicata* of the judicial decision which was responsible for the damage.' Köbler, paras 39–40.

[16] Case C-416/17 Commission v. France ECLI:EU:C:2018:811.

[17] This litigation was a result of a previous case (Case C-310/09 Ministre du budget, des comptes publics et de la fonction publique v. Accor [2011] ECR I-08115) and the interpretation of this decision by the French Conseil d'État. See analysis in 5.2.2.

prompt enough as a result of protracted domestic procedures. It is no secret that in the EU there are many types of legislators: proactive, reactive or simply inactive. Therefore, the developments may not be rapid or homogenous. This also raises the problem of potential lack of level playing field and inequality of treatment between Member States. Some Member States may be penalised for their proactiveness and their ultimate commitment to the EU whereas others would be indirectly rewarded for their inactivity and potentially incompatible rules.

Furthermore, interpretative difficulties may arise if the national courts continue to develop principles pertaining to the previous (incompatible) legislation in an effort to wind up existing cases. What is more, amendments to legislation are not immune from subsequent attacks at the Court of Justice. This generates further delays, expenses and legal uncertainty.

In any case, most of the important principles of EU direct tax law are the result of either the Commission's infringement proceedings or a national court's request for a preliminary reference. The question tends to be phrased as follows. There is an acknowledgement that the Union lacks competence in direct tax matters and that Member States are thought to have retained their powers in that field. However, these powers must still be exercised compatibly with EU law.[18] The Court of Justice is called upon to decide whether the incumbent Member State has indeed exercised its powers in such manner. The cases that get to the Court of Justice are invariably cases where a national tax provision is considered to be incompatible with the Treaty's fundamental freedoms, or state aid. As a result, even in such areas where the Union lacks competence altogether, there are substantial developments derived from the case law of the Court of Justice, thus forcing further integration.

To an extent, this has generated what this author described elsewhere[19] as 'reverse subsidiarity': the situation whereby in exercising their technically exclusive powers, Member States find themselves significantly constrained by EU law.[20] The author has argued that the ability of a Member State to apply reverse subsidiarity – that is, to exercise their tax powers without infringing EU law – depends on a number of

[18] Case C-279/93 Finanzamt Köln-Altstadt v. Roland Schumacker [1995] ECR I-225, para 21. See, for example, dicta in Case C-80/94 GHEJ Wielockx v. Inspecteur der Directe Belastingen [1995] ECR I-2493, para 16; Case C-107/94 PH Asscher v. Staatssecretaris van Financiën [1996] ECR I-3089, para 36; Case C-391/97 Frans Gschwind v. Finanzamt Aachen-Außenstadt [1999] ECR I-5451, para 20; Case C-294/97 Eurowings Luftverkehrs AG v. Finanzamt Dortmund-Unna [1999] ECR I-7447, para 15 and in many more cases.
[19] See Christiana HJI Panayi, 'Reverse subsidiarity and cross-border loss relief: Can Member States be left to their own devices?' [2010] 3 British Tax Review, 267–301.
[20] The principle of subsidiarity is derived from the field of EU external relations. Under this principle, in areas in which the EU has non-exclusive competence, it shall only act 'if and in so far as the objectives of the proposed action cannot be sufficiently achieved by the Member States, either at central level or at regional and local level, but can rather, by reason of the scale or effects of the proposed action, be better achieved at Union level': Art 5(3) TEU. Subsidiarity, therefore, addresses the question of whether the EU should exercise its non-exclusive powers or whether it should defer to Member State action. The issue of subsidiarity can never, de jure, arise in an area in which the EU has no competence.

factors. Firstly, it depends on the clarity and consistency of the judgments of the Court of Justice in a given area – whether pursuant to an infringement proceeding or a reference for preliminary ruling. The more coherent the judgments are, the stronger their precedential value. Secondly, it depends on the ability of national courts to adopt and interpret the Court's jurisprudence. Thirdly, it depends on the willingness of national legislatures to adapt to and comply with this jurisprudence.

The following chapters mainly deal with the first factor: the jurisprudence of the Court of Justice in areas where Member States impose tax obstacles to the cross-border movement of companies. It is illustrated that in some cases the problematic nature of the Court's precedents acts as a deterrent for the development of a coherent body of corporate tax law that can easily be followed by national courts and legislatures.

The remainder of this chapter considers the general methodology of the Court of Justice in direct tax cases. Subsequent chapters examine specific themes in greater detail.

3.2 FUNDAMENTAL FREEDOMS AND DIRECT TAXATION

The four fundamental freedoms[21] are the free movement of goods, persons, services and capital. Non-discrimination is at the heart of these provisions. The fundamental freedoms are, in fact, thought of as giving specific expression to the general prohibition against discrimination on grounds of nationality, enshrined in Article 18 TFEU. The fundamental freedoms are directly applicable.[22] Therefore, they cover all legal areas, including taxation. This is irrespective of the fact that application in the tax field is not expressly stipulated in the wording of the Treaties and the Union does not have competence in that field.

3.2.1 Free Movement of Goods

The free movement of goods includes the abolition of customs duties and similar charges,[23] the prohibition of quantitative restrictions,[24] the prohibition of discriminatory internal taxation on imported goods[25] and state monopolies of a commercial character.[26] The free movement of goods was the first freedom to be used extensively, being linked with harmonisation measures on customs, excise duties and VAT. This freedom is mostly relevant to indirect taxes and is not examined further in this chapter, nor in this book.

---

[21] See, generally, Christiana HJI Panayi, 'EU Tax Law and Companies: Principles of the Court of Justice' (ch 19) in *Gore-Browne on EU Company Law* (London: LexisNexis, 2020).
[22] Case C-1/93 Halliburton Services BV v. Staatssecretaris van Financiën [1994] ECR I-1137, para 16.
[23] Arts 28 to 32 TFEU.
[24] Arts 34 to 36 TFEU.
[25] Arts 110 to 113 TFEU.
[26] Art 37 TFEU.

3.2.2 Free Movement of Persons

The free movement of persons covers the free movement of workers[27] as well as the freedom of establishment for persons[28] and for companies.[29]

Under the free movement of workers provision, EU workers are to be protected against 'discrimination based on nationality between workers of the Member States as regards employment, remuneration and other conditions of work and employment'.[30] Specific rights are also included in this freedom such as the right to accept offers of employment in another Member State or to reside in the Member State of employment, subject to exceptions in respect of public policy, public security, public health and employment in the public service.[31] Member States are free to determine their national public policy requirements but these are to be interpreted strictly. A public policy ground must be an acknowledged one and proved in each case.

In the direct tax field, this freedom has been used in cases where a non-resident worker was taxed more heavily or was not given the same benefits as a resident worker. For example, in de Groot[32] the Court of Justice found that Dutch legislation that disallowed part of the personal expenses of an individual in the country of residence on the ground that he had also received income in other Member States violated the free movement of workers. In Biehl,[33] the Court of Justice found that Luxembourg legislation that allowed refunds of withholding tax overpayments only to people who were resident for the whole year in Luxembourg, and not for part of the year, violated the free movement of workers. In Renneberg[34] Dutch legislation that prevented the taking into account of negative rental income relating to immovable property located in Belgium after a worker transferred his residence from the Netherlands to Belgium infringed the free movement of workers. In another case, the Court of Justice found that Estonia violated the free movement of workers by not granting a personal income tax exemption to non-residents who earned small amounts of income in Estonia.[35]

In Kieback,[36] the Court of Justice ruled that a Member State can refuse to grant a tax advantage to a non-resident worker despite the fact that the requirements for taxation as a resident were met during part of the year. This was on the basis that, although he received in that Member State all or almost all his income from that

---

[27] Art 45 TFEU.
[28] Art 49 TFEU.
[29] Art 54 TFEU.
[30] Art 45(2) TFEU.
[31] See Art 45(3) and (4) TFEU.
[32] Case C-385/00 FWL de Groot v. Staatssecretaris van Financiën [2002] ECR I-11819.
[33] Case C-175/88 Klaus Biehl v. Administration des contributions du grand-duché de Luxembourg [1990] ECR I-1779.
[34] Case C-527/06 Renneberg v. Staatssecretaris van Financiën [2008] ECR I-07735.
[35] See Case C-39/10 Commission v. Estonia, ECLI:EU:C:2012:282.
[36] See Case C-9/14 Kieback, ECLI:EU:C:2015:406.

period, that income did not form the major part of his taxable income for the entire year in question.

The free movement of workers was also used to tackle Luxembourg tax law, whereby a tax credit was granted to resident pensioners receiving pension income, subject to the condition that they have a certificate of deduction of Luxembourg tax. In other words, the tax credit was, in effect, limited to Luxembourg pensions. The Court of Justice held that by not granting the credit in respect of pensions received in connection with previous employment in the Netherlands, Luxembourg restricted the free movement of workers.[37]

In an important later case, the Court of Justice examined a multi-state situation whereby the worker earned income in many states. It was held that as the residence state could not take into account the personal and family situation, the personal and family tax benefits should be allocated on a pro rata basis.[38]

The Court of Justice has also found that Belgian tax rules that subjected the exemption of employment income received by a Belgian resident in another Member State to the condition that the income-generating activity was actually performed in that Member State were in line with the free movement of workers.[39] Perhaps this is a sign that the Court of Justice is beginning to be swayed more by territoriality arguments than it used to be.[40]

Article 45 TFEU covers employed persons only. Self-employed persons can only be protected under freedom of establishment, which is enshrined in Article 49 TFEU.[41] This provision specifically guarantees nationals of any Member State the freedom 'to take up and pursue activities', including the setting-up and managing of companies, in any Member State under the same conditions as those that apply to the Member State's nationals.

Under Article 54 TFEU, the right of establishment is extended to companies and firms formed in accordance with the law of a Member State and having their registered office, central administration or principal place of business within the Union. For companies, the registered office, central administration or principal place of business serve as connecting factors with the legal system of a particular Member State, like nationality for natural persons. As the Court of Justice reiterated in the *Oy AA* case, '[t]o accept that the Member State of establishment may freely apply different treatment solely because the registered office, central administration

---

[37] Case C-300/15 Kohll and Kohll-Schlesser, ECLI:EU:C:2016:361
[38] Case C-283/15 X v. Staatssecretaris van Financiën, ECLI:EU:C:2017:102. For commentary, see Isabella de Groot, 'Case X (C-283/15) and the Myth of "Schumacker's 90% Rule"' (2017) 45(8/9) *Intertax* 567; Hannelore Nieste, 'Case X v. Staatssecretaris van Financiën: Fractional Allocation of Personal and Family Tax Benefits for EU Resident Individuals with Multi-State Income' (2017) 4 *EC Tax Review* 201.
[39] See Case C-602/17 Benoît Sauvage, Kristel Lejeune v. État belge, ECLI:EU:C:2018:856.
[40] For an overview of the case law and recent trends, see Niels Bammens, 'Free movement of citizens and family taxation', in Christiana HJI Panayi, Werner Halsehner, Edoardo Traversa (eds), *Research Handbook on European Union Taxation Law* (Cheltenham: Edward Elgar Publishing, 2020), ch 8.
[41] However, the rulings of the Court of Justice under the free movement of workers provision are frequently relevant to the interpretation of the freedom of establishment.

or principal place of business of a company is situated in another Member State would deprive [the freedom of establishment] of its substance.'[42] Therefore, in so far as companies are concerned, freedom of establishment is 'designed to guarantee the benefit of national treatment in the host Member State, by prohibiting all discrimination based on the place where the registered office, central administration or principal place of business of a company is situated'.[43]

Freedom of establishment encompasses the right to take up and carry on activities as a self-employed person and to set up and manage undertakings. It protects the right to set up a primary establishment (new undertaking) or a secondary one (agency or branch or subsidiary). The concept of establishment is a broad one, 'allowing a Community national to participate, on a stable and continuous basis, in the economic life of a Member State other than his State of origin and to profit therefrom, so contributing to economic and social interpenetration within the Community, in the sphere of activities of self-employed persons'.[44] As Advocate General Darmon noted in the Daily Mail case, 'establishment within the meaning of the Treaty involves two factors: physical location and the exercise of an economic activity, both, if not on a permanent basis, at least on a durable one'.[45]

Similar to the free movement of workers, the rights enshrined under Articles 49 and 54 TFEU 'shall not prejudice the applicability of provisions laid down by law, regulation or administrative action providing for special treatment for foreign nationals on grounds of public policy, public security or public health'.[46]

Freedom of establishment has been used extensively in the direct tax field and especially vis-à-vis companies. It has been used to strike down national tax laws that treated resident companies and branches of non-resident companies differently,[47] laws that taxed a parent company on the profits of its subsidiary if set up in a low-tax jurisdiction,[48] or that more readily recharacterised interest payments to non-resident companies compared to resident companies,[49] regimes that taxed outbound or inbound dividends more heavily than domestic dividends,[50] or that made a non-resident's right to deductions on business income conditional upon the exercise of an option to be taxed as residents,[51] or that allowed group parent companies to

---

[42] Case C-231/05 Oy AA [2007] ECR I-6373, para 30. Citing, inter alia, Case 270/83 Commission of the European Communities v. France ('Avoir Fiscal') [1986] ECR 273, para 18; Case C-330/91 Commerzbank [1993] ECR I-4017, para 13.
[43] Case C-231/05 Oy AA, para 30.
[44] Case C-55/94 Gebhard (Reinhard) v. Consiglio dell'Ordine degli Avvocati e Procuratori di Milano [1995] ECR I-4165, para 25.
[45] Case 81/87 R. v. HM Treasury and Customs and Excise Commissioners, ex parte Daily Mail and General Trustplc [1988] ECR 5483, para 3 (Advocate General).
[46] Art 52 TFEU.
[47] See Chapter 4.
[48] See Chapters 4 and 7.
[49] See Chapter 7.
[50] See Chapter 5.
[51] Case C-440/08 Gielen v. Staatssecretaris van Financiën [2010] ECR I-2323.

amortise the goodwill from the acquisition of a domestic group company only,[52] or that prevented the deduction of expenses relating to a dwelling situated in the Member State of the taxpayer's residence, by the Member State where the taxpayer exercised professional activities[53] and so on.

Progressive turnover taxes have been scrutinised in several cases, with interesting results. In Hervis, a special tax imposed on the turnover of store retail trade was found to be in breach of the freedom of establishment.[54] This was because taxable legal persons that were linked undertakings under the legislation had to aggregate their turnover before applying a steeply progressive rate and dividing the resulting amount of tax among them in proportion to their actual turnover. As a result, an undertaking could be liable to an average rate of taxation considerably higher than that which would have applied if the turnover of its own stores only was taken into consideration. This restricted the freedom of establishment because the application of the steeply progressive scale to a consolidated tax base was liable to disadvantage undertakings linked, within a group, to companies established in another Member State.

However, in later cases, the Court of Justice found that steeply progressive turnover taxes which targeted the retail and telecommunication sectors were not contrary to the freedom of establishment.[55] This was notwithstanding the fact that the actual burden of the tax was mainly borne by undertakings controlled directly or indirectly by nationals of other Member States or by companies that had their registered office in another Member State. As the Court of Justice held in the *Vodafone* case, 'the fact that the greater part of such a special tax is borne by taxable persons owned by natural persons or legal persons of other Member States cannot be such as to merit, by itself, categorisation as discrimination'.[56]

3.2.3 Freedom to Provide Services

Freedom to provide services is set out in Articles 56 to 62 TFEU. By contrast to freedom of establishment, which requires the pursuit of an economic activity from a fixed base for an indefinite period, this freedom includes the carrying-out of an economic activity for a temporary period, so long as a national of a Member State having an establishment in the Union offers services in another Member State or to nationals of another Member State.

Freedom to provide services requires a cross-border element. Natural and legal persons may enjoy this freedom if they have a place of establishment in a Member

---

[52] See Case C-66/14 Finanzamt Linz v. Bundesfinanzgericht, Außenstelle Linz, ECLI:EU:C:2015:66.
[53] Case C-283/15 X v. Staatssecretaris van Financiën, ECLI:EU:C:2017:102.
[54] Case C-385/12 Hervis v. Hungary, ECLI:EU:C:2014:47.
[55] Case C-323/18 Tesco-Global Áruházak Zrt v. Nemzeti Adó- és Vámhivatal Fellebbviteli Igazgatósága, ECLI:EU:C:2020:140 and Case C-75/18 Vodafone Magyarország Mobil Távközlési Zrt. v. Nemzeti Adó- és Vámhivatal Fellebbviteli Igazgatósága, ECLI:EU:C:2020:139.
[56] Case C-75/18 Vodafone, para 52.

State other than the one in which the service is provided,[57] but are not required to have permanent physical presence in the host state (i.e. the state in which the service is provided). It is settled case law that Article 56 TFEU confers rights not only on the provider of services but also on the recipient of services,[58] even though this is not expressly set out in the wording of the freedom.

In order to be protected under this freedom, services must be 'normally provided for remuneration'.[59] A generic list of services that may be protected is set out in Article 57 TFEU, though this is not exhaustive.[60] It has been held that this freedom protects the provision of a wide variety of services such as banking,[61] insurance,[62] legal,[63] media[64] and so on.

Similar to the other freedoms, freedom to provide services is without prejudice to national laws 'providing for special treatment for foreign nationals on grounds of public policy, public security or public health'.[65] The Council has the power to extend the provisions of this freedom to third-country nationals who provide services and who are established in the EU. It has not done so yet. This proved to be decisive in some cases, where the service provider was a third-country national.[66] As a result, the protection offered by the freedom could not be extended to such providers.

Some confusion has been generated by the wording of Article 57 TFEU, which stipulates that 'services' shall be considered services for the purposes of Article 56 TFEU if they are not covered by the other freedoms. In the Fidium Finanz case,[67] the Court of Justice reiterated that this paragraph only related to the definition of the notion of 'services' and did not establish a priority rule. Therefore, the provision of some services, especially services involving capital movements such as banking and insurance, may be covered by freedom of establishment, the free movement of capital and freedom to provide services.

In the direct tax field, freedom to provide services has been used to strike down national legislation that imposed heavier taxes on residents leasing property from

---

[57] Case 205/84 Commission v. Germany [1986] ECR 3755, para 25 and Case C-180/89 Commission v. Italy [1991] ECR 709, para 15.
[58] See, in particular, Joined Cases 286/82 and 26/83 Luisi and Guiseppe Carbone [1984] ECR 377; Case C-204/90 Bachmann [1992] ECR I-249; Case C-158/96 Kohll [1998] ECR I-1931; Case C-224/97 Ciola [1999] ECR I-2517; and Case C-294/97 Eurowings.
[59] Art 57 TFEU.
[60] As stated in Art 57 TFEU, services shall in particular include (a) activities of an industrial character; (b) activities of a commercial character; (c) activities of craftsmen; and (d) activities of the profession.
[61] Case C-484/93 Svensson and Gustavsson [1995] ECR I-3955, para 11; Case C-222/95 Parodi [1997] ECR I-3899, para 17.
[62] Case C-118/96 Safir [1998] ECR I-1897, para 22.
[63] Case C-3/95 Reisebüro Broede [1996] ECR I-6511, para 38.
[64] Joined Cases C-34/95, 35/95 and 36/95 De Agostini [1997] ECR I-3843, para 50.
[65] Art 62 TFEU.
[66] See Case C-452/04 Fidium Finanz [2006] ECR I-9521; Case C-290/04 FKP Scorpio Konzertproduktionen [2006] ECR I-9461. See Christiana HJI Panayi, 'The protection of third-country rights in recent EC case law' (19 February 2007) 45(7) *Tax Notes International*, 659–66.
[67] Case C-452/04 Fidium Finanz, para 32.

non-resident lessors than from resident lessors,[68] or made it more difficult to deduct foreign professional expenses against the taxable income of service recipients,[69] or taxed foreign lottery winnings but exempted domestic winnings,[70] or refused an investment growth premium to a lessor when the lessee used the leased asset in another Member State,[71] or when a Member State only allowed domestic financial institutions and business trustees to be appointed as tax representatives of investment funds or property investment funds,[72] or when a Member State restricted a tax credit on income from loans granted for the acquisition of assets in the national territory only,[73] or when a Member State limited the benefits of the investment tax credit to domestic investments,[74] or when a Member State required third party economic operations to incorporate and to have a minimum share capital of €10 m in order to be entitled to collect local taxes,[75] or when a Member State imposed more onerous tax obligations on a company using workers seconded by temporary employment agencies in another Member State,[76] or when a Member State imposed irrecoverable default interest on withholding tax only in relation to cross-border payments,[77] and so on.

Also, as shown in Chapter 5, this freedom was used to strike down the Portuguese withholding tax on interest paid to non-resident financial institutions because it was imposed on the gross amount of the interest paid, whereas resident financial institutions were taxed on their net income.[78]

In the recent Google Ireland case,[79] the Court of Justice found that that the obligation to submit a tax declaration imposed on non-resident companies for the purposes of Hungarian advertisement tax on turnover did not constitute a restriction on the freedom to provide services. However, the penalty system was in breach of this freedom, on proportionality grounds. For non-resident companies, the fine was

---

[68] Case C-294/97 Eurowings.
[69] Case C-55/98 Skatteministeriat v. Bent Vestergaard [1999] ECR I-7641.
[70] Case C-42/02 Diana Elisabeth Lindman v. Skatterättelsnämnden [2003] ECR I-13519. See also Case C-153/08 Commission v. Spain [2009] ECR I-9735, where it was found to be incompatible with the freedom to provide services for a Member State to refuse a tax exemption to winnings from lotteries, games and betting organised abroad where such tax exemption was applicable to domestic winnings.
[71] Case C-330/07 Jobra Vermögensverwaltungs-Gesellschaft mbH v. FinanzamtAmstetten Melk Scheibbs [2008] ECR I-9099.
[72] Case C-387/10 Commission v. Austria [2011] ECR I-00142. Also see Case C-678/11 Commission v. Spain, ECLI:EU:C:2014:2434, where this freedom was used to strike down national rules that required non-resident pension funds and insurance companies to designate a tax representative who was resident in the jurisdiction.
[73] See Case C-09/11 Waypoint Aviation v. Belgium [2011] ECR I-11405.
[74] Case C-287/10 Tankreederei I SA v. Directeur de l'Administration des Contributions Directes [2010] ECR I-14233.
[75] See Joined Cases C-357/10 to C-359/10 Duomo Gpa Srl and Others v. Comune di Baranzate and Others, ECLI:EU:C:2012:283.
[76] Joined Cases C-53/13 and C-80/13 Strojírny Prostějov v. Czech Republic, ECLI:EU:C:2014:2011.
[77] See Case C-48/15 NN International, ECLI:EU:C:2012:521, para 59 and the case-law cited therein.
[78] Case C-18/15 Brisal, ECLI:EU:C:2016:549.
[79] Case C-482/18 Google Ireland v. Hungarian Tax Administration, ECLI:EU:C:2020:141.

issued within several days and the amount increased exponentially. This was without the competent authority giving the affected suppliers of services the time necessary to comply with their obligations or the opportunity to submit their observations. The fine on resident companies was significantly less and did not increase in the same way.

3.2.4 Free Movement of Capital

The free movement of capital and payments is set out in Articles 63 to 66 TFEU. Under these provisions, all restrictions on the movement of capital and payments between Member States and between Member States and third countries are prohibited. This is without prejudice to the right of Member States 'to apply the relevant provisions of their tax law which distinguish between taxpayers who are not in the same situation with regard to their place of residence or with regard to the place where their capital is invested'[80] and 'to take all requisite measures to prevent infringements of national law and regulations, in particular in the field of taxation'.[81] This, however, cannot be done by means of 'arbitrary discrimination or a disguised restriction on the free movement of capital and payments as defined in Article 63'.[82] In the current version of Article 63 TFEU, movements of capital within the Union and to or from a third country are on an equal footing.[83] However, the TFEU now contains amendments that expressly permit the different tax treatment of third-country nationals.[84] These amendments

---

[80] Art 65(1)(a) TFEU.
[81] Art 65(1)(b) TFEU.
[82] See Art 65(3) TFEU, which is effectively a codification of the rule of reason developed by the Court of Justice.
[83] Free movement of capital did not initially encompass the rights of third-country nationals. In addition, as it was phrased in the form of guidelines rather than in absolute terms, with a significant degree of discretion left to the Member States, it was not considered as having direct effect. Therefore, not even Member State nationals could derive protection from this freedom. Various Directives were subsequently enacted, but they only made provision for partial liberalisation. It was not until 1990 that the free movement of capital was significantly liberalised as a result of the enactment of Council Directive 88/361/EEC for the implementation of Art 67 of the EEC Treaty, OJ 1988 L178/5. This Directive provided new impetus in the area of capital movements by abolishing all restrictions on capital movements between persons resident in Member States. It also provided a non-exhaustive indicative list of capital movements to facilitate the application of the Directive. The liberalisation of capital movements corresponded to the first stage of the economic and monetary union. Council Directive 88/361 was withdrawn when the Maastricht Treaty entered into force, introducing the new version of the free movement of capital under Art 73B. The new Article, which became effective from 1 January 1994, provided for full liberalisation of capital movements, not only within the European Community (as it then was), but also in relation to third countries. It was also recognised as having direct effect. See, for example, Joined Cases C-358/93 and 416/93 Bordessa [1995] ECR I-361; Joined Cases C-163/94, C-165/94 and C-250/94 Sanz de Lera [1995] ECR I-4821.
[84] See para 4 of Art 65, which reads as follows: 'In the absence of measures pursuant to Article 64(3), the Commission or, in the absence of a Commission decision within three months from the request of the Member State concerned, the Council, *may adopt a decision stating that restrictive tax measures*

codify earlier case law, which established that justifications to restrictions involving a third country may carry more weight.[85]

In the A case the Court of Justice emphasised that the concept of restriction per se under Article 63 TFEU applied in the same way for capital movements between Member States and third countries, and for capital movements between Member States only. In other words, a restriction was a restriction, regardless of where the movement of capital took place.[86] However, the same may not be said in so far as justifications to restrictions to the free movement of capital are concerned. This is because it has been widely acknowledged in a number of cases and in the Commission's Communication on anti-abuse measures[87] that justifications to restrictions affecting capital movement from third countries may be more readily available than justifications to restrictions affecting capital movement within the EU/EEA.[88] Of course, this is not an automatic conclusion. It ought not to be assumed that movement of capital to or from third countries will always enjoy less protection than movement of capital within the EU/EEA. Each case should be decided on its facts. For example, in the CFC Group Litigation case, the third-country element was relevant in finding justification to a restriction,[89] but in the Orange European Smallcap Fund case it was not.[90]

Capital movement is not defined in the TFEU (or in previous treaties), but reference is usually made to the non-exhaustive list in Annex I to Council

---

adopted by a Member State concerning one or more third countries are to be considered compatible with the Treaties in so far as they are justified by one of the objectives of the Union and compatible with the proper functioning of the internal market. The Council shall act unanimously on application by a Member State' (emphasis added). Other derogations to the free movement of capital (but not the movement of payments) are sanctioned under Art 66 TFEU. Furthermore, derogations to the free movement of capital and payments are sanctioned under Art 75 TFEU based on ex-Art 60 EC. As for the difference between the two, see Joined Cases 286/82 and 26/83 Luisi and Giuseppe Carbonne, para 21. 'Payment' refers to a consideration for the underlying transaction/service, whereas 'capital' has more of an investment element. The distinction is perhaps no longer important within the EU but may be important in the context of external agreements.

[85] See Christiana HJI Panayi, 'The fundamental freedoms and third countries' (2008) 48(11) *European Taxation*, 571–82; Karoline Spies, 'The external dimension of the fundamental freedoms and taxation', in Christiana HJI Panayi, Werner Halsehner, Edoardo Traversa (eds), *Research Handbook on European Union Taxation Law* (Elgar Publishing, 2020), ch 26.

[86] This was also confirmed in Case C-194/06 Orange European Smallcap Fund [2008] ECR I-374, para 87. The case is also examined in Chapter 5.

[87] Communication from the Commission to the Council, the European Parliament and the European Economic and Social Committee, *Direct Taxation: Communication on the Application of Anti-abuse Measures – within the EU and in Relation to Third Countries*, COM(2007) 725 (*Communication on the Application of Anti-Abuse Measures*).

[88] Ibid.

[89] Case C-201/05 Test Claimants in the CFC and Dividend Group Litigation v. Commissioners of Inland Revenue [2008] ECR I-02875, paras 95–7.

[90] Case C-194/06 Orange European Smallcap Fund, paras 95–7. Here a justification based on the third-country element was not accepted because the relevant restriction affected all the shareholders of the collective investment enterprise without distinction, whether resident or established in the EU or in third countries. In other words, the restrictive ambit of the legislation was not sufficiently targeted against third-country shareholders. See also analysis in 5.2.2.

Directive 88/361/EEC.[91] The capital movements listed in Annex I include direct investments,[92] operations in securities, investment in real estate, loans and credits, sureties, guarantees and other items. In numerous cases the Court of Justice has recognised the nomenclature annexed to this Council Directive as having important indicative value.[93]

The EC Treaty contained some express derogations to the free movement of capital, an important one being the standstill clause found in ex-Article 57(1) EC. The standstill clause ensured that some pre-1994 restrictions on the movement of capital between Member States and third countries were grandfathered. These were restrictions 'involving direct investment – including in real estate – establishment, the provision of financial services or the admission of securities to capital markets'.[94] In the TFEU the standstill clause is preserved and a similar grandfathering provision is inserted for restrictions existing under national law in Bulgaria, Estonia and Hungary, the relevant date being 31 December 1999.[95]

The standstill clause proved to be decisive in *Holböck*, where the Court of Justice interpreted Austrian rules on dividend taxation as being in existence at the cut-off date of 31 December 1993.[96] As a result, no protection could be offered under EU law, even though the Court of Justice had found these rules to constitute a restriction to the free movement of capital.[97] In addition, in the A case[98] the Court of Justice left it to the national court to decide whether the standstill provision applied to the Swedish legislation, as it was unclear from the facts of the case. In the Orange European Smallcap Fund case[99] the Court of Justice repeated its earlier findings and added that 'direct investment' refers to 'investments of any kind undertaken by natural or legal persons and which serve to establish or maintain lasting and direct

---

[91] This Directive was adopted under ex-Art 67 of the EEC Treaty.
[92] Para I of Annex I, entitled: 'Direct Investments'.
[93] See, for example, Case C-222/97 Trummer and Mayer [2005] ECR I-1661, para 21; Case C-98/01 Commission v. UK [2003] ECR I-4641, paras 39–40; Joined Cases C-282/04 and C-283/04 Commission v. Netherlands [2006] ECR I-09141, para 19.
[94] Ex-Art 57(1) EC. The Council could, acting by qualified majority on a proposal from the Commission, adopt measures on the movement of capital to or from third countries. Unanimity was required for measures that constituted a step back in Community law as regards the liberalisation of the movement of capital to or from third countries. See ex-Art 57(2) EC. This has now moved to para 3 of Art 64 TFEU.
[95] Art 64(1) TFEU.
[96] See Case C-157/05 Holböck [2007] ECR I-4051, para 43. See Axel Cordewener, Georg Kofler and Clemens Philipp Schindler, 'Free movement of capital and third countries: exploring the outer boundaries with Lasertec, A and B and Hölbock' (2007) 47(8/9) *European Taxation*, 371–6.
[97] Case C-157/05 Holböck, para 30. The standstill clause was also considered in Case C-524/04 Test Claimants in the Thin Cap Group Litigation v. Commissioners of Inland Revenue [2007] ECR I-2107. The Court of Justice concluded that it was up to the national court to decide whether the national measure fell within this derogation: see para 196. Whether or not a restriction existing prior to 1994 affected direct investment was a question for the referring court, in Case C-101/05 A [2007] ECR I-11531.
[98] Case C-101/05 A.
[99] Case C-194/06 Orange European Smallcap Fund.

links between the persons providing the capital and the undertakings to which that capital is made available in order to carry out an economic activity'.[100] Therefore, portfolio investment was unlikely to be covered under the standstill clause.

In a later case, the Court of Justice dealt with the standstill clause, and its application to the Dutch extended time period for recovering third-country tax debts.[101] Here, the Court of Justice gave a broad interpretation to Article 64(1) and held, contrary to the findings of the Dutch referring court, that the exception was not limited to restrictions on the movement of capital that related solely to the categories referred to in Article 64(1). As such, it could apply to general measures, such as the extended time-period for the recovery of tax on foreign income, provided that the particular case involved one of the prescribed types of capital movement – that is, provided that the extended recovery period created a link between the movement of capital and the provision of financial services.

More recently,[102] the Court of Justice considered the German CFC rules and the applicability of the standstill clause in the context of reforms. It was found that the clause applied even if the rules were later extended to cover shareholdings that did not involve direct investments. More specifically, it was found that German reform introduced in 2000–1 which reduced the shareholding threshold for passive intermediary companies qualifying as CFCs from 10 per cent to 1 per cent did not in itself affect the applicability of the standstill clause.

The broad definition of capital movements can lead to situations falling under more than one Treaty freedom. For example, there could be an overlap between freedom of establishment and the free movement of capital when a branch or subsidiary is established.[103] Similarly there could be an overlap with freedom to provide services when there is a transfer of an insurance contract[104] or the provision of banking services.[105] There could also be an overlap of all three freedoms. For example, in the Cadbury Schweppes and the Thin Cap Group Litigation cases the national court referred a question of incompatibility with freedom of establishment, freedom to provide services and the free movement of capital.[106]

Therefore, it is not always immediately apparent which freedom is applicable in a given setting. In fact, the possibility of overlap is expressly acknowledged in the wording of some of these freedoms. For example, under Article 49 TFEU the fact

---

[100] Ibid, para 102.
[101] Case C-317/15 X v. Staatssecretaris van Financiën, ECLI:EU:C:2017:119.
[102] Case C-135/17 X-GmbH v. Finanzamt Stuttgart – Körperschaften, ECLI:EU:C:2019:136.
[103] See subpara I of Annex I (Direct Investments: Establishment and extension of branches or new undertakings belonging solely to the person providing the capital and the acquisition in full of existing undertakings) in Council Directive 88/361/EEC.
[104] Ibid, para X of Annex I (Transfers in Performance of Insurance Contracts).
[105] Ibid, para VI of Annex I (Operations in Current and Deposit Accounts with Financial Institutions) and para VIII (Financial Loans and Credits).
[106] See analysis in Chapter 7.

that freedom of establishment applies does not mean that the freedom relating to the movement of capital cannot also apply.[107] In other words, the fact that there is an exercise of an establishment does not preclude the movement of capital; and vice versa.[108] There are no priority or exclusion rules.[109]

Let us take as an example the holding of capital by nationals of a Member State in a company established in another Member State. Which freedom applies – freedom of establishment or free movement of capital? In *Baars*[110] the Court of Justice gave a qualified answer. If the holding gives the Member State national 'definite influence over the company's decisions and allows him to determine its activities' then the situation is covered by freedom of establishment.[111] By analogy, if the holding does not confer on the Member State national definite influence, then free movement of capital applies.

This is not always an easy distinction to make, increasing the possibility of overlap of these freedoms.[112] In the first edition to this book, it was noted that when this analysis was used by the Court of Justice in cases involving third-country residents, the free movement of capital was often eschewed in favour of the other freedoms whose scope was solely intra-EU.[113] However, as shown in 3.3.1, in later cases, this trend has not been followed, as the Court of Justice now takes into account factors other than just whether the legislation applied exclusively to situations in which the

---

[107] See Art 49 TFEU, which reads as follows: 'Freedom of establishment shall include the right to take up and pursue activities as self-employed persons and to set up and manage undertakings ... under the conditions laid down for its own nationals by the law of the country where such establishment is effected, *subject to the provisions of the chapter relating to* capital' (emphasis added).

[108] See Art 65(2) TFEU: 'The provisions of this chapter shall be *without prejudice to the applicability of restrictions on the right of establishment* which are compatible with the Treaties' (emphasis added). See also Art 58(2) TFEU, where an express provision is made to the fact that '[t]he liberalisation of banking and insurance services connected with movements of capital shall be effected in step with the liberalisation of movement of capital'.

[109] As for the interpretation of Art 57(1) TFEU, which stipulates that 'services' shall be considered services for the purposes of Art 56 TFEU if they are not covered by the other freedoms, see analysis above and Case C-452/04 Fidium Finanz, para 32.

[110] Case C-251/98 C Baars v. Inspecteur der Belastingdienst Particulieren/Ondernemingen Gorinchem [2000] ECR I-2787.

[111] Ibid, para 22.

[112] The distinction seems to have been further blurred in a non-tax case. See, for example, the Golden Shares case (Joined Cases C-282/04 and C-283/04 Commission v. Netherlands [2006] ECR I-9141), where the Court of Justice clarified that for the purposes of ex-Art 56 EC, movement of capital includes 'in particular direct investments in the form of participation in an undertaking through the holding of shares which confers the possibility of effectively participating in its management and control ('direct' investments) and the acquisition of shares on the capital market solely with the intention of making a financial investment without any intention to influence the management and control of the undertaking ('portfolio' investments)': Joined Cases C-282/04 and C-283/04 Commission v. Netherlands, para 19.

[113] See Christiana HJI Panayi, 'Thin capitalisation GLO et al – a thinly concealed agenda?' [2007] 35(5) *Intertax*, 298–309; HJI Panayi, 'The protection of third-country rights in recent EC case law'; Axel Cordewener, Georg Kofler and Clemens Philipp Schindler, 'Free movement of capital in third country relations and national tax law: an emerging issue before the ECJ' (2007) 47(3) *European Taxation*, 107–19; HJI Panayi, 'The fundamental freedoms and third countries'.

parent company exercised decisive influence over the company paying the dividends.

It is also noteworthy to mention the Prunus case,[114] where the Court of Justice held that OCTs (Overseas Countries and Territories) such as the British Virgin Islands are to be treated as non-Member States for the purposes of the free movement of capital. Since there was no express reference to movements of capital between Member States and OCTs in the Treaties,[115] OCTs could only benefit from the liberalisation of the movement of capital provided for in Article 63 TFEU in their capacity as non-Member States.[116] In this case the standstill clause in Article 64(1) was found to operate and the restrictive French tax provision was grandfathered.

Whether the same approach should apply between a Member State and its own OCT was left unanswered but the issue was finally settled in the X BV and TBG case.[117] Here, the Dutch dividend withholding tax was levied on dividend distributions made by companies resident in the Netherlands to their parent companies in the Netherlands Antilles. It was questioned whether this was a breach of the free movement of capital.

Advocate General Jääskinen had argued that OCTs should be treated as third countries for the purposes of the free movement of capital, even the OCTs of Member States. The Court of Justice followed a different approach. Although there was no provision relating to the free movement of capital under the Council's OCT Decision[118] applicable to the Netherlands Antilles, Article 47 of this Decision was similar as it prohibited, inter alia, 'restrictions on the acquisition of shares in companies and the repatriation of benefits stemming therefrom'.[119] Article 55(2) of the OCT Decision, however, included a tax carve-out expressly aimed at preventing tax avoidance.[120] The Court of Justice found that the withholding tax was covered by this provision as the tax measure was intended to prevent excessive capital flows towards the Netherlands Antilles and to counter its appeal as a tax haven. Whether this objective was pursued in an effective and proportionate manner was a matter for the referring court to assess.[121]

---

[114] Case C-384/09 Prunus SARL, Polonium SA v. Directeur des Services Fiscaux [2011] ECR I-000, [2011] STC 1392.
[115] Ibid, para 30.
[116] Ibid, para 31.
[117] Joined Case C-24/12 and Case C-27/12 X BV and TBG Ltd v. Staatssecretaris van Financiën, ECLI: EU:C:2014:1385. For an overview of the external dimension of the fundamental freedoms, including the free movement of capital, see Karoline Spies, 'The external dimension of the fundamental freedoms and taxation'.
[118] Council Decision 2001/822/EC of 27 November 2001 on the association of the overseas countries and territories with the European Community (OJ 2001 L314/1).
[119] Case C-24/12 X BV and Case C-27/12 TBG, para 49.
[120] Ibid, para 51.
[121] Ibid, para 53.

Overall, in the direct tax field the free movement of capital has been used to strike down an Austrian stamp tax levied on loans taken with foreign lenders but not Austrian lenders,[122] discriminatory taxation of inbound and outbound dividends,[123] tax reliefs and deferrals limited to resident investors or domestic investments,[124] different capital gains taxes levied on resident and non-resident individuals,[125] different taxation of annuities paid by non-residents on domestically sourced income,[126] restrictions to tax deductions for donations to science and research institutions located outside Austria,[127] or rules that provided for a longer limitation period for inheritance tax claims relating to assets situated outside the country,[128] or that imposed a flat rate tax on income from non-transparent foreign investment funds,[129] or that imposed a lower inheritance tax allowance for non-resident individuals,[130] and so on.

3.3 METHODOLOGY OF THE COURT OF JUSTICE

Over the years some trends and ad hoc rules seem to have developed in the case law of the Court of Justice. Whilst one would hesitate to conclude that these have led to a consistent and predictable methodology followed by the Court of Justice, certain patterns appear to be emerging.

3.3.1 Finding the Relevant Freedom

As already mentioned in section 3.2.4, a certain activity could be covered – and protected – under more than one fundamental freedom. In the first edition to this book it was noted that in the last few years, the Court of Justice had begun to eschew the simultaneous application of many freedoms, choosing to base its decisions on the freedom that is *predominantly or primarily* relevant. Restrictions under the other applicable freedoms were seen as an unavoidable or inevitable consequence of the restriction to that predominant freedom. Invariably, when the overlap was between the free movement of capital and the freedom of establishment, the Court of Justice focused on whether there was a holding giving the

---

[122] Case C-439/97 Sandoz GmbH v. Finanzlandesdirektion für Wien, Niederösterreich und Burgenland [1999] ECR I-7041.
[123] See Chapter 5.
[124] See Case C-436/00 X and Y v. Riksskatteverket [2002] ECR I-10829; Case C-242/03 Ministre des Finances v. Jean-Claude Weidert and Élisabeth Paulus [2004] ECR I-07379.
[125] See Case C-562/07 Commission v. Kingdom of Spain [2009] ECR I-9553. Here the Court of Justice found that Spain was in breach of its obligations under ex-Art 56 EC and Art 40 EEA for treating differently, until 31 December 2006, the capital gains of resident and non-resident individuals.
[126] See Case C-450/09 Ulrich Schröder v. Finanzamt Hameln [2011] ECR I-2497.
[127] See Case C-10/10 Commission v. Austria [2011] ECR I-5389.
[128] Case C-132/10 Halley et al v. Belgium [2011] ECR I-08353.
[129] Case C-326/12 Rita van Caster and Patrick van Caster v. Germany, ECLI:EU:C:2014:2269.
[130] Case C-479/14 Hünnebeck, ECLI:EU:C:2016:412.

Member State national definite influence over the company's decisions and allowing him to determine its activities. In subsequent cases, additional tests were put forward by the Court of Justice in assessing which freedom was primarily relevant.

Initially, the freedom that tended to be subordinated under this approach was the free movement of capital.[131] This had very important implications in so far as third-country nationals are concerned, as the free movement of capital is the only freedom available to them. For example, in Fidium Finanz the subordination of the free movement of capital meant that the third-country service provider could not benefit from protection under EU law because the freedom to provide services did not extend to such nationals.[132] Similarly in Lasertec, only freedom of establishment was found to be applicable in assessing the German thin capitalisation rules. This meant that a Swiss company caught by the strict thin capitalisation rules could not seek protection under EU law.[133] Furthermore, in Stahlwerk the Court of Justice found that although German legislation that prevented losses of a US branch to be set off against the profits of the German head office had restrictive effects on the free movement of capital, such effects were an unavoidable consequence of the restriction to the freedom of establishment.[134] As the latter freedom could not be invoked by third-country undertakings such as the US branch, the German provision was compatible with EU law.[135] In Scheunemann,[136] a case on German inheritance tax rules, the Court of Justice found that the relevant freedom was the freedom of establishment and not the free movement of capital. Here a tax-free amount was allowed for a substantial shareholding in a company registered in a Member State but not for a shareholding in a company registered in a non-EU country. As freedom of establishment could not cover situations concerning a shareholding in a company registered in a third country, there was no breach.

This trend of subordinating the free movement of capital had also been confirmed in the Commission's 2007 Communication on the application of anti-abuse measures in the area of direct taxation.[137] In this Communication the Commission reiterated that the centre of gravity in respect of some anti-abuse rules, for example

---

[131] See Case C-452/04 Fidium Finanz [2006] ECR I-9521; Case C-196/04 Cadbury Schweppes and Cadbury Schweppes Overseas [2006] ECR I-7995; Case C-524/04 Thin Cap Group Litigation; Case C-464/05 Maria Geurts, Dennis Vogten v. Belgian State [2007] ECR I-9325; Case C-492/04 Lasertec Gesellschaft für Stanzformen mbH v. Finanzamt Emmendingen [2007] ECR I-3775; Case C-102/05 Skatteverket v. A and B [2007] ECR I-3871; Case C-311/08 Société de Gestion Industrielle v. Belgian State [2010] ECR I-487.

[132] Case C-452/04 Fidium Finanz. Contrast with Advocate General Stix-Hackl's analysis, where he considered the case as falling under both the freedom to provide services and the free movement of capital.

[133] Case C-492/04 Lasertec.

[134] See order made by the Court of Justice in Case C-415/06 Stahlwerk Ergste Westig GmbH/Finanzamt Düsseldorf-Mettmann [2007] ECR I-152, para 16 et seq.

[135] See also Chapter 4.

[136] Case C-31/11 Marianne Scheunemann v. Germany, ECLI:EU:C:2012:481.

[137] Communication on the Application of Anti-Abuse Measures, pp 8–9.

CFC rules and thin capitalisation rules,[138] lies clearly within freedom of establishment. Therefore, 'Community law does not impose any particular requirements on the legitimacy of the application of such [rules] to transactions outside the EU'.[139] It is only when the application of such rules is not confined to situations and transactions between companies where one has definite influence over the other, that the free movement of capital (and its protective scope vis-à-vis third-country nationals) may be entertained.[140] It was emphasised that[141] 'Community law does not require Member States to avoid discrimination in relation to the establishment of their nationals outside the Community, or the establishment of third-country nationals in a Member State'.[142]

In later cases, the trend of eschewing the free movement of capital in favour of other freedoms (and especially the freedom of establishment) was not so easily followed because the Court of Justice started to focus not only on the existence of definite influence and control, but also the purpose of the legislation. For example in the FII Group Litigation II case,[143] it was found that when the tax legislation affected both establishment and the movement of capital, a third-country national could use the free movement of capital, even in circumstances where there was in fact a controlling interest. This was because the UK tax rules applied irrespective of whether or not the shareholder exerted decisive influence over the company paying the dividends.[144] In order to determine whether there was a predominantly relevant freedom, it was important to look at the purposes of the legislation.[145] Where it was apparent for the purposes of national legislation that it could *only* apply to shareholdings that enabled the holder to exert a definite influence on the decisions of the company concerned and to determine its activities, then free movement of capital could not be relied on.[146] By contrast, national rules relating to the tax treatment of dividends from a third country that did *not* apply exclusively to situations in which the parent company exercised decisive influence over the company paying the dividends must be assessed in light of the free movement if capital.

In another case, Kronos,[147] the importance of looking at the purpose or intention of the legislation was reiterated. Here, it was held that the 10 per cent shareholding threshold of the legislation 'admittedly serves to exclude from the scope of the

---

[138] For an analysis of these types of regimes, see Chapter 7.
[139] *Communication on the Application of Anti-Abuse Measures*, p 8.
[140] Ibid.
[141] See MEMO/07/558 released on 10 December 2007: 'Direct taxation: Communication on the application of anti-abuse measures – within the EU and in relation to third countries – Frequently Asked Questions'.
[142] Ibid, p 4.
[143] Case C-35/11 Case C-35/11 Test Claimants in the FII Group Litigation, ECLI:EU:C:2012:707. The case is also considered in Chapter 5. See 5.2.2.
[144] Ibid, para 104.
[145] Ibid, para 90.
[146] Ibid, para 98.
[147] Case C-47/12 Kronos International Inc v. Finanzamt Leverkusen, ECLI:EU:C:2014:2200.

exemption shareholdings acquired solely with the intention of making a financial investment without any intention to influence the management and control of the undertaking'.[148] However such a threshold did not in itself make the exemption applicable only to those shareholdings that enabled the holder to exert a definite influence on the company's decisions and to determine its activities. National rules setting such a threshold could fall within the ambit of both freedom of establishment and the free movement of capital. In order to establish which of these freedoms prevailed in this case, the purpose of national legislation had to be delineated.[149]

In Bouanich II,[150] the Court of Justice neatly summarised its previous case law on this point:

> [N]ational legislation intended to apply only to those shareholdings which enable the holder to exert a definite influence on a company's decisions and to determine its activities falls within the scope of Article 49 TFEU on freedom of establishment ... On the other hand, national provisions which apply to shareholdings acquired solely with the intention of making a financial investment without any intention to influence the management and control of the undertaking must be examined exclusively in the light of the free movement of capital.[151]

The Court of Justice clarified that when it could not be determined from the legislation that the rules fell predominantly within the scope of one freedom or another, then the rules had to be examined on the basis of *both* freedoms.[152]

This was confirmed more recently in the EV v. Finanzamt Lippstadt case.[153] Here, it was found that a shareholding of 15 per cent did not necessarily imply that the shareholder exercised definite influence over the company.[154] There was sufficient information to establish that the relevant national rules did not apply solely to situations in which the parent company had a shareholding which enabled it to exercise a definite influence over the decisions of its subsidiary and to determine its activities. As such, the free movement of capital was applicable.[155]

3.3.2 *Discrimination and Restriction Approach*

How are the fundamental freedoms, whichever ones may be applicable, actually used in the direct tax field? How does the Court of Justice assess whether a tax measure is in breach of the fundamental freedoms?

---

[148] Ibid, para 33.
[149] Ibid, paras 36–8.
[150] Case C-375/12 Margaretha Bouanich v. Directeur des services fiscaux de la Drôme, ECLI:EU:C:2014:138.
[151] Case C-375/12 Bouanich, para 28.
[152] Ibid, paras 29–31.
[153] Case C-685/16 EV v. Finanzamt Lippstadt, ECLI:EU:C:2018:743.
[154] Ibid, para 40.
[155] Ibid, para 41. See also 5.2.2.

Discrimination and restriction are the key concepts. In assessing whether a tax measure is in breach of the fundamental freedoms, the Court of Justice initially approached the question from a non-discrimination perspective.

Under the non-discrimination approach, a comparison is essential. Discrimination consists of dissimilar treatment of comparable situations. 'Dissimilar' means disadvantageous for the person treated differently.[156] Differentiation based on objective criteria is permissible, but any unjustified difference of treatment constitutes discrimination. Differentiation encompasses not only increased tax burdens but also procedural disadvantages.

A distinction is often made between direct (overt) and indirect (covert) discrimination. Direct discrimination involves differentiation according to nationality, whereas indirect discrimination is thought to involve differentiation according to other criteria leading to non-nationals being treated less favourably than nationals. For example, a distinction based on residence, even though equally applicable to nationals and non-nationals, can be a covert form of discrimination because non-residents are mainly non-nationals.[157]

By contrast, as mentioned in Chapter 1, a distinction based on residence is in fact the norm in international tax practice. Although under the non-discrimination provision of the OECD Model Tax Convention (Article 24) discrimination on grounds of nationality is forbidden, this clause does not extend to non-residents, even if they are in a comparable situation to residents.[158] The OECD Model Tax Convention starts from the assumption that residents and non-residents are 'usually not in the same circumstances for the purposes of paragraph 1'[159] unless residence is totally irrelevant for the purposes of the provision or administrative measure under consideration.[160] Indirect/covert discrimination on the basis of residence is not accepted. This was reiterated in the OECD's discussion document on the non-discrimination principle.[161] In fact, in this discussion document the OECD expressly acknowledged the possibility of divergence with EU law.[162]

---

[156] Case C-175/88 Biehl, para 13.
[157] Case 152–73 Giovanni Maria Sotgiu v. Deutsche Bundespost [1974] ECR 153.
[158] See analysis in Chapter 1. See also Frans Vanistendael, 'Taxation and non-discrimination, a reconsideration of withholding taxes in the OECD' (2010) 2(2) *World Tax Journal*, 175–91; Mary C. Bennett, 'Non-discrimination in international tax law: a concept in search of a principle' (2005–6) 59(4) *Tax Law Review*, 439–85; Hugh J. Ault and Jacques Sasseville, 'Taxation and non-discrimination: a reconsideration' (2010) 2(2) *World Tax Journal*, 101–25; Kees van Raad, 'Non-residents – personal allowances, deduction of personal expenses and tax rates' (2010) 2(2) *World Tax Journal*, 154–61; Malcolm Gammie, 'Non-discrimination and the taxation of cross-border dividends' (2010) 2(2) *World Tax Journal*, 162–74; Ruth Mason, 'Tax discrimination and capital neutrality' (2010) 2(2) *World Tax Journal*, 126–38.
[159] See Commentary to para 1 of Art 24 of the OECD Model Tax Convention, para 18.
[160] Ibid, see examples in paras 19–25.
[161] OECD, *Application and Interpretation of Article 24 (Non-Discrimination)* (OECD, 2007).
[162] Ibid, Annex, p 29. For a comparison between the two approaches, see Christiana HJI Panayi, 'Recent Developments regarding the OECD Model Convention and EC Law' (2007) 47(10) *European Taxation*, 452–66. See also Frans Vanistendael, 'Taxation and Non-discrimination' and

3.3 Methodology of the Court of Justice

The implications of this divergence of approach in EU and international tax law are crucial in a number of areas of corporate tax law. For example, the non-discrimination test, as interpreted by the Court of Justice, prevents host states from treating permanent establishments and subsidiaries differently if they are in a comparable situation. Similarly, it prevents the levying of more onerous taxes on profit distributions when paid to non-residents, or when received by residents if the profit was distributed by a non-resident, and so on. These and other issues are examined in the following chapters.

After the early cases, the Court of Justice moved from the non-discrimination to the non-restriction approach, without abandoning the former. Under the restriction approach, national measures that apply indiscriminately to all persons but which in fact hinder intra-EU trade are prohibited. All measures that prohibit, impede or render less attractive, the exercise of a freedom are regarded as restrictions.

To an extent the restriction approach is tautologous to the indirect discrimination test, as both seem to scrutinise general measures that prima facie do not distinguish between residents and non-residents. However, the emphasis of the two tests is different. Under the indirect discrimination approach, the focus is on the fact of discrimination of non-residents, whereas under the restriction approach the focus is on the fact that EU persons (residents and non-residents alike) are prevented from exercising their EU freedoms.[163] Under the restriction approach, there also seems to be less insistence on making comparisons, as restrictions apply indiscriminately to all. It is the fact that a restriction affects cross-border movements, that is, 'it imposes a specific disadvantage on operators desirous of moving or establishing themselves within the Community',[164] that is reprehensible.

It was initially thought that whether or not a case was decided as an instance of discrimination or restriction was important, not only in terms of the necessity to satisfy the comparability test, but also in terms of justification. If it were discrimination, then this could only be justified by mandatory requirements in the public interest as expressly laid down in the EC Treaty (now TFEU), namely public health, public security and public policy.[165] Economic aims could not constitute grounds for public policy. Generally, these grounds were rarely satisfied in direct tax cases. If it was a restriction, the following conditions had to be satisfied: (a) the restriction was applied in a non-discriminatory manner; (b) it was justified by imperative

---

Silke Bruns, 'Taxation and non-discrimination: clarification and reconsideration by the OECD' (2008) 48(9) *European Taxation*, 484–92.

[163] Arguably, an indirect discrimination is almost always a restriction, but not vice versa.

[164] Case C-446/03 Marks & Spencer, para 28 (Advocate General).

[165] Some of these provisions have already been referred to above. In so far as free movement of workers is concerned, see Art 45(3) TFEU. In so far as freedom of establishment and freedom to provide services are concerned, see Art 52 TFEU. In so far as free movement of capital is concerned, see Art 65(1)(b) TFEU. See Case 352/85 Bond van Adverteerders and others v. The Netherlands State [1988] ECR 2085, para 24; and Case C-288/89 Stichting Collectieve Antennevoorziening Gouda and others v. Commissariaat voor de Media [1991] ECR I-4007, paras 13–14.

requirements in the general interest; (c) it was suitable for securing the attainment of the objective pursued; and (d) it did not go beyond what was necessary in order to attain this objective.[166]

In dealing with justifications to restrictions, a substantial part of the Court's analysis was devoted to the second condition, namely the imperative requirements in the general interest. Examples of imperative requirements that have been accepted[167] are the following: the need for fiscal control and supervision,[168] the need to combat tax fraud,[169] the need to preserve the fiscal cohesion of the domestic tax system,[170] the need to safeguard the allocation of tax jurisdiction,[171] the need to prevent the double use of losses and loss trafficking,[172] the need to protect creditors[173] and in the case of a merger, the need to protect minority shareholders and employees.[174] Some suggested grounds have failed – for example loss of revenue and erosion of the tax base,[175] and the availability of administrative remedies[176] or of counterbalancing advantages.[177]

In so far as justifications are concerned, the third-country element ought not to be neglected. A restriction affecting third-country nationals may be more justifiable than a restriction affecting EU nationals, as explained in 3.2.4.[178]

---

[166] Case C-19/92 Kraus v. Land Baden-Wurttemberg [1993] ECR I-1663, para 32; and Case C-55/94 Gebhard, para 37.
[167] Even if these grounds are accepted, they are to be narrowly construed.
[168] Case C-250/95 Futura Participations SA v. Administration des Contributions [1997] ECR I-2471.
[169] Case C-367/96 Kefalas [1998] ECR I-2843; Case C-264/96 Imperial Chemical Industries plc (ICI) v. Kenneth Hall Colmer (Her Majesty's Inspector of Taxes) [1998] ECR I-4695; Case C-9/02 Hughes de Lasteyrie du Saillant [2004] ECR I-02409.
[170] Case C-204/90 Bachmann. This ground was not successfully invoked in subsequent cases. See, for example, Case C-80/94 Wielockx; Case C-484/93 Svensson and Gustavsson; Case C-35/98 Staatssecretaris van Financiën v. BGM Verkooijen [2000] ECR I-4071; Case C-436/00 X and Y v. Riksskatteverket [2002] ECR I-10829; and Case C-324/00 Lankhorst-Hohorst GmbH v. Finanz Steinfurt [2002] ECR I-11779. However, in later cases the protection of fiscal cohesion was again successfully invoked. See Case C-418/07 Société Papillon v. Ministère du budget, des comptes publics et de lafonction publique [2008] ECR I-8947, paras 46–51; Case C-157/07 Finanzamt für Körperschaften III in Berlin v. Krankenheim Ruhesitz am Wannsee-Seniorenheimstatt GmbH [2008] ECR I-8061, para 45. Some of these cases are analysed in Chapter 4.
[171] Much emphasis has been placed on this justification in Case C-446/03 Marks & Spencer [2005] ECR I-10837 and other later cases. See Case C-231/05 Oy AA; Case C-470/04 N v. Inspecteur van de Belastingdienst Oost/Kantoor Almelo [2006] ECR I-7409.
[172] Case C-446/03 Marks & Spencer; Case C-231/05 Oy AA.
[173] In the Centros case, a non-tax case, the Court of Justice thought that this ground was a valid justification but was not applicable on the facts of the case. Case 212/97 Centros Ltd v. Erhvervs-og Selskabsstyrelsen [1999] ECR I-01459, para 35.
[174] See also Case C-411/03 SEVIC Systems AG [2005] ECR I-10805.
[175] See, for example, Case C-264/96 ICI, para 28; Case C-307/97 Compagnie de Saint-Gobain, Zweigniederlassung Deutschland v. Finanzamt Aachen-Innerstadt [1999] ECR I-6161, para 50; Case C-385/00 De Groot, para 103.
[176] See, for example, Case C-175/88 Biehl; Case C-118/96 Safir [1998] 1998 I-01897.
[177] See, for example, Case 270/83 Avoir Fiscal; Case C-107/94 Asscher; Case C-330/91 Commerzbank.
[178] See also the analysis of the dividends case law in Chapter 5.

3.3 Methodology of the Court of Justice

This argument was first mooted in the FII Group Litigation case.[179] Here the Court of Justice showed some readiness to consider that 'where companies making distributions are established in non-member countries, it may be more difficult to determine the tax paid by those companies in the state in which they are resident than in a purely Community context'.[180] The Court expressly acknowledged that it was true that:

> because of the degree of legal integration that exists between Member States of the Union, in particular by reason of the presence of Community legislation which seeks to ensure cooperation between national tax authorities ... *the taxation by a Member State of economic activities having cross-border aspects which take place within the Community is not always comparable to that of economic activities involving relations between Member States and non-member countries.*[181]

The Court of Justice agreed with its Advocate General in that a Member State may demonstrate that a restriction on capital movements to or from third countries 'is justified for a particular reason in circumstances where that reason would not constitute a valid justification for a restriction on capital movements between Member States'.[182] According to the Court, the UK government had not succeeded in establishing this.[183]

The Court of Justice seized upon this argument in the A case,[184] where a restriction affecting inbound dividends from non-EU countries was justified on the grounds of effectiveness of fiscal supervision. Where the legislation of a Member State made the grant of a tax advantage dependent on satisfying requirements, compliance with which could be verified only by obtaining information from the competent authorities of a third country, 'it is, in principle, legitimate for that Member State to refuse to grant that advantage if, in particular, because that third country is not under any contractual obligation to provide information, it proves impossible to obtain such information from that country'.[185] The Court of Justice left it to the national court to decide whether this was indeed the situation in this case.

In the CFC Group Litigation case[186] the third-country element was relevant in accepting the justification to a restriction, but in the Orange European Smallcap Fund case[187] it was not. In the Commission *v.* Italy

---

[179] Case C-446/04 Test Claimants in the FII Group Litigation *v.* Commissioners of Inland Revenue [2006] ECR I-11753, paras 169–72.
[180] Ibid, para 169.
[181] Ibid, para 170, emphasis added.
[182] Ibid, para 171.
[183] Ibid, para 172.
[184] Case C-101/05 A.
[185] Ibid, para 63.
[186] Case C-201/05 CFC Group Litigation case.
[187] Case C-194/06 Orange European Smallcap Fund, paras 95–7. Here a justification based on the third-country element was not accepted because the relevant restriction affected all the shareholders of the collective investment enterprise without distinction, whether resident or established in the EU or in non-member countries. See also the analysis in 5.2.2.

case,[188] a restriction to the free movement of capital was justified vis-à-vis EEA companies but not vis-à-vis Member State companies. The same conclusion was reached by Advocate General Jääskinen and the Court of Justice in the Rimbaud case.[189] In many more cases, especially in the context of dividend taxation, the Court of Justice took into account the third-country element.[190]

Finally, it ought to be pointed out that lately the distinction between discrimination and restriction seems to have been obliterated. When it comes to justification, at least in a tax-related context, the Court of Justice (and at times the referring courts or tribunals)[191] tend to merge the discrimination and restriction concepts. Sometimes, when indirect discrimination is alleged, the Court of Justice justifies it under a rule of reason that pertains to the restriction approach,[192] whereas in other cases it does not. Advocate General Maduro in Marks & Spencer asked the Court of Justice 'to put an end to these uncertainties',[193] but the Court of Justice did not address the issue.

The difficulty in delineating the precise ambit of indirect discrimination compared to a restriction is obvious. If a comparison is not strictly necessary for either concepts and there is convergence in the justification stage, then perhaps the distinction between the two will become a matter of semantics. Advocate General Geelhoed went even further in the ACT Group Litigation case, when he claimed that there was no practical difference between the manner of formulation of a restriction and discrimination, without distinguishing direct and indirect discrimination.[194] In a more recent case, the Hornbach-Baumarkt case, Advocate General Bobek revisited some of the difficulties in applying the discrimination and the restriction approach,[195] though unfortunately the discussion was not followed up by the Court of Justice, as shown in Chapter 7.

One cannot help but wonder whether these are merely analytical tools used by the Court of Justice in order to reach the desired results.

---

[188] Case C-540/07 Commission v. Italy [2009] ECR I-10983. See the analysis in 5.3.3.
[189] Case C-72/09 Établissements Rimbaud SA v. Directeur général des impôts and Directeur des services fiscaux d'Aix en Provence [2010] ECR I-10659.
[190] See, for example, Case C-190/12 Emerging Markets Series of DFA Investment Trust Company, ECLI:EU:C:2014:249; Case C-641/17 College Pension Plan of British Columbia v. Finanzamt München Abteilung III, ECLI:EU:C:2019:960. See 5.3.2.
[191] For example, in the Cadbury Schweppes case the UK Special Commissioners questioned the compatibility of the national controlled foreign company rules with EU law both in terms of the discrimination approach and the restriction approach. See Case C-196/04 Cadbury Schweppes, para 10.
[192] See, for example, Case C-204/90 Bachmann, a case of indirect discrimination in which fiscal cohesion was accepted as a justification. See also Case C-80/94 Wielockx, para 26.
[193] Case C-446/03 Marks & Spencer, para 33 (Opinion).
[194] Case C-374/04 Test Claimants in Class IV of the ACT Group Litigation v. Commissioners of Inland Revenue [2006] ECR I-11673, para 36. The Advocate General rephrased the enquiry as involving two types of restrictions: quasi-restrictions, which result inevitably from the coexistence of different national systems and true restrictions, which are restrictions going beyond those resulting inevitably from the co-existence of national tax systems. He gave examples for each category.
[195] See Case C-382/16 Hornbach-Baumarkt AG v. Finanzamt Landau, ECLI:EU:C:2018:366.

3.3.3 Tax Treaties and Double Taxation

Under ex-Article 293 EC, Member States were encouraged to enter into negotiations with each other so as to secure for their nationals, inter alia, the abolition of double taxation in the Community.[196] This provision did not have direct effect, that is it did not 'confer on individuals any rights on which they might be able to rely before their national courts'.[197] Ex-Article 293 EC has somehow disappeared from the TFEU. Although it is debatable what this change means,[198] case law does not seem to suggest that it makes a difference.

Before analysing the status of tax treaties in the EU,[199] some basic concepts of international tax law need to be explained.

Firstly, let us consider jurisdiction to tax. In theory, a country is free to adopt whatever rules of fiscal jurisdiction it wishes to adopt, no matter how wide-ranging their scope. However, in practice jurisdiction to tax is effective only if there is some link, a connecting factor, between the country asserting the jurisdiction and the taxpayer or the income sought to be taxed. Residence and source are the basic connecting factors.[200]

A country exerts source-based taxation when it taxes all income arising or having an economic nexus with the source country,[201] irrespective of whether such income accrues to residents or non-residents. By contrast, under the residence principle, persons resident within the country's territorial jurisdiction are taxed on their worldwide income, irrespective of the source of the income and irrespective of any concurrent residence in another country. Pursuant to both of these principles, extraterritorial taxing jurisdiction is often asserted. For example, under the residence principle jurisdiction is extended over the foreign-sourced income of residents. Under the source principle jurisdiction is extended over the source country income of non-residents. This may lead to juridical double taxation, a phenomenon also mentioned in Chapter 1, whereby a person is being taxed twice on the same income. Such tax burden would not have existed in the absence of the cross-border element.[202]

---

[196] Luc Hinnekens, 'The uneasy case and fate of Article 293 Second Indent EC' (2009) 37(11) *Intertax*, 602–9.
[197] Case C-336/96 Gilly [1998] ECR I-2793, para 16.
[198] See Martii Nieminen, 'Abolition of double taxation in the Treaty of Lisbon' (2010) 64(6) *Bulletin for International Taxation*, 330–5.
[199] For a comprehensive discussion, see Christiana HJI Panayi, *Double Taxation, Tax Treaties, Treaty Shopping and the European Community* (Kluwer Law International, 2007).
[200] See Angel Schindel and Adolfo Atchabahian, 'General Report', *Source and Residence: New Configuration of their Principles*, Cahiers de droit fiscal international, Volume 90a (The Hague: Kluwer Law International, 2005); HJI Panayi, *Double Taxation, Tax Treaties, Treaty Shopping and the European Community*, ch 1.
[201] In this book the terms host state and home state are used instead of source country and country of residence respectively, but the terminology used in international tax literature is source and residence.
[202] See also the analysis in Chapters 4–5. This is not the same as economic double taxation, which, as explained in Chapter 1, can also arise in a purely domestic context. Nevertheless, the combination of

Furthermore, if an individual is a dual resident then the two jurisdictions in which he or she is resident may seek to tax his or her profitable activities (residence/residence clash). Or if two jurisdictions consider certain income as having its source in their territory, they may both seek to tax it (source/source clash). Very frequently, there is a residence/source clash. For example, when dividends are paid by a company in the host state to a shareholder in the home state, those dividends may be subject to source country taxes (e.g. a withholding tax) and residence country taxes (e.g. income tax). Therefore, the shareholder would be subject to juridical double taxation in respect of those dividends.

Countries use unilateral and/or bilateral methods to eliminate or reduce double taxation. Unilaterally, countries may exempt the foreign-sourced income or tax it and give a credit. These unilateral methods are often complemented by bilateral methods: tax treaties (also called double taxation conventions). Tax treaties are international agreements between states. They are invariably of a bilateral nature, though there are a few multilateral tax treaties.[203] Tax treaties, like contracts, create rights and obligations between the contracting states. They cannot create rights or obligations for a third state, not being a contracting state, without its consent.

In tax treaties the contracting states agree how to allocate or share tax jurisdiction over certain cross-border income (e.g. dividends, royalties, branch profits) so as to avoid juridical double taxation. Tax treaties tend to follow the OECD Model Tax Convention in laying down distributive and priority rules for different types of income and capital taxes. Some of these distributive rules will be examined in the following chapters of this book.

In so far as the interface between tax treaties and EU tax law is concerned, there are a few important issues to note.

Member States retain power to enter into tax treaties. As held in an older case, Gilly, in the absence of any unifying or harmonising measures adopted in the Community context under the now abolished Article 293 EC, Member States retain competence to define the criteria for allocating their powers of taxation as between themselves, with a view to eliminating double taxation.[204] Here the Court of Justice had to examine whether France violated the free movement of workers provision by not fully crediting the German taxes paid by Mrs Gilly against her French tax bill. Under the France–Germany tax treaty, France was to grant a credit equal to the tax that would have been payable in France as if the taxpayer earned the income in

---

the two types of double taxation may increase the costs of cross-border investment substantially. See HJI Panayi, *Double Taxation, Tax Treaties, Treaty Shopping and the European Community*, ch 2.

[203] See, for example, the 1971 Model Convention for the Avoidance of Double Taxation between Member Countries and Other Countries outside the Andean Sub-region; the Convention for the Avoidance of Double Taxation within the Andean Group; the Nordic Convention on Income and Capital entered into by Denmark, Finland, Iceland, Norway and Sweden, concluded in 1983 and replaced in 1987, 1989 and 1996.

[204] Case C-336/96 Gilly, para 30.

France. As French tax rates were lower than German rates, not all the German tax paid could have been credited. As a result, a frontier worker resident in France and working in Germany was, by reason of the tax treaty credit mechanism taxed more heavily in France than persons whose occupational activity was pursued exclusively in France.

The Court of Justice decided that France did not violate the EC Treaty. To the Court, this was the result of different rates being allowed to apply under the relevant tax treaty and the allocation of tax jurisdiction decided by the contracting states. This allocation of powers of taxation, whether by unilateral means or tax treaties, was to be respected by Community (now Union) law. In other words, if a Member State chose the credit method to give relief for double taxation, Community law could not demand that it adopted the exemption method, unless the chosen method was not consistently used. In addition, as explained above, safeguarding the balanced allocation of taxing powers was an imperative requirement that could go towards justifying a restriction if the other conditions were fulfilled.[205]

Gschwind was decided in the same way. Here the Court of Justice held that denying income-splitting to a non-resident couple not meeting the requirements of the host state legislation was compatible with free movement of workers. The Court of Justice respected the allocation of taxing rights under the relevant tax treaty.[206]

However, in the exercise of fiscal competence, whether through national law or tax treaties, the Court of Justice insists that Member States still have to comply with EU law. The distinction between allocation of tax powers and exercise of fiscal competence is not always an easy one to make.

In Saint-Gobain[207] the Court of Justice found that the refusal to grant concessions to German branches of companies established in other Member States violated the freedom of establishment when similar benefits were available to German companies under tax treaties between Germany and non-Member States. Germany had to extend benefits *unilaterally* to German branches of companies resident in other Member States. However, the Court of Justice refrained from explaining why this unilateral extension did not affect the pre-agreed allocation of tax powers.

By contrast, in the D case[208] the Court of Justice found that the Netherlands was not obliged to extend to a German resident the treaty benefits given to Belgian residents. The Germany–Netherlands tax treaty did not provide for the same allowances as the Belgium–Netherlands tax treaty. This was a question of pre-agreed allocation of tax powers between these Member States. The relevant treaties were

---

[205] See 3.3.2. For a later case, see Case C-241/14 Bukovansky v. Finanzamt Lörrach, ECLI:EU:C:2015:766, in the context of the EU-Switzerland Agreement.
[206] Case C-391/97 Gschwind.
[207] Case C-307/97 Saint-Gobain. The case is also considered in Chapter 4. See 4.3.2.
[208] Case C-376/03 D v. Rijksbelastingdienst [2005] ECR I-5821.

not to be interfered with by extending benefits given to Belgian residents also to German residents.

It is not easy to reconcile these and other judgments.[209] Later cases, however, seem to suggest that the Court of Justice is paying more deference to tax treaties and to the OECD Model Tax Convention, on which Member States rely in concluding tax treaties.[210]

In Bouanich the Court of Justice held that the France–Sweden tax treaty, as interpreted in light of the commentaries of the OECD Model Tax Convention, was to be taken into account in interpreting EU law.[211] Similarly, in van Hilten the Court of Justice, in line with Advocate General Léger's comments, found that 'for the purposes of the allocation of powers of taxation, it is not unreasonable for the Member States to find inspiration in international practice and, particularly, the model conventions drawn up by the [OECD]'.[212]

Lidl Belgium[213] is another case where the Court of Justice deferred to the OECD Model Tax Convention. In this case the Court had to decide whether German legislation that prevented the losses incurred by a foreign branch of a German company to be set off against the profits of this company was compatible with freedom of establishment. The Court of Justice found that the German legislation restricted freedom of establishment, but this restriction was justified. Once again, the Court showed its respect for basic concepts of international tax law as encapsulated in the OECD Model Tax Convention[214] by giving enhanced support to the tax treaty allocation argument.[215] It stated:

> [T]he Court has recognised the legitimate interest which the Member States have in preventing conduct which is liable to undermine the right to exercise the powers of taxation which are vested in them. In this connection, where a double taxation convention has given the Member State in which the permanent establishment is situated the power to tax the profits of that establishment, to give the principal

---

[209] For a comprehensive analysis on this earlier case law, see ch 4 in HJI Panayi, *Double Taxation, Tax Treaties, Treaty Shopping and the European Community.*

[210] Case C-513/03 van Hilten-van der Heijden [2006] ECR I-1957, para 48. See also Case C-346/04 Conijn [2006] ECR I-6137, para 17; Case C-470/04 N, para 45; and Case C-231/05 Oy AA, para 50 (Advocate General Kokott).

[211] Case C-265/04 Bouanich [2006] ECR I-923, para 51.

[212] Case C-513/03 van Hilten, paras 47 and 82 (Advocate General).

[213] Case C-414/06 Lidl Belgium GmbH & Co KG v. Finanzamt Heilbronn [2008] ECR I-3601.

[214] See para 22: 'That definition of a permanent establishment as an autonomous fiscal entity is consonant with international legal practice as reflected in the model tax convention drawn up by the Organisation for Economic Cooperation and Development (OECD), in particular Articles 5 and 7 thereof. The Court has already held that, for the purposes of the allocation of fiscal competence, it is not unreasonable for the Member States to draw guidance from international practice and, particularly, the model conventions drawn up by the OECD.' The Court of Justice cited Case C-336/96 Gilly, para 31, and Case C-513/03 van Hilten, para 48.

[215] Under the relevant tax treaty, profits of the foreign branch were exempt from the tax base of the German head office but losses could not be included either. See analysis in 4.3.5.

company the right to elect to have the losses of that permanent establishment taken into account in the Member State in which it has its seat or in another Member State would seriously undermine a balanced allocation of the power to impose taxes between the Member States concerned.[216]

Therefore, even though the OECD Model Tax Convention has not been used to interpret or modify EU law,[217] the Court's respect and deference to it is obvious and understandable. If the tax treaty network were to be dismantled, there would be nothing there which could replace it.

One of the strongest endorsements of tax treaties to date is the Court's decision in Damseaux.[218] The case is also discussed in Chapter 5.[219] Here the Court of Justice rejected arguments that the country of residence of a shareholder receiving foreign-sourced dividends was obliged to eliminate juridical double taxation. The disadvantages that could arise 'from the parallel exercise of tax competences by different Member States, to the extent that such an exercise is not discriminatory, do not constitute restrictions prohibited by the EC Treaty'.[220]

In this case, under the relevant tax treaty, dividends distributed by a French company to a Belgian resident were liable to be taxed in both Member States. When both the Member State in which the dividends were paid (host state) and the Member State in which the shareholder resided (home state) taxed those dividends, 'to consider that it is necessarily for the Member State of residence to prevent that double taxation would amount to granting a priority with respect to the taxation of that type of income to the Member State in which the dividends are paid'.[221] Whilst such attribution of powers may be reflected under the OECD Model Tax Convention, Community law did 'not lay down any general criteria for the attribution of areas of competence between the Member States in relation to the elimination of double taxation within the Community'.[222] Therefore, the attribution of powers under the relevant tax treaty was respected, even if it led to juridical double taxation. An EU method of attribution of powers could not be imposed and the Member State of residence was not obliged, under Community law, to prevent the disadvantages that arose from the exercise of competence as attributed by the two Member States in their tax treaty.[223]

---

[216] Case C-414/06 Lidl Belgium, para 51, citing Case C-231/05 Oy AA, para 55.
[217] See Thomas Dubut, 'The Court of Justice and the OECD Model Tax Conventions or the uncertainties of the distinction between hard law, soft law, and no law in the European case law' (2012) 40(1) *Intertax*, 2–12.
[218] Case C-128/08 Jacques Damseaux v. Etat Belgique [2009] ECR I-6823. For commentary, see Christiana HJI Panayi, 'Tax treaties *post-Damseaux*' [2009] *Tax Journal*, 996, 9–11; Luca Cerioni, 'Double taxation and the internal market: reflections on the ECJ's decisions in *Block* and *Damseaux* and the potential implications' (2009) 63(11) *Bulletin for International Taxation*, 543–56.
[219] See 5.2.3.
[220] Case C-128/08 Damseaux, para 27.
[221] Ibid, para 32.
[222] Ibid, para 33.
[223] Ibid, para 34.

This case was followed in the judgments of the Court of Justice in Haribo & Salinen[224] and in Block.[225] Incidentally, the principle that Member States are not obliged to adapt their own tax systems to different Member State tax systems in order to eliminate double taxation has been extended in that Member States are not required to adapt their tax legislation to enable taxpayers to benefit from a tax advantage granted by another Member State.[226]

Furthermore, in the Commission v. Italy case,[227] tax treaties were taken into account in assessing whether the difference in treatment generated by the Italian dividend tax rules was compensated for under tax treaties. The Court of Justice found that the application of the tax treaties did not always compensate the difference in treatment in full.[228] In addition, as Italy had not concluded a tax treaty with all Member States (e.g. Slovenia), this argument could not, therefore, in any event succeed in relation to dividends distributed to companies in Slovenia.[229] This case was followed in Commission v. Spain.[230] Both cases are analysed in Chapter 5.

Overall, notwithstanding the fact that the tax treaty powers (in addition to the domestic tax powers) of Member States are partly constrained as a result of EU law, nevertheless, an analysis of the case law relating to tax treaties suggests that tax treaties and, to an extent, the OECD Model Tax Convention which they tend to replicate, are largely tolerated within the EU legal order, even though asymmetrical benefits may be derived therefrom.[231] It is becoming obvious that the Court of Justice is trying to protect Member States' allocation of taxing powers and is resisting the de facto multilateralisation of tax treaties, beyond what is required by existing EU law (Directives and case law). The Court's respect and deference to the OECD Model Tax Convention is understandable. If the tax treaty network were to be dismantled, there is currently nothing there which could adequately replace it. The closest we have to some ad hoc multilateralisation of tax treaties is the recently signed OECD Multilateral Instrument,[232] which, however, only deals with some of the OECD/G20's BEPS recommendations and minimum standards. It does not set out to be a multilateral instrument for the allocation of taxing rights.

---

[224] Joined Cases C-436/08 and C-437/08 Haribo & Österreichische Salinen [2011] ECR I-00305. See analysis in Chapter 5.
[225] Case C-67/08 Margarete Block v. Finanzamt Kaufbeuren [2009] ECR I-883, para 31.
[226] See Case C-157/10 Banco Bilbao Vizcaya Argentaria (BBVA) v. Administracion General del Estado [2011] ECR I-13023.
[227] Case C-540/07 Commission v. Italy.
[228] Ibid, para 37.
[229] Ibid, para 41.
[230] Case C-487/08 Commission v. Spain [2010] ECR I-4843.
[231] Christiana HJI Panayi, 'The relationship between EU and international tax law', in Christiana HJI Panayi, Werner Halsehner, Edoardo Traversa (eds), *Research Handbook on European Union Taxation* (Elgar Publishing, 2020), p 119.
[232] See the OECD's Multilateral Convention to Implement Tax Treaty Related Measures to Prevent BEPS, www.oecd.org/tax/treaties/multilateral-convention-to-implement-tax-treaty-related-measures-to-prevent-BEPS.pdf.

There have been attempts in the past, both by the OECD and the Commission, to consider the divergences between EU law and the OECD approach in various areas and possible ways of alignment,[233] though nothing coordinated and concrete has come out of these attempts. The fact that the Commission has wholeheartedly supported[234] the proposals on Action 6 of the BEPS Action Plan which deals with prevention of tax treaty abuse suggests that we might eventually see some alignment between OECD and EU policies in this area. This is notwithstanding the fact that, as has been argued elsewhere, some of these proposals may not be technically compatible with the principles set out by the Court of Justice in seminal cases.[235]

It is hoped that there will be clearer guidance as regards the position of tax treaties in the EU context.

3.3.4 Overall or Per-Country Approach?

There is one crucial question on the Court's methodology that has been left open: in examining whether a certain national tax rule is discriminatory or restrictive, can out-of-state benefits or burdens be taken into account in assessing in-state tax treatment (the so-called 'overall approach')? Or is tax treatment from only one Member State perspective to be considered (the so-called 'per-country' or 'single state' approach)? In other words, what is to be taken into account in considering whether the Treaty rights of an EU national – and also in the case of the free movement of capital of a third-country national – are violated?

Case law is not consistent on this point. In examining whether or not a national tax measure is compatible with EU law, either under the discrimination or the restriction approach, the Court of Justice does not always take into account the overall context in which the measure is applied. In fact, the Court of Justice tends to consider the impugned treatment in one Member State only. Tax benefits in the other Member State are irrelevant and cannot offset any fiscal hindrances in the Member State concerned.[236]

---

[233] A European Commission workshop on EU Law and Tax Treaties took place in 2005. From an OECD perspective, see the Annex to the OECD report on non-discrimination discussed in OECD, *Application and Interpretation of Article 24 (non-discrimination), Public discussion draft* (2006), www.oecd.org/tax/treaties/38516170.pdf.

[234] See the Recommendation on Tax Treaties, which was part of the Commission's Anti-Tax Avoidance Package released in January 2016. The Recommendation advised Member States to reinforce their tax treaties against abuse by aggressive tax planners, in an EU-law compliant way, without really giving any guidance as to how to do so. Commission Recommendation of 28.1.2016 on the implementation of measures against tax treaty abuse, COM(2016) 271 final (28.01.16)

[235] See Christiana HJI Panayi, *Advanced Issues in International and European Tax Law* (Hart Publishing 2015), ch 6, and later updated version in Christiana HJI Panayi, 'The Compatibility of the OECD/ G20 Base Erosion and Profit Shifting Proposals with EU Law', 70 [2016] 1/2 *Bulletin for International Taxation* 95–112.

[236] In the context of the freedom to provide services, the Eurowings and Danner cases unequivocally held that 'any tax advantage resulting for providers of services from the low taxation to which they are

There have been calls for the Court of Justice to reassess its stance on this point. Advocate General Geelhoed urged the Court to adopt the overall approach in a number of high profile cases. In the ACT Group Litigation case he opined that, for the purposes of the free movement provisions, obligations in the countries of residence and source should be seen *as a whole*, 'or as achieving a type of equilibrium'.[237] This was because '[e]xamination of the situation of an individual economic operator in the framework of just one of these States – without taking into account the [freedom of establishment] obligations of the other State – may give an unbalanced and misleading impression, and may fail to capture the economic reality in which that operator is acting'.[238] The Advocate General made similar comments in his opinions in Kerckhaert–Morres,[239] Denkavit[240] and the Thin Cap Group Litigation cases.[241] So far, the Court of Justice has not given a clear answer on this point. In none of these cases did it accept the Advocate General's approach. Then again, it did not reject it either.[242]

Another related question is whether tax treaties are to be taken into consideration in assessing whether a national tax rule is compatible with EU law. Tax treaties are very important in assessing the actual tax burden of a cross-border activity or investment. Certain foreign income may be exempt from taxation in the country of residence under the provisions of the relevant tax treaty, or a withholding tax imposed by a country of source may be reduced to the rates of the relevant tax treaty. Should tax treaties not be part of the equation in considering whether a certain measure is compatible with EU law?

In Bouanich[243] the Court of Justice held that tax treaties were part of such equation. The Court was examining whether or not the Swedish tax legislation on share repurchases breached EU law. For resident shareholders, a repurchase of shares was taxed as a capital gain and the cost of acquisition of the repurchased shares could be deducted. The gain was taxed at the rate of 30 per cent. For non-resident shareholders (in the case in question Mrs Bouanich, who was a French

subject in the Member State in which they are established cannot be used by another Member State to justify less favourable treatment in tax matters given to recipients of services established in the latter State'. Case C-136/00 Rolf Dieter Danner [2002] ECR I-8147, para 56, citing Case C-294/97 Eurowings, para 44. In the free movement of capital context, Case C-35/98 Verkooijen, para 61 and Case C-315/02 Anneliese Lenz v. Finanzlandesdirektion für Tirol [2004] ECR I-7063, para 41, contain similar dicta.

[237] Case C-374/04 ACT Group Litigation case, para 72 (Advocate General).
[238] Ibid.
[239] Case C-513/04 Kerckhaert-Morres [2006] ECR I-10967, para 26 (Advocate General).
[240] Case C-170/05 Denkavit [2006] ECR I-11949, para 37 (Advocate General).
[241] Case C-524/04 Thin Cap Group Litigation case, para 69 (Advocate General).
[242] These judgments are examined in greater detail in Chapter 5. For general commentary, see Maria Cruz Barreiro Carril, 'National tax sovereignty and EC fundamental freedoms: the impact of tax obstacles on the internal market' (2010) 38(2) *Intertax*, 105–13, 109–11; Ruth Mason, 'Made in America for European tax: the internal consistency test' (2008) 49(4) *Boston College Law Review*, 1, 277–326, 1, 304.
[243] Case C-265/04 Bouanich.

resident) the repurchase was treated as a distribution of a dividend and the acquisition cost could not be deducted. The Court of Justice held that the France–Sweden tax treaty had to be taken into account in determining whether or not the tax legislation was consistent with EU law, that is whether resident shareholders were in fact treated more favourably than non-resident shareholders. It was for the national court to make the assessment.[244]

A similar line was taken in the ACT Group Litigation case.[245] Here the Court of Justice, citing the Bouanich case, stated that it was for the national court to determine whether, on the given factual and legal matrix, the obligation to treat resident and non-resident companies in the same way has been complied with, 'taking account, where necessary, of the provisions of the [tax treaty] that that Member State has concluded with the State in which the shareholder company is resident'.[246]

Even more explicitly, in Amurta[247] Advocate General Mengozzi opined that whilst the underlying tax treaty *was* relevant in assessing whether the Dutch tax rules on outbound dividends were discriminatory, national tax treatment in the country of the recipient of the dividends (i.e. unilateral domestic tax treatment) was *not* relevant. The Court of Justice agreed. Since the relevant tax treaty formed part of the legal background to the main proceedings and had been presented as such by the national court, the Court of Justice had to take it into account in order to give an interpretation of EU law that was relevant to the national court.[248] It was for the national court to establish whether account should be taken of the tax treaty and, if so, to determine whether it neutralised the effects of the restriction on the free movement of capital.[249]

By contrast, in the Orange European Smallcap Fund case the Court of Justice found that the existence of a tax treaty, the application of which would have eliminated the disparity caused by the Dutch legislation between resident and non-resident shareholders of investment funds, could not alter the finding of restriction to the free movement of capital.[250]

The Court of Justice did not follow this stance in the Commission v. Italy case[251] and the Commission v. Spain case mentioned above.[252] Here tax treaties were taken into account in assessing whether the differences in treatment generated by the Italian and Spanish dividend tax rules were compensated for under tax treaties. The Court of Justice found that the application of the tax treaties did not always compensate the difference in treatment or in full.

---

[244] Ibid, para 55.
[245] Case C-374/04 ACT Group Litigation case.
[246] Ibid, para 71. See also Case C-170/05 Denkavit.
[247] Case C-379/05 Amurta SGPS v. Inspecteur van de Belastingdienst [2007] ECR I-9569.
[248] Ibid, para 80.
[249] Ibid, para 84.
[250] Case C-194/06 Orange European Smallcap Fund, paras 112–114.
[251] CaseC-540/07 Commission v. Italy.
[252] See Case C-487/08 Commission v. Spain.

In the BBVA case[253] the Court of Justice took note of the tax treatment in the other Member State but only for the purposes of justifying the denial of the foreign tax credit on foreign taxes that were never levied. No positive obligation was imposed. Here a Spanish bank, Banco Bilbao Vizcaya Argentaria, earned interest in Belgium that was exempt from tax at source under Belgian legislation. BBVA wanted (from Spain) a credit for the 10 per cent tax that the Belgium–Spain tax treaty permitted Belgium to impose. Spanish legislation denied a foreign tax credit for taxes accrued but not paid because of the exemption in Belgium. The matter was referred to the Court of Justice.

The Court of Justice held that the alleged disadvantage suffered by BBVA was not double taxation of the interest received, as that interest was taxed solely in Spain, but the fact that it was not possible to benefit, for the purposes of calculating the tax due in Spain, from the tax advantage in the form of the exemption granted under Belgian law. This was a disadvantage that arose from the parallel exercise of tax competences by different Member States. To the extent that such an exercise was not discriminatory, it did not constitute a restriction.[254]

As the Court of Justice held, if, as case law establishes,[255] Member States are not obliged to adapt their own tax systems to the different systems of tax of the other Member States in order to eliminate double taxation, 'a fortiori, those States are not required to adapt their tax legislation to enable taxpayers to benefit from a tax advantage granted by another Member State in the exercise of its powers in tax matters, so long as their rules are not discriminatory'.[256] To the extent that the Spanish legislation was not discriminatory as compared with the treatment applied to interest obtained in that Member State, it was compatible with the free movement of capital. Whether or not there was discrimination was for the national court to establish.

In Bouanich II,[257] the Court of Justice held that failure to take into account or partially taking into account the tax paid in the other Member State for the calculation of the tax cap was in breach of the freedom of establishment and the free movement of capital. In this case, Ms Bouanich received dividends from a Swedish company. The dividends were subject to 15 per cent withholding tax. Under the French rules applicable at the time, a tax shield applied whereby the overall French tax burden could not be more than 50 per cent or 60 per cent. Furthermore, there was a right to restitution of the portion of tax that exceeded the threshold.

In Ms Bouanich's case, foreign withholding taxes on income were not taken into account for the purposes of the tax shield. She argued that the tax shield penalised income from foreign-sourced dividends.[258] Since the withholding tax levied outside

---

[253] Case C-157/10 BBVA.
[254] Ibid, paras 37–8.
[255] The Court of Justice cited Case C-67/08 Block, para 31.
[256] Case C-157/10 BBVA, para 39.
[257] Case C-375/12 Margaretha Bouanich v. Directeur des services fiscaux de la Drôme, ECLI:EU:C:2014:138.
[258] Ibid, para 32.

3.3 Methodology of the Court of Justice

France was not taken into account, or was taken into account only partially, in the calculation of the income tax that may be reimbursed to her, the amount corresponding to the foreign withholding tax remained permanently chargeable to the taxpayer. This systematically increased the tax burden on foreign-sourced dividends as opposed to that on French dividends.[259]

The Court of Justice distinguished this case from the earlier Kerckhaert and Morres case.[260] The Bouanich II case did not relate to the prevention of double taxation but to the domestic (French) tax treatment of dividends distributed by a company established in Sweden, for the purposes of applying a mechanism capping various direct taxes. Here, there was different treatment of a resident taxpayer receiving domestic dividends and a resident taxpayer receiving foreign-sourced dividends taxed in both states – 'the double taxation being regulated by the imputation in the Member State of residence of a tax credit of an amount corresponding to the tax paid in the State of the distributing company'.[261] By contrast, in the Kerckhaert and Morres case, French legislation did not make any distinction between domestic and foreign-sourced dividends, as it imposed a uniform rate of taxation on the dividends. The adverse consequences were a result of the parallel exercise of taxing powers between Member States.[262]

The Court of Justice also emphasised that there was a difference between the granting of a tax credit under the France-Sweden tax treaty and the application of the tax shield. The granting of a tax credit was a result of the relevant tax treaty and was part of the parallel exercise of taxing powers by these jurisdictions. The tax shield was unrelated to the parallel exercise of tax jurisdiction and only concerned France's tax jurisdiction. That tax provision had the purpose and effect of reducing the level of taxation of the income on which that Member State exercised its powers of taxation.[263]

The Court of Justice found that there was a restriction to the freedom of establishment and the free movement of capital. This could not be justified on the basis of the balanced allocation of tax rights between Member States. As the Court of Justice pointed out, the restitution of tax granted under the tax shield was a tax advantage provided for by the French legislation, which limited the tax burden of taxpayers by applying a system of capping, as such, guaranteeing the restitution of tax paid above a certain percentage. Such a tax-capping mechanism did not affect the possibility of the French government taxing the activities carried on in its territory, nor did it restrict the possibility of that Member State taxing income acquired in another Member State.[264]

---

[259] Ibid, para 33.
[260] Case C-513/04 Kerckhaert and Morres.
[261] Case C-375/12 Bouanich II, para 38.
[262] Ibid, para 39.
[263] Ibid, paras 40–2.
[264] Ibid, para 85.

This is a very interesting result. While the reasoning vis-à-vis the cap mechanism is relatively straightforward, the application of the ruling to refund mechanisms may prove troublesome in cases where the only income of a resident is foreign-sourced dividends.

Overall, it could be argued on the basis of the above cases that, at least in the tax treaty context, the Court of Justice may have started to look more broadly when assessing the compatibility of national provisions. Whilst there is a general reluctance to adhere to the overall approach and take into account tax treatment in another Member State, tax treaties are more readily considered in deciding whether a taxpayer's fundamental freedoms are breached. It is still unclear whether measures imposed unilaterally by one Member State (i.e. not in the context of a tax treaty, or when the tax treaty is irrelevant) can be taken into account to assess the discriminatory effect of tax laws of another Member State. Perhaps to the extent that this does not lead to a positive obligation in one Member State (usually the home state) to eliminate double taxation arising from the exercise of competence of the two Member States, as in Damseaux, then the tax treatment in the other Member State (usually the host state) may be taken into account. Case law here is still not settled.

3.4 CONCLUSION

Despite the limitations of the European Treaties in the area of direct taxes, the Court of Justice has inadvertently been put in a position of filling in some of the gaps arising from the lack of harmonising or coordinating action. Using general Treaty provisions, the Court of Justice has established important principles affecting national tax systems. Companies engaging in cross-border activities, or investing abroad, have been greatly affected by these principles and in many cases benefited from the ensuing changes in domestic legislation. At the same time, as shown in subsequent chapters, in areas where the Court's judgments are not consistent with each other, or in situations when Member States extended rules applicable to transactions with non-residents also to transactions between residents, for domestic groups, compliance costs may have increased without necessarily any gain.

This chapter examined what appears to be the basic approach of the Court of Justice in direct tax cases and the methodology it uses. It was shown that although the Court has adopted an expansive interpretation of the Treaty freedoms, nevertheless a number of issues that might affect the result of a case remain unresolved. It will be shown in the following chapters that this has an impact on the degree of difficulty that Member States may have in exercising their tax competence compatibly with EU law – that is in the application of reverse subsidiarity, as discussed in section 3.1. It also has an impact on the ability of national courts to police and enforce the application of reverse subsidiarity domestically. The limitations of the judicial approach constitute an all-pervasive theme of this book and are revisited in Chapter 9.

The following chapters examine selected areas of case law and, wherever relevant, a comparison with the treatment under international tax law and the OECD Model Tax Convention is made. It will be shown that although the flexible use of the notion of precedent by the Court of Justice has led to the creation of pockets of case law, much work is still needed for a coherent body of EU corporate tax law to be established.

4

Tax Obstacles to the Cross-Border Movement of Companies: Direct Investment

As explained in previous chapters, there is no competence to harmonise corporate taxes in the European Union. Basic issues such as the test of company residence for tax purposes, the tax rates, the rules on the taxable base, loss relief, attribution of profits and expenses and so on are not regulated by EU law. It is only when national tax rules discriminate against foreign nationals or restrict EU nationals from exercising their freedoms, or distort competition in a prohibited way, that there can be an intervention at EU level.

While at this juncture, textbooks based on national tax law would devote much space on the structure of their corporate tax systems, this is where a book on EU corporate tax law is largely silent – being an issue pertaining to tax harmonisation. So far, the most substantial initiative to provide some uniform rules has been the CCTB/CCCTB, which was discussed in Chapter 2. Other than that, an investor wishing to set up a company (or group of companies) in the EU is faced with twenty-seven corporate tax regimes. This chapter looks at some of the tax obstacles faced by single companies, group companies and branches[1] in the context of direct investment.

4.1 COMPANY RESIDENCE

States invariably use corporate residence as the connecting factor for imposing taxes on companies, that is for exercising their tax jurisdiction. This is also enshrined in the OECD Model Tax Convention, pursuant to which companies are taxed on the basis of tax residence.[2] Outside of the tax field, residence does not tend to be very relevant[3] and is an indeterminate connecting factor. As a result, states often prescribe

---

[1] In this chapter and throughout this book, unless stated otherwise, the terms 'branch' and 'permanent establishment' are used interchangeably.
[2] See Art 4 OECD Model Tax Convention.
[3] As mentioned in an English case, '[r]esidence is not a concept for company law purposes of any importance; it is very important for taxation purposes but for purposes of control of the statutory books such as the share register it is of no significance whatever'. International Credit and Investment Co v. Adham [1994] 1 BCLC 66. Corporate residence may also be important for ascertaining the

additional criteria or tests in determining corporate tax residence, for example, place of incorporation, place of registered seat, place of management and so on. These are very similar to the connecting factors used in determining the applicable company law,[4] but they should not be confused as they serve different purposes. Tax residence links a company with the tax jurisdiction of a state. If used as a connecting factor in company law, corporate residence links the 'proper law' of a company (*lex societatis*) with the (non-tax) laws of a state. The existence of the one does not presuppose the existence of the other.[5]

EU law shows no preference for any specific connecting factor (or criteria in delineating a connecting factor) either for corporate law[6] or direct tax law purposes.[7] As discussed in Chapter 3, Article 54 TFEU extends entitlement to freedom of establishment to 'companies or firms formed in accordance with the law of a Member State and having their registered office, central administration or principal place of business within the Union'. Therefore, all types of connecting factors under company law are included in this description.

Unsurprisingly in a treaty that does not purport to deal with tax matters, corporate tax residence is not discussed. As a matter of fact, corporate tax residence is not at all relevant. It has been reiterated numerous times by the Court of Justice that the allocation of tax jurisdiction – and as a corollary, the criteria for establishing residence for tax purposes – falls within the domain of Member State competence. As Advocate General Geelhoed stated in the ACT Group Litigation case, 'the power to choose criteria of, and allocate, tax jurisdiction lies purely with Member States (as governed by international tax law)'.[8]

Member States have the power to determine their own tests and criteria that would allow them to exercise their tax jurisdiction. Some Member States may choose an objective test (e.g. place of incorporation or place of registered office),

---

company's amenability to jurisdiction. See AV Dicey and JH Morris, *The Conflict of Laws* (London: Stevens, 1974), Rule 160(2).

[4] For example, nationality, domicile, residence, legal seat, place of incorporation, place of management, place of registration, place of registered office, etc. See Peter Behren, 'General Principles on Residence of Companies', Chapter 1 in Guglielmo Maisto (ed), *Residence of Companies under Tax Treaties and EC Law*, EC and International Tax Law Series, Vol 5 (Amsterdam: IBFD, 2009).

[5] Christiana HJI Panayi, 'Exit Taxation as an Obstacle to Corporate Emigration from the Spectre of EU Tax Law', in Catherine Barnard and Okeoghene Odudu (eds), *Cambridge Yearbook of European Legal Studies 2010–2011*, Vol 13 (Oxford: Hart Publishing, 2012).

[6] This is particularly relevant in the context of corporate mobility. For the lack of harmonisation of the definition of seat in corporate law, see European Commission DG/LSE, *Study on the Law Applicable to Companies: Final Report* (2016). Also see Edoardo Traversa, 'Corporate Tax Residence at the Crossroads between International Competition and Convergence: Outlining the Debate', in *Corporate Tax Residence and Mobility* (EATLP 2017), p 12.

[7] As regards the allocation of taxing rights in the VAT legislation, see Rita de la Feria, 'Place where the Supply/Activity is Effectively Carried Out as an Allocation Rule: VAT v. Direct Taxation', in Michael Lang, Peter Melz, Eleonor Kristoffersson and Thomas Ecker (eds), *Value Added Tax and Direct Taxation – Similarities and Differences* (Amsterdam: IBFD, 2009).

[8] Case C-374/04 Test Claimants in Class IV of the ACT Group Litigation (2006) ECR I-11673, para 52.

other states may choose a subjective test (e.g. place of management), while others may choose a combination of the two.[9] Moreover, the domestic definition of corporate residence may be qualified under tax treaties, in so far as the application of treaty rights as agreed between contracting states are concerned.[10]

To this extent, one would think that the treatment of corporate tax residence under EU law is straightforward: it is the Member States that determine whether a company falls under their tax jurisdiction and they can agree between themselves (or with a third country) on how to allocate this tax jurisdiction. EU law does not prescribe what connecting factors a Member State ought to have. Neither does it prescribe how tax jurisdiction is to be shared. Furthermore, as shown in Chapter 3, some cases, the high-water mark of which is the D case,[11] seem to suggest that the Court of Justice is paying more deference to tax treaties and the OECD Model Tax Convention, on which the Member States rely in concluding their tax treaties.

One may argue that a company incorporated in the home state cannot demand from the host state where its place of management is located to consider it tax resident if the host state adopts the incorporation test for tax residence. The host state is not in breach of its obligations under EU law to refuse to recognise the company as a tax resident.

This statement is deceptively simple. The protective scope of EU law does not end where the Member State's power to determine tax residence begins. While formally that power remains intact, in reality, in some instances it is circumscribed. This is because, irrespective of whether a Member State recognises a company as (tax) resident, to the extent that the company is in a comparable situation to a (tax) resident company, it cannot be treated in a discriminatory manner. As with everything else left within the competence of Member States, what EU law *does* demand is that whatever rules are chosen, they should not be applied in a discriminatory manner. Therefore, if a French-resident company is given certain tax reliefs and these are not extended to the permanent establishment of a non-resident company in an objectively comparable situation with a resident company, there could be a question of incompatibility. This, however, has no effect on how a Member State (in our example, France) chooses to define who is tax resident and who is not. It is a question of how national tax legislation applies to resident and non-resident persons after these are categorised as resident and non-resident according to domestic rules. Nevertheless, it could be argued that even if residence is respected as a connecting factor, by requiring the extension of national benefits linked to it to non-residents, this takes away some of its essence.

---

[9] The UK follows this approach. See, generally, Christiana HJI Panayi. 'UK Report', Ch 22 in Guglielmo Maisto (ed), *Residence of Companies under Tax Treaties and EC Law*, EC and International Tax Law Series, Vol 5 (Amsterdam: IBFD, 2009).
[10] Art 4 OECD Model Tax Convention.
[11] Case C-376/03 D v. Rijksbelastingdienst [2005] ECR I-5821.

A notable exception where residence is given heightened importance is within tax treaties. It has been shown that the fact that treaty benefits are restricted to residents of contracting states is not a breach of EU law.[12] There is no EU obligation to extend those benefits to residents of the other Member States that are not a party to the tax treaty, as those benefits are an integral part of the treaty. The Court of Justice has refused to enter into a discussion of whether a resident of a third Member State can ever be in a comparable situation to a resident of one of the contracting states to a tax treaty. Therefore, it would seem that there is nothing per se wrong in restricting tax treaty benefits to residents of contracting states – notwithstanding the bilateralism of this approach. Even some Directives limit their scope to Member State resident companies, though these instruments are multilateral.[13]

Overall, while the importance of residence for the attainment of certain benefits in a tax system may effectively have been eroded, it still remains important as a connecting factor when it comes to treaty benefits and entitlement under some direct tax directives.

4.2 ISSUES WITH THE TAXATION OF CORPORATE GROUPS

EU law has had a substantial impact on domestic rules imposed by the Member States on company structures and strategies. This is not only a result of the direct tax Directives, examined in Chapter 2, but also – and perhaps primarily – through negative integration. As mentioned above, EU law does not impose any immediate obligations on the Member States on how to structure their corporate tax system in terms of rates, taxable base, depreciation and so on. What it does is to prevent the Member States from imposing rules that restrict the ability of companies to exercise their fundamental freedoms or that discriminate between resident and non-resident companies when they are in an objectively comparable situation. Therefore, national tax rules affecting a single company cannot be subject to scrutiny under EU law, unless there is a cross-border element to these rules that falls within the scope of the fundamental freedoms, as considered in Chapter 3.

The most important freedom for the establishment of companies and, generally, for direct investment, is freedom of establishment. As with the other freedoms, this freedom has an outbound (home state) angle and an inbound (host state) angle. From an outbound perspective, a home state must not impose obstacles to nationals who are exercising their freedom to set up and have an establishment in another Member State. This reflects capital export neutrality concerns.[14] From an inbound

---

[12] See 3.3.3.
[13] For example, the Parent-Subsidiary Directive applies to companies resident in a Member State under domestic law and subject to taxation there. The Interest and Royalties Directive and the Merger Directive contain similar requirements. See Chapter 2.
[14] For a discussion of capital export neutrality and capital import neutrality, and the literature on these principles, see Christiana HJI Panayi, *Double Taxation, Tax Treaties, Treaty Shopping and the European Community* (Kluwer Law International, 2007), Ch 1.

perspective, a host state has to give national treatment to persons from other Member States, whether they are organised as a primary establishment or a secondary establishment through a branch, agency or subsidiary. This reflects capital import neutrality concerns. As shown in this chapter and subsequent chapters, a Member State may be under different obligations as a home state or a host state.

Typically, therefore, there are two types of obstacles: the home state obstacles where a resident company is hindered by its national rules from carrying on its business in another Member State, and the host state obstacles where a non-resident company is hindered by another Member State's rules from carrying on its business there in a similar way to domestic companies. Depending on the scope of the business activities, that is whether an establishment is involved such as a branch or agency or subsidiary in which a company has definite influence and control or whether it is an instance of portfolio investment, freedom of establishment or the free movement of capital are triggered.

Examples of home state obstacles discussed in this book are where a parent company is not able to deduct costs or expenses or losses relating to a foreign subsidiary or foreign branch where such items would have been deductible in case of a domestic subsidiary or branch, or where a parent company is taxed more heavily as a result of controlling a foreign company in a low-tax jurisdiction rather than a resident company, or where higher taxes are imposed on foreign-sourced payments of dividends or interest or royalties, or where a company is taxed more heavily when it transfers assets to a foreign group company or a foreign branch than a domestic one, or where exit taxes are imposed on a company transferring its tax residence abroad and so on.

Host state obstacles arise where a non-resident company, either through its branch or on its own, is taxed more heavily than a resident company. This could be as a result of the non-resident company being taxed on its profits on a gross basis rather than net basis, or when it is subject to higher tax rates, or where stricter depreciation rules apply, or where returns from foreign investments are taxed more heavily or receive less beneficial treatment and so on.

As with most principles arising under negative integration, the Court of Justice does not take a structured approach. Often it cannot do so, due to the unsystematic nature of negative integration, as discussed in 3.1. An implication of this is that the Court of Justice does not adopt a different approach according to whether the national tax rules affect a single company or a group or a branch. While such factors may be relevant when it comes to comparability or justifications, they do not pre-empt the Court's restriction or discrimination analysis. By contrast, because of some characteristics of group companies (e.g. separate legal entity), whether a rule relates to such companies or branches may be an important consideration in international tax law. Some of these issues are examined in this chapter and the following chapters. Throughout the analysis, a comparison is made with the

4.2.1 Expenses in Foreign Holdings

There have been a few cases dealing with the non-deductibility of expenses or charges incurred by parent companies in relation to shareholdings in cross-border subsidiaries. In international tax law, this is an issue that tends to fall under each country's expense allocation rules. Within the EU, these non-deductibility rules have to conform to fundamental freedoms.

The Bosal case[15] has already been mentioned in Chapter 2. Here a Dutch parent company, which carried on holding, financing and licensing royalty-related activities, borrowed funds to invest in the share capital of subsidiaries in nine other Member States. The Dutch tax authorities refused deduction for the interest on the funds because the dividends received from these subsidiaries were exempt. The Dutch legislation made the deductibility of costs connected with a company's shareholding in a subsidiary in another Member State conditional on those costs being indirectly instrumental in making profits taxable in the Netherlands. Had the funds been invested in a Dutch subsidiary, interest would have been deductible, even if domestic dividends were effectively exempt. The option to deny the parent company's holding costs was a common practice at the time, also permitted under the Parent-Subsidiary Directive.[16]

Notwithstanding this, the Court of Justice found the rules to be incompatible with freedom of establishment. By allowing costs to be deducted only if they were instrumental in taxable profits being made in the Netherlands, the legislation hindered the exercise of the freedom of establishment, as it penalised the establishment of subsidiaries in another Member State. A parent company would be dissuaded from carrying on its activities through the intermediary of a subsidiary established in another Member State as such subsidiaries did not usually generate profits that were taxable in the Netherlands.[17]

The restriction was not justified. As far as the coherence of the tax system was concerned, the Court of Justice found that there was no direct link between, on the one hand, the granting of a tax advantage (the right to deduct costs connected with holdings in the capital of their subsidiaries from their taxable profit) to parent companies established in the Netherlands and, on the other, the tax system relating to the subsidiaries of parent companies where the latter were established in that Member State.[18] Interestingly in this context, the Court of Justice emphasised that '[u]nlike operating branches or establishments, parent companies and their

---

[15] Case C-168/01 Bosal Holding BV v. Staatsecretaris van Financiën [2003] ECR I-9409.
[16] See Art 4(2) of the Parent-Subsidiary Directive and the analysis in Ch 2.
[17] Case C-168/01 Bosal, para 27.
[18] Ibid, para 31.

subsidiaries are distinct legal persons, each being subject to a tax liability of its own, so that a direct link in the context of the same liability to tax is lacking and the coherence of the tax system cannot be relied upon'.[19]

The Court of Justice also rejected the argument that the different tax treatment of parent companies was justified because subsidiaries that made profits taxable in the Netherlands and those that did not were not in comparable situations. This was not the right comparator test. Instead, the difference in tax treatment concerned parent companies according to whether or not they had subsidiaries making profits taxable in the Netherlands, even though those parent companies were all established in that Member State.[20]

A similar approach was followed in later cases. In Keller,[21] the Court of Justice found that German rules that precluded the deductibility of shareholder expenses on foreign tax-exempt dividends were not compatible with freedom of establishment. In this case, a German-resident company, Keller Holdings, owned a German subsidiary, which had a substantial holding in an Austrian company. Dividends distributed by the Austrian subsidiary to the German subsidiary were tax exempt under the Germany-Austria tax treaty. Dividends further distributed by the German subsidiary to Keller Holdings were also tax exempt. Keller Holdings tried to deduct the interest on loans raised to acquire the participation in its German subsidiary and other administrative expenses. The German tax authorities refused to deduct these expenses on the basis that they had an immediate economic connection with tax-exempt income (i.e. the income from the Austrian company).

The Court of Justice found this treatment to be incompatible with freedom of establishment under the EC Treaty and the EEA Agreement.[22] Even though the issue was whether the German group parent company could deduct costs incurred in respect of its shareholding in a German subsidiary, this was not considered to be an internal situation. As the disallowance of the deduction was linked to the receipt of dividends from a second-tier Austrian subsidiary, the case fell within the scope of the EC and EEA Treaties.[23]

The Court of Justice thought that a German parent company with a German subsidiary was in a comparable situation to a German parent with a foreign subsidiary. This was because in so far as the dividends received by the German parent were concerned, they were, in reality, all exempt from taxation whether paid by a German or foreign subsidiary.[24] However, holding costs could only be deducted in a domestic situation because of the economic link requirement. As a result, the tax position of a company with an indirect subsidiary in Austria was less favourable than that of

---

[19] Ibid, para 32.
[20] Ibid, para 39.
[21] Case C-471/04 Keller Holding [2006] ECR I-2107.
[22] The claim arose between 1993 and 1995. As Austria did not join the Community until 1 January 1995, this case was examined under the provisions of both the EC Treaty and the EEA Agreement.
[23] Case C-471/04 Keller Holding, paras 23–4.
[24] Ibid, para 31.

a company with an indirect subsidiary in Germany.[25] This difference in treatment could dissuade a parent company from carrying on its activities through direct or indirect subsidiaries established in the other Member States.[26] The Court of Justice concluded that the restriction could not be justified.

Similarly, in Rewe,[27] the Court of Justice found that German rules restricting depreciation of holdings in non-resident subsidiaries violated EU law. Under German tax law applicable at the time of the case, write-downs on resident participations were immediately tax deductible, irrespective of the nature of the participation (passive or active). By contrast, write-downs on non-resident participations were only immediately tax deductible if the company generated active income abroad or held an interest of at least one quarter in another foreign company that generated active income.[28]

The Court of Justice found there was a restriction to the freedom of establishment.[29] The tax situation of a German parent company with non-resident subsidiaries was more onerous than if it had resident subsidiaries.[30] Even if the loss derived from the non-resident subsidiary could be set off against subsequent profits, the immediate deduction of a write-down constituted a cash-flow advantage.[31] It was found that German parent companies were in a comparable situation as regards losses suffered from the depreciation of their shareholdings in subsidiaries. These were losses suffered by the German parent company and not the subsidiary. In addition, the profits of the subsidiaries – whether resident or non-resident – were not taxable in the hands of the parent companies.[32] This difference of treatment gave rise to a tax disadvantage.[33] A parent company might be dissuaded from carrying on its activities through subsidiaries established in the other Member States.[34] The Court of Justice concluded that the German rules restricted the freedom of establishment and were not justified.[35]

In the Glaxo Wellcome case,[36] the judgment of the Court of Justice was more nuanced. Here, German law disallowed a deduction of losses arising from a write-down on the value of participations acquired from non-resident shareholders.[37] The Court of Justice found that the German legislation was not in breach of the free

---

[25] Ibid, para 34.
[26] Ibid, para 35.
[27] Case C-347/04 Rewe Zentralfinanz eG [2007] ECR I-2647.
[28] Ibid, para 10.
[29] The relevant subsidiaries were wholly owned by Rewe.
[30] Ibid, para 30.
[31] Ibid, para 29.
[32] Ibid, para 34.
[33] Ibid, para 31.
[34] Ibid.
[35] Ibid, para 70.
[36] Case C-182/08 Glaxo Wellcome GmbH & Co. KG v. Finanzamt München II [2009] ECR I-8591.
[37] In this case, the reduction in value of shares as a result of a dividend distribution did not affect the basis of assessment for a resident taxpayer when that taxpayer had acquired shares in a resident company from a non-resident shareholder. Had those shares been acquired from a resident shareholder, such a reduction in value would have reduced the acquirer's basis of assessment. Ibid, paras 3–10.

movement of capital, even though such write-down was allowed for resident participations. This legislation was put in place under the former imputation system to prevent a non-resident taxpayer from benefiting economically from the imputation credit in case of a disposal of shares to a resident shareholder.[38]

Although the legislation restricted the free movement of capital, this restriction could be justified by the need to maintain a balanced allocation of the power to impose taxes between the Member States.[39] It was also justified by the need to prevent wholly artificial arrangements that did not reflect economic reality and whose only purpose was to obtain a tax advantage unduly.[40] It was for the national court to examine whether the legislation at issue in the main proceedings was limited to what was necessary in order to attain those objectives.[41]

Notwithstanding the conclusion in the Glaxo Wellcome case, the important point to note in all of these cases is that the Court of Justice had no qualms about requiring the depreciation of the value of a foreign subsidiary or the deduction of financing costs to be taken into account in the home state. The Court of Justice looked at it as a home state restriction: a parent company was dissuaded from establishing subsidiaries abroad. The fact that the different treatment was because the home state could not tax the profits of the non-resident subsidiary was not relevant.

Arguably, in all of the above cases there was some – limited – jurisdictional nexus: the loss/expense was that of a resident parent company, albeit suffered as a result of the non-resident subsidiary or investment in the non-resident subsidiary. What if there is absolutely no jurisdictional link? What if the loss is of the non-resident subsidiary? Could it be set off against the profits of the resident parent company, even if that company could not normally tax the profits of the non-resident subsidiary? This issue was addressed in group relief cases, discussed next.

4.2.2 Cross-Border Loss Relief

Group relief, that is the possibility of losses incurred by one company being set off against the profits of another company of the same group is very important. Domestic relief of losses within a group of companies is available in most Member States under specific circumstances. In such circumstances, the group is effectively treated as an economic unit. However, most Member States conferring domestic relief require that the surrendering and the receiving group companies be resident companies or that the losses are domestic losses. As a result, loss relief is rarely available in cross-border situations. This may lead to over-taxation and create obstacles to cross-border movement. While the unavailability of cross-border loss

---

[38] For a discussion of the classical and imputation systems of taxation, see Chapter 5.
[39] Case C-182/08 Glaxo Wellcome, para 88.
[40] Ibid, para 92.
[41] Ibid, paras 94–8.

relief is not treated as discrimination under the OECD Model Tax Convention,[42] the unavailability or limitation of cross-border loss relief is thought to be especially problematic in the EU context. It influences business decisions on whether and how to enter a new market, creating 'a barrier to entering other markets, which perpetuates the artificial segmentation of the internal market along national lines'.[43]

The issue of cross-border loss relief between group companies was considered by the Court of Justice in Marks & Spencer plc v. IRC.[44] Before this case is analysed, it is important to explain the precursor to the UK tax legislation that was at issue in that case.

In ICI v. Colmer, the Court of Justice looked into the UK group relief rules applicable at the time. These rules allowed tax relief between consortium members when the business of the holding company (owned by the consortium) consisted wholly or mainly in the holdings of shares in UK subsidiaries. Here ICI and Wellcome Foundation Ltd were resident in the UK and had formed a consortium through which they owned respectively 49 and 51 per cent in a UK holding company. The sole business of the UK holding company was to hold shares in twenty-three trading companies. Four of these subsidiaries were resident in the UK, six in other Member States and thirteen in non-Member States. For a given accounting period, ICI tried to set off 49 per cent of one of the UK subsidiary's losses as against its chargeable profits. The UK tax authorities denied the relief on the basis that the majority of the holding company's subsidiaries were non-resident companies, and the case was eventually referred to the Court of Justice. The Court found the residence requirement to be in breach of freedom of establishment. Companies belonging to a resident consortium that had, through a holding company, exercised their right to freedom of establishment in order to set up subsidiaries in other Member States, were denied tax relief on losses incurred by a resident subsidiary where the majority of the subsidiaries controlled by the holding company were not resident in the UK.[45]

Following this case, the UK loss relief rules were amended, and the focus of the new legislation shifted from the surrendering company's ownership structure to the location of the loss. Under the amended legislation, broadly, group relief could only be granted for losses considered within the scope of UK taxation. As a result, losses made by a UK branch of a non-resident company could be surrendered to another group company for offset against its UK taxable profits. In addition, a UK group company's losses could be surrendered to the UK branch of a non-resident company for offset against any UK branch profits.

---

[42] See discussion on Art 24(5) OECD Model Tax Convention below.
[43] Communication from the Commission to the Council, the European Parliament and the European Economic and Social Committee, *Tax Treatment of Losses in Cross-Border Situations*, COM(2006) 824, p 3.
[44] Case C-446/03 Marks & Spencer plc v. IRC [2005] ECR I-10837.
[45] Case C-264/96 ICI [1998] ECR I-4695, para 22.

In Marks & Spencer, the condition that the surrendering and claimant companies be resident or carrying on economic activity in the UK was challenged. This case is one of the most high-profile and extensively discussed cases in the jurisprudence of the Court of Justice.[46] In this case, the profitable UK parent company, Marks & Spencer plc, claimed group tax relief in respect of losses incurred by its French, Belgian and German subsidiaries. These non-resident subsidiaries had no UK branch and had never traded in the UK. As a result, they were not within the scope of the UK group relief rules. The tax inspector, therefore, refused group relief and Marks & Spencer's appeal was rejected by the Special Commissioners.[47] Marks & Spencer appealed that decision before the High Court, which decided to stay the proceedings and refer the matter to the Court of Justice for a preliminary ruling.

The Court of Justice decided that the non-availability of group relief for losses from foreign subsidiaries prima facie hindered cross-border groupings. Group relief constituted a tax advantage for the companies concerned, as it speeded up the relief of the losses of the loss-making companies by allowing them to be set off immediately against the profits of other group companies.[48] The exclusion of such an advantage led to the different treatment of losses incurred by a UK-resident subsidiary and by a non-resident subsidiary with no UK branch. This deterred parent companies from setting up subsidiaries in the other Member States and restricted freedom of establishment.[49]

This restriction could be justified on the following grounds, taken together.[50] Firstly, there was a need to preserve the allocation of taxing rights between the Member States. Giving companies the option to have their losses taken into account in different Member States would significantly jeopardise the balanced allocation of a Member State's power to impose taxes.[51] Secondly, it was necessary to prevent double relief of losses both in the Member State of the subsidiary and the Member State of the parent company.[52] Thirdly, the risk of tax avoidance would exist if companies were free to

---

[46] See, for example, Mark Persoff, 'Marks & Spencer: more questions than answers' [2005] 3 *British Tax Review*, 260–6; Timothy Lyons, 'Marks & Spencer: something for everyone?' [2006] 1 *British Tax Review*, 9–14, 12; Michael Lang, 'The Marks & Spencer case: the open issues following the ECJ's final word' (2006) 46(2) *European Taxation*, 54–67.

[47] Decision SpC 00352, reported at [2003] STC (SCD) 70.

[48] Case C-446/03 Marks & Spencer, para 32.

[49] Ibid, para 33.

[50] Ibid, para 51. In subsequent cases, the Court of Justice held that this was not a cumulative requirement. See, for example, Case C-470/04 N v. Inspecteur Van de Belastingdienst Oost/ Kantoor Almelo [2006] ECR I-7409, para 42; Case C-231/05 Oy AA [2007] ECR I-6373, paras 51–60; and Case C-379/05 Amurta SGPS v. Inspecteur van de Belastingdienst [2007] ECR I-9569, paras 57–9. In a later case, Case C-311/08 Société de Gestion Industrielle v. Belgian State [2010] ECR I-487, the Court of Justice reverted to the position that the two justifications (preservation of balanced allocation of taxing powers and prevention of tax avoidance) are to be taken together. See Christiana HJI Panayi, 'Reverse subsidiarity and EU tax law: Can Member States be left to their own devices?', [2010] 3 *British Tax Review*, 267–301, 278; Mathieu Isenbaert, *EC Law and the Sovereignty of the Member States in Direct Taxation*, IBFD Doctoral Series, Vol 19 (Amsterdam: IBFD, 2010), pp 543–4.

[51] Marks & Spencer, paras 43–6.

[52] Ibid, paras 47–8.

transfer losses from Member States with lower levels of taxation to those with higher levels of taxation, thus increasing the value of the losses.[53]

However, for the restrictive measure to be justified, it could not go beyond what was necessary to attain the essential part of the objectives pursued. In other words, the restriction had to be proportional. In order to assess the proportionality of the restrictive measure, the Court of Justice took into account whether the non-resident subsidiary had exhausted all possibilities for relief available in its Member State of residence. The possibilities were set out in paragraph 55 of the judgment. The Court of Justice considered that the restrictive measure went beyond what was necessary to attain the essential part of the objectives pursued where:

> the non-resident subsidiary has exhausted the possibilities available in its State of residence of having the losses taken into account for the accounting period concerned by the claim for relief and also for previous accounting periods, if necessary by transferring those losses to a third party or by offsetting the losses against the profits made by the subsidiary in previous periods, and ... there is no possibility for the foreign subsidiary's losses to be taken into account in its State of residence for future periods either by the subsidiary itself or by a third party, in particular where the subsidiary has been sold to that third party.[54]

Therefore, the availability of carry-back, current year relief against other local profits or carry-forward, either by the subsidiary or a third party to which those losses were transferred or sold, meant that not all possibilities for relief had been exhausted. It was only when the resident parent company demonstrated to the tax authorities of its Member State that those conditions were fulfilled (i.e. that all possibilities for relief had been exhausted) that it became contrary to freedom of establishment to preclude the possibility for the parent company to deduct from its taxable profits in that Member State the losses incurred by its non-resident subsidiary.[55] The Court of Justice emphasised that the Member States were free to adopt or maintain in force rules having the specific purpose of precluding from a tax benefit wholly artificial arrangements whose purpose was to circumvent or escape national tax law.[56]

This decision forced the UK to amend its group relief rules once again. In the Finance Act 2006, entitlement to claim group relief for EU losses was finally granted, but under strict conditions. Broadly, the amended legislation allowed non-resident group companies without a UK branch to surrender losses to a UK company in the same group when certain conditions were fulfilled.[57] However, the Commission found that the amended legislation was still restrictive and not aligned with the spirit of the Court's decision in the Marks & Spencer case.[58] The issue was eventually

---

[53] Ibid, paras 49–50.
[54] Ibid, para 55.
[55] Ibid, para 56.
[56] Ibid, para 57.
[57] For an analysis of the new legislation, see HJI Panayi, 'Reverse subsidiarity and EU tax law', 289ff.
[58] IP/09/1461, 8 October 2009. The Commission's case ref no is 2007/4026.

referred to the Court of Justice.[59] In her opinion, Advocate General Kokott advised the Court of Justice to reverse the Marks & Spencer case and more specifically, to reverse the terminal losses test, as it was impractical and did not protect the interests of the internal market.[60] The test was 'also not a less onerous means of guaranteeing the fiscal sovereignty of Member States as it does not facilitate the activity of cross-border groups but rather constitutes a virtually inexhaustible source of legal disputes between taxpayers and the Member States' tax administrations.'[61] While the Court of Justice did not follow the reasoning in the Advocate General's opinion, it still found that there was no breach as the Commission had not shown that the UK legislation made it virtually impossible in practice for a resident parent company to obtain cross-border group relief.

In Oy AA,[62] a case decided shortly after the Marks & Spencer case, the Court of Justice seemed to pay more deference to Finnish legislation, which prevented a resident company from deducting an intra-group transfer unless the recipient company was also resident in Finland. Under Finnish law, an intra-group transfer was tax deductible for the contributor and taxable income for the recipient, if both the contributor and the recipient of the group were domestic companies.[63] Here Oy AA, a Finnish-resident company, was a wholly-owned indirect subsidiary of a UK-resident company. Oy AA wanted to make a group contribution to the UK parent company. All other requirements set out in the Finnish legislation were satisfied, other than the requirement that the contributor and recipient be Finnish companies.

The Court of Justice found that the Finnish legislation constituted a restriction to the freedom of establishment. The difference in treatment between resident subsidiaries according to the seat of the parent company made it less attractive for companies established in the other Member States to exercise their freedom of establishment in Finland. Parent companies could 'refrain from acquiring, creating or maintaining a subsidiary in the State which adopts that measure'.[64]

According to the Court of Justice, the restriction was justified on the basis of safeguarding the balanced allocation of the power to tax between the Member States and the prevention of tax avoidance, taken together. The Court of Justice concluded that the Finnish group contribution regime was suitable for the attainment of these objectives. Rather surprisingly, the Court found that 'taken as a whole'[65] the Finnish regime was proportional, even though not specifically designed to prevent purely

---

[59] Case C-172/13 Commission v. UK, ECLI:EU:C:2015:50.
[60] For the reasoning of the Advocate General, see paras 42–53 of her opinion (Case C-172/13 Commission v. UK, ECLI:EU:C:2014:2321).
[61] Ibid, para 44.
[62] Case C-231/05 Oy AA.
[63] The parent company had to hold at least 90 per cent of the shares of the subsidiary or both had to be held by a joint parent company that held 90 per cent in these companies.
[64] Case C-231/05 Oy AA, para 39.
[65] Ibid, para 63.

4.2 Taxation of Corporate Groups

artificial arrangements.[66] In this statement, the Court of Justice not only deviated from its previous judgments on anti-abuse provisions,[67] but it was also conspicuously silent vis-à-vis the Marks & Spencer's exhaustion of possibilities test.

Obviously, the Court of Justice was concerned that Finland would lose the power to tax the transferred profit if the recipient was a non-resident company.[68] However, why was the inability to tax the profit a relevant concern for profit contribution regimes (or for this specific regime) when the inability to reincorporate a terminal loss was not a concern in the Marks & Spencer case? Given the similarities of profit contribution and loss relief regimes,[69] one would have thought that similar conclusions ought to apply. In fact, in Sweden, a group contribution regime similar to the Finnish regime was found by national courts to be contrary to freedom of establishment if contributions for final losses of subsidiaries could not be deducted.[70] In this case, the Marks & Spencer's exhaustion of possibilities test was applied though, again, not in its full rigour.[71]

Société Papillon[72] was another important case dealing with the French integration regime. Here the French parent company, Société Papillon, included in its tax group French subsidiaries indirectly held through a Dutch company. The French tax authorities did not allow tax consolidation because the shares in the French company were held through a non-resident (Dutch) company without a French branch. The Conseil d'État referred the question of the compatibility of this regime with freedom of establishment.

The judgment of the Court of Justice was along similar lines to the opinion of the Advocate General. The Court of Justice found that the situation of a parent company that was resident in a Member State and held sub-subsidiaries in that Member State through a resident subsidiary was comparable to the situation of a parent company with sub-subsidiaries resident in the same Member State but held through a non-resident subsidiary.[73] The French legislation aimed to treat, as far as possible,

---

[66] Ibid.
[67] See analysis in Chapter 7.
[68] Case C-231/05 Oy AA, paras 64–5.
[69] Under a profit contribution arrangement, there is an intra-group transfer of profits, whereas under a loss relief arrangement there is an intra-group transfer of losses. Under both regimes, the transfer is on an ad hoc and bilateral basis. Group companies retain their separate tax bases, and a single group tax base is not created. On the variety of tax rules dealing with groups, see, inter alios, Yoshihiro Masui, 'General Report', *Group Taxation*, Cahiers de droit fiscal international, Vol 89b (Kluwer Law International, 2004), p 21; Ioanna Mitroyanni, *Integration Approaches to Group Taxation in European Internal Market* (Kluwer Law International, 2008), pp 122–6.
[70] See advance rulings of the Swedish National Board in Dnr 206-04/D and Dnr 193-04/D, 29 September 2006. On appeal to the Swedish Supreme Court, the decision of the National Board was confirmed on 11 March 2009. See analysis in HJI Panayi, 'Reverse subsidiarity and EU tax law', p 17.
[71] In these Swedish cases, a deduction was allowed for final losses suffered only by EU/EEA subsidiaries and only if such subsidiaries were dissolved through liquidation.
[72] Case C-418/07 Société Papillon v. Ministère du budget, des comptes publics et de la fonction publique [2008] ECR I-08947.
[73] Case C-418/07 Société Papillon, para 29.

a group company in the same way as an undertaking with a number of permanent establishments, by allowing the results of each company to be consolidated.[74] Therefore, the French consolidation regime led to unequal treatment of French parent companies depending on whether they held their lower-tier subsidiaries through intermediary companies established in France or abroad.[75] This was a restriction to the freedom of establishment.[76]

The Court of Justice agreed with its Advocate General in that the restriction could be justified by the need to preserve the coherence of the French group tax system. The tax integration regime provided for the tax consolidation of companies and, to offset this, neutralisation of certain transactions between group companies.[77] In other words, a direct link existed between the tax integration regime (the tax advantage) and the elimination of internal transactions (the compensating disadvantage). The neutralisation of transactions internal to the group avoided losses being used twice: the deduction of a loss at the level of the sub-subsidiary as an ordinary loss and the deduction at the level of the parent company as a loss of the parent company for the depreciation of its holding in the subsidiary.[78]

However, internal transactions would not be neutralised, and the losses would be taken into account twice when the intermediary subsidiary was a non-resident company. This was because a non-resident company was not subject to the tax integration regime.[79] In such circumstances, resident companies would enjoy the advantages of the tax integration regime, as regards the consolidation of results and the immediate taking into account of the losses of all the companies subject to that regime, without the losses of the subsidiary and the provisions made by the parent company being capable of being neutralised.[80] As a result, the direct link between the tax advantage and the compensating disadvantage would be eliminated, thus affecting the coherence of the regime.[81]

Even if the restriction was justified, the Court of Justice stated that it still had to be proportional. The French government had argued that the rules were necessary due to the difficulties the French tax authorities had in ascertaining whether losses would be used twice.[82] The Court of Justice pointed out that practical difficulties could not themselves justify the infringement of a freedom.[83] In a domestic situation, the risk of multiple deductions of losses would have been prevented by the elimination of

---

[74] Ibid, para 28.
[75] Ibid, para 31.
[76] Ibid, paras 31–2.
[77] Ibid, para 45.
[78] Ibid, para 47.
[79] Ibid, para 48.
[80] Ibid, para 49.
[81] Ibid, para 50.
[82] Ibid, para 53.
[83] Ibid, para 54.

4.2 Taxation of Corporate Groups

internal transactions. The Mutual Assistance Directive[84] could have been used to obtain information regarding the intermediate EU entity.[85] Furthermore, France could have asked for such documents from the French parent company as was necessary to determine whether the provisions made by that company for the losses in the share value in the subsidiary could be explained indirectly by a loss of the sub-subsidiary through the provisions of that subsidiary.[86]

Therefore, the Court of Justice found the outright prohibition of the French rules to be disproportional.[87] As a corollary, the French consolidation regime was incompatible with freedom of establishment. Arguably, this was not a representative case on consolidation systems because here, the parent company was not asking to consolidate with the intermediate Dutch company. Rather, it challenged the French rules that prevented it from forming a consolidated group with its other French sub-subsidiaries due to those sub-subsidiaries being held by a non-resident company. Therefore, there was no question of foreign losses being offset by French taxable profits.

In X Holding,[88] a case dealing with the Dutch fiscal unity regime, the Court of Justice was specifically asked whether a Dutch parent company should be allowed to form a consolidated group with non-resident subsidiaries. Under the Dutch regime, resident group companies could be treated as a fiscal unity if the parent company owned at least 95 per cent of the shares in the subsidiary and only for overlapping accounting periods. Non-resident subsidiaries could not be included in a fiscal unity unless they had a Dutch permanent establishment to which the shares in the subsidiary were attributed. When a fiscal unity was formed, then a subsidiary was effectively treated as a permanent establishment of the parent company. The profits and losses of companies within the fiscal unity were calculated on a fully consolidated basis, intercompany transactions were ignored, and only one corporate income tax return was filed for the entire entity.

In this case, a Dutch parent, X Holding BV, was prevented from forming a fiscal unity with its wholly owned Belgian subsidiary, F NV, as the latter did not have a Dutch permanent establishment. The Netherlands Supreme Court questioned whether the inability to form a cross-border fiscal unity violated the freedom of establishment. Advocate General Kokott and the Court of Justice found that it did not. Although the regime restricted the freedom of establishment,[89] the restriction was justified on the basis of safeguarding the allocation of the power to impose taxes.[90]

---

[84] At that time, the previous version of the Directive applied (Council Directive 77/799/ EEC). However, the new Directive on Administrative Cooperation (Council Directive 2011/16/EU), which replaced this, would equally apply to the circumstances of the case. See Ch 2.
[85] Case C-418/07 Société Papillon, para 55.
[86] Ibid, para 56.
[87] It is noteworthy that although the Advocate General also doubted whether the regime was proportional, she left it to the national court to decide whether there were less restrictive means to deny inclusion of a sub-tier subsidiary for tax group purposes. See para 67 of the opinion.
[88] See Case C-337/08 X Holding BV [2010] ECR I-1215.
[89] Ibid, para 19.
[90] Ibid, para 33.

The optional nature of the arrangement, combined with the ability to alter the fiscal unity on a yearly basis,[91] raised concerns that the tax base of the unity would be manipulated. The parent company could choose to consolidate with loss-making foreign subsidiaries in one year and exclude them from the fiscal unity in the following year when they become profitable. Conversely, the parent company could choose to exclude profitable foreign subsidiaries from the fiscal unity in one year and include them in the following year when they make losses. Therefore, the Court of Justice thought that the restriction was justified on the basis of safeguarding the allocation of the power to impose taxes between the Member States.

Moreover, the restriction did not go beyond what was necessary to achieve this objective.[92] The Court of Justice followed the Advocate General's interpretation of proportionality. Even though non-resident subsidiaries were completely excluded from a fiscal unity, this did not render the regime disproportionate. The fact that a more proportional recovery arrangement applied to foreign permanent establishments was not a relevant consideration because permanent establishments and subsidiaries were not in a comparable situation regarding the allocation of the power to impose taxes.[93] Hence, the Netherlands was under no obligation to extend this advantage to foreign subsidiaries.[94]

To an extent, these remarks were made somewhat pre-emptively, as the arguments used to justify non-comparability between the two legal forms were very general ones, not tailored to the specific facts of the case. Both the Advocate General and the Court of Justice refrained from explaining why permanent establishments and subsidiaries were not in this instance in a comparable situation, given that when a fiscal unity was formed, domestic subsidiaries were effectively treated as if they were domestic permanent establishments. It is noteworthy that this comparability point was raised by the Dutch Advocate General Wattel in the Netherlands Supreme Court.[95] It was also an issue raised by Advocate General Maduro in his opinion in the Marks & Spencer case.[96] Perhaps Advocate General Kokott and the Court of Justice did not want to get embroiled in this debate, preferring to conclude that 'the Member State of origin is not obliged to apply the same tax scheme to non-resident subsidiaries as that which it applies to foreign permanent establishments'.[97]

Following a Commission reasoned opinion,[98] there was another request for a preliminary ruling on the Dutch fiscal unity regime's compatibility with the

---

[91] Ibid, para 32.
[92] Ibid, para 42.
[93] Ibid, paras 36–8.
[94] Ibid. The Dutch Supreme Court followed the Court's judgment in its final decision on the case on 7 January 2011.
[95] See case comment by Dennis Weber in (2010) 1 *Highlights & Insights on European Taxation*.
[96] Case C-446/03 Marks & Spencer, para 48 (Advocate General).
[97] Case C-337/08 X Holding, para 40.
[98] See IP/11/719 of 16 June 2011.

freedom of establishment. This was the SCA Group Holding BV case.[99] Under the Dutch regime, a group of companies was allowed to file a single tax return and calculate the Netherlands corporate income tax on a consolidated basis. However, fiscal consolidation was not permitted between a Dutch parent company and a Dutch second-tier (or lower) subsidiary held by one or more EU intermediary companies, nor was it possible for two Dutch subsidiary companies held by an EU parent company to form a fiscal unity together.

The Advocate General opined that these rules were not compatible with the freedom of establishment. The Court of Justice agreed. It was irrelevant that, even in a purely internal situation, no parent company could form a tax entity with sub-subsidiaries without also including the intermediate subsidiary.[100] There was an interesting discussion as to whether the restriction could be justified by the need to preserve the coherence of the Dutch tax system, as regards the prevention of the double use of losses. The Court of Justice dismissed this argument. The Dutch participation exemption prevented the Dutch parent company from taking a loss on its subsidiary.[101] Therefore, the participation exemption prevented the double use of losses.[102] It was through 'this general exemption – and not specific provisions for the neutralisation of certain transactions, as in the system at issue in the case giving rise to the judgment in Société Papillon – that the Netherlands tax system seeks to prevent the double use of losses within a tax entity'.[103] As such, the Court of Justice found that this case was distinguishable from Société Papillon. Here, no direct link could be established between the granting of the tax advantage linked to the formation of a tax entity and the offsetting of that advantage by a particular tax.[104] The same reasoning applied as far as sister companies were concerned.

In later cases, the Court of Justice continued to struggle in applying the Marks & Spencer's exhaustion of possibilities test.

In the A Oy case,[105] a loss-making Swedish company merged with its Finnish parent company. The activities of the Swedish company ceased to exist. If these companies were Finnish companies and the merger was not executed purely to benefit from the loss carry-forward, A Oy would have been entitled to take over the

---

[99] See Case C-39/13 Inspecteur van de Belastingdienst Noord/kantoor Groningen v. SCA Group Holding BV, ECLI:EU:C:2014:1758. Also, see two other requests made by the same court on the same date in X AG and Others v. Inspecteur van de Belastingdienst Amsterdam (Case C-40/13) and Inspecteur van de Belastingdienst Holland-Noord/kantoor Zaandam v. MSA International Holdings BV, MSA Nederland BV (Case C-41/13). The cases were joined.

[100] Case C-39/13 SCA Group Holding, para 25.

[101] Ibid, para 37.

[102] In fact, as emphasised in para 39, the holding exemption mechanism was designed so that a resident parent company could never take into account a loss linked to a holding in one of its subsidiaries, even where that subsidiary had its seat in another Member State.

[103] Ibid, para 38.

[104] Ibid, para 40.

[105] Case C-123/11 A Oy, ECLI:EU:C:2013:84.

tax losses of the subsidiary. The Court of Justice found there was a breach of the freedom of establishment. The fact that the merger was motivated solely by tax considerations was not in itself capable of making freedom of establishment inapplicable.[106] The restriction was justified on the basis of the three justifications set out in the Marks & Spencer case. As far as proportionality was concerned, the Court of Justice applied the exhaustion of possibilities test. Swedish law provided for the possibility of taking the taxpayer's losses into account in future tax years for the purposes of calculating the taxable basis. However, here, the Swedish company would be liquidated, and there would be no subsidiary or permanent establishment left. It was for the national court to decide whether the exhaustion of possibilities test had been satisfied.

By contrast, in the K case,[107] the Court of Justice did not follow the exhaustion of possibilities test. Here, Finnish tax authorities did not allow K, a Finnish tax resident, to deduct losses he sustained on the sale of immovable property in France from income charged to tax in Finland. The losses could be deducted if the immovable property was in Finland. The Court of Justice found this to be a restriction to the free movement of capital, but it was justified on the basis of the need to safeguard the balanced allocation of the power to impose taxes between Finland and France and the need to ensure the cohesion of the Finnish tax system. The refusal to allow the deduction of losses arising from the sale of immovable property situated in France safeguarded the symmetry between the right to tax profits and the right to deduct losses. The measure also contributed to the objective of ensuring a balanced allocation of the power to impose taxes between the Member States.[108]

As far as proportionality was concerned, the Court of Justice found that K could not be regarded as having exhausted all possibilities available for loss relief in the Member State in which the property was situated because such possibilities never existed in France.[109] Free movement of capital could not be understood as meaning that a Member State is required to adjust its tax rules on the basis of the tax rules of another Member State in order to ensure, in all circumstances, that all disparities are removed, given that the decisions made by a taxpayer as to investment abroad may be to the taxpayer's advantage or not, according to circumstances.[110] Therefore, these tax rules were considered to be proportional.[111] As such, there was no breach.

In the Felixstowe case,[112] the companies seeking to claim consortium relief and the surrendering company were UK-resident companies. The surrendering company was owned by a consortium. One member of this consortium, a Luxembourg

[106] Ibid, para 26.
[107] Case C-322/11 K case, ECLI:EU:C:2013:716.
[108] Ibid, para 55.
[109] Ibid, paras 76–7.
[110] Ibid, para 80.
[111] Ibid, para 82.
[112] Case C-80/12 Felixstowe Dock & Railway Company and Others, ECLI:EU:C:2014:200.

company, was the link company (for consortium relief purposes) with the claimant companies. Under the UK tax legislation at the time, the surrendering of losses was not possible when the company that acted as the link company was resident in another Member State. The national court questioned whether the restriction on claiming consortium relief through a non-resident link company was in breach of the freedom of establishment and the free movement of capital. The referring court also asked whether the situation was any different in terms of EU law, if the link between companies passed through companies in third countries.

The Court of Justice found that the legislation was in breach of the freedom of establishment. The analysis was not affected by the fact that the ultimate parent company of the group and the consortium, and certain intermediate companies in the chain of interests, were established in a third country.[113] The Court of Justice noted that '[s]uch a circumstance has no effect on the application of the freedom of establishment of the companies capable of benefiting from the tax advantage provided for by national legislation'.[114]

Agreeing with its Advocate General, the Court of Justice emphasised that the origin of the shareholders, be they natural or legal persons, of companies resident in the European Union did not affect the right of those companies to rely on freedom of establishment.[115] '[T]he status of being a European Union company is based, under Article 54 TFEU, on the location of the corporate seat and the legal order where the company is incorporated, not on the nationality of its shareholders'.[116] This was an important pronouncement at the time, with an impact on anti-abuse rules which focus on beneficial ownership and/or control. Whether or not the Felixstowe case should now be read in light of the Danish tax cases,[117] analysed in Chapter 2, is uncertain as those cases dealt with dividend/interest payments and conduit structures. It could be argued that the Felixstowe case confirmed the right of EU companies to benefit from the freedom of establishment irrespective of the origin of the shareholders, while the Danish tax cases explored the limits of this right in situations of possible abuse such as with conduit structures. Another interesting point is that in Felixstowe, the Court of Justice noted that a restrictive measure might be justified by the objective of combating tax havens. This was the first time the justification had ever been used.[118] Nevertheless, it does seem to buttress the point that there are limits to freedoms, however expansive their scope.

---

[113] Ibid, para 37.
[114] Ibid, para 38.
[115] Ibid, para 40.
[116] Ibid.
[117] Joined Cases C-115/16, C-118/16, C-119/16 and C-299/16, N Luxembourg 1 (C-115/16), X Denmark A/S (C-118/16), C Danmark I (C-119/16), Z Denmark ApS (C-299/16), ECLI:EU:C:2019:134 and Joined Cases C-116/16 and C-117/16, T Danmark (C-116/16), Y Denmark Aps (C-117/16), ECLI:EU: C:2019:135.
[118] See para 32, Case C-80/12 Felixstowe.

In a later case, the Groupe Steria case,[119] the Court of Justice considered the French tax integration rules. Under French law, dividends received by a parent company from a qualifying affiliate were tax exempt, except for a lump sum amount corresponding to 5 per cent of the dividends which remained taxable. This amount was deemed to represent the tax-deductible expenses incurred for the management of the participation, referred to as the portion of costs and expenses. When the tax consolidation regime applied, that is, between French resident companies meeting various conditions including a direct or indirect 95 per cent ownership or French permanent establishments, this 5 per cent add-back was neutralised for the computation of the group taxable result, leading to a full exemption of intra-group dividends.

The Court of Justice found the legislation to be in breach of the freedom of establishment. Under the French rules, only resident companies could be part of a tax-integrated group and, as such, the tax advantage was reserved for domestic dividends.[120] To exclude from the benefit of such an advantage a parent company that owned a subsidiary established in another Member State was liable to make it less attractive for that parent company to exercise its freedom of establishment, as it would be deterred from setting up subsidiaries in other Member States.[121]

The difference in treatment could not be justified on the grounds of the balanced allocation of taxing powers. The X Holding case was qualified as it could not be inferred from that judgment that any difference in treatment between companies belonging to a tax-integrated group, on the one hand, and companies not belonging to such a group, on the other hand, was compatible with freedom of establishment:[122]

> In that judgment, the Court merely examined the residence condition as a condition of access to a tax integration scheme, and held that that condition was justified, taking into account the fact that such a scheme allows losses to be transferred within the tax-integrated group. As regards tax advantages other than the transfer of losses within the tax-integrated group, a separate assessment must therefore be made ... as to whether a Member State may reserve those advantages to companies belonging to a tax-integrated group and consequently exclude them in cross-border situations.[123]

In the Groupe Steria case, the difference in treatment concerned only incoming dividends, received by resident parent companies. Therefore, what was at stake was the fiscal sovereignty of the same Member State, as in the Papillon case.[124] The

---

[119] Case C-386/14 Groupe Steria SCA v. Ministère des Finances et des Comptes publics, ECLI:EU:C:2015:524.
[120] Ibid, paras 18–19.
[121] Ibid, para 20.
[122] Ibid, para 27.
[123] Ibid, paras 27–8.
[124] Ibid, para 29.

Court of Justice concluded that the rule was incompatible with the freedom of establishment.

In a later case, the Court of Justice examined other aspects of the Dutch fiscal unity regime and their compatibility with the freedom of establishment. Namely, the Court of Justice was asked to consider the rules on interest deduction and on deduction of foreign exchange losses on EU participations.[125]

The first case concerned a Dutch company that borrowed funds from the Swedish top holding company of a group of which it was a member and then used those funds to make a share contribution in an Italian subsidiary. This subsidiary, in turn, used these funds to purchase shares in another Italian company. According to the Dutch rules, the Dutch tax authorities denied the deductibility of the interest paid by the Dutch entity to the Swedish lending company. The borrower argued that its freedom of establishment was restricted as the interest would have been deductible if the company was allowed to form a fiscal unity with its Italian subsidiary.

The Court of Justice held that the situation of a parent company wishing to form a fiscal unity with a non-resident subsidiary was objectively comparable to that of a parent company wishing to form a fiscal unity with a domestic subsidiary. The difference in treatment was an infringement of the freedom of establishment.[126]

As for justifications, the Court of Justice rejected the need to preserve the division of taxing rights between the Member States, noting that the rules at issue did not appear to depend on where the income corresponding to the deduction claimed was taxed.[127] Regarding the need to safeguard the coherence of the Dutch tax system, the Court of Justice found that the Dutch government failed to prove a direct link between the disputed tax deduction and a corresponding tax benefit.[128] As for the justification of preventing tax evasion and fraud and conduct involving the creation of wholly artificial arrangements, this was rejected again. The Court of Justice noted that the likelihood of tax evasion was the same in a purely internal case as it was in a cross-border situation.

> When a parent company finances the purchase of shares in a subsidiary by a loan taken out with another related company, the risk that that loan does not reflect a genuine economic transaction and is intended simply to create a deductible charge artificially is no less if the parent company and the subsidiary are both resident in the same Member State and together form a single tax entity than if the subsidiary is established in another Member State and is not, therefore, permitted to form a single tax entity with the parent company.[129]

---

[125] Joined cases Case C-398/16 and C-399/16 X BV and X NV v. Staatssecretaris van Financiën, ECLI:EU:C:2018:110.
[126] Ibid, para 37.
[127] Ibid, paras 39–42.
[128] Ibid, paras 43–5.
[129] Ibid, para 50.

The Court of Justice concluded that the Dutch legislation was contrary to freedom of establishment.

The second case concerned a Dutch parent company of a fiscal unity that wanted to deduct a foreign exchange loss on a UK shareholding as a result of group reorganisation. The application of the Netherlands participation exemption rules meant that such foreign exchange losses were non-deductible. Because of the holding exemption, both the increases and decreases in value stemming from changes in the exchange rate of a foreign currency in which the value of that holding was expressed were not taken into account to determine profit. Therefore, the Dutch parent company could not deduct from its taxable profits the currency loss sustained on the amount of its investment, as a shareholder, in its UK subsidiary. The Dutch parent company argued the losses would have been deductible if it had been allowed to form a fiscal unity with the UK subsidiary and, as such, this was contrary to the freedom of establishment.

Here, the Court of Justice found that the situation of a Dutch parent company investing in a resident subsidiary and that of a Dutch parent company investing in a non-resident subsidiary were not comparable, as foreign exchange losses would not arise in a purely domestic situation.[130] Even if the situations were comparable, the difference in treatment was still questionable.[131] This was because the Dutch parent company would not be able to deduct any losses resulting from the impairment of its interest in a resident subsidiary with which it forms a tax group.

According to the Court of Justice, it could not be inferred from the provisions of freedom of establishment that a Member State would be required to exercise, asymmetrically, its taxation powers so as to permit the deduction of losses from operations whose results, if they were positive, would not, in any event, be taxed.[132] As such, the Dutch rules were not in breach of the freedom of establishment.

In two later cases, the emphasis was placed again on the exhaustion of possibilities test. In the Memira[133] and Holmen cases,[134] the Swedish Supreme Administrative Court had referred two cases dealing with final losses. Both cases involved Swedish parent companies that sought to deduct losses accrued by their non-resident subsidiaries. In both cases, the Court of Justice found that, notwithstanding the legal limitations on the use of losses under the tax regimes of the Member State where the subsidiary was resident, tax losses could not be regarded as final if the parent company did not provide evidence that it was impossible to use such losses economically.

The Memira case entailed a cross-border merger between a loss-making German subsidiary and a Swedish parent company. The German subsidiary had incurred tax

---

[130] Ibid, para 56.
[131] Ibid, para 57.
[132] Ibid, para 58.
[133] Case C-607/17 Memira, ECLI:EU:C:2019:510.
[134] Case C-608/17 Holmen, ECLI:EU:C:2019:511.

losses exceeding its profits of previous tax years and could not use such losses in Germany or Sweden. The Court of Justice was asked to clarify whether the German losses would be deductible in Sweden after the merger had been finalised.

Here, the Court of Justice emphasised that the fact that the subsidiary's Member State of establishment did not allow the losses of one company to be transferred, in the event of a merger, to another company liable for corporation tax, whereas such a transfer was allowed in the event of a merger between resident companies, was not decisive unless the parent company showed that it was impossible for it to deduct those losses by ensuring, in particular by means of a sale, that they were fiscally taken into account by a third party for future tax periods.[135]

The Holmen case dealt mainly with questions regarding whether tax losses arising in indirectly held Spanish subsidiaries could be deductible for the Swedish parent company upon liquidation of the Spanish companies. The losses of the Spanish subsidiaries could no longer be used in Spain, because under Spanish laws, tax losses could be neither carried back nor transferred to other taxpayers. Under Swedish law, a parent company could, under certain conditions, deduct definitive losses incurred by a wholly and directly-owned foreign subsidiary. In this case, the loss-making Spanish subsidiary was held through an intermediate Spanish resident company with which it formed a consolidated tax group. Liquidation of the sub-subsidiary could not result in recognition of final losses at the level of the intermediate company, as this was not possible in Spain.

Here, the Court of Justice conceded that in the context of final losses of a non-resident subsidiary, direct ownership was generally a requirement, as it aimed to prevent the double use of losses and the cherry picking of Member States in which to use the losses. However, while the direct ownership requirement was justified in principle, it was disproportionate for Sweden to preclude the possibility for the parent company to take into account the final losses of a non-resident subsidiary if the intermediate subsidiaries between the Swedish parent and Spanish sub-subsidiary were all established in the same Member States, as it was in this case. If any of the intermediate companies were resident in a different Member State, there would have been a risk that tax losses could be used twice.

To assess the finality of the non-resident subsidiary's losses, within the meaning of paragraph 55 of the Marks & Spencer case, the fact that the Member State of the subsidiary (i.e. Spain) did not allow the losses of one company to be transferred to another company in the year of liquidation was not decisive, unless the parent company showed that it was impossible for it to deduct those losses by ensuring, in particular by means of a sale, that they were taken into account by a third party for future periods.[136] As such, restrictions relating to the offsetting of losses and loss carry-forwards in Spain

---

[135] Case C-607/17 Memira, para 28.
[136] Case C-608/17 Holmen, para 40.

were irrelevant in assessing whether the losses were final and could be deducted by the parent company.[137]

Although these two cases revived the exhaustion of possibilities test, a later case seems to have put another nail to the coffin of the Marks & Spencer case. In Aures Holdings,[138] a Dutch company incurred tax losses in the Netherlands in 2007. In 2009, the company transferred its place of effective management to the Czech Republic, becoming tax resident therein. After the tax residence change, the company sought to use the losses incurred in the Netherlands to offset Czech taxable income. The Czech tax authorities denied the use of the losses arguing that Czech tax law only allowed the use of losses originating in the Czech Republic and as computed in accordance with Czech tax law.

In a referral to the Court of Justice, no breach of the freedom of establishment was found. Although the denial to use the losses incurred while the company was resident in another Member State constituted a difference in the tax treatment, when compared against the tax treatment of a Czech resident company that incurred losses in the same tax year,[139] however, there was no comparability. More specifically, these situations were not comparable in light of the objectives pursued by the Czech tax rules; namely, preserving the allocation of taxing power between the Member States and preventing the risk of double deduction of losses.[140] As the Court of Justice held:

> where the host Member State has no tax jurisdiction over the tax year during which the loss at issue arose, the situation of a company, which has transferred its tax residency to that Member State and subsequently claims a loss there previously incurred in another Member State, is not comparable to that of a company the turnover of which was subject to the tax powers of the previous Member State on the basis of the tax year during which that company incurred that loss.[141]

Otherwise there is a risk of double use of losses in both Member States.[142] The same conclusion was reached even if the losses were final. Symmetry seemed to have been crucial to the Court of Justice: the new Member State of residence of the company did not have jurisdiction over the losses that had accrued while the company was subject to the jurisdiction of another Member State. As such, the Court of Justice concluded that the Member State to which a company transfers its place of effective management cannot be required to take into account a loss incurred before that transfer which related to tax years in respect of which that company was not tax resident in that Member State.[143] With this statement, the Court of Justice appears to

---

[137] Ibid, para 44.
[138] Case C-405/18 AURES Holdings, ECLI:EU:C:2020:127.
[139] Ibid, paras 33–4.
[140] Ibid, para 38.
[141] Ibid, para 41.
[142] Ibid, para 42.
[143] Ibid, para 52.

reject the exhaustion of possibilities test on the basis of the territoriality argument. Interestingly, this is what the Special Commissioners had argued in the Marks & Spencer case at first instance.[144]

In another recent case, B and Others,[145] the Court of Justice examined the compatibility of various aspects of the Luxembourg tax consolidation regime with the freedom of establishment. The case involved Luxembourg companies controlled by a French parent company and which were part of a consolidated group in Luxembourg. The Luxembourg tax authorities rejected a request by the Luxembourg companies to carry out a horizontal tax integration – that is, to include in their integrated group their sister companies which were companies controlled by the same French parent company. This was because under Luxembourg rules, the tax consolidation of sister companies was allowed only insofar as the non-resident controlling entity had a permanent establishment in Luxembourg, which held the shareholdings in the controlled companies.

The Court of Justice found that in this case a non-resident company with a permanent establishment in a Member State and a non-resident company without a permanent establishment were in comparable situations. The different treatment resulted in a restriction to the freedom of establishment which could not be justified.

The Court of Justice also considered the Luxembourg rules dealing with changes in the composition of the integrated group. The rules forced a parent company established in another Member State to end a pre-existing vertical tax integration between one of its subsidiaries and some of the resident sub-subsidiaries in order to allow that subsidiary to carry out a horizontal tax integration with other resident subsidiaries of such parent company. This interruption could have led to an adjustment of the tax position of the companies in the integrated group. In a domestic situation, changes in the composition of a tax consolidation arose when a controlled entity entered for the first time in the tax consolidation (or withdrew at the end of the minimum period fixed under Luxembourg law) and did not lead to an interruption of the integrated group. The fact that the Luxembourg rules required an immediate interruption when a sister company became part of an existing consolidation with a non-resident controlling entity was not compatible with the freedom of establishment.

The above cases, especially the more recent ones, show the selective and variable application of the principles set out in the Marks & Spencer case, as well as the various justifications. It could be argued – and the author has argued elsewhere[146] and in the first edition to this book – that the Court's approach (or lack of it) creates imbalances and that EU legislative action may be a better and fairer method of dealing with these issues. In fact, the developments in the case law go much further than what was envisaged in a Draft Directive on Cross-Border Loss

---

[144] See Decision SpC 00352, reported at [2003] STC (SCD) 70.
[145] Case C-749/18 B and Others, ECLI:EU:C:2020:370. At the time of writing, this decision was not available in English.
[146] HJI Panayi, 'Reverse subsidiarity and EU tax law'.

Relief,[147] as well as the 2007 Commission Communication on the Tax Treatment of Losses in Cross-Border Situations.[148]

For example, under the Draft Directive on Cross-Border Loss Relief, cross-border loss relief was available under stringent qualifying conditions.[149] Member States were able to ensure that loss relief was only temporary and reversible. Subsequent profits of the surrendering subsidiary were reincorporated in the tax base of the claimant company. There were also provisions allowing automatic reincorporation[150] and the application of domestic anti-abuse rules.[151] The Commission's approach in its Communication was similar but more nuanced to take into account the Marks & Spencer judgment. As for group losses, to which most of the Communication was devoted, the Commission suggested targeted measures for effective and immediate once-only deduction of losses at least in a vertical context. It was argued that these measures should not normally result in a definite shift of income from one Member State to another unless the losses were terminal and there was no possibility for relief in the state in which such losses were incurred.[152] It is obvious that the Communication was not confined to the exhaustion of possibilities test. The Commission stressed 'the need for effective systems to provide cross-border loss relief within the EU'[153] and showed its preference for clear rules and temporary loss relief.

By contrast, under the case law of the Court of Justice, the rules are not clear and do not provide for temporary solutions. Later case law suggests a shift away from the exhaustion of possibilities test, with the Court of Justice showing more willingness to support territoriality arguments.

---

[147] Proposal for a Council directive concerning arrangements for the taking into account by enterprises of the losses of their permanent establishments and subsidiaries situated in other Member States, COM(90) 595 final. See the brief discussion in 1.2.5.

[148] Communication from the Commission to the Council, the European Parliament and the European Economic and Social Committee, *Tax Treatment of Losses in Cross-Border Situations*, SEC(2006) 1690.

[149] Group relief was available between group companies (only upstream losses allowed) when they satisfied a minimum capital holding requirement. Only 75 per cent of direct subsidiaries qualified – indirect shareholdings were not covered. However, Member States could allow a lower minimum holding. See Art 2. Relief was by credit, although Member States were not prevented from 'maintaining or introducing other methods of taking into account the losses of subsidiaries of its enterprises located in the other Member States, including the consolidated profit method'. Art 12. See analysis in HJI Panayi, 'Reverse subsidiarity and EU tax law', pp 269–72.

[150] Member States were given the option of providing for automatic reincorporation under specific circumstances, for example, when reincorporation had not occurred within five years of the loss becoming deductible, where the subsidiary was sold, wound up or transformed into a permanent establishment and where the enterprise's holding in the capital of the subsidiary had fallen below the minimum level laid down by the Member State in which the enterprise was situated. See Art 10.

[151] Draft Loss Relief Directive, Art 13. The application of the deduction and reincorporation method also precluded the tax recognition of value adjustments to shareholdings. See Art 11. Therefore, double deduction of losses at the subsidiary and parent company level was prevented.

[152] *Loss Relief Communication*, p 8.

[153] Ibid, p 10.

The developments in the case law are also in stark contrast with the treatment of group relief or consolidation regimes under the OECD Model Tax Convention, where the unavailability of cross-border loss relief is not treated as discrimination, even if loss relief is available domestically. While Article 24(5) of the OECD Model Tax Convention forbids a contracting state to give less favourable treatment to an enterprise, the capital of which is owned by one or more residents of the other contracting state, '[t]his provision, and the discrimination which it puts an end to, relates to the taxation only of enterprises and not of the persons owning or controlling their capital'.[154] The aim of this provision, according to the OECD Commentary, is to ensure equal treatment for taxpayers residing in the same state, and not subject foreign capital to identical treatment to that applied to domestic capital.[155] Therefore, as expressly stated in the Commentary to Article 24(5), this paragraph 'cannot be interpreted to extend the benefits of rules that take account of the relationship between a resident enterprise and other resident enterprises (e.g. rules that allow consolidation, transfer of losses or tax-free transfer of property between companies under common ownership)'.[156] The underlying rationale seems to be that a subsidiary is a separate legal person from the parent company. As the parent company is not taxed on the profits of the subsidiary, it should not be required to absorb the subsidiary's losses. This is especially important in an international context, where taxable profits and unusable losses arise in different jurisdictions.

In any case, as far as group relief is concerned, not only have the judgments of the Court of Justice challenged and eroded established principles in international tax law, but they also seem to have gone much further than what was originally intended by the Commission. Similar but perhaps not as controversial conclusions are reached in the context of loss relief within the same company examined in 4.3.5.

4.2.3 *Controlled Foreign Companies*

In order to prevent a situation whereby the profits of a company in a high-tax jurisdiction are sheltered in a controlled subsidiary in a low-tax jurisdiction, the profits of the foreign subsidiary are often subject to taxation in the state of the parent company. Such rules fall within the scope of Controlled Foreign Company (CFC) regimes, the rationale of which is explained in greater detail in Chapter 7. Until recently, EU law imposed serious (taxpayer-friendly) constraints on the discretion of Member States to draft their CFC regimes, following the Cadbury Schweppes case.[157]

---

[154] OECD Commentary to Art 24, para 76.
[155] Ibid.
[156] Ibid, para 77. See, however, JF Avery Jones et al, who have argued that this is too widely stated and that it may not apply to some grouping provisions, depending on their details and structure. See JF Avery Jones et al, 'Art 24(5) of the OECD Model in relation to intra-group transfers of assets and profits and losses' (2011) 3(2) *World Tax Journal*, 179–225.
[157] Case C-196/04 Cadbury Schweppes [2006] ECR I-07995.

However, with the advent of the Anti-Tax Avoidance Directive, Member States had to adopt common CFC rules as a *de minimis* standard. The combined effect of the relevant case law and the legislative provisions in this area is examined in Chapter 7.

4.3 ISSUES WITH THE TAXATION OF PERMANENT ESTABLISHMENTS

4.3.1 *Defining Permanent Establishments*

Under the OECD Model Tax Convention, the technical (treaty) term for a branch is 'permanent establishment'. This is defined in Article 5 of the OECD Model Tax Convention for the purposes of the allocation of taxing rights when an enterprise of one state derives business profits from another state. There is no definition or description of the terms 'branch' or 'permanent establishment' in the European Treaties. Under freedom of establishment, the term 'establishment' is used in a much broader and generic way, covering agencies, branches and subsidiaries. There is no express requirement for physical presence or specific types of activities, as in Article 5 of the OECD Model Tax Convention.

Permanent establishments are defined in the context of the Parent-Subsidiary Directive and the Interest and Royalties Directive, though the definitions are not identical with that under the OECD Model Tax Convention, as explained in Chapter 2. The concept of permanent establishment features in the Merger Directive,[158] but as it is not defined, it is likely to be interpreted according to national law or the underlying tax treaty of the relevant Member States. Therefore, it is safe to say that there does not appear to be a uniform concept of permanent establishment in the context of EU direct tax law.[159]

The importance of a permanent establishment under EU law is not so much how it is defined or applied but rather how it is to be treated for taxation purposes. While the norm under international tax law is for a host state to be able to treat permanent establishments differently from resident companies, in EU law, there are certain limitations to this approach, as shown below.

---

[158] Under the Merger Directive relief in the form of deferral depends on the assets remaining connected with a permanent establishment in the Member State of the transferring company. See Chapter 6.

[159] Contrast the situation under VAT case law, where the Court of Justice developed the concept of 'fixed establishment' in a more uniform way. See analysis in Rita de La Feria, 'Permanent Establishments in Indirect Taxation', in Giulia Gallo and Irene JJ Burgers (eds), *Permanent Establishments* (Amsterdam: IBFD, 2016); Emiliano Zanotti, 'Taxation of inter-company dividends in the presence of a PE: the impact of the EC fundamental freedoms (Part One)' (2004) 44(11) *European Taxation*, 493–505; Peter Cussons and Eric Fitzgerald, 'EU Report', *The Attribution of Profits to Permanent Establishments*, Cahiers de droit fiscal international, Vol 91b (Kluwer Law International, 2006), 69–88, 73–5. See, also, the decision of the Court of Justice in Case C-547/18 Dong Yang Electronics, ECLI:EU:C:2020:350.

4.3.2 The Different Treatment of Permanent Establishments and Companies

Tax rules can disrupt the principle of neutrality of legal form. If permanent establishments are taxed differently from subsidiaries, this could create an incentive to trade through one vehicle rather than another. When there is a cross-border element to this, neutrality of legal form and market access may be impeded. This is because if the permanent establishment of a non-resident company is taxed more heavily than a resident company, this means that the non-resident company is potentially restricted from trading in the host state through that type of establishment. However, in some circumstances, there could be legitimate reasons why the permanent establishment (and effectively the non-resident company) is subject to a different tax burden compared to a resident company. The permanent establishment and the resident company may not be in a comparable situation and, therefore, by taxing them differently, neutrality would not be disturbed.

From a general perspective, freedom of establishment has been interpreted as guaranteeing the neutrality of legal form in a cross-border situation. As such, a Member State national should not be restricted in choosing whether to trade in another Member State through a subsidiary (resident) company or a permanent establishment. The creation and the outright ownership by a natural or legal person established in one Member State of a permanent establishment not having a separate legal personality situated in another Member State is considered as falling within the scope of the application of freedom of establishment.[160] National tax rules, including rules that differentiate between a resident company and a permanent establishment, have been scrutinised to that effect.

The Court's case law on discrimination of permanent establishments does not really indicate a de jure or de facto categorisation of a permanent establishment as regards the whole enterprise. Neither do any of the EU tax instruments in which the permanent establishment concept features suggest how this is to be taxed. So far, the focus of the Court of Justice has been on the comparability of a subsidiary with a recognised permanent establishment – however, this is defined under national law.

In many cases where the comparability point was addressed, the Court of Justice assimilated the permanent establishment to a hypothetical subsidiary: it found a resident company and a non-resident company (through its permanent establishment) to be in a comparable situation. This, however, was not done automatically. In all of the cases, the Court of Justice first examined the comparability of the permanent establishment and a subsidiary on the facts of each case.

In the first important case decided on direct tax matters, the Avoir Fiscal case,[161] the Court of Justice had to deal with discriminatory taxation of French branches of

---

[160] See dicta in Case C-414/06 Lidl Belgium [2008] ECR I-3601, para 15; Case C-18/11 HMRC v. Philips Electronics UK Ltd, ECLI:EU:C:2012:532, para 19 (Advocate General).
[161] Case 270/83 Commission v. France (Avoir Fiscal) [1986] ECR 273.

non-resident companies. Under French tax law, branches of foreign insurance companies were not given the same tax credit (the Avoir Fiscal) as French companies. The Court of Justice found this treatment to be incompatible with freedom of establishment. It expressly acknowledged 'that a distinction based on the location of the registered office of a company or the place of residence of a natural person may, under certain conditions, be justified in an area such as tax law'.[162] However, on the facts of the case resident and non-resident insurance companies were in a comparable situation. This was because a foreign insurance company, through its French branch, was subject to taxation in the same way as a French insurance company. As the Court of Justice stated, French tax law did not 'distinguish, for the purpose of determining the income liable to corporation tax, between companies having their registered office in France and branches and agencies situated in France of companies whose registered office is abroad'.[163] Therefore, the different treatment of the two entities was discriminatory. By refusing the tax credit to the branch when this credit was available to a resident company, the foreign company's choice of legal form was restricted, contrary to freedom of establishment.[164]

Commerzbank[165] was decided in a similar way. Here a UK rule restricted the so-called 'repayment supplement' for late tax refunds to UK companies. A German company, Commerzbank, through its UK branch, granted loans to US companies. Commerzbank paid tax in the UK on the interest received from those US companies. Subsequently, it sought repayment of that sum from the UK tax authorities, on the basis that the interest was exempt from UK tax under the then applicable USA–UK[166] tax treaty. Commerzbank received a refund of the overpaid tax. However, it also claimed the repayment supplement. The UK tax authorities refused the repayment supplement on the basis that Commerzbank was not tax resident in the UK.

The Court of Justice found that the refusal to grant the repayment supplement to the UK branch of a German company was incompatible with freedom of establishment. This was a case of indirect discrimination. As the Court explained, although the rule applied independently of the company's seat, 'the use of the criterion of fiscal residence within national territory for the purpose of granting repayment supplement on overpaid tax [was] liable to work more particularly to the disadvantage of companies having their seat in other Member States'.[167] Non-resident companies were worse off channelling their loans through a UK branch rather than a UK subsidiary. This restricted the choice of legal form that non-resident

---

[162] Ibid, para 19.
[163] Ibid, para 19.
[164] Ibid, para 22.
[165] Case C-330/91 Commerzbank [1993] ECR I-4017.
[166] Convention of 2 August 1946 between the Government of the United Kingdom of Great Britain and Northern Ireland and the Government of the United States of America for the Avoidance of Double Taxation and the Prevention of Fiscal Evasion with respect to Taxes on Income (SR & O 1946, No 1327), as amended by a Protocol of 20 September 1966 (SI 1966 No 1188).
[167] Case C-330/91 Commerzbank, para 15.

companies had in structuring their activities in the UK. The domestic provision could not be justified by the fact that the exemption from tax that gave rise to the refund was available only to non-resident companies. This was 'a rule of a general nature withholding the benefit'.[168] The fact that Commerzbank would not have been exempt from tax had it been resident was of no relevance to the Court of Justice.

In Halliburton,[169] the Court of Justice considered a Dutch concession on transfer tax that was restricted to transfers of immovable property between Dutch-resident companies. In this case, a US company, Halliburton Inc, had a German and a Dutch subsidiary. The German subsidiary had a branch in the Netherlands, through which it owned immovable property. As part of an internal European reorganisation scheme, the German subsidiary transferred its Dutch branch (and, as a corollary, the immovable property) to the Dutch subsidiary. The Dutch tax authorities levied land transfer tax on the Dutch subsidiary. Had this transfer been between two Dutch companies, it would have been exempt from transfer tax.

Again, the Court of Justice found this to be a covert form of discrimination, contrary to freedom of establishment. The conditions for the sale of property owned by a non-resident (through its branch) were more onerous than for residents.[170] It is noteworthy that in Halliburton, the Dutch subsidiary received the assets of the former German company that successfully claimed the relief from transfer tax charged on it, even though it had not exercised any Community (at the time) rights. As pointed out by the Court of Justice, it was the actual vendor who was 'in a distinctly less favourable position than if it had chosen the form of a public or private limited company instead of that of a permanent establishment for its business in the Netherlands'.[171] Even if the difference in the treatment had only an indirect effect on the Dutch transferee company, this was enough to find discrimination.[172] Therefore, a person other than the one who directly enjoyed the fundamental freedom could also benefit from it.[173]

In other cases, the Court of Justice held that the taxation of branches at a higher rate than resident companies could violate freedom of establishment. In Royal Bank of Scotland,[174] Greece effectively imposed a higher tax rate on foreign companies

---

[168] Ibid, para 19.
[169] Case C-1/93 Halliburton Services BV v. Staatssecretaris van Financiën [1994] ECR I-1137.
[170] Ibid, para 19.
[171] Ibid, para 19.
[172] Ibid, para 20.
[173] Although Advocate General Kokott in her opinion in Case C-18/11 Philips Electronics, para 83 assumed that, following this and other cases, it did not matter who challenged the application of the legislation provided the person bringing the challenge was affected, perhaps not too much should be read into this at least in the Halliburton case. In Halliburton, the point was not argued, and both the transferor and transferee companies were subsidiaries of a US company that was treated as if it were a Dutch company under the ownership non-discrimination provision of the USA-Netherlands tax treaty. See also comments made by the First-Tier Tax Tribunal in Philips Electronics UK Ltd v. HMRC [2009] UKFTT 226 (TC) p 12, 10–15.
[174] Case C-311/97 Royal Bank of Scotland v. Elliniko Dimosio [1999] ECR I-2651.

carrying on banking activities in Greece through a branch rather than through a resident company.[175] This was found to be unjustifiably discriminatory. It was not important to the Court of Justice that resident companies were taxed on the basis of their worldwide income, and non-resident companies were taxed only on the income generated domestically. As the basis of assessment for taxation was calculated in the same way for both companies, they were in an objectively comparable situation.

In Saint-Gobain[176] the Court of Justice even went as far as to require the extension of tax treaty benefits to branches when such treaty benefits were only applicable to resident companies. Here the Court of Justice had to decide whether the refusal to grant concessions to German branches of companies established in the other Member States was compatible with the freedom of establishment when similar benefits were available to German companies under tax treaties between Germany and third countries. The Court of Justice found that as far as the grant of the tax concession was concerned, the German branch and the German company were in a comparable situation because they were both taxed on the dividends received in the same way. Even though in this case a resident and a non-resident company were taxed on a different basis (worldwide and limited basis, respectively), what was important was the fact that as regards the taxation of dividends received, they were in a comparable situation. As a result, the refusal to grant those tax concessions, which primarily affected non-residents, made it less attractive for such companies to have inter-corporate holdings through branches in the Member State concerned.[177] Therefore, it violated freedom of establishment. Germany had to extend benefits (unilaterally) to German branches of companies resident in other Member States.

It could be argued that following this case when dividend relief is available for intra-group distributions, relief may have to be extended to permanent establishments in respect of dividends from holdings forming part of their assets. This should be contrasted with the situation under the OECD Model Tax Convention, which does not currently impose such an obligation on states, leaving it up to them to decide whether to provide for such extension of relief to permanent establishments.[178]

In another case, the Court of Justice held that the Member States must not apply a higher tax on branch profits compared to the rate applicable to the *distributed* profits of resident companies. In CLT-UFA SA,[179] under the then applicable German split-rate system, profits of German branches were subject to corporate income tax at a rate of 42 per cent. The retained profits of German companies were

---

[175] Although the same tax rate applied to both foreign and domestic companies, only domestic companies could qualify for a reduced tax rate because of conditions relating to the legal form and the nature of shares to be issued.
[176] Case C-307/97 Compagnie de Saint-Gobain, Zweigniederlassung Deutschland v. Finanzamt Aachen-Innenstadt [1999] ECR I-6161. The case was also discussed in 3.3.3.
[177] Ibid, para 42.
[178] See Art 24(3) of the OECD Model Tax Convention.
[179] Case C-253/03 CLT-UFA SA [2006] ECR I-01831.

subject to corporate income tax at a rate of 45 per cent. If these profits were distributed to the parent company by 30 June 1996, the tax rate was reduced to 33.5 per cent.[180] If the profits were distributed after that date, they were taxed at 30 per cent. The Court of Justice found that these rules were incompatible with freedom of establishment. The effect of the split-rate system was that for a foreign company, forming a branch was less attractive than forming a subsidiary. This restricted the foreign company's freedom to choose the appropriate legal form in which to pursue cross-border economic activities.[181]

The German government tried to argue that a branch and a subsidiary were not in an objectively comparable situation with regard to profit distributions. A subsidiary no longer owned the profits distributed to its parent company while the profits transferred by a branch to its head office continued to be internal assets of the same company.[182] The Court of Justice disagreed with this argument. The only real difference between profit distributions by subsidiaries and profit transfers by branches was that the former but not the latter presupposed the existence of a formal decision to that effect.[183] According to the Court of Justice, this was a mere technicality that did not nullify the comparable situation between the two vehicles. Having found that freedom of establishment precluded such national rules, the Court of Justice left it to the referring court to decide the rate that should apply on German branches.[184]

It is important to stress that in all of the above cases, the Court of Justice did not say that residents and non-residents are always in a comparable situation. Therefore, it should not be assumed that, for EU tax law purposes, subsidiaries are always assimilated to permanent establishments and entitled to the same tax treatment, although, arguably, an effort is made to that effect in some of the Directives.[185] One issue to bear in mind is that, currently, the comparability exercise is undertaken from a tax perspective only. In other words, only the tax rules applying to the permanent establishment and the subsidiary are considered by the Court of Justice. However, is this approach right? What about other non-tax differences (e.g. the availability of limited liability, separate legal entity, different accounting obligations) or other general regulatory differences that may be the underlying reason for the different tax treatment in the host state – that is the state where the permanent establishment is set up? While it may not be easy to take into account the whole regulatory

---

[180] Under the transitional provisions of the Parent-Subsidiary Directive, Germany was allowed to levy a 5 per cent withholding tax on dividends until 30 June 1996.
[181] Ibid, para 14.
[182] Ibid, paras 19–20.
[183] Ibid, para 23. In the case of a subsidiary, even if the distributed profits were no longer part of its assets, those profits could still be made available to that subsidiary by its parent company in the form of share capital or shareholder loan. Ibid, para 24.
[184] Ibid, para 37.
[185] As stated in Chapter 2, there are certain provisions in the Interest and Royalties Directive and the Parent-Subsidiary Directive that seek to ensure that permanent establishments benefit from these Directives in the same way as companies.

framework that applies to a resident company and the permanent establishment of a non-resident company, one cannot help but wonder whether confining the comparability exercise to the tax factors (always) produces an accurate and fair result.

In any case, this appears to be the Court's stance so far. Permanent establishments are not always assimilated to subsidiaries – it all depends on the facts of the case.[186] Nevertheless, when it comes to a non-resident company claiming equal tax treatment in the host state, the comparability criterion tends to be satisfied when the permanent establishment – whether itself or on the basis of profit distributions received – is taxed in a similar way to resident companies. Other regulatory differences are not to be taken into account. In such circumstances, the host state has to ensure equal treatment of resident companies and permanent establishments of non-resident companies.

This should be contrasted with the position taken under the OECD Model Tax Convention. As mentioned a few times in this book, the protective scope of the non-discrimination provision of the OECD Model Tax Convention does not extend to non-residents, even if they are in a comparable situation to residents. The OECD Model Tax Convention starts from the assumption that residents and non-residents are not in a comparable situation unless residence has no relevance whatsoever with respect to the different treatment under consideration. Therefore, the starting point is that indirect/covert discrimination on the basis of residence is not accepted.

However, the non-discrimination provision of the OECD Model Tax Convention provides some limited protection to permanent establishments by requiring that '[t]he taxation on a permanent establishment which an enterprise of a Contracting State has in the other Contracting State shall not be less favourably levied in that other State than the taxation levied on enterprises of that other State carrying on the same activities'.[187] Under this provision, discrimination on the basis of different taxation is not impugned, as long as this different taxation is not more burdensome. States may, therefore, apply specific mechanisms only for the purposes of determining profits attributable to the permanent establishment, or rules and administrative practices that seek to determine the profits that are attributable to it, as long as taxation is not less favourable than that levied on a domestic enterprise carrying on similar activities.[188]

In calculating the tax rate on the permanent establishment's profits, the host state might take into account the profits of the whole enterprise. However, it is only the actual profits attributed according to Article 7(2) of the OECD Model Tax Convention that can be taxed. The Commentary clarifies that paragraph 3 of Article 24 of the OECD Model Tax Convention is restricted to the taxation of profits

---

[186] For a recent overview, see Alexandre Maitrot de la Motte, 'Taxation of business in the EU: General issues', in Christiana HJI Panayi, Werner Halsehner, Edoardo Traversa (eds), *Research Handbook on European Union Taxation Law* (Elgar Publishing, 2020).

[187] Art 24(3) OECD Model Tax Convention.

[188] OECD Commentary to Art 24, para 34.

from the activities of the permanent establishment itself and does not extend to the taxation of the enterprise as a whole.[189] As a corollary, if the more burdensome taxation relates to the whole enterprise, this is not discriminatory. It is only discriminatory under Article 24(3) when it relates to the taxation of the permanent establishment – that is if the net profits of a permanent establishment are taxed at a higher rate than the net profits of a resident taxpayer.

Sometimes the two situations may not be distinguishable. The Commentary to the OECD Model Tax Convention gives the examples of branch tax and branch level interest tax. These are effectively additional taxes imposed on branch profits to compensate for the fact that no dividend withholding tax can be levied on such profits when repatriated to the non-resident head office. The branch tax is considered to be contrary to Article 24(3), being a (supplementary) tax levied on the profits of the activities of the permanent establishment itself and not a tax on the enterprise in its capacity as owner of the permanent establishment.[190] By contrast, the branch level interest tax is considered to be a tax on the enterprise and as such compatible with Article 24(3) of the OECD Model Tax Convention. Although, as argued, this is a tax on amounts that would be deducted in computing the profits of the permanent establishment, for instance, interest, ultimately it is a tax on the enterprise to which the interest is considered to be paid.[191] The reasoning of the OECD Commentary on this point is not very convincing and has been criticised.[192]

Notwithstanding the limitations of the Commentary, it still seems to be the underlying assumption of the OECD Model's non-discrimination provision (which remains unchanged following the BEPS project) that, to the extent that it is the non-resident company that is being taxed detrimentally, this is not a problem. It is only when profits of the permanent establishment are taxed in a more burdensome way that Article 24(3) of the OECD Model Tax Convention may offer some protection.

EU law does not make such a distinction. Even though a permanent establishment is frequently compared to a resident subsidiary as if it is a separate legal entity, the Court of Justice does not seem to exclude the effect of taxation on the profits of the enterprise as a whole in assessing compatibility with the freedom of establishment. In other words, the Court of Justice does not (yet) seem to draw distinctions between tax rules affecting profits of the permanent establishment per se compared to tax rules affecting the enterprise in its capacity as owner of the permanent establishment. If anything, the protection tends to be sought by the non-resident company that exercises its freedom of establishment by setting up a permanent

---

[189] Ibid, para 59.
[190] Ibid, para 60.
[191] Ibid, para 61.
[192] See, for example, Luc Hinnekens and Philippe Hinnekens, 'General Report', *Non-Discrimination at the Crossroads of International Taxation*, Cahiers de droit fiscal international, Vol 93a (Kluwer Law International, 2008), p 29; Mary C Bennett, 'Non-discrimination in international tax law: a concept in search of a principle' (2005–6) 59(4) *Tax Law Review*, 439–85.

establishment. The aim is not of itself to neutralise the taxation of companies and permanent establishments. In other words, the aim is not unconditional neutrality of legal form. The aim is to lift restrictions in choosing the legal form of a secondary establishment, to the extent that this entails discrimination based on the location of the corporate seat. The same approach is followed as regards the attribution of profits, considered next.

4.3.3 Rules for the Attribution of Profits and Expenses

The case law above shows how much more difficult it has become for the Member States to tax permanent establishments (of non-resident companies) in a more burdensome way than resident companies. Rules on the attribution of profits to permanent establishments, set out in Article 7 of the OECD Model Tax Convention, may have been affected in a similar way.

Following the 2010 update to the OECD Model Tax Convention, which adopted the Authorised OECD Approach (AOA) for the purposes of Article 7, the profit attribution rule of the OECD Model Tax Convention is to be interpreted in accordance with the arm's length principle, irrespective of the fact that a permanent establishment is not a legal entity distinct from the head office. This amendment aimed to align the rules on taxing business profits under Article 7 of the OECD Model Tax Convention with the transfer pricing rules of Article 9 by allocating profits to permanent establishments as if they were separate legal entities. Under Article 7(2) of the OECD Model Tax Convention, the profits that are attributable to the permanent establishment in the host state are the profits that it might be expected to make, in particular in its dealings with other parts of the enterprise, if it were a separate and independent enterprise engaged in the same or similar activities under the same or similar conditions, taking into account the functions performed, assets used and risks assumed by the enterprise through the permanent establishment and other parts of the enterprise.

EU law does not seem to interfere with the separate entity approach and the application of the AOA. The issue of attribution of profits is not as developed and is perceived as a question of allocation of taxing powers. By way of example, in the SGI case[193] the Court of Justice refrained from striking down the Belgian transfer pricing rules on the allocation of expenses between related companies, even if they restricted the freedom of establishment in a rather pre-emptive manner. The Court of Justice found the rules to be justified on the basis of preventing tax avoidance, taken together with the need to preserve the balanced allocation of the power to impose taxes between the Member States. This case, as well as a later one decided in a similar way,[194] are analysed in greater detail in Chapter 7.

---

[193] Case C-311/08 Société de Gestion Industrielle (SGI) v. État belge [2010] ECR I-487.
[194] Case C-382/16 Hornbach-Baumarkt AG v. Finanzamt Landau, ECLI:EU:C:2018:366.

Neither has the EU (yet) imposed by way of legislation any rules dealing with attribution of profits. As discussed in Chapter 2, there is the Arbitration Convention that seeks to establish an arbitration procedure that eliminates double taxation in the course of transfer pricing disputes, including disputes on profit attributions between Member States. The Arbitration Convention is based on the arm's length principle. Also, as the Tax Dispute Resolution Mechanisms Directive deals with tax treaty disputes, the arm's length principle is likely to be enshrined in those tax treaties. Therefore, the issue of attribution of profits has so far remained within the ambit of the powers of the Member States, notwithstanding the Commission's attempts to carve out an EU interpretation of the arm's length principle in the context of the state aid prohibition.[195]

There is one aspect of attribution of profits where EU law might be relevant – the allocation of expenses. Under Article 7(3) of the OECD Model Tax Convention, expenses incurred by an enterprise for the purposes of the permanent establishment[196] will be directly deducted in determining its profits. In addition, other expenses attributed to another part of the enterprise for functions performed for the benefit of the permanent establishment (e.g. overhead expenses) may be reflected in a notional charge to the permanent establishment.[197] As a result of these rules, companies have an incentive to manipulate their tax bases by allocating expenses where profits are taxed or where profits are taxed at higher rates. Both host and home states may impose limits on such practices.[198] For example, as the host state, the state of the permanent establishment may refuse to take into account all expenses incurred by the permanent establishment or expenses that seem to be linked to the carrying on of the business by both the permanent establishment and the head office. However, even if the host state treatment is compliant with Article 7(3) and the AOA approach, it still has to be questioned whether it is compatible with EU law.

Guidance can be sought from case law in the context of the cross-border provision of services where the issue of expenses was addressed. In Gerritse,[199] a Dutch musician who performed in Germany was not allowed to deduct business expenses unless they exceeded 50 per cent of the receipts. On this point, the Court of Justice found that the inability of a non-resident to deduct business expenses was incompatible with the freedom to provide services. The Court of Justice noted that business

---

[195] See Chapter 8.
[196] It should be pointed out that this is not the same as saying that the expenses have been incurred as part of the activity carried on through the permanent establishment, which is the test for taking into account payments received by a permanent establishment. Therefore, expenses incurred in carrying on activities through a permanent establishment are not deducted unless the expenses have been incurred for the purposes of the permanent establishment. See discussion in Peter Harris and David Oliver, *International Commercial Tax* (Cambridge University Press, 2010), pp 159–60.
[197] OECD Commentary to Art 7, para 34.
[198] See also analysis in 5.1.
[199] Case C-234/01 Arnoud Gerritse v. Finanzamt Neukolln-Nord [2003] ECR I-5945.

expenses were 'directly linked to the activity that generated the taxable income in Germany, so that residents and non-residents [were] placed in a comparable situation in that respect'.[200] As the rule risked operating mainly to the detriment of nationals of other Member States, it constituted indirect discrimination on the grounds of nationality.[201] Gerritse was followed in the Centro Equestre case,[202] where the facts were very similar. Giving some guidance on the concept of direct economic connection, the Court of Justice noted that operating expenses directly connected to the income received in the Member State in which the activity was pursued must be understood as being expenses with a direct economic connection to the provision of services giving rise to taxation in that state and inextricably linked to those services, such as travel and accommodation costs.[203] The place and time at which the costs were incurred were immaterial.[204]

Although these cases were in the context of the freedom to provide services and dealt with non-resident individuals and companies without a permanent establishment in the host state (i.e. the state of activity), there is no reason why the principles set out by the Court of Justice cannot be applied in this context too. If anything, the existence of the permanent establishment of the non-resident individual or company in the host state lends further support to the argument that these non-resident persons are in a comparable situation with a resident person and, as such, deserve to have their expenses deducted in a similar way. Even though the non-resident person in the above cases was seeking to deduct the expenses it incurred in the host state from *its* taxable base and not that of its permanent establishment, the fact remains that the expenses were linked to the host state. While the two situations are not identical, arguably the effect is rather similar. Furthermore, the requirement for direct economic connection may not be too dissimilar with the current approach in Article 7(3) of the OECD Model Tax Convention, to the extent that the host state follows this approach. It may be more difficult to decide this point if the host state consolidates the profits and losses of permanent establishments and uses formulary apportionment, as the link between the taxable base and the host state becomes more tenuous than before.

Home state restrictions on expense allocation may be more fine-tuned. In the context of exemption countries,[205] as the allocation of expenses to a foreign permanent establishment reduces the (exempt) foreign income, this creates an incentive for a company to allocate the expenses to its domestic taxable profits. Home states may not recognise such expenses or deem them to have arisen in the host state. To the extent that these expenses are linked with the company's business in the home state,

[200] Ibid, para 27.
[201] Ibid, para 28.
[202] Case C-345/04 Centro Equestre da Leziria Grande Lda v. Bundesamt fürFinanzen [2007] ECR I-1425.
[203] Ibid, para 25.
[204] Ibid.
[205] For discussion on the exemption and credit methods of relief, see 1.1 and 5.1.

this may lead to a restriction of the freedom of establishment. By having a foreign permanent establishment, the resident company cannot use up (some of) its expenses.

The allocation of foreign expenses may also give rise to home state issues even if that state imposes worldwide taxation, as the expense allocation might impact the amount of foreign tax relief given. This is because the deductibility of foreign expenses reduces the foreign tax payable and, as a corollary, limits the amount of foreign tax credit that a home state may be obliged to give.[206] To the extent that rules on expense allocation reduce the allowable foreign tax credit, they create a disincentive for setting up a permanent establishment in another Member State, contrary to freedom of establishment.

This issue was encountered in the Seabrokers case.[207] Here one of the questions that the EFTA Court had to deal with was whether Norway was in breach of its obligations under the EEA Agreement for apportioning part of the debt interest expenses of a Norwegian company to its UK branch when those expenses were linked to the company's business activities in Norway (the home state). As this led to a reduction of the maximum credit allowance given by the home state, it restricted the Norwegian company's freedom of establishment.[208]

The EFTA Court distinguished three situations. Firstly, when expenses were linked to the income of a company's branch in the host state (here another EEA state) and not linked to the company's income in the home state, such company was not in a comparable situation to a company whose expenses were all incurred in the home state. Therefore, such company could not expect the same tax treatment by the home state with regard to expenses related to the branch in the host state. To the extent that the host state did not grant a deduction for expenses relating solely to the income of the branch, the resulting burden for the taxpayer was simply a consequence of the two states exercising their different tax regimes in parallel.[209]

The same conclusions followed when expenses were not linked to any particular business activities of a company in the home or host state (through its branch) and expenses were attributed in proportion to the parts of the global net income earned in these two states. Again, the company was not in a comparable situation to one whose expenses arose solely in the home state. If the host state did not grant a similar proportional deduction for expenses when calculating the tax on the income of the branch, the resulting burden for the company was simply a consequence of the disparity from the exercise of tax powers of the two states.[210]

---

[206] For the mechanisms of this, see 5.1.
[207] Case E-7/07 Seabrokers v. Norway [2008] EFTA Court Report 171.
[208] The EFTA Court also examined the treatment of deductible group contributions and decided the question the same way as for interest expenses.
[209] Ibid, para 54.
[210] Ibid, para 55.

By contrast, a company conducting all its business in its home state and having all its debt interest expenses linked to that state was in a comparable situation to a company conducting its business in its home state and through a branch in the host state but having all its debt interest expenses linked to the home state. Therefore, these companies had to receive the same tax treatment in the home state.[211] Here, as the different treatment led to a reduction of the maximum credit allowance given by Norway, there was a restriction to the freedom of establishment.[212] The EFTA Court did not assess justifications to these restrictions, as none were given.[213]

4.3.4 Notional Payments and Expenses

What may be even more problematic in the EU context is the taxation of notional payments and the allocation of (notional) expenses resulting from internal dealings between the permanent establishment and the head office. In the current OECD Commentary, the AOA – the separate and independent enterprise approach – only applies to determine the profits attributable to the permanent establishment for the purposes of Articles 7, 23A and 23B and does *not* change the nature of the income derived by the enterprise.[214] Therefore, notional payments for internal dealings between the head office and the permanent establishment or between permanent establishments do not give rise to taxation.

Nevertheless, if states decide to extend the separate and independent enterprise fiction beyond these confines, then internal dealings can be recognised.[215] In that case, notional charges for dealings will be deducted in computing the profits of the permanent establishment in the same way as a payment made by a subsidiary to its parent company would be deducted. This would not lead to the creation of notional income for the enterprise that a state could tax under another provision.[216]

While the Commentary discusses the possibility of notional payments/expenses in the context of Articles 6 and 11 of the OECD Model Tax Convention,[217] in some states this approach may be extended to other tax-deductible (notional) income such as royalties. As a result, withholding taxes could be imposed on such notional rents, interest and royalties. This may even be extended to dividends considered a notional return on 'free' capital, having a similar effect to branch profit taxes.[218] Arguably, the

---

[211] Ibid, para 56.
[212] Ibid, paras 56–7.
[213] Ibid, para 69.
[214] OECD Commentary to Art 7, para 28.
[215] Ibid, para 29.
[216] For example, rent under Art 6 of the OECD Model Tax Convention when the economic ownership of a building used by a permanent establishment is attributed to the head office or interest under Art 11.
[217] See para 28.
[218] See 4.3.2. Also, Georg W. Kofler and Servaas Van Thiel, 'The "authorized OECD approach" and European tax law' (2011) 51(8) *European Taxation*, 327–33, 331–2.

limitations of Article 10 of the OECD Model Tax Convention would not apply in this situation, as they do not apply to intra-company dividend payments.

In the first edition of this book, the compatibility of such notional payments with EU law was questioned. It was noted that the Directives would not apply as they can only cover payments between two companies (albeit with the insertion of permanent establishments in some cases) – that is, not intra-company payments. It was argued that fundamental freedoms might be applicable. If the comparability analysis focuses on the payment and the discriminatory withholding tax on it, then case law on withholding taxes on outbound payments by companies may be relevant.[219] If the comparability analysis focuses on the discriminatory taxation of a permanent establishment in the host state, then the case law examined in this chapter is relevant.[220] The latter analysis was indeed applied in a case that assessed the application of freedom of establishment in situations where notional interest deduction rules were less favourable to foreign permanent establishments compared to domestic permanent establishments.

In the Argenta Spaarbank case,[221] Argenta Spaarbank NV (henceforth, Argenta) was unable to take into account the assets of its Dutch permanent establishment in calculating its notional interest deduction. The notional interest deduction was a tax deduction calculated as a fictitious interest expense on the adjusted equity of the company. The regime was effectively based on a percentage of corporate equity and meant to allow Belgian corporate income taxpayers a deduction reflecting the economic cost of the use of capital equal to the cost of long-term risk-free financing. As far as companies with foreign permanent establishments were concerned, there were limitations to their ability to deduct notional interest where the permanent establishment was in a country with which Belgium had entered into a tax treaty that exempted from Belgian tax the profits derived through that permanent establishment. The referring court questioned whether the Belgian tax legislation was in breach of the freedom of establishment.

As the Court of Justice stated, it was obvious that in this case, to calculate the deduction for risk capital, there was different treatment between the assets of foreign permanent establishments, the income from which was not taxable in Belgium, and the assets of Belgian permanent establishments.[222] In the former case, the assets were not taken into account when calculating the risk capital serving as a basis for the calculation of the deduction, whereas the assets attributed to permanent establishments situated in Belgium were taken into account for that purpose.[223]

Agreeing with the opinion of the Advocate General, the Court of Justice found that taking into account the assets of a permanent establishment in order to calculate

---

[219] See analysis in 5.3.
[220] See above, 4.3.2.
[221] Case C-350/11 Argenta Spaarbank NV v. Belgische Staat, ECLI:EU:C:2013:447.
[222] Ibid, para 22.
[223] Ibid, para 23.

the deduction for risk capital of a company subject to corporation tax in Belgium constituted a tax advantage since this helped to reduce the effective rate of the corporation tax that such a company must pay in that Member State.[224] This tax advantage was denied when the Belgian company had a foreign permanent establishment the profits of which were not taxable in Belgium due to a tax treaty.[225] This disadvantageous treatment was not the result of the parallel exercise of the fiscal sovereignty of different Member States and, therefore, it restricted the freedom of establishment.

The Court of Justice did not accept a justification based on the need to safeguard the coherence of the tax system. Although it was true that the advantage was granted only where the profits generated by the permanent establishment were taxable in Belgium, however, there was no direct link between the advantage calculated by taking account of the permanent establishment's assets and the taxation of the return generated by them.[226] The Belgian legislation only required that any income generated by the permanent establishment must be taxable in Belgium, 'without making the grant of the advantage in question conditional on such income actually being generated or actually being taxed'.[227]

As far as the balanced allocation of taxing powers was concerned, this justification was also rejected. The Court of Justice emphasised that the attribution of taxing powers under the tax treaty could not systematically justify any refusal to grant an advantage to the Belgian company.[228] This justification could be accepted, in particular, where the system in question was designed to prevent conduct capable of jeopardising the right of a Member State to exercise its powers of taxation in relation to activities carried out in its territory.[229] However, in this case, conferring the tax advantage would jeopardise neither Belgium's right nor the Netherlands' right to exercise their power to tax concerning activities carried out in its territory and would not result in the shifting of income normally taxable in one of those Member States to the other.[230] Therefore, the restriction could not be justified and there was a breach of the freedom of establishment.

Overall, this case, although factually complex, set an important precedent as far as notional expenses were concerned.

---

[224] Ibid, para 24.
[225] Ibid, para 25.
[226] Ibid, paras 45–6.
[227] Ibid, para 47. In fact, the assets of the permanent establishment could be taken into account for deduction purposes where the income from a permanent establishment was taxable in Belgium, even if the permanent establishment had not generated income there.
[228] Ibid, para 51.
[229] Ibid, para 53.
[230] Ibid, para 55.

4.3.5 Cross-Border Loss Relief

The problematic treatment of cross-border group relief was examined in 4.2.2. Intra-company loss relief is just as problematic. While relief is almost always available if both the head office and the permanent establishment are in the same state, if they are not, relief may be available but often subject to conditions. Here the issue is not whether there has been proper allocation of the expenses to the foreign branch. Rather, the issue is whether the branch losses (effectively, the excess of expenses over proceeds),[231] which are foreign losses, can be used by the head office. There are broadly two different approaches to this in international tax law. Either both foreign branch profits and losses are always exempt without exceptions, or foreign branch losses are included in the domestic tax base but recaptured when the branch becomes profitable. The OECD Model Tax Convention, together with its Commentary, does not take a position on this point and leaves the choice to the contracting states.[232]

In two cases, the Court of Justice looked at the reverse scenario: profits of foreign branches being used to reduce losses of the head office. The Court of Justice examined this from a host state perspective in the Futura case[233] and a home state perspective in the AMID case.[234]

In the first case, Futura was a French company that wanted to carry-forward losses against the profits of its Luxembourg branch. Under Luxembourg law, local branches of non-resident companies could only carry-forward losses if these losses were economically linked to the branch, provided that resident taxpayers did not receive more favourable treatment.[235] The branch was also required to keep accounts according to Luxembourg law. The Luxembourg tax authorities refused relief because they considered the losses to be attributable to the French head office rather than to the Belgian branch.

The Court of Justice found that the source (host) state rule restricting the loss carry-forward to losses that had an economic link with income earned in that state could be justified under the territoriality principle. As the Court of Justice stated, '[s]uch system, which is in conformity with the fiscal principle of territoriality, cannot be regarded as entailing any discrimination, overt or covert, prohibited by the Treaty'.[236] Nevertheless, the requirement for the Luxembourg branch to keep accounts according to Luxembourg law was held to be disproportionate.

In any case, Futura stands for the proposition that a host state (i.e. the state of the permanent establishment) cannot be obliged to set off the losses of the foreign head

---

[231] See CFE, Opinion Statement of the CFE ECJ Taskforce on Losses Compensation within the EU for Individuals and Companies Carrying Out Their Activities through Permanent Establishments, July 2009, p 1.
[232] OECD Commentary to Arts 23A and 23B, para 44.
[233] Case C-250/95 Futura Participations SA v. Administration des Contributions [1997] ECR I-02471.
[234] Case C-141/99 AMID v. Belgian State [2000] ECR I-11621.
[235] Case C-250/95 Futura, para 43.
[236] Ibid, para 22.

office against the permanent establishment's profits due to territoriality concerns. There is nothing to prevent the host state from requiring evidence of the economic nexus of the losses with the branch. While Futura may have been seen as a logical decision, following the Marks & Spencer case, its strength as a precedent has been questioned. If in certain circumstances a parent company was forced to absorb the losses of its foreign subsidiary – a completely separate entity – then why was the profitable part of one company not also to be forced to absorb losses of another (foreign) part of the same company? If anything, the latter appears more justifiable, as there is no separate entity and no piercing of the corporate veil involved. Furthermore, the qualification of the Court of Justice in Futura that the host state can ignore foreign losses provided its resident taxpayers do not receive more favourable treatment[237] (i.e. Luxembourg companies being able to use foreign branch losses) suggests that the territoriality justification is not absolute.

In AMID, the Court of Justice examined the situation from the perspective of the home state and reached a different conclusion from that in Futura. The Court of Justice found that a Belgian company with a Belgian branch was in a comparable situation to a Belgian company with a Luxembourg branch. There was a difference in treatment in so far as the deduction of losses was concerned. Losses incurred in Belgium could be carried forward by companies established exclusively in Belgium. By contrast, if the loss-making Belgian company had a profit-making foreign branch, then these losses had to be set off against the branch profits (here the Luxembourg branch) even though the profits were tax exempt under the applicable tax treaty between the two Member States.

The Court of Justice found that, by setting off domestic losses against profits exempted by the tax treaty, the Belgian legislation established a differentiated tax treatment between companies incorporated under national law having domestic establishments only and those having establishments in another Member State. Those companies were likely to suffer a tax disadvantage that they would not have suffered if all their establishments were situated in the same Member State.[238] This difference in treatment was not justified. Therefore, the home state was prevented from demanding the offsetting of domestic losses against (exempt) income of the foreign branch before the carry-forward of unrelieved losses could be allowed.

There has been much criticism that the reasoning in this case was flawed. The problem with the Court's analysis in AMID is that the same tax treatment would have occurred in a domestic context. Losses of the head office would have been set off against the profits of a domestic branch first, before being carried forward.[239] Therefore, Belgian companies with Belgian branches were treated the same way as Belgian companies with Luxembourg branches.

---

[237] Ibid, para 43.
[238] Case C-141/99 AMID, para 23.
[239] See analysis of legislation in para 4 in Case C-141/99 AMID.

Furthermore, the Court of Justice ignored the fact that foreign branch profits and foreign branch losses were in essence, treated symmetrically under Belgian law. By allowing the carry-forward, Belgium would have given relief domestically for foreign branch losses even if branch profits were exempt. Nevertheless, this asymmetrical treatment was not a relevant consideration.[240] To an extent, other than the comparability argument, which was misapplied, the Belgian government had not made an effort to justify the difference in treatment – a point raised by the Court of Justice.[241] This does not, however, change the fact that the reasoning was flawed.

Perhaps AMID was the Court's (wrong) reaction to the Futura case. As the host state (i.e. the state of the permanent establishment) was not obliged to absorb the losses of the foreign head office following Futura, if no obligation was imposed on the home state, then losses may have gone unrelieved. The problem with this approach, though, is that it shifts the burden onto the home state. While this could have been permissible as regards losses that could never be relieved elsewhere (e.g. if the Belgian company ceased trading and its losses were final, a reverse Marks & Spencer scenario), this was not the situation in AMID. Here the taxpayer did not complain of unrelieved losses – it complained that it did not have the choice of carrying forward those losses rather than setting them off against profits of the branch.

Arguably, a better approach would have been to question whether, by taking into account exempt branch profits that were also taxed in the host state, the home state created unrelieved double taxation. Following Kerckhaert–Morres and Damseaux, however, this argument is more likely to fail, being the result of disparities from the exercise in parallel of the fiscal sovereignty by two Member States.[242] Neither is it likely that the host state will be required to take into account the Belgian treatment of the Luxembourg branch profits, especially since this was contrary to the underlying tax treaty – that is the allocation of taxing powers between those states. If anything, with hindsight it seems the most appropriate way to deal with such a situation would have been to seek redress in the home state for the treaty override, if any.

It is uncertain whether AMID's end result is more appropriate in the context of a home state that adopts a credit system for taxing foreign profits.[243] The argument is as follows: if domestic losses have to be set against foreign branch profits first and cannot be carried forward, this will lead to fewer losses being carried forward and more excess foreign tax credits. As excess foreign tax credits are more difficult to use than carried-forward losses, this leads to detrimental treatment. While there is some logic in this argument, the Court of Justice may be reluctant to get embroiled in the

---

[240] Ibid, para 24.
[241] Ibid, para 32.
[242] See 3.3.3 and 5.2.3.
[243] See John Avery Jones, 'A comment on "AMID: the wrong bridge or a bridge too far?"' (2001) 41(7/8) European Taxation, 251.

controversy of whether restrictions on the use of excess foreign tax credits, an inherent feature of sophisticated credit systems, breach EU law.

Subsequent cases dealt with the inability to set off foreign branch losses vis-à-vis domestic profits.

In Lidl Belgium,[244] German legislation prevented losses incurred by the Luxembourg branch of a German company from being set off against the profits of the company.[245] The Court of Justice found this to be a restriction to the freedom of establishment. A provision that allowed losses incurred by a branch to be taken into account in calculating the profits and taxable income of the head office was a tax advantage.[246] This tax advantage was only available to companies with domestic branches.[247] Therefore, the tax situation of a German company with a branch established in another Member State was less favourable than it would be if the branch were established in Germany. This restricted the freedom of establishment of the German company.[248]

The Court of Justice found the restriction to be justified on the basis of two of the Marks & Spencer grounds: the preservation of allocation of taxing powers and the prevention of double relief of losses.[249] There was no need for all three justifications to be applicable.[250] The restriction was also sufficiently targeted and proportional.[251] The Court of Justice found that the exhaustion of possibilities test[252] had not been satisfied. This was because the branch losses were not terminal losses. The Luxembourg tax legislation provided for the possibility of deducting the branch losses in future tax years.[253] The branch had benefited from this provision in 2003, when it generated profits.[254] Therefore, there was no need for an immediate deduction of losses and future recapture.

The Court of Justice reiterated the importance of respecting the allocation of taxing powers attained in the tax treaty between Germany and Luxembourg.[255] It concluded that the German rule was not in breach of the freedom of establishment even if the unavailability of immediate loss relief led to cash-flow disadvantages.

---

[244] Case C-414/06 Lidl Belgium. A similar case dealing with a non-EU branch was dismissed by the Court of Justice for not falling within the protective scope of freedom of establishment: Case C-415/06 Stahlwerk Ergste Westig GmbH/Finanzamt Düsseldorf-Mettmann [2007] ECR I-152.

[245] This is because under the tax treaty with Luxembourg, Germany exempted both profits and losses of foreign branches. Therefore, both profits and losses of a Luxembourg branch were removed from the taxable base of the German company.

[246] Case C-414/06 Lidl Belgium, para 23.

[247] Ibid, para 24.

[248] Ibid, para 25.

[249] Ibid, paras 30–7.

[250] Ibid, paras 40–1. The Court of Justice referred to the Oy AA judgment, where again only two of the Marks & Spencer grounds for justification were applicable. Case C-231/05 Oy AA, para 60.

[251] Case C-414/06 Lidl Belgium, para 43.

[252] See para 55 of the judgment in Case C-446/03 Marks & Spencer.

[253] Case C-414/06 Lidl Belgium, para 49.

[254] Ibid, para 50.

[255] Ibid, para 52.

4.3 Taxation of Permanent Establishments

The judgment should be contrasted with Advocate General Sharpston's opinion, where the unavailability of immediate loss relief was decisive. The Advocate General thought that there were less restrictive means of attaining the objective of the legislation, such as allowing the deduction of losses while providing for the recapture of the loss relief in future profitable periods,[256] with a provision for automatic reincorporation after a certain amount of time or if the permanent establishment ceased to exist in that form.[257] The carry-forward of the losses was not an acceptable substitute. Compared to the immediate offsetting of losses and subsequent recapture of profits, the carry-forward resulted in a cash-flow disadvantage.[258]

This opinion was not surprising given Advocate General Sharpston's earlier opinion in the Deutsche Shell case.[259] Here, in a slightly different context but looking at the same issues, the Advocate General opined that the non-deductibility of foreign currency losses in respect of foreign permanent establishments was incompatible with freedom of establishment. In Deutsche Shell, the profits of an Italian permanent establishment of a German company were tax exempt in Germany. Currency losses in respect of the Italian permanent establishment were non-deductible under German law, as this was an expense directly linked to exempt income. The Advocate General found this to be an unjustified restriction to the freedom of establishment. What was crucial to her analysis was the fact that the currency loss could only be taken into account in Germany.[260] In other words, in this case, the exhaustion of possibilities test was satisfied.

The Court of Justice reached the same conclusion but without relying on the Marks & Spencer case.[261] In so far as the restriction was concerned, the Court of Justice acknowledged the argument of allocation of taxing powers. A Member State was not required to take account of the negative results of a foreign permanent establishment just because those negative results were not capable of being taken into account for tax purposes in the host state.[262] However, the Court of Justice distinguished this situation from that arising as a result of a mere disparity between national tax rules. It focused on the fact that the tax disadvantage concerned related to a specific operational factor that was capable of being taken into consideration only by the German tax authorities. A currency loss was not the same as a typical loss of a permanent establishment. This

---

[256] Ibid, para 24 (Advocate General).
[257] Ibid. This was in fact what the German legislation provided until 1999 when it was repealed.
[258] Ibid, para 28 (Advocate General).
[259] Case C-293/06 Deutsche Shell [2008] ECR I-1129.
[260] Ibid, paras 50–1. This loss was invisible in Italy as at the time Italy operated in Italian lira. Therefore, all computations for tax purposes were carried out solely in that currency. The currency loss only appeared when the sums were converted to the German mark.
[261] In fact, Case C-446/03 Marks & Spencer was only cited once, on a general proposition. By contrast to the reasoning of Advocate General Sharpston, the Marks & Spencer justification test was not referred to explicitly.
[262] Case C-293/06 Deutsche Shell, para 42.

was not a loss that could ever be suffered by the permanent establishment – it was a loss of the head office.[263] Therefore, to exclude it from the tax base of the head office, when it could never be deducted in the Member State of a permanent establishment, was an unjustifiable restriction to the freedom of establishment.

In any case, the facts in Deutsche Shell are much more distinct than in Lidl Belgium, and the former case is unlikely to provide a stronger precedent than the latter case. What seemed to be decisive in both cases was the availability (or unavailability) of loss relief in the host state. However, in a later case, Krankenheim,[264] the Court of Justice showed reluctance to interfere with the home state practice of recapturing a previously deducted loss, irrespective of whether the host state provided relief for this loss.

In this case, a German-resident company had a branch in Austria. The Austrian branch had incurred losses from 1982 but generated profits from 1991 until 1994. Under the Germany–Austria tax treaty, the branch was exempt in Germany and only taxed in Austria. In addition, under German law at the time, a German company was allowed to deduct the losses of its branch, whether domestic or foreign. However, in the case of foreign branches, there was provision for subsequent recapture if they became profitable. In other words, the losses of a foreign branch would later be reintegrated in the tax base of the German company if such branch subsequently made profits.

Austria allowed carry-forward of branch losses unless, after taking its worldwide income into account, the company made an overall profit.[265] In this case, as the worldwide income of the German company exceeded the losses of its Austrian branch, no carry-forward was allowed in Austria. Germany allowed the deduction of the branch losses but then recaptured them. The Austrian Federal Finance Court referred the case to the Court of Justice, asking whether this recapture mechanism was compatible with the freedom of establishment as set out in Article 31 of the EEA Agreement.[266]

The Court of Justice found that the recapture mechanism for foreign branches restricted the freedom of establishment. Although Germany gave a tax advantage – loss relief – to both German and foreign branches, this advantage was withdrawn in the case of foreign branches as a result of the recapture mechanism. Therefore, a German company with an Austrian branch was in a less favourable situation than a German company with a German branch, thus discouraging such a company from carrying on its business through an Austrian branch.[267] Nevertheless, this restriction

---

[263] Ibid, para 44.
[264] Case C-157/07 Finanzamt für Körperschaften III in Berlin v. Krankenheim Ruhesitz am Wannsee-Seniorenheimstatt [2008] ECR I-8061.
[265] This was irrespective of the fact that the losses may not have been deductible in the state of the head office.
[266] As the recapture occurred in 1994, before Austria had acceded to the EU, the EEA Agreement was applicable. See para 26.
[267] Case C-157/07 Krankenheim, para 38.

4.3 Taxation of Permanent Establishments

could be justified by the need to guarantee the coherence of the German tax system. As held:

> the reintegration of losses provided for by the German tax system at issue in the main proceedings cannot be dissociated from their having earlier been taken into account. That reintegration, in the case of a company with a permanent establishment in another State in relation to which that company's State of residence has no power of taxation, as the referring court indicates, reflects a logical symmetry. There was thus a direct, personal and material link between the two elements of the tax mechanism at issue in the main proceedings, the said reintegration being the logical complement of the deduction previously granted.[268]

The Court of Justice found the restriction appropriate to achieve this objective because it 'operate[d] in a perfectly symmetrical manner, only deducted losses being reintegrated'.[269] Moreover, the restriction was entirely proportionate to the objective pursued, since the reintegrated losses were reintegrated only up to the amount of the profits made.[270]

The fact that the recapture mechanism applied even though the German company was unable to set off the losses in Austria as a result of the Austrian tax rules did not affect this conclusion. As the Court of Justice stated, in the absence of any unifying or harmonising Community measures, Member States retained the power to define the criteria for taxing income and wealth with a view to eliminating double taxation, by means of tax treaties if necessary.[271] This competence also implied that a Member State was not required to take account, for the purposes of applying its tax law, of the possible negative results arising from particularities of legislation of another Member State (here the Austrian rules on the carry-forward of losses).[272] Therefore, host state rules were ignored, and Germany could apply the recapture mechanism. The Court of Justice refused to strike down an established practice in international tax law.[273]

This approach was aligned with the treatment of losses of a foreign permanent establishment under the Draft Cross-Border Loss Relief Directive,[274] discussed above.[275] In the Draft Directive, two methods were available to home states: the

---

[268] Ibid, para 42.
[269] Ibid, para 44.
[270] Ibid, para 45.
[271] Ibid, para 48.
[272] Ibid, para 49.
[273] This is the so-called asymmetric approach, whereby losses of a foreign permanent establishment can be included in the domestic tax base but are recaptured in future years. Under the symmetric approach, profits and losses of a foreign permanent establishment are always exempt. See Tigran Mkrtchyan, 'In search of Ariadne's Thread: permanent establishments and losses in the European Union' (2009) 63(12) *Bulletin for International Taxation*, 586–99; CFE, 'Opinion Statement – Lidl Belgium'.
[274] Proposal for a Council directive concerning arrangements for the taking into account by enterprises of the losses of their permanent establishments and subsidiaries situated in other Member States, COM(90) 595 final.
[275] See 4.2.2.

credit method and the method of deduction of losses and subsequent reincorporation of profits.[276] Furthermore, home states were given the option of providing for automatic reincorporation under specific circumstances.[277] This suggests that under the Draft Directive, no relief would have been allowed for terminal losses of a permanent establishment. By contrast, under some of the earlier case law on losses of a foreign permanent establishment, relief could only be permitted if the losses were final. Krankenheim seems to deviate from this line of reasoning by allowing the recapture mechanism to remain in place irrespective of the ability of the permanent establishment to set off the losses in the host state. Moreover, by ignoring the tax treatment in the host state, an assessment of terminal losses could no longer be made. In other words, Krankenheim brought us closer to the approach of the Draft Directive.

The host state may also be required to ignore home state rules as suggested in the opinion of Advocate General Kokott and the Court of Justice's judgment in Philips Electronics.[278] This was a preliminary reference questioning the compatibility of the UK's group relief rules on permanent establishments with freedom of establishment. Under UK law the profits and losses of a company incorporated and tax resident in another Member State were taxable in the UK to the extent that the profits were attributed to a business carried on in the UK through a permanent establishment. However, UK losses of a UK permanent establishment of a non-resident company could not be surrendered to a UK company by way of group relief where any part of those losses or any amount brought into account in computing them 'corresponds to, or is represented in, any amount which, for the purposes of any foreign tax is (in any period) deductible from or otherwise allowable against non-UK profits of the company or any person'.[279]

In this case, Philips Electronics UK Ltd, the UK taxpayer, made various consortium claims for group relief in its tax returns, in respect of losses incurred by the UK permanent establishment of a Dutch company, which was also the parent company of the taxpayer. The claims were refused on the basis that the losses could have been taken into account in the Netherlands. The referring court questioned whether this refusal was compatible with the freedom of establishment. In essence, this was not a case of foreign loss relief but rather a case of inability to use domestic losses, as the permanent establishment that incurred them was of a non-resident company.

Advocate General Kokott and the Court of Justice found the rules to be incompatible with freedom of establishment. The UK legislation imposed certain conditions on the possibility of transferring, by means of group relief to a resident company, losses sustained by the permanent establishment of a non-resident company situated in that Member State, while the transfer of losses sustained in that

---

[276] Ibid, Arts 5–7.
[277] Ibid, Art 8.
[278] Case C-18/11 HMRC v. Philips Electronics UK Ltd, ECLI:EU:C:2012:532.
[279] Ibid, paras 4 and 10.

4.3 Taxation of Permanent Establishments

Member State by a resident company was not subject to any equivalent conditions. This difference in treatment made it less attractive for companies having their seat in other Member States to exercise the right to freedom of establishment through a branch. Therefore, the UK legislation restricted the freedom to choose the appropriate legal form in which to pursue activities in another Member State.[280]

The Court of Justice found that a foreign company with a UK permanent establishment was in an objectively comparable situation to a UK company. This was even though a non-resident company with a permanent establishment in the UK was taxable only on the amount of profits generated in the UK and attributable to that permanent establishment, whereas a resident company was taxable on its worldwide income. Comparability was assessed only as regards losses – that is the possibility of transferring, by means of group relief, losses sustained in the UK to another company in that group.[281]

The restriction could not be justified by preserving the allocation of taxing powers since only UK losses were to be surrendered against the profits of the UK taxpayer. Such losses, as well as profits, were within the scope of UK tax.[282] This justification ground was designed to safeguard the symmetry between the right to tax profits and the right to deduct losses. However, in this case, it was irrelevant to safeguarding the UK's power of taxation that the losses to be surrendered could also be taken into account in the Netherlands. The power of the host state to impose taxes was not affected by the possibility of transferring, by group relief and to a resident company, the losses sustained by a permanent establishment situated in its territory.[283] As Advocate General Kokott noted, the UK's power of taxation would only be impaired if foreign losses were to be taken into account, because such losses would reduce the tax revenue of the UK while the (foreign) profits from the activity could not be taxed.[284]

Neither was the restriction justified by the need to prevent the double use of losses. Although there was a risk of double use of losses (both in the host state where the permanent establishment was situated and also in the Member State where the non-resident company had its seat), the host state's power of taxation was not affected.[285] The UK's tax revenue was the same irrespective of whether losses of the permanent establishment were also taken into account in the Member State of the head office. In any case, the Court of Justice argued that prevention of the double use of losses did not constitute an autonomous justification – it had to be in combination with another justification.[286] In this case, the restriction could not be justified by these grounds, whether on their own or combined.[287]

---

[280] Ibid, paras 15–16.
[281] Ibid, paras 17–20.
[282] Under Art 7 of the UK-Netherlands tax treaty, the UK was able to tax the income of domestic companies and that of UK permanent establishments of Dutch companies. See para 47 of opinion.
[283] Ibid, para 25 (Court of Justice).
[284] Ibid, para 50 (Advocate General). See also the Court's judgment, para 26.
[285] Ibid, paras 30–1 (Court of Justice).
[286] Ibid, para 33 (Court of Justice) and para 67 (Advocate General).
[287] Ibid, para 35 (Court of Justice).

The Advocate General argued that the restriction was not proportional. The surrender of losses was ruled out even where only a part of the losses was allowable in the host state.[288] Moreover, the provision did not differentiate according to how the losses were taken into account for the purposes of the foreign tax, whether host state loss relief was temporary or permanent.[289] The Court of Justice saw no need to address the proportionality issue, given that the restriction could not be justified.[290]

It was also irrelevant to the Court of Justice that it was not the freedom of establishment of the UK-resident company that had been unjustifiably restricted, but rather that of the non-resident company with a permanent establishment in the UK. In order to be effective, freedom of establishment had to extend the benefit of group relief to such situations.[291] The Advocate General explained this point further. While it was the Dutch parent company that exercised the freedom, it was the UK taxpayer who suffered the disadvantage. The restriction for the Dutch company lay in the fact that its contracting partner – the UK taxpayer – was denied an advantage, itself suffering disadvantages as a result.[292] The freedom of establishment of the Dutch parent company could only be guaranteed if its contracting partner was accorded the advantage. Only that company could invoke the advantage of surrendering losses.[293]

This case suggested an endorsement of the per-country approach, which seems to have been watered down in the more recent case of Bevola, which is discussed below. Later cases also focused more on proportionality issues, as well as justifications based on the coherence of the tax system and the balanced allocation of taxing powers.

In the Nordea Bank Denmark case,[294] Advocate General Kokott and the Court of Justice dealt with the circumstances under which a Member State may prevent a resident company from fully recapturing the losses of a foreign permanent establishment. Here, the referring court asked whether Danish legislation was compatible with the freedom of establishment by allowing a resident company to deduct from its taxable profits the losses incurred by a foreign permanent establishment but applying a recapture mechanism on the losses in the event of total or partial transfer of the permanent establishment's activities to a company belonging to the same group and established in the same state as the permanent establishment.

Nordea Bank was the legal successor to a Danish bank, which held bank branches (i.e. permanent establishments) in Sweden, Finland and Norway. These branches made losses, which were set off against Danish profits. Following a cross-border merger, the Danish bank branches were closed, and the activities were transferred to affiliated companies in Sweden, Finland and Norway. The acquiring banks could not deduct

[288] Ibid, para 73 (Advocate General).
[289] Ibid, para 74 (Advocate General).
[290] Ibid, para 36 (Court of Justice).
[291] Ibid, para 39.
[292] Ibid, para 85 (Advocate General).
[293] Ibid.
[294] Case C-48/13 Nordea Bank Danmark A/S v. Skatteministeriet, ECLI:EU:C:2014:2087.

4.3 Taxation of Permanent Establishments

the losses of the closed branches from their profits. The Danish tax authorities regarded this event as a partial transfer, which triggered a recapture of the loss relief granted. The referring court questioned whether this recapture rule was compatible with the freedom of establishment.

The Court of Justice found that the rule restricted the freedom of establishment. It examined whether the restriction could be justified by the need to preserve the balanced allocation of taxing powers in connection with the objective of preventing tax avoidance. This would exist where companies transferred a previously loss-making permanent establishment to a group company in another state to realise the profits outside the Danish tax jurisdiction.[295] If Denmark was denied the power to reincorporate the losses deducted into the taxable profits of the Danish company carrying out the transfer, when it has lost the power to tax any future profits, this would artificially erode Denmark's tax base and, therefore, affect the allocation of the power to impose taxes resulting from the Nordic Convention.[296]

However, the Court of Justice found that the legislation went beyond what was necessary to attain this objective.[297] The balanced allocation of taxing powers had the objective of safeguarding the symmetry between the right to tax profits and the right to deduct losses. The need to safeguard that symmetry meant 'that the losses deducted in respect of the permanent establishment must be capable of being offset by taxation of the profits made by it under the tax jurisdiction of the Member State in question, that is to say, both the profits made throughout the period when the permanent establishment belonged to the resident company and those made at the time of the permanent establishment's transfer'.[298] Therefore, this objective only allowed Denmark to tax the profits and gains over the assets of the permanent establishment that had accrued during the period that it was a permanent establishment of the Danish transferring company. Recapturing, in addition, all of the previously deducted losses was considered to be disproportional.

This conclusion was not altered by the fact that it would be difficult for Denmark, in the event of an intra-group transfer to verify the market value of the business transferred in another Member State.[299] 'Such difficulties are not specific to cross-border situations since the Danish authorities necessarily already carry out similar checks when a business is sold in the context of an intragroup transfer of a resident establishment.'[300] In any event, the Danish authorities always had the power to request from the transferring company the necessary documents to verify whether the value of the business adopted to calculate the gain on a transfer of a foreign establishment was the same as the market value.[301]

[295] Ibid, para 29.
[296] Ibid, para 30.
[297] Ibid, para 31.
[298] Ibid, para 33.
[299] Ibid, para 37.
[300] Ibid, para 38.
[301] Ibid, para 39.

In another important case, the Timac Agro case,[302] the Court of Justice was asked to consider the compatibility of the German rules on the recapturing of tax losses of a foreign permanent establishment with the principle of freedom of establishment. Here, what was at issue was the recognition of foreign permanent establishment losses where the loss-making permanent establishment was sold to another group entity.

In general, profits and losses of a foreign permanent establishment to which the tax exemption method applied under a tax treaty were not included in the domestic tax assessment. Until the assessment period in 1998, German law stipulated that losses incurred by a foreign permanent establishment could, as an exception, be deducted from the domestic assessment basis when they could not be recognised in the country where the foreign permanent establishment was located. Correspondingly, the amount was added back in subsequent years, insofar as the foreign permanent establishment generated profits. The deducted amounts were also added back if the permanent establishment was reorganised, transferred or discontinued in subsequent years. In the case of reorganisations, transfers or discontinuations, the amounts had to be added back irrespective of whether a profit was generated.

The legislation was repealed in 1999. Thereafter, losses of a foreign permanent establishment were deductible only in the country where the foreign permanent establishment was located and not for domestic tax purposes.

The Court of Justice agreed with its Advocate General and held that Germany might limit the use of losses from an Austrian permanent establishment of a German company where, as in the Austria-Germany tax treaty, Austrian permanent establishment income was exempt from German taxation if that income was subject to tax in Austria. For the period 1997/1998, the Court of Justice considered that the situations of a foreign and a domestic permanent establishment were comparable because Germany had exercised a taxing right through the recapture rule. This rule formed a logical symmetry with the previous loss deduction. In line with the Krankenheim decision, the rule was coherent and necessary to preserve the balanced allocation of taxing powers. It was up to the referring court to determine whether the recapture rule was also proportionate, that is, whether Timac Agro could prove that the losses incurred were final. If so, they should be deductible.

For the period of 1999 and onwards, the Court of Justice distinguished the application of the exemption method from the recapture rule applicable in earlier years. As Germany now exempted foreign permanent establishment income symmetrically via the exemption method of the underlying tax treaty, the situations of a foreign and a domestic permanent establishment were not objectively comparable anymore. Therefore, there was no breach. This case showed the importance placed

---

[302] Case C-388/14 Timac Agro Deutschland GmbH v. Finanzamt Sankt Augustin, ECLI:EU:C:2015:829.

by the Court of Justice on the symmetrical treatment of profit and losses of a foreign permanent establishment.

In the Bevola case,[303] the Court of Justice was asked to assess the compatibility of the Danish loss relief rules with EU law. The case dealt with a Danish resident company that decided to close its Finnish permanent establishment. Upon cessation of its activities, the Finnish permanent establishment incurred losses for which no relief was available in Finland. Relying on the Marks & Spencer case, the taxpayer tried to deduct these losses in Denmark. The Danish tax authorities denied the deduction claiming that, under Danish law, such a deduction would be permitted only where the Danish taxpayer had applied for the international joint taxation regime. This was an optional regime that provided for the combined taxation in Denmark, for at least ten years, of all profits and losses realised by foreign subsidiaries and permanent establishments.

The Advocate General found that the Danish rules were in breach of the freedom of establishment, as they prevented a Danish company from deducting the final losses incurred by its permanent establishment in Finland. The Court of Justice agreed with the Advocate General. While foreign permanent establishments and domestic permanent establishments were generally not in a comparable situation with regard to measures aimed at preventing double taxation, nevertheless, in relation to the prevention of the double deduction of losses, foreign permanent establishments that incurred final losses had to be considered to be comparable to domestic permanent establishments.[304]

Although the Court of Justice found that the restriction could be justified by the need to ensure a balanced allocation of taxing rights between the Member States, by the need to preserve the coherence of the Danish tax system and by the need to avoid the double use of losses, nevertheless, the rule was disproportional to the extent that the foreign permanent establishment had incurred final losses.[305] Relying on the Marks & Spencer case, the Court of Justice held that the burden of proof was on the taxpayer to provide evidence that the losses should be considered as final. The criterion of final losses was met only if it was established that the foreign permanent establishment no longer had income in its Member State of residence.[306] 'So long as that subsidiary continues to be in receipt of even minimal income, there is a possibility that the losses sustained may yet be offset by future profits made in the Member State in which it is resident.'[307]

It is interesting to note that the Court of Justice accepted a justification based on the preservation of the coherence of a Member State's tax system in situations where the general ability of a resident company to set off losses of its resident permanent

---

[303] Case C-650/16 A/S Bevola and Jens W Trock ApS v. Skatteministeriet, ECLI:EU:C:2018:424.
[304] Ibid, paras 37–8.
[305] Ibid, para 59.
[306] Ibid, para 64.
[307] Ibid.

establishment was correlated to the inclusion in its taxable results of any profits made by that permanent establishment.[308] This went beyond the interpretation of this justification given in the Krankenheim case, where the Court of Justice had strictly linked the reintegration of losses at the level of the German head office to the fact that they had previously been taken into account.

In the NN A/S case,[309] a Danish resident company (NN A/S) had a subsidiary in Sweden that was the head office of a permanent establishment in Denmark. In 2008, NN A/S sought to offset the tax losses of the Danish permanent establishment against its profits. The tax authorities rejected the request arguing that losses incurred by the Danish permanent establishment of a non-resident company could only be offset against the profits of a Danish tax group to the extent that these losses could not be used in the jurisdiction of the permanent establishment's head office. On the contrary, in a purely domestic situation, the possibility to offset the losses of a permanent establishment against the group's profits was not subject to any conditions. NN A/S appealed the decision, arguing that based on the Philips Electronics case, this difference in treatment constituted a restriction to the freedom of establishment that could not be justified. The case was referred to the Court of Justice.

Advocate General Campos found that Danish permanent establishments were comparable to Danish companies for the purposes of the fiscal unit regime.[310] As such, the different treatment under Danish legislation restricted the freedom of establishment. However, the restriction could be justified on the basis of prevention of double deduction of losses. Referring to the efforts made by the EU to prevent base erosion and profit shifting and the adoption of anti-hybrid rules in the Anti-Tax Avoidance Directive, the Advocate General concluded that the objective to prevent the double deduction of losses should be considered as appropriate justification, independent from the prevention of tax fraud. Whether or not the restriction went beyond what was necessary to attain the objective pursued was for the national court to assess.

The Court of Justice reached the same conclusion but with different reasoning, as far as justifications were concerned. As regards the allocation of taxing powers, the Court of Justice noted that the fact that the losses could be used both in Denmark and Sweden did not favour either of the two Member States to the detriment of the other. Therefore, the balanced distribution of powers of taxation between these two Member States would not be affected.[311]

The Court of Justice then assessed whether the restriction might be justified by the prevention of double deduction of losses. Referring to previous case law, the right of Member States to prevent the risk of losses being taken into account twice was

---

[308] See paras 46–7.
[309] Case C-28/17 NN A/S v. Skatteministeriet, ECLI:EU:C:2018:526.
[310] Case C-28/17 NN A/S v. Skatteministeriet, ECLI:EU:C:2018:86.
[311] Case C-28/17 NN A/S, case, para 40 (Court of Justice).

confirmed.³¹² However, this could not simply be inferred from the fact that two Member States concurrently exercised their power of taxation over the profits of the same permanent establishment. Consideration had to be given to the provisions of the underlying tax treaty between Denmark and Sweden. In fact, here, the arrangement was regulated by the Nordic Convention.³¹³

The Court of Justice found that under Article 25 of the Nordic Convention, the double taxation of a permanent establishment's profits was prevented by the tax credit mechanism. Therefore, the possibility to deduct the losses of such a permanent establishment twice would amount to an unjustified advantage for cross-border situations over purely domestic situations. The Danish legislation specifically intended to prevent the group concerned from exploiting the same loss twice. Therefore, the restriction was justified on the basis of the prevention of double deduction of losses.³¹⁴

As regards proportionality, the Court of Justice considered whether the Danish rules deprived the taxpayer of any possibility to offset the losses incurred by the Danish permanent establishment. This would be the case, for instance, where it was impossible to use the losses in the state of residence of the subsidiary (i.e. Sweden).³¹⁵ The principle of proportionality would be respected, if the Danish legislation allowed the losses of a Danish permanent establishment to be offset in Denmark, as far as the group could show evidence that such loss could not effectively be deducted in another Member State. In the case at hand, the Court of Justice left it to the referring court to assess whether the losses incurred by the Danish permanent establishment could be offset in Sweden.³¹⁶

The Court of Justice concluded that the Danish legislation restricted the freedom of establishment. However, such restriction could be justified by the prevention of the double deduction of losses in cases where there was a tax treaty between Denmark and the relevant Member State where the subsidiary was situated that effectively mitigated the risk of double taxation of the permanent establishment's profits.

Interestingly, although this case is very similar to the Philips Electronics case, the Court of Justice reached a different conclusion. As discussed above, in the Philips Electronics case, the Court of Justice rejected a justification based on the prevention of the double use of losses, stating that the fact that the losses could be used both in the UK and the Netherlands did not affect the UK's power to tax. In contrast, in this case, the Court of Justice relied on domestic law and its interaction with the Swedish

---

[312] Ibid, para 41.
[313] Ibid, paras 44–5.
[314] Ibid, paras 47–8.
[315] As explained in para 53, the loss was the result of the merger of two Danish branches in the group and the choice made by the group – as permitted by Swedish law – that the merger should be treated for tax purposes as a restructuring of activities, and, as such, not be subject to tax in Sweden. Consequently, it was impossible, in practice, to set those losses off against the Swedish subsidiary's profits.
[316] Ibid, paras 55–6.

tax system (under the Nordic Convention) in finding that the existence of provisions preventing the double taxation of the permanent establishment's profits, could justify the restriction on the basis of the prevention of the double use of losses. Arguably, the Court of Justice seems to imply that had there been no mechanism to prevent double taxation of the permanent establishment's profits, then this restriction may not be justified on this ground (i.e. on the basis of preventing the double use of losses). Although this is a shift in the reasoning of the Court of Justice compared to previous case law, it remains to be seen how it will be applied to final losses, which was the scenario referred to it and bounced back to the national court to determine. The Memira and Holmen cases discussed in section 4.2.2 seem to suggest a higher burden of proof as regards final losses. Arguably, the more recent cases discussed in this section suggest greater reliance on the Marks & Spencer's exhaustion of possibilities test for losses relating to foreign permanent establishments, compared to non-resident subsidiaries. Whether this pattern will be reversed, remains to be seen.

The next chapter continues the analysis by examining obstacles arising from the taxation of portfolio investment.

5

Tax Obstacles to Cross-Border Portfolio Investment

The previous chapter examined tax obstacles to direct investment in the context of group relationships and within the same company. This chapter focuses on the taxation of passive income. The taxation of such income is very important, irrespective of whether it arises from portfolio or non-portfolio investment, as it could give rise to both economic and juridical double taxation. It will be shown that, especially in the context of EU law, the amount and type of tax imposed on passive income is not the only relevant consideration. Rather, the availability of reliefs to mitigate or eliminate juridical and economic double taxation is crucial.

5.1 DOUBLE TAXATION RELIEF MECHANISMS

In Chapters 1 and 3 the concepts of juridical and economic double taxation were discussed briefly. It was explained that whilst the OECD Model Tax Convention tries to deal with juridical double taxation, recognising its harmful effects, it does not deal with economic double taxation, as the latter requires fundamental reform of tax systems. In the post-BEPS world, dealing with economic double taxation does not seem to be a priority anyway.

The OECD Model Tax Convention provides guidelines for dealing with juridical double taxation. As far as cross-border dividends, interest and royalties are concerned, there are some ad hoc priority rules. For example, as explained in Chapter 2, the Dividends Article of the OECD Model Tax Convention, Article 10, gives to the home state a prima facie but non-exclusive right to tax with an additional right to the host state, subject to limitations. Interest is treated in a similar way in Article 11. Article 12 gives the home state an exclusive right to tax. However, taxes already levied on dividends, interest or royalties as part of the corporate profits of the distributing company – the underlying taxes – are not taken into account, nor do the methods for relieving double taxation under Article 23A and 23B cover such taxes. Whilst these provisions give relief for withholding taxes thus mitigating, to a great extent but not completely eliminating, juridical double taxation, there is no relief for the underlying taxes. Therefore, these provisions do not prevent recurrent taxation on the profits distributed to the parent company at the level of the subsidiary and at the level of the parent company.

However, economic double taxation is just as problematic as juridical double taxation, because, inter alia, it distorts the form of the investment (i.e. whether the business is conducted through corporate or non-corporate vehicles), the choice between debt or equity (the former being deductible, the latter not), the timing and character of profit distributions and so on.[1] States, in their capacity as either host states or home states, frequently adopt relief mechanisms either at corporate level or at shareholder level, independently of the OECD Model Tax Convention.

At corporate level, dividends can be deducted as business expenses, thus also reducing the bias towards debt financing.[2] Alternatively, there can be two different tax rates for retained profits and distributed profits, the latter being taxed at a lower rate.[3] At shareholder level, dividends may be excluded from the personal income tax base of the shareholder[4] or they may be taxed at a lower rate. Shareholders may also be granted a dividend tax credit for the corporate tax suffered on the dividends, which can be used to reduce the personal income tax base. Pursuant to this relief mechanism, the tax credit may be full or partial. Dividend relief is usually found in imputation systems.[5]

One crucial restrictive factor of shareholder-level relief mechanisms is that they are usually limited to resident shareholders in resident companies. The relief is rarely extended to foreign shareholders and there is nothing to prevent this under the non-discrimination principle of the OECD Model Tax Convention. Article 24(5) forbids a contracting state to give less favourable treatment to an enterprise, the capital of which is owned or controlled, wholly or partly, directly or indirectly, by one or more residents of the other contracting state.[6] However, this provision relates to the taxation *only* of enterprises and does not extend to their shareholders. As stated in the Commentary, withholding tax obligations that are imposed on a resident company with respect to dividends paid to non-resident shareholders but not with respect to dividends paid to resident shareholders is not in breach of Article 24(5).[7]

The situation could not be more dissimilar under EU law, where the host state exclusion of non-residents from the benefit of certain reliefs to mitigate economic double taxation given to resident shareholders is often found incompatible with EU

[1] See Walter Hellerstein, Georg W. Kofler and Ruth Mason 'Constitutional restraints on corporate 62(1) tax integration' (2008) *Tax Law Review*, 1–66, 6.
[2] This is often called the dividend deduction method.
[3] This is called the split-rate system. Also see discussion in Chapter 1.
[4] This is called dividend exemption or dividend exclusion.
[5] In some of the case law of the Court of Justice, the terms 'credit' and 'imputation' appear to be used interchangeably. See, for example, Joined Cases C-436/08 and C-437/08 Haribo Lakritzen Hans Riegel BetriebsgmbH & Österreichische Salinen AG v. Finanzamt Linz, discussed in 5.2.2.
[6] OECD Commentary to Art 24, para 76.
[7] Ibid, para 78.

law. Similarly, the home state exclusion of reliefs on foreign-sourced income may also be incompatible with EU law. The salient question is twofold: how should the host state treat foreign shareholders, and how should the home state treat domestic shareholders as regards corporate taxes paid abroad? Whilst host states and home states were never required under customary international tax law to extend shareholder credits to either inbound or outbound dividends, they have been forced to do so in many cases examined in this chapter.

In addition, a number of issues arise as far as relief mechanisms for *juridical* double taxation are concerned. A home state may provide foreign tax relief for host state taxation either unilaterally or through tax treaties. The most common methods are exemption and credit,[8] which are also enshrined in Articles 23A and 23B of the OECD Model Tax Convention, as a means of alleviating juridical double taxation only. Under the exemption method, the home state does not tax host state income. Under the credit mechanism, income is taxed in both states but the home state, unilaterally or through tax treaties, grants a credit for the host state taxes against its own.[9] The home state may allow a full credit[10] or an ordinary credit.[11]

As far as passive income is concerned, these methods exempt or give credit for the tax levied on the income itself – usually a withholding tax. There is no provision for the underlying foreign taxes relating to the passive income, that is for the taxes paid by the distributing company on the profits out of which the dividends were paid, leading to economic double taxation. This may not be much of a problem for interest and royalties as these tend to be deductible at (host state) corporate level anyway. As dividends are not usually deductible, corporate taxes levied on that income remain unrelieved in the home state if no credit is given for such taxes, leading to cascading taxes and economic double taxation. As far as non-portfolio dividends are concerned, some states grant an indirect tax credit for the underlying foreign taxes, but there is no provision for such credit under the OECD Model Tax Convention.

One question arising is whether the credit and the exemption methods yield the same result for EU tax law purposes. In other words, if a home state exempts domestic dividends but gives a credit for foreign tax on inbound dividends, does it

---

[8] See also 1.1. In addition, there is the deduction method mentioned above, according to which the foreign taxable income is deducted as an expense. This is a method of partial relief and does not fully remove the burden of double taxation. It is not considered further in this book. See generally Gauthier Blanluet and Philippe Durand, 'General Report', *Key Practical Issues to Eliminate Double Taxation of Business Income*, Cahiers de droit fiscal international, Vol 96b (Kluwer Law International, 2011).

[9] See Art 23B of the OECD Model Tax Convention and Commentary, paras 15–16.

[10] That is a deduction of the total amount of foreign taxes paid on all the income tax due. This may lead to excess foreign tax credits or a refund if the foreign taxes paid are more than the home state taxes. See, for example, Commentary on Arts 23A and 23B, para 16. See Blanluet and Durand, 'General Report', p 20.

[11] Here the home state may allow an ordinary credit, in that deduction is restricted to that part of its own tax that is attributable to the foreign source income with no refund if the foreign tax paid exceeds the domestic charge.

treat the two types of dividends in the same way? Much would depend on whether the conferral of the tax credit is subject to limitations under national law. The tax credit is usually provided for foreign income taxes of a similar nature,[12] or even for foreign taxes from a specific country or region. There could be a limitation as to the member of the group against the profits of which the credit can be set off. The home state may also require information to be disclosed, or prescribe a time at which the foreign tax becomes eligible for credit and so on. These limitations can be especially problematic in cases where there are excess foreign credits, that is where host state taxation exceeds home state taxation. The equivalence of the credit and the exemption mechanisms for relief is an issue that the Court of Justice has examined in a number of cases, as shown in this chapter.

The allocation of deductions/expenses is also relevant to the tax credit mechanism.[13] As foreign tax credit limitations tend to be computed on a net basis, expenses are taken into account anyway.[14] The allocation of deductions/expenses to domestic income increases the foreign tax credit limitation (as there is more taxable foreign income) and allocation of deductions/expenses to foreign income reduces the limitation (as there is less taxable foreign income).[15] Therefore, in a credit system an over-allocation of expenses to foreign sources reduces the foreign tax credit limitation.[16] The OECD Model Tax Convention and Commentary are silent on this issue and contain no guidance on how expenses should be allocated between domestic and foreign income.

As the misallocation of expenses reduces the allowable foreign tax credit, this creates a disincentive to invest in another Member State, which could fall foul of the EU's fundamental freedoms. Matters are more complicated in the context of group companies making intra-group distributions, as the allocation of expenses could be even more difficult to delineate if an attempt is made to allocate part of the underlying expenses (e.g. the parent company's expenses attributable to the holding).[17] This chapter reviews several cases where some of these issues arose (e.g. the taxation of outbound dividends on a gross basis rather than a net basis,

[12] There could be an item-by-item limitation or a type of income limitation, in which case the home state may be restrictive as to the type of domestic income against which the foreign tax can be set off. For example, foreign tax credits may only be set off against domestic corporate income tax, even though the home state may impose substantial additional taxes such as trade tax. See Blanluet and Durand, 'General Report', p 41. In addition, the nature of the foreign levy may be examined – that is, whether the levy is compulsory or optional, discretionary as to rate, whether it is imposed on a gross or net basis, whether the foreign country allows a similar credit, etc.
[13] Expense allocation was examined by the EFTA Court in the context of permanent establishments. See Case E-7/07 Seabrokers v. Norway [2008] EFTA Court Report 171, analysed in Chapter 4.
[14] Blanluet and Durand, 'General Report', p 27.
[15] Ibid.
[16] In the context of exemption states, there is an incentive for companies to allocate the expenses to the domestic taxable profits as foreign profits are exempt. Home states tend to impose restrictions on this practice. See also analysis in 5.3.5.
[17] See Peter Wattel, 'Taxation of Intercompany Dividends and EU Law: Three Surprising Aspects of the Recent Case Law of the European Court', in Guglielmo Maisto (ed), *Taxation of Intercompany*

restrictions on deductibility of expenses relating to outbound or inbound dividends or interest payments).

In general, the approach of the OECD Model Tax Convention and Commentary on home state or host state relief mechanisms is rather limited. Whilst the focus of the OECD Model Tax Convention is on juridical double taxation, even for that the solutions offered are not satisfactory, nor sufficient to eliminate it. There is no attempt to deal with economic double taxation and the international tax community defers to countries' choices of dealing with it. In a cross-border context, limitations of home state or host state mechanisms for relieving juridical or economic double taxation may have implications under EU law. However, as will be shown in this chapter, the Court of Justice has not taken a very consistent approach in dealing with juridical and economic double taxation, displaying an unwillingness to deal with the former but not the latter. It is questioned whether the Court's jurisprudence on the taxation of passive income and mainly dividends is defendable, or whether it still 'fails to hold together substantively, functionally, and rhetorically', as has been argued in the past.[18]

The remainder of this chapter focuses on the taxation of *portfolio* investment in the EU, from a home state and a host state perspective. The principles of the Court's case law may, however, also be relevant in cases of non-portfolio investment, when the requirements of the Parent-Subsidiary and Interest and Royalties Directives are not satisfied.[19]

5.2 THE TAXATION OF INBOUND DIVIDENDS

With the exception of the Parent-Subsidiary Directive, which applies to profit distributions related to non-portfolio holdings, dividend taxation is governed by national laws and tax treaties. However, as with all areas in which the Member States have retained legislative competence, this competence still has to be exercised consistently with EU law. The principles that apply as regards the taxation of inbound and outbound dividends are quite similar but not identical.

As far as non-portfolio shareholdings are concerned, under specific circumstances examined in Chapter 2, profit distributions are not to be taxed either at home state or at host state level, to the extent that they have already been taxed at corporate level (i.e. before being distributed). Therefore, the Parent-Subsidiary Directive seeks to eliminate economic double taxation under certain circumstances. It prevents the Member State in which a subsidiary company is resident from imposing a withholding tax on profits distributed to its parent company. Furthermore, the Directive prevents the Member

---

Dividends under Tax Treaties and EU Law, EC and International Tax Law Series, Vol 8 (Amsterdam: IBFD, 2012), p 48.

[18] See Michael J. Graetz and Alvin Warren, 'Dividend taxation in Europe: when the ECJ makes tax policy' (2007) 44(6) *Common Market Law Review*, 1, 577–623, 1, 622.

[19] See Chapter 2.

State in which the parent company is resident from taxing such distributed profits. If the Member State of the parent company *does* tax such profits, then it has to allow the parent company to deduct from the amount of tax due that fraction of the corporation tax paid by the subsidiary that relates to those profits. Clearly, the Directive allows Member States to choose whether they will exempt distributed profits or tax them but give credit for the underlying tax. The same provisions apply as regards permanent establishments receiving the distributed profits. Member States have the option to provide that any charges relating to the holding and losses resulting from the distribution of the profits of the subsidiary may not be deducted from the taxable profits of the parent company,[20] as such costs relate to exempt income.

As for portfolio dividends and profit distributions not falling under the scope of the Parent-Subsidiary Directive, the fundamental freedoms are relevant. It ought to be remembered that, even in situations falling under the scope of a Directive, compatibility with fundamental freedoms is also required. Furthermore, the Court of Justice does not tend to distinguish in its judgments between portfolio and non-portfolio holdings.

For inbound dividends the general principle is that shareholders (corporate or non-corporate) receiving foreign-sourced dividends should be treated the same way as shareholders receiving domestic dividends if they are in an objectively comparable situation, unless different treatment is justified. If the country of residence of the shareholder (the home state) chooses to provide reliefs for domestic dividends, then it must provide the same reliefs at least for EU-sourced dividends.[21] However, not all types of reliefs have to be extended in that way – only reliefs for economic double taxation. The seminal cases on this point are Verkooijen,[22] Lenz[23] and Manninen.[24] Although these cases dealt with individuals, the same principles were subsequently applied in a corporate context.

5.2.1 *The Early Cases: Individual Shareholders*

In Verkooijen, a Dutch national who was resident in the Netherlands, Mr Verkooijen, acquired shares through stock options in a Belgian company. The dividends received from the Belgian company were subject to home state taxation in the hands of Mr Verkooijen. Had the dividends been received from a resident company, they would have been exempt from tax up to a certain amount, to reflect the fact that the distributing company had already paid corporation tax in the Netherlands.

---

[20] Parent-Subsidiary Directive, Art 4(2).
[21] Non-EU-sourced dividends may not warrant the same treatment. See below.
[22] Case C-35/98 Staatssecretaris van Financiën v. BGM Verkooijen [2000] ECR I-4071.
[23] Case C-315/02 Anneliese Lenz v. Finanzlandesdirektion für Tirol [2004] ECR I-7063.
[24] Case C-319/02 Petri Manninen [2004] ECR I-7477.

5.2 The Taxation of Inbound Dividends

The Court of Justice found that the Dutch legislation restricted the free movement of capital, as it dissuaded Dutch nationals from investing in companies that had their seat in another Member State.[25] In addition, for companies having their seat in another Member State, the Dutch legislation constituted an obstacle to the raising of capital in the Netherlands. The dividends paid to Dutch residents by such non-resident companies received less favourable tax treatment than domestic dividends, making an investment in such companies less attractive.[26] The restriction was not justified. The Court of Justice reiterated the point that unfavourable tax treatment contrary to a fundamental freedom could not be justified by the existence of other tax advantages in the other state.[27] This is an example of a case where the per-country approach, discussed in 3.3.4, was followed.

In Lenz[28] the Court of Justice followed the same approach. Under Austrian tax laws Austrian residents receiving dividends from Austrian companies benefited from a more favourable tax treatment on those dividends[29] than if they had received the dividends from a non-resident company. This was incompatible with the free movement of capital.

In Manninen[30] a Finnish imputation tax credit was only given to domestic dividends. By contrast to the Lenz case, here the Finnish tax legislation had a mechanism that tried to ensure that the imputation credit reflected the amount of corporation tax actually payable by the Finnish company. If the tax paid by a Finnish company by way of corporation tax turned out to be less than 29/71ths of the amount of dividends that it had decided to distribute during the tax year in question, then the difference was charged to that company by means of an additional tax. Nevertheless, this fact could not exonerate the Finnish tax legislation.[31] There was an infringement of the free movement of capital.

It has been argued that this decision is slightly different from Lenz and Verkooijen, in that it does not really follow the per-country approach. In Manninen the obligation to extend the imputation credit depended on whether the host state relieved economic double taxation. If it did, then the credit would not be extended.[32] Arguably, in none of these cases did the Court of Justice really consider corporate and shareholder taxes separately. The different treatment resulted from the combination of these taxes. A shareholder who was refused an imputation credit would not be treated in a less advantageous way if the credit was in fact not needed, that is if the distributed profits received had not been subject to

---

[25] Case C-35/98 Verkooijen, para 34.
[26] Ibid, para 35.
[27] Ibid, para 61.
[28] Case C-315/02 Lenz.
[29] Fixed rate of 25 per cent or 'half rate'.
[30] Case C-319/02 Manninen.
[31] Ibid, paras 54-5.
[32] See Graetz and Warren, 'Dividend taxation in Europe', 1, 589. They argue that this is an important departure from the Court's previous refusal to consider corporate and shareholder taxes together.

taxation at host state level or if relief was given there. Arguably, the per-country approach still applies to the extent that *other* host state benefits are ignored – benefits not related to the host state tax which can be neutralised by the imputation credit. If no underlying tax was levied on those profits, it would be difficult for the shareholder to demand an imputation credit from the home state. In Manninen the Court of Justice simply recognised the relevance of the tax treatment of the underlying corporate profits in the host state to the appropriate tax treatment of the dividends in the home state.

What ought to be noted is that in these cases the country of residence of the shareholders receiving domestic dividends had, in essence, chosen to *give* relief to the shareholders for the economic double taxation suffered on those dividends. If *no* such relief from economic double taxation had in fact been given for domestic dividends, then resident shareholders could not have demanded such relief for inbound dividends. The Kerckhaert–Morres[33] and Damseaux[34] cases illustrate this point well and are examined in 5.2.3.

5.2.2 *Later Cases: Corporate Shareholders*

The FII Group Litigation case[35] was the first important case to deal with corporate shareholders receiving foreign-sourced dividends. In this case the UK, inter alia, applied a different tax treatment according to whether a UK-resident company received dividends from a resident company or a non-resident company. Domestic dividends were *exempt* from taxation in the hands of the UK (corporate) recipient. By contrast, foreign-sourced dividends were subject to UK corporation tax (a home state tax), but a *credit* was granted for any withholding tax levied by the host state. Credit was also given for any underlying tax paid by the company distributing the dividend, if the recipient company held a 10 per cent shareholding in it.

On this point[36] the Court of Justice found that the UK's exemption/credit system did not contravene the EC Treaty (ex-Articles 43 and 56 EC), so long as it provided the same treatment for domestic and foreign-sourced dividends. Whilst the Member State retained the power to organise its system for taxing distributed profits,[37] the Court of Justice considered that equal treatment of domestic and foreign-sourced dividends would be achieved:

> provided that the tax rate applied to foreign-sourced dividends is not higher than the rate applied to nationally-sourced dividends and that the tax credit is at least equal to

---

[33] Case C-513/04 Mark Kerckhaert and Bernadette Morres v. Belgian State [2006] ECR I-10967.
[34] Case C-128/08 Jacques Damseaux v. Etat Belgique [2009] ECR I-6823.
[35] Case C-446/04 Test Claimants in the FII Group Litigation v. Commissioners of Inland Revenue [2006] ECR I-11753, para 46.
[36] Many issues were referred to the Court of Justice. Only the ones relevant to the discussion in this chapter are mentioned.
[37] Ibid, para 47.

the amount paid in the Member State of the company making the distribution (i.e. the underlying corporate income tax), up to the limit of the tax charged in the Member State of the company receiving the dividends.[38]

This was ultimately a question for the national court.[39] In applying this principle, the Court of Justice found that to the extent that the UK dividend taxation rules did not give any credit for the underlying tax in respect of EU-sourced dividends where the holding was less than 10 per cent, but did so when the holding was at least 10 per cent, this was against the free movement of capital. A credit for the underlying tax had to be available even if the holding was less than 10 per cent.[40] The fact that the underlying tax was a foreign (host state) tax and the UK, as the home state, was asked to give relief for it was not a relevant consideration.

This was an important judgment in this area, which consolidated the principles of earlier case law and extended them to corporate shareholders receiving foreign-sourced dividends, despite some interpretative uncertainties on peripheral points.[41] The principles from this case were later on applied to more complex settings, such as the one in the Orange European Smallcap Fund case.[42]

Here the Dutch referring court questioned whether home state restrictions on the granting of relief to Dutch investment funds for (foreign) withholding tax on inbound dividends were compatible with the free movement of capital. In this case the profits of a resident investment fund were subject to 0 per cent corporate income tax. Distributed profits were to be taxed in the hands of the shareholders. If the fund received dividends from resident companies, then it was entitled to a full refund of the Dutch withholding tax levied on those dividends. As the fund was taxed at 0 per cent, the tax deducted at source from the dividends received by the fund had to be refunded to the fund.

The aim of the legislation was to neutralise the tax burden on investments through a fund so that the tax treatment would be the same as with income from direct investment. If the fund received dividends from non-resident companies, then relief was also given for the foreign withholding tax. However, this relief was subject to two important limitations. Firstly, the relief was limited to the amount a resident individual would be entitled to under the relevant tax treaty had the investment been direct. Secondly, the relief was to be granted only to the extent that the shareholders of the fund were Dutch residents. If the shareholders were non-residents, then this relief was reduced proportionately to the Dutch resident participation.

---

[38] Ibid, para 57.
[39] Ibid, para 56.
[40] Ibid, see analysis of question 1, paras 33–74.
[41] Upon returning to the UK's High Court, the latter made a further reference to the Court of Justice for a preliminary ruling to clarify references to tax rates and different levels of taxation made in the original case. See Case C-35/11 Test Claimants in the FII Group Litigation, ECLI:EU:C:2012:707, discussed further down.
[42] Case C-194/06 Staatssecretaris van Financiën v. Orange European Smallcap Fund NV [2008] ECR I-374.

In this case the Orange European Smallcap Fund (OESF) received dividends from companies in a number of countries, including Portugal and Germany. At the relevant time there was no tax treaty between the Netherlands and Portugal and the treaty with Germany did not provide for a credit. In addition, some of shareholders of the OESF were resident in other Member States and third countries. The relief for foreign withholding tax on these dividends was restricted and reduced proportionately.

The Court of Justice found only the first rule to be compatible with the free movement of capital. The legislation did not impose any corporation tax on the fund, regardless of whether it received dividends from Germany, Portugal or the Netherlands. Therefore, dividends received from Portugal and Germany were treated the same way as dividends received from Dutch companies. By refraining from taxing dividends from other Member States, the Netherlands avoided the imposition of a series of charges to tax arising from the exercise of its own fiscal powers, just as it did in respect of dividends paid by resident companies.[43]

The Court of Justice also disagreed with the Commission's contention that the Netherlands, in its capacity as the Member State of residence of the recipient of the dividends, had to offset the foreign tax burden on those dividends in the same way as it did for Dutch dividends.[44] The situations were not comparable. The greater burden imposed on Portuguese and German dividends received by the fund did not arise as a result of a difference in treatment attributable to the tax regime in the Netherlands. Rather it stemmed from the decision of Germany and Portugal to make a deduction at source from those dividends, and from the decision of the Netherlands not to tax those dividends.[45]

The fact that in some tax treaties the Netherlands had to extend this concession (i.e. the refund of the foreign withholding tax) but in others it did not, or that in some cases there was no tax treaty, did not alter this conclusion. This was because the aim of the legislation was to equalise, as much as possible, the tax treatment of investment through a fund and investment directly by a natural person. Therefore, if the tax treaty concession was not extended to situations where the investment was through a fund, then 'the decision to invest through the intermediary ... runs the risk of being less advantageous to a shareholder who is a natural person than direct investment'.[46] By contrast, if the concession was refused in cases where there was no underlying tax treaty conferring this benefit, then 'the decision, by a natural person, to invest through the intermediary of such an enterprise does not involve the risk of losing a benefit which he could have enjoyed if he had chosen to invest directly in those Member States'.[47] Therefore, the situations were not objectively comparable.

---

[43] Ibid, para 35.
[44] Ibid, para 38.
[45] Ibid, para 42.
[46] Ibid, para 62.
[47] Ibid, para 63.

As for the second limitation, the Court of Justice agreed with the Advocate General that this was incompatible with free movement of capital. The limitation on the concession meant that the profit to be distributed to the shareholders of the fund in proportion to their interest was also reduced. Therefore, this reduction of the concession for foreign tax adversely affected all the shareholders of the fund, since it had the effect of reducing the total amount of profit for distribution.[48] Consequently, under the Dutch regime it was of greater benefit for a fund to attract resident shareholders, 'since the smaller the interest in that enterprise of shareholders who are resident or established in other Member States, the greater will be the profit available for distribution to shareholders'.[49] The effect of this was that non-residents were deterred from investing in Dutch funds. Dutch funds were also restricted from raising capital abroad.

The Netherlands taxed dividends distributed by the fund to resident *and* non-resident shareholders. Therefore, a fund whose shareholders were partly resident and partly non-resident shareholders was in a comparable situation to a fund whose shareholders were all resident. As soon as the Netherlands had decided to grant to funds a concession for tax deducted abroad and to exercise its fiscal sovereignty over all dividends distributed by such funds to their shareholders, resident and non-resident, it had to extend that benefit to funds whose shareholders included non-residents.[50] There was a restriction on the free movement of capital which was not justified. The fact that *some* fund shareholders were third-country residents was not a relevant justification since all shareholders were affected by the restrictive relief. This was because the (proportionately) reduced relief of foreign dividend withholding tax depleted the fund's profit distributions for *all* shareholders, not just third-country shareholders.[51] Arguably, the Court of Justice may have reached a different conclusion if *all* the shareholders of the fund were third-country resident or resident in a state that did not have a tax treaty with the Netherlands.

Overall, the case law of the Court of Justice up to this point in time suggests the following: if the home state chooses to relieve economic double taxation on domestic dividends, then it must provide the same relief for foreign-sourced dividends, even if this means giving relief for foreign underlying taxes. Non-EU-sourced dividends may not merit the same treatment, but this has to be specifically proved in each case. The principles derived from this case law were followed in a number of subsequent cases.[52] Later cases also dealt with the compatibility of different methods for relieving double taxation as well as with the administrative burdens imposed.

---

[48] Ibid, paras 71–2.
[49] Ibid, para 73.
[50] Ibid, paras 78–9.
[51] Ibid, para 136.
[52] See, for example, Case C-101/05 Skatteverket v. A [2007] ECR I-11531; Case C-201/05 The Test Claimants in the CFC and Dividend Group Litigation v. Commissioners of Inland Revenue [2008] ECR I-02875; Case C-406/07 Commission v. Greece [2009] ECR I-62.

In the Haribo and Salinen cases,[53] under Austrian law domestic dividends were exempt regardless of the size of the holding, whereas inbound dividends were exempt if the holding was at least 10 per cent. For EU/EEA portfolio dividends (i.e. below 10 per cent), the shareholder had to fulfil certain formal conditions for the exemption method to apply. In practice, the conditions for the application of the exemption method (mainly information on the underlying corporate income tax paid by the distributing company) could not or could hardly be fulfilled by the shareholder. In that case there was a switch from the exemption method to the credit method, but again the conditions for the application of the credit method either could not be fulfilled by the shareholder or could only be fulfilled with difficulty. For portfolio dividends paid by EEA companies there was an additional condition that there must be comprehensive arrangements for mutual assistance and cooperation. There were no provisions for relieving economic double taxation on dividends paid from third countries.

In Haribo the referring court questioned the compatibility of the above provisions with the free movement of capital. In Salinen the issue was whether a tax credit for portfolio income could ever alleviate double taxation when the parent company receiving the tax credit was loss-making. As Austria did not allow tax credits to be carried forward, the credit method would only serve to reduce the losses in the year of receipt of the dividend income. Therefore, no credit could be granted for the underlying corporate income tax and the withholding tax. Following a preliminary reference, the Court of Justice was called to determine whether these rules were compatible with the free movement of capital.

The Court of Justice found that Austria was not in breach of the free movement of capital for switching from the exemption method to the credit method under certain circumstances.[54] To the extent that the mechanism for preventing or mitigating distributed profits from being liable to a series of charges to tax led to equivalent results, there was no incompatibility.[55] However, the administrative burdens imposed on the recipient company in order to qualify for such a credit could not be excessive. The fact that the national tax authority demanded information from the recipient company relating to the tax that had actually been charged on the profits of the distributing company was an intrinsic part of the operation of the credit method and did not affect the equivalence between the exemption and credit methods.[56] This suggests that the credit method may be compatible with the fundamental freedoms, even if it is very difficult for a taxpayer to determine the amount of the underlying corporate income tax paid on the distributed dividends. The burden of proof remains with the taxpayer. As a result,

---

[53] Joined Cases C-436/08 and C-437/08 Haribo & Salinen.
[54] Ibid, para 141.
[55] Ibid, para 143.
[56] Ibid, para 147. The Court of Justice used the term 'imputation method' rather than 'credit method', treating them as synonymous.

economic double taxation is not always removed. As shown further down, the position as regards information requirements was watered down in subsequent case law.

The Court of Justice found that the Austrian legislation restricted the free movement of capital but was justified by overriding reasons in the public interest that were connected with the effectiveness of fiscal supervision and combating tax evasion.[57] As far as proportionality was concerned, whilst it was permissible for a Member State to make an exemption for dividends from an EEA state conditional on the existence of mutual assistance between the two states, only such mutual assistance requirement was necessary. Requiring an agreement for mutual assistance not only at the administrative level, but also with regard to enforcement was disproportional,[58] since Austria was to collect the tax from resident shareholders.

Furthermore, in answering the questions in Salinen, the Court of Justice held that, in the application of the credit method, the unavailability of carry-forward of the credit for the tax paid abroad was incompatible with Article 63 TFEU.[59] By contrast, a Member State was not required to give a credit for withholding tax paid on dividends in another Member State or in a non-Member State in order to prevent *juridical* double taxation. This was the result of two Member States choosing 'to exercise their fiscal competence and to subject those dividends to taxation in the hands of the shareholder'.[60] The disadvantages that may arise from the parallel exercise of the powers of taxation by different Member States, in so far as such an exercise was not discriminatory, did not constitute a restriction to the free movement of capital.[61]

To an extent, this judgment may erode the power of Member States as home states not to allow a full credit. Whilst the Court of Justice in Salinen did not require a refund for the foreign tax credit that could not be used in that year, arguably by requiring the carry-forward of the tax credit, Austria was effectively asked to confer more than an ordinary credit.

There have been two further references to the Court of Justice dealing with similar issues. In Accor[62] the Court of Justice was asked to deal with the pre-2005 French system of dividend taxation. Under this system, all dividends received by a French parent company from subsidiaries, resident and non-resident, were exempt from tax. If the parent company redistributed those dividends to its shareholders, it

---

[57] Ibid, para 69.
[58] Ibid, paras 71–3, 75.
[59] Under the Austrian imputation system, dividends distributed by non-resident companies were included in the tax base of the company receiving them, thereby reducing the amount of that loss by the amount of the dividends received when a loss was recorded for the tax year in question. The amount of the loss that could be carried forward to subsequent tax years was thus also reduced to the same extent. By contrast, dividends from resident companies, which were exempt, did not affect the tax base of the company receiving the dividends or any losses that it may be able to carry forward. Ibid, para 157.
[60] Ibid, para 168.
[61] Ibid, paras 169, 173.
[62] Case C-310/09 Ministre du budget, des comptes publics et de la fonction publique v. Accor [2011] ECR I-08115.

had to pay advance corporation tax. A tax credit was given for advance payments relating to redistributed profits originating from French subsidiaries. This tax credit could be set off against the advance payment due, which effectively cancelled it out. No credit was given if the redistributed profits originated from non-resident subsidiaries.

The Court of Justice agreed with the opinion of its Advocate General and found the legislation to be contrary to the freedom of establishment and the free movement of capital.[63] The principles of equivalence and effectiveness did not preclude the reimbursement of the advance payments from being subject to the condition that the parent company furnishes evidence relating to the tax rate and the tax actually paid on the profits made by the non-resident subsidiaries. Production of that evidence may, however, be required only if it did not prove virtually impossible or excessively difficult to furnish proof of payment of the tax by the non-resident subsidiaries. It was for the national court to determine whether those conditions were met.[64] This case was subject to further litigation with some interesting results.[65]

In Meilicke II[66] similar issues were addressed. The Court of Justice held that equivalent treatment was required and that the national system had to be transposed, to the fullest extent possible, to cross-border situations.[67] For example, where it was not possible to take account of indirect prior charges to corporation tax at national level, such charges were not to be taken into account as regards dividends paid to residents by non-resident companies.[68] The calculation of the tax credit had to be made in relation to the rate of corporation tax on the distributed profits applicable to the dividend paying company according to the laws of its Member State of establishment (i.e. the host state).[69] However, the amount to be imposed could not exceed

---

[63] Ibid, paras 59 and 67.
[64] Ibid, para 102.
[65] Following this judgment, the French Conseil d'État delivered two decisions in December 2012, which set out the conditions for the reimbursement of advance payments made in breach of EU law. See judgments of 10 December 2012 (Rhodia: FR:CESSR:2012:317074.20121210) and of 10 December 2012 (Accor: FR:CESSR:2012:317075.20121210). Inter alia, the taxation suffered by non-resident sub-subsidiaries was not taken into account and the refunded amounts were limited to one-third of the dividends distributed. The Commission took the view that the interpretation of the Accor decision by the French Conseil d'État was contrary to EU law and referred France to the Court of Justice in 2016. See Case C-416/17 Commission v. France, ECLI:EU:C:2018:811. Indeed, the Court of Justice found the French rules to be in breach of EU law and the evidentiary obligations imposed by the French Supreme Court for a refund to be disproportionate. As also mentioned in 3.1, the Court of Justice also found that France had failed to fulfil its obligations under Art 267 TFEU, because the French Supreme Court did not refer the matter to the Court of Justice, as it should have done.
[66] Case C-262/09 Wienand Meilicke and Others v. Finanzamt Bonn-Innenstadt, ECLI:EU:C:2011:438. This case was a continuation of the first Meilicke case (Case C-292/04 Meilicke and Others [2007] ECR I-1835) where it was held that the imputation credit should be extended to residents receiving foreign-sourced dividends and not just domestic dividends. The national court referred further questions to the Court of Justice regarding the application of this credit.
[67] Ibid, para 31.
[68] Ibid.
[69] Ibid, para 34.

the amount of income tax payable by the shareholder on the dividends in its home state.[70] In other words, this was an ordinary credit.

It was also questioned whether Germany could make the grant of a tax credit subject to submission of a special corporate tax certificate, without any opportunity for the shareholder to show, by means of other factors and relevant information, the tax actually paid.[71] Although the Court of Justice noted that it was 'inherent in the principle of the fiscal autonomy of Member States that they determine what is, according to their own national system, the evidence required in order to benefit from such a tax credit',[72] the exercise of this fiscal autonomy had to be carried out compatibly with EU law and could not be conducted too formalistically.

The provision of documentary evidence by the shareholder enabling the Member State to ascertain, clearly and precisely, whether the conditions for obtaining a tax credit were met without having to make an estimate of that tax credit should suffice, even if this information was not in the form of the corporate tax certificate.[73] Only if the shareholder concerned produced no information could the relevant tax authorities refuse the tax advantage sought.[74] The fact that the Member State had recourse to the mechanism of mutual assistance under Directive 77/799 did not mean that it 'would be required to spare the company receiving dividends the necessity of providing them with proof of the tax paid in another Member State by the company making the distribution'.[75] This Directive enabled Member States to require information, but did not *oblige* them to do so.[76]

This is a very interesting development in the case law. Until then, the existence of the Mutual Assistance Directive (now superseded by the Directive on Administrative Cooperation 2011/16/EU) seemed to be regarded as a panacea by the Court of Justice. Now its judgments are more nuanced and try to balance the duty of taxpayers to provide information with the duty of the Member States to extend reliefs on the provision of such information, with a heavier compliance burden being placed on taxpayers. There is still reliance on mutual assistance on exchange of information and in general exchange of information agreements but in a less prescriptive manner.

Another remarkable development is that the Court of Justice appears to treat the exemption and the credit methods as equivalent. The technical argument is as follows. The credit method enables dividends from non-resident companies to be accorded treatment equivalent to that accorded, by the exemption method, to dividends paid by resident companies.[77] As a corollary, the use of both methods –

---

[70] Ibid.
[71] Ibid, para 40.
[72] Ibid, para 37.
[73] Ibid, para 46.
[74] Ibid, para 47.
[75] Ibid, para 50.
[76] Ibid, paras 50–1.
[77] Joined Cases C-436/08 and C-437/08 Haribo & Salinen, para 89.

one for domestic dividends and the other for inbound dividends – does not lead to discrimination. In other words, the Court of Justice is not really saying that the methods are equivalent *in abstracto*, something that would be very difficult to argue given the long-standing dichotomy also enshrined under the OECD Model Tax Convention.[78] What the Court of Justice *is* saying is that they are equivalent in these types of cases, because the application of the credit method to dividends from non-resident companies makes it possible to ensure that foreign-sourced and nationally-sourced portfolio dividends bear the same tax burden.[79]

Even in situations where host state taxation does not exceed home state taxation, the administrative burden for complying with the credit method – an intrinsic part of its operation as accepted in Haribo & Salinen and subsequent cases – may be very heavy. Although the Court of Justice has stated that administrative burdens imposed on the recipient company in order to qualify for such a credit must not be excessive, later case law suggests that the Court of Justice is reluctant to interfere with Member State evidentiary requirements, especially as regards foreign underlying taxes, unless they are too formalistic.

There is a further dimension to this. The Court of Justice often justifies a finding of equivalence of the two relief mechanisms on the basis that exempting the inbound dividends would give taxpayers who have invested in foreign holdings an advantage compared to those having invested in domestic holdings. Indeed, the credit method neutralises the advantage from investing in another Member State. Is this not, however, a goal of the Internal Market? How is this method of offsetting tax advantages abroad any different from that in, inter alia, Eurowings[80] and Danner,[81] where the Court of Justice emphasised that any tax advantage from low taxation in one state cannot be used by another Member State to justify more onerous tax treatment? It is difficult to make a distinction between these cases.

There was a further referral dealing with the issue of equivalence between the exemption method and the credit method, following the judgment in the original FII Group Litigation case.[82] In the FII Group Litigation II case,[83] the Court of Justice noted that the exemption method and the imputation/credit method were in fact equivalent provided that 'the tax rate applied to foreign-sourced dividends is not higher than the rate applied to nationally-sourced dividends and that the tax credit is at least equal to the amount paid in the State of the company making the distribution, up to the limit of the tax charged in the Member State of the company receiving the dividends.'[84] The equivalence of the exemption and imputation methods would be compromised in the following circumstances.

---

[78] The differences between the two methods were briefly considered in 5.1.
[79] Ibid.
[80] Case C-294/97 Eurowings [1999] ECR I-7447, para 44.
[81] Case C-136/00 Danner [2002] ECR I-8147, para 56.
[82] Case C-446/04 FII Group Litigation.
[83] Case C-35/11 Test Claimants in the FII Group Litigation, ECLI:EU:C:2012:707, para 39.
[84] Ibid, para 39.

If the paying company is subject to a nominal rate of tax below the nominal rate of tax to which the resident recipient company is subject, the exemption of the nationally-sourced dividends from tax in the hands of the latter company would give rise to lower taxation of the distributed profits than if the imputation method applied to foreign-sourced dividends received by the same resident company.[85] In this situation, the application of the exemption method would give rise to taxation of the distributed (nationally-sourced) profits at the lower nominal rate of tax applicable to the company *paying* dividends, while the application of the imputation method to foreign-sourced dividends will give rise to taxation of the distributed profits at the higher nominal rate of tax applicable to the company *receiving* dividends.[86]

If the imputation method takes account of the effective level of taxation of the profits in the Member State of origin, then again it would cease to be equivalent to the exemption method if the profits of the company that pays dividends are subject in the Member State of residence to an effective level of taxation lower than the nominal rate of tax.[87] As a result, the tax exemption of domestic dividends would give rise to *no* tax liability for recipients irrespective of the effective level of taxation to which the profits out of which the dividends had been paid were subject. By contrast, application of the imputation method to foreign-sourced dividends would lead to *additional* tax liability for the recipient if the effective level of taxation to which the profits of the company paying the dividends was subject falls short of the nominal rate of tax to which the profits of the resident company receiving the dividends was subject.[88] The Court of Justice concluded that '[u]nlike the exemption method, the imputation method therefore does not enable the benefit of the corporation tax reductions granted at an earlier stage to the company paying dividends to be passed on to the corporate shareholder.'[89]

In assessing the equivalence of the two methods in this context, the referring court had to take into account both the applicable nominal rates of tax and the effective levels of taxation. The 'tax rates' to which the original judgment (more specifically, paragraph 56) referred related to the nominal rate of tax and the 'different levels of taxation ... by reason of a change to the tax base' related to the effective levels of taxation. The effective level of taxation may be lower than the nominal rate of tax by reason, in particular, of reliefs reducing the tax base.[90]

As regards any difference between the nominal rate of tax and the effective level of taxation to which the resident company paying dividends was subject, the Court of Justice found that the exemption and imputation methods did not immediately

---

[85] Ibid, para 44.
[86] Ibid, para 45.
[87] Ibid, para 46.
[88] Ibid, para 47.
[89] Ibid, para 48.
[90] Ibid, para 49.

cease to be equivalent as soon as exceptional cases existed in which nationally-sourced dividends were exempt, although the profits out of which those dividends were paid had not been subject in their entirety to an effective level of taxation corresponding to the nominal rate of tax. It was left to the referring court to determine whether the difference between the effective level of taxation and the nominal rate of tax was exceptional in nature.[91] In this case, the difference between the two rates was not by way of exception and, therefore, there was a restriction on freedom of establishment and on capital movements.[92]

The restriction could be justified on the basis of ensuring the coherence of the tax system. Here, a direct link existed between, on the one hand, the tax advantage granted (i.e. the tax credit in the case of foreign-sourced dividends and the tax exemption for nationally-sourced dividends), and, on the other hand, the tax to which the distributed profits had already been subject.[93] Very importantly, the Court of Justice found that an imputation system would have been proportionate if, unlike the UK system, a credit given for the foreign corporation tax was set at the UK nominal rate of tax rather than the tax actually paid.[94]

The Court of Justice still refused to demand a full credit. It was acknowledged that in applying the imputation method to foreign-sourced dividends, even on the basis of the nominal rate of tax, this may still lead to less favourable tax treatment compared to domestic dividends, as a result in particular of the existence in the Member States of different rules relating to the determination of the basis of assessment for corporation tax.[95] However, it was stressed that, when unfavourable treatment of that kind arises, 'it results from the exercise in parallel by different Member States of their fiscal sovereignty, which is compatible with the Treaty.'[96]

In a later case, the Kronos case,[97] the Court of Justice followed the same approach of deference towards the home state's method for eliminating double taxation of profits distributed by resident and non-resident subsidiaries. Until 2001, domestic dividends received by a German corporate taxpayer were fully taxable in Germany. A certain amount of corporate tax paid by the subsidiary was credited/refunded at the level of the parent company. By contrast, under certain circumstances such as a participation of at least 10 per cent, foreign dividends were exempt from taxation. As such, a credit/refund of foreign corporate tax was not possible.

Kronos was a holding company of a group of companies, with its statutory seat in the US, but its effective place of management in Germany. Kronos was set up in order to undertake the integrated management of the group's European and Canadian subsidiaries. It held different participations (90–100 per cent) in

---

[91] Ibid, para 50.
[92] Ibid, paras 53 and 54.
[93] Ibid, para 59.
[94] Ibid, paras 61 and 62.
[95] Ibid, para 64.
[96] Ibid.
[97] Case C-47/12 Kronos International Inc v. Finanzamt Leverkusen, ECLI:EU:C:2014:2200.

subsidiaries resident in Member States and in third countries. In the years in dispute (1991–2001) Kronos received various dividends from its subsidiaries and made both profits and losses in Germany.

As far as domestic distributions were concerned, a German recipient company that had incurred tax losses could obtain a refund of the underlying corporate income tax paid by the (German) distributing company. Kronos requested reimbursement of the foreign corporation tax levied on its foreign subsidiaries in the respective source countries. The German tax authorities denied the refund on the basis that the related dividend income was exempt from tax in Germany under the applicable tax treaties.

As to the compatibility of different mechanisms adopted to eliminate double taxation with the free movement of capital,[98] the Court of Justice very importantly reiterated that applying the exemption method for domestic dividends and the imputation method for foreign dividends was acceptable as these were in principle equivalent mechanisms.[99] Each Member State remained free to organise its system for taxing distributed profits and prevent the imposition of a series of charges to tax on those profits, provided, however, that the system in question did not entail discrimination.[100]

The Court of Justice noted that in the situation where the company receiving dividends incurs tax losses, reimbursement of the tax paid by the distributing company could be regarded as a cash-flow advantage.[101] However, the refusal to grant a refund and the difference in treatment could be explained by an objective difference in the situations at hand. A (loss-making) company such as Kronos receiving foreign-sourced dividends was not in a comparable situation to that of a company receiving domestic dividends.[102] 'The difference between those situations stems, first, from the fact that the Federal Republic of Germany, following the conclusion of double taxation conventions with other Member States and with third States, waived the exercise of its powers of taxation over the dividends distributed by companies resident in those States.'[103] Therefore, the obligations of the Member State of residence of the company receiving dividends when it did not exercise its own powers of taxation over those dividends were different, from the obligations owed by it when it elected to tax those dividends. In the latter situation, it must take

---

[98] For a discussion on overlapping freedoms, see 3.3.1.
[99] See para 66, where it was clarified that the two methods were in fact equivalent provided, however, that the tax rate applied to foreign-sourced dividends was not higher than the rate applied to nationally-sourced dividends and that the tax credit was at least equal to the amount paid in the state of the company making the distribution, up to the limit of the tax charged in the Member State of the company receiving the dividends. Citing FII Group Litigation II case, para 39.
[100] Kronos, paras 67–8.
[101] Ibid, para 79.
[102] Ibid, para 81.
[103] Ibid, para 82.

into account, within the limits of its own taxation, the tax burden resulting from the exercise of the tax powers of the other Member State.[104]

The refund requested by Kronos was in the context of the imputation method, the logical corollary of taking the dividends into account and of the previous reduction of the losses that could be carried forward. Without such a refund, the taking of the dividends into account and the reduction of the losses of the company receiving them were liable to result in economic double taxation of those dividends in subsequent tax years when the results of the company receiving the dividends were positive.[105] By contrast, in the context of the exemption method, as the losses were not reduced, there was no risk of economic double taxation of the dividends received. The lack of a refund was counterbalanced by not taking the dividends into account when determining the basis of assessment.[106] Therefore, the German rules were found to be compatible with the free movement of capital.

In The Trustees of the BT Pension Scheme v. HMRC,[107] it was questioned whether the refusal by the UK tax authorities to grant a tax credit to resident shareholders receiving UK-sourced dividends, when those dividends originated from foreign-sourced profits, was in breach of the free movement of capital. The Court of Justice ruled that the free movement of capital was the relevant freedom, as the acquisition of shares on the capital market was solely with the intention of making a financial investment without any intention to influence the management and control of the undertakings.[108] There was a restriction to this freedom as the dividends received by the trustees were not entitled to a tax credit. This had the effect of discouraging those shareholders from investing in the capital of UK-resident companies that received dividends from non-resident companies, and favouring investments in UK-resident companies that received dividends from other UK-resident companies.[109]

This was not a purely internal situation[110] – the different treatment arose precisely because the dividends originated from foreign-sourced profits. Therefore, the free movement of capital covered this situation, irrespective of the fact that the shareholders receiving dividends could be resident in the same Member State as the company distributing the dividends. The Court of Justice found that there was a restriction to the free movement of capital which could not be justified.

In EV v. Finanzamt Lippstadt,[111] the Court of Justice was asked to consider the tax treatment of dividends received by German companies from non-EU subsidiaries for the purposes of the German business tax. Under the German legislation,

[104] Ibid, para 86.
[105] Ibid, para 87.
[106] Ibid, para 88.
[107] Case C-628/15 The Trustees of the BT Pension Scheme, ECLI:EU:C:2016:1002.
[108] Ibid, paras 30–1.
[109] Ibid, para 36.
[110] Ibid, para 39.
[111] Case C-685/16 EV v. Finanzamt Lippstadt, ECLI:EU:C:2018:743.

dividends from domestic shareholdings were exempt from German business tax, subject to a 15 per cent minimum shareholding requirement. By contrast, as regards foreign shareholdings, the exemption was subject to stricter rules, such as an active business test at the level of the distributing subsidiary. The German referring court asked if these rules were in breach of the free movement of capital. Both Advocate General Wathelet and the Court of Justice found the German regime incompatible with the free movement of capital.

There was a different treatment of dividends distributed by a resident company and of dividends distributed by a non-EU company. This constituted a restriction to the free movement of capital.[112] As regards the applicability of the standstill clause under Article 64 TFEU, it was noted that although the German legislation applied to direct investments, both its material and personal scope had been significantly modified since 1993.[113] As such, the restriction was not covered by the standstill clause. Furthermore, the restriction could not be justified by the objective of combating tax avoidance and evasion. This was because the German rules introduced an irrebuttable presumption of fraud and abuse and were not targeted exclusively against wholly artificial arrangements, which did not reflect economic reality.[114]

The Court of Justice concluded that the German legislation restricted the free movement of capital, because it provided stricter requirements for exempting dividends received from a non-resident company, than those applicable when the paying company was a German resident. This judgment is likely to have a significant practical impact on the tax treatment of non-EU sourced dividends for German business tax purposes.

5.2.3 *Economic and Juridical Double Taxation – The Home State Perspective*

It has been shown above that, as far as economic double taxation is concerned, the extent to which this is prevented under EU law depends on whether the home state takes measures to mitigate it domestically but does not extend such measures in a cross-border situation. However, if domestic and inbound dividends are treated the same way by the home state, then there is no discrimination. The Court of Justice often finds that economic double taxation has to be tackled but juridical double taxation cannot be interfered with, being a consequence of the parallel exercise of tax competences by different Member States.

In Kerckhaert–Morres[115] two Belgian residents, Mr Kerckhaert and Ms Morres, received a dividend from a French-resident company. French law granted an imputation credit (the *avoir fiscal*) of 50 per cent on this dividend but also imposed

---

[112] Ibid, para 64.
[113] Ibid, para 79.
[114] Ibid, paras 95–9.
[115] Case C-513/04 Kerckhaert–Morres.

a 15 per cent withholding tax on both the dividend and the imputation credit. The dividend was also taxed according to Belgian tax law at 25 per cent. The taxpayers requested that the withholding tax be credited against the Belgian tax due, as a fixed quota of foreign tax.[116] The Belgian tax authorities did not allow this and the issue was referred to the Court of Justice.

The Court of Justice decided that the Belgian legislation was compatible with the free movement of capital. It noted that the Belgian tax was fixed and that Belgian tax legislation did not make any distinction between domestic and EU-sourced dividends.[117] The fact that Belgium did not give relief for French withholding tax was a result of the exercise in parallel by two Member States of their fiscal sovereignty.[118] This problem was to be mitigated through a concerted effort from both Member States 'by applying, in particular, the apportionment criteria followed in international tax practice. The purpose of the France–Belgium Convention is essentially to apportion fiscal sovereignty ... in those situations'.[119]

Similarly, in Damseaux[120] the Court of Justice found that Belgium was not in breach of the free movement of capital in failing to prevent (juridical) double taxation of dividends paid by a company resident in another Member State. In this case, under the relevant tax treaty, dividends distributed by a French company to a Belgian resident were liable to be taxed in both Member States. The Court of Justice pointed out that this was a situation where juridical double taxation arose. The Court of Justice stated that it had no jurisdiction to rule whether Belgium's inaction in entering (or amending) its tax treaties to avoid double taxation was in breach of EU law. Nor could it examine the relationship between a national measure and the provisions of a tax treaty such as the one at issue.[121] The disadvantages arose from the parallel exercise of tax competences by different Member States. To the extent that such an exercise was not discriminatory, there was no restriction prohibited by EU law.[122]

Whilst the OECD Model Tax Convention set out rules for the attribution of taxing rights between contracting states, EU law did 'not lay down any general criteria for the attribution of areas of competence between the Member States in relation to the elimination of double taxation within the Community'.[123] The Member State of residence was not obliged, under EU law, to prevent the disadvantages that could arise from the exercise of competence by the two

---

[116] Broadly, under Art 19A(1)(2) of the France-Belgium tax treaty, any Belgian withholding tax or fixed quota of foreign tax was to be credited against the Belgian dividend tax.
[117] Case C-513/04 Kerckhaert–Morres, para 17.
[118] Ibid, para 20.
[119] Ibid, para 23.
[120] Case C-128/08 Damseaux.
[121] Ibid, para 22.
[122] Ibid, para 27.
[123] Ibid, para 33.

Member States.[124] Therefore, Belgium was not in breach of its obligations under EU law.

It should be noted that both in Kerckhaert–Morres and Damseaux what was at stake was a non-creditable (final) withholding tax applicable to both domestic and foreign-sourced dividends. Therefore, at the time it was decided, it was not clear whether the same conclusion would follow in the case of a creditable withholding tax. If domestic withholding taxes were credited at home state level, would foreign withholding taxes also be credited to avoid different treatment of domestic and inbound dividends? Arguably, there was much logic in this argument, the reasoning of which was analogous to the reasoning examined in 5.2.1 and 5.2.2. A home state that gives shareholders receiving domestic dividends a tax credit for underlying corporation taxes is forced to give a similar credit for foreign underlying corporation taxes to shareholders receiving foreign-sourced dividends. If the home state gives shareholders a credit for domestic withholding taxes paid on the dividends, should not the same be extended to foreign withholding taxes?

Not necessarily so, following Haribo & Salinen[125] discussed above. Here, under Austrian tax law, the domestic withholding tax was credited against the domestic income tax of the shareholder. The Court of Justice reiterated that a Member State was not required to give a credit for withholding taxes paid on dividends in another Member State or in a non-Member State in order to prevent juridical double taxation. This was the result of two Member States choosing 'to exercise their fiscal competence and to subject those dividends to taxation in the hands of the shareholder'.[126] Article 63 TFEU could not be interpreted as obliging a Member State to provide, in its tax legislation, that a credit be granted for the withholding tax levied on dividends in another Member State in order to prevent juridical double taxation.[127] The fact that in a domestic scenario the withholding tax would have been creditable did not appear to be a relevant consideration to the Court of Justice. In fact, it was not even mentioned in the Court's reasoning on this point. Therefore, the different stance of the Court of Justice as regards economic and juridical double taxation appears to persist, irrespective of whether the tax burden on foreign dividends is the same.

Obviously, here the approach is diametrically opposed to that of the OECD Model Tax Convention, which focuses on the elimination of juridical double taxation but not economic double taxation. Whilst the OECD's stance is understandable given the limitations of a non-binding instrument, it is difficult to understand the approach of the Court of Justice. Why should the home state be responsible for the host state's corporation tax (by forcing the home State to extend relief for the host state's underlying tax) but not for the host state's

---

[124] Ibid, para 34.
[125] Joined Cases C-436/08 and C-437/08 Haribo & Salinen.
[126] Ibid, para 168.
[127] Ibid, para 171.

withholding tax? Certainly, what matters to the shareholder is the double tax burden – whether this is called economic or juridical.[128]

What is even more perplexing is the Court's excuse for this result – it involves the exercise in parallel by two Member States of their fiscal sovereignty. Is that not what generates multiple tax burdens in most situations? It is difficult to see how juridical double taxation results from the exercise in parallel of fiscal sovereignty but not economic double taxation. Perhaps the Court of Justice was wary of interfering with the OECD's mechanisms for the alleviation of *juridical* double taxation. It did not have similar qualms as regards the methods chosen by Member States to alleviate *economic* double taxation – something the OECD refrains from dealing with anyway. If this is the case, then it would seem that the Court of Justice is more respectful of the OECD, an influential organisation with non-binding powers, than the Member States' (internally) binding rules. Otherwise, it is difficult to understand and justify the end result of these cases from a purely technical interpretation of the fundamental freedoms. This is neither the most satisfactory nor logical result, especially since the Court of Justice does not appear to be very strict with this distinction as far as outbound dividends are concerned, as shown in 5.4.

5.3 THE TAXATION OF OUTBOUND DIVIDENDS

Case law on the taxation of outbound dividends starts from a similar premise to that on inbound dividends, although there are some subtle differences. The state of the distributing company (i.e. the host state) has to ensure equal tax treatment of resident and non-resident recipients of dividends if they are in a comparable situation. From a host state perspective, resident and non-resident shareholders are in a comparable situation if they are both subject to host state taxes. In other words, a tax imposed by the host state only on outbound dividends, or a relief from economic double taxation only available to resident shareholders, could be discriminatory if the non-resident shareholder is also subject to tax on those dividends in the host state.

5.3.1 *The Early Cases*

The first important case in this area was Fokus Bank,[129] decided by the EFTA Court. In this case, dividends paid by a Norwegian company to shareholders residing in Norway were taxable as general income in the hands of those shareholders. In order to avoid economic double taxation, Norwegian shareholders were granted an imputation tax credit that corresponded to the amount of tax paid by the distributing

---

[128] Ibid. See also Wattel, 'Taxation of Intercompany Dividends and EU Law', p 44.
[129] Case E-1/04 Fokus Bank ASA v. The Norwegian State, represented by Skattedirektoratet (The Directorate of Taxes) [2004] EFTA Court Report 1.

company on the dividends. This meant that the dividends were effectively tax-free. Dividends paid out to non-resident shareholders were subject to withholding tax. No imputation tax credit was given for such dividends.

The EFTA Court decided that the Norwegian tax rules restricted the free movement of capital, as enshrined in Article 40 of the EEA Agreement. The restriction was twofold. Firstly, there was a restriction at shareholder level. As non-resident shareholders were treated less favourably than resident ones, they could be deterred from investing in Norwegian companies. There was also a restriction at company level. The Norwegian tax rules made it less attractive for non-residents to invest in Norwegian companies. Therefore, Norwegian companies were hindered from raising capital outside of Norway.[130] The restriction was not justified. The EFTA Court emphasised that this unfavourable tax treatment could not be justified by the existence of tax advantages in the country of residence of the shareholder. One country could not shift its obligation to comply with the EEA Agreement to another country by relying on the latter country to make good the disadvantages of its own legislation.[131]

It ought to be pointed out that in Fokus Bank the non-resident shareholders receiving the dividends were subject to Norwegian dividend withholding tax of 15 per cent in a *similar* way to resident shareholders.[132] Arguably, to that extent only (i.e. the 15 per cent withholding tax) the foreign shareholders were in a comparable situation to resident shareholders. In other words, Norway should have allowed the imputation credit to the foreign shareholders to the extent necessary to extinguish the 15 per cent withholding tax only.

This interpretation of the judgment is reconcilable with the principles set out in the ACT Group Litigation case.[133] Here the Court of Justice examined aspects of the UK's imputation regime, in force until 6 April 1999. Under this regime a group income election was permitted only between UK resident companies. If a UK company paid dividends to a UK parent company when a group income election was in place, the paying company did not have to account for advance corporation tax (ACT) on the dividends. If, however, a UK company paid dividends to a non-UK parent company, it had to account for ACT in the quarter in which the dividends were paid and could not offset that ACT against any corporation tax due, or obtain a repayment, until nine months after the year end. Accordingly, companies with non-UK parent companies suffered a cash-flow disadvantage.

Under this regime tax credits were also available for dividends paid by UK companies to certain UK shareholders, and these could be used to offset their tax liabilities or be refunded in cash. This credit was not generally available to non-

---

[130] Ibid, para 26.
[131] Ibid, para 37.
[132] The withholding tax for residents was higher (28 per cent), but this was immediately offset with an imputation credit.
[133] Case C-374/04 Test Claimants in Class IV of the ACT Group Litigation [2006] ECR I-11673.

residents such as the claimants. However, since a non-resident corporate shareholder was not entitled to a tax credit, such shareholder was effectively not liable to any UK income tax on the distribution. Some of the UK's tax treaties granted a full or partial tax credit to shareholders resident in the other contracting state, in which case such shareholders *were* liable to UK income tax on the UK dividends. Some of these tax treaties contained a limitation on benefits (LOB) clause,[134] which removed the entitlement of foreign corporate shareholders to a tax credit if these shareholders were owned by a company resident in a country whose tax treaty with the UK did not confer a tax credit on companies receiving UK dividends.

The Court of Justice agreed with the decision of Advocate General Geelhoed, in that it was not contrary to freedom of establishment and free movement of capital for the UK to confer an entitlement to a tax credit to resident (company) recipients of UK-sourced dividends when it did not grant such a tax credit to non-resident recipients of such dividends. To the Court of Justice these situations were not comparable. It was the exercise of host state taxing jurisdiction over the recipient of the dividends that created the basis for establishing comparability.[135] In the absence of such exercise of tax jurisdiction, resident and non-resident recipient companies were not comparable.

Therefore, the key distinction according to the Court of Justice was the fact that the non-resident recipient company was not liable to tax *in the UK* on those dividends. In such circumstances the UK was not obliged to confer a tax credit. It was only when such dividends fell within the UK tax net – whether because of legislation or pursuant to a tax treaty – that the non-resident company was entitled to a tax credit and was in a comparable situation to a resident company. If this was the case, then the host state was 'obliged to ensure that, under the procedures laid down by its national law in order to prevent or mitigate a series of liabilities to tax, non-resident shareholder companies [were] subject to the same treatment as resident shareholder companies'.[136] It was for the national court to determine, in each case, whether that obligation had been complied with, 'taking account, where necessary, of the provisions of the [tax treaty] that that Member State has concluded with the state in which the shareholder company was resident'.[137]

It is noteworthy that, if no UK tax was levied on those dividends, the fact that the dividends may have been subject to tax in the country of the recipient (the home state) was irrelevant. The resident and the non-resident recipient would still not be in a comparable situation. In establishing comparability, the Court of Justice only looked at tax treatment from the perspective of the UK as a host state. In other words,

---

[134] For an analysis of LOBs at that point in time, see ch 2 in Christiana HJI Panayi, *Double Taxation, Tax Treaties, Treaty Shopping and the European Community* (Kluwer Law International, 2007).
[135] Case C-374/04 ACT Group Litigation, at para 68.
[136] Ibid, para 70.
[137] Ibid, para 71, citing Case C-265/04 Bouanich [2006] ECR I-923, paras 51–5.

it followed the per-country approach.[138] The tax treatment in the home state was irrelevant.

The same reasoning was applied to LOBs. The reciprocity of rights and obligations was an inherent consequence of bilateral tax treaties. When the LOB of the underlying tax treaty was triggered, then no tax credit was given to the shareholders claiming under the tax treaty. As there was no tax credit, there was no UK tax liability. By contrast, when the LOB was inapplicable, then shareholders claiming under that tax treaty were entitled to the dividend tax credit and were subject to tax on it. Therefore, shareholders claiming reliefs under different tax treaties were not in a comparable situation, as they were not all subject to UK tax liability. The Court of Justice concluded that there was no question of incompatibility with freedom of establishment and free movement of capital.

The Denkavit case,[139] decided two days after the judgment in the ACT Group Litigation case was delivered, followed the same trend. Here France imposed a withholding tax[140] on dividends paid by French subsidiaries to non-resident parent companies. Dividends paid to resident companies were almost fully exempt from taxation. The Court of Justice stated that although non-resident dividend recipients were not generally in a comparable situation to resident recipients, nevertheless, as soon as a Member State, either unilaterally or by way of a tax treaty, imposed a charge to tax on them, their situation became comparable.[141] The Court of Justice concluded that imposing a liability to tax on dividends paid to a non-resident parent company and allowing resident parent companies to be almost fully exempt from such tax was discriminatory and incompatible with freedom of establishment.[142]

The Dutch dividend withholding tax regime was also subject to scrutiny in the Amurta case.[143] Here the Court of Justice followed the opinion of Advocate General Mengozzi in that the Dutch tax treatment of dividends distributed to non-resident parent companies was incompatible with the free movement of capital. Similar to the facts in Denkavit, here dividends distributed by Dutch companies to non-resident companies were subject to a 25 per cent withholding tax. By contrast, dividends distributed to resident companies were exempt from withholding tax. Following Denkavit and the ACT Group Litigation case, the Court of Justice in Amurta concluded that residents and non-residents were in a comparable situation when the host state exercised its tax jurisdiction over non-residents unilaterally or by way of a tax treaty.[144] If that were the case and the host state then decided to give relief

---

[138] See 3.3.4.
[139] Case C-170/05 Denkavit [2006] ECR I-11949.
[140] A 5 per cent withholding tax was imposed in accordance with French domestic tax law and the Netherlands-France tax treaty. The statutory rate was 25 per cent. At the time in question (1987–8) the Parent-Subsidiary Directive had not yet come into force.
[141] Case C-170/05 Denkavit, paras 34–5.
[142] Ibid, para 41.
[143] Case C-379/05 Amurta SGPS v. Inspecteur van de Belastingdienst [2007] ECR I-9569.
[144] Ibid, paras 27–8.

to its own residents for economic double taxation by exempting dividends received from withholding tax, non-residents should also benefit from such exemption.[145]

The case law set out in this section suggests that, overall, the free movement of capital and the freedom of establishment require equal tax treatment to be granted to residents and non-residents in receipt of dividends from the host state, if they are both subject to host state taxes on those dividends. If they are not, then a non-resident recipient is not in an objectively comparable situation to a resident recipient. In such a case it is not discriminatory for the host state to refuse the extension of reliefs to a non-resident recipient. Furthermore, for outbound dividends the Court of Justice seems to be focusing on the tax treatment in the host state. The fact that these dividends may also be subject to tax in the state of the recipient shareholder (the home state) is irrelevant. This approach is similar to that applied on inbound dividend cases, with the exception of reliefs relating to underlying (host state) taxes. This is the only situation where the Court of Justice requests from the home state to extend a relief to foreign-sourced dividends received by a resident shareholder, as explained in 5.2.1.

5.3.2 *Later Cases – Consolidation of the Court's Principles*

Following the earlier cases discussed in the previous section, the Court of Justice was called to examine the compatibility of withholding taxes on passive income paid to non-resident persons in two high-profile cases. The judgments centred on whether a resident and a non-resident recipient of interest in one case, and dividends in another case, were in a comparable situation.

In a judgment released relatively soon after the ground-breaking cases discussed in 5.3.1, the Court of Justice appeared to approach withholding taxes on interest payments differently compared to its position on withholding taxes on dividends. In Truck Center[146] the Court of Justice found that imposing a withholding tax on outbound payments of interest but exempting such domestic payments was not in breach of EU law, because resident and non-resident recipient companies were not in a comparable situation. The Court's reasoning was not very convincing though. It appeared to be based on the fact that residents were taxed on a residence basis and non-residents on a source basis and that the recipient company was subject to different arrangements vis-à-vis the recovery of the tax. The reasoning is examined in greater detail in 5.4 below. Suffice to say that the Court of Justice concluded that the different treatment did not constitute a restriction to the freedom of establishment.[147] The same conclusion applied in relation to the free movement of capital.

---

[145] Ibid, paras 39–41.
[146] Case C-282/07 État belge – SPF Finances v. Truck Center SA [2008] ECR I-10767.
[147] Ibid, para 50.

By contrast, in the Aberdeen Property case[148] both Advocate General Mazák and the Court of Justice found that freedom of establishment was infringed when withholding taxes were levied on dividends paid from a Finnish company to a Luxembourg SICAV,[149] because no such withholding taxes were levied on dividends paid to a resident company or fund. This was an important case, as it consolidated the principles first set out in the ACT Group Litigation case and removed any doubts as to the applicability of Truck Center, at least in the context of dividends.

The Court of Justice found that the Luxembourg SICAV was in a comparable situation to a Finnish company or investment fund. This finding was based on the following grounds. Differences between the legal form of the funds did not justify the different treatment,[150] nor did the fact that the income of the SICAV was not taxed in Luxembourg.[151] The non-taxation of the income in the home state (i.e. the state of the members of the SICAV, Luxembourg) did not make it more legitimate for the host state (i.e. the state of the SICAV, Finland) to tax such income, since Finland had chosen not to exercise its tax jurisdiction over such income when received by resident companies.[152] Just because income of a SICAV was not taxed and the imposition of a series of charges to tax took place at the level of the members of the SICAV rather than the SICAV itself, this did not mean that the home state should take measures to avoid these charges to tax. It was the host state that, 'by subjecting to withholding tax income that has already been taxed at the level of the distributing company, creates the series of charges to tax, a series which that Member State chose to prevent in the case of dividends distributed to resident companies'.[153]

The Court of Justice found the restriction to the freedom of establishment not to be justified. The argument concerning prevention of tax avoidance was rejected. The Finnish tax rules did not specifically target wholly artificial arrangements lacking economic reality and designed to circumvent the legislation of the Member State concerned.[154] The argument concerning the balanced allocation of the power to tax was also rejected. Since Finland chose not to tax recipient companies in its territory in respect of this kind of income, it could not rely on the argument to justify the taxation of outbound dividends.[155] The fact that the tax treaty between Finland and Luxembourg reserved to Finland the right to exercise its tax jurisdiction over dividends paid to Finnish companies was of no relevance.[156] The Court of

---

[148] Case C-303/07 Aberdeen Property Fininvest Alpha Oy [2009] ECR I-5145.
[149] A SICAV (Société d'Investissement À Capital Variable) was an open-ended collective scheme that derived its value by the number of participating investors. It was not an entity included in the list annexed to the Parent-Subsidiary Directive.
[150] Ibid, para 50.
[151] Ibid, para 51.
[152] Ibid, para 52.
[153] Ibid, para 54.
[154] Ibid, paras 64–5.
[155] Ibid, para 67.
[156] Ibid, para 68.

Justice reiterated the principle that '[a] Member State cannot rely on a double taxation convention in order to avoid its obligations imposed under the Treaty'.[157]

Neither did the argument concerning the coherence of the Finnish tax system succeed. There was no direct link between the tax advantage concerned and the offsetting of that advantage by a particular tax levy.[158] The withholding tax exemption was not subject to the condition that the dividends received by the share company were distributed onward by it and that their taxation in the hands of the shareholders in the company allowed the exemption from withholding tax to be offset.[159] Consequently, there was no direct link between the exemption from withholding tax and the taxation of those dividends as income of the shareholders in a share company.[160] Therefore, it was concluded that the Finnish rules were incompatible with freedom of establishment.

Subsequent cases showed that the Aberdeen Property case, which was more faithful to the principles set out by the Court of Justice in the ACT Group Litigation case, was to be followed rather than Truck Center, both in the context of dividends and interest.[161] The same principles would seem to apply vis-à-vis EEA distributions, though the different legal context in which these distributions arise may be an exonerating factor at the justification stage.

In Commission v. Netherlands[162] the Court of Justice found that by not exempting from withholding tax dividends paid to companies established in Iceland or Norway under the same conditions as dividends paid to Dutch companies, there was a breach of the free movement of capital of the EEA Agreement. Under Dutch law, dividends paid by subsidiaries to their parent companies were subject to 15 per cent withholding tax. If the dividends were paid to a Dutch or EU company that had a participation of no less than 5 per cent in the distributing company, then there was an exemption from withholding tax. For this exemption to apply to Icelandic or Norwegian companies, they had to have participations of respectively 10 per cent or 25 per cent.[163] Therefore for Icelandic and Norwegian shareholders, the host state made the benefit of an exemption subject to the holding of a higher stake in the capital of the distributing company.

Whilst the Court of Justice emphasised the importance of consistent application of the rules under the EC Treaty and the EEA Agreement, the inapplicability of the Mutual Assistance Directive was taken into account. Nevertheless, this was not enough to justify the restriction.[164] This higher capital holding requirement bore

---

[157] Ibid, para 69.
[158] Ibid, para 72.
[159] Ibid, para 73.
[160] Ibid, para 74.
[161] See analysis in 5.4.
[162] Case C-521/07 Commission v. Netherlands [2009] ECR I-4873.
[163] This was on the basis of the Netherlands-Iceland tax treaty, signed on 25 September 1997 and the Netherlands-Norway tax treaty, signed on 12 January 1990.
[164] Case C-521/07 Commission v. Netherlands, para 47.

'no relation to the conditions otherwise required from all companies in order to be entitled to that exemption'.[165] Therefore, the Netherlands had failed to fulfil its obligations under the EEA Agreement.[166]

In the past few years, there has been an influx of cases on dividend withholding taxes – some more straightforward than others.

In Commission v. Portugal,[167] the Court of Justice found that Portugal had violated the free movement of capital by taxing dividends paid to a non-resident pension fund at a higher rate than dividends paid to a Portuguese pension fund. Furthermore, in Secilpar[168] the Court of Justice issued an order in which it held that in light of the Portugal–Spain tax treaty, Portugal's rules on the deduction at source of corporate income tax for a non-resident company violated the free movement of capital.

In the Santander case[169] the Court of Justice clarified some aspects of its existing case law. Under French tax law, dividends distributed by French companies to non-resident investment funds (UCITS)[170] were subject to withholding tax, whereas when paid to French investment funds there was no withholding tax. Multiple claims filed by non-resident investment funds for refunds of French withholding taxes were rejected by the French tax authorities and the cases were referred to the Court of Justice. One question referred was whether the situation of the shareholders must be taken into account together with that of the funds in determining whether resident and non-resident funds were treated differently.

The Court of Justice found that the French rules restricted the free movement of capital. Dividends distributed by a resident company to a non-resident UCITS, irrespective of whether the UCITS was established in another Member State or a non-Member State, were taxed at the rate of 25 per cent by way of withholding tax, whereas such dividends were not taxed when paid to a resident UCITS.[171] This different treatment discouraged non-resident UCITS from investing in resident companies and discouraged resident investors from acquiring shares in non-resident UCITS.[172]

---

[165] Ibid, para 48.
[166] Ibid, para 52.
[167] Case C-493/09 Commission v. Portugal [2011] ECR I-09247.
[168] Case C-199/10 Secilpar – Sociedade Unipessoal SL v. Fazenda Publica [2010] ECR I-00154.
[169] Joined Cases C-338/11 to C-347/11 Santander Asset Management SGIIC SA, on behalf of FIM Santander Top 25 Euro Fi v. Directeur des résidents à l'étranger et des services généraux and Santander Asset Management SGIIC SA, on behalf of Cartera Mobiliaria SA SICAV and Others v. Ministre du Budget, des Comptes publics, de la Fonction publique et de la Réforme de l'État, ECLI:EU:C:2012:286.
[170] UCITS are undertakings for collective investments in transferable securities. The applicants in the main proceedings were Belgian, German, Spanish and American UCITS investing, inter alia, in shares in French companies and receiving dividends from those shares.
[171] Joined Cases C-338/11 to C-347/11 Santander, para 16.
[172] Ibid, para 17.

The Court of Justice examined whether resident and non-resident UCITS were in a comparable situation. Although it was up to each Member State to organise, compatibly with EU law, its system for taxing distributed profits, where national tax legislation established a distinguishing criterion for the taxation of distributed profits, 'account must be taken of that criterion in determining whether the situations are comparable'.[173] However, only the relevant distinguishing criteria established by the legislation in question had to be taken into account. Accordingly, where a Member State chose to exercise its tax jurisdiction over dividends distributed by resident companies on the sole basis of the place of residence of the recipient UCITS, the tax situation of the latter's shareholders was irrelevant for the purpose of determining whether or not that legislation is discriminatory.[174]

In this case the tax legislation established a distinguishing criterion based on the UCITS' place of residence only, in that it only subjected non-resident UCITS to withholding taxes on dividends which they received.[175] There was no link between the non-taxation of dividends received by resident UCITS and the taxation of those dividends in the hands of its shareholders. Indeed, the tax exemption enjoyed by resident UCITS was not conditional on their shareholders being taxed on the income distributed to them.[176] Nor did the legislation take account of the tax situation of shareholders in UCITS that distributed dividends received.[177] The Court of Justice pointed out that it was not always the case that the shareholders of resident UCITS were resident in France and the shareholders of non-resident UCITS were resident in the state of establishment of the UCITS.[178] Although some tax treaties between France and the Member State or the non-Member State concerned provided that the state of residence of such shareholders was to take account of the withholding tax applied in France, it could not be inferred from this that the tax situation of such shareholders would be taken into account under the French legislation. On the contrary, it was the shareholders' state of residence that, under such tax treaties, was to take account of the tax treatment of the dividends in France in respect of the UCITS.[179]

In light of the distinguishing criterion of the legislation, that is the UCITS' place of residence, the situations could only be compared at the level of the investment vehicle in order to determine whether that legislation was discriminatory.[180] As such,

[173] Ibid, para 27.
[174] Ibid, para 28.
[175] Ibid, para 29.
[176] Ibid, para 30.
[177] Ibid, para 32.
[178] Ibid, para 33.
[179] Ibid, para 37.
[180] Ibid, para 39. The case was distinguishable from Case C-194/06 Orange European Smallcap where the tax exemption enjoyed by the investment funds was conditional on the requirement that all the profits of those funds be distributed to their shareholders, in order to make the tax burden on investment proceeds through fiscal investment enterprises the same as that on direct investments by private investors. See analysis in 5.2.2.

5.3 The Taxation of Outbound Dividends

the different treatment of resident UCITS and non-resident UCITS could not be justified by a relevant difference in their situations.[181] In other words, there was a different treatment of resident and non-resident UCITS that were in a comparable situation.

The Court of Justice rejected the justifications put forward by the French government. Since France had chosen not to tax resident funds on domestic dividends, the restriction could not be justified by the need to safeguard the balanced allocation of taxing rights[182] or by the need to guarantee the effectiveness of fiscal supervision.[183] Nor could it be justified by the necessity to ensure the coherence of the French tax system, as it lacked a direct link between the tax advantage concerned and the compensation of that advantage by a particular tax levy.[184] The Court of Justice saw no need to consider whether the restriction on movements of capital to or from non-Member States was justified, as the reference for a preliminary ruling did not address this.[185] The Court of Justice also rejected the French government's request for a temporal limitation of its judgment because there was no uncertainty regarding the legal position.[186]

Although the judgment brought some clarity as regards the comparability exercise, the Court's treatment of tax treaties generated confusion. One could question why the underlying tax treaties were not considered to be part of the relevant legal framework of the host state and taken into account in the comparability exercise, as was done in Denkavit, Amurta and other cases that are further discussed below in 5.3.3. Technically, this case does not overrule previous case law. It ought to be remembered that in Santander the Court of Justice emphasised that the tax legislation established a distinguishing criterion based on the UCITS' place of residence only and decided the case on that basis. The place of residence of the shareholders was irrelevant. However, the underlying tax treaties were relevant to the taxation of the shareholders and *not* that of the UCITS. Therefore, these tax treaties could not be taken into account in assessing whether the foreign UCITS (and not its shareholders) was discriminated against. Arguably, the result would have been different had the tax treaties provided for relief of the UCITS itself, as in certain circumstances tax treaties are taken into account for the neutralisation of host state taxes, as shown in section 5.3.3.

There have been many cases involving pension funds following the Santander case. In Emerging Markets Series of DFA,[187] the Polish tax rules were challenged for denying a tax exemption to dividends paid by Polish companies to investment funds established in a third country – in this case, the US. It was argued that a Member

---
[181] Ibid, para 44.
[182] Ibid, para 48.
[183] Ibid, para 49.
[184] Ibid, paras 50–2.
[185] Ibid, para 54.
[186] Ibid, para 61.
[187] Case C-190/12 Emerging Markets Series of DFA Investment Trust Company, ECLI:EU:C:2014:249.

State could not exclude from a tax exemption dividends paid to an investment fund in a third country if the states had a mutual administrative assistance agreement.

The Court of Justice found that the Polish tax rules restricted the free movement of capital. The different tax treatment of dividends paid to resident and non-resident investment funds could discourage, on the one hand, investment funds established in a non-member country from investing in companies established in Poland, and, on the other hand, investors resident in Poland from acquiring shares in non-resident investment funds.[188] The Court of Justice found that the non-resident investment funds were in a situation that was objectively comparable to that of investment funds whose registered office was in Poland. This was because the tax legislation adopted as a distinguishing criterion the place of residence of investment funds.[189]

As far as justifications were concerned, the Court of Justice rejected arguments based on the coherence of the Polish tax system and the balanced allocation of taxing rights.[190] The Polish government's request for a temporal limitation of the effect of the ruling was also rejected.[191] However, the justification based on the need to maintain the effectiveness of fiscal supervision was accepted. This was only where the legislation of a Member State made entitlement to a tax advantage dependent on the satisfaction of conditions compliance with which could be verified only by obtaining information from the competent authorities of a non-Member State and where, because that non-Member State was not bound by an agreement to provide information, it proved impossible to obtain that information from it.[192]

In this case, there was a regulatory framework of mutual administrative assistance established between Poland and the USA, which permitted the exchange of information that may be required for the application of the Polish tax legislation.[193] Therefore, it could not be ruled out a priori that US investment funds would not be able to provide relevant documentary evidence to enable the Polish tax authorities to determine whether those investment funds operated under conditions equivalent to those applicable to EU investment funds.[194] It was for the referring court to decide whether the existing regulatory framework in fact enabled the Polish tax authorities to verify this.[195]

In another case, the Fidelity Funds case,[196] the Court of Justice found that the Danish withholding tax on dividends distributed to non-resident investment funds

---

[188] Ibid, paras 42–3.
[189] Ibid, paras 58–70.
[190] Ibid, paras 89–105.
[191] Ibid, paras 106–13.
[192] Ibid, para 84.
[193] Ibid, para 85. See Art 23 of the US-Poland tax treaty of 1974 and the OECD/Council of Europe Mutual Administrative Assistance Convention 1988. See para 86.
[194] Ibid, para 87.
[195] Ibid, para 88.
[196] Case C-480/16 Fidelity Funds v. Skatteministeriet, ECLI:EU:C:2018:480.

5.3 The Taxation of Outbound Dividends

was in breach of the free movement of capital. In this case, a UK registered and a Luxembourg resident UCITS with portfolio investments in Denmark that did not exceed 10 per cent of the share capital of the participations held, received dividends that were subject to Danish withholding tax at a rate of 25 per cent in 2000, rising to 28 per cent between 2001 and 2009. Had the dividends been paid to a Danish UCITS, they would be exempt from withholding tax, under the condition that they must elect the status of distributing fund and make a minimum distribution to its investors. There was a corresponding obligation for the investment fund to act as withholding agent on behalf of its investors. The taxpayers argued that this different treatment was contrary to the free movement of capital and requested a refund of the withholding tax levied. They also argued that the minimum distribution requirement was contrary to the freedom to provide services. The Court of Justice found that there was a restriction to the free movement of capital.

The resident and non-resident funds were found to be in a comparable situation in light of the objective of the legislation to avoid economic double taxation by only taxing the members of the investment fund.[197] If both the investment funds and their members were taxed, economic double taxation would occur.[198] The restriction was justified based on the need to safeguard the coherence of the tax system.[199] Since the Danish rules made the tax exemption conditional on an (actual or technical) minimum distribution to investors, which was subject to Danish withholding tax, the advantage granted to resident UCITS in the form of a withholding tax exemption was offset by the subsequent taxation of the dividends distributed onwards, in the hands of their investors. However, the restriction went beyond what was necessary in order to safeguard the coherence of the Danish tax system. A less restrictive measure would be to allow non-resident UCITS to benefit from the withholding tax exemption, provided they paid a tax equivalent to that which Danish funds were liable to levy on the minimum distribution required.[200] The Court of Justice concluded that the Danish legislation was contrary to the free movement of capital.

In a later case, the Sofina case,[201] the Court of Justice examined the compatibility of the French withholding tax levied on dividends paid by French companies to non-resident companies with the free movement of capital. In this case, three loss-making Belgian companies received French-sourced dividends that were subject to a 15 per cent withholding tax under the France-Belgium tax treaty. As the companies were loss-making, the withholding tax resulted in a non-recoverable expense. Had the recipient companies been French, then they would only have been taxed on the dividends once they became profitable again. The Belgian companies argued that

---

[197] Ibid, paras 52–3.
[198] Ibid, para 55.
[199] Ibid, paras 79–81.
[200] Ibid, paras 83–5.
[201] Case C-575/17 Sofina SA v. Ministre de l'Action et des Comptes publics, ECLI:EU:C:2018:943.

this less favourable tax treatment was in breach of EU law and requested a refund of the tax levied.

The Court of Justice agreed that there was a difference in treatment. The dividends paid to a non-resident company were subject to immediate and definitive taxation, whereas the tax imposed on dividends paid to a resident company depended on whether the latter's financial year was net loss-making or net profit-making.[202] 'Thus, where losses are made, the taxation of those dividends is not only deferred to a subsequent profit-making year, thus procuring a cash-flow advantage for the resident company, but is also thereby uncertain, since that tax will not be levied if the resident company ceases trading before becoming profitable.'[203] In other words, a deferral of taxation resulted in definitive exemption of the dividends paid to a resident company if the latter did not become profitable before it ceased trading.

The Court of Justice found that the exclusion of a cash-flow advantage in a cross-border situation when it was granted in an equivalent domestic situation constituted a restriction on the free movement of capital.[95] As such, the Court of Justice found that the French legislation was liable to give rise to an advantage for loss-making resident companies, since it gave rise, at the very least, to tax deferral, or even an exemption in the event of that company ceasing trading. By contrast, non-resident companies were subject to immediate and definitive taxation irrespective of their results.[204] It was emphasised that the tax disadvantage borne by the non-resident recipient company could not be compensated by another advantage such as a reduced withholding tax rate (i.e. lower than what was the applicable rate to residents),[205] or by the fact that the legislation did not treat resident and non-resident recipients of dividends differently when such companies were profitable.[206]

The Court of Justice found that this restriction was not justified. A justification based on the balanced allocation of taxing rights between Member States was rejected.[207] It was also emphasised that the loss of tax revenue resulting from the non-imposition of withholding tax on dividends distributed to non-resident loss-making companies ceasing their activities could not be regarded as an appropriate justification, as 'the French State consents to such losses when resident companies cease trading without returning to profitability'.[208]

Furthermore, a justification based on the need to ensure the effective collection of taxes was rejected.[209] This was because the existing mutual assistance mechanisms (Directive 2010/24/EU) provided the French tax authorities with a framework

---

[202] Ibid, para 28.
[203] Ibid.
[204] Ibid, para 34.
[205] Ibid, para 38.
[206] Ibid, para 39.
[207] Ibid, paras 56–64.
[208] Ibid, para 63.
[209] Ibid, para 78.

of cooperation and assistance that allowed them to recover a tax liability in the Member State of residence of the Belgian companies.[210] If the advantage associated with the deferral of withholding taxes was extended to loss-making non-resident companies, then the restriction would be eliminated without raising obstacles to the achievement of the aim pursued by the national legislation.[211] Therefore, the French rules were in breach of the free movement of capital.[212]

This judgment opens up many possibilities as regards withholding taxes. There is no reason why the judgment cannot apply to other types of payments on which withholding taxes are levied, such as interest, royalties, or even capital gains. Furthermore, as the judgment is based on the free movement of capital, then it may also affect dividends paid to non-resident companies established in a third country, though of course the justification grounds may be stronger in that scenario.

This case, however, has been criticised in that the Court of Justice may have extended the standard of comparability, by requiring to take into consideration the (foreign) non-dividend income of the recipient company when comparing the tax treatment of domestic and outbound dividends,[213] thus leaning towards an overall approach rather than a per-country approach which has been followed so far. It has also been criticised that the judgment may go beyond withholding taxes and dividend taxation by attaching a 'no-loss' condition to all source state taxing rights.[214] Whether or not, in fact, this case will have such far reaching implications remains to be seen.

In a later case, the *College Pension Plan* case,[215] the Court of Justice reviewed the German withholding tax rules relating to dividends paid to foreign pension funds. A Canadian pension fund that held shareholdings lower than 1 per cent in German resident companies, received dividends from those companies. These dividends were subject to a 15 per cent withholding tax. The pension fund applied for a refund of the withholding tax, arguing that it was discriminatory and hindered the free movement of capital, as German pension funds were de facto subject to more favourable taxation with regard to dividends received from German companies. This was because German pension funds were subject to a 25 per cent

---

[210] Ibid, paras 75–6.
[211] Ibid, para 77.
[212] The Court of Justice did not address the net taxation argument, as it was not necessary to do so. This was the final question referred by the French court and focused on whether the fact that non-residents could not deduct expenses directly linked to the collection of dividends was justified by the difference in tax rates between the income tax paid by residents and the withholding tax paid by non-residents. Ibid, para 21.
[213] For an interesting critique, see the CFE opinion statement submitted to the EU institutions on 10/10/2019: Opinion Statement ECJ-TF 3/2019 on the CJEU decision of 22 November 2018 in Case C-575/17, Sofina, on withholding taxes, losses and territoriality.
[214] Ibid.
[215] Case C-641/17 College Pension Plan of British Columbia v. Finanzamt München Abteilung III, ECLI:EU:C:2019:960.

withholding tax, which, however, could be credited against the 15 per cent German corporate tax, the excess being refundable. In addition, German pension funds had to book a technical reserve for an amount corresponding to almost the entire value of the dividends. The amount booked was deductible for corporate tax purposes. As such, resident pension funds paid no or very low taxes on dividends received from German companies. The German tax authorities denied the refund and the Canadian pension fund appealed the decision before the Fiscal Court of Munich. The case was eventually referred to the Court of Justice, which found that there was a breach of the free movement of capital.

The Court of Justice held that the application of the withholding tax to foreign pension funds was discriminatory if the foreign pension funds and the domestic pension funds were in comparable situations. Under German tax law, there was a direct link between the receipt of the dividends and the creation of the technical reserve, which was deductible. The Court of Justice found that a non-resident pension scheme that allocated dividends received to its provisions for pensions, whether voluntarily or as a result of regulatory requirements, was in a comparable situation to a German pension fund. However, it was for the referring court to assess whether this was the case in the situation at hand and whether this condition was met.

The Court of Justice found that the restriction could not be justified by overriding reasons in the public interest. It rejected justifications based on the need to ensure a balanced allocation of taxing rights, the need to safeguard the coherence of the German tax system, and the need to ensure the effectiveness of fiscal supervision. It was also found that the discrimination was not covered by the standstill clause provided by Article 64(1) TFEU. Although the rules imposing the application of the withholding tax were already in force prior to the cut-off date, the rules granting the de facto exemption to German pension funds were introduced afterwards. Moreover portfolio investments did not fall within the material scope of the standstill clause, as they did not qualify as direct investments. Shareholdings representing less than 1 per cent of the capital of the issuer could not qualify as direct investments for the purposes of this clause. Nor did the present case qualify as the provision of financial services, as investment in shares made by a pension fund did not amount to the provision of financial services. It was, therefore, concluded that the German legislation constituted an unjustified restriction to the free movement of capital that did not fall within the scope of the standstill clause.

In another recent case, the Deka case,[216] the Court of Justice found that the inability of a non-resident investment fund to reclaim withholding tax levied in the Netherlands due to the distribution requirements of the Dutch legislation was contrary to the free movement of capital. Under Dutch tax law, dividend distributions to both resident and non-resident investment funds were subject to a 15 per cent

---

[216] Case C-156/17 Köln-Aktienfonds Deka v. Staatssecretaris van Financiën, ECLI:EU:C:2020:51.

5.3 The Taxation of Outbound Dividends

withholding tax. However, Dutch funds that elected to be treated as fiscal investment enterprises (FIEs) were in the years in question entitled to a refund of the dividend withholding tax they had paid, provided that they met certain profit distribution and shareholder requirements. As these requirements were not met by foreign investment funds, the Dutch withholding tax on dividend distributions was a final tax burden.

Deka, a German investment fund, received dividends from its Dutch portfolio investments which were subject to Dutch dividend withholding tax. Deka applied for a refund of this withholding tax, considering itself comparable to a Dutch FIE. This application was rejected on the basis that the shareholder requirement and the distribution requirement were not met.

Under the shareholder requirement, there were participation thresholds which were not to be exceeded by holders of shares or certificates of participation in a fund in order to qualify for the FIE regime. Deka had argued that it was difficult to prove that it met the shareholder requirement because its shares were publicly traded via an electronic trading system and as such, had no information on the identity of its shareholders.[217] However, the Court of Justice found that the non-resident fund's difficulty in providing supporting evidence that it fulfilled this requirement was not a problem for which the Netherlands should have to answer[218] and, as a corollary, this requirement did not restrict the free movement of capital. However, it was for the referring court to determine whether the conditions imposed did not de facto disadvantage non-resident investment funds.[219]

Under the distribution requirement, the fund's taxable profits had to be distributed within eight months following the end of the fiscal year. The Court of Justice found that the denial of the benefit to a non-resident fund whose profits were subject to tax in its state of residence, irrespective of whether such profits had been distributed or not, could constitute a restriction on the free movement of capital. The Court of Justice took into account the fact that in the Member State of establishment of the investment fund (Germany), 'the proceeds of its investments which have not been distributed are deemed to have been distributed or are taken into account in the tax which that Member State levies on shareholders or participants as though that profit had been distributed.'[220] Therefore, this method of distribution and taxation seemed to have a similar objective as the distribution requirement of the Dutch FIE regime. However, this was for the referring court to verify in order to determine whether a resident investment fund which made an actual distribution of its profits (as per the regime's requirement), and a non-resident investment fund whose profits were not distributed but were deemed to have been distributed and were taxed as

---

[217] Ibid, para 63.
[218] Ibid, para 65.
[219] Ibid, para 67.
[220] Ibid, para 68.

such at shareholder level (as per the German rules), were in an objectively comparable situation.[221]

The Dutch Government did not provide any possible justifications for the restriction. The Court of Justice concluded that the Dutch rules were contrary to the free movement of capital in cases where it was impossible or excessively difficult for a non-resident fund to comply with the requirement, and the fund's profits were subject to tax in its state of residence, irrespective of whether the profits had actually been distributed to the non-resident fund's shareholders.

This is another important judgment. The Court of Justice established that a German fund which did not actually distribute its profits to its shareholders was not in an automatically incomparable situation to that of a Dutch FIE, because of the objective pursued by the underlying legislation. To an extent, the Court of Justice suggests that a tax imposed in the state of residence of the fund (i.e. the home state) could be considered equivalent to a tax imposed in the source jurisdiction from which the dividend payment was made (i.e. the host state) for the purposes of determining whether the two situations are objectively comparable. Moreover, this judgment suggests that in the comparability exercise, the Court of Justice examines what is in fact the legal position in the *other* Member State. Arguably, in this case, the Court of Justice did not adopt an overall approach as there was no assessment on the basis of the combined effect of the German and Dutch rules, but a rather modified version of the per-country approach. Here, the Court of Justice examined whether the non-resident fund was in a comparable situation to a Dutch FIE because of the similarity of its home state tax regime (to the host state regime) and not because of the simultaneous application of the two regimes.

It could also be argued that as a result of this decision, the requirement for distributions to actually be made may no longer be relevant. This could be significant for non-distributing accumulation funds, where investors are taxable on the basis of a deemed yield rather than distributions received.

5.3.3 The Relevance of Tax Treaties – Neutralisation of Host State Taxes?

The relevance of tax treaties in finding whether there is discrimination was examined in 3.3.3. Tax treaties have been particularly important in the dividends case law, especially in the context of outbound dividends. In the Denkavit[222] and Amurta[223] cases considered above, the Court of Justice examined whether the host state tax burden for which provision for relief was made in the underlying tax treaty was in *fact* relieved. This apparent treaty-based overall approach allows for the neutralisation of a discriminatory withholding tax in the host state by the provision of a treaty-based tax

---

[221] Ibid, paras 81–2.
[222] Case C-170/05 Denkavit.
[223] CaseC-379/05 Amurta.

5.3 The Taxation of Outbound Dividends

credit in the taxpayer's home state.[224] To an extent, it also qualifies the per-country approach.

In Amurta it was emphasised that only neutralisation as a result of an underlying tax treaty was relevant. A Member State could ensure compliance with its obligations under the Treaty through the conclusion of a tax treaty with another Member State.[225] The existence of a tax credit granted unilaterally by a Member State did not suffice. The difference between a treaty-based tax credit and a unilateral one was that the tax system resulting from the tax treaty formed part of the legal background of the proceedings and had been presented as such by the national court. The Court of Justice had to take it into account in order to give an interpretation of EU law that was relevant to the national court.[226] It was for the national court to identify the law applicable to the main proceedings and whether account should be taken of the tax treaty. It was also up to the national court to decide whether the tax treaty ultimately neutralised the effects of the restriction on the free movement of capital.[227]

Subsequent cases further highlighted the significance of tax treaties in the compatibility analysis. In Commission v. Italy[228] Italy's withholding tax regime had been found to be in breach of EU law but compatible with the EEA Agreement.[229] It was undisputed that the Italian legislation subjected outbound dividends to a higher rate of taxation than domestic dividends.[230] Italy had argued that account should be taken of tax treaties and of the Italian tax system as a whole in assessing this difference in treatment. Outbound dividends were not in reality treated differently from domestic dividends, since tax treaties allowed the tax withheld at source in Italy to be set off against that due in the other Member State.[231] However, the Court of Justice found that the application of the tax treaties did not always compensate the difference in treatment. For this to happen, the Italian withholding tax had to be set off against the tax due in the other Member State *in full*.[232] This set-off was not

---

[224] See Georg Kofler, 'Tax treaty "neutralisation" of source state discrimination under the EU fundamental freedoms?', [2011] 65(12) *Bulletin for International Taxation*, 684–90, 685.
[225] Case C-379/05 Amurta, para 79.
[226] Ibid, para 80.
[227] Ibid, paras 82–4.
[228] Case C-540/07 Commission v. Italy [2009] ECR I-10983.
[229] Under Italian tax law in force until 31 December 2007, outbound dividends were subject to 27 per cent withholding tax, unless they fell within the scope of the Parent-Subsidiary Directive. Four-ninths of the withholding tax at most could be subsequently repaid on application. This withholding tax could also be reduced if tax treaties were in place, though the rate remained higher than that imposed on dividends distributed to resident companies. For dividends paid to domestic companies, 95 per cent of the amount was excluded from tax, with the result that domestic dividends were taxed on only 5 per cent of their gross amount at the ordinary tax rate of 33 per cent. The effective tax rate was 1.65 per cent. The Commission argued that the Italian tax regime violated the free movement of capital and freedom of establishment, referring the case to the Court of Justice. See ibid, para 32.
[230] Case C-540/07 Commission v. Italy, para 33.
[231] Ibid, paras 35, 43.
[232] Ibid, para 37.

guaranteed if the dividends were not sufficiently taxed in the Member State of the recipient,[233] or if Italy had not concluded tax treaties with all Member States, as was the case with Slovenia.[234]

The Italian rules therefore restricted the free movement of capital and were not justified on the basis of preserving the coherence of the tax system, maintaining a balanced distribution of the power to tax and the need to fight tax evasion.[235] The Mutual Assistance Directive 77/799 could have been invoked by a Member State in order to obtain from the competent authorities of the other Member State all the information necessary to enable it to establish the amount of taxes due.[236] In so far as the EEA Agreement was concerned, the Court of Justice found that the restriction was justified by the overriding reason in the public interest regarding the fight against tax evasion.[237] This was because the Mutual Assistance Directive only applied between EU Member States.[238] Italy and Liechtenstein did not have an arrangement for tax information exchange[239] and Italy's tax treaties with Norway and Iceland did not contain provisions laying down an obligation to supply information.[240]

This case illustrates the importance of looking at the precise context in which the movement of capital takes place when assessing compatibility with EU law. It has been followed in Commission v. Spain,[241] a case where the threshold for the participation exemption was much higher for non-resident companies than for resident companies. Here the Court of Justice reiterated that it was possible that a Member State might succeed in ensuring compliance with its EU obligations by concluding tax treaties with another Member State.[242] However, it 'was necessary for that purpose that application of such a convention should allow the effects of the difference in treatment under national legislation to be compensated for'.[243] The Court of Justice emphasised that the difference in treatment between domestic and outbound dividends did not disappear 'unless the tax withheld at source under national legislation can be set off against the tax due in the other Member State in the full amount of the difference in treatment arising under the national legislation'.[244]

In this case most of the Spanish tax treaties provided that the amount deducted or set off in respect of tax withheld in Spain could not exceed the fraction of the tax paid by the recipient company in the home state, calculated before the deduction,

[233] Ibid, para 38.
[234] Ibid, para 41.
[235] Ibid, paras 56–9.
[236] Ibid, para 60.
[237] Ibid, para 68.
[238] Ibid, para 70.
[239] Ibid, para 71.
[240] Ibid.
[241] Case C-487/08 Commission v. Spain [2010] ECR I-4843.
[242] Ibid, para 58.
[243] Ibid, para 59.
[244] Ibid.

corresponding to taxable income in Spain.²⁴⁵ In other words, the Spanish tax treaties tended to limit the amount that could be deducted or offset. Furthermore, the difference in treatment could be neutralised only where the dividends from Spain were sufficiently taxed in the other Member State.²⁴⁶ Therefore, the actual taxation of dividends depended not only on the Spanish tax rules but also on the tax rules in the other Member States. It was concluded that Spain was wrong to argue that tax treaties always neutralised the different treatment.²⁴⁷ Since Spain did not present any justifications for this unequal treatment, the Commission's claim succeeded in so far as EU nationals were concerned.²⁴⁸ In so far as compatibility with Article 40 of the EEA Agreement was concerned, the Court of Justice found this part of the claim inadmissible because the Commission failed to provide enough information.²⁴⁹

Overall, the Court of Justice presents the tax treaty neutralisation approach as an extension of the per-country approach. It is only to the extent that the home state tax credit is part of the legal framework of the host state, being interwoven in the underlying tax treaty, that it is relevant and only to the extent that it neutralises the discriminatory effect of host state rules. The (unilateral) home state rules per se are not relevant.

Later cases raised the question whether the requirement for the full amount of the difference in treatment to be neutralised requires the conferral of a full credit.²⁵⁰ This method of relief, which is not required under the OECD Model Tax Convention,²⁵¹ may not necessarily be required in this context either. The Court of Justice focuses on whether the restriction is *in fact* neutralised as a result of the tax treaty arrangements of the host state. This means that the results may not always be consistent. Much would depend on whether the dividends are sufficiently taxed in the home state for an ordinary credit to absorb the host state withholding tax. The mere existence of a full treaty credit that in practice does not lead to neutralisation of the discriminatory tax would, arguably, not be sufficient either. In any case, in the absence of an effective arrangement for neutralisation, the obligation of the host state not to tax the outbound dividends in a discriminatory manner persists. There is no transfer of the host state's obligation to the home state simply because there is a tax treaty.

---

²⁴⁵ Ibid, para 61.
²⁴⁶ Ibid, para 62.
²⁴⁷ Ibid, para 64. One issue raised was that Spain had not concluded a tax treaty with Cyprus. Even though Cyprus offered a general exemption on dividends received from other Member States and there was in effect no double taxation, a Member State could not 'rely on the existence of a tax advantage granted unilaterally by another Member State in order to escape its obligations under the Treaty'. See para 66.
²⁴⁸ Ibid, paras 68–9.
²⁴⁹ Ibid, paras 70–5.
²⁵⁰ See scholarship on this point listed in Kofler, 'Tax treaty "neutralisation" of source state discrimination', 688.
²⁵¹ See discussion in 5.1.

Arguably, the Court's tax treaty neutralisation approach is also a necessary measure to preserve tax treaties. As most Member States have tax treaties that would neutralise discriminatory withholding taxes on dividends by placing an obligation on home states to credit such taxes, the case law of the Court of Justice seems to support the allocation of taxing powers under tax treaties, rather than undermine it.

5.3.4 Economic and Juridical Double Taxation – The Host State Perspective?

Although in an inbound scenario the Court of Justice has refused to force Member States to relieve juridical double taxation, the same cannot be said in an outbound scenario. As discussed in 5.2.3, in Kerckhaert–Morres and Damseaux the Court was unequivocal in that juridical double taxation caused by the parallel exercise of tax competences by different Member States was not incompatible with the fundamental freedoms. This was confirmed in Haribo & Salinen. A home state was not obliged to give to shareholders a credit for a foreign withholding tax, irrespective of whether it gave such credit for domestic withholding taxes.

However, some cases suggest that the Court of Justice does not make the distinction between economic and juridical double taxation in the context of outbound dividends. As such, the treatment of host state obligations does not seem to be symmetrical compared to the obligations imposed on the home state, though this is not always obvious in the judgment.

In Commission v. Germany,[252] the Court of Justice found that German laws imposing a higher tax burden on dividends paid to companies registered in another Member State or in the EEA than on dividends paid to German companies was incompatible with the free movement of capital. Here, however, the higher tax burden was a result of unrelieved *juridical* double taxation rather than economic double taxation, though this was not immediately apparent from the description of the legislative framework. Even though dividends distributed were subject to a 26.375 per cent withholding tax irrespective of the residence of the recipients, as a result of a participation exemption, dividends distributed to domestic corporate shareholders were generally eligible for an effective 95 per cent exemption.[253] A domestic company was granted a tax credit for the withholding tax levied. This tax credit was reimbursed to the taxpayer to the extent that the amount of income tax to be paid was less than the amount of the tax credit. Therefore, resident companies receiving dividends suffered no tax burden as a result of the withholding tax.[254] No such credit was granted to a non-resident shareholder, so the withholding tax became a final tax burden.

---

[252] Case C-284/09 Commission v. Germany [2011] ECR I-09879.
[253] The dividends were treated as exempt, with 5 per cent treated as a non-deductible business expense. Dividends distributed to German companies were also not taken into account in calculating such recipients' income.
[254] Ibid, para 49.

5.3 The Taxation of Outbound Dividends

The Court of Justice dismissed Germany's argument that domestic and foreign shareholders were not in a comparable position. Germany clearly chose to exercise its power of taxation over dividends distributed to companies resident in other Member States. Non-resident companies in receipt of those dividends thus found themselves in a situation comparable to that of resident companies as regards the risk of a series of charges to tax on dividends distributed by resident companies.[255] The fact that only profits redistributed by German companies were liable to suffer over-taxation in Germany, since Germany could only tax the income of the shareholders of resident companies, was irrelevant.[256]

It was argued that the presence of local income taxes imposed on resident corporate shareholders justified the different tax treatment of dividends. This argument was rejected. Unfavourable tax treatment contrary to a fundamental freedom could not be regarded as compatible with EU law because of the existence of other advantages, even assuming such advantages exist.[257]

It was also argued that tax treaties with other EU and EEA Member States limited the risk of double taxation as the withholding tax could be set off against the tax due in the home state. This was not enough, according to the Court of Justice. Although it could not be ruled out that a Member State may succeed in ensuring compliance with its EU obligations by concluding a tax treaty with another Member State,[258] it was necessary that the application of such tax treaty allowed the effects of the difference in treatment under national legislation to be compensated for.[259] Here Germany's tax treaty reductions on the withholding tax were not enough to compensate for this different treatment.[260] Neither was the application of the set-off method enough. If the dividends were not taxed, or not sufficiently taxed in the home state, the German withholding tax could not be set off.[261]

There was therefore a restriction to the free movement of capital that could not be justified by the need to ensure a balanced allocation of the power to tax and the need to maintain the coherence of the tax system.

The peculiarity of this decision is that, in essence, it dealt with juridical double taxation though as mentioned above, this may not have been discernible from the description of the legislative framework. The German system gave relief for the dividend withholding tax and not for the underlying corporation tax. The result seems to be at odds with the case law of the Court of Justice on juridical double taxation from an inbound perspective, discussed in 5.2.3. There it was shown that home states are under no obligation to extend a credit given for domestic withholding taxes to foreign withholding taxes, as they are under no obligation to relieve

---

[255] Ibid, para 58.
[256] Ibid, para 59.
[257] Ibid, para 71.
[258] Ibid, para 62.
[259] Ibid, para 63.
[260] Ibid, para 65.
[261] Ibid, paras 66–8.

juridical double taxation. By contrast, in this case the Court of Justice has imposed such an obligation but on *host* states. It is difficult to understand why the host state is required to prevent juridical double taxation on outbound dividends but not the home state on inbound dividends. In both contexts, isn't juridical double taxation the result of the parallel exercise of taxing powers by two Member States?

Whether or not this was an intentional result or whether the Court of Justice did not realise it was dealing with juridical double taxation is not certain. It would seem, however, that later cases involving investment funds, especially the Deka case analysed in more detail in section 5.3.2, might also follow this approach as the Court of Justice does not seem to be insistent on a distinction between economic and juridical double taxation. In other words, in comparing the tax treatment of domestic and outbound dividends the Court of Justice does not seem to exclude reliefs from juridical double taxation, in contrast with the position analysed in 5.2.3.

5.3.5 *Taxation on Gross Basis or Net Basis and Other Deductions*

Outbound dividends and interest are usually subject to taxation at source on a gross basis, whereas domestic dividends may be subject to taxation on a net basis. It is debatable whether this leads to discrimination.

As mentioned in 4.3.3, the Court of Justice has looked at expenses in the context of the cross-border provision of services. In Gerritse,[262] the inability of a non-resident musician to deduct business expenses in Germany where he was performing was incompatible with the freedom to provide services. To the extent that the business expenses were directly linked to the activity that generated the taxable income in Germany, residents and non-residents were in a comparable situation. Therefore, they had to be given the same opportunity to be taxed on a net basis. The same conclusion was reached in Centro Equestre.[263]

Tax treaties may be a relevant consideration in deciding whether host state taxation of non-residents on a gross basis is compatible with EU law. In Bouanich[264] the Court of Justice was asked to examine whether or not the Swedish tax legislation on share repurchases breached the free movement of capital. For resident shareholders a repurchase of shares was taxed as a capital gain and the cost of acquisition of the repurchased shares could be deducted. The gain was taxed at the rate of 30 per cent. For non-resident shareholders the repurchase was treated as a distribution of a dividend and the cost of acquisition could not be deducted. Mrs Bouanich, a French resident shareholder, was taxed at 15 per cent on this amount.[265]

---

[262] Case C-234/01 Arnoud Gerritse v. Finanzamt Neukolln-Nord [2003] ECR I-5945.
[263] Case C-345/04 Centro Equestre da Lezíria Grande Lda v. Bundesamt für Finanzen [2007] ECR I-1425.
[264] Case C-265/04 Margaretha Bouanich v. Skatteverket [2006] ECR I-923.
[265] Ibid, para 17.

5.3 The Taxation of Outbound Dividends

The Court of Justice found that it was incompatible with the free movement of capital for a share repurchase payment to a non-resident shareholder to be taxed as a dividend without a right to deduct the acquisition cost of the shares, whereas the same payment made to a resident shareholder was taxed as a capital gain with a right to deduct the acquisition cost.[266] As the cost of acquisition was directly linked to the payment made on the share repurchase, residents and non-residents were in a comparable situation. There was no objective difference between the two situations to justify the different treatment.[267] The Court of Justice further held that the France–Sweden tax treaty had to be taken into account in determining whether or not the tax legislation was consistent with EU law.[268] It was for the national court to make the assessment.[269]

What is interesting is the fact that, although the comparison was between the tax treatment of an outbound dividend and a capital gain, the Court of Justice was willing to entertain the question whether the gross basis of taxation for non-resident taxpayers made their situation less favourable compared to resident taxpayers. There is no reason why a comparison cannot be made between a domestic dividend and an outbound dividend as far as the basis of taxation is concerned.

An attempt was made to address this issue in Commission v. Portugal,[270] a case on outbound interest payments. Here interest payments to non-resident financial institutions were subject to 20 per cent withholding tax on the gross amount, reduced to 15 per cent, 12 per cent and 10 per cent under tax treaties. Interest payments to resident financial institutions were taxed at 25 per cent on net profit. The Commission argued that the legislation was in breach of the freedom to provide services and the free movement of capital. The Court of Justice dismissed the action because the Commission had failed to provide sufficient evidence that non-resident financial institutions were in fact taxed more heavily than Portuguese financial institutions. It was essential to show that the higher tax rate linked with a narrower tax base for resident institutions compared to the lower tax rate linked with a broader tax base for non-resident institutions led to different treatment. Evidence borne out of actual facts was needed. The arithmetical example given, conceded by the Commission to be a theoretical one, was not enough.[271]

This case suggested, perhaps in a rather inconclusive way, that it may be contrary to fundamental freedoms and especially the free movement of capital to impose withholding taxes on a gross basis for outbound dividends and on a net basis for domestic dividends. For a case to succeed, the heavier tax burden on outbound

---

[266] Ibid, para 43.
[267] Ibid, para 40.
[268] Ibid, para 51.
[269] Ibid, para 55.
[270] Case C-105/08 Commission v. Portugal.
[271] Ibid, paras 29–30.

dividends would have to be shown on the basis of concrete evidence rather than theoretical examples.

Of course, matters get more complicated if a host state does not tax outbound dividends on a gross basis but rather imposes a method for attributing costs that is different from the one applied to domestic dividends. Earlier case law was not at all prescriptive as to what was required for ensuring that a non-resident taxpayer's costs with a direct economic connection to the host state income were deductible.[272] Later cases confirmed that a host state should allow the deduction of costs with an economic connection to outbound dividends, when that host state allowed such costs for domestic dividends.

In the Commission v. Finland case,[273] the Court of Justice found the legislation that allowed resident pension funds to reduce the taxes payable on dividends received through permissible deductions but did not provide a similar mechanism for non-resident pension funds was in breach of the free movement of capital. Resident pension funds were authorised to deduct the amounts reserved in order to meet their obligations as regards pensions, which, in fact, gave rise to a tax exemption on those dividends. Therefore, dividends received by resident pension funds were, in effect, exempt or partially exempt from income tax as a result of the provisions of national law, but the dividends received by non-resident pension funds were taxed at 19.5 per cent, or at 15 per cent, or less under tax treaties concluded by Finland. This restriction could not be justified. Therefore, the Finnish rules were found to be in breach of the free movement of capital.

By contrast, in Commission v. Germany,[274] the Court of Justice reached a different conclusion. German tax laws allowed resident pension funds to deduct operating costs but prohibited a deduction for non-resident funds. Although the Court of Justice found that the regime restricted the free movement of capital, there was no breach. The Commission based its case on administrative operating costs, such as banking fees, transaction costs and the costs of employees handling the investments of the pension fund. The Court of Justice found that it had not been shown that such operating costs could be directly linked to identifiable dividends or interest income.

---

[272] See Case C-234/01 Gerritse, para 27; Case C-345/04 Centro Equestre da Lezíria Grande, paras 23 and 25. This issue was mentioned in Case C-105/08 Commission v. Portugal by Advocate General Kokott, who thought that 'the question must remain open as to whether non-residents' costs have a direct economic connection with their income in the host State only in the case where they can also be attributed *individually* to the income or whether, perhaps, a pro rata apportionment of global costs is required' (para 54). It has been argued that the former method would be more precise but also more difficult to apply, while the latter method would be less precise but more practical. See Philippe Martin, 'Dividends and Withholding Taxes', in Guglielmo Maisto (ed), *Taxation of Intercompany Dividends under Tax Treaties and EU Law*, EC and International Tax Law Series, Vol 8 (Amsterdam: IBFD, 2012), p 31.

[273] Case C-342/10 Commission v. Finland, ECLI:EU:C:2012:688.

[274] Case C-600/10 Commission v. Germany, ECLI:EU:C:2012:737.

5.3 The Taxation of Outbound Dividends

In another important case, Miljoen et al, the Court of Justice dealt with the tax treatment of foreign shareholders receiving dividends from a Dutch source.[275] Two cases[276] concerned Belgian individual shareholders, whereas one case[277] concerned a French corporate shareholder. In all these cases, the foreign shareholders receiving dividends were subject to Dutch dividend withholding tax. Dividend distributions to resident shareholders would also have been subject to this tax, but those shareholders would, in the end, have been subject to personal or corporate income tax, in which case the withholding tax was no more than a pre-levy.

In order to assess whether the withholding tax was compatible with EU law, the Court of Justice first assessed whether the foreign shareholders ultimately bore a heavier tax burden in the Netherlands than residents on the same dividends. In comparing the tax burden of foreign and resident shareholders, individual shareholders were distinguished from corporate shareholders. For individual shareholders, the tax burden had to be calculated on the basis of the calendar year, taking into account all shares in Dutch companies and the tax-free sum that resident shareholders enjoyed.[278] For corporate shareholders, 'only expenses which were directly linked to the actual payment of the dividends could be taken into account for the purposes of comparing the tax burden of companies'.[279] Financing costs concerning the ownership of the shares per se and pre-acquisition dividends were not included. As such, the application of a withholding tax of 15 per cent on the dividends of non-resident taxpayers resulted in them having to bear in the Netherlands a final tax burden which was greater than that borne by residents on the same dividends. This difference in the tax treatment of taxpayers was liable to deter non-resident taxpayers from investing in companies established in the Netherlands, and therefore constituted a restriction on the free movement of capital.[280]

This restriction could be justified by the effects of the relevant tax treaties between the host state and the home states, but only if the difference in treatment between resident and non-resident shareholders ceased to exist. On the facts of these cases, the Court of Justice argued that the restriction could not be regarded as justified, but ultimately left it to the referring court to decide.[281]

In the Pensioenfonds Metaal case,[282] the Court of Justice followed the Miljoen case. Although it was found that the Swedish tax legislation was not in breach of the free movement of capital for taxing dividends paid to non-resident pension funds,[283]

---

[275] Joined Cases C-10/14 JBGT Miljoen, C-14/14 X and C-17/14 Société Générale SA v Staatssecretaris van Financiën; ECLI:EU:C:2015:608.
[276] Cases C-10/14 and C-14/14.
[277] Case C-17/14.
[278] Ibid, para 54.
[279] Ibid, para 59.
[280] Ibid, para 61.
[281] Ibid, para 90.
[282] Case C-252/14 Pensioenfonds Metaal en Techniek v. Skatteverket, ECLI:EU:C:2016:402.
[283] Under Swedish legislation, only dividends paid to non-resident pension funds were subject to the Swedish withholding tax of 30 per cent on the gross amount (here, the treaty rate was 15 per cent).

nevertheless, referring to Miljoen, it was emphasised that under the free movement of capital, non-resident funds should not be prevented from taking into account professional expenses linked directly with the receipt of dividends, if such deductions were allowed in the tax base of resident funds. It was up to the referring court to decide whether the Swedish tax legislation prevented non-resident funds from taking into account such expenses.

In Brisal,[284] there was a reference to the Court of Justice regarding the compatibility of the Portuguese withholding tax on non-resident financial institutions, which prohibited deductions against interest payable to non-resident lenders. The Court of Justice found the legislation to be in breach of the freedom to provide services.[285] In light of recent case law, it was reiterated that in relation to the *deduction* of business expenses that have a direct connection to the activity pursued, resident providers and non-resident providers were in a comparable situation. The freedom to provide services precluded national tax legislation, which, as a general rule, took into account gross income when taxing non-residents, without deducting business expenses, whereas residents were taxed on their net income, after deduction of those expenses.[286] The same conclusion applied to the provision of financial services – these could not be treated differently from the provision of services in other areas.[287]

The restriction was not justified by the fact that non-resident financial institutions were subject to a tax rate that was lower than the rate applicable to resident financial institutions.[288] Nor was it justified by the preservation of the balanced allocation of taxing powers between Member States, as there was 'nothing which can explain in what way the allocation of taxation powers require that non-resident financial institutions, with regard to the deduction of business expenses directly related to their taxable income in that Member State, must be treated less favourably than resident financial institutions'.[289] As regards the need to prevent double deduction of

---

Dividends paid to resident pension funds were not subject to withholding tax, but were subject to the Swedish capital yield tax, computed on a fictitious basis. A resident pension fund was effectively taxed at a flat rate of 15 per cent on the gross dividend. The objective of the system was to ensure that the capital yield tax levied on resident pension funds was neutral from the point of view of the form of investment. The tax rate was aimed at covering the tax on all capital yield; that is, not only dividends but capital gains and interest as well. Although the Swedish withholding tax restricted the free movement of capital, it was found that a non-resident pension fund was not in a situation comparable to that of a resident pension fund. See analysis up to para 63.

[284] Case C-18/15 Brisal – Auto Estradas do Litoral SA v. Portugal, ECLI:EU:C:2016:549.
[285] As regards the first question referred, it was found that the freedom to provide services did not preclude national legislation under which a *procedure* for withholding tax at source was applied to the income of non-resident financial institutions in the Member State in which the services were provided, whereas the income received by financial institutions resident in that Member State was not subject to such withholding tax, if this was justified and did not go beyond what was necessary to attain the objective pursued. Ibid, para 22.
[286] Ibid, para 23.
[287] Ibid, para 27.
[288] Ibid, para 33.
[289] Ibid, para 37.

5.3 The Taxation of Outbound Dividends

business expenses, the Mutual Assistance Directive 77/799 (as amended and in force at the relevant time) could be used to address these concerns.[290] A justification based on the need to ensure the effective collection of tax was also rejected.

As regards what business expenses were directly related to interest income arising from a financial loan agreement, the Court of Justice reiterated that business expenses directly related to the income received in the Member State in which the activity was pursued must be understood as expenses occasioned by the activity in question.[291]

> With regard to the service at issue in the main proceedings, that is to say, the granting of a loan, it must be noted that the performance of that service necessarily gives rise to business expenses such as, for example, travel and accommodation expenses, and legal or tax advice, for which it is relatively easy both to establish the direct link with the loan in question and to prove the actual amount involved. Since taxpayers with limited liability must be able to enjoy the same treatment as taxpayers with unlimited liability, they must be granted, as regards those expenses, the same opportunities to make deductions, whilst being subject to the same requirements as regards, in particular, the burden of proof.[292]

There could be financing costs that were necessary to the pursuit of the activity, but in respect of which it may prove more difficult to establish a direct link with a given loan or the actual amount involved (e.g. the fraction of the general expenses of the financial institution, which may be regarded as necessary for the granting of a particular loan).[293] However, the mere fact that the evidence was more difficult to provide could not authorise a Member State to deny categorically to non-resident taxpayers a deduction that it grants to resident ones. It could not be ruled out that a non-resident taxpayer would be able to provide relevant documentary evidence enabling the tax authorities to ascertain, clearly and precisely, the nature and genuineness of the business expenses in respect of which the deduction was sought. Nothing prevented the tax authorities from requiring from a non-resident taxpayer to provide such proof as they may consider necessary.[294] Therefore, the Portuguese tax rules were found to be in breach of EU law.

The guidance given by the Court of Justice in this case is very important not just in the context of outbound dividends but also in the context of outbound interest.

5.3.6 Other Developments

Arguably, this is one of the few areas of case law where the principles set out by the Court of Justice have been largely followed in later cases. What is also evident is that the Commission has played a pivotal role in the development of these principles. In addition

---

[290] Ibid, para 38.
[291] Ibid, para 46.
[292] Ibid, para 47.
[293] Ibid, para 48.
[294] Ibid, paras 49–50.

to instigating litigation through infringement proceedings, the Commission has also produced valuable soft law. As early as 2004 it issued a Communication providing guidance to Member States on the taxation of dividends received by individuals as portfolio shareholders, based on the case law of the Court of Justice up to that time.[295]

The Commission also adopted a recommendation that outlined how Member States could facilitate non-resident investors claiming withholding tax relief on dividends, interest and other securities income received from other Member States.[296] The Commission recommended, inter alia, that Member States should provide relief at source rather than any refund of withholding tax, should apply quick and standardised refund procedures if relief at source was not given, should accept alternative proofs of investors' entitlement to tax relief besides certificates of residence and should allow claims to be filed electronically. The Commission also made suggestions as to how Member States could involve financial intermediaries in making claims on behalf of investors.

Furthermore, in 2011, the Commission published a public consultation paper, examining the tax problems arising when dividends were distributed to cross-border portfolio and individual investors.[297] The Commission suggested several options as proposed solutions.[298] The advantages and disadvantages of these options were listed in the consultation paper. Only the last option addressed both juridical and economic double taxation. The other options focused on juridical double taxation only.[299]

At the time, it was thought to be politically unfeasible for the Commission to force Member States to choose one of these options by renouncing their own method of taxing dividends. In the first edition to this book, it was questioned whether the ongoing litigation would make it so costly for Member States that this resistance would eventually wither away. Whilst, as explained above, the case law of the Court of Justice in this area has moved consistently without major deviations from the earlier case law, nevertheless, there have been no attempts to harmonise withholding taxes in the EU. In fact, a 2017 soft law initiative was not even as ambitious as the 2011 consultation document, focusing on best practices on withholding tax procedures in the context of

---

[295] Communication from the Commission to the Council, the European Parliament and the European Economic and Social Committee, *Dividend Taxation of Individuals in the Internal Market*, COM (2003) 810 final.

[296] See IP/09/1543: *Securities income: Commission recommends simplified procedures for claiming cross-border withholding tax relief.*

[297] See Public Consultation Paper, *Taxation Problems that Arise when Dividends Are Distributed across Borders to Portfolio and Individual Investors and Possible Solutions* (Commission, 28 January 2011).

[298] The suggested options were as follows: (a) the abolition of withholding taxes on cross-border dividend payments to portfolio/individual investors; (a) the conferral (by the home state) of a full credit for the withholding taxes levied in the host state; (c) net rather than gross taxation in the host state; (d) the application of a general EU-wide reduced rate of withholding tax with information exchange; and (e) limitation of both source and residence taxation of dividend income.

[299] For commentary, see Christoph Spengel and Lisa Evers, 'The cross-border taxation of dividends in the case of individual portfolio investors: issues and possible solutions' (2012) 21(1) *EC Tax Review*, 17–32. The authors recommended the abolition of withholding taxes combined with automatic exchange of information: ibid, p 27.

a code of conduct.³⁰⁰ Whilst in the aftermath of the BEPS project there were suggestions to impose a withholding tax on all profit distributions to non-EU recipients,³⁰¹ this does not seem to have been followed up, at least not yet.

In any case, it should be emphasised that the principles derived from the Court's case law, as analysed in 5.2 and 5.3, do not appear to be restricted to portfolio holdings. They may be relevant to non-portfolio holdings in situations where the Parent-Subsidiary Directive is inapplicable. Even if the Directive applies, national tax rules still have to be compatible with fundamental freedoms, as discussed in previous chapters. Arguably, the reverse also applies, in that principles derived from the case law relating to the Parent-Subsidiary Directive might also be relevant in the context of portfolio holdings. For example, the guidelines set out in the Danish tax cases³⁰² might be relevant in situations where there are anti-treaty shopping rules at host state level reinstating withholding taxes on otherwise exempt dividends. Furthermore, in cases of abuse, the general anti-abuse rule of the Anti-Tax Avoidance Directive could be relevant.³⁰³ The next generation of dividend cases will most likely explore these overlaps.

5.4 THE TAXATION OF INTEREST AND ROYALTIES

An issue left unaddressed at the time of the first edition to this book was whether the principles examined above were limited to dividend payments or whether they could also be applied to interest and royalty payments. This issue seems to have been settled now, with the Court of Justice approaching the taxation of dividend payments and interest payments in the same way.³⁰⁴ Although there have been no cases on royalties, there is no prima facie reason why the case law on dividends and interest cannot also apply by analogy to royalties. The focus of the case law in general is on the different tax treatment of domestic and foreign-sourced dividends or interest causing discrimination. The same analysis should apply vis-à-vis royalties, unless a different treatment is justified.

---

[300] Code of Conduct on Withholding Tax, European Commission, 20 November 2017, Ref Ares(2017) 5654449.
[301] See the European Parliament's report prepared by the Special Committee on Tax Rulings and Other Measures Similar in Nature or Effect (TAXE2). The report contained recommendations to make corporate taxation fairer and clearer and to tackle tax evasion and aggressive tax planning. One of the recommendations was a withholding tax on profits leaving the EU. See also European Parliament resolution of 6 July 2016 on tax rulings and other measures similar in nature or effect (2016/2038(INI)).
[302] Joined Cases C-115/16, C-118/16, C-119/16 and C-299/16 N Luxembourg 1, X Denmark A/S, C Danmark I, Z Denmark ApS, ECLI:EU:C:2019:134 and Joined Cases C-116/16 and C-117/16 T Danmark, Y Denmark Aps, ECLI:EU:C:2019:135. See analysis in Chapter 2 and especially 2.1.5.
[303] See discussion in 2.6.
[304] The only exception so far was in Case C-282/07 Truck Center, which as explained in this section, was not followed in later case law.

A few issues to note. Although the EU Directives impose different obligations on home states for inbound dividends and for inbound interest and royalties,[305] the reliefs are similar. Furthermore, even if the Interest and Royalties Directive applies, this does not mean that the protective scope of the fundamental freedoms is excluded. The Directive lays down the conditions for the host state to be obliged to exempt the interest or royalty payment, one of which is that the payment should be taxed in the home state. Technically, however, the Directive does not deal with the taxation of the payment in the home state. As a corollary, it does not preclude the extension of home state reliefs to inbound interest and royalties when such reliefs are given to domestic interest and royalties. What types of reliefs could be encompassed though?

Here the case law on dividends is not very coherent. It was illustrated in this chapter that as far as reliefs for economic double taxation are concerned, the Court of Justice demands the extension of such reliefs to non-resident shareholders. By contrast, the Court of Justice has been reluctant to interfere with methods of relieving juridical double taxation on inbound dividends, but the position as regards outbound dividends is less clear. This has been criticised in 5.3.4.

Arguably, the case law allowing extension of reliefs for *economic* double taxation may not be of much relevance in this context because interest and royalties, being deductible,[306] are not usually subject to economic double taxation. Assume, however, that for whatever reason an interest or royalty payment is not deductible and a tax credit is given only for domestic payments or only to resident recipients by the home state or the host state, respectively. Here, to the extent that economic double taxation *does* arise, there is no reason why the case law on dividends cannot apply, forcing the home state to extend the tax credit to resident recipients of foreign (interest or royalty) payments or the host state to extend the tax credit to foreign recipients of these payments, subject to the same caveats on comparability and justifications. As illustrated in the analysis of the case law in this chapter, each Member State has obligations only to relieve (economic) double taxation with respect to double taxation it imposes itself, and only when it relieves such double taxation on domestic dividends. Where for whatever reasons economic double taxation arises on cross-border interest and royalties, the case law on dividends ought to be applied by analogy.

In the Truck Center case,[307] the Court of Justice suggested that interest payments could be treated differently compared to dividends. In this case, under Belgian law

---

[305] As shown in Chapter 2, under the Parent-Subsidiary Directive the home state must either exempt inbound dividends, or if it taxes them, it must give a credit for the underlying (host state) tax. By contrast, the Interest and Royalties Directive does not prohibit home state taxation on inbound interest and royalties, to the extent that the recipient is the beneficial owner. If anything, home state taxation is a prerequisite for the host state exemption.

[306] See also discussion in 2.3.

[307] Case C-282/07 Truck Center.

interest paid or payable to non-resident companies was subject to withholding taxes. No withholding taxes were imposed on interest paid or payable to resident companies. In addition, under the Belgium–Luxembourg tax treaty, Belgium could impose a maximum of 15 per cent withholding tax on interest paid by a Belgian company to a Luxembourg company, if the Luxembourg company owned at least 25 per cent of the shares in the Belgian company.

The Court of Justice found that imposing a withholding tax on outbound payments of interest but exempting such domestic payments was not in breach of the freedom of establishment and the free movement of capital. The Court's judgment was centred on the rather flawed argument that resident and non-resident payee companies were not in a comparable situation but without really giving a convincing explanation why.[308] Even less convincingly, the Court of Justice argued that resident companies were not necessarily in an advantageous situation compared to non-resident companies. Resident companies were obliged to make advanced payments of corporation tax. The rate of withholding tax was also significantly lower than the corporation tax charged on the income of resident companies.[309] Therefore, there was no breach.

As explained in 5.3.2, it is not easy to reconcile the Court's judgment in Truck Center with that in the Aberdeen Property case[310] which followed shortly after – albeit in the context of economic double taxation. It was certainly not aligned with later cases. Whilst the inherent difference between interest and dividends – deductibility from the underlying corporate profits – could have justified a different result, this argument was not raised in Truck Center. Rather, the judgment appears to be based on spurious grounds.

Although Truck Center was never officially overruled, it is no longer considered good authority. In Commission v. Portugal,[311] a case on outbound interest payments, Advocate General Kokott and the Court of Justice appeared to take a similar approach to the issues as under the dividends case law. Here interest payments to non-resident financial institutions were subject to 20 per cent withholding tax on a gross basis, but reduced under tax treaties. Interest payments to resident financial institutions were taxed at 25 per cent on net profit. The Commission argued that the Portuguese legislation was in breach of the freedom to provide services and the free movement of capital. The Court of Justice, following the recommendation of its Advocate General, dismissed the action because the Commission had failed to provide sufficient evidence that Portugal taxed interest paid to non-resident financial institutions more heavily than interest paid to Portuguese financial institutions. Despite the inconclusiveness of this case, what is noteworthy is that here the non-comparability

---

[308] See analysis in paras 42–8.
[309] Case C-282/07 Truck Center, para 49.
[310] Case C-303/07 Aberdeen Property Fininvest Alpha Oy.
[311] Case C-105/08 Commission v. Portugal.

of resident and non-resident financial institutions in receipt of interest payments was not assumed, as it was in Truck Center.[312]

In later cases, the Court of Justice more clearly aligned the tax treatment of interest and dividend payments. In Tate & Lyle Investments,[313] the Court of Justice examined Belgian legislation that allowed resident investment companies an imputation credit on their corporate taxes for the 10 per cent withholding tax that had been levied on Belgian-sourced interest and dividend payments received. No imputation credit was allowed for such interest and dividend payments made to non-resident companies. The Court of Justice found this to be incompatible with EU law. Also, in Commission v. Belgium,[314] the Court of Justice treated withholding taxes on dividends and interest distributed by a Belgian company to resident and non-resident investment funds the same way, in finding a breach of the freedom of establishment and the free movement of capital under TFEU and EEA Agreement.

This case law supports the argument made in the first edition to this book, that there is no immediately apparent reason why dividends, interest and royalties should be treated any differently in this context. Not only that, but as regards the tax treatment of payments arising from non-portfolio relationships, the Parent-Subsidiary and the Interest and Royalties Directives show a clear convergence of approach.

It is a welcome development that in subsequent cases, the Court of Justice seems to have moved away from the Truck Center case and streamlined the principles applicable to dividends and interest payments.

---

[312] The Commission had relied on an arithmetical example and theoretical calculations but this was not enough. The onus was on the Commission to establish that the figures on which its calculations were based reflected economic reality, by furnishing, inter alia, statistical data or information concerning the level of interest paid on bank loans and relating to the refinancing conditions in order to support the plausibility of its calculations.
[313] Case C-384/11 Tate & Lyle Investments, ECLI:EU:C:2012:463.
[314] Case C-387/11 Commission v. Belgium, ECLI:EU:C:2012:670.

6

Reorganisations under EU Tax Law

Business restructurings[1] are a common phenomenon for multinationals in recent years, often being a necessary reaction to market demands and competition. As stated in the OECD Transfer Pricing Guidelines, there is no legal or universally accepted definition of business restructurings.[2] It is stated that for the purposes of the Guidelines, the term 'refers to the cross-border reorganization of the commercial or financial relations between associated enterprises, including the termination or substantial renegotiation of existing arrangements'.[3] Business restructurings are thought of as maximising synergies and economies of scale, streamlining the management of business lines and improving their efficiency.[4] Overall, business restructurings aim to contribute to the optimal allocation of resources. However, the tax issues pertaining to business restructurings, especially cross-border ones, are numerous and complex.

The taxation of capital gains and fiscal reserves and the taking back, in full or in part of the provisions made, is a recurrent problem. These gains and reserves are not usually taxed unless realised through the disposal of the underlying assets or the liquidation of the company owning the assets. However, a cross-border corporate reorganisation such as a merger may require the winding-up of one of the companies to be merged. This could trigger the taxation of unrealised capital gains and fiscal reserves, affecting not only the merged company but also its shareholders and increasing the costs of the merger. Furthermore, previous year losses may not be carried over to the newly created or reorganised entity, especially if these are foreign losses and/or there has been a substantial change in the business. The absence of cross-border loss relief could seriously inhibit the reorganisation.[5] Cross-border reorganisations could also lead to expenses such as financing costs becoming non-deductible. If there is debt

---

[1] In this chapter, the terms 'business restructurings' and 'reorganisations' are used interchangeably.
[2] OECD Transfer Pricing Guidelines, Ch IX, para 9.1.
[3] Ibid.
[4] Ibid, para 4.
[5] On cross-border loss relief, see also Chapter 4.

financing, then interest deductibility restrictions could also apply.[6] Many other problems may arise.[7]

In so far as domestic reorganisations are concerned, national laws invariably provide for tax deferral on qualifying assets and stock or the carry-over of losses. Therefore, there is no immediate taxation imposed on unrealised gains or fiscal reserves. Moreover, financing costs and interest payments tend to be deductible. This treatment is, however, rarely extended to cross-border reorganisations, thus leading to their disadvantageous treatment.

EU law has gone some way in addressing these problems, but many issues remain unresolved. This chapter focuses on the impact of EU law on aspects of corporate reorganisations. For the purposes of this chapter, the term 'corporate reorganisation' is used in a generic way, encompassing, inter alia, the types of transactions covered under the Merger Directive, transfers of the seat and internal transfers of assets (i.e. within a company).

6.1 CORPORATE REORGANISATIONS AND THE MERGER DIRECTIVE

The Merger Directive[8] introduces tax rules aimed at ensuring, as much as possible, that cross-border restructuring operations would not be at a disadvantage compared to similar domestic operations. As stated in the Preamble to the Directive, such operations may be necessary to create in the EU conditions analogous to those of an Internal Market and ensure the effective functioning of such an Internal Market.[9] Therefore, corporate reorganisations ought not to be hampered by restrictions, disadvantages or distortions arising in particular from Member State tax provisions.[10] The Directive contains specific rules on how to attain this objective.

6.1.1 *The Scope of the Merger Directive*

The Directive applies to certain transactions involving companies from two or more Member States.[11] A company must be of a legal form set out in the Annex to the Directive and be resident in a Member State. Therefore, the cross-border element is essential. Two companies from the same Member State cannot benefit from the Directive even if the transferring company has foreign branches of activities to be

---

[6] On interest deductibility restrictions and thin capitalisation, see Chapter 7.
[7] For example, depreciation allowances may be lost and there may be disagreement as to the valuation of assets; VAT and stamp duties may be incurred, etc.
[8] See Council Directive 2009/133/EC of 19 October 2009 on the common system of taxation applicable to mergers, divisions, partial divisions, transfers of assets and exchanges of shares concerning companies of different Member States and to the transfer of the registered office of an SE or SCE between Member States (codified version) [2009] OJ L310/34 (Merger Directive).
[9] Ibid, para 2 of the Preamble.
[10] Ibid.
[11] Ibid, Art 1.

6.1 Corporate Reorganisations and the Merger Directive 251

transferred. As with the other Directives examined in Chapter 2, the Merger Directive does not apply if pursuant to a tax treaty with a non-Member State, the company is resident outside of the EU. Only certain types of transactions enjoy the protection of the Merger Directive:[12] namely mergers, divisions, partial divisions, exchange of shares, transfers of assets and transfers of the registered office of a Societas Europaea (SE) or a Societas Cooperativa Europaea (SCE).[13]

A 'merger' as defined in Article 2(a) of the Merger Directive includes mergers into an existing company[14] or into a new company.[15] In these situations, the merging companies[16] must be dissolved without going into liquidation. They must also transfer all their assets and liabilities either to the existing (absorbing) company or a newly formed company. In exchange for such transfer, the existing or newly formed company must issue to the shareholders of the transferring company or companies securities representing their capital. A cash payment not exceeding 10 per cent of the value of those securities may additionally be made to the transferring company or companies. In Kofoed,[17] the Court of Justice held that if a profit distribution had not been agreed in a binding manner prior to the exchange of shares, a profit distribution taking place after the exchange was not part of the cash payment.

Upstream mergers are also encompassed in the Directive's definition of 'merger'.[18] Here a company, on being dissolved without going into liquidation, must transfer all its assets and liabilities to the company holding all the securities representing its capital.

A division is defined as an operation whereby a company transfers all its assets and liabilities to two or more existing or new companies on being dissolved without going into liquidation, in exchange for the pro rata issue to its shareholders of securities representing the capital of the companies receiving the assets and liabilities.[19] In other words, in return for the assets and liabilities received, the receiving company (or companies) issues shares to the (former) shareholders in the disappearing company (or companies). Again, a cash payment of not more than 10 per cent may be made. A partial division or split-off is similarly defined, with the

---

[12] Ibid, Art 1(a) and (b).
[13] Technically, the transfer of the registered office of an SE or SCE has nothing to do with merging or demerging but rather falls in the field of corporate migration. There was no need for this provision to be included in the Merger Directive, especially since the SE and SCE Regulations already provide for the transfer of the registered office of an SE or SCE from one Member State to another, without winding up or creating a new legal person.
[14] Merger Directive, Art 2(a)(i).
[15] Ibid, Art 2(a)(ii).
[16] In the case of a merger into an existing company (Art 2(a)(i)), one or more companies may be the transferring company. In the case of a merger into a new company (Art 2(a)(ii)), at least two companies must be the transferring companies.
[17] See Case C-321/05 Hans Markus Kofoed v. Skatteministeriet (2007) ECR I-5795. See analysis in 6.1.3.
[18] Merger Directive, Art 2(a)(iii).
[19] Ibid, Art 2(b).

difference being that here a company transfers one or more branches of activity to one or more existing or new companies, leaving at least one branch of activity in the transferring company.[20] This transfer is in exchange for shares to be issued by the receiving companies to the shareholders of the transferring company and not the transferring company itself.[21]

A transfer of assets is defined as an operation whereby a company transfers one or more branches of activity to another company in exchange for shares in the receiving company.[22] No cash payment is allowed for the transfer of assets. The transferring company is not dissolved. As a result of the issuing of shares, the receiving company becomes a subsidiary of the transferring company. This is effectively a transaction between companies without any tax consequences for shareholders.

An exchange of shares is an operation whereby a company acquires a holding in the capital of another company, thus obtaining a majority of the voting rights in that company.[23] The shares of the acquiring company are exchanged for shares in the other company, and a maximum of 10 per cent cash payment may be made. Therefore, the target company becomes a subsidiary of the acquiring company.

There are a number of limitations to this Directive. Firstly, only merging companies or transfers of assets between companies fall within its scope. In contrast to the Parent-Subsidiary and the Interest and Royalties Directives, permanent establishments of transferring or acquiring companies do not enjoy any protection under the Merger Directive. In addition, transfers of non-EU branches of activities of Member State companies or EU branches of activities of non-EU companies are not covered. Furthermore, the Merger Directive does not offer protection to bona fide company restructuring operations if they do not fall under the types of transactions covered and do not comply with the strict requirements of the Directive. For example, transfers of assets by individuals owning a business that does not operate as a company are not covered by the Directive.

It is also questioned whether the 'subsidiarisation' of the branch of a company is covered by the Merger Directive – that is the transfer of a permanent establishment located in a Member State to a new company established in the same Member State.[24] Although the Commission takes the view that given the Directive's purpose, the conversion of permanent establishments into subsidiaries cannot be excluded from its scope, especially since it does not affect the taxation rights of the state where the former permanent establishment was located, technically, the

---

[20] Ibid, Art 2(c).
[21] This would be covered by a transfer of assets.
[22] Merger Directive, Art 2(d).
[23] Or if the acquiring company already has such majority holding, it acquires a further holding. See Art 2(e).
[24] This is done through a transfer of assets. A company headquartered in one Member State with a permanent establishment in another Member State transforms this permanent establishment into a company of that other Member State.

Directive does not seem to cover this situation as there is no cross-border transfer of assets.[25]

6.1.2 Reliefs under the Merger Directive

The Merger Directive seeks to ensure that, when one of these eligible operations occurs, there will be no taxation of the capital gains arising from the transfer of assets and liabilities. However, the assets and liabilities of the transferring company must be effectively connected to a permanent establishment of the receiving company in the Member State of the transferring company and play a part in generating the profits or losses taken into account for tax purposes.[26] This ensures that gains arising from the future realisation of the deferred capital gains will be part of the tax base allocated to the Member State of the transferring company. There is no definition or further description of this remaining permanent establishment requirement, and the Directive does not specify for how long the transferred assets must be connected with it.

In reality, therefore, the Merger Directive does not establish a system of exemption from taxation of capital gains that result from qualifying transactions but rather a common system of deferral of such taxes.[27] The relief applies only if the receiving company computes any new depreciation and any gains or losses in respect of the assets and liabilities transferred according to the rules that would have applied to the transferring company or companies had the transaction not taken place.[28] In addition, the Member State of the transferring company must refrain from recapturing any provisions or reserves formed by the transferring company in respect of assets or liabilities transferred, as long as these provisions or reserves are carried over to the permanent establishment of the receiving company in the Member State of the transferring company.[29] Furthermore, the Member State of the transferring company must allow a carry-over of these tax-free provisions/reserves to the (remaining) permanent establishment of the receiving company.[30]

As for losses, if national law allows these to be carried over to the merged entity, then the same treatment must be extended to the permanent establishment of the receiving company, as long as it is situated in the Member State of the transferring

---

[25] 'Company Taxation in the Internal Market', SEC(2001), 236, analysed in 1.4.
[26] Merger Directive, Art 4(1)(b).
[27] See also dicta by Advocate General Jääskinen in para 37 of Case C-207/11 3D I Srl v. Agenzia delle Entrate Direzione Provinciale di Cremona, ECLI:EU:C:2012:818 discussed below at 6.1.3.
[28] Merger Directive, Art 4(3).
[29] Ibid, Art 5.
[30] There is an exception where the provisions/reserves are in connection with assets and liabilities of a foreign permanent establishment of the transferring company. As a result of the transfer, that foreign permanent establishment becomes a foreign permanent establishment of the receiving company, which therefore cannot be subject to tax in the Member State of the transferring company if those assets are later sold. See Art 10.

company.[31] If there is no remaining permanent establishment, freedom of establishment and the case law examined in Chapter 4 might still be relevant.

If the receiving company already has a holding in the transferring company prior to the merger, the participation is cancelled. Any gains accruing to the receiving company on the cancellation of its holding are not liable to any taxation.[32]

The Merger Directive contains provisions that seek to defer taxation in respect of capital gains arising from the shares exchanged by the shareholders, whether corporate bodies or individuals, as long as the allotted shares received by these shareholders are not subsequently alienated.[33] The deferral only applies if the shareholders do not attribute to the shares received a value for tax purposes higher than the value of the exchanged shares immediately before the merger, division or exchange of shares.[34] Furthermore, the deferral applies in respect of taxes arising after the exchange of shares by shareholders. Technically, a tax imposed prior to the exchange of shares may not be prevented, though the Commission has argued that this is not fully aligned with the spirit of Article 8 of the Directive.[35]

In case of an exchange of shares, the Member State of the acquired company cannot impose as a precondition for deferral the continuation of book values by the acquiring company. In the A.T. case,[36] German legislation required the carry-over of the historical book value of the shares transferred, otherwise the shareholders of the acquired company would be taxed on the capital gains arising from the transfer. The capital gain was deemed to correspond to the difference between the initial cost of the shares and their market value unless the acquiring company carried over the historical book value of the shares transferred in its own tax balance. The Court of Justice found this to be in breach of Articles 8(1) and (2) of the Merger Directive.

The Merger Directive does not contain rules on the valuation of shares. In addition, gains arising out of the subsequent transfer of shares may be taxed by the Member States.[37] This can lead to double taxation if the host state, upon the subsequent disposal of shares received by an acquiring company in exchange for transferred assets or shares from the transferring company, adopts the book value of

---

[31] Ibid, Art 6.
[32] Ibid, Art 7(1). There is an exception to this where the receiving company has a holding of less than 10 per cent in the capital of the transferring company. This is to prevent the tax-free distribution of profits through mergers of subsidiaries into their parent companies when the requirements of the Parent-Subsidiary Directive are not satisfied.
[33] Ibid, Art 8(1). The Directive provides that the transfer of the registered office of an SE or an SCE shall not, of itself, give rise to any taxation of the income, profits or capital gains of the shareholders (see Art 14(1) and para 11 of the Preamble). Technically, such provision was not needed because the migration of an SE/SCE does not involve any substitution, allotment or acquisition of shares.
[34] Ibid, Art 8(4). For partial divisions, the relief will only apply if the shareholders do not attribute to the sum of the securities received and those held in the transferring company a value for tax purposes higher than the value that the securities held in the transferring company had immediately before the partial division.
[35] 'Company Taxation in the Internal Market', pp 237–8.
[36] See Case C-285/07 A.T. v. Finanzamt Stuttgart-Körperschaften [2008] ECR I-9329.
[37] Merger Directive, Art 8(6).

the assets transferred or the shares exchanged. At the time of transfer, both the transferring company and acquiring company would be taxed on the same capital gain; in the case of the former, this would be the deferred tax, as a result of Article 8(1), and in the case of the latter this would be the subsequently realised tax, as a result of Article 8(6). As the Merger Directive does not interfere with valuation and does not require a step-up, it does not seem to prevent this situation.[38] Nevertheless, as shown in the Jacob and Lassus cases discussed in 6.1.3, freedom of establishment may provide some protection to affected taxpayers.[39]

Issues also arise in triangular situations. Where the transferred assets include a permanent establishment in a third Member State,[40] the Member State of the transferring company cannot levy a tax on that permanent establishment.[41] However, the Member State of the transferring company may reinstate any losses of that permanent establishment previously set off against the taxable profits of the transferring company in that Member State and not recovered. Other than that, the Member States of the permanent establishment and the receiving company have to apply the provisions of the Directive to such transfer as if the permanent establishment were in the Member State of the transferring company (i.e. no taxation of unrealised gains).[42]

Shareholders of fiscally transparent entities (whether of the transferring or receiving company) enjoy the same benefits and are not, therefore, taxed on unrealised gains on transferred assets.[43] Member States of shareholders of a fiscally transparent transferring/acquired company have the option not to apply the provisions of this Directive when taxing a direct or indirect shareholder of that company in respect of the income, profits or capital gains of that company.[44] However, they must give relief for the notional tax that the company could have paid on the transfer if the Directive did not apply.[45] The same applies to shareholders of a fiscally transparent receiving/acquiring company – their Member States may not apply the relief under Article 8.[46]

---

[38] 'Company Taxation in the Internal Market', pp 238–9.
[39] Joined Cases C-327/16 and C-421/16 Marc Jacob and Ministre des Finances et des Comptes publics v. Ministre des Finances et des Comptes publics and Marc Lassus, ECLI:EU:C:2018:210.
[40] The same rules apply if the permanent establishment is situated in the Member State of the receiving company.
[41] Merger Directive, Art 10(1).
[42] Ibid, Art 10(2) contains derogations for the Member States of transferring companies applying the credit method. Such a Member State has the right to tax any profits or capital gains of the foreign permanent establishment on the condition that it gives relief for the tax that, but for the provisions of this Directive, would have been charged in the Member State of the permanent establishment, in the same way, and the same amount as it would have done if that tax had actually been charged and paid.
[43] See Arts 4(3) and 8(3) applicable to a fiscally transparent transferring company and a fiscally transparent receiving company, respectively.
[44] Ibid, Art 11(1). The characterisation of a company as fiscally transparent by the Member State of the shareholders must be based on an assessment of the legal, not the fiscal, characteristics of that company arising from the law under which it is constituted.
[45] Ibid, Art 11(2).
[46] Ibid, Art 11(3).

If this situation arises, then they should treat these shareholders as if the receiving/acquiring company were resident there.[47]

The Directive also contains an anti-abuse provision. A Member State is allowed to refuse to apply or to withdraw the benefit of all or any part of the Directive where it appears that the operation:

> has as its principal objective or as one of its principal objectives tax evasion or tax avoidance; the fact that one of the operations referred to in Article 1 is not carried out for valid commercial reasons such as the restructuring or rationalisation of the activities of the companies participating in the operation may constitute a presumption that the operation has tax evasion or tax avoidance as its principal objective or as one of its principal objectives.[48]

The Court of Justice was asked to interpret some of these provisions in a number of cases, examined below.

6.1.3 Case Law on the Merger Directive

In Leur-Bloem[49] the Court of Justice examined the definition of 'exchange of shares' when dealing with a merger between two Dutch companies.[50] The Court of Justice held that it was clear from the provision itself and the general scheme of the Directive that the common tax rules laid down by the Directive applied without distinction to all mergers, divisions, transfers of assets or exchanges of shares. This was irrespective of the reasons behind these operations, whether financial, economic or simply fiscal.

The Directive was capable of applying even if the acquiring company did not itself carry on business.[51] Furthermore, it was not necessary to have a permanent merger of the business of the two companies into a single unit. This was, however, subject to the Directive's anti-abuse provision. The fact that the transaction was not carried out for valid commercial reasons, such as the restructuring or rationalisation of the activities of the companies involved, could raise a presumption of abuse.

However, to determine whether a particular operation had the principal objective of tax evasion or tax avoidance, the tax authorities could not confine themselves to applying pre-determined general criteria but instead had to subject each particular case to a general examination that was open to judicial review. The concept of valid commercial reasons involved more than the attainment of a purely fiscal advantage.

---

[47] Ibid, Art 11(4).
[48] Ibid, Art 15(1).
[49] Case C-28/95 Leur-Bloem v. Inspecteur de Belastingdienst/Ondernemiger Amsterdam 2 [1997] ECR I-4161.
[50] Here, as Dutch law was identical to the provisions of the Merger Directive, the Court of Justice held that it had jurisdiction to consider a merger between two Dutch companies.
[51] In this case, the same natural person who was the sole shareholder and director of the acquired companies became the sole shareholder and director of the acquiring company.

Further points emerged from Andersen og Jensen,[52] a case dealing with the transfer of assets. Danish law provided an exemption from capital gains on a transfer of assets if the transferring and receiving companies were both companies from a Member State, as defined in Article 3 of the Directive. The exemption was, however, subject to the prior authorisation of the Danish tax authority, which had the power to impose certain conditions.

Two employees of an existing Danish company ('Oldco') subscribed for shares in a new Danish company ('Newco'). The assets of Oldco were to be transferred to Newco in exchange for shares. Before the transfer took place, Oldco took a loan. The liability in respect of this loan (but not the amount borrowed) was to be transferred by Oldco to Newco. Newco arranged to obtain credit from a bank to finance its future cash requirements. A condition of this credit was that the bank should have a lien over the shares in Newco. These arrangements were intended to facilitate a generation change. The Danish tax authorities ruled that the transfer of assets by Oldco to Newco should be classified as a transfer of assets, avoiding taxation on capital gains, only if both the proceeds of the loan and the related debt liability were retained by Oldco (or the proceeds and the liability were both transferred to Newco), and no lien was granted in respect of Newco by its shareholders, including Oldco. The case was referred to the Court of Justice.

Here the Court of Justice held that the Directive covered only transfers of assets that encompassed all the assets and liabilities relating to a branch of activity. The transfer of the liability by Oldco to Newco, leaving the sum borrowed with Oldco, did not, therefore, satisfy the terms of the Directive.[53]

The Court of Justice had also been asked whether Newco could be said to be capable of functioning by its own means, as required by the Directive if the lien over its shares were necessary for it to carry on its activities. The Court of Justice said that this issue had to be determined by the national court because it depended on the specific circumstances of the case. In this respect, the independent operation of the business had to be determined primarily from a functional point of view and only secondarily from a financial point of view. The assets transferred had to be capable of operating as an independent undertaking without requiring additional investment. The fact that a company receiving a transfer took out a bank loan under normal market conditions could not in itself mean that the transferred business was not independent. This was true even if the loan was guaranteed by the shareholders of the receiving company, who provided their shares in that company as security for the loan.

Even if national legislation complies with the provisions of the Merger Directive, or is not caught by the Directive at all,[54] it may still fall foul of the fundamental freedoms. In

---

[52] Case C-43/00 Andersen og Jensen ApS v. Skatteministeriet [2002] ECR I-379.
[53] It was irrelevant that Oldco – the transferring company – retained a small number of shares in a third company.
[54] For example, if the relevant entity is not included in the list of companies to which the Merger Directive applies. See Art 3(a) and the Annex to the Directive.

the SEVIC case,[55] a German company was prevented from merging with a Luxembourg company.[56] The German Commercial Register refused the registration of this merger because the German Merger Code applied only to entities with a registered seat in Germany. Had this proposed merger been an internal one, it would have been registered.

The Court of Justice found this refusal to be a restriction to the freedom of establishment. A merger was an example of an activity falling within the ambit of this freedom. According to the Court, cross-border merger operations, like other company transformation operations, responded to the needs for cooperation and consolidation between companies established in different Member States. As such, they constituted particular methods of exercise of the freedom of establishment.[57] Agreeing with its Advocate General, the Court of Justice pointed out that a merger such as the one at issue in the main proceedings constituted an effective means of transforming companies in that it made it possible, 'within the framework of a single operation, to pursue a particular activity in new forms and without interruption, thereby reducing the complications, times and costs associated with other forms of company consolidation such as those which entail, for example, the dissolution of a company with liquidation of assets and the subsequent formation of a new company with the transfer of assets to the latter'.[58]

As recourse to such means of company transformation was limited to domestic companies, companies were treated differently according to the internal or cross-border nature of the merger.[59] This was likely to deter the exercise of freedom of establishment. Although the restriction could be justified by imperative grounds in the public interest,[60] it had to be appropriate for ensuring the attainment of the objectives pursued and could not go beyond what was necessary to attain them.[61] The general refusal of the German Commercial Register prevented the realisation of cross-border mergers even if the interests of creditors, minority shareholders, employees and so on were not threatened. This went beyond what was necessary to protect these legitimate interests.[62]

In Kofoed[63] the Court of Justice dealt with the concept of cash payments. It was held that a dividend distribution that took place shortly after the exchange of shares was not to be regarded as a cash payment calculated for the purposes of the

---

[55] Case C-411/03 SEVIC Systems AG [2005] ECR I-10805.
[56] The Luxembourg company was to be absorbed by the German company through dissolution without liquidation.
[57] Case C-411/03 SEVIC, para 19.
[58] Ibid, para 21.
[59] Ibid, para 22.
[60] Here, the protection of the interests of creditors, minority shareholders and employees, the preservation of the effectiveness of fiscal supervision and the fairness of commercial transactions. See, para 24.
[61] Case C-411/03 SEVIC, paras 28–9.
[62] Ibid, para 30.
[63] Case C-321/05 Kofoed.

10 per cent threshold. This was even though the parties agreed upon the dividend distribution in a non-legally binding manner when exchanging shares.

In this case, taxpayers exchanged all the shares in a Danish company for the shares in an Irish company. Four days later, the taxpayers received a substantial dividend. The Danish government assessed this distribution as part of the cash payment. The Court of Justice disagreed. A monetary payment made by an acquiring company to the shareholders of the acquired company could not be classified as a cash payment merely because of a certain temporal or another type of link to the acquisition, or possible fraudulent intent.[64] Instead, it was necessary to 'ascertain in each case, having regard to the circumstances as a whole, whether the payment in question had the characteristics of binding consideration for the acquisition'.[65] For the dividend distribution to be considered part of the cash consideration, it had to form an integral part of the consideration for the acquisition.[66]

The Court of Justice also examined whether a possible abuse of rights may be taken into account. It held that the anti-abuse provision of the Directive reflected 'the general Community law principle that abuse of rights is prohibited'.[67] Individuals could not improperly or fraudulently take advantage of provisions of EU law. The application of EU legislation could not be extended to cover abusive practices, that is 'transactions carried out not in the context of normal commercial operations, but solely for the purpose of wrongfully obtaining advantages provided for by Community law'.[68] The Court of Justice concluded that the exchange of shares would be taxable if national rules on abuse of rights, tax evasion or tax avoidance could be interpreted in accordance with the Directive's anti-abuse provision. This was a question to be decided by the national court.[69]

It is noteworthy that in this decision, the Court of Justice talked about a general Community law principle of abuse of rights in the tax context. However, the fact that for the transaction to be penalised, national anti-abuse rules had to be interpreted in accordance with the Directive's anti-abuse provision suggests that the Court of Justice was, at this point, reluctant to impose a free-standing (EU) principle of abuse of rights. This judgment is revisited in Chapter 7.

In Zwijnenburg[70] the Court of Justice found that if a certain tax was not prohibited under the Merger Directive, then national anti-abuse rules relating to that tax would be allowed and the merger transaction could be affected. In this case, Mr Zwijnenburg operated a clothes store at two separate buildings in the Netherlands.

---

[64] Ibid, para 31.
[65] Ibid.
[66] Ibid, para 33.
[67] Ibid, para 38.
[68] The Court cited Case C-212/97 Centros [1999] ECR I-1459, para 24; Case C-255/02 Halifax and Others [2006] ECR I-1609, paras 68–9; Case C-456/04 Agip Petroli [2006] ECR I-3395, paras 19–20; and Case C-196/04 Cadbury Schweppes and Cadbury Schweppes Overseas [2006] ECR I-7995, para 35.
[69] Case C-321/05 Kofoed, para 46.
[70] Case C-352/08 Modehuis A. Zwijnenburg BV v. Staatssecretaris van Financiën [2010] ECR I-4303.

One of the buildings was owned by the Dutch company Zwijnenburg BV, which was ultimately owned by Mr Zwijnenburg. The other building was leased from Zwijnenburg Beheer BV; a property management company owned indirectly by Mr Zwijnenburg's parents. In order to consolidate the two buildings in a single company and transfer ownership of the building, the entire enterprise of Zwijnenburg BV was merged into Zwijnenburg Beheer BV in a share exchange transaction. The remaining shares in Zwijnenburg Beheer BV were then purchased by Zwijnenburg BV, with no transfer tax on the buildings. Had the property simply been transferred directly, the Dutch 6 per cent real estate transfer tax would otherwise have been due.

Here the Court of Justice held that the Netherlands could not deny the benefits of the Merger Directive where a merger was undertaken to avoid the Dutch real estate transfer tax, as that type of tax was not within the scope of the Directive. Only for the taxes expressly referred to in the Merger Directive could there be reliefs and, therefore, be liable to come within the exception provided in the anti-abuse provision.[71] There was nothing in the Directive to suggest that it intended to extend the benefit of its provisions to other taxes, such as the Dutch transfer tax.[72] Such a case was regarded as falling within the scope of the fiscal powers of the Member States.[73]

The anti-abuse provision of the Merger Directive was again considered in the Foggia case,[74] where the concept of valid commercial reasons was explained in the context of business restructurings. Here the Court of Justice reiterated established case law in that the concept involves more than the attainment of a purely fiscal advantage. A merger by way of exchanging shares having only such an aim could not have a valid commercial reason.[75] A merger operation based on several objectives, which may also include tax considerations, could have a valid commercial reason provided that those considerations were not predominant.[76] Where the merger operation had the sole aim of obtaining a tax advantage and was not carried out for valid commercial reasons, such a finding could constitute a presumption that the operation had tax evasion or avoidance as one of its principal objectives.[77]

In order to determine this, there had to be a general examination of the case, taking into account aspects mentioned by the national court, such as the fact that on the date of the merger, the acquired company was no longer carrying out any management activity, no longer had any financial holdings and the acquiring company intended to

---

[71] Ibid, para 50.
[72] Ibid, para 52.
[73] Ibid, para 53.
[74] Case C-126/10 Foggia – Sociedade Gestora de Participações Sociais SA v. Secretário de Estado dos Assuntos Fiscais [2011] ECR I-10923.
[75] Ibid, para 34, citing Case C-28/95 Leur-Bloem.
[76] Ibid, para 35.
[77] Ibid, para 36.

take over the acquired company's losses not yet exhausted for tax purposes.[78] However, none of these factors could be considered decisive. As the Court of Justice held:

> a merger or restructuring carried out in the form of the acquisition of a company that does not carry on activity and that does not contribute assets to the acquiring company may, nevertheless, be considered by the latter to have been carried out for valid commercial reasons.[79]

Since Article 6 of the Merger Directive made express reference to the transferring of losses, it could not be ruled out that a merger by acquisition of a company holding such losses may have valid commercial reasons.[80] However, the fact that those tax losses were very substantial, and their origin had not been determined could constitute an indicator of tax evasion or avoidance.[81]

It was questioned whether, drawing on the terms 'restructuring' and 'rationalisation', the positive effect on the group's cost structure resulting from the reduction of the administrative and management costs could constitute a valid commercial reason within the meaning of the Directive's anti-abuse provision.[82] The Court of Justice commented that the concepts of restructuring and rationalisation must be understood as involving more than the attainment of a purely fiscal advantage. Any operation of restructuring and rationalisation having only such an aim could not constitute a valid commercial reason.[83]

While valid commercial reasons were not precluded where the restructuring/rationalisation of a group allowed its administrative and management costs to be reduced, this was not the case here. It was clear that having regard to the magnitude of the anticipated tax benefit, the saving made by the group in terms of the cost structure was relatively marginal.[84] Cost savings resulting from the reduction of administrative and management costs were inherent in any operation of a merger by acquisition as this implied a simplification of the structure of the group.[85] However, automatically accepting that such saving constitutes a valid commercial reason would entirely deprive the anti-abuse provision of its purpose.[86]

As in Kofoed, the Court of Justice stated that the anti-abuse provision of the Directive reflected the general principle of EU law that abuse of rights was prohibited. The application of EU legislation could not be extended to cover abusive practices, that is transactions carried out not in the context of normal commercial operations, but solely for the purposes of wrongfully obtaining advantages provided

---

[78] Ibid, para 38.
[79] Ibid, para 40.
[80] Ibid, para 41.
[81] Ibid, para 42.
[82] Ibid, para 43.
[83] Ibid, para 46.
[84] Ibid, para 47.
[85] Ibid, para 48.
[86] Ibid, para 49.

for by that legislation.[87] It was for the referring court to determine whether the constituent elements of tax evasion or avoidance within the meaning of the anti-abuse provision were present in the context of the dispute.[88]

The guidelines given by the Court of Justice in this case are important. To sum up, firstly, to the extent that the tax considerations are not predominant, then a valid commercial reason could be established for the purposes of the Directive's anti-abuse provision. Secondly, a merger by acquisition of a company holding tax losses may have valid commercial reasons, though the amount of the losses may be indicative of tax evasion. Thirdly, the concepts of restructuring and rationalisation must be understood as involving more than the attainment of a purely fiscal advantage but not necessarily more than the reduction of administrative and management costs, unless such costs are marginal.

Despite the inapplicability of the Merger Directive to EEA undertakings, freedom of establishment as set out in the EEA Agreement could be applicable. The Court of Justice decided this in the context of a reference from the Finnish Supreme Court dealing with the tax treatment of a cross-border exchange of shares between a Finnish limited liability company and a Norwegian LLC.[89] As the Merger Directive did not apply to such reorganisations, the Finnish court questioned whether freedom of establishment applied and whether the exchange of shares should be tax neutral, as would be the case with companies established in EU Member States.

The Court of Justice found that freedom of establishment was applicable. The Finnish rules that treated the exchange of shares as a taxable transaction restricted this freedom.[90] The restriction could not be justified by the need to combat tax evasion. The mere fact that, in an exchange of shares, the acquiring company had its place of management in a third country that was a party to the EEA Agreement could not constitute a general presumption of tax evasion.[91] The need to safeguard the effectiveness of fiscal supervision could be a valid justification. However, if an agreement on mutual administrative assistance in the field of taxation provided for the exchange of information between the national authorities that was as effective as that provided under the Mutual Assistance Directive 77/799,[92] then the justification would not be applicable.[93] It was for the national court to decide whether the existing information exchange mechanisms were as effective.[94]

It is obvious on the basis of this case law that, despite the limitations of the Merger Directive, freedom of establishment can be used as a backstop to ensure that a wider range of reorganisation operations are protected. Later cases explored some

---

[87] Ibid, para 50.
[88] Ibid, paras 51–2.
[89] See Case C-48/11 Veronsaajien Oikeudenvalvontayksikkö v. A Oy, ECLI:EU:C:2012:485.
[90] Ibid, para 29.
[91] Ibid, para 32.
[92] Now superseded by the Directive on Administrative Cooperation 2011/16/EU.
[93] Case C-48/11 Veronsaajien, para 39.
[94] Ibid.

technical issues pertaining to the Merger Directive, as well as the application of the fundamental freedoms in reorganisation scenarios.

In the 3D I Srl case,[95] the Court of Justice held that the Merger Directive did not prevent national laws which, in order to allow for tax deferral on the transfer of assets, required that the transferring company carries over in its own balance sheet an appropriate reserve fund equivalent to the capital gain arising on that transfer. In this case, the Court of Justice held that while the Merger Directive set out the conditions governing the deferral of the taxation of the capital gains relating to the business transferred, it did not establish the conditions that governed the transferring company's ability to benefit from the deferral of taxation of the capital gains relating to the securities of the receiving company issued in exchange for the transfer of assets.[96] 'In particular, it does not address the question as to what value the transferring company must attribute to those securities'.[97] The Merger Directive left it to the discretion of Member States to decide.

In the Euro Park Service case,[98] the Court of Justice considered the conditions that a Member State could impose for the purposes of applying the anti-abuse provision of the Merger Directive. Here, the French tax authorities did not defer the taxation of capital gains realised on a French company's assets at the time of its merger with a company established in another Member State, on the basis that the merging companies had not sought prior approval from the French tax authority and that the merger was not for 'valid business reasons' but for the purposes of tax evasion or tax avoidance.

The Court of Justice held that the anti-abuse provision of the Merger Directive allowed the Member States to provide for a presumption of tax evasion or tax avoidance in cases where the merger was not carried out for valid commercial reasons.[99] As far as the exercise of that option and the application of that presumption, in the absence of more detailed EU law provisions, it was for the Member States, observing the principle of proportionality, to determine the conditions needed for the purposes of applying this provision.[100] The anti-abuse provision of the Directive was not intended, as regards the measures designed to counter tax evasion and avoidance, to achieve exhaustive harmonisation at EU level.[101]

As regards the existence of a preliminary procedure, it was noted that the Merger Directive did not contain any procedural requirements with which the Member States had to comply in order to benefit from the tax advantages provided.[102] In any case, the procedure set out in national law was not compatible with the

---

[95] Case C-207/11 3D I Srl.
[96] Ibid, para 29.
[97] Ibid.
[98] Case C-14/16 Société Euro Park Service, venant aux droits et obligations de la société Cairnbulg Nanteuil v. Ministre des finances et des comptes publics, ECLI:EU:C:2017:177.
[99] Ibid, para 23.
[100] Ibid, para 24.
[101] Ibid, paras 25–6.
[102] Ibid, para 34.

Directive.[103] The national rules had to be sufficiently precise, clear and foreseeable to enable taxpayers to precisely understand their rights to ensure that they can benefit from tax advantages under the Directive and rely on them, if necessary, before the national courts.[104] Instead, the legislation at issue in the main proceedings did not specify any detailed rules for the application of the preliminary procedure. Also, the legislation did not appear to be sufficiently precise, clear and foreseeable to enable taxpayers to ascertain their rights, particularly since some of the procedural rules could change at the discretion of the tax authority.[105] It was concluded that the national procedural rules failed to satisfy the requirement of legal certainty and, therefore, the legislation was not consistent with the principle of effectiveness.[106]

Even assuming that the Merger Directive allowed the Member States to provide for such a condition, the requirement laid down by the legislation was found to be incompatible with the Directive. The anti-abuse provision had to be interpreted restrictively, and the Member States should not rely on a general presumption of tax evasion or tax avoidance.[107]

Similar issues were raised in the A Oy case.[108] Here, a Finnish resident company transferred its Austrian permanent establishment to an Austrian resident company in exchange for shares of the receiving company. The gain realised upon the transfer was immediately taxable in Finland, and the collection of the tax could not be deferred. By contrast, in an equivalent domestic situation, the capital gains would not have been taxed until the disposal of the transferred assets.

The Court of Justice found that the Finnish legislation was compatible with Art 10(2) of the Merger Directive. Therefore, Finland could tax the transfer of the foreign permanent establishment but had to give the transferring company a notional tax credit for the corporation tax that Austria would have charged on the gain if the Merger Directive had not prevented Austria from doing so.[109] However, neither this provision nor any other provision of the Merger Directive contained rules as to when the collection of the tax due was to take place. It was up to the Member States to set out the provisions for collection, in compliance with EU law.[110]

The Court of Justice found that the Finnish rules restricted freedom of establishment because, in a comparable domestic situation, the transfer of a permanent establishment to another Finnish resident company would not have been taxed.[111] Referring to prior case law and particularly to the Verder

---

[103] Ibid, para 35.
[104] Ibid, para 40.
[105] Ibid, para 41–2.
[106] Ibid, para 46.
[107] Euro Park Service, paras 47–57.
[108] Case C-292/16 A Oy, ECLI:EU:C:2017:888.
[109] Ibid, paras 19–21.
[110] Ibid, paras 21–2.
[111] Ibid, para 27.

case[112] discussed in more detail below, the Court of Justice found that the restriction to the freedom of establishment could be justified by the need to preserve the balanced allocation of taxing powers between the Member States and by the principle of fiscal territoriality.[113] However, the immediate taxation of the gains arising from the transfer of the permanent establishment and the collection of this tax was not proportionate to the extent that the taxpayer was not given an option to defer the payment of the tax.[114] Compliance with Article 10(2) of the Merger Directive did not affect this conclusion as the rule on notional tax credit dealt only with the determination of the tax due and not with the time of collection.[115] Very importantly, the Court of Justice confirmed that the legislation was disproportional not because of 'the amount of tax due but from the fact that it makes no provision for the taxpayer to defer the time at which it is collected'.[116]

The interaction between the Merger Directive and the principles of the Court of Justice in the area of exit taxes was further explored in the Jacob and Lassus cases.[117] Here, the Court of Justice was asked to examine the compatibility of the French exit tax rules with the Merger Directive. More specifically, it was questioned whether Article 8(1) of the Merger Directive prevented a mechanism that allowed the deferral of taxation of the capital gain established upon an exchange of shares until the subsequent disposal of those shares. The Court of Justice was further asked whether the Merger Directive prevented a Member State from levying the deferred tax if, at the time of the subsequent transfer, the assets exchanged fell outside its tax jurisdiction. The Lassus case also dealt with the question whether disallowing the offsetting of a loss arising on the subsequent disposal of the shares was in breach of the freedom of establishment, as such offsetting would have been allowed in a purely domestic situation.

In the Jacob case, a French taxpayer exchanged shares held in a French company for shares in another French company in 1996. The capital gain arising from the exchange of shares was subject to optional tax deferral. As such, the gain was established at the moment of exchange, but the tax was only charged and collected upon the subsequent disposal of the shares received. In 2004, Jacob moved his tax residence to Belgium, and in 2007, he sold the shares. Following this, the capital gain that was subject to deferred taxation was taxed by the French tax authorities together with default interest and a 10 per cent surcharge. It was irrelevant that the taxpayer was no longer tax resident in France. The taxpayer argued that according to the Merger Directive, the exchange of shares was not, in itself, a chargeable event and that the subsequent transfer of the shares should have been the event that gave

---

[112] Case C-657/13 Verder LabTec GmbH & Co KG v. Finanzamt Hilden, ECLI:EU:C:2015:331.
[113] Case C-292/16 A Oy, paras 31–3.
[114] Ibid, paras 35–7.
[115] Ibid, para 38.
[116] Ibid.
[117] Joined Cases C-327/16 and C-421/16 Jacob and Lassus.

rise to the capital gain. The taxpayer also argued that the sale of the shares should not have been taxable in France since he was no longer resident there.

In the Lassus case, Mr Lassus, a UK tax resident, in 1999, exchanged shares held in a French company with those held in a Luxembourg company. This gave rise to a capital gain for which the taxpayer was subject to tax in France according to the France-UK tax treaty, even though he was tax resident in the UK. The capital gain was deferred in accordance with the French legislation at the time. In 2002, the taxpayer sold 45 per cent of his holding in the Luxembourg company, which, in the view of the French tax authorities, triggered the taxation of the corresponding part of the capital gain subject to deferred taxation, established in 1999. The taxpayer incurred a loss on the transfer of the shares, which the French tax authorities refused to offset against the capital gain from the exchange of shares. It was argued that France had lost its fiscal competence over the relevant capital gain, as the transfer fell within the UK's fiscal competence.

The Court of Justice found the questions referred to be admissible.[118] In considering whether the French deferral mechanism was prohibited by the Merger Directive, the Court of Justice noted that, although the Directive provided for a fiscal neutrality requirement under Article 8(1),[119] it also safeguarded the financial interests of the Member State of the acquired entity or transferring company, including the power to tax the capital gain in respect of shares existing before the exchange.[120] In other words, the objective of this provision was not to prevent the Member States from ever taxing the gain arising from the subsequent transfer of shares.[121]

For the purposes of Article 8(1), fiscal neutrality meant that an exchange of shares could not by itself give rise to the taxation of the capital gain resulting from that transaction (i.e. the initial share exchange would not be considered as a chargeable event). However, fiscal neutrality was not aimed at preventing this capital gain from ever being taxed by the Member State with fiscal competence.[122] It was emphasised that the Member States had some latitude as regards the implementation of Article 8 of the Merger Directive. A national measure which established the capital gain when the exchange of shares occurred but did not tax the gain until the year in which the event putting an end to the deferral of taxation occurred (i.e. the subsequent transfer of the shares received in the exchange) respected the principle of fiscal neutrality as set out in Article 8(1) of the Merger Directive.[123]

---

[118] Regarding the Jacob case, the French legislation applied the same approach in a purely domestic exchange of securities as provided for under the Merger Directive (paras 36–7). As regards the Lassus case, it was found that the fact that the taxpayer was resident in another Member State than that of the acquired or the acquiring company did not exclude the situation from the scope of the Merger Directive, as the residence of the taxpayer holding the shares was irrelevant (paras 38–43).
[119] Ibid, para 47.
[120] Ibid, para 48.
[121] Ibid, para 49.
[122] Ibid, para 50.
[123] Ibid, paras 51–6.

The Court of Justice went on to consider France's powers to tax the gain resulting from the exchange. It was found that France could still tax this gain.[124] The Court of Justice noted that the Merger Directive did not harmonise the criteria for allocating taxing powers between the Member States and as such, Member States retained the power to define these criteria, by treaty or unilaterally, with a view to eliminating double taxation.[125] Consequently, Article 8 of the Merger Directive was interpreted as allowing French rules that provided for the taxation of the deferred capital gain, upon a subsequent transfer of the shares received in exchange, even though that transfer did not fall within the fiscal competence of that Member State.[126]

Finally, the Court of Justice examined whether or not the loss realised upon the subsequent transfer of the shares had to be taken into account by France when assessing the capital gain resulting from the exchange. The Court of Justice found that this question did not fall within the scope of the Merger Directive but could be assessed in light of the freedom of establishment. It was observed that, unlike Mr Lassus, a resident taxpayer would have been able to offset the loss incurred upon the transfer against the deferred capital gain resulting from the (initial) exchange. Such a difference in treatment was liable to impede corporate restructuring transactions covered by the Merger Directive and render them less attractive to non-resident taxpayers holding securities. As such, it restricted the freedom of establishment.[127] This difference in treatment could not be justified by the allocation of powers to tax between the Member States, since only the fiscal competence of France was concerned.[128]

The Court of Justice emphasised that the circumstances, in this case, were different from those under exit tax cases, such as the National Grid Indus case, which is discussed in 6.2.3. That case related to the deferral of the collection of tax, which had been definitively determined by the date when the taxpayer transferred its tax residence.[129] In that context, 'a possible omission by the host Member State to take account of decreases in value does not impose any obligation on the Member State of origin to revalue, at the time of the definitive transfer of the new shares, a tax debt which was definitively determined on the date when the taxpayer, because of [its] transfer of residence, ceased to be subject to tax in the Member State of origin'.[130] By contrast, this case related to the deferral of actual taxation. In Jacob and Lassus, the capital gain established at the time of the exchange was taxed at the

---

[124] Ibid, paras 58–9.
[125] Ibid, paras 60–1.
[126] Ibid, para 66.
[127] Ibid, para 76.
[128] Jacob and Lassus, para 81. As explained earlier on, at the date of the exchange of shares, Mr Lassus was tax resident in the UK. However, under the France-UK tax treaty, he was treated as French tax resident. As such, the capital gains resulting from that exchange of shares fell within the fiscal competence of France.
[129] Ibid, para 82.
[130] Ibid.

date of the subsequent transfer of shares. This meant that the Member State in question exercised its fiscal competence in respect of that capital gain at the time when the capital loss at issue arose. Therefore, the taking into account of such a capital loss 'form[ed] part of the obligation of the Member State seeking to exercise its fiscal competence in respect of that same capital gain, which actually becomes taxable on the date of that transfer'.[131]

In conclusion, the French legislation was found to be compatible with the Merger Directive but not with the freedom of establishment, because capital losses occurring upon the subsequent transfer of shares were not taken into account. As EU law did not provide detailed rules for the offset and calculation of the capital loss, it was for the Member States to provide such EU-compliant rules.[132]

Overall, in this judgment, the Court of Justice provided some very useful guidance on the interpretation of the Merger Directive's principle of fiscal neutrality. Furthermore, the distinction made between general exit tax mechanisms and the fiscal neutrality requirement of the Merger Directive is likely to prove very important in the future.

Later cases gave further guidance on the principle of fiscal neutrality of the Merger Directive. In the AQ and DN case,[133] the Court of Justice found that (deferred) capital gains from securities exchanged, and capital gains resulting from the subsequent transfer of those securities should be treated equally as regards the tax rate and the application of tax allowances. Therefore, if at the time of the initial exchange the domestic law provided for a holding period relief, the deferred capital gain should also benefit from such a relief and under the same conditions.[134] Here, the Court of Justice deduced a positive rule on how deferred capital gains should be taxed on the basis of the fiscal neutrality principle. As was noted, in implementing this principle, Member States had a certain degree of latitude.[135]

However, it would seem that this latitude can be exercised in a restrictive way when it comes to domestic anti-abuse rules. In a case decided shortly before the AQ and DN case, it was found that interest deductibility restrictions might be acceptable in the context of the Merger Directive. In the Galeria Parque case,[136] the Court of Justice examined the compatibility of the Portuguese rules on mergers and acquisitions and more specifically, the interest deduction limitations for reverse mergers. Here, Portuguese law prevented taxpayers from deducting interest on loans taken out to finance the acquisition of shares, upon the merger of the borrower with the target. Such costs would have been deductible if the reverse merger had not taken

---

[131] Ibid, para 83.
[132] Ibid, para 85.
[133] Joined Cases C-662/18 and C-672/18 AQ and DN v. Ministre de l'Action et des Comptes publics, ECLI:EU:C:2019:750.
[134] Ibid, paras 41–4.
[135] Ibid, para 41.
[136] Case C-438/18 Galeria Parque Nascente-Exploração de Espaços Comerciais SA v. Autoridade Tributária e Aduaneira, ECLI:EU:C:2019:619.

place. The Court of Justice found these rules to be compatible with the Merger Directive.

As was noted, 'in view of the principle of fiscal autonomy, it is the prerogative of the EU Member States, within the limits of EU Law, to determine if and under what conditions the expenses incurred by a company may be deducted against its taxable income'.[137] As such, the Merger Directive did not prevent the Member States from enacting a law whereby costs that were considered tax deductible in the hands of the incorporated company before the merger, and would have been tax deductible had the merger not taken place, were not considered tax deductible in the hands of the incorporating company after a merger.

This decision has been criticised for cancelling out the neutrality requirement of the Merger Directive.[138] It remains to be seen whether the Court of Justice will follow this restrictive approach in assessing all domestic measures which affect the principle of fiscal neutrality, or whether this restrictive approach will be relevant only in the context of specific anti-abuse rules.

6.2 CORPORATE MIGRATION AND EXIT TAXES

The previous section examined reorganisation operations falling under the scope of the Merger Directive, whereby a company undergoes a substantial change as a result of transferring all its assets and liabilities or a substantial branch of activity, or when it exchanges shares. This section looks at the situation where a company transfers its tax residence to another country. From the perspective of the home state (outbound migration), exit taxes are invariably imposed. From the perspective of the host state (inbound migration), the transfer and setting-up of an establishment there, that is the migrating company, may mean that the host state has an obligation to provide national treatment. Host state issues arising as a result of this obligation have been examined throughout this book. This part of the chapter focuses on the home state perspective and more specifically exit taxes.

6.2.1 Exit Taxes

Exit taxes are all types of charges imposed on a person upon the transfer of their tax residence. They are usually imposed on the unrealised gains over the assets of a person who becomes non-resident or over assets transferred to another state. The rationale behind exit taxes is that the home state (i.e. the state of the emigrating person or transferred asset) preserves its taxing rights over gains accruing but not yet realised in its territory. This is because under customary international tax law, as

---

[137] Ibid, para 50.
[138] Filipe Romão, Cláudia Reis Duarte & Raquel Maurício, 'Comment on Galeria Parque Nascente (Case C-438/18) Regarding the Deductibility of Interest in the Context of a Neutral Merger', 60 [2020] 2/3 *European Taxation* 76–84, 84.

encapsulated in the OECD Model Tax Convention, capital gains on movable property tend to be taxed in the home state of the alienator.[139] Therefore, in the absence of exit taxes, the home state is likely to lose the right to tax gains accrued prior to emigration but realised after that event. This is especially problematic and could lead to tax avoidance if the host state (i.e. the state of immigration) does not impose any taxes on such gains, or the tax burden is much lower there. Some countries ignore emigration altogether and do not treat it as a taxable event. This is usually the case if these countries do not levy capital gains taxes. Other countries recognise emigration but do not impose any exit taxes.

Practices in countries that have exit taxes follow a variety of patterns. Some countries levy general exit taxes on accrued gains in all items of appreciated property, others limit taxes on accrued gains in specific items of appreciated property,[140] others impose trailing taxes or prefer clawbacks of deductions and tax deferrals and so on.[141] Furthermore, exit taxes can be imposed in different ways. They can be included in specific tax treaty provisions between the countries or treated as a domestic transaction to which tax treaties do not apply, as the deemed disposal 'occurs' immediately before emigration.

Arguably, exit taxes are restrictive measures as they hinder a person's ability to move to another Member State. These taxes only apply to a person moving their tax residence abroad. A person remaining a tax resident is taxed on a realisation basis, rather than an accruals basis. This different treatment could constitute an obstacle to free movement.

There are other issues affecting an emigrating person. Very importantly, the imposition of exit taxes may lead to double taxation of both post- and pre-emigration gains on assets held by the emigrating person. Post-emigration gains will be taxed twice both by the home and host state if both states consider they have jurisdiction to tax the full gain upon disposal.[142] Even if the home state taxes the gains accrued up to the moment of emigration, if the host state does not provide for a step-up according to the deemed disposal value, then the pre-emigration gains would be taxed twice. The same consequence will follow if neither state grants a tax credit for the tax levied by the other, or if neither state takes into account decreases in value.

---

[139] See Art 13 of the OECD Model Tax Convention. Also see Stefano Simontacchi, *Taxation of Capital Gains under the OECD Model Convention, With Special Regard to Immovable Property* (Kluwer Law, 2007).

[140] For example, on shares and securities.

[141] For different types of regimes, see Luc De Broe, 'General Report', *The Tax Treatment of Transfer of Residence by Individuals*, Cahiers de droit fiscal international, Vol 87b (Kluwer Law International, 2002).

[142] This could be the case, for example, if the home state deems the emigrating person to continue to be tax resident, or if both the home and host state claim jurisdiction over the capital gains of a former resident and a resident respectively, or if the underlying movable asset remains in the home state.

6.2 Corporate Migration and Exit Taxes

Moreover, the home state may exercise its taxing rights on existing reserves and/or may take back, in full or in part, the provisions made upon the act of emigration. Unless the host state provides for the creation of similar reserves or provisions and allows deductions, then double taxation would occur.

In cases where there is a transfer of assets, double taxation could result from mismatches in valuation methods. For example, if an asset is transferred from a home state that exercises its taxing rights at the moment of transfer (at market value) to a host state that values the transferred asset at book value but subsequently taxes any increase in value upon the disposal of the asset, this could lead to double taxation. The reverse of these scenarios could lead to double non-taxation.[143]

In its 2006 Communication on exit taxation,[144] the Commission recognised the problematic nature of exit taxes on cross-border movement and urged the Member States to coordinate their exit tax policies. The Commission suggested several ways to ensure coordination and resolve mismatches leading to double taxation or double non-taxation. For example, the home state could give a credit for host state taxes and vice versa, or the two states could divide taxing rights on the gains with decreases in value to be taken into account by either state, or the host state could be required to allow a step-up based on the market value established in the home state, or each Member State could continue to value the assets according to their rules but provide for a procedure to resolve valuation disputes.[145]

The Commission emphasised that all these methods depend on effective administrative cooperation and mutual recognition. It was also recognised that these methods could offer 'scope for tax arbitrage in that taxpayers may seek to exploit differences in valuation practices between [Member States] to maximise the amount of gains taxed in the [Member States] with the lower corporate tax rate'.[146] The Commission expressed its willingness to assist the Member States in developing guidance to remove discrimination and double taxation and, at the same time, prevent unintended non-taxation, abuse and tax base erosion.

Following this Communication, the European Council also adopted a resolution[147] with some guiding principles for the transfer of economic activities[148] between Member States. Similar to the Commission's Communication, the emphasis was

---

[143] For example, if the home state refrains from taxing the gains and the host state provides a step-up, or if neither state takes into account the pre-emigration gain, or if both states take into account decreases in value.

[144] Communication from the Commission to the Council, the European Parliament and the European Economic and Social Committee, *Exit Taxation and the Need for Co-ordination of Member States' Tax Policies*, COM(2006) 825.

[145] Ibid, pp 5–7.

[146] Ibid, p 7.

[147] Council Resolution 16412/08 of 2 December 2008.

[148] This was defined in the resolution as any operation whereby a taxpayer subject to corporation tax or a natural person engaged in a business ceases to be subject to corporate or personal income tax in a Member State (the exit state) while at the same time becoming subject to corporate or personal income tax in another Member State (the host state); or transfers a combination of assets and

on symmetrical treatment: the host state had to allow a step-up in the base cost when the home state taxed unrealised gains. Therefore, both the Commission and the Council preferred a holistic approach: the home state and the host state had to cooperate to remove impediments to cross-border movement as a result of exit taxation.

As shown below, the Court of Justice does not appear to follow this approach in its case law on exit taxes on individuals, nor in its case law on exit taxes on companies. Although, the Court of Justice initially appeared to be protective of emigrating individuals, its stance hardened in later years. This approach seems to have been solidified in later case law and is in fact now incorporated in the Anti-Tax Avoidance Directive.

6.2.2 *The Early Exit Tax Cases on Individuals*

Initially, the Court of Justice dealt with cases challenging exit taxes imposed on individuals.

In Hughes de Lasteyrie du Saillant,[149] a taxpayer transferring his residence from France to Belgium was required by French legislation to pay tax on the unrealised increases in the value of his shareholding.[150] The tax payment could be suspended until the taxpayer actually sold the shares, but only if the taxpayer provided a guarantee sufficient to ensure recovery of the tax. The tax would also be waived if, after five years, the taxpayer still owned the shares.

According to the Court of Justice, freedom of establishment prohibited the home state from restricting the ability of its own nationals to exercise their freedom of establishment in another Member State,[151] even if the restriction was of limited scope or minor importance.[152] Here, although the French rules did not prevent French taxpayers from exercising their right of establishment, they had a dissuasive effect, as taxpayers wishing to transfer their tax residence outside France were subject to disadvantageous treatment in comparison with persons who maintained their residence in France. Taxpayers became liable, simply by reason of such transfer, to tax on gains that had not yet been realised whereas, if they remained in France, increases in value would become taxable only when, and to the extent that, they were actually realised. This difference in treatment was likely to discourage taxpayers from carrying out such a transfer.[153]

---

liabilities from a head office or a permanent establishment in the exit state to a permanent establishment or a head office in the host state. Ibid, p 3.

[149] Case C-9/02 Hughes de Lasteyrie du Saillant [2004] ECR I-02409.
[150] The taxpayer held either directly or indirectly with members of his family securities conferring entitlement to more than 25 per cent of the profits of a company subject to corporation tax and established in France.
[151] Case C-9/02 Hughes de Lasteyrie, para 42.
[152] Ibid, para 43.
[153] Ibid, paras 45–6.

Although it was possible to benefit from the suspension of payment, that was not automatic and was in fact subject to strict conditions,[154] including, in particular, conditions as to the setting-up of guarantees. Those guarantees in themselves had a restrictive effect, in that they deprived the taxpayer of the enjoyment of the assets given as a guarantee.[155] Therefore, there was a restriction that was not justified and as such, constituted a breach of freedom of establishment.

In the N case,[156] the Court of Justice examined the Dutch exit tax rules. Here, substantial shareholders (i.e. shareholders owning at least a five per cent interest in a non-transparent entity) who transferred their place of residence outside the Netherlands were subject to an exit tax. Under certain circumstances, taxpayers were granted a ten-year extension to pay ('conservative tax assessment') on the provision of security. If the ten-year period expired without any disposal of shares, taxpayers were acquitted from their liability and the security was released.

Mr N emigrated from his permanent residence in the Netherlands to the UK. He was the sole shareholder of three Dutch companies, the management of which had since that date been transferred to the Netherlands Antilles. As a result of the old rules, Mr N received a conservative tax assessment. He complained that the Dutch rules restricted his freedom of movement.

Citing Hughes de Lasteyrie, the Court of Justice found that the Dutch rules constituted an obstacle to the freedom of establishment.[157] Although it was possible to benefit from the suspension of payment, this was not automatic and was subject to conditions, such as the provision of guarantees. Those guarantees had a restrictive effect, in that they deprived taxpayers of the enjoyment of the assets given as a guarantee.[158] Another point made by the Court of Justice was that as a result of the Dutch rules, decreases in value occurring after the transfer of residence were not taken into account in order to reduce the tax debt. As such, the tax on the unrealised increase in value could have exceeded what Mr N would have had to pay if the disposal had taken place on the same date, without him transferring his residence abroad.[159] Moreover, the tax declaration required at the time of the transfer of residence was an additional formality likely to hinder the taxpayer's freedom of establishment further.[160]

The Court of Justice then examined whether the Dutch rules pursued legitimate objectives in the public interest. Rather than looking at the justification grounds considered in Hughes de Lasteyrie, the Court of Justice focused on the preservation

---

[154] The taxpayer had to lodge a specific application for deferment within a certain time period. The taxpayer also had to designate a tax representative with power to represent him vis-à-vis the tax authorities. Furthermore, he had an annual obligation to send the tax authorities a statement of changes in the (unrealised) capital gains in question. Any delay in doing so could lead to forfeiture of the deferral. See paras 36–8 of Advocate General's opinion.
[155] Case C-9/02 Hughes de Lasteyrie, para 47 (Court of Justice).
[156] Case C-470/04 N v. Inspecteur Van de Belastingdienst Oost/Kantoor Almelo [2006] ECR I-7409.
[157] Ibid, para 39.
[158] Ibid, para 37.
[159] Ibid, para 37.
[160] Ibid, para 38. See also Advocate General's opinion, para 79.

of taxing powers between the Member States, namely the power to tax increases in the value of company holdings.[161] As the Court of Justice explained, in the absence of any unifying or harmonising Community measures, Member States retained the power to define, by treaty or unilaterally, the criteria for allocating their powers of taxation with a view to eliminating double taxation. In so doing, Member States could find inspiration in international practice and in particular the OECD Model Tax Convention.[162]

An interesting argument made by the Advocate General to show the coherence of the Dutch rules was that in addition to the tax liability on emigrating taxpayers with substantial shareholdings, the rules provided a corresponding step-up for immigrating taxpayers at the time of immigration. According to the Advocate General, this method was consistent with the principle of territoriality because it took account only of the profit that had arisen during the period of residence within the territory.[163] The Court of Justice did not address this point. The argument could not have succeeded in any case, and double taxation would not have been avoided if the host state did not allow or provide for a step-up – which was, in fact, the case here as the UK–Netherlands tax treaty did not impose such a step-up obligation.[164] However, it is noteworthy that the Court of Justice refrained from examining the tax treatment of the emigrating shareholder in the host state in assessing the compatibility of the exit tax rule in the home state.

In any case, the Court of Justice found the Dutch rules to be suitable for attaining their objective[165] and proceeded to examine the issue of proportionality. The conservative assessment was allowed, as long as there was no immediate tax collection and no requirement for the provision of guarantees. The obligation to provide guarantees was disproportional as there were methods less restrictive of the fundamental freedoms, such as using the Mutual Assistance Directives (now superseded by new legislation).[166] In addition, the Dutch exit tax rules had to take full account of any reductions in value capable of arising after the transfer of residence by the taxpayer concerned, unless such reductions had already been taken into account in the host Member State.[167] The release of the security by the Dutch government could not have amounted to a retrospective lifting of the costs associated with the giving of a guarantee.[168]

---

[161] Ibid, para 41. The use of this justification on a stand-alone basis was rather novel at the time. In Case C-446/03 Marks & Spencer plc v. IRC [2005] ECR I-10837 this justification was to be considered together with two other grounds (preventing double relief of losses and tax avoidance). See para 51.
[162] Case C-470/04 N, para 46.
[163] See para 107 of the Advocate General's opinion.
[164] See Oliver Gutman, 'Cartesio Oktato es Szolgaltato bt – the ECJ gives its blessing to corporate exit taxes', [2009] 4 *British Tax Review*, 385–95, 390.
[165] Case C-470/04 N, para 47.
[166] See analysis in Chapter 2, at 2.7.
[167] Ibid, paras 53–5.
[168] As regards costs, the deposit of company shares by way of security may have reduced confidence in the solvency of their owner, to whom less favourable credit conditions might have applied. Ibid, para 57. The decision of the Court of Justice was confirmed by the Dutch Supreme Court when the case

Therefore, in the earlier case law on emigrating individuals, the Court of Justice readily viewed the imposition of immediate exit taxes as a restriction to the freedom of establishment. The obligation for a tax declaration at the time of transfer and the obligation to give a guarantee for deferral to be allowed were also viewed as restrictive measures. The restriction could be justified,[169] but it had to be proportional. Any home state exit tax mechanism also had to take into account reductions in value arising after the transfer of tax residence, unless such reductions had already been taken into account in the host state.

It was questioned at the time whether the above principles also applied to emigrating companies. In the first case dealing with such taxes, the National Grid Indus case,[170] the Court of Justice paved the way for a new approach, without expressly overruling the principles set out in the case law so far.

6.2.3 *The National Grid Indus Case and Its Aftermath*

National Grid Indus BV was a company incorporated under Dutch law which had its place of effective management in the Netherlands. Since 1996, it had a claim expressed in sterling against National Grid Company plc, a company established in the UK. Following the rise in the value of the pound sterling against the Dutch guilder, an unrealised exchange rate gain was generated on that claim. In 2000, National Grid Indus transferred its place of effective management to the UK and, by virtue of the relevant tax treaty, after the transfer, it was deemed to be UK tax resident. The Dutch tax authorities imposed a final settlement on the unrealised capital gains existing at the time of the transfer of the place of management and demanded immediate payment of the tax.

National Grid Indus contested the final settlement, claiming that it was contrary to freedom of establishment. Eventually, the case was referred to the Court of Justice. The referring court asked whether a company incorporated under the laws of a Member State, which transferred its real company seat to another Member State, could invoke freedom of establishment if a final settlement tax was imposed by the first Member State in respect of that transfer. If that were the case, the referring

---

went back to it. Mr N was compensated for the cost of providing the guarantee, but the preliminary tax assessment stayed intact, with the caveat that future decreases in the value of the shares should be taken into account upon collection. See Hoge Raad, 20 February 2009, no 07/12314, V-N 2009/11.9. See also Charlotte Bornhaupt, 'Dutch Supreme Court upholds exit tax on shareholder', (16 March 2009) 53(11) *Tax Notes International*, 942–4; Dennis Weber and Mark Persoff, 'Case law – the Netherlands, UK', (2009) 18(3) *EC Tax Review*, 138–40.

[169] For a critical assessment of the justification grounds used in these cases, see Christiana HJI Panayi 'Exit Taxation as an Obstacle to Corporate Emigration from the Spectre of EU Tax Law', [2011] *Cambridge Yearbook of European Legal Studies* 245–82, Pt IV.

[170] Case C-371/10 National Grid Indus BV v. Inspecteur van de Belastingdienst Rijnmond/kantoor Rotterdam [2011] ECR I-12273. For commentary, see Christiana HJI Panayi, 'National Grid Indus BV v Inspecteur de Belastingdienst Rijnmond/kantoor Rotterdam: Exit taxes in the European Union revisited' [2012] 1 *British Tax Review*, 41–9.

court questioned if it was contrary to freedom of establishment for the final settlement tax to be applied without deferment and the possibility of taking into consideration subsequent decreases in value, or whether this could be justified by the necessity of allocating the power to impose taxes between the Member States.

The Court of Justice largely agreed with the decision of its Advocate General and found that the charging of tax on unrealised capital gains over the assets of a company when it transfers its place of management to another Member State restricted the freedom of establishment.[171] This restriction was justified on the basis of ensuring the preservation of the allocation of powers of taxation between the Member States.[172] A Member State was entitled to tax the economic value generated by an unrealised capital gain in its territory.[173]

As far as proportionality was concerned, the Court of Justice distinguished between the ascertainment of the amount of tax and the recovery of the tax. The immediate ascertainment and recovery of the tax when the company transferred its place of management, without the company being given the possibility of deferred payment of the tax, was disproportional. By contrast, the immediate ascertainment of the amount of tax but with the possibility of deferred payment, even without taking into account decreases in value, was not disproportional.

In this case, the Court of Justice clearly deviated from some of the principles laid down in its earlier exit tax case law on individuals. Contrary to the N case, decreases of value were not to be taken into account for the establishment of the exit tax. As the Court of Justice reasoned, the tax due on the unrealised capital gains was determined when the power of the Member State of origin to tax the company ceased to exist; here at the time of the transfer of the company's place of management.[174] The fact that the final settlement tax related to a (currency) profit that accrued under the tax jurisdiction of the Netherlands and that the profit could not be reflected in the host Member State was irrelevant. This was in accordance with the principle of fiscal territoriality.[175] A possible omission by the host Member State to take account of decreases in value did not impose any obligation on the Member State of origin to revalue, at the time of realisation of the asset concerned, the tax debt definitively determined when the company in question ceased to be subject to tax in the latter Member State because

---

[171] Case C-371/10 National Grid Indus, paras 40–1. Contrary to the submissions of Member States, the fact that the gain was in effect an exchange rate gain that disappeared when the place of effective management was transferred to the UK did not mean that the gain had been realised. The Court of Justice also conceded that it made no difference to its analysis that the unrealised gains taxed related to exchange rate gains 'which cannot be reflected in the host Member State under the tax system in force there'. Ibid, para 64.

[172] Ibid, paras 46–51. The need to maintain the coherence of the national tax system, as a justification, was considered to coincide with the balanced allocation of powers of taxation. See paras 80–2. The risk of tax avoidance as a justification also failed as the mere transfer of residence to another Member State could not give rise to a general presumption of tax evasion. See paras 83–4.

[173] Ibid, para 49.

[174] Ibid, para 59.

[175] Ibid, para 60.

6.2 Corporate Migration and Exit Taxes

of the transfer of its place of effective management.'[176] It was emphasised that the Treaty offered no guarantee to a company covered by Article 54 TFEU in that transferring its place of effective management to another Member State would be neutral as regards taxation.[177] Therefore, in so far as the deferred recovery option was concerned, the claim was already ascertained'[178] and decreases in value were not to be taken into account.

Following this case, home states were allowed to give taxpayers the following option: either pay the exit tax immediately (and suffer in terms of cash-flow and forego decreases in value) or defer the payment (and suffer the administrative burden in connection with the tracing of the assets and *still* not have decreases in value taken into account). The deferred payment of the amount of tax would be 'possibly together with interest in accordance with the applicable national legislation'.[179] Furthermore, contrary to its earlier case law,[180] provision of a bank guarantee as insurance against the risk of non-recovery of the tax was accepted by the Court of Justice.[181]

After this decision, there was concern that the National Grid Indus case made the emigration of companies more cumbersome and costly than the emigration of individuals. In the first edition of this book, the author argued that there was no reason why the two situations should be treated differently. Later judgments confirmed that the two situations should be approached in the same way, but in line with the National Grid Indus precedent and not the earlier case law discussed in 6.2.2.

In Commission v. Spain,[182] a case on emigrating individuals, the Court of Justice looked at deferral of realised but not yet taxable income. Here under Spanish law, where taxpayers became non-resident, any income not previously brought into charge to income tax was charged in the last tax year in which they were considered residents. The difference between this case and the earlier cases on emigrating individuals was that the Spanish legislation only dealt with the taxation of income that had already been realised but not charged to tax prior to emigration. The Commission sought a declaration that this was incompatible with the principle of free movement of persons laid down in the citizenship provision, the free movement of workers and the freedom of establishment.

---

[176] Ibid, para 61.
[177] Ibid, para 62.
[178] See, for example, para 72 ('tracing of the individual assets for which a capital gain was ascertained at the time when the company transferred its place of effective management to another Member State'), para 77 ('the tracing of assets relates only to the recovery of the tax debt, not to its ascertainment'), para 78 ('the assistance of the host Member State will concern not the correct ascertainment of the tax but only its recovery').
[179] Ibid, para 73.
[180] See analysis in 6.2.2.
[181] Ibid, para 74.
[182] Case C-269/09 Commission v. Spain, ECLI:EU:C:2012:439.

The Court of Justice looked at the issues first in light of the latter two freedoms, rather than the citizenship provision.[183] Although the Spanish legislation did not prevent a taxpayer resident in Spain from exercising his right to freedom of movement, it was 'capable none the less of restricting the exercise of that right by exerting, at the very least, a deterrent influence on taxpayers wishing to settle in another Member State'.[184] It was acknowledged that the taxpayer was not subject to an additional tax at the time of transferring his residence as the taxable income had already been realised, but he was still deprived of an advantage that could facilitate the payment of the debt.[185] The withdrawal of that advantage constituted a clear disadvantage in terms of cash-flow.[186] The measure was liable to obstruct the exercise of the free movement of workers and freedom of establishment.[187]

The restriction could not be justified by the need to ensure the effective recovery of the tax debt. Relying on the distinction between recovery and ascertainment of a tax debt set out in the National Grid Indus case, the Court of Justice argued that since the tax debt was definitively determined at the time of emigration, the assistance required from the host state would be sufficiently covered by the existing EU cooperation mechanisms.[188] Although these mechanisms did not always function in an efficient and satisfactory manner, this could not justify the restriction.[189] As far as the justification of preserving the balanced allocation of taxing powers between the Member States was concerned, this was rejected on similar grounds. Here what was at issue was the immediate recovery of the tax debt at the time of the transfer of residence and not the determination of the tax debt – the latter only being relevant to the allocation of taxing powers between the Member States.[190] As for the need to preserve the coherence of the Spanish tax system, this was also rejected as no other Member State had sought to tax the income realised in Spain.[191]

The same conclusions applied in the context of the citizenship provision.[192] However, the Court of Justice concluded that there was no violation of the EEA Agreement. Although there was a restriction, this was justified on the basis of ensuring the effectiveness of fiscal supervision and the prevention of tax avoidance. This was because of the different legal context applicable to EEA States and because there may not be agreements for the exchange of information between some Member States and some EEA States.[193]

---

[183] Ibid, para 50.
[184] Ibid, para 56.
[185] Ibid, para 58.
[186] Ibid, para 59.
[187] Ibid, para 61.
[188] Ibid, paras 68–9.
[189] Ibid, para 72.
[190] Ibid, paras 81–2.
[191] Ibid, paras 85–6.
[192] Ibid, paras 91–3.
[193] Ibid, paras 96–7.

The Court of Justice, however, refrained from discussing whether Spain was allowed to require guarantees and/or to calculate interest, as suggested in National Grid Indus. In Commission v. Portugal,[194] a case dealing with the Portuguese exit tax provisions,[195] Advocate General Mengozzi addressed these issues. He argued that, in accordance with the principle of equivalence, if in its national legislation generally applicable to the recovery of tax claims, the home state provided that the option of deferred payment came together with interest, there was no objective reason to exclude from it the situation of an emigrating company, whose tax debt in the home state was ascertained at the time of that transfer.[196]

However, as far as bank guarantees were concerned, Advocate General Mengozzi was not as permissive as the Court of Justice in the National Grid Indus case. The Advocate General thought that the systematic application of such a requirement with a view to ensuring the recovery of tax in the context of deferred payments could have an equally restrictive effect as immediate payment at the time of emigration since it was likely to deprive the taxpayer of the enjoyment of the assets provided as a guarantee.[197] A strict interpretation of the requirement for bank guarantees had to be given,[198] and such guarantees should only be required if there was a genuine and serious risk of non-recovery of the tax claim.[199]

The Court of Justice largely followed the opinion of its Advocate General in finding that almost[200] all the national tax provisions violated the freedom of establishment. However, it refrained from discussing the issue of interest for late payment and guarantees. A few years later, the Commission again successfully pursued infringement proceedings against Portuguese exit tax rules affecting individuals.[201]

Notwithstanding the criticism of some of the above cases, it would seem that the judgments of the Court of Justice on exit taxes could address some of the limitations of the Merger Directive. The DI. VI. case[202] provides a good example of this. In this

---

[194] Case C-38/10 Commission v. Portugal, ECLI:EU:C:2012:521.
[195] Here what was at issue was the immediate taxation of unrealised capital gains relating to (1) assets of Portuguese companies transferring their registered office and effective management to another Member State or a state party to the EEA Agreement; (2) assets assigned to a Portuguese permanent establishment of a non-resident company in the case of the cessation of that company's activity in Portuguese territory; and (3) assets transferred out of Portuguese territory assigned to a Portuguese permanent establishment of a non-resident company. It was questioned whether the Portuguese legislation was compatible with freedom of establishment.
[196] Ibid, para 77 (Advocate General).
[197] Ibid, para 78 (Advocate General).
[198] Ibid, para 81 (Advocate General).
[199] Ibid, para 82 (Advocate General).
[200] There was no restriction of freedom of establishment in cases where there was taxation as a result of the cessation of activity of a Portuguese permanent establishment. What caused the taxation was not the transfer of all the activities related to a Portuguese permanent establishment to another Member State but the actual cessation of activities. Ibid, para 30 (Court of Justice).
[201] Case C-503/14 Commission v. Portugal, ECLI:EU:C:2016:979.
[202] Case C-380/11 DI. VI. Finanziaria di Diego della Valle & C. Sap A v. Administration des contributions en matière d'impôts, ECLI:EU:C:2012:552.

case, Luxembourg rules that made the granting of a reduction in capital tax conditional on the taxpayer remaining liable to Luxembourg capital tax for the next five tax years was found to be incompatible with freedom of establishment. DADV was a company incorporated under Luxembourg law that transferred its seat to Italy, where it was absorbed by an Italian company, DI. VI., by means of a merger. Two years prior to the transfer of its seat, DADV had received a capital tax reduction and had since maintained the required reserve in its balance sheet. As a result of the transfer, the capital tax reduction was withdrawn. Had the company remained in Luxembourg, the benefit of the capital tax reduction would only have been withdrawn if the reserve provided for in the legislation was used, before the expiry of the five-year period, for purposes other than the capitalisation of the company.[203]

The Court of Justice found that the different treatment had negative repercussions on the assets of companies wishing to transfer their seat outside Luxembourg and was liable to deter them from doing so during the five-year period following the conferral of the capital tax reduction.[204] This difference in treatment could not be justified by the need to ensure a balanced allocation of tax powers between Member States. Withdrawing the capital tax reduction and requiring immediate payment when the company transferred its seat to another Member State did not ensure Luxembourg's powers of taxation or the balanced allocation of the powers of taxation between the Member States.[205] Furthermore, as there was no direct link between the tax advantage granted and the offsetting of that advantage by a particular tax levy, the legislation could not be justified by the need to ensure the coherence of the national tax system.[206]

Following this case, Member States that impose conditions on merging companies for the tax deferral of assets and preservation of fiscal reserves may have to reassess their rules. Whether or not conditions such as the Merger Directive's remaining permanent establishment condition would also be caught is yet to be seen. On the one hand, the judgments of the Court of Justice are broad enough for such a condition to be considered restrictive. On the other hand, such a condition could be interpreted as being akin to the requirement of a guarantee accompanying deferral of taxation – something that the Court of Justice approved in National Grid Indus.

In Arcade Drilling,[207] a Norwegian limited liability company was deemed (by the Norwegian tax authorities) to have relocated outside Norway.[208] As a result, an obligation to liquidate under domestic company law was imposed, giving rise to liquidation taxes. The Norwegian tax authorities also claimed that failure to meet

---

[203] Ibid, para 35.
[204] Ibid, para 36.
[205] Ibid, paras 44–5.
[206] Ibid, paras 46–8.
[207] Case E-15/11 Arcade Drilling AS v. The Norwegian State [2013] 1 CMLR 416.
[208] This was because all board meetings were held in the UK from 2001 and, as from December 2002, all board members were UK resident.

the obligation to liquidate still led to liquidation taxation based on a general anti-avoidance rule. This was disputed by the Norwegian company as it had not technically been liquidated.

The EFTA Court decided that, even though the Norwegian company relocated its head office to the UK, it was still a company established under Norwegian company law. As such, it could rely on freedom of establishment. In the absence of clear provisions in national law, the relocation of its head office did not take away the company's right to rely on the freedom of establishment. The EFTA Court found that the liquidation tax restricted the freedom of establishment. Following the National Grid Indus case, the restriction could be justified on the basis of maintaining the balanced allocation of the power to impose taxes between the EEA States, but the legislation may have been disproportionate.

The EFTA Court accepted that the national authorities were entitled to establish the final amount of the tax at the time of relocation but held that it was disproportionate to require the immediate payment of the tax. The immediate payment could give rise to a significant disadvantage for the company relocating its head office in terms of cash-flow, and in some cases, it could force it into liquidation.[209] This problem could be avoided by deferring the recovery of the tax debt until the assets in respect of which a tax amount was established by the authorities of the EEA State on the occasion of the relocation of a company's place of head office to another EEA State were actually realised.[210]

The EFTA Court followed the judgment of the Court of Justice in the National Grid Indus case in stating that national authorities may take certain measures in order to secure the eventual payment of the amount of tax, provided that there was a genuine and proven risk of non-recovery.[211] This risk was essentially 'dependent on the nature and extent of the company's tax positions, and the sources of information available to the national authorities regarding these tax positions, inter alia, through cooperation with and the exchange of information with the authorities of other EEA States'.[212] If it were easy to trace the individual assets, capital and other positions for which a tax amount was ascertained, then the company could be offered a choice in the EEA State of origin between immediate payment of the amount of tax, which created a disadvantage for that company in terms of cash-flow but freed it from subsequent administrative burdens, and deferred payment of the amount of tax. The latter option could entail interest and would involve an administrative burden for the company in connection with tracing the relocated assets.[213] However, this would be less harmful to the freedom of establishment.

---

[209] Ibid, para 100.
[210] Ibid.
[211] Ibid, para 101.
[212] Ibid, para 102.
[213] Ibid, para 103.

According to the EFTA Court, account also had to be taken of the risk of non-recovery of the tax, which increased over time.[214] Such risk could be taken into account by Norway through measures such as the provision of a bank guarantee. In these specific circumstances, a bank guarantee could be unnecessary if the risk of non-recovery was covered by the personal liability of the shareholders for the outstanding tax debts of the company.[215]

The National Grid Indus case was also followed in Commission v. Netherlands,[216] a case dealing with exit tax rules imposed on both emigrating individuals and legal entities on the relocation of their businesses' place of effective management from the Netherlands to another country. If there were a remaining permanent establishment, the exit tax did not apply to assets and liabilities attributable to such permanent establishment. The Court of Justice ruled that the Dutch rules breached the freedom of establishment – the remaining permanent establishment provision was not enough. What is interesting is that during the infringement proceedings, the Netherlands announced that it would change its exit tax rules with retroactive effect. In fact, the Minister of Finance published a policy statement giving taxpayers the option to defer payment of tax under some conditions if relocation was to another EU/EEA State. However, it was irrelevant to the Commission and later to the Court of Justice that the law had already changed. The proceedings were upheld.

In Commission v. Spain,[217] the Court of Justice again followed the new line of reasoning. Here, Spanish legislation imposed an immediate exit tax on the unrealised gains accrued by Spanish resident companies and Spanish permanent establishments of non-resident entities when a Spanish company transferred its tax residence abroad without allocating its assets to a remaining (Spanish) permanent establishment (situation a). An immediate exit tax was also levied where a permanent establishment located in Spain ceased its activities (situation b) or transferred its assets outside of Spain (situation c). The Court of Justice found that there was a breach of freedom of establishment in situations (a) and (c) but not (b), as in the latter situation there was no different treatment between a cross-border situation and a purely domestic one.

The restriction could be justified by the need to ensure the balanced allocation of taxing powers among the Member States and the coherence of their tax systems. However, it was found that the Spanish rules went beyond what was necessary to ensure these objectives were achieved because there were mechanisms in place within the EU that enabled Spain to collect the exit tax (e.g. mutual assistance for the recovery of claims under Directive 2010/24/EU). Furthermore, as regards Spanish rules that allowed the deferral of tax debts in case of temporary treasury

---

[214] Ibid, para 105.
[215] Ibid.
[216] Case C-301/11 Commission v. Netherlands, ECLI:EU:C:2013:47
[217] Case C-64/11 Commission v. Spain, ECLI:EU:C:2013:264.

constraints, these were not accepted by the Court of Justice as constituting an adequate deferral mechanism for exit taxes.

In Commission v. Denmark,[218] it was held that the Danish rules on exit taxation of cross-border transfers of assets within a company were contrary to EU law. Under Danish tax law, an internal (i.e. within the company) but cross-border transfer of assets was regarded as a sale and taxed as such at market value in the year of transfer. The tax liability arose at the time of exit and was payable immediately regardless of whether the underlying gain was actually realised. A transfer of assets between a company's different establishments within Denmark was not taxed. The Court of Justice found that these rules were contrary to the freedom of establishment.

Denmark had argued that National Grid Indus only applied to financial assets disposed of or intended to be disposed of after the cross-border transfer. It was proportionate to impose taxation on unrealised non-financial assets at the time of transfer if the assets were used in a business and were subject to depreciation. Otherwise, taxpayers would be able to avoid taxation completely. The Court of Justice dismissed the argument that only immediate taxation would preserve Denmark's taxation rights on the unrealised capital gains if these assets were not sold afterwards. In contrast, Denmark was allowed to tax capital gains attributable to when the assets were subject to the Danish tax jurisdiction and to determine the amount of tax at the time of the transfer, but the immediate recovery of such tax was disproportionate.

The Court of Justice further clarified that the ruling in National Grid Indus applied to assets used for business purposes even if such assets depreciated over time and could never be disposed of. The proportionality test set out in that case was also applied to these types of non-financial assets. If the assets were such that they were not going to be disposed of, then the Member States were free to define another trigger for taxation (other than realisation/actual sale), to ensure the gain was taxed. However, the trigger for such taxation must constitute a measure less harmful to the freedom of establishment than the immediate recovery of the tax at the time of transfer. The Court of Justice did not give any guidance as to what that trigger might be.

Later cases followed the National Grid Indus case, but the Court of Justice gave even more latitude to the Member States. In the DMC case,[219] the Austrian corporate partners in a German limited partnership exchanged their partnership interests with a German company in return for shares in that company. The partnership had only one partner after the transfer and ceased to exist. The German tax authorities considered that the transfer gave rise to a taxable gain, based on the going concern (market) value of the partnership interests rather than the lower book value at which

---

[218] Case C-261/11 Commission v. Denmark, ECLI:EU:C:2013:480.
[219] Case C-164/12 DMC, ECLI:EU:C:2014:20.

they had been transferred. As a result, there was immediate taxation of unrealised capital gains.

A continuation of the book value would have been possible under German law if the shares received were taxable in Germany but not if Germany could not tax the unrealised gain as in this case.[220] Therefore, the Austrian partners had to pay tax on the hidden reserves included in the contributed assets. German law provided the option to pay the tax over a five-year period without interest but subject to providing security. The referring court questioned whether the inability to transfer at book value was in breach of the free movement of capital. It was questioned whether the immediate taxation of unrealised capital gains in certain reorganisation scenarios could be justified on the basis that the Member State of origin may no longer exercise its powers of taxation in relation to those capital gains at the time when the gain was realised.

This case was examined under the free movement of capital, as the application of the relevant legislation did not depend on the extent of an investor's interest in the limited partnership.[221] It was found that the inability to transfer at book value and the mandatory revaluation constituted a restriction that could be justified by the objective of preserving the balanced allocation of the power to impose taxes between the Member States.[222] However, the restriction could not go beyond what was necessary to attain this objective. The Court of Justice held that by giving the taxpayer a choice between immediate recovery of the tax due or recovery spread over five years, the legislation was proportionate. Where the taxable person elected for deferred payment, the requirement to provide a bank guarantee would only be imposed on the basis of the actual risk of non-recovery of the tax. A prior assessment of this risk was necessary before a guarantee was demanded.[223]

This case was crucial as it was the first time that the Court of Justice accepted a phased deferral of exit taxes, finding that the distribution of payments in instalments over a period of years was not disproportional. The DMC case was followed in the Verder case,[224] which dealt with the application of exit taxes on the transfer of assets from a German partnership to its Dutch permanent establishment. Verder LabTec was a limited partnership under German law established in Germany. From May 2005, the partnership dealt exclusively with the administration of its patent, trademark and model rights. By a contract of 25 May 2005, it transferred those rights to its permanent establishment located in the Netherlands. Due to the transfer of the various intangibles from the German partnership to its Dutch permanent

---

[220] It was stated by the referring court that under the Austria-Germany tax treaty, only Austria could tax the issued shares.
[221] Ibid, para 34.
[222] Ibid, para 56.
[223] Ibid, para 67.
[224] Case C-657/13 Verder LabTec GmbH & Co KG v. Finanzamt Hilden, ECLI:EU:C:2015:331.

establishment, the German tax authorities assumed a realisation of built-in gains of the transferred assets and imposed an exit tax. The tax authorities allowed payment of the exit tax in ten yearly instalments. The German partnership complained that this was in breach of its freedom of establishment.

The Court of Justice acknowledged that had this transfer been within Germany, there would be no taxation since unrealised capital gains were not taxed. This difference in treatment was likely to result in a disadvantage in liquidity for a German company wishing to transfer assets to a permanent establishment located in another Member State.[225] There was a restriction to the freedom of establishment,[226] but it was justified on the basis of ensuring the preservation of the allocation of powers of taxation between the relevant Member States and was suitable to that effect.[227]

As regards the proportionality of the legislation, it was noted at the outset that it was proportionate for a Member State to determine the amount of the tax due on the unrealised capital gains at the time of the cross-border transfer of the assets at issue.[228] Referring to its judgment in the DMC case, which dealt with an exit tax bill spread over five annual payments, a staggered recovery of tax on unrealised capital gains over ten annual instalments could also be considered proportionate to attain the objective of preserving the balanced allocation of taxing powers.[229] Therefore, the German exit tax legislation was compatible with EU law.

The Verder case confirmed the Court's acceptance of a phased deferral of exit taxes first set out in the DMC case, upon which the exit tax provision of the Anti-Tax Avoidance Directive was based. Some issues remained unsettled, such as whether this phased deferral was only allowed if no interest was payable, or whether the dicta of the Court of Justice on guarantees were limited to bank guarantees or whether they could extend to all types of guarantees. Another issue not addressed was whether reductions in value were to be taken into account and if so, how, and by which Member State. Some guidance can be found on these issues in Article 5 of the Anti-Tax Avoidance Directive, analysed in 6.2.4.

The principles developed by the Court of Justice in this area have also been applied to situations involving a trust. In the Trustees of the Panayi Settlements case,[230] the Court of Justice was asked to assess the imposition of a UK tax on capital gains as a result of the majority of the trustees of the UK trust becoming non-resident. Under UK law, when the trustees of a UK trust became non-resident, a disposal followed by immediate re-acquisition at market value was deemed to have taken place. The legislation did not allow for the deferral of the tax.

---

[225] Ibid, para 37.
[226] Ibid, para 39.
[227] Ibid, paras 41–7.
[228] Ibid, para 48.
[229] Ibid, paras 51–2.
[230] Case C-646/15 Trustees of the Panayi Settlements, ECLI:EU:C:2016:1000.

The Court of Justice concluded that the trust could rely on the fundamental freedoms.[231] The trustees had the right and the obligation to manage and dispose of the assets placed in the trust, in accordance with the trust instrument and UK law. The activity of the trustees – in relation to the trust's assets – was inextricably linked to the trust itself. As such 'the trust and its trustees constitute an indivisible whole'.[232] The Court of Justice concluded that the UK legislation restricted the freedom of establishment, but it was justified by the need to preserve the allocation of the powers of taxation between the Member States.[233] However, by only allowing the immediate payment of the tax due without the possibility of deferral, the legislation went beyond what was necessary to achieve that objective and was not proportionate. The UK legislation was, therefore, in breach of the freedom of establishment.[234]

The same principles have also been applied to scrutinise exit taxes arising upon the transfer of residence to Switzerland. In the Wächtler case,[235] it was questioned whether the German exit tax rules were compatible with the EU-Switzerland Agreement on the free movement of persons. Under the exit tax rules, unrealised appreciations in the value of company rights were taxed (without deferral) when a German national transferred his residence to Switzerland. Both Advocate General Wathelet and the Court of Justice concluded that the German legislation infringed the right of establishment as enshrined under the EU-Switzerland Agreement.

6.2.4 *The Exit Tax Provision of the Anti-Tax Avoidance Directive*

As mentioned, the Anti-Tax Avoidance Directive includes a provision on exit taxes – Article 5. This provision applies in situations where a taxpayer moves assets from its head office to its permanent establishment (and vice versa)[236] or the taxpayer moves its tax residence out of the tax jurisdiction of a state,[237] or the taxpayer transfers the

---

[231] Although under UK law trusts were not deemed to be companies or firms for the purposes of the freedom of establishment, agreeing with the Advocate General, the Court of Justice found that trusts could be covered by the concept of 'other legal persons'. Ibid, paras 29–30.
[232] Ibid, para 32.
[233] Both the Advocate General and the Court of Justice had rejected the argument that since the beneficiaries remained resident in the UK and would be liable to tax on any payments received from the trust, the UK did not lose the right to tax. The Court of Justice noted that such a possibility to tax was not sufficient to preserve the UK's power of taxation since it would depend on the decisions of the trust or beneficiaries (i.e. whether to make payments to the beneficiaries or for the latter to remain resident in the UK). This could not be regarded as sufficient to preserve the powers of that Member State to tax capital gains accruing within its territory. Ibid, para 55.
[234] Interestingly, when the case went back to the referring court, the parties could not reach an agreement as to how to apply the judgment. In a further hearing to the UK's First-Tier Tribunal, the judge chose to interpret the judgment by ruling that the exit charges could be paid by annual instalments over the minimum period available (five years) even where trust assets were sold in the meantime. See Trustees of the Panayi A&M Trusts Nos 1–4 *v.* HMRC [2019] TC 7406.
[235] Case C-581/17 Martin Wächtler *v.* Finanzamt Konstanz, ECLI:EU:C:2019:138.
[236] Art 5(1)(a) & (b) of the Anti-Tax Avoidance Directive.
[237] Art 5(1)(c).

business carried on by its permanent establishment from a Member State to another Member State or an EEA country.[238] Under this provision, an exit tax is applicable requiring the Member State of origin to levy a tax on the market value less their value for tax purposes (i.e. the book value).[239] For transfers from a Member State to another Member State or in a country party to the EEA Agreement, the tax could be paid in instalments over five years[240] or until a third party disposal, if that is earlier.[241] Interest can be charged and, when there is a demonstrable and actual risk of non-recovery, guarantees could be demanded.[242] The Directive prohibits the levying of a guarantee where the legislation of the Member State concerned provides for the possibility of recovery of the tax debt through another taxpayer which is a member of the same group and is tax resident in that Member State.[243]

The receiving Member State has to accept the market value established by the Member State of the taxpayer or the permanent establishment as the starting value of the assets for tax purposes (i.e. there is a step-up).[244] The Preamble to the Directive states that in order to compute the relevant amount, 'it is critical to fix a market value for the transferred assets at the time of exit of the assets based on the arm's length principle'.[245] It is not clear if the arm's length principle referred to here is the one derived from Article 9 of the OECD Model Tax Convention and the OECD Transfer Pricing Guidelines.[246] Arguably, much would depend on the interpretation and application of this principle in the home Member State (or Member State of origin).

A literal reading of the text[247] would suggest that the obligation to grant a step-up only applies in case of intra-EU transfers. (Host/receiving) Member States are free to refuse such step-up with regard to transfers from third countries.[248] It is obvious from the Directive that intra-EU/EEA transfers are treated differently vis-à-vis third

---

[238] Art 5(1)(d).
[239] Art 5(1).
[240] It is not entirely clear if the five-year period is a minimum or a maximum. See Hein Vermeulen, 'Entrepreneurial, Corporate and Asset Emigration in Exit Taxation in the ATAD', in Pasquale Pistone and Dennis Weber (eds), *The Implementation of Anti-BEPS Rules in the EU: A Comprehensive Study* (Amsterdam: IBFD, 2018) 298, who argues that the Member State of origin cannot make use of a period longer than five years.
[241] Art 5(2) of the Anti-Tax Avoidance Directive.
[242] Art 5(3).
[243] Ibid.
[244] See Art 5(5).
[245] Preamble of the Anti-Tax Avoidance Directive, para 10.
[246] See Chapter 8. Also see Hein Vermeulen, 'Entrepreneurial, Corporate and Asset Emigration in Exit Taxation in the ATAD', p 295.
[247] See Art 5(5): 'Where the transfer of assets, tax residence or the business carried on by a permanent establishment is to *another Member State*, that Member State shall accept the value established by the Member State of the taxpayer or of the permanent establishment as the starting value of the assets for tax purposes, unless this does not reflect the market value.' (Emphasis added.)
[248] See also Paloma Schwarz, 'The Exit Tax Rule (Article 5 ATAD)', in Werner Haslehner, Katerina Pantazatou, Georg Kofler and Alexander Rust (eds), *A Guide to the Anti-Tax Avoidance Directive* (Elgar Publishing, 2020), at 5.48.

country transfers.[249] (Home) Member States are obliged to offer taxpayers the choice between immediate payment and phased deferral only as regards intra-EU/EEA transfers. This is notwithstanding the fact that in the DMC case[250] discussed in the previous section, exit taxes were found to infringe the free movement of capital and not only the freedom of establishment.

It is interesting to note that the preamble to this Directive clarifies 'that transfers of assets, including cash, between a parent company and its subsidiaries fall outside the scope of the envisaged rule on exit taxation'.[251] Arguably, in such circumstances, the default position would be the case law of the Court of Justice, discussed above. In any case, what is remarkable with this quasi-codification of the case law is that the EU has gone from scrutinising the exit tax provisions of a home state to demanding from a home state to impose exit taxes.

6.3 TRANSFER OF ASSETS WITHIN THE SAME COMPANY

This section examines tax issues arising from the cross-border transfer of assets within the same company – i.e. between a head office and its permanent establishment. As a permanent establishment is part of the same legal entity as the head office, when there is a transfer of assets between the two, technically, there is no change of ownership and no actual disposal of the asset.[252] Invariably, in a domestic setting, such transfers are considered as internal transactions (or intra-company dealings) not giving rise to an actual gain or loss. However, when the transfer of assets is cross-border, most states consider such transfers as giving rise to a deemed disposal, as the state from which the assets are transferred risks losing its jurisdiction to tax gains from a subsequent (actual) disposal of the assets.[253]

The OECD Model Tax Convention does not impose any restrictions on the right of the home state (i.e. the state from which the assets are transferred) to tax any (unrealised) gains on the transfer of assets to a permanent establishment or a head office in the host state. The fact that no similar charge would have been levied had this been a domestic transfer or internal dealing is not discriminatory under Article 24(3) OECD Model Tax Convention.[254] Neither does the OECD Commentary

---

[249] See, especially, Art 2(d) and analysis in Schwarz, 5.55–5.56.
[250] Case C-164/12 DMC.
[251] Preamble of the Anti-Tax Avoidance Directive, para 10.
[252] See also 4.3.3 and 4.3.4.
[253] This will be the case not only if the state of the head office (assuming a transfer of assets from a head office to a foreign permanent establishment) uses the exemption method but also if it uses the credit method for taxing gains of foreign permanent establishments. This is because once the asset is transferred to the permanent establishment, then under Art 13 of the OECD Model Tax Convention, the state of the permanent establishment has the primary right to tax gains arising from subsequent disposal of the asset to a third party. If the state of the permanent establishment exercises this right, then the state of the head office has to give credit for that tax under Art 23B. See Peter Harris and David Oliver, *International Commercial Tax* (Cambridge University Press, 2010), p 419.
[254] See OECD Commentary to Art 24, para 35.

6.3 Transfer of Assets within the Same Company

impose an obligation on the host state to recognise the deemed disposal at the home state and give a step-up (or step down) to the market value. This could lead to double taxation or non-taxation.[255]

It was argued in the first edition of this book that this situation created an impediment to this type of cross-border reorganisations and, as a corollary, a restriction to the freedom of establishment. In light of recent case law discussed in section 6.2.3, the imposition of exit taxes on cross-border transfers of assets within the same company is governed by the same principles as those derived from the National Grid Indus line of case law. More in point, in Commission v. Denmark,[256] it was held that the Danish rules on exit taxation of cross-border transfers of assets within a company were contrary to the freedom of establishment. Similarly, in the Verder case,[257] what was at stake was the transfer of assets from a German partnership to its Dutch permanent establishment and the taxation of the built-in gains over those assets. As explained, the Court of Justice approved the recovery of exit taxes over ten annual instalments, and as such, the restriction to the freedom of establishment was justified and proportional.

This position is now confirmed in the Anti-Tax Avoidance Directive, which imposes an obligation on the home State to ensure that a taxpayer is subject to tax at an amount equal to the market value of the transferred assets when there is a transfer of assets from its head office to its permanent establishment in another Member State or a third country and vice versa.[258] As noted above in section 6.2.4., this tax can be deferred if the transferee is in another Member State or an EEA country. However, it still has to be paid in five yearly instalments,[259] and interest may be charged,[260] as well as a guarantee requested.[261] To an extent, this position is somewhat aligned with the treatment under the OECD Model Tax Convention, with the difference that under the Directive, the host state has a positive obligation to provide a step-up in value under certain circumstances. As explained in 6.2.4, for intra EU/EEA transfers, the Directive requires the host state to accept the value established by the home state as the starting value of the assets for tax purposes, 'unless this does not reflect the market value'.[262]

Compared to earlier case law, there is now much more limited protection offered to taxpayers regarding the imposition of exit taxes. In certain circumstances, exit taxes are now compulsory for home states. Although the collection of this tax may be deferred, it could still be payable under instalments over a few years, even if the gains

---

[255] See also 6.2.3.
[256] Case C-261/11 Commission v. Denmark.
[257] Case C-657/13 Verder.
[258] Art 5(1)(a) & (b).
[259] Art 5(2).
[260] Art 5(3).
[261] Ibid.
[262] Art 5(5).

are never materialised. There is even less protection if a taxpayer is emigrating from a third country, as a step-up in value may not be recognised by an EU host state. Moreover, as already discussed in 6.2.4, if a taxpayer is emigrating from a Member State to a third country, under the Directive the home Member State is not obliged to offer a choice between immediate payment of the exit tax and deferral. This state of affairs, combined with the limited reliefs offered under the Merger Directive, suggest that the European Union still has a long way to go in order to facilitate corporate reorganisations in the Internal Market.

7

Tax Avoidance and EU Law

This chapter examines various types of anti-abuse regimes, their compatibility with EU law and the impact of the Anti-Tax Avoidance Directive. Here an attempt is made to assess the judgments of the Court of Justice in this area and to consider whether the principles derived from these judgments when analysed in the current legislative context provide a uniform body of law. Before examining specific anti-abuse regimes, it is important to consider the prior question of whether there is a general concept of tax abuse for the purposes of EU law.

7.1 AN EU PRINCIPLE OF ABUSE OF TAX LAW?

There are two ideas that seem to be universal. One is that taxpayers are free to structure their affairs in such a way as to limit their tax liability. The other is the idea that Member States are entitled to put measures in place to prevent certain types of arrangements that they consider abusive. It has been debated for some time whether there is one coherent principle of abuse of EU law and, as a corollary, whether Member States are entitled or under an obligation to combat abusive tax practices. In the first edition to this book, it was argued that on the basis of the Court's jurisprudence up to that point in time, it was difficult to conclude that there was an EU principle of tax abuse, overriding any domestic principles. The inconsistent terminology of the Court of Justice using the terms 'abuse', 'evasion', 'avoidance' and 'fraud' interchangeably in the tax case law and the linguistic discrepancies in the translations of the judgments[1] were not helpful either. Furthermore, the various terms could have different meanings in different jurisdictions and/or their boundaries could be unclear. Up to very recently, on the basis of the case law, it was thought that EU law did not provide a general principle of abuse of rights in the field of direct taxation, being a non-harmonised area, by contrast to the area of VAT.

---

[1] Opinion Statement of the CFE ECJ Task Force on the Concept of Abuse in European Law, based on the Judgments of the European Court of Justice Delivered in the Field of Tax Law (November 2007).

In Halifax[2] the Court of Justice first showed signs of accepting a freestanding principle of abuse of law in the tax context.[3] This case dealt with an aggressive and complex VAT planning scheme intended to locate the place of supply of services outside the EU. The UK tax authorities challenged this scheme. Eventually, a reference was made by the VAT and Duties Tribunal to the Court of Justice to interpret the rules of the Sixth VAT Directive on the place of supply of services. More importantly, the Court of Justice was also asked to determine whether there was a principle of abuse of rights disallowing such schemes.

The Court of Justice decided that the transactions encompassed supplies of services for the purposes of the VAT legislation and therefore were subject to it. In any case, the application of Community legislation could 'not be extended to cover abusive practices by economic operators, that is to say transactions carried out not in the context of normal commercial operations, but solely for the purpose of wrongfully obtaining advantages provided for by Community law'.[4]

Applying the principle of abuse of law to the Sixth VAT Directive, the Court of Justice held that an abusive practice occurs where, firstly, the transaction results in a tax advantage that would be contrary to the purpose of the provisions formally applied, and secondly, the essential aim of the transaction was to obtain a tax advantage.[5] To the Court of Justice, objective criteria and respect of legal certainty were essential.[6] For the purposes of the second part of the test, the Court of Justice stated that, in determining the real substance and significance of the transactions, national courts could consider factors such as the purely artificial nature of those transactions and the legal, economic and/or personal links among operators involved in the tax avoidance scheme.[7] If an abusive practice was found to exist, then the transactions involved had to be redefined so as to re-establish the situation that 'would have prevailed in the absence of transactions constituting that abusive practice'.[8]

Although the Halifax case was hailed as a groundbreaking decision for the purposes of VAT legislation, it was not entirely clear whether guidance could be derived for other areas such as direct tax law. Later cases seemed to support the idea that the principle would only be relevant to VAT cases.

---

[2] Case C-255/02 Halifax plc Leeds Permanent Development Services Ltd and County Wide Property Investments Ltd v. Commissioners of Customs & Excise [2006] ECR I-1609.

[3] In the non-tax context, the origins of such principle are traced back to earlier cases and mainly Case C-110/99 Emsland-Stärke GmbH v. Hauptzollamt Hamburg-Jonas [2000] ECR I-1569. See Rita de la Feria, 'Prohibition of abuse of (Community) law: the creation of a new general principle of EC law through tax', (2008) 45(2) *Common Market Law Review*, 395–441, 408.

[4] Case C-255/02 Halifax, para 69.

[5] Ibid, paras 74–5.

[6] Ibid, para 72.

[7] Ibid, para 81.

[8] Ibid, para 94.

In Part Service, another VAT case,[9] the Halifax two-pronged test was applied and refined. The Court of Justice clarified that to find an abusive practice for the purposes of the Sixth VAT Directive it was enough that the accrual of a tax advantage was the *principal* aim of the transaction or the transactions in question, and not the *sole* aim pursued, to the exclusion of other economic objectives.[10] This was for the national court to assess, taking account of the purely artificial nature of the transaction and the links of a legal, economic and/or personal nature between the operators involved.[11]

In Weald Leasing[12] the Court of Justice dealt with an asset-leasing transaction, the purpose of which was the deferment of the VAT liability by spreading on rental payments. Here the existence of the tax advantage was not enough. It had to be shown that this advantage was contrary to the purposes of the VAT legislation.[13] The Court of Justice emphasised that a taxable person could not be criticised for choosing a leasing transaction that procured him the advantage of spreading the payment of his tax liability.[14] It was up to the national court to determine, firstly, whether the contractual terms of the leasing transactions were contrary to the Sixth VAT Directive and of the national legislation transposing it. That would be the case particularly if the rentals were set at levels that were unusually low or did not reflect any economic reality – that is if they were not at arm's length.[15] A finding that there was an abusive practice was inferred from the object and effects of the impugned transactions, as well as their purpose.[16] The fact that the undertaking did not usually engage in such transactions was irrelevant.[17] If the transaction was abusive, then it had to be redefined so as to re-establish the situation that would have prevailed in the absence of the elements of those contractual terms that were abusive.[18]

Weald Leasing was important as the Court of Justice openly embraced the arm's length principle as a means of delineating elements that could go towards establishing the abusive nature of a transaction.[19] It also clarified that a finding of abuse did not nullify the transaction but paved the way for its recharacterisation.

---

[9] Case C-425/06 Ministero dell'Economiae delle Finanze, formerly Ministero delle Finanze v. Part Service Srl, company in liquidation, formerly Italservice Srl [2008] ECR I-897.
[10] Ibid, para 45.
[11] Ibid, para 62.
[12] Case C-103/09 The Commissioners for Her Majesty's Revenue and Customs v. Weald Leasing Ltd [2010] ECR I-13589.
[13] Ibid, para 33.
[14] Ibid, para 34.
[15] Ibid, para 39.
[16] Ibid, para 44.
[17] Ibid, para 45.
[18] Ibid, para 53.
[19] See also para 50 in Case C-277/09 The Commissioners for Her Majesty's Revenue & Customs v. RBS Deutschland Holdings GmbH [2010] ECR I-13805, where the fact that the various transactions concerned took place between two parties that were legally unconnected was decisive.

Apart from VAT cases, the idea of a general principle of abuse of tax law was initially discussed in cases under the Merger Directive, considered in Chapter 6. In Kofoed[20] the Court of Justice first toyed with the idea that the anti-abuse provision of the Directive reflected the general Community law principle that abuse of rights is prohibited. Similar statements were made by Advocate General Kokott in her opinion in Kofoed[21] and in Zwijnenburg.[22] The Court of Justice in Zwijnenburg, however, did not follow this approach, preferring a strict interpretation of the provision.[23] In Foggia,[24] another case on the Merger Directive, the Court of Justice followed Kofoed. Here the Court of Justice was asked to delineate the contours of the anti-abuse provision of the Directive and the extent to which tax savings from restructuring operations were caught. The Court of Justice repeated its statement in Kofoed, that there was a general principle of EU law that abuse of rights is prohibited.[25] Citing previous case law,[26] it was reiterated that '[t]he application of EU legislation may not be extended to cover abusive practices, that is to say, transactions carried out not in the context of normal commercial operations, but solely for the purpose of wrongfully obtaining advantages provided for by that law'.[27]

Although the statements in these cases suggested a free-standing principle of abuse of rights, up to that point in time it was still uncertain whether the Court of Justice would have reached the same conclusion had these cases not been in the context of a Directive – an area where there was ad hoc harmonisation. It was questioned whether a general principle of abuse of rights applied to *all* tax areas, whether harmonised or not.

In the 3 M Italia case[28] the Court of Justice found that it did not. What was at stake here was the transfer of the right of usufruct over the shares in an Italian company (3 M Italia) from a US company to another Italian company, in order to benefit from a lower withholding tax and a tax credit. The Italian tax authorities took the view that this was a sham transaction designed to evade tax and that the dividends distributed by 3 M Italia had in fact been received by the US company. The case was referred to the Court of Justice. One of the questions[29] asked was whether the principle of the prohibition of abuse of rights, as defined in the Halifax and Part Service cases, could

---

[20] Case C-321/05 Hans Markus Kofoed v. Skatteministeriet [2007] ECR I-05795, para 38. See 6.1.3 and Katrina Petrosovich, 'Abuse under the Merger Directive' (2010) 50(12) *European Taxation*, 558–67.
[21] See C-321/05 Kofoed, para 57 (Advocate General).
[22] Case C-352/08 Modehuis A. Zwijnenburg BV v. Staatssecretaris van Financiën [2010] ECR I-04303, para 61 (Advocate General).
[23] Ibid, para 46 of the Court's decision and the analysis in 6.1.3.
[24] Case C-126/10 Foggia – Sociedade Gestora de Participagdes Sociais SA v. Secretário de Estado dos Assuntos Fiscais [2011] ECR I-10923.
[25] Ibid, para 50.
[26] Case C-212/97 Centros [1999] ECR I-1459, para 24; Case C-255/02 Halifax, paras 68 and 69; and Case C-321/05 Kofoed, para 38.
[27] Case C-126/10 Foggia, para 50.
[28] Case C-417/10 Ministero dell'Economia e delle Finanze, Agenzia delle Entrate v. 3M Italia SpA, ECLI:EU:C:2012:184.
[29] The main question was whether the Italian litigation amnesty procedure (amnesty in exchange for a levy of 5 per cent of the taxable amount) was compatible with EU law, and more specifically the

only apply in the field of harmonised taxes and in matters governed by provisions of secondary EU law, or whether it extended, as a category of abuse of fundamental freedoms, to matters involving non-harmonised taxes such as direct taxes.

In its judgment the Court of Justice rejected the argument that the principle of prohibition of abuse of rights as set out in Halifax and Part Service could be extended to the field of non-harmonised taxes. To the Court, it was clear that no general principle existed in EU law that might entail an obligation on Member States to combat abusive practices in the field of direct taxation.[30] At the time, the judgment also put to rest arguments that there was a free-standing general anti-avoidance rule for the purposes of EU tax law or that there should be one.[31]

This case law should now be read in light of the Danish tax cases,[32] discussed in Chapter 2. In all these cases, the Danish companies requested an exemption of the Danish withholding tax levied on the payments made to the EU company, under the Interest and Royalties Directive and the Parent-Subsidiary Directive. This request was denied by the Danish tax authorities on the basis that this was a conduit structure and the company receiving the income was not the beneficial owner of the payment. In these cases, the Court of Justice made some important pronouncements, which were analysed in detail in Chapter 2.

One important point arising was that the non-transposition of the anti-abuse provision of the Parent-Subsidiary Directive into Danish tax law did not prevent Denmark from relying on domestic or treaty-based provisions to combat an abuse of this Directive. This was because, according to the Court of Justice, EU law prohibited abusive practices as a general principle. It was found to be settled case law that 'there is, in EU law, a general legal principle that EU law cannot be relied on for abusive or fraudulent ends'.[33] This conclusion was irrespective of whether the Member States implemented domestic or treaty-based anti-abuse provisions in their domestic tax systems.[34] It is obvious that on this point, the Court of Justice has moved away from the 3 M Italia case discussed above and no longer limits the application of this general principle of EU law to harmonised areas.[35] The

---

fundamental freedoms, the principle of non-discrimination, the EU general principle of effectiveness and state aid. The Court of Justice found that the legislation was compatible with the above. See analysis in Adam Zalasinski, 'The principle of prevention of (direct tax) abuse: scope and legal nature – remarks on the 3M Italia Case', (2012) 52(9) *European Taxation*, 446–54.

[30] Ibid, para 32.
[31] See, for example, Greg Sinfield, 'The Halifax principle as a universal GAAR for tax in the EU' [2011] 3 *British Tax Review* 235–46.
[32] Joined Cases C-115/16, C-118/16, C-119/16 and C-299/16 N Luxembourg 1, X Denmark A/S, C Danmark I, Z Denmark ApS, ECLI:EU:C:2019:134 and Joined Cases C-116/16 and C-117/16 T Danmark, Y Denmark Aps, ECLI:EU:C:2019:135.
[33] Ibid, para 96.
[34] See analysis from para 95 et seq.
[35] See analysis in Roland Ismer, 'Abuse of Law as a General Principle of European Union (Tax) Law', in Werner Halsehner, Katerina Pantazatou, Georg Kofler and Alexander Rust (eds), *A Guide to the Anti-Tax Avoidance Directive* (Elgar Publishing, 2020).

principle seems to apply even when a Member State has omitted to incorporate an anti-abuse provision of a Directive.

As also mentioned in Chapter 2, in the Danish tax cases the Court of Justice gave very useful guidance on indicia which the national court should consider in assessing whether an arrangement was structured in such a way as to obtain improper entitlement to an exemption, and in particular whether the immediate recipient only played a conduit role.[36] If the national court found that there was abuse, the Member State was not required to identify the person it regarded as being the beneficial owner of the income, as it may be impossible for the national authorities to provide this information.[37] In the judgment, the Court of Justice also reviewed the concept of 'beneficial ownership' in the context of the Interest and Royalties Directive, as well as other important interpretative points.[38]

Notwithstanding this important development – i.e. extending the EU prohibition of abuse of rights in a non-harmonised area – a finding of abuse of tax laws or tax avoidance was never completely irrelevant as far as the compatibility of national tax legislation was concerned. As shown in previous chapters, depending on the term used by Member States or the Court of Justice, the prevention of tax abuse or tax avoidance or tax evasion was often advanced as a justification for national measures restricting fundamental freedoms. Sometimes it was enough to justify the restriction but sometimes it was not.

One could argue that in the Danish tax cases, the Court of Justice was influenced by the fact that by the time the judgment was made, the Parent-Subsidiary Directive contained a general anti-abuse rule (GAAR).[39] There was also a GAAR in the Anti-Tax Avoidance Directive.[40] This meant that even if a Member State now chose not to incorporate the anti-abuse provisions of the Parent-Subsidiary Directive into domestic law, the GAAR of the Anti-Tax Avoidance Directive would nevertheless be applicable. Of course, since the adoption of either GAARs did not have retroactive effect, they were not relevant to the questions referred to the Court of Justice in the Danish tax cases. However, in light of this legislative evolution, whether or not there was a general EU principle of abuse of law had to an extent become a moot point by the time of the judgment. Not only was there now a GAAR in the Parent-Subsidiary Directive, but also a self-standing GAAR in the Anti-Tax Avoidance Directive.

---

[36] Ibid, para 132.
[37] Ibid, paras 143–5.
[38] See analysis in Chapter 2.
[39] See amended Art 1(2) introduced by Council Directive (EU) 2015/121 of 27 January 2015 amending Directive 2011/96/EU on the common system of taxation applicable in the case of parent companies and subsidiaries of different Member States. For the background to this amendment, see Christiana HJI Panayi, *Advanced Issues in International and European Tax Law* (Hart Publishing, 2015), ch 5.
[40] See Art 6 of the Anti-Tax Avoidance Directive.

The remainder of this chapter examines how the Court of Justice dealt with various regimes aimed at preventing certain types of tax abuse and, whenever relevant, the impact of the Anti-Tax Avoidance Directive.

7.2 CONTROLLED FOREIGN COMPANIES

Before analysing the Court of Justice cases in this area, some of which are considered as landmark cases,[41] it is important to examine the rationale behind controlled foreign companies (CFC) rules.

Whilst most countries tax their residents on a worldwide basis, technically a group company is not taxed on the profits of another group company, whether resident or not, as they are separate legal entities.[42] Taxation is deferred until the subsidiary's profits are distributed to the parent company or the parent company disposes of its shares in the subsidiary. This deferral is especially beneficial to shareholders in non-resident companies located in low-tax jurisdictions or tax havens. If the non-resident company is located in such jurisdiction and is controlled by the parent company, then the parent company could effectively avoid paying domestic corporation tax by diverting profits to that subsidiary.

CFC regimes, sometimes called anti-deferral regimes, are often put in place to prevent such arrangements by taxing resident shareholders of CFCs on their pro rata share of some or all of the undistributed income of the CFC.[43] A CFC is typically described as a non-resident company controlled by residents (individuals or companies) that is subject to a much lower level of taxation by being established offshore.[44] Therefore, the main focus of CFC rules is thought to be to prevent or limit the ability of residents of a country to use foreign companies in tax havens or low-tax jurisdictions to avoid or defer domestic tax.[45] The importance of CFC rules in combating harmful tax competition was reiterated

---

[41] See, Christiana HJI Panayi, 'Cadbury Schweppes and Cadbury Schweppes Overseas (2006) – CFC Rules Under EU Tax Law', in John Snape and Dominic de Cogan, *Landmark Cases in Revenue Law* (Hart Publishing, 2019).

[42] Some countries have rules that allow consolidation of profits between group companies for tax purposes.

[43] For an overview, see OECD, Controlled Foreign Company Legislation (1996); Brian Arnold, *The Taxation of Controlled Foreign Corporations: An International Comparison* (Toronto: Canadian Tax Foundation, 1986), pp 1ff; Michael Lang, Hans-Jörgen Aigner, Ulrich Scheuerle and Markus Stefaner (eds), *CFC Legislation, Tax Treaties and EC Law* (The Hague: Kluwer Law, 2004). See also Brian Arnold and Patrick Dibout, 'General Report', in *Limits on the Use of Low-Tax Regimes by Multinational Businesses: Current Measures and Emerging Trends*, Cahiers de droit fiscal international, Vol 86b (Kluwer Law International, 2001).

[44] See Arnold and Dibout, 'General Report', pp 38ff; Office of Tax Policy, *The Deferral of Income Earned through US Controlled Foreign Corporations – A Policy Study* (Department of Treasury Office, 2000), chs 1 and 2.

[45] See Arnold and Dibout, 'General Report'. See also Office of Tax Policy, *The Deferral of Income Earned through US Controlled Foreign Corporations*, ch 3.

and emphasised by the OECD in its influential 1998 report on harmful tax competition[46] and, fifteen years later, in Action 3 of the BEPS Action Plan.[47]

In so far as the technical details and the focus of CFC regimes are concerned, these vary across countries. There is a diversity of techniques for defining CFCs, encompassing criteria such as control, effective level of taxation, activity and type of income of the CFC. There is also a diversity of methods for the identification of low-tax regimes, ranging from objective criteria to a system of lists, or both.[48] Under Action 3 of the BEPS Action Plan, recommendations regarding the design of CFC rules were to be developed. The recommendations in the Discussion Draft[49] and the Final Report[50] on Action 3 were in the form of building blocks that were necessary for the design of effective CFC rules. These recommendations were not minimum standards, but were, rather, designed to ensure that jurisdictions that chose to implement them would have rules that effectively prevent taxpayers from shifting income to foreign subsidiaries.

The Final Report specifically recommended that CFC rules should only be applied to foreign companies that were subject to an effective tax rate which was meaningfully lower than that applied in the parent company jurisdiction. On the basis of these guidelines, countries were expected to find a balance between having effective rules that do not result in double taxation, and rules that do not unduly increase the administrative burdens and compliance costs for taxpayers. It was acknowledged that, while the recommendations developed under Action 3 had to be broad enough to be effective in countering base erosion and profit shifting, they also had to be adaptable, where necessary, to enable Member States to comply with their obligations under EU law.[51] Although in the first edition to this book the question of compatibility of CFC regimes with EU law was considered to be somewhat settled, this should now be read in light of the Anti-Tax Avoidance Directive, as well as more recent case law.

7.2.1 *CFCs in EU Tax Case Law*

Notwithstanding the rationale of CFC rules, as a result of their application the parent company is effectively penalised for having invested in foreign low-tax jurisdictions. This is, arguably, a home state restriction. As the Commission recog-

---

[46] OECD, *Harmful Tax Competition – An Emerging Global Issue* (1998), pp 40ff. See also analysis in 1.3.
[47] OECD (2013), Action Plan on Base Erosion and Profit Shifting, OECD Publishing. Available at: http://dx.doi.org/10.1787/9789264202719-en.
[48] See Arnold and Dibout, 'General Report', pp 29–34.
[49] OECD, *Discussion Draft: Strengthening CFC Rules* (OECD 2015), available at www.oecd.org/ctp/aggressive/discussion-draft-beps-action-3-strengthening-CFC-rules.pdf.
[50] OECD, *Action 3 Final Report 2015 – Designing Effective Controlled Foreign Company Rules* (OECD, 2015), available at http://dx.doi.org/10.1787/9789264241152-en.
[51] Ibid, at para 19, p 17.

nised in its Communication on the application of anti-abuse measures in the area of direct taxation,[52] '[the] main purpose of CFC rules is to prevent resident companies from avoiding domestic tax by diverting income to subsidiaries in low tax countries'.[53] This treatment raises issues of discrimination because the profits of a subsidiary receive different tax treatment for the sole reason that the subsidiary is resident in another Member State. Equally, the inclusion of the profits of a foreign subsidiary in the taxable profits of the resident parent company constitutes an obstacle to the ability of the latter to establish itself in another Member State through a subsidiary.[54]

The seminal case in this area is Cadbury Schweppes.[55] Here the focus was on the UK CFC legislation, according to which a resident company was subject to corporation tax on its worldwide profits, which included the profits of a foreign branch *but not* the profits of a foreign subsidiary. Outside of the CFC legislation, a UK parent company was taxed on the profits of the foreign subsidiary only when they were distributed to it as dividends. Where the CFC legislation applied,[56] the profits of a foreign subsidiary were attributed to the UK parent company at the time when these profits arose and were taxed with a credit for the foreign tax paid by the subsidiary. If the subsidiary subsequently distributed a dividend, this tax could be credited against the tax payable by the parent company on the dividend.

In this case Cadbury Schweppes, a UK company, indirectly held 100 per cent of the shares of two Irish subsidiaries. These subsidiaries were subject to a 10 per cent corporate tax rate under the now abolished International Financial Services Centre regime in Dublin. This was lower than the UK tax rate. As none of the exemptions under the CFC legislation applied, Cadbury Schweppes was taxed by the UK tax authorities on the profits of its Irish subsidiaries. Cadbury Schweppes appealed to the Special Commissioners,[57] arguing that the UK CFC regime was in breach of freedom of establishment, freedom to provide services and the free movement of capital. The Special Commissioners decided to stay the proceedings and refer the question to the Court of Justice.

[52] Communication from the Commission to the Council, the European Parliament and the European Economic and Social Committee, *Direct Taxation: Communication on the Application of Anti-Abuse Measures – within the EU and in Relation to Third Countries*, COM(2007) 725 (Anti-Abuse Communication).
[53] Ibid, p 7.
[54] Ibid, p 7.
[55] Case C-196/04 *Cadbury Schweppes* [2006] ECR I-7995.
[56] Broadly, the UK CFC rules at the time applied if a subsidiary was resident outside the UK and was subject to a lower level of taxation. A lower level of taxation was deemed to exist if, for any accounting period, the tax paid by the foreign subsidiary was less than three-quarters of what would have been payable had this been a UK subsidiary. The UK CFC rules did not apply if the subsidiary made sufficient distributions as defined (acceptable distribution policy test); the subsidiary derived exempt income as defined (exempt activities test); the subsidiary met a stock exchange quotation test (public quotation requirement); the subsidiary's profits did not exceed £50,000 (de minimis test); and a motive test was satisfied.
[57] This was, at the time, the first instance appeal body for decisions of the UK tax administration.

The Court of Justice held that the UK legislation had to be examined in light of freedom of establishment only. The legislation applied to resident companies that had a controlling holding in their subsidiary established outside the UK. This gave the resident company definite influence on the subsidiary's decisions and allowed it to determine the subsidiary's activities. Although the rules had restrictive effects on the free movement of services and the free movement of capital, such effects were an unavoidable consequence of any restriction on freedom of establishment and did not justify an independent examination.[58]

The Court of Justice found that the UK CFC rules restricted freedom of establishment. This was because profits of a controlled company were only attributed to the UK parent company when this controlled company was incorporated in a low tax Member State (within the meaning of the UK CFC rules). Profits were not attributed to the UK parent if the controlled company was UK resident.[59] This difference of treatment dissuaded UK-resident companies from establishing, acquiring or maintaining a subsidiary in a Member State with such lower level of taxation, and therefore constituted a restriction to the freedom of establishment.[60]

The Court of Justice then examined whether this restriction was justified. Any advantage resulting from the low taxation in the Member State of the subsidiary could not by itself authorise the Member State of the parent company to offset that advantage by less favourable tax treatment of the parent company.[61] The need to prevent the reduction of tax revenue was also not an acceptable justification.[62]

Prevention of tax avoidance and evasion as a justification to this restriction were also considered. The Court of Justice emphasised that the mere fact that a resident company established a secondary establishment such as a subsidiary in another Member State could not justify a general presumption of tax evasion.[63] A national measure restricting freedom of establishment could only be justified where it specifically targeted wholly artificial arrangements aimed at circumventing the application of the legislation of the Member State concerned.[64] In this case the specific objective of the restrictive rules had to be to prevent conduct involving the creation of wholly artificial arrangements that did not reflect economic reality, with a view to escaping the tax normally due on the profits generated by activities carried out on national territory.[65]

According to the Court of Justice, the UK CFC rules were suitable for the attainment of this objective. However, they also had to be proportional. More

---

[58] Case C-196/04 Cadbury Schweppes, paras 31–3. This is an example of a case where, although many freedoms were relevant, the case was decided on the basis of one freedom only. See 3.3.1.
[59] Ibid, para 44.
[60] Ibid, para 45.
[61] Ibid, para 49.
[62] Ibid.
[63] Ibid, para 50.
[64] Ibid, para 51.
[65] Ibid, para 55.

specifically, the CFC rules had to exclude from their scope situations whereby, despite the existence of tax motives, the incorporation of a CFC reflected economic reality. In determining whether or not economic reality existed, in addition to the subjective element that consisted of the intention to obtain a tax advantage, objective factors had to be taken into account.[66] These objective factors, which were ascertainable by third parties, included, in particular, the extent to which the CFC physically existed in terms of premises, staff and equipment.[67] However, the fact that the activities that corresponded to the profits of the CFC could just as well have been carried out by a UK company did not lead to the conclusion that this was a wholly artificial arrangement.[68] Furthermore, for the UK CFC rules to be proportional, the UK parent company had to be given an opportunity to produce evidence that the arrangement was genuine.[69]

The Court of Justice concluded that it was for the national court to determine whether the UK CFC legislation was confined to wholly artificial arrangements.

Cadbury Schweppes was followed in the CFC Group Litigation case.[70] In this case the Court of Justice again looked at the UK CFC rules.[71] An important feature of this case was that the Court of Justice found certain compliance requirements (where the resident company sought exemption from taxes already paid on CFC profits) *not* to be prohibited, as long as their aim was to verify that the CFC was actually established and that its activities were genuine and did not entail undue administrative constraints.[72] The Court of Justice also held that the resident company was best placed to establish that it had not entered into wholly artificial arrangements that did not reflect economic reality.[73] It was up to the national court to determine whether the motive test of the UK CFC legislation lent itself to an interpretation that enabled the CFC charge to be restricted to wholly artificial arrangements.[74]

---

[66] Ibid, paras 64–5.
[67] Ibid, para 67. Advocate General Léger had explained in greater detail some relevant criteria in establishing artificiality. Firstly, the degree of physical presence of the subsidiary, i.e. examining whether or not the subsidiary has the premises, staff and equipment necessary to carry out the services provided to the parent company. Secondly, the genuine nature of the activity provided by the subsidiary, i.e. considering the competence of the subsidiary's staff in relation to the services provided and the level of decision-making in carrying out those services. Thirdly, the economic value of that activity with regard to the parent company and the entire group, i.e. whether or not the value reflects the exercise of genuine activities in the State of the subsidiary. Case C-196/04 Cadbury Schweppes, paras 111–14 (Advocate General).
[68] Ibid, para 69 (Court of Justice).
[69] Ibid, para 70.
[70] Case C-201/05 The Test Claimants in the CFC and Dividend Group Litigation v. Commissioners of Inland Revenue [2008] ECR I-02875.
[71] The Court of Justice also looked at the UK rules on the taxation of inbound dividends and followed established case law.
[72] Case C-201/05 CFC Group Litigation, paras 82 and 85.
[73] Ibid, para 82.
[74] Incidentally, in Vodafone 2 v. HMRC [2008] EWHC 1569 (Ch), in the High Court, Mr Justice Evans-Lombe found that the UK CFC legislation was incompatible with EU law because its motive test did

In 2010, ECOFIN adopted a resolution on the coordination of Member States' tax policies with regard to anti-abuse provisions.[75] The resolution recommended that Member States, when applying CFC and thin capitalisation rules within the EU that are not applicable in similar domestic situations, should follow some guidelines. The guidelines included a non-exhaustive list of indicators suggesting that profits may have been artificially diverted to CFCs.[76] The importance of administrative cooperation was also stressed.

It should be noted that one type of anti-deferral legislation – switch-over clauses – were considered to be less problematic by the Court of Justice which found that those clauses did not restrict fundamental freedoms. The case in question is Columbus Container.[77] In this case the claimant was a Belgian limited partnership with German resident partners. The activities of the partnership consisted, inter alia, of financing subsidiaries and branches. The partnership's profits and assets were, under German domestic tax law, assessed as foreign branch profits and assets of the German partners. In Belgium the partnership was treated as a company and enjoyed the status of a Belgian Coordination Centre. According to the Belgium–Germany tax treaty, the profits from the net assets of a Belgian partnership were exempt in Germany. However, German anti-abuse rules provided for a switch from the exemption method to the tax credit method in respect of certain passive branch profits subject to low taxation abroad. The key question was whether or not this switch-over clause, technically a treaty override, was compatible with freedom of establishment and the free movement of capital.

---

    not ensure that only wholly artificial arrangements would be caught by the regime. Therefore, the UK CFC rules had to be disapplied. This decision was reversed at the Court of Appeal (Vodafone 2 v. HMRC [2009] EWCA Civ 446), which held that the CFC rules should be interpreted as if there was a new additional exception applying with retrospective effect. This new exception would apply to companies that are actually established in the EU/EEA area and that carry on genuine economic activities there. The concept of genuine economic activities was not defined. For companies established outside the EU/EEA area and for companies established in the EU/ EEA area but without genuine economic activities, the normal CFC rules would apply. It is understood that the case has now been settled. See David Stewart, 'Vodafone Settles Dispute with HMRC Over Controlled Foreign Corporations', reported in Tax Analysts 2010 WTD 142-2. David Klass, 'Rereading UK legislation to reflect ECJ decisions', (17 May 2010) 58(7) *Tax Notes International*, 543–6.

[75] See Draft Council resolution contained in 10597.10 FISC 58, dated 2 June 2010. The resolution was adopted by ECOFIN on 8 June 2010.

[76] The list of indicators read as follows (see ibid, p 4): 'a. there are insufficiently valid economic or commercial reasons for the profit attribution, which therefore does not reflect economic reality; b. incorporation does not essentially correspond with an actual establishment intended to carry on genuine economic activities; c. there is no proportionate correlation between the activities apparently carried on by the CFC and the extent to which it physically exists in terms of premises, staff and equipment; d. the non-resident company is overcapitalised, it has significantly more capital than it needs to carry on its activity; e. the taxpayer has entered into arrangements which are devoid of economic reality, serve little or no business purpose or which might be contrary to general business interests, if not entered into for the purpose of avoiding tax.'

[77] Case C-298/05 Columbus Container Services BVBA & Co. v. Finanzamt Bielefeld-Innenstadt [2007] ECR I-10451.

The Court of Justice, contrary to Advocate General Mengozzi's opinion,[78] held that the switch-over clause did not constitute a restriction to the freedom of establishment or the free movement of capital. The effect of the switch-over clause was that investors who invested in low-tax jurisdictions were brought to the same position as investors who invested in Germany in so far as tax rates were concerned. The German legislation did not make any distinction between taxation of income derived from the profits of German partnerships and taxation of income derived from the profits of partnerships established in another Member State that subjects those profits to a rate of tax below 30 per cent. Accordingly, there was no difference of treatment and no discrimination, as 'partnerships such as Columbus [did] not suffer any tax disadvantage in comparison with partnerships established in Germany'.[79] Therefore, the switch-over clause did not breach any fundamental freedoms.

This judgment was at odds with Cadbury Schweppes, even though chronologically the two cases were not far apart. In both cases the impugned home State rules ensured that persons investing in low-tax jurisdictions were brought to the same position as persons investing at home. In Cadbury Schweppes this was not a relevant consideration to rebut the argument of different treatment, but in Columbus Container it was. As a result, in the latter case the Court of Justice did not have to explain why a switch-over clause that did not target wholly artificial arrangements was compatible with EU law, nor did it have to assess the proportionality of the restriction. While there is some inconsistency in the judgments, this can, perhaps, be attributed to the fact that the Court of Justice did not want to tamper with switch-over clauses and get embroiled in a discussion of whether relief by credit and relief by exemption offer the same protection.[80]

In a later case, Commission v. United Kingdom,[81] the Court of Justice followed Cadbury Schweppes. Here, the UK was subject to infringement proceedings on its rules on the transfer of assets abroad and the attribution of gains to members of non-resident close[82] companies. In this respect, this case was not about CFC legislation but was relevant to aspects of it.[83] The measures at issue provided that UK-resident participators in a non-resident close company with at least a 10 per cent shareholding in that close company were liable to immediate taxation on the capital gains realised

---

[78] Advocate General Mengozzi had opined that the German switch-over clause restricted freedom of establishment and the free movement of capital. He devoted most of his opinion to examining whether or not the restriction was justified – a question ultimately left for the national court.

[79] Case C-298/05 Columbus Container, para 40.

[80] See also analysis in 5.1 and the case law in Chapter 5.

[81] Case C-112/14 European Commission v. The United Kingdom of Great Britain and Northern Ireland, ECLI:EU:C:2014:2369.

[82] Under UK law at the time, a close company was a company under the direct (or indirect) control of a limited number of shareholders, or those with an interest in the company's capital or income.

[83] Regarding the referral of the UK rules on the transfer of assets abroad, see European Commission Press Release IP/12/1147 (24 Oct. 2012). Regarding the referral of the UK rules on the attribution of gains to members of non-resident companies, see European Commission Press Release IP/12/1146 (24 Oct. 2012).

on disposals of company assets, regardless of whether they actually received the proceeds. Where a UK-resident close company disposed of assets and made taxable gains, tax was charged only in the event of the distribution of the gains to participators or if the participators disposed of their interests in the company. Furthermore, the tax was based on the amount actually received by the participators and not on the amount of the gains made by the company itself.

The Court of Justice concluded that this difference in tax treatment discouraged UK-resident taxpayers from investing in non-resident close companies and made it more difficult for such companies to attract capital.[84] Here, there was a restriction of the free movement of capital, which could be justified on the basis of combating tax evasion and tax avoidance. However, following Cadbury Schweppes, the national rule went beyond what was necessary to achieve this objective.[85] This rule was not confined to targeting wholly artificial arrangements which did not reflect economic reality and were carried out for tax purposes alone, but also affected conduct whose economic reality could not be disputed.[86] Furthermore, the UK legislation did not allow the taxpayer to provide evidence to show the economic reality of their participation in the company in question.[87] The national legislation was therefore in breach of the free movement of capital.[88]

More recently, in the X case,[89] the Court of Justice considered Germany's former CFC rules as applicable to third countries and reviewed the application of the wholly artificial arrangements test in the context of the free movement of capital. The case concerned a German parent company holding a 30 per cent participation in its Swiss subsidiary. This subsidiary, having mainly passive income, qualified as a CFC according to the German legislation. As such, the parent company's profits were increased by the tax authorities. The taxpayer challenged this assessment arguing that the German rules were contrary to the free movement of capital.

The Court of Justice found that the German CFC rules constituted a restriction to the free movement of capital that may be justified by overriding reasons in the public interest, in particular the need to prevent tax evasion.

Interestingly, the referring court had asked whether the interpretation of the concept of wholly artificial arrangements as adopted by the Court of Justice in

---

[84] Case C-112/14 Commission v. United Kingdom, para 20.
[85] Ibid, paras 26–9.
[86] Ibid, para 28.
[87] Ibid.
[88] Although both this freedom and the freedom of establishment were applicable, as the Commission primarily sought a declaration that the United Kingdom had failed to fulfil its obligations under Art 63 TFEU and Art 40 EEA Agreement, the Court of Justice confined itself to examining the case from the point of view of the free movement of capital (ibid, at para 17).
[89] Case C-135/17 X-GmbH v. Finanzamt Stuttgart – Körperschaften, ECLI:EU:C:2019:136.

Cadbury Schweppes could be applied to the situation in the main proceedings, which involved the free movement of capital and not the freedom of establishment.[90] It was also asked what qualitative and quantitative requirements must the shareholding held by a resident taxpayer in the third-country company satisfy in order for it not to be regarded as wholly artificial.[91]

The Court of Justice reiterated that the free movement of capital was not meant to frame the conditions under which companies can establish themselves within the Internal Market but to liberalise cross-border movements of capital.[92] Therefore, in the context of the free movement of capital, the concept of wholly artificial arrangements could not be limited to the indications of Cadbury Schweppes[93] as to when the establishment of a company did not reflect economic reality, 'since the artificial creation of the conditions required in order to escape taxation in a Member State improperly or enjoy a tax advantage in that Member State improperly can take several forms as regards cross-border movements of capital'.[94] It was conceded that those indications may also amount to evidence of the existence of a wholly artificial arrangement for the purposes of applying the rules on the free movement of capital, 'in particular when it proves necessary to assess the commercial justification of acquiring shares in a company that does not pursue any economic activities of its own'.[95]

However, in the context of the free movement of capital, the concept of wholly artificial arrangement was also capable of covering any scheme which had as its *primary objective* or *one of its primary objectives* the artificial transfer of the profits made by way of activities carried out in the territory of a Member State to third countries with a low tax rate.[96] Furthermore, the Court of Justice emphasised that the case law concerning restrictions on the exercise of the freedoms of movement within the EU could not be transposed in its entirety to movements of capital between Member States and third countries, since such movements took place in a very different legal context.[97]

The Court of Justice noted that the German legislation introduced an irrebutable presumption of abuse, which was not proportionate.[98] Germany's obligation to offer taxpayers an opportunity to provide commercial justifications for their arrangements had to be assessed in light of the availability of administrative and legislative measures permitting, if necessary, the accuracy of such evidence to be verified by the German

---

[90] Ibid, paras 81–2.
[91] Ibid, para 83.
[92] Ibid, para 83.
[93] The Court of Justice cited paras 67–9 of Cadbury Schweppes.
[94] Case C-135/17 X, para 84.
[95] Ibid, para 84.
[96] Ibid.
[97] Ibid, paras 89–90.
[98] Ibid, para 88.

tax authorities.[99] It was for the referring court to assess whether a legal framework existed between Germany and Switzerland that genuinely empowered the German tax authorities to verify the accuracy of any information that may be provided about the Swiss CFC.[100]

Whilst the Court of Justice in this case reiterated the Cadbury Schweppes test of wholly artificial arrangements, references to 'one of the primary objectives' could be perceived as a significant loosening of this, being closer to the principal purpose test of the OECD Model Tax Convention,[101] as well as the GAAR of the Anti-Tax Avoidance Directive and of the Parent-Subsidiary Directive. Whether this broader interpretation of the wholly artificial arrangements test is restricted to situations involving the free movement of capital only[102] or whether it will be followed in later cases across both the freedom of establishment and the free movement of capital remains to be seen.

Overall, in the cases analysed in this section, the Court of Justice reviewed the compatibility of domestic anti-deferral rules (mostly CFC rules) with the fundamental freedoms. Therefore, the focus of these cases was on what Member States were *prevented* from doing, as regards their national rules. With the advent of the Anti-Tax Avoidance Directive, a de minimis CFC rule has now become obligatory. In other words, the focus has now shifted from what Member States *must not* do, to what they *must* do. This point is revisited below.

7.2.2 *CFCs and the Anti-Tax Avoidance Directive*

One of the most contentious provisions of the proposed Anti-Tax Avoidance Directive which to an extent delayed its adoption was the CFC provision. It is noteworthy that the initial version of the Anti-Tax Avoidance Directive contained a provision on a switch-over clause and on CFCs.[103] However, the switch-over clause was deleted from the final version of the Directive but the CFC provision remained in the final and approved version, with amendments.

---

[99] Ibid, para 91.
[100] Ibid para 94.
[101] See Art 29 of the OECD Model Tax Convention (para 9). This was introduced as a result of Action 6 of the BEPS Action Plan, which considered measures to prevent treaty abuse. See also Art 7 of the OECD's Multilateral Instrument (Multilateral Convention to Implement Tax Treaty Related Measures to Prevent BEPS).
[102] See comments made in CFE Opinion Statement ECJ-TF 4/2019 on the CJEU decision of February 26, 2019, in Case C-135/17, X-GmbH, concerning the application of the German CFC legislation in relation to third countries, dated 12 December 2019.
[103] See Arts 6 and 7–8 of Proposal for a Council Directive laying down rules against tax avoidance practices that directly affect the functioning of the internal market, COM(2016) 26 final. The final (and adopted) version of the Anti-Tax Avoidance Directive is found in Council Directive 2016/1164 of 12 July 2016 Laying Down Rules against Tax Avoidance Practices that Directly Affect the Functioning of the Internal Market, [2016] OJ L 193.

7.2 Controlled Foreign Companies

Article 7(1) of the Anti-Tax Avoidance Directive stipulates that the Member State of a taxpayer shall treat an entity, or a permanent establishment of which the profits are not subject to tax or are exempt from tax in that Member State, as a CFC if two cumulative conditions are satisfied: an ownership percentage test[104] and a difference in corporate tax paid test.[105] If the two cumulative conditions are satisfied, then there is a further stipulation that the Member State of the taxpayer (i.e. of the parent company) *shall* include the non-distributed income of the CFC in its tax base on the basis of either the entity/categorical approach,[106] or the transactional approach.[107] In the implementation of this Directive, it was left to Member States to decide which approach to adopt as far as taxing the non-distributed income of the CFC.

Under the entity/categorical approach, the Anti-Tax Avoidance Directive lists several categories of income that would qualify as non-distributed income for the purposes of this provision. These are the typical categories of passive income that would be treated as tainted for the purposes of a CFC provision. This provision does not apply where the CFC carries on a substantive economic activity supported by staff, equipment, assets and premises, as evidenced by relevant facts and circumstances. Where the CFC is resident or situated in a third country that is not a party to the EEA Agreement, Member States have discretion *not* to apply this provision – in other words, the more mechanical entity/categorical approach would apply without exclusion for substantive economic activities. Arguably, as the X case[108] discussed in 7.2.1 was decided after this Directive came into force, the principles set out in this judgment should be taken into account in implementing the Directive into national law.[109]

Under the transactional approach, the Member State of the taxpayer shall include in its tax base the non-distributed income of the entity or permanent establishment arising from non-genuine arrangements that have been put in place for the essential purpose of obtaining a tax advantage. For the purposes of this provision,

> an arrangement or a series thereof shall be regarded as non-genuine to the extent that the entity or permanent establishment would not own the assets or would not have undertaken the risks which generate all, or part of, its income if it were not controlled by a company where the significant people functions, which are relevant

---

[104] Art 7(1)(a).
[105] Art 7(1)(b).
[106] Art 7(2)(a).
[107] Art 7(2)(b).
[108] Case C-135/17 X.
[109] Also see Alexander Rust, 'Controlled Foreign Company Rule (Articles 7 and 8 ATAD)', in Werner Halsehner, Katerina Pantazatou, Georg Kofler and Alexander Rust (eds), *A Guide to the Anti-Tax Avoidance Directive* (Elgar Publishing, 2020), pp 195–6. Rust argues that Art 7(2)(a) will have to be adapted so that the taxpayer must be given the opportunity to show, without being subject to undue administrative constraints, any commercial justification for an investment in the country of the CFC if the information can be verified by the tax administration of the third country. He repeats this argument at p 210, in that the taxpayer has to be given such opportunity, if the Member State of the taxpayer has concluded a tax treaty containing an exchange of information clause with the residence state of the CFC.

to those assets and risks, are carried out and are instrumental in generating the controlled company's income.[110]

Arguably, Member States opting for the transactional approach would not seem to go beyond a transfer pricing rule.[111]

There are opt-outs for both approaches. Under the entity/categorical approach, a Member State may opt not to treat an entity or permanent establishment as a CFC if one-third or less of the income accruing to the entity or permanent establishment falls within the categories listed under Article 7(2)(a). Furthermore, a Member State may opt not to treat financial undertakings as CFCs if one-third or less of the entity's income from the listed categories comes from transactions with the taxpayer or its associated enterprises.[112] As regards the transactional approach, Member States have the discretion to exclude an entity or permanent establishment with accounting profits of no more than €750,000, and non-trading income of no more than €75,000,[113] or of which the accounting profits amount to no more than 10 per cent of its operating costs for the tax period.[114]

The computation rules are set out in Article 8 of the Anti-Tax Avoidance Directive. The income to be included in the tax base under the previous provision is calculated 'in accordance with the rules of the corporate tax law of the Member State where the taxpayer is resident for tax purposes or situated'.[115] Losses are to be carried forward according to national law and are not included in the tax base.[116]

Furthermore, the income is calculated in proportion to the taxpayer's participation in the CFC entity.[117] The income to be included in the tax base of the taxpayer is limited to amounts generated through assets and risks that were linked to significant people functions carried out by the controlling company.[118] As an express endorsement to the OECD's work, the Directive states that '[t]he attribution of controlled foreign company income is calculated in accordance with the arm's length principle'.[119]

The income is included in the tax period of the taxpayer in which the tax year of the entity ends.[120] The Directive provides for the subsequent distribution or subsequent disposal of a participation in the CFC, whereby there is deduction for any taxes previously paid in the CFC jurisdiction to ensure there is no double taxation.

It is debatable whether the CFC provision of the Anti-Tax Avoidance Directive, which was heavily influenced by the conclusions of the OECD/

---

[110] Art 7(2)(b).
[111] See Rust, 'Controlled Foreign Company Rule (Articles 7 and 8 ATAD)', p 198.
[112] See Art 7(3).
[113] Art 7(4)(a). For the purpose of the transactional approach, the operating costs may not include the cost of goods sold outside the country where the entity is resident, or the permanent establishment is situated, for tax purposes and payments to associated enterprises.
[114] Art 7(4)(b).
[115] Art 8(1).
[116] Ibid.
[117] Art 8(3).
[118] Art 8(2).
[119] Ibid.
[120] Art 8(4).

G20 on Action 3 of the BEPS project,[121] is aligned with EU law, and more specifically the established case law of the Court of Justice in this area.[122] From a purely EU law perspective, several questions arise.

Firstly, it is questionable whether the non-genuine arrangements to which the Directive refers in the transactional approach are the same as the wholly artificial arrangements test established in Cadbury Schweppes. In that case, the threshold for finding that national CFC rules were compatible with freedom of establishment was very high. Only wholly artificial arrangements could justify CFC rules which were restrictive in nature. Here, it would appear that the threshold is lower. Under the Directive, non-genuine arrangements seem to be equated with arrangements where the parent company does not carry out significant people functions, relevant to the assets and risks generating the CFC income.[123] There is no mention of artificiality or usurpation of power.

Similarly, in the entity/categorical approach, the exclusion of a CFC carrying on 'a substantive economic activity supported by staff, equipment, assets and premises, as evidenced by relevant facts and circumstances',[124] seems to lower the threshold compared to the wholly artificial arrangements test of the Cadbury Schweppes case. Is artificiality the same as not carrying on a substantive economic activity? How about ancillary economic activities? These are issues which ought to be addressed. Arguably, if the principal purpose test set out by the Court of Justice in the X case is not restricted to situations falling under the free movement of capital, the divergence of approach between case law and the Directive might be somewhat bridged.

A further concern is whether the treatment of third countries under the Anti-Tax Avoidance Directive is compatible with EU law. As mentioned, Member States are entitled to apply the entity/categorical approach without an exception for substantive economic activities when the CFC is in a third country. One could argue that, as the legislation is intended to apply only to those shareholdings which enable the holder to exert a definite influence on a company's decisions and to determine its activities, then freedom of establishment is the predominantly relevant freedom and not the free movement of capital. As freedom of establishment does not protect third-country nationals, then applying the CFC provisions to such nationals in a more restrictive way than to EU nationals is not in breach of EU law.

However, this last argument assumes that in this context, the predominantly relevant freedom will always be the freedom of establishment and never the free movement of

---

[121] See the ECOFIN General Approach Paper (9432/16) of 24 May 2016, p 5.
[122] For the author's views, see Christiana HJI Panayi, 'The ATAD CFC rule and its impact on the existing regimes of EU Member States', in Pasquale Pistone & Dennis Weber (eds) *The Implementation of the Anti-BEPS in the European Union: A Comprehensive Study* (Amsterdam: IBFD, 2018); Christiana HJI Panayi, 'Cadbury Schweppes and Cadbury Schweppes Overseas (2006) – CFC Rules Under EU Tax Law', in John Snape and Dominic de Cogan (eds) *Landmark Cases in Revenue Law* (Hart Publishing, 2019).
[123] See also Art 7(2)(b) of the Anti-Tax Avoidance Directive.
[124] Ibid, Art 7(2)(a).

capital. It was shown in the X case that the free movement of capital may also be applicable in the context of Member State CFC rules. Furthermore, this argument ignores the fact that the provisions of the Anti-Tax Avoidance Directive, themselves quite controversial, are considered to be de minimis harmonisation rules and that some Member States may opt for stricter rules that do not just focus on definite influence and control. Precluding the parent company of a third-country CFC which engages in substantive economic activities, from ever benefiting from the protection of EU law is an assumption that the Court of Justice never made in Cadbury Schweppes.

As also discussed above, what is obvious is that since Cadbury Schweppes was decided, the emphasis has shifted from having the Court of Justice scrutinise CFC (and other anti-abuse) regimes, to requiring from Member States to introduce de minimis anti-abuse rules through this Directive. The case of CFC rules is even more striking because almost half of the Member States had no such rules at the time that the Anti-Tax Avoidance Directive was enacted.[125] This should have raised concerns regarding (lack of) EU competence.

It should be pointed out that the CFC provisions in the Anti-Tax Avoidance Directive are not even fully aligned with the proposals of the OECD in the context of Action 3 of the BEPS Action Plan. The OECD's Final Report on Action 3 left considerable leeway for countries to implement CFC rules, recognising that there is no 'one size fits all' solution. By contrast, the CFC provisions of the Directive have forced Member States to adopt CFC rules with a one-size-fits-all approach that extends to arrangements with third countries, going much further than the BEPS recommendations. It is becoming more and more evident that the Commission is pushing its own agenda in this area.

7.3 INTEREST DEDUCTIBILITY RESTRICTIONS

Debt is often preferred over equity because, as already mentioned,[126] interest payments are invariably deductible in the hands of the payer/borrower company whereas dividends are not and are payable from taxable profits. Using related party and third party debt to achieve excessive interest deductions or to finance the production of exempt or deferred income and other financial payments that are economically equivalent to interest payments, was seen under the BEPS project as one of the simplest profit-shifting techniques available in international tax planning.[127] Excessive interest deductions on intra-group loans of a group operating internationally may create competitive distortions between such group and one operating domestically.[128] This may also have a negative

---

[125] See, for example, the Study on aggressive tax planning, produced in the context of the Anti-Tax Avoidance Package which recognised that many Member States had no CFC rules or had ineffective CFC rules. Also see Commission Communication on the Anti-Tax Avoidance Package: Next steps towards delivering effective taxation and greater tax transparency in the EU, COM/2016/023 final.
[126] See 2.3.
[127] OECD, *Limiting Base Erosion Involving Interest Deductions and Other Financial Payments, Action 4 – 2015 Final Report* (OECD Publishing, 2015) para 1, p 15.
[128] Ibid, para 3.

impact on capital ownership neutrality, 'creating a tax preference for assets to be held by multinational groups rather than domestic groups'.[129]

Action 4 of the BEPS project set out to develop recommendations in the form of best practices for the design of rules to prevent base erosion and profit shifting by way of interest expenses. The primary concern appeared to be that multinational groups could claim total interest deductions that significantly exceeded their actual third-party interest expense. Such deductible payments could give rise to double non-taxation in both inbound and outbound investment scenarios.

The Interest Deductions Discussion Draft[130] examined methods of limiting excessive interest expense deductions: namely, a group-wide rule, which would limit a company's net interest deductions to a proportion of the group's actual net third party interest expense; and a fixed ratio rule, which would apply irrespective of the level of debt of a group and which would limit a company's interest deductions to an amount determined by applying a fixed benchmark ratio to an entity's earnings, assets or equity. In the Final Report on Action 4, the OECD endorsed the fixed ratio proposal limiting intercompany and third party interest expense in respect of net interest of 10 per cent to 30 per cent of earnings before interest, tax, depreciation and amortisation (EBITDA), applied to net, including third party, interest at an entity level.[131] There was also a recommendation for a group ratio rule to enable groups that were more highly leveraged with third party debt to apply the worldwide ratio rather than the country's fixed ratio rule, i.e. a possible 10 per cent uplift to prevent double taxation. Countries could apply a different rule based on a relevant financial ratio, or could choose not to apply any group ratio rule, provided that the fixed ratio rule was applied to both multinational and domestic groups.

In the EU context, most of the earlier case law discussed in this area dealt with national thin capitalisation rules. However, the principles derived from this case law can also apply to other types of rules restricting interest deductibility (such as earnings-stripping rules or fixed debt/equity safe havens). This case law is considered below.

7.3.1 Thin Capitalisation in EU Tax Case Law

Thin capitalisation is the practice whereby related companies have a high proportion of debt in relation to equity,[132] obviously to benefit from the deductibility of

---

[129] Ibid.
[130] OECD, Discussion Draft on Interest Deductions and Other Financial Payments (OECD, 2014).
[131] This approach was criticised in the run-up to the Final Report, because of its rejection of the arm's length test and the fact that it would most likely incentivise groups to increase third-party funding, which could give rise to further economic distortions. See analysis in Christiana HJI Panayi, 'The Compatibility of the OECD/G20 Base Erosion and Profit Shifting Proposals with EU Law', 70 [2016] 1/2 *Bulletin for International Taxation* pp 95–112, pt 3.4.
[132] For a general analysis, see James Gadwood and Paul Morton, 'General Report', *Interest deductibility: The Implementation of BEPS Action 4*, Cahiers de droit fiscal international, Vol 104A (Rotterdam: International Fiscal Association, 2019); Brian Arnold, 'General Report', *Deductibility of Interest and*

interest. In its Communication on anti-abuse measures, the Commission considered the background to thin capitalisation rules and explained the reasons why debt finance seems to be more attractive in a cross-border context.

> Debt and equity financing attract different tax consequences. Financing a company by means of equity will normally result in a distribution of profits to the shareholder in the form of dividends, but only after taxation of such profits at the level of the subsidiary. Debt financing will result in a payment of interest to the creditors (who can also be the shareholders), but such payments generally reduce the taxable profits of the subsidiary. Dividend and interest may also attract different withholding tax consequences. The difference in treatment between debt and equity financing under national tax law (and at bilateral level), as a result of which the source state's taxing rights on interest are generally more limited than those on dividends, make debt financing considerably more attractive in a cross-border context and can therefore lead to the erosion of the tax base in the state of the subsidiary.[133]

National rules designed to prevent thin capitalisation practices have been scrutinised by the Court of Justice.[134] The first important case in this area was Lankhorst-Hohorst,[135] where the Court of Justice examined the German thin capitalisation rules. Under German tax law, interest paid by a corporation on debt to its shareholders that exceeded a statutory debt-to-equity ratio was recast as covert dividends if the shareholders were not entitled to the corporation tax credit. Non-resident shareholders were not entitled to such credit. This meant that interest payments made to non-resident shareholders were almost always recast as covert dividends. The purpose of the provision was to combat tax evasion by shareholders seeking to remove profits from the corporation as tax-deductible interest, rather than taxable dividends. The provision was also meant to discourage the under-capitalisation of German companies.

Here the Dutch ultimate parent to the German company Lankhorst-Hohorst made a loan to it to enable it to reduce its bank interest payments. The German tax authorities recast the interest payment by Lankhorst-Hohorst to the Dutch parent as a covert distribution of profits and levied a tax of 30 per cent. Following a reference for a preliminary ruling, the Court of Justice found that the German rules restricted the freedom of establishment. The argument that the restriction was

---

other Financing Charges in Computing Income, Cahiers de droit fiscal international, Vol 79a (The Hague: Kluwer Law International, 1994); Detlev Piltz, 'General Report', *International Aspects of Thin Capitalization*, Cahiers de droit fiscal international, Vol 81b (The Hague: Kluwer Law International, 1996); Pascal Hinny, 'General Report', *New Tendencies in Tax Treatment of Cross-Border Interest of Companies*, Cahiers de droit fiscal international, Vol 93b (The Hague: Kluwer Law International, 2008).

[133] *Anti-Abuse Communication*, p 7.
[134] Following the Scheuten Solar case, it was clarified that interest limitation rules are not contrary to the Interest and Royalties Directive. See Case C-397/09 Scheuten Solar Technology GmbH v. Finanzamt Gelsenkirchen-Süd [2011] ECR I-06455 and analysis in Chapter 2, at 2.3.3.
[135] See Case C-324/00 Lankhorst-Hohorst GmbH v. Finanz Steinfurt [2002] ECR I-11779.

justified because it was designed to prevent thin capitalisation and tax evasion was rejected. This was because the legislation was very general and could catch situations such as the present one, where no abuse had been shown.

Following the Lankhorst-Hohorst case, a number of claims were made in the UK's High Court challenging the compatibility of the UK thin capitalisation rules. This was the Thin Cap Group Litigation case.[136] Generally, until 1995 the UK tax rules provided that any interest paid to any non-UK resident lender that was a member of the same group was treated as a distribution. This treatment was modified by the provisions of certain tax treaties concluded by the UK. In 1995 the UK rules were amended to provide that interest paid between group members was treated as a distribution to the extent that it exceeded the arm's length amount, except if both the payer and the payee were subject to UK corporation tax. In 1998 the transfer pricing rules, which applied to companies under common control, were extended to cover interest payments. These rules did not apply if both the payer and the payee were subject to UK corporation tax. In 2004 this carve-out was removed and the transfer pricing regime was extended to transactions between parties within the charge to UK corporation tax.

In the Thin Cap Group Litigation case various test cases were referred to the Court of Justice by the High Court. Broadly, each of the test cases at issue involved a UK resident subsidiary that was, directly or indirectly, at least 75 per cent owned by a non-UK resident parent company in which either the parent or another non-UK resident group company had made a loan to the UK subsidiary. Most of the questions referred were answered in a similar way by the Advocate General and the Court of Justice.

In so far as the applicable freedom was concerned, the Court of Justice[137] agreed with the Advocate General's opinion in that only freedom of establishment was relevant. As the Court noted, the UK legislation affected intra-group loans in respect of which the parent and/or the intermediate group companies had a definite influence or control over subsidiary companies. Therefore, the legislation primarily affected freedom of establishment and was to be examined in light of that freedom only. Although the legislation may also have had 'restrictive effects on the freedom to provide services and the free movement of capital, such effects must be seen as an unavoidable consequence of any restriction on freedom of establishment and [did] not justify independent examination'.[138]

This conclusion was decisive as regards cases involving non-member countries. When the lending company and the common parent company were resident in a non-member country, freedom of establishment was not applicable. Similarly,

---

[136] Case C-524/04 Test Claimants in the Thin Cap Group Litigation v. Commissioners of Inland Revenue [2007] ECR I-02107. See Christiana HJI Panayi, 'Thin Capitalisation GLO, et al – a thinly concealed agenda?' (2007) 35(5) *Intertax*, 298–309.

[137] Case C-524/04 Thin Cap Group Litigation, para 28.

[138] Ibid, para 34.

when the (EU) lender company did not have a controlling shareholding in the (EU) borrowing company and both the lender and the borrower were controlled by a common parent in a non-EU country, then freedom of establishment was not applicable. In such situations no protection could be offered under EU law.

The Court of Justice, agreeing with its Advocate General, found that the UK thin capitalisation legislation prima facie restricted freedom of establishment. The recharacterisation of interest as distribution meant that the borrowing company was unable to deduct that interest from its taxable profits. This effectively made (the repayment of) loans granted by non-resident companies *more* expensive compared to those granted by resident companies.[139] This was not a case of allocation of tax jurisdiction between the UK and its tax treaty partners. The recharacterisation of interest under the then applicable UK rules 'represented a unilateral choice on the part of the United Kingdom legislature'.[140]

Interestingly, the Court of Justice recognised that the fact that under some UK tax treaties the recharacterisation of interest was to be matched by a corresponding reduction in taxable profits in the state of the lender could have been relevant in assessing discrimination.[141] However, on the facts of the case as presented before the Court, it could not have been shown that the tax disadvantage resulting from the recharacterisation was always matched by a corresponding advantage in the state of the lender. The Court of Justice refused to impose an obligation on the Member State to coordinate with the other Member State prior to recharacterising the interest. This is understandable, given that a Member State's assertion of its tax jurisdiction (here the protection of its tax base) could not depend on the assertion of tax jurisdiction by another Member State.

The cohesion of the tax system was examined as a justification but rejected, as no direct link could be established between the tax advantage and the offsetting of that advantage by a tax charge. According to the Court of Justice, it had not been shown that, after recharacterisation, any upward adjustment to the taxable profits of the borrowing company would be offset by the grant of a tax advantage to the recipient company.[142]

The Court of Justice also considered the anti-abuse justification. It was noted that companies had the right to structure their affairs as they wish and they should be allowed to finance their subsidiaries by equity or debt. However, as the Advocate General also pointed out, 'this possibility reaches its limit when the company's choice amounts to abuse of law'.[143] As in Cadbury Schweppes, the Court of Justice stated that a national measure restricting freedom of establishment may be

---

[139] In addition to the non-deductibility of the recharacterised distribution, the company could also have become liable to advanced corporation tax on such distribution. Ibid, para 39.
[140] Ibid, para 51.
[141] Ibid, para 54.
[142] Case C-524/04 Thin Cap Group Litigation, para 69.
[143] Ibid, para 66 (Advocate General).

7.3 Interest Deductibility Restrictions

justified where it specifically targets wholly artificial arrangements that do not reflect economic reality, in order to escape the legislation of the Member State concerned. A general presumption of abuse did not suffice to justify the restriction.[144]

The Court of Justice found that the UK thin capitalisation rules were sufficiently targeted against thin capitalisation arrangements.[145] It was also found that this legislation was an appropriate means of attaining the objective underlying its adoption, namely enabling the UK to prevent practices the sole purpose of which was to avoid the tax payable on profits generated by UK-sourced activities.[146]

In so far as the proportionality requirement was concerned, again, similar to Cadbury Schweppes, it was important for the UK thin capitalisation rules to provide for a consideration of objective and verifiable elements that could be used to determine whether a transaction represented a purely artificial arrangement. More specifically, national legislation had to satisfy two requirements. Firstly, the taxpayer had to be given the opportunity, without being subject to undue administrative constraints, to provide evidence of any commercial justification that there may have been for the impugned arrangement.[147] Secondly, the recharacterisation of interest paid as a distribution was limited to the proportion of that interest which exceeded what would have been paid had the relationship between the relevant companies been at arm's length.[148]

In Thin Cap Group Litigation case there were a number of sub-scenarios in which the loan finance was provided by a group company (sometimes EU/EEA resident or third-country resident) and the common parent of the lending company and the borrowing company was a third-country resident. Here the Court of Justice thought that it was irrelevant that the loan was actually granted by an EU/EEA group company or the branch of such company. What was crucial was the fact that the common parent company of the borrowing and lending companies was not resident in the EU/EEA area. This was because the UK thin capitalisation legislation 'affects freedom of establishment, not as regards the lending company, but only as regards the parent company which enjoys a level of control over each of the other companies concerned allowing it to influence the funding decisions of those companies'.[149] Therefore, whenever the parent company was in a third country, there was no protection under freedom of establishment, *regardless of where the company lending the funds was actually resident* (within the EU/EEA or in a third country). As free movement of capital was inapplicable, not being the predominantly relevant freedom, then no protection could be sought by group companies whose common parent was resident in a third country.

---

[144] Ibid, paras 72–4 (Court of Justice).
[145] Ibid, para 76.
[146] Ibid, para 77.
[147] Ibid, para 82.
[148] Ibid, para 83.
[149] Ibid, para 99.

Inevitably, this decision had important financing implications for groups owned by non-EU/EEA parents. Intra-group loans for such groups could be subject to stricter thin capitalisation rules, irrespective of the actual residence of the lender.

While the importance of the Thin Cap Group Litigation case as a precedent is undeniable, one crucial question was left open: the relationship between the Court's commercial justification test and the OECD's arm's length principle. From an international tax perspective, the two concepts cannot be equated as there are inherent differences – commercial justification connoting a subjective standard, not necessarily aligned with the OECD's more objective arm's length standard. In the first edition to this book it was questioned whether, following the Thin Cap Group Litigation case, the existence of a commercial justification could enable taxpayers to escape thin capitalisation rules even in the absence of an arm's length arrangement. Later cases discussed in the context of transfer pricing rules would suggest that the Court of Justice might not be confined by the OECD's interpretation of the arm's length principle.[150] This also seems to be buttressed by the Commission's Anti-Abuse Communication.[151]

In Lasertec[152] the Court of Justice dealt with the partial recharacterisation of interest payments made by a German 50 per cent subsidiary to its Swiss parent. Here Lasertec, a German limited liability company, received a loan in 1995 from its Swiss-resident parent company that exceeded the then applicable debt-to-equity ratio. The German tax authorities denied a deduction for the interest expense. The German referring court asked whether this violated the free movement of capital. It also asked whether the German legislation was covered by the standstill provision.[153]

The Court of Justice reiterated the point that 'national provisions relating to holdings giving the holder a definite influence on the decisions of the company concerned and allowing him to determine its activities come within the material scope of the Treaty provisions on freedom of establishment'.[154] The German legislation satisfied these criteria since the legislation applied when the non-resident lending company had a substantial holding (i.e. more than 25 per cent) in the

---

[150] See 7.4. Contrast with the decision of the English Court of Appeal in the Thin Cap Group Litigation case, discussed in 7.4, which found that in light of subsequent cases, the UK was only required to apply an arm's length test and *not* an additional commercial justification test.

[151] The Commission emphasised that the application of thin capitalisation rules must be confined to purely artificial arrangements. 'This may be achieved by ensuring that the terms of the debt financing arrangements between related companies remain within the limits of what would have been agreed upon between unrelated parties or that they are based on otherwise valid commercial reasons'. See p 7. Although the language used here was reminiscent of the arm's length principle, the Commission nevertheless acknowledged that Member States could not operate effective tax systems unless they were able to ensure that their tax bases were not eroded through non-commercial arrangements between associated companies. Ibid.

[152] Case C-492/04 Lasertec Gesellschaft für Stanzformen mbH v. Finanzamt Emmendingen [2007] ECR I-3775.

[153] The legislation had been passed before the 1 January 1994 cut-off date for the purposes of ex-Art 57(1) EC but did not come into effect until after that date.

[154] Case C-492/04 Lasertec, para 20.

capital of the borrowing company.¹⁵⁵ Moreover, as Lasertec, the lending company, held two thirds of the nominal capital in the borrowing company, such a holding unquestionably conferred on Lasertec a definite influence on the borrower's decisions and activities.¹⁵⁶

It was found that the German legislation constituted a restriction to the freedom of establishment, which did not extend protection to third-country nationals. As such, Germany was entitled to restrict the deduction of interest where the loan was provided by a non-EU/EEA company. Once again, the exclusion of the free movement of capital meant that no protection could be offered under EU law.¹⁵⁷

In Lammers and Van Cleeff¹⁵⁸ the Court of Justice followed the principles of its earlier case law in finding Belgian thin capitalisation rules incompatible with the freedom of establishment. In this case, interest paid to a non-resident director (individual or company), of a Belgian company was recharacterised as dividends if the interest exceeded the market rate, or the total of the interest-bearing loans was higher than the paid-up capital and taxed reserves at the beginning of the taxable period. The recharacterised interest was not tax deductible and could be subject to withholding tax. Interest paid to directors that were Belgian resident companies was not recharacterised, even if these limits were exceeded.

Here the Belgian subsidiary of a Dutch parent company appointed three directors, including the Dutch parent company. Interest paid to the Dutch parent was recharacterised by the Belgian tax authorities as dividends. After a preliminary reference, the Court of Justice found that the Belgian legislation restricted the freedom of establishment and that this restriction was not justified. Furthermore, the restriction was disproportional as recharacterisation could occur even in transactions that were not to be regarded as purely artificial arrangements.¹⁵⁹ Interest payments made to non-resident companies were recharacterised as dividends as soon as they exceeded the statutory limit. Therefore, the Court of Justice once again confirmed that thin capitalisation rules are not per se objectionable, as long as they target wholly artificial arrangements and are proportional.

In a later case, the Itelcar case,¹⁶⁰ the Court of Justice found the Portuguese thin capitalisation rules to be in breach of the free movement of capital. In this case, a national rule that denied a tax deduction for excessive interest paid to a lender in a third country was examined. Under Portuguese law, excessive debt was found when the debt-to-equity ratio was above 2:1. Non-deductibility of the excessive interest would arise when a Portuguese entity owed excessive debt to an entity in

---

[155] Ibid, para 21.
[156] Ibid, para 23.
[157] See also analysis in 3.3.1.
[158] Case C-105/07 NV Lammers and Van Cleeff [2008] ECR I-00173.
[159] Ibid, para 33.
[160] Case C-282/12 Itelcar – Automóveis de Aluguer Lda v. Fazenda Pública, ECLI:EU:C:2013:629.

a third country and had a special relationship with that entity. Interest was deductible when it was paid to a Portuguese resident lending company with which the borrower had a special relationship.

Although the legislation was found to be restrictive, the Court of Justice decided that it could be justified on the basis of preventing tax avoidance. Nevertheless, the legislation was found to be disproportionate, because the definition of the term 'special relation' did not require the lender to be a shareholder in the Portuguese entity. As a result, where the lender was not a shareholder, any credit arrangement would be caught. This broad presumption of tax avoidance was impermissible.

Therefore, the Court of Justice concluded that the Portuguese thin capitalisation rules were incompatible with EU law. The Court of Justice also noted that the Portuguese tax rules did not make it possible, from the outset, to determine their scope with sufficient precision. As such, they were in breach of the requirement for legal certainty.[161]

In the Masco Denmark case, the Court of Justice looked at taxation from the perspective of the recipient parent (lender) company.[162] Danish corporate tax rules provided an exemption from tax for interest income on loans given by a Danish resident company to its Danish affiliated companies, if the corresponding interest deduction was denied to the debtor company because of the application of thin capitalisation rules. This exemption from tax was not given when the affiliated debtor company was resident in another Member State. In other words, the tax exemption was given to the recipient parent company only to offset the effect of the Danish thin capitalisation rules.

In this case, a Danish company owned a subsidiary in Germany. The German subsidiary had economic difficulties and incurred losses. The Danish parent company provided loans to the German subsidiary, which resulted in the subsidiary being unable to deduct its interest expenses due to the application of the German thin capitalisation rules. As such, the tax exemption was not available to the Danish parent company. Contrary to the opinion of the Advocate General, the Court of Justice decided that the Danish legislation was in breach of the freedom of establishment, as it was liable to render less attractive the exercise by a Danish parent company of its freedom of establishment by deterring it from setting up subsidiaries in other Member States as opposed to setting up Danish subsidiaries.[163] Again, contrary to the opinion of the Advocate General, the Court of Justice found that this restriction resulted solely from the Danish rules.[164]

---

[161] Ibid, paras 44–5.
[162] Case C-593/14 Masco Denmark ApS and Damixa ApS v. Danish Ministry of Taxation, ECLI:EU:C:2016:984.
[163] Ibid, paras 26–7.
[164] Ibid, para 28.

7.3 Interest Deductibility Restrictions

As the situations were comparable,[165] the Danish rules restricted the freedom of establishment. Although this restriction could be justified by the need to ensure a balanced allocation of taxing powers between Member States, the Court of Justice ruled that the Danish legislation went beyond what was necessary in order to attain the objective of the Danish rules, which was to eliminate double taxation of interest income.[166]

A less restrictive way would have been for Denmark to allow part of the exemption. Where a parent company in one Member State has a subsidiary in another Member State with more stringent rules on thin capitalisation, the granting, by the Member State of the parent company, of a tax exemption to that parent company for interest paid by its subsidiary up to the amount that the subsidiary was not entitled to deduct under the thin capitalisation rules of its own Member State would not call into question the balanced allocation of the power to impose taxes and would constitute a measure less restrictive of freedom of establishment than that provided under the Danish legislation.[167]

As regards the prevention of tax avoidance, the Court of Justice noted that in order for this justification to succeed, the specific objective of the measure had to be to prevent wholly artificial arrangements. However, the Danish legislation did not have such a specific objective, as it was generally applied.[168] Furthermore, on the facts of the case, here the parent company had given the loan to finance its subsidiary which was 'in major financial difficulties at the material time, and therefore, a priori, those losses did not appear to constitute a wholly artificial arrangement entered into for tax reasons alone'.[169]

The Court of Justice, therefore, concluded that the legislation was in breach of the freedom of establishment. It is noteworthy that the Court of Justice agreed with the Advocate General's opinion that freedom of establishment could not be understood as meaning that a Member State is required to draw up its own tax rules on the basis of, or as a response to, those in another Member State so as to ensure that any disparities arising from national tax rules are ultimately removed. However, the Court of Justice disagreed with the Advocate General's opinion that the difference in treatment was in effect a disparity due to the combination of the Danish and German rules and that granting a tax exemption would call into question the balanced allocation of the power to impose taxes.

It was found that the difference arose solely as a result of the Danish rules and the Court of Justice in effect applied the principle derived from the Manninen case.[170] This

---

[165] According to the Court of Justice, in each of the two situations the interest income received by the parent company would be subject to economic double taxation or to a series of charges, which was what the Danish legislation sought to avoid. Therefore, there was comparability. See paras 29–30.
[166] Ibid, para 39 et seq.
[167] Ibid, para 43.
[168] Ibid, paras 44–5.
[169] Ibid, para 46.
[170] See Case C-319/02 Petri Manninen [2004] ECR I-07477, analysed in Chapter 5.

aspect of the decision is important and may have implications for other Member States that confer tax benefits to offset a tax charge only in situations where the tax charge arises under domestic tax law and not under foreign tax law. Furthermore, the reiteration of the Cadbury Schweppes principle in this case which was decided a few months after the Anti-Tax Avoidance Directive was adopted, suggests that the Court of Justice still considers that case to be prevailing law, notwithstanding the different approach of the Directive's interest deductibility limitation rule.[171]

However, as discussed in Chapter 6, a more recent case law suggests that Member States have some discretion in determining if and under what conditions the expenses incurred by a company may be deducted against its taxable income, even in a situation covered by the Merger Directive. In the Galeria Parque case,[172] Portuguese law prevented taxpayers from deducting interest on loans taken out to finance the acquisition of shares, upon the merger of the borrower with the target. Such costs would have been deductible if the merger had not taken place. The Court of Justice found these rules to be compatible with the Merger Directive. With this ruling, the Court of Justice opens up the way for more implied anti-abuse provisions to be introduced in the Merger Directive.[173]

7.3.2 Interest Deductibility Limitation Rule and the Anti-Tax Avoidance Directive

The Anti-Tax Avoidance Directive contains a provision that limits interest deductions under certain circumstances. Article 4 of this Directive states that exceeding borrowing costs[174] are deductible in the tax period in which they are incurred up to an amount of 30 per cent of the taxpayer's[175] EBITDA or up to an amount of €3,000,000.[176] This rule is applicable to all entities that are subject to corporate income tax,[177] irrespective of the legal form of the entity, or its shareholders, or their tax residence.

---

[171] See 7.3.2.
[172] See Case C-438/18 Galeria Parque Nascente-Exploração de Espaços Comerciais SA v. Autoridade Tributária e Aduaneira, ECLI:EU:C:2019:619, analysed in Chapter 6.
[173] See analysis in 6.1.3.
[174] Art 2(2) of the Anti-Tax Avoidance Directive defines exceeding borrowing costs as the amount by which the deductible borrowing costs of a taxpayer exceed taxable interest revenue and other economically equivalent taxable revenue that the taxpayer receives according to national law. For the definition of borrowing costs, see Art 2(1).
[175] For the purposes of this provision, Member States may also treat as a taxpayer an entity that is permitted or required to apply the rules on behalf of a group, as defined according to national tax law; and an entity in a group, as defined according to national tax law, which does not consolidate the results of its members for tax purposes (Art 4(1), second subsection, paras (a) & (b)). In such circumstances, exceeding borrowing costs and the EBITDA may be calculated at the level of the group and comprise the results of all its members (Art 4(1), third subsection).
[176] Art 4(3)(a). If a tax group exists as per Art 4(1), then the amount of €3,000,000 applies for the entire group.
[177] Art 1.

Member States may (but are not obliged to) allow the following important exception to the interest limitation rule:[178] taxpayers that are part of a group can fully deduct their net interest if they can demonstrate that the ratio of their equity over their total assets is equal to or higher than the equivalent ratio of the group.[179] For the purposes of this provision, the consolidated group consists of all entities which are included in audited consolidated statements drawn up in accordance with the accounting rules that apply in a Member State or the International Financial Reporting Standards.[180] The taxpayer may also be given the right to deduct exceeding borrowing costs fully if the taxpayer is a standalone entity.[181]

The EBITDA of a tax year that is not fully absorbed by the net interest incurred by a taxpayer in that or previous tax years may be carried forward indefinitely and will increase the relevant EBITDA of the following year. Similarly, interest that cannot be deducted because of the EBITDA limitation may be carried forward to subsequent years. Carry-back is limited to three to five years.[182]

The deductibility rate is set at the top end of the scale at 10–30 per cent as recommended by the OECD under Action 4 of the BEPS project.[183] Member States are allowed to implement stricter rules.[184] A fixed net interest/earnings ratio was considered to be robust against tax avoidance planning as it was not easy to manipulate and as it linked interest deductions to taxable earnings.[185] The Directive allows Member States to exclude from the scope of this provision exceeding borrowing costs incurred on loans concluded before the 17 June 2016, but the exclusion does not extend to any subsequent modification of such

---

[178] See Art 4(5).
[179] The taxpayer ratio is considered equal to the ratio of the group if the taxpayer ratio is lower by up to 2 per cent and all assets and liabilities are valued using the same method as in consolidated financial statements. See Art 4(5).
[180] The taxpayer is allowed to use consolidated financial statements prepared under other accounting standards. See Art 4(8).
[181] Art 4(3)(b).
[182] Art 4(6). For an analysis of how some Member States have applied this provision, see Daniel Gutmann, 'The Interest Limitation (Article 4 ATAD)', in Werner Halsehner, Katerina Pantazatou, Georg Kofler and Alexander Rust (eds), *A Guide to the Anti-Tax Avoidance Directive* (Elgar Publishing, 2020), p 124, at 4.47 et seq.
[183] Art 4(5) of the Anti-Tax Avoidance Directive.
[184] See a study which investigated the economic consequences and the effectiveness of Art 4 of the Anti-Tax Avoidance Directive on an EU-wide basis. It was found that the economic consequences of this rule were fairly small. Based on a sample of 492,977 firms from 21 EU Member States, it was found that without an allowance and an exemption for stand-alone firms, between 13.97 per cent and 17.29 per cent of all EU firms would be affected by the interest barrier. This percentage decreased substantially, to between 0.51 per cent and 0.81 per cent, if an allowance of €3,000,000 was granted. The study concluded that in evaluating the effectiveness of the interest barrier, the results showed that this provision was effective in aligning interest deductibility with real economic activity in the vast majority of EU Member States. See M. Petutschnig, M. Rechbauer and S. Rünger, 'Assessment of the Interest Barrier Rule of Art 4 of the EU Anti-Tax Avoidance Directive for a Sample of European Firms', 11 [2019] 3 *World Tax Journal* 347–77.
[185] W. E. C. Heyvaert and E. Moonen, 'ATAD Implementation in Belgium: An Analysis of the New Interest Limitation Rule', 59 [2019] 7 *European Taxation* 354–60, 354.

loans.[186] Member State may also exclude financial undertakings from the scope of this provision, even when such undertakings are part of a consolidated group.[187]

The Anti-Tax Avoidance Directive permits Member States that have national rules which are equally effective to the interest limitation rule to apply those rules at the latest until 1 January 2024.[188]

The Preamble to this Directive states that Member States could, in addition to this interest deductibility limitation rule, also use targeted rules against intra-group debt financing, in particular thin capitalisation rules.[189] This statement is confusing, as thin capitalisation rules are an example of interest limitation rules – to an extent, thin capitalisation rules are akin to safe harbor debt-to-equity ratios. One could argue that with this statement, the Commission is trying to exclude scrutiny of Article 4 of the Directive on the basis of the principles of the case law analysed in 7.3.1. Regardless of how one interprets this statement, there is no reason why these principles should not also apply to the interest deductibility limitation rule of the Directive. As shown in the analysis of case law on other Directives,[190] the provisions of every Directive have to be implemented and applied by Member States in a way which is also compatible with fundamental freedoms. Certainly, the mechanical nature of the rules under Article 4 of the Directive and the absence of any commercial justification test suggest that an interpretation in line with the Cadbury Schweppes wholly artificial arrangements test – also reiterated in the more recent Marco Denmark case – would be difficult to achieve. However, there is no reason why affected taxpayers cannot challenge the implementation of Article 4 by their Member States on the basis of the fundamental freedoms.

7.4 TRANSFER PRICING

Transfer pricing is the practice of setting the prices for goods and services sold between related parties. When the related parties are based in different jurisdictions, there can be manipulation of the prices to ensure that more profits arise in the low-tax jurisdiction than in the high-tax jurisdiction. Most countries follow the arm's length principle in assessing whether the prices set out by the related parties are correct. Pursuant to this principle, the prices set for

---

[186] See Art 4(4)(a). Member States are also allowed to exclude from the scope of this provision costs incurred on loans used to fund a long-term public infrastructure project where the project operator, borrowing costs, assets and income are all in the Union. See Art 4(4)(b).
[187] See Art 4(7).
[188] See Art 11(6). Also see Commission Notice setting out that interest deductibility limitation rules by France, Greece, the Slovak Republic, Slovenia and Spain are equally effective for the purposes of the purposes of this provision. Commission Notice, *Measures considered equally effective to Art 4 of the Anti-Tax Avoidance Directive* [2018] OJ C 441/1.
[189] Preamble, para 6.
[190] See Chapter 2.

related party transactions should be comparable to those that would have been agreed between independent parties. As such, related parties are treated as separate and independent entities, ignoring the group relationship. Guidance for the application of the arm's length principle is often sought in the OECD's Transfer Pricing Guidelines,[191] which are regularly updated but still a non-binding instrument just like the OECD Model Tax Convention.

In the EU context, there is a combination of soft law and hard law for the regulation of transfer pricing. For a long time, the Arbitration Convention was a key instrument in this area. This instrument dealt with the elimination of double taxation arising from transfer pricing adjustments and settlement disputes between Member State competent authorities on the basis of the arm's length principle.[192] Guidance was given on the implementation of the Arbitration Convention through soft law instruments, many of which were produced by the Commission's Joint Transfer Pricing Forum.[193] The new Tax Dispute Resolution Mechanisms Directive does not officially replace the Arbitration Convention but certainly provides a more efficient route for taxpayers to take in resolving their tax disputes with competent authorities.[194]

So far, the Court of Justice has considered transfer pricing issues in two cases referred to it. Both cases were decided in a rather conservative way but not fully aligned with either previous case law or the OECD Model Tax Convention and the OECD Transfer Pricing Guidelines. In the first case, the SGI case,[195] it was questioned whether the Belgian rules were compatible with the non-discrimination provision, the freedom of establishment and the free movement of capital. Under Belgian law, exceptional or gratuitous benefits given by a Belgian company to a non-resident company were automatically added to the taxable base of the Belgian company, if the recipient company was, directly or indirectly, in a relationship of interdependence with the Belgian company. In similar circumstances, if the recipient company was a Belgian company, such benefit was not automatically added back.

Here a Belgian holding company, Société de Gestion Industrielle SA (SGI), made an interest-free loan to a French subsidiary. It also paid management expenses to a Luxembourg corporate shareholder, who was also the director and managing director of SGI. For the interest-free loan, the Belgian tax authorities added an amount of income to SGI's tax base, corresponding to a notional interest payment from the French subsidiary. As for the management fees, the tax authorities refused

---

[191] The latest version was released in 2017. See OECD Transfer Pricing Guidelines for Multinational Enterprises and Tax Administrations (OECD, 2017).
[192] See analysis in Chapter 2, at 2.4.
[193] Ibid.
[194] See analysis in Chapter 2, at 2.5.
[195] Case C-311/08 Société de Gestion Industrielle (SGI) v. État belge [2010] ECR I-487.

to allow a business expense deduction. SGI challenged these assessments and the case was referred to the Court of Justice.

The Court of Justice agreed with Advocate General Kokott in that freedom of establishment was the relevant freedom[196] and the Belgian legislation constituted a restriction to this freedom.[197] This restriction was, however, justified on the basis of preserving the balanced allocation of taxing powers between Member States.[198] This was because to give companies the right to elect to have their losses or profits taken into account in their Member State or in another Member State, could seriously undermine the balanced allocation of the power to impose taxes between the Member States, since the tax base would be increased in one of the Member States, and reduced in the other, by the amount of the losses or profits transferred.[199]

The Belgian legislation was also justified on the basis of preventing tax avoidance. Even though the national legislation was not specifically designed against purely artificial arrangements, the Court of Justice thought that it was justified by the objective of preventing tax avoidance, taken together with that of preserving the balanced allocation of the power to impose taxes between Member States.[200] In subsequent paragraphs the Court of Justice again emphasised that the two justifications were to be taken together.[201] It is surprising that the Court of Justice reverted to the Marks & Spencer position, requiring justifications to be taken together, when this was no longer insisted upon in subsequent case law.[202] It is also surprising that the Court of Justice did not place more emphasis on the fact that the Belgian legislation was not targeted against wholly artificial arrangements. In fact, the Court of Justice was inconsistent in using terms to identify tax avoidance.[203]

For the legislation to be proportional, two grounds had to be satisfied. Firstly, for each occasion where there was a suspicion that a transaction went beyond what the companies would have agreed under fully competitive conditions, the taxpayer had to be given an opportunity, without being subject to undue administrative constraints, to provide evidence of any commercial justification that there may have been for that transaction.[204] Secondly, where the consideration of such evidence led to the conclusion that the transaction in question went beyond what the companies would have agreed under fully competitive conditions, the corrective tax measure had to be confined to the part that exceeded what would have been agreed if the

---

[196] Ibid, para 37.
[197] Ibid, para 55.
[198] Ibid, paras 60–4.
[199] Ibid, para 62.
[200] Ibid, para 66.
[201] Ibid, paras 69–70.
[202] See 4.2.2.
[203] The Court of Justice initially used the term 'wholly artificial arrangements' (para 65), then 'purely artificial arrangements' (para 66) and later just 'artificial arrangements' (para 67). See Opinion Statement of the CFE on the case law of the European Court of Justice on transfer pricing related to loans (decision of 21 January 2010 in Case C-311/08, SGI), para 10.
[204] Case C-311/08 SGI, para 71.

companies did not have a relationship of interdependence.[205] The Court of Justice concluded that it was for the referring court to decide whether the Belgian legislation went beyond what was necessary to attain the objectives pursued by the legislation, taken together.[206]

Following this decision, the status of the wholly artificial arrangements test as a standard for assessing whether national transfer pricing rules were sufficiently targeted was uncertain. Whilst it was the litmus test in CFC and thin capitalisation cases,[207] the SGI case cast doubt on it. In this case, even though the Belgian legislation was not targeted against wholly artificial arrangements, it was still found to be compatible with EU law.

The judgment further perpetuated the uncertainty over the status of the arm's length principle in EU law. In the previous case law of the Court of Justice, the focus was not so much on the arm's length principle, but rather on objective and verifiable elements that could be used to determine whether a transaction represented a purely artificial arrangement. Evidence of any commercial justification was an important factor in justifying the different treatment of resident and non-resident companies. The problematic nature of the concept of commercial justification as an alternative to the arm's length principle was also explained in 7.3.1.

The issue was directly raised in UK courts when the Thin Cap Group Litigation case returned. Reversing the decision of Mr Justice Henderson,[208] the Court of Appeal[209] found the UK thin capitalisation rules to be lawful. The majority in the Court of Appeal followed HMRC's argument in finding that the Court of Justice's test in the Thin Cap Group Litigation case, interpreted in light of subsequent cases such as the SGI case, only required the UK to apply an arm's length test and *not* an additional commercial justification test. To an extent, the Court of Appeal decided

---

[205] Ibid, para 72.
[206] Ibid, para 75.
[207] See analysis in 7.2.1 and 7.3.1.
[208] Mr Justice Henderson had found the UK thin capitalisation rules to be incompatible with freedom of establishment, in so far as they restricted tax deductions for interest paid on loans to UK subsidiaries of group companies based in other EU Member States and not covered by bilateral income tax treaties. According to Justice Henderson, the UK arm's length test could not be interpreted as importing, or as itself being subject to, a further subjective test of commercial justification. Since a conforming interpretation was not possible, the UK thin capitalisation rules had to be disapplied in relation to transactions that had a genuine commercial justification. Justice Henderson held that tax authorities should bear the burden of proving the lack of commercial justification by positive evidence. Also, taxpayers were entitled to repayment of taxes that a Member State imposed in breach of EU law. See Test Claimants in the Thin Cap Group Litigation v. Commissioners for Her Majesty's Revenue and Customs [2009] EWHC 2908 (Ch). For commentary, see Paul Farmer and Kelly Coutinho, 'Marleasing versus disapplication: thin cap – a return to legal principle?', (23 November 2009) 1006 *Tax Journal*, 17–19; Michael Anderson and Philippe Freund, 'Thin Cap GLO judgment', (23 November 2009) 1006 *Tax Journal*, 5–7.
[209] See Test Claimants in the Thin Cap Group Litigation v. Commissioners for Her Majesty's Revenue and Customs [2011] EWCA Civ 127. Lady Justice Arden dissented in the Court of Appeal. The UK's Supreme Court refused leave to appeal the Court of Appeal's decision. Furthermore, a second panel of the Supreme Court also refused to re-refer the issues to the Court of Justice.

that the application of the arm's length test was sufficient justification for discriminating against non-resident parent companies, without needing to prove further commercial justification. This stance was more aligned with the OECD Model Tax Convention's approach. It also equated the arm's length test with the question of whether there was a wholly artificial arrangement, similar to what the Court of Justice effectively did in the SGI case,[210] watering down the latter rather than the former.

In the first edition to this book, it was questioned whether this interpretation of the wholly artificial arrangements test should be followed by the Court of Justice, in order to help prevent a conflict with the OECD Model Tax Convention and ensure more consistency within the case law. It was also questioned whether the wholly artificial arrangements test might end up not applying to transfer pricing rules. Later case law suggests that indeed the wholly artificial arrangements test is modified in this area. However, the Court of Justice has not abandoned the concept of commercial justification, leaving the possibility open for a potentially different approach vis-a-vis the OECD's arm's length principle.

In the Hornbach-Baumarkt case,[211] it was questioned whether the German transfer pricing legislation was compatible with the freedom of establishment. The legislation applied only to cross-border situations and did not allow the taxpayer to rely for justification on commercial reasons resulting from its status as a shareholder of the foreign subsidiary. In this case, a German parent company had given guarantees and letters of comfort to banks with respect to loans made to foreign subsidiaries but without requiring any payment or consideration. The German tax authorities adjusted the profits of the parent company upwards and the parent company challenged this decision. The case was eventually referred to the Court of Justice, which concluded that there was no breach of EU law.

The Court of Justice found that the transfer pricing legislation restricted the freedom of establishment.[212] This restriction was justified by the need to preserve the balanced allocation of taxing rights between Member States, provided that the transfer pricing legislation was aimed at preventing profit shifting via transactions that were not in accordance with market conditions. The Court of Justice did not consider whether the restriction was justified on the basis of preventing tax avoidance, as no such argument had been advanced.[213]

The Court of Justice went on to examine the proportionality of the German transfer pricing legislation and to clarify the meaning of the concept of commercial

---

[210] Philip Baker, 'Transfer pricing and Community law: the SGI case' (2010) 38(4) *Intertax*, 194–6, 195. Also see Opinion Statement of the CFE on the case law of the European Court of Justice on transfer pricing related to loans (decision of 21 January 2010 in Case C-311/08, SGI), para 16.
[211] Case C-382/16 Hornbach-Baumarkt-AG v. Finanzamt Landau, ECLI:EU:C:2018:366.
[212] Ibid, para 35.
[213] As pointed out by the Court of Justice, the German government neither identified a wholly artificial arrangement within the meaning of the case law, nor a desire on the part of the applicant in the main proceedings to reduce its taxable profit in Germany: ibid, para 55.

7.4 Transfer Pricing

justification. It was questioned whether this concept included economic reasons resulting from the very existence of a relationship of interdependence between the parent company and its subsidiaries which were resident in another Member State.[214] The Court of Justice found that there may be a commercial justification by virtue of the fact that the taxpayer was a shareholder in the foreign group companies, which would justify the conclusion of the transaction under non-arm's length terms.[215] As the gratuitous granting of comfort letters containing a guarantee statement could be explained by the economic interest of the shareholder in the financial success of the foreign group subsidiaries, this could be sufficient commercial justification. This being the case, the German legislation did not go beyond what was necessary to achieve the objective pursued, to the extent that 'the authorities responsible for the enforcement of that legislation afford the resident taxpayer the opportunity to prove that the terms were agreed on for commercial reasons which could result from its status as a shareholder in the non-resident company, which is a matter for the referring court to assess'.[216]

This is a very important decision. Contrary to the opinion of the Advocate General, the Court of Justice did not rely on tax avoidance or profit shifting reasons to justify the restrictive legislation. Rather, its acceptance of commercial justification and what that encompasses could pave the way for what the Advocate General warned to be 'a blunt and full exclusion of any business transactions with subsidiaries from the application of the [arm's length] principle, because a parent will always have interest in seeing its subsidiary prosper'.[217]

By not insisting on wholly artificial arrangements, both the SGI and Hornbach-Baumarkt cases seem to suggest that the Court of Justice is taking a different approach from that taken under other anti-abuse rules. Perhaps this is understandable, as there is much more developed international soft law – or at least international consensus on some concepts – which is set out in the OECD's Transfer Pricing Guidelines. However, this does not mean that the Court of Justice will eschew any discussion or challenge over national transfer pricing rules, even if those rules emanate from established OECD principles. It would seem that this is actually encouraged by the Commission, if one considers the state aid challenges over the transfer pricing rulings of some Member States, which are discussed in Chapter 8. Although the recent decision of the General Court in the Apple[218] case seems to curtail the Commission's ambitions in developing a free-standing EU arm's length principle, the SGI and Hornbach-Baumarkt cases suggest that the Court of Justice will not hesitate to (indirectly) interfere with the arm's length principle if that is

---

[214] Ibid, para 51.
[215] Ibid, para 56.
[216] Ibid, para 58.
[217] Ibid, para 113 (Advocate General).
[218] Cases T-778/16 and T-892/16 Apple Sales International and Apple Operations Europe v. Commission, ECLI:EU:T:2020:338.

necessary for the application of EU law. This should perhaps act as a warning not to blindly follow any OECD initiatives in the context of the digital economy.

7.5 OTHER ANTI-ABUSE PROVISIONS

In addition to the above anti-abuse rules, it was shown in Chapters 2 and 6 that anti-abuse clauses have long existed in the context of the Parent-Subsidiary Directive, the Merger Directive and the Interest and Royalties Directive.[219] The aim of these clauses is to prevent the reliefs provided under the Directives from being abused. For example, the Parent-Subsidiary Directive and the Interest and Royalties Directive allow domestic or agreement-based provisions for the prevention of fraud or abuse.[220] The Parent-Subsidiary Directive now also has a GAAR,[221] as well as a provision which prevents reliefs from being granted in situations of mismatches in the tax treatment of profit distributions which would lead to double non-taxation.[222] Furthermore, under the Tax Dispute Resolution Mechanisms Directive, a Member State may deny access to a dispute resolution procedure in cases where penalties were imposed in that Member State in relation to adjusted income or capital for tax fraud, wilful default and gross negligence.[223]

Very importantly, as mentioned in 7.1 and in Chapter 2, the Anti-Tax Avoidance Directive also has a GAAR. The GAAR in the Anti-Tax Avoidance Directive was aimed at formulating a coordinated response to abusive tax practices within the EU, forcing Member States to adopt a common standard.[224] It was meant to fill in the gaps of domestic legislation[225] and, in fact, some Member States did not implement it as they already had rules deemed to have the same (or a broader) scope.[226]

The GAAR of the Anti-Tax Avoidance Directive targets an arrangement or a series of arrangements in which the main purpose or one of the main purposes is to obtain a tax advantage and which (arrangement or a series of arrangements) are not genuine having regard to all relevant facts and circumstances.[227] It is further clarified that the arrangement or series of arrangements shall be regarded as non-genuine to the extent

---

[219] See Art 1(4) of the Parent-Subsidiary Directive; Art 5 of the Interest and Royalties Directive; Art 15 of the Merger Directive.
[220] See Art 1(4) of Parent-Subsidiary Directive; Art 5 of Interest and Royalties Directive.
[221] See Art 1(2) of Parent-Subsidiary Directive.
[222] Ibid, Art 4(1)(a).
[223] Art 16(6) of Tax Dispute Resolution Mechanisms Directive.
[224] Andreas Perdelwitz, 'Developing a Common Framework against Tax Avoidance in the European Union', in Pasquale Pistone and Dennis Weber (eds), *The Implementation of Anti-BEPS Rules in the EU: A Comprehensive Study* (Amsterdam: IBFD, 2018) 330.
[225] Preamble to the Anti-Tax Avoidance Directive, para 11.
[226] For example, Belgium, Bulgaria, Croatia, Finland, Germany, Greece, Ireland, Italy, the Netherlands, Portugal, Spain, Sweden and the United Kingdom. Daniel Gutmann, Andreas Perdelwitz, Emmanuel Raingeard de la Blétière, René Offermanns, Marnix Schellekens, Giulia Gallo, Adrián Grant Hap and Magdalena Olejnicka, 'The Impact of the ATAD on Domestic Systems: A Comparative Survey', 57 (2017) 1 *European Taxation* 2–20, p 9.
[227] Art 6(1) of Anti-Tax Avoidance Directive.

that they are not put into place for valid commercial reasons which reflect economic reality.[228] The actual language of the provision suggests that this GAAR is to be interpreted in an extensive way, taking into account both tax motives and non-tax motives in determining whether there are non-genuine arrangements.[229] Therefore, the non-tax objectives can be very general, in applying this provision.

Overall, the GAAR of the Anti-Tax Avoidance Directive seems to have been designed in a very vague and broad manner, so that it would function as a deterrent for taxpayers.[230] Nevertheless, the lowering of the standard of tax abuse seems to go against earlier judgments of the Court of Justice discussed in this chapter.

In the Anti-Tax Avoidance Directive, there is now also a complex legal framework addressing hybrid mismatches. As explained in the preamble to this Directive, hybrid mismatches are the consequence of differences in the legal characterisation of payments (financial instruments) or entities and those differences surface in the interaction between the legal systems of two jurisdictions.[231] For a long time, this type of mismatches were unregulated at EU level and it was up to Member States to address the issue, if at all.

The first EU-wide mismatch rule was the aforementioned provision of the Parent-Subsidiary Directive which was introduced to tackle hybrid loans and mismatches as a reaction to Action 2 of the BEPS project.[232] This rule, however, was not sufficient to meet the concerns set out in Action 2. Therefore, a more comprehensive solution was introduced in the Anti-Tax Avoidance Directive, which broadly provided that one of the two jurisdictions in a mismatch should deny the deduction of a payment leading to such an outcome.[233] This provision was criticised for covering intra-EU mismatches only. Following an amendment to the Directive,[234] the territorial scope of the rules has been extended to third countries. The amending legislation also extended the scope of operation of the rules, in order to address hybrid entity mismatches, hybrid financial instrument mismatches, hybrid permanent

---

[228] Ibid, Art 6(2).
[229] Maartens Floris de Wilde, 'Is the ATAD's GAAR a Pandora's Box?', in Pasquale Pistone and Dennis Weber (eds), *The Implementation of Anti-BEPS Rules in the EU: A Comprehensive Study* (Amsterdam: IBFD, 2018).
[230] Błażej Kuźniacki, 'The GAAR (Art 6 ATAD)', in Werner Halsehner, Katerina Pantazatou, Georg Kofler and Alexander Rust (eds), *A Guide to the Anti-Tax Avoidance Directive* (Elgar Publishing, 2020), p 150, at 6.4.
[231] Preamble to the Anti-Tax Avoidance Directive, para 13.
[232] See Council Directive 2014/86/EU of 8 July 2014 amending Directive 2011/96/EU on the common system of taxation applicable in the case of parent companies and subsidiaries of different Member States, [2014] OJ L219. The amending legislation introduced what is now Art 4(1)(a) of the Parent-Subsidiary Directive.
[233] See Art 9 of Anti-Tax Avoidance Directive. For commentary, see Leopoldo Parada, 'Hybrid Financial Instruments and Anti-Hybrid Rules in the EU ATAD (Article 9 ATAD)', in Werner Halsehner, Katerina Pantazatou, Georg Kofler and Alexander Rust (eds), *A Guide to the Anti-Tax Avoidance Directive* (Elgar Publishing, 2020).
[234] Council Directive 2017/952 of 29 May 2017 amending Directive (EU) 2016/1164 as regards hybrid mismatches with third countries, [2017] OJ L144.

establishments mismatches/disregarded permanent establishments, imported mismatches, reverse hybrid mismatches, tax residency mismatches and hybrid transfers. The current scope of the hybrid mismatch rules of the Anti-Tax Avoidance Directive is now very technical and much more aligned with the recommendations under Action 2 of the BEPS project. It will not be examined further in this book.[235]

[235] For more information, see Oana Papa, 'Recent Measures to Counter Hybrid Mismatch Arrangements at the EU Level', (2017) 9 *European Taxation* 401–6; Konstantin Karainov, 'The ATAD 2 Anti-Hybrid Rules versus EU Member State Tax Treaties with Third States: Is Override Possible?' (2019) 2/3 *European Taxation* 52–9; Tomas Balco, 'ATAD 2: Anti-Tax Avoidance Directive', (2017) 4 *European Taxation* 127–36; Gijs Fibbe, 'Hybrid Mismatch Rules under ATAD I & II', in Pasquale Pistone and Dennis Weber (eds), *The Implementation of Anti-BEPS Rules in the EU: A Comprehensive Study* (Amsterdam: IBFD, 2018) 409–18; Karoline Spies, 'Hybrid Entities and Anti-Hybrid Rules in the EU ATAD (Article 9 and 9a ATAD)', in Werner Halsehner, Katerina Pantazatou, Georg Kofler and Alexander Rust (eds), *A Guide to the Anti-Tax Avoidance Directive* (Elgar Publishing, 2020).

8

State Aid and Taxation

As far as negative harmonisation is concerned, the focus of the case law has long been on the impact of fundamental freedoms on national tax rules. The various types of corporate tax rules that were affected were discussed in Chapters 4–7. However, the fundamental freedoms are not the only benchmark against which national tax measures are to be assessed. The state aid prohibition is another critical provision, which, as shown in this chapter, could affect the design of a country's tax system and certain aspects of its administration.

8.1 INTRODUCTION

The state aid prohibition is enshrined in Article 107(1) TFEU, which reads as follows:

> Save as otherwise provided in this Treaty, any aid granted by a Member State or through State resources in any form whatsoever which distorts or threatens to distort competition by favouring certain undertakings or the production of certain goods shall, in so far as it affects trade between Member States, be incompatible with the common market.

Article 107(1) TFEU does not have a direct effect.[1] There has to be an aid in the sense of a benefit or advantage,[2] granted by a Member State or through Member State resources. This encompasses regional or local authorities and public bodies.[3] Most importantly, the aid must favour certain undertakings or the production of certain goods (the 'selectivity' principle),[4] distort or threaten to distort competition, and must be capable of affecting trade between Member States.

---

[1] Case 74/76 Ianelli & Volpi SpA v. Meroni [1977] ECR 557. See also Case 78/76 Steinike und Weinlig v. Germany [1977] ECR 595; Case C-354/90 Fédération National de Commerce Extérieur des Produits et al (FNCEPA) v. France [1991] ECR I-5505.

[2] The salient question is whether the recipient of the advantage is receiving a benefit which it would not have otherwise received under normal market conditions.

[3] For example, Case C-323/82 Intermills v. Commission [1984] ECR 3809; Case C-177/98 Pigs and Bacon Commission v. McCarren [1979] ECR 2161.

[4] A measure can be selective even if it applies to a large number of undertakings. See, for example, Case C-143/99 Adria-Wien Pipeline [2001] ECR I-8365 and Case C-148/04 Unicredito Italiano [2005] ECR I-11137 etc.

The concept of state aid is wider than that of a subsidy, embracing not only positive benefits, such as subsidies but 'also interventions which, in various forms, mitigate the charges which are normally included in the budget of an undertaking and which, without therefore being subsidies in the strict meaning of the word, are similar in character and have the same effect'.[5]

Reductions in the tax base,[6] tax exemptions,[7] tax credits,[8] deferment of the payment of taxes[9] and cancellation or even special rescheduling of tax debt are examples of state aid.[10] Such tax measures are considered to be granted by the Member State or through its resources. This is because a tax exemption mitigates the charge that would normally be recoverable from the undertaking. Therefore, the Member State loses tax revenue. This loss of tax revenue is equivalent to the consumption of state resources in the form of fiscal expenditure.[11] The fact that legislation is in breach of one of the fundamental freedoms does not mean that it cannot also fall foul of the state aid prohibition.[12]

---

[5] Case C-387/92 Banco Exterior de Espana SA v. Ayuntamiento de Valencia [1994] ECR I-877, para 13, citing the judgment in Case 30/59 De Gezamenlijke Steenkolenmijnen in Limburg v. High Authority of the European Coal and Steel Community [1961] ECR 1. This case was decided in the context of the European Coal and Steel Community Treaty.

[6] For example, by means of special deductions, special or accelerated depreciation arrangements or the entering of reserves on the balance sheet. Case C-66/02 Italy v. Commission of the European Communities [2005] ECR I-10901, para 78; Case C-222/04 Ministero dell'Economia e delle Finanze v. Cassa di Risparmio di Firenze SpA [2006] ECR I-289, para 132.

[7] Case C-387/92 Banco Exterior de España SA [1994] ECR I-00877; Joined Cases C-465/09P to C-470/09P Territorio Historico de Vizcaya – Diputacion Foral de Vizcaya et al v. Commission [2011] ECR I-00083.

[8] See Cases T-92/00 and T-103/00 Territorio Historico de Alava – Diputacion Foral de Alava [2002] ECR II-1385.

[9] Case C-156/98 Federal Republic of Germany v. Commission of the European Communities [2000] ECR I-6857; Case C-66/02 Italy v. Commission of the European Communities, para 78.

[10] See, generally, Commission Notice on the notion of state aid as referred to in Art 107(1) of the Treaty on the Functioning of the European Union (C/2016/2946), [2016] OJ C 262; Notice on the Application of the State Aid Rules to Measures Relating to Direct Business Taxation, [1998] OJ C384/3. Wolfgang Schön, 'Taxation and state aid law in the European Union' (1999) 36(5) *Common Market Law Review*, 911–36; Frans Vanistendael, 'Fiscal support measures and harmful tax competition' (2000) 9(3) *EC Tax Review*, 152–60.

[11] Notice on the Application of the State Aid Rules to Measures Relating to Direct Business Taxation, para 10.

[12] See the case of the Sardinian regional tax on tourist stopovers by aircraft and boats, which was levied on those domiciled outside Sardinia. The Court of Justice found this tax to be incompatible with the freedom to provide services and with the state aid prohibition. Case C-169/08 Presidente del Consiglio dei Ministri v. Regione Sardegna [2009] ECR I-10821. More recently, see A-Fonds case, on the domestic court's jurisdiction in cases concerning state aid regimes that also violate fundamental freedoms. Here, the Court of Justice found that the domestic court had no jurisdiction to rule on the refund of a tax in case of breach of the free movement of capital if that refund constituted a state aid scheme. This was because, under the provisions of the TFEU, the Commission had exclusive competence to assess the existence of unlawful state aid. Case C-598/17 A-Fonds, ECLI:EU:C:2019:352. See also Roland Ismer and Sophia Piotrowski, 'Relationship of fiscal State aid and the fundamental freedoms', in Christiana HJI Panayi, Werner Halsehner, Edoardo Traversa (eds), *Research Handbook on European Union Taxation Law* (Elgar Publishing, 2020).

8.1 Introduction

The first edition of this book questioned whether tax credits or exemptions conferred under tax treaties could be regarded as state aid.[13] The author argued that these treaty benefits, which reduce or eliminate double taxation only for certain undertakings or industries satisfying specific criteria, to the extent that they could be considered selective for the purposes of Article 107 TFEU, could be a form of state aid.[14] This would mean that a Member State's ability to offer tax incentives through tax treaties may be restricted. While the Parent-Subsidiary and the Interest and Royalties Directives have in certain circumstances streamlined host state taxes for the avoidance of double taxation, as tax treaties are still applicable with potentially more generous provisions, the risk of falling foul of the state aid prohibition should not be ignored. The judgment of the Court of Justice in the World Duty Free case would seem to support this position.[15] In that case, it was held that a tax provision could be contrary to the state aid prohibition even if the number of undertakings able to claim entitlement was large.

Certain types of aid, such as aid of a social character[16] or aid to help in the alleviation of a natural disaster[17] are deemed to be compatible with the common market.[18] Furthermore, aid may be compatible with the common market if it falls within any of the six derogations laid down in Article 107(3) TFEU. These derogations have been strictly construed, though some of them proved essential at times of financial crises. More recently, the flexibility predicted in Article 107(3)(b) was used by the Commission to adopt a Temporary Framework to enable the Member States to support their economies during the Covid-19 outbreak.[19] One of the five types of reliefs allowed was elective tax advantages to a company for up to €800,000 to address its urgent liquidity needs.[20]

---

[13] For my earlier views on this point, see Christiana HJI Panayi, 'Limitation on Benefits and state aid' (2004) 44(2) *European Taxation*, 83–98 and ch 4 of Christiana HJI Panayi, *Double Taxation, Tax Treaties, Treaty Shopping and the European Community* (Alphen aan den Rijn: Kluwer Law International, 2007).

[14] This can be shown with the example of reduced withholding tax rates on dividends. Assuming the Parent-Subsidiary Directive is inapplicable, Member State A, as a host state, might have agreed under tax treaty A/B to levy 15 per cent withholding tax on dividends paid by SubCoB to its ParentCoB in Member State B. However, Member State A may have agreed under tax treaty A/C to levy 5 per cent withholding tax on dividends paid by a SubCoC to its ParentCoC in Member State C. Compared to SubCoB, SubCoC gets a tax reduction of 10 per cent, which could be construed as state aid if the criteria for the tax reduction are sufficiently selective. See HJI Panayi, *Double Taxation, Tax Treaties, Treaty Shopping and the European Community*, ch 4, pp 172–3.

[15] Case C-20/15P European Commission v. World Duty Free Group SA and Others, ECLI:EU:C:2016:981. See analysis in 8.4.

[16] Art 107(2)(a) TFEU.

[17] See Art 107(2)(b) TFEU.

[18] Art 107(2) TFEU.

[19] See Communication from the Commission, *Temporary Framework for state aid measures to support the economy in the current COVID-19 outbreak*, C(2020) 1863 final (19 March 2020).

[20] Ibid, p 5, Member States were required to show that the state aid measures notified to the Commission under this Communication were necessary, appropriate and proportionate to remedy a serious

Another important provision is Article 109 TFEU, which empowers the Council, acting by a qualified majority on a proposal from the Commission, and after consulting the European Parliament to make any appropriate regulations to apply state aid provisions. This Article has provided the basis for Council action empowering the Commission to make regulations exempting certain categories of aid.[21]

Whether or not a given measure is state aid is a question that the courts both at European and national level have the competence to decide. However, whether such state aid is compatible or not with the common market is a question that the national courts do not have the competence to determine.[22] As far as the definition of state aid, the Commission has historically preferred a broad brush approach and examined each aid on its own merits.[23] The salient question is whether the recipient of the advantage is receiving a benefit which it would not have otherwise received under normal market conditions.[24] The benefit should improve the undertaking's financial position or reduce the costs that it would have to bear. The Commission does not need to prove that trade will be affected.[25] It is sufficient to show that the measure threatens competition,[26] that intra-EU trade may be affected and not necessarily permanently.[27] In such circumstances, distortion of competition may

---

disturbance in the economy of the Member State concerned and that all the conditions of this Communication were fully respected. Ibid, p 4. For example, see the UK's Coronavirus Business Interruption Loan Scheme, approved on 6 April 2020, which provided support to small and medium-sized enterprises in the context of the coronavirus outbreak.

[21] For example, under the General Block Exemption Regulations, the Commission declared specific categories of state aid compatible with the Treaty if they fulfilled certain conditions. See Council Regulation (EC) No 994/98 of 7 May 1998 on the application of Arts 92 and 93 of the Treaty establishing the European Community to certain categories of horizontal state aid ([1998] OJ L142/1). This was amended by Council Regulation No 733/2013 of 22 July 2013 amending Regulation (EC) No 994/98 on the application of Arts 92–3 of the Treaty establishing the European Community to specific categories of horizontal state aid ([2013] OJ L 204/11).

[22] See below 8.3.

[23] Conor Quigley, 'The Notion of State Aid in the EEC' [1988] *EL Rev* 242–56.

[24] Case C-39/94 SFEI v. La Poste [1996] ECR I-3547, para 60; Case C-241/95P Tiercé Ladbroke v. Commission [1997] ECR I-7007, para 35; Case T-67/94 Ladbroke Racing v. Commission [1998] ECR II-1, para 52.

[25] See Cases T-298, 312, 313, 315, 600–7/97 Alzetta Mauro v. Commission [2000] ECR II-2319, paras 76–90.

[26] Case T-288/97 Regione Autonoma Friuli Venezia Giia v. Commission [2001] ECR II-1169, paras 49–50; Case T-35/99 Keller SpA v. Commission [2002] ECR II-261 para 85.

[27] In Case T-211/05 Italy v. Commission [2009] ECR II-02777, the General Court examined the compatibility of tax incentives for companies involved in initial public offering procedures with the state aid prohibition. The General Court argued that the Commission was not obliged to show that competition was undermined permanently; or to carry out a more detailed investigation of the substantial impact of the measures on the recipients' competitive position. The decision of the General Court was followed by the Court of Justice upon appeal. See Case C-458/09P Italy v. Commission [2011] ECR I-00179.

be easily inferred.[28] The above requirements form part of a global question. Essential guidance on the constituent elements of the state aid prohibition can be found in the 2016 Commission Notice on the notion of state aid.[29]

Initially, the Commission attacked the more obvious types of state aids such as direct grants, subsidiaries, state guarantees and loans. In the last few years, it has turned its attention to more indirect forms of state aid, emphasising social and fiscal measures. State aid has become very important in the tax field.[30] According to the Commission, the measures which relieve the recipients of charges that are normally borne from their budgets,[31] such as reductions in the tax base,[32] total or partial reduction in the amount of tax (exemption or tax credit), deferment, cancellation or even special rescheduling of tax debt are examples of state aid. Such tax measures are thought to be granted by the state or through state resources. This is because a tax exemption mitigates the charge that would normally be recoverable from the undertaking. Therefore, the state loses tax revenue. This loss of tax revenue is equivalent to the consumption of state resources in the form of fiscal expenditure.[33]

A company may be affected by the state aid prohibition, whether it is the recipient of aid or the competitor of the recipient. The aid given to a company may have to be repaid if it is unlawful or has not been properly notified or approved by the Commission. If repayment is demanded, the recipient of the aid will have to reimburse within four months the full amount of the financial benefit received, including interest, up to a maximum of ten years prior to the start of an investigation. No recovery is necessary when the unlawful aid was paid more than ten years before the Commission's investigation.[34] Competitor companies may also trigger

---

[28] Case C-730/79 Philip Morris v. Commission [1980] ECR 2671, para 11; Case C-53/00 Ferring SA v. ACOSS [2001] ECR I-9067, para 21; Case C-234/84 Belgium v. Commission [1986] ECR 2263, para 22. See also a more recent case: Case C-522/13 Ministerio de Defensa and Navantia SA v. Concello de Ferrol, ECLI:EU:C:2014:2262. Here, the Court of Justice found a property tax exemption for state-owned land made available to a private company that traded goods and services within the EU constituted state aid.

[29] Commission Notice on the notion of state aid referred to in Art 107(1) of the Treaty on the Functioning of the European Union (2016).

[30] See Conor Quigley, *European State Aid Law* (3rd edn, Hart Publishing, 2015); Pierpaolo Rossi-Maccanico, 'Commentary of state aid review of multinational tax regimes' [2007] 1 *European State Aid Law Quarterly* 25; Christiana HJI Panayi, 'State Aid and Tax: The Third Way?' 32 [2004] 6/7 *Intertax* 287–311; Michael Rydelski, 'Distinction between State Aid and General Tax Measures', 19 [2010] 4 *EC Tax Review* 149.

[31] Commission Notice on the application of the state aid rules to measures relating to direct business taxation [1998] OJ C 384/3–9, para 9. For a commentary on the 1998 Notice, see Commission, *Report on the implementation of the Commission notice on the application of the state aid rules to measures relating to direct*, COM(2004)434. This has now been superseded by the 2016 Commission Notice on the notion of state aid.

[32] For example, by means of special deductions, special or accelerated depreciation arrangements or the entering of reserves on the balance sheet.

[33] Notice on the application of the state aid rules to measures relating to direct business taxation (1998), para 10.

[34] It has been noted that almost any communication about the aid between the Member State and the Commission, which need not be known to the beneficiary can restart the ten-year limitation period.

investigations by lodging complaints with the Commission. In fact, when the Commission has doubts about the compatibility of a proposed aid measure, it invites interested parties to submit comments and opens a formal investigation procedure. Furthermore, it has now been held that competitors of the beneficiaries of a state aid measure may bring a direct action against a Commission decision.[35]

8.2 THE ROLE OF THE COMMISSION AND MEMBER STATES

The Commission has a pivotal role in the application of the state aid prohibition. Member States are required to notify the Commission as to any plans to grant state aid or alter existing state aid – i.e. aid that was already notified and approved.[36] The Court of Justice has interpreted this Article as if it imposes a standstill obligation on the Member States during the Commission's review period.[37] The Commission must reach a decision within two months otherwise, the standstill obligation comes to an end.

During the notification procedure, the Commission applies a balancing test; it balances the positive effects of the aid for achieving a common interest objective and its negative effects on competition and trade. This test includes an economic evaluation of the aid. If the Commission finds that the aid (whether existing or new) is incompatible with Article 107 TFEU, 'it shall decide that the State concerned shall abolish or alter such aid within a period of time to be determined by the Commission'.[38] This procedure is meant to intensify cooperation between the Commission and Member States. The Commission may also ask the Court of Justice to order a Member State to recover illegal state aid.

Broadly, the Commission keeps a constant review of existing aids offered by the Member States[39] and aids that have not been properly notified to the Commission. It should be pointed out that when the Commission initiates a formal state aid investigation procedure, the Member State concerned must suspend the implementation of the measure under investigation. The Commission can impose a suspension injunction where it can show that the Member State concerned is not planning to suspend the aid at issue.

Member States may challenge a Commission decision under Article 263 TFEU. This challenge may relate to a review of the legality of the Commission's or the Council's decision or an application for annulment of any binding act taken by Community institutions. The Commission may also bring an action against

---

See George Peretz, 'The Consequences of Unlawful State Aid', (2015) *Tax Journal* 11–13 (6 March 2015) p 11, citing Case C-276/03P Scott [2005] ECR I-8437.
[35] See Joined Cases C-622/16P to C-624/16P Scuola Elementare Maria Montessori Srl v. European Commission and Others, ECLI:EU:C:2018:873.
[36] Art 108(3) TFEU.
[37] Case C-120/73 Gebrüder Lorenz Gmbh v. Germany [1973] ECR 1471.
[38] Art 108(2) TFEU.
[39] See Art 108(1) TFEU.

a Member State under Article 108(2) TFEU. This action is to enforce a negative decision – i.e. when the Member State has not recovered aid previously determined incompatible by the Commission. The Commission may also commence proceedings under general law for failure to act,[40] but these provisions are more cumbersome.

Furthermore, a person individually and directly concerned may bring an action under Article 263 TFEU against decisions prohibiting aid. The Court of Justice insists on some tangible connection between the aid and the recipient and not just for the recipient to belong to a group that could benefit from the prohibited aid.[41] The decision must affect them because of certain attributes peculiar to them, or by reason of circumstances in which they are differentiated from other persons.[42]

Similarly, an action may be brought by a competitor of the recipient, but the competitor needs to show that there are specific circumstances which allow them to be singled out from a potentially large group of competitors of the recipient of the aid.[43] As mentioned above, direct action against a Commission decision brought by competitors of the beneficiaries of a state aid measure was allowed in Scuola Elementare Maria Montessori.[44] In the recent Tesco case,[45] it was clarified that taxpayers might not rely on the argument that an exemption from tax (which benefitted competitors) was illegal state aid in order to avoid payment of that tax or obtain repayment of the tax paid. As stated, the possible unlawfulness of an exemption from a certain tax is not capable of affecting the lawfulness of the tax itself.[46] In other words, if the exemption is found to be illegal state aid, then there has to be recovery from the beneficiaries but the other undertakings which did not benefit from such exemption must (continue to) pay the tax.

8.3 THE ROLE OF NATIONAL COURTS

National courts also play a significant role in applying the state aid prohibition.[47] They can rule that a given aid is state aid within the meaning of Article 107(1) TFEU

---

[40] Arts 258–60 TFEU.
[41] Case 67/85 Van Der Kooy and others v. Commission [1988] ECR 219.
[42] See the Plaumann test in Case 25/62 Plaumann v. Commission [1963] ECR 95.
[43] Case 10 and 18/68 Eridania Zuccherifici and others v. Commission [1969] ECR 459. Also, see Case C-198/91 Cook v. Commission [1993] ECR I-2487; Case C- 313/90 CIRFS v. Commission [1993] ECR I-1125.
[44] See Joined Cases C-622/16P to C-624/16P Scuola Elementare Maria Montessori Srl v. European Commission and Others, ECLI:EU:C:2018:873.
[45] Case C-323/18 Tesco-Global Áruházak Zrt v. Nemzeti Adó- és Vámhivatal Fellebbviteli Igazgatósága, ECLI:EU:C:2020:140.
[46] Ibid, para 40.
[47] See Notice on Cooperation between national courts and the Commission in the state aid field [1995] OJ C312/07, replaced by Notice on the Enforcement of State Aid Law by National Courts [2009] OJ C85/1. Also see Commission Handbook on Enforcement of EU state aid law by national courts (2010), http://ec.europa.eu/competition/publications/state_aid/national_courts_booklet_en.pdf.

but cannot rule on the compatibility of the aid with the common market; only the Commission can do this. In applying Article 107(1) TFEU, the Commission urges national courts to refer preliminary questions to the Court of Justice under Article 267 TFEU when in doubt.[48] National courts can rule that a given aid is illegal when it has not been properly notified and can order interim injunctive measures to prevent or suspend the granting of unlawful aid. Furthermore, national courts have the power to assess ex officio whether the state aid rules have been infringed, even if the argument has not been brought by the parties.[49]

When the Commission decides pursuant to Article 108(2) TFEU that an aid is incompatible with the common market and requires repayment of the aid, the national authorities have a duty to seek recovery without delay.[50] National courts may also order remedial action when there is unlawful aid without a Commission decision.

A recovery decision is addressed to the Member State that granted the unlawful aid and not to the beneficiary. However, the Member State must implement the recovery decision by seeking reimbursement from the beneficiary. Recovery is limited to ten years from the day the aid was awarded to the beneficiary. Where a beneficiary refuses to repay the aid, the Member State must commence enforcement proceedings in national courts, and this obligation overrides any domestic procedural rules which preclude recovery. In fact, national courts are obligated to apply all appropriate devices and remedies to protect the rights conferred on individuals under Article 108(3) TFEU. Such course of action may include setting aside any conflicting provisions of national law, repayment of aid, granting orders for interim relief, re-establishing the pre-existing competitive position of the relevant parties and even awarding damages to parties whose interests were harmed.[51]

The amount to be recovered is calculated on the basis of a comparison between the tax actually paid and the amount that would have been paid if the generally applicable rule had applied, irrespective of the fact that a beneficiary would not have entered into the transaction absent the aid. Interest may also be ordered on the amount repayable, and this could be on a compound basis.[52] It is only in exceptional circumstances that the recovery of unlawful state aid would not be appropriate; for example, if it is absolutely impossible[53] or if legitimate expectations have been generated by the Commission justifying non-recovery or if it is contrary to the

---

[48] Notice on enforcement of state aid law by national courts (2009), paras 89–96.
[49] Ibid.
[50] Council Regulation 2015/1589 of 13 July 2015 laying down detailed rules for the application of Art 108 of the Treaty on the Functioning of the European Union, [2015] OJ L 248. Also see Notice on the enforcement of state aid law by national courts (2009), paras 30–6.
[51] Notice on the enforcement of state aid law by national courts (2009), paras 28–62.
[52] See Council Regulation 2015/1589 and Notice on the enforcement of state aid law by national courts, para 41.
[53] As was held, '[t]he condition that it be absolutely impossible to implement a decision is not fulfilled where the defendant Member State merely informs the Commission of the legal, political or practical difficulties involved in implementing the decision, without taking any real steps to recover the aid from the undertakings concerned, and without proposing to the Commission any alternative

general principles of EU law.⁵⁴ These grounds are to be strictly construed. The Commission and the Member State must work together in good faith with a view to overcoming any difficulties of recovery.

Statements or other reassurances by the Member States are irrelevant, only legitimate expectations generated by the Commission or other EU institutions can be accepted. The beneficiary must also have received precise assurances from the Commission or other EU institutions to justify these expectations. This is rarely the case if the fiscal measure had not been notified to the Commission.⁵⁵ In many instances, the Commission recognised that previous decisions in which a tax scheme was approved might have created legitimate expectations for beneficiaries of similar tax schemes.⁵⁶

The recovery process has been further clarified following the publication of the Commission's 2019 Notice on the implementation of Commission decisions ordering the Member States to recover unlawful and incompatible state aid,⁵⁷ which replaced a previous notice.⁵⁸ The new Recovery Notice provides specific Member State guidance on the quantification of the aid to be recovered and the identification of beneficiaries. There are also detailed provisions on the implementation of recovery in case of tax reliefs, insolvency proceedings and restructuring.

8.4 STATE AID AND TAXES

State aid law began to be systematically applied in the area of taxation in the past twenty years.⁵⁹ Reductions in the tax base,⁶⁰ tax exemptions,⁶¹ tax

---

arrangements for implementing the decision which could have enabled those difficulties to be overcome'. Case C-214/07 Commission v. France [2008] ECR I-08357, para 46.

⁵⁴ Notice on the enforcement of state aid law by national courts (2009), paras 32–3. Also, see Case C-332/98 France v. Commission [2000] ECR I-4833.

⁵⁵ See Margarida Afonso, 'Recovery of Fiscal Aid', in Alexander Rust and Claire Micheau (eds), *State Aid and Tax Law* (Kluwer, 2013), p 67. Also, see George Peretz, 'The Consequences of Unlawful State Aid', p 11.

⁵⁶ See, for example, Decision C54/2001 on Ireland's aid relief for foreign income, [2003] OJ L 204/51, recitals 54–7 and Commission Decision 2011/5/EC on the tax amortisation of financial goodwill for foreign shareholding acquisitions implemented by Spain, [2011] OJ L 7, recitals 158–69.

⁵⁷ See Communication Notice on the recovery of unlawful and incompatible state aid, C/2019/5396, [2019] OJ C247/1–23.

⁵⁸ Notice from the Commission, *Towards an effective implementation of Commission decisions ordering Member States to recover unlawful and incompatible State aid*, [2007] OJ C 272/4–17.

⁵⁹ Peter J. Wattel, 'Interaction of State Aid, Free Movement, Policy Competition and Abuse Control in Direct Tax Matters', 2 (2013) *World Tax Journal* 128–44; Wolfgang Schön, 'Taxation and State Aid Law in the European Union' (1999) 36 *Common Market Law Review* 911.

⁶⁰ For example, by means of special deductions or accelerated depreciation arrangements. See Case C-66/02 Italy v. Commission, para 78; Case C-222/04 Ministero dell' Economia e delle Finanze v. Cassa di Risparmio di Firenze SpA [2006] ECR I-289, para 132.

⁶¹ See, inter alia, Case C-387/92 Banco de Crédito Industrial SA, now Banco Exterior de España SA v. Ayuntamiento de Valencia [1994] ECR I-877; Joined Cases C-465/09P to C-470/09P Comunidad Autónoma de La Rioja v. Territorio Histórico de Álava – Diputación Foral de Vizcaya and Others [2011] ECR I-83.

credits,[62] deferment of the payment of taxes,[63] cancellation or even special rescheduling of tax debts, a favourable tax regime for the restructuring of banks,[64] the conversion of tax debt into share capital,[65] the cancellation of tax debts in bankruptcy proceedings[66] and specific tax amnesties[67] have been found to be prohibited state aid.

In 1998, the Commission had issued a Notice on the application of state aid rules to measures relating to direct business taxation.[68] In the 1998 Notice, it was emphasised that tax measures that reduce a firm's tax burden in various ways[69] could be considered to be granted by the state or through state resources, as they mitigate the charge normally due from the undertaking.[70] Therefore, the state loses tax revenue, and this loss of tax revenue is equivalent to the consumption of state resources in the form of fiscal expenditure.[71] As for the criterion of affecting competition and trade between Member States, in the 1998 Notice it was emphasised that this 'presupposes that the beneficiary of the measure exercises an economic activity, regardless of the beneficiary's legal status or means of financing'.[72] The mere fact that the aid strengthens the firm's position compared to that of other firms that are competitors in intra-Community trade was enough to allow the conclusion that such trade was affected. The fact that aid was relatively small and the recipient was moderate in size did not alter this conclusion.[73]

The 1998 Notice also discussed the concept of selectivity. The following test, consolidating existing case law at the time, was set out:

> The main criterion in applying [Art 107(1) TFEU] to a tax measure is therefore that the measure provides in favour of certain undertakings in the Member State an exception to the application of the tax system. The common system applicable should thus first be determined. It must then be examined whether the exception to the system or differentiations within that system are justified 'by the nature or general scheme' of the tax system, that is to say, whether they derive directly from the basic or guiding principles of the tax system in the Member State concerned. If this is not the case, then State aid is involved.[74]

---

[62] See Cases T-92/00 and T-103/00 Territorio Historico de Alava – Diputacion Foral de Alava [2002] ECR II-1385.
[63] Case C-156/98 Federal Republic of Germany v. Commission of the European Communities [2000] ECR I-6857; Case C-66/02 Italy v. Commission, para 78.
[64] Case C-452/10P BNP Paribas v. Commission, ECLI:EU:C:2012:318.
[65] Case C-124/10P Commission v. EDF, ECLI:EU:C:2012:318.
[66] Case C-73/11P Frucona Košice a.s. v. Commission, ECLI:EU:C:2013:32.
[67] See Case C-417/10 Ministero dell'Economia e delle Finanze, ECLI:EU:C:2012:184 and Commission Decision of 11 July 2012 on the tax amnesty measure notified by Latvia, S.A. 33183, [2013] OJ C 1/6.
[68] See, generally, Notice on the application of the state aid rules (1998).
[69] Ibid, para 9.
[70] Ibid, paras 10–11.
[71] Ibid, para 10.
[72] Ibid, para 11.
[73] Ibid.
[74] Ibid, para 16.

8.4 State Aid and Taxes

In other words, it is important to identify the general system and the derogation. As a second step, if the tax measure is found to be a derogation, then it must be examined whether it is justified by or inherent in the logic of the system.

The application of this test has proved quite challenging at times, as shown in subsequent case law.[75] The 1998 Notice has now been replaced by the more general Commission 2016 Final Notice on the notion of aid,[76] which has given updated guidance on the essential elements of state aid on the basis of later case law. However, the selectivity test is broadly the same.

In the Paint Graphos case,[77] the Court of Justice reiterated that a derogation could be justified if it resulted directly from the basic or guiding principles of the tax system. Tax exemptions resulting from an objective that was unrelated to the tax system of which they formed part could not circumvent the state aid prohibition.[78] It was necessary to ensure compliance with the requirement that a benefit must be consistent with the inherent characteristics of the tax system in question and the manner in which that system was implemented.[79] Member States had to introduce and apply appropriate control and monitoring procedures in order to ensure that the tax measures introduced were consistent with the logic and general scheme of the tax system.[80] Furthermore, tax exemptions had to be consistent with the principle of proportionality and not go beyond what was necessary to pursue the objective.[81]

As for the condition relating to the effect on trade between Member States and the distortion of competition, again, the Court of Justice gave some useful guidance. Here, there was no need to show the real effect on trade and actual distortion of competition. It was enough that aid was liable to affect such trade and distort competition.[82] In particular, when aid granted by a Member State strengthened the position of an undertaking compared with other undertakings competing in intra-Community trade, the latter must be regarded as affected by that aid.[83] It was not necessary that the undertaking benefiting from the aid was involved in intra-Community trade.

One of the most important and controversial cases in the area of fiscal state aids is the Gibraltar case,[84] which dealt with the UK's proposed corporate tax reform in

---

[75] See Commission Notice on the notion of state aid (2016); *Report on the Implementation of the Commission Notice on the Application of the State Aid rules to measures relating to Direct Business Taxation*, C(2004)434, dated 9 February 2004.
[76] Commission Notice on the notion of state aid (2016), para 229.
[77] Joined Cases C-78/08 & C-79/08 & C- 80/08 Paint Graphos [2011] ECR I-07611.
[78] Ibid, para 70.
[79] Ibid, para 73.
[80] Ibid, para 74.
[81] Ibid, paras 74–5.
[82] Ibid, para 78. Citing, inter alia, Case C-372/97 Italy v. Commission [2004] ECR I-3679, para 44; Case C-148/04 Unicredito Italiano [2005] ECR I-11137, para 54.
[83] Paint Graphos case, para 79.
[84] Joined Cases C-106/09P & C-107/09P Commission v. Gibraltar and UK [2011] ECR I-11113. For commentary, see, inter alios, Pierpaolo Rossi-Maccanico, 'The Gibraltar Judgment and the Point on Selectivity in Fiscal Aids', [2009] 2 *EC Tax Review* 67–75; Raymond Luja, '(Re)shaping fiscal state aid: selected recent cases and their impact', 40 (2012) 2 *Intertax* 120–31; John Temple Lang, 'The Gibraltar

Gibraltar. In this case, the UK had notified the Commission of its plans to replace profit-based taxation with a general payroll tax and a business property occupation tax both capped at 15 per cent of business profits. In its decision,[85] the Commission found that the scheme was materially and regionally specific – the assumption, for the latter, being that Gibraltar is a mere UK region and not an independent territory for tax purposes.[86] The case was appealed, and the decision reversed by the Court of First Instance in its entirety,[87] on the basis that the reference framework corresponded exclusively to the geographical limits of the territory of Gibraltar. As such, no comparison could be made between the tax regime applicable to companies established in Gibraltar and that applicable to UK companies for the purpose of establishing a selective advantage.[88] This meant that the tax reform proposals were not regionally selective, nor materially selective.

The Court of Justice reversed the Court of First Instance's judgment.[89] In doing so, the Court of Justice also went against Advocate General Jääskinen's opinion, who had agreed with the Court of First Instance. More specifically, the Court of Justice found the regime to be materially selective. Its basic features – i.e. the payroll tax and the business property occupation tax as sole bases of assessment – excluded from the outset any taxation of offshore companies, since these companies had no employees and also did not occupy business properties.[90] The classification of a tax system as selective was not conditional upon that system being designed so that all undertakings were subject to the same tax burden, but some benefitted from derogating provisions.[91] Furthermore, for a tax system to be classifiable as selective, it did not need to be designed in accordance with a certain regulatory technique. Otherwise, national tax rules would fall, from the outset, outside the scope of control of state aid merely because they were adopted under a different regulatory technique although they produced the same effects.[92]

The Court of Justice held that the reference system, although founded on criteria that were of a general nature, discriminated in practice between companies in a comparable situation with regard to the objective of the tax reform.[93] The measure was, therefore, de facto selective. The fact that the offshore companies were not

---

State aid and taxation judgment – A "methodological revolution"'(2012) 4 *European State Aid Law Quarterly* 805–12.

[85] Commission Decision of 30/3/2004, OJ (EC) L 85/1, 2/4/2005.
[86] See Cases T-211/04 and T-215/04 Commission v. Gibraltar and UK. For an analysis, see Christiana HJI Panayi, *Advanced Issues in International and European Tax Law* (Hart Publishing, 2015), ch 7.
[87] Cases T-211/04 and T-215/04 Government of Gibraltar and United Kingdom v. Commission [2008] ECR II-3745.
[88] Ibid, para 115.
[89] Joined Cases C-106/09P and C-107/09P Commission and Spain v. Government of Gibraltar and United Kingdom [2011] ECR I-11113.
[90] Ibid, paras 100–2.
[91] Ibid, para 91.
[92] Ibid, para 92.
[93] Ibid, para 101.

8.4 State Aid and Taxes

taxed was not a random consequence of the regime. Rather, it was the inevitable consequence of the fact that the bases of assessment were specifically designed so that offshore companies, which by their nature have no employees and do not occupy business premises, have no tax base under the bases of assessment adopted in the proposed tax reform.[94]

Even though there was no derogation from the normal tax regime, the Court of Justice still found the regime selective. What was determinative was that the general tax system was too narrowly defined from the outset and discriminated in practice between companies which were in a comparable situation. It is interesting to note that the Commission's views that the Gibraltar tax system had an inherently discriminatory character (and the relevance of this) had been discussed and rejected by the Advocate General in his opinion, as to accept such an approach would be tantamount to triggering a methodological revolution in the application of the state aid rules.[95] The Advocate General had also argued that this measure was, in fact, an example of harmful tax competition between Member States which 'clearly does not fall within the mechanism for controlling State aid established by the Treaty, even though there are cases where measures are liable to amount both to harmful tax competition and to State aid incompatible with the common market.'[96] In this case, the measure could only be addressed under the code of conduct on business taxation and not under the state aid provision.[97] According to the Advocate General, the legitimate objective of combating harmful tax competition could not justify distortion of the EU's legal framework in relation to state aid, or the adoption of ad hoc solutions.[98]

Although the Gibraltar case has been widely criticised, it has not been overruled by later case law. In fact, the judgment was reiterated by the Commission in its 2016 Notice on state aid.[99] Later case law has been to an extent conflicting as regards the selectivity requirement.

In the World Duty Free Group case,[100] the Court of Justice followed the decision of the Advocate General and reversed the conclusion of the General Court, by finding that selectivity does not depend on whether a specific group of undertakings can be identified that benefits from the tax advantage. According to Spanish tax laws, where a company taxable in Spain acquired a shareholding in a 'foreign company'[101]

---

[94] Ibid, para 106.
[95] See paras 201–2 of the opinion.
[96] Ibid, para 134.
[97] See para 134 of the opinion.
[98] Ibid.
[99] Commission Notice on the notion of state aid (2016), para 130.
[100] Joined Cases C-20/15P and C-21/15P World Duty Free. The case was formerly known as the Spanish amortisation case: see Cases T-219/10 and T-399/11 Autogrill España SA v. Commission, and Banco Santander SA and Santusa Holding SL v. Commission, ECLI:EU:T:2018:784.
[101] In order to qualify as a 'foreign company', a company had to be subject to a similar tax to the tax applicable in Spain and its income had to be derived mainly from business activities carried out abroad.

of at least 5 per cent and held it without interruption for at least one year, the goodwill resulting from that shareholding could be deducted through amortisation. This did not apply to goodwill resulting from the acquisition of a shareholding in a company established in Spain. In two in-depth investigations,[102] the Commission found the Spanish tax regime incompatible with the state aid prohibition. Following these decisions, three affected undertakings established in Spain (Autogrill España, Banco Santander and Santusa Holding) appealed the Commission decisions. The General Court annulled these decisions, finding that the Commission had failed to establish the selective nature of the relevant tax measure. The Spanish regime was not aimed at any particular category of undertakings or the production of goods but, instead at a type of economic transactions. No categories of undertakings were excluded from taking advantage of it since the application of the rules was independent of the nature of an undertaking's activity.

Advocate General Wathelet had criticised the reasoning of the General Court as being excessively formalistic and restrictive. The Court of Justice found that there was state aid. The tax measure was selective, even though the tax advantage was accessible to all undertakings that were tax resident in Spain. Therefore, a measure may be selective even if the difference in treatment was based on a distinction between undertakings choosing to perform the transaction covered by the measure and those choosing not to perform it. The fact that the number of undertakings able to claim entitlement under a national measure was very large or that those undertakings belonged to various economic sectors, was not sufficient to call into question the selective nature of that measure and its classification as state aid.[103]

By finding selectivity even though there was a rather large category of beneficiaries, this decision suggests considerable leniency in interpreting the requirement of selectivity. In a later case, the Heitkamp case,[104] however, the Court of Justice followed a restrictive interpretation of the selectivity requirement, more aligned with previous case law. Here, the Court of Justice annulled the decision of the General Court,[105] which looked at the compatibility of the German tax provisions dealing with the carry-forward of tax losses in the case of restructuring of companies in difficulty (*Sanierungsklausel*). Under German legislation, loss carry-forward was permitted unless the ownership of the loss-making company had changed to a significant extent after the losses had been incurred (loss forfeiture rule). In such

---

[102] One decision related to the acquisition of EU shareholdings and the other to the acquisition of non-EU shareholdings. See Decision 2011/5/EC of 28 October 2009 on the tax amortisation of financial goodwill for foreign shareholding acquisitions C-45/07 (ex NN 51/07, ex CP 9/07) implemented by Spain ([2011] OJ L7/48) and Decision 2011/282/EU of 12 January 2011 on the tax amortisation of financial goodwill for foreign shareholding acquisitions C-45/07 (ex NN 51/07, ex CP 9/07) implemented by Spain ([2011] OJ L135/1).
[103] Joined Cases C-20/15P and C-21/15P World Duty Free, para 67.
[104] Case C-203/16P Dirk Andres v. European Commission, ECLI:EU:C:2018:505.
[105] Case T-287/11 Heitkamp BauHolding v. Commission, ECLI:EU:T:2016:60.

8.4 State Aid and Taxes

circumstances, losses could only be carried forward in the case of restructuring of companies in difficulty (the restructuring clause).

The Commission found that the restructuring clause constituted state aid. Being an exception to the loss forfeiture rule, it conferred a selective advantage to the eligible entities, which were in a comparable factual and legal situation to those not eligible for it. The General Court agreed with this analysis, but the Court of Justice annulled the decision, on the basis that the loss forfeiture rule was not the correct system of reference.[106] As the Court of Justice argued, the selectivity of a tax measure could not be assessed on the basis of a reference framework that included only a limited set of provisions that were artificially taken from a broader legislative framework. It was found that the general rule of loss carry-forward was the correct reference system.[107] The Court of Justice reiterated that the regulatory technique used by the legislator could not be decisive for the purposes of determining the reference framework.

This case shows that the proper identification of the reference framework remains crucial to the Court of Justice, which insists on looking at the whole picture (i.e. the broader legislative framework) rather than just extracting some specific rules. A later case suggests that the Court of Justice might even take into account the existence of the group relationship in determining whether a group of companies and independent companies are in a comparable situation for the purposes of selectivity.

In the A-Brauerei case,[108] the Court of Justice examined the compatibility of the German real estate transfer tax with the state aid prohibition. The applicable transfer tax was not charged on taxable acquisitions involving a restructuring within a group of companies. Both the Advocate General and the Court of Justice found that the German legislation did not constitute prohibited state aid. The selective nature of the measure had to be examined in light of the objective pursued by the tax system concerned. From that standpoint, the selectivity requirement was not satisfied as companies in the same group and independent companies were not in a comparable situation. The Court of Justice argued that the distinction was justified since it sought to avoid double taxation if transfers of real property were taxed within the same group.

On the basis of these recent judgments, it is difficult to predict how the Court of Justice will deal with the pending high-profile tax ruling investigations examined below. The World Duty Free judgment suggests a level of leniency as far as selectivity is concerned. On the other hand, the insistence for an expansive interpretation of the reference framework in Heitkamp and A-Brauerei might also make it more difficult for the Commission to show that the tax rulings were not inherent in the logic of the system. Arguably, the recent cases analysed in this section are distinguishable as they were about aid schemes and not about individual aid, such

---

[106] Case 203/16P Dirk Andres para 102.
[107] Ibid, para 103.
[108] Case C-374/17 Finanzamt B v. A-Brauerei, ECLI:EU:C:2018:1024.

as the tax ruling cases. In any case, the General Court in the Apple judgment[109] did not cite any of these cases, showing that the focus was on technical issues.

8.5 TAX RULINGS, ADVANCE PRICING AGREEMENTS AND STATE AID

In the midst of the BEPS project, several state aid Commission investigations were launched, which examined the transfer pricing tax rulings received by some MNEs leading to significant tax reductions in violation of the state aid prohibition. The MNEs and jurisdictions involved were initially Apple in Ireland, Starbucks in the Netherlands and Fiat in Luxembourg. The Commission later launched more investigations.

What was objectionable to the Commission in each of these cases was that the tax rulings given by the Member States allowed the MNE beneficiaries to depart from market conditions in setting the commercial conditions of intra-group transactions. The Commission argued that, as a result, the Member States renounced taxable revenues and state resources. The premise of the Commission's opening decisions in most of these cases seemed to be that the existence of advantage and selectivity was satisfied when there was no compliance with the arm's length principle. To an extent, in most of the preliminary decisions in these investigations, the Commission rejected the economic rationale underlying the tax rulings and the way the arm's length principle and various comparability methods had been applied.[110] It showed preference for some methods of finding comparables and substituted its own judgment and calculations.[111]

Questioning discretionary practices of tax administrations is not something new in the area of state aid. As stated in the Commission's 1998 Notice, treating economic agents on a discretionary basis may mean that the individual application of a general measure takes on the features of a selective measure, in particular where the exercise of the discretionary power goes beyond the simple management of tax revenue by reference to objective criteria.[112] While the Commission acknowledged that in daily practice tax rules need to be interpreted, nevertheless, they 'cannot leave room for a discretionary treatment of undertakings'.[113] More specifically regarding administrative rulings, if these merely contain an interpretation of general rules, they do not give rise to a presumption of aid. However, if these administrative rulings are very obscure and leave room for manoeuvre, then there may be such a presumption.[114] In any case,

---

[109] See 8.5.3.
[110] Dimitrios Kyriazis, 'From Soft Law to Soft Law through Hard Law: The Commission's Approach to the State Aid Assessment of Tax Rulings' (2016) 15 *European State Aid Law Quarterly* 428.
[111] See Christiana HJI Panayi, *Advanced Issues in International and European Tax Law* (Hart Publishing, 2015), ch 7.
[112] Commission Notice on the application of the state aid rules to measures relating to direct business taxation (1998), para 21, citing Case C-241/94 France v. Commission (Kimberly Clark Sopalin) [1996] ECR I-4551.
[113] Ibid, para 22.
[114] Ibid.

8.5 Tax Rulings, Advance Pricing Agreements and State Aid

this does 'not make Member States any less able to provide their taxpayers with legal certainty and predictability on the application of general tax rules'.[115] The cases investigated almost twenty years later suggest that the distinction between straightforward interpretation of rules and opaque interpretation is still not always easy to apply in practice.

In the 2016 Notice, it was emphasised that the function of a tax ruling was to establish in advance the application of the ordinary tax system to a particular case in view of its specific facts and circumstances.[116] The importance of pricing intra-group transactions at arm's length was repeated several times.[117] It was noted that 'a tax ruling which endorses a transfer pricing methodology for determining a corporate group entity's taxable profit that does not result in a reliable approximation of a market-based outcome in line with the arm's length principle confers a selective advantage upon its recipient'.[118] Reiterating the assertion first made in the Belgian Excess Profits final decision in early 2016,[119] the Commission argued that the 'arm's length principle necessarily forms part of the Commission's assessment of tax measures granted to group companies under Article 107(1) of the Treaty, independently of whether a Member State has incorporated this principle into its national legal system and in what form'.[120] This argument was to be repeated in many of the Commission final decisions discussed below.

In its Working Paper on state aid and tax rulings[121] released in June 2016, the Commission set out its preliminary views after examination of the Member States' tax ruling practices. There was a short analysis on how some transfer pricing arrangements do not seem to reflect the arm's length principle when the outcome manifestly deviated from a reliable approximation of a market-based outcome.[122] It was also stated that the Commission's focus would be on cases where there was a manifest breach of the arm's length principle.[123]

The US has shown its strong disagreement with the Commission investigations, many of which affect US multinationals. In August 2016, the US Department of the Treasury released a White Paper on the Commission's state aid investigations of transfer pricing rulings.[124] The White Paper acknowledged the shared view of the US

---

[115] Ibid.
[116] Commission Notice on the notion of state aid (2016), para 169.
[117] See paras 169–73.
[118] Ibid, para 171.
[119] See, for example, Belgian Excess Profits case, in 8.5.1.
[120] Ibid, para 172.
[121] See DG Competition Working Paper on state aid and tax rulings, available at: https://ec.europa.eu/competition/state_aid/legislation/working_paper_tax_rulings.pdf.
[122] See para 14 et seq.
[123] Ibid, para 23.
[124] See *The European Commission's Recent State Aid Investigations of Transfer Pricing Rulings* – US Department of the Treasury White Paper, www.treasury.gov/resource-center/tax-policy/treaties/Documents/White-Paper-State-Aid.pdf.

Treasury and the Commission on tax avoidance by multinational companies, but also outlined the US Treasury's concerns with the Commission's approach; namely, that the Commission's approach was new and departed from prior case law and its decisions, that the Commission should not seek retroactive recoveries under the new approach and that the new approach was inconsistent with international norms and undermined the international tax system.[125] These concerns were arguably exacerbated following the Commission's final decision in the Apple case, discussed below.[126]

In the remainder of this section, some of the pending investigations will be examined.

8.5.1 The Belgian Excess Profits Regime

One of the first regimes which the Commission investigated was the Belgian Excess Profits regime.[127] Under this regime, multinational companies were allowed to reduce their tax base through binding tax rulings, which were typically valid for four years and could be renewed. In such tax rulings, the actual recorded profit of a multinational was compared with the hypothetical average profit that a stand-alone company in a comparable situation would have made. The alleged difference in profit was deemed to be 'excess profit' by the Belgian tax authorities, and the multinational's tax base was reduced proportionately. This was based on the premise that multinational companies made 'excess profits' due to being part of a multinational group, for example, due to synergies, economies of scale, reputation, client and supplier networks, access to new markets etc. In practice, the actual recorded profit of companies concerned was usually reduced by more than 50 per cent and in some cases by up to 90 per cent.

In its preliminary decision,[128] the Commission found that the Belgian rules resulted in unlawful state aid. The exemptions allowed under the excess profit ruling system were not extended to all undertakings and as such were considered as derogating from the reference system. Although such derogation could be justified by the nature and general scheme of the tax system, for example, to avoid double taxation, the Commission argued that the transfer pricing guidelines and double tax treaties already provided a sufficient basis to avoid double taxation. Hence, the Belgian regime was not necessary to achieve the desired goal.

In its final decision, the Commission largely confirmed its preliminary conclusions. It was in the press release of 11 January 2016[129] that the Commission first used

---

[125] Ibid, p 2.
[126] See analysis in 8.5.3.
[127] SA.37667 Excess Profit exemption in Belgium.
[128] State aid – Belgium – state aid SA.37667 (2015/C) (ex 2015/NN) – Excess profit tax ruling system in Belgium – Art 185§ 2(b) CIR92 – Invitation to submit comments pursuant to Art 108(2) of the Treaty on the Functioning of the European Union, [2015] OJ C 188/24–65.
[129] IP/16/42.

8.5 Tax Rulings, Advance Pricing Agreements and State Aid

the terms 'arm's length principle under EU state aid rules'. The Commission found that the regime derogated from normal practice under Belgian company tax rules and the arm's length principle under EU state aid rules. As such, the legislation provided unlawful fiscal state aid, which had to be recovered.

The Commission did not elaborate on what was meant by the arm's length principle under EU state aid rules in the press release. Nor was the analysis in the non-confidential version of this decision any more illuminating.[130] In a rather unconvincing manner, the Commission talked about the arm's length principle as forming part of its assessment under Article 107(1) of the TFEU,[131] wording which also featured in the 2016 Commission Notice.[132] For the avoidance of any doubt, the Commission argued that 'the arm's length principle that the Commission applies in its State aid assessment is not that derived from Article 9 of the OECD Model Tax Convention and the OECD [Transfer Pricing] Guidelines, which are non-binding instruments, but a general principle of equal treatment in taxation falling within the application of Article 107(1) of the Treaty, which binds the Member States and from whose scope the national tax rules are not excluded'.[133]

This approach attracted criticism but, from that point forward, was followed up in all the other Commission decisions. Under this approach, the Commission avoided the complexities that would have ensued if it had fully aligned itself and followed the arm's length principle as enshrined in the OECD Transfer Pricing Guidelines. Not only was this principle not binding but, as in the Apple case,[134] may not have been incorporated into domestic law at the time of some of these tax rulings.

Following an appeal by the Belgian government, the General Court annulled the final decision of the Commission, finding that the latter had erred in qualifying the measure as an aid scheme.[135] The General Court rejected Belgium's argument that the Commission encroached upon its tax jurisdiction. While Belgium had the competence to adopt measures in order to avoid double taxation, the Member States had to exercise their tax competences in accordance with EU law,[136] including the state aid prohibition.[137]

The General Court found that the Belgian tax authorities had a margin of discretion over all the essential elements of the exemption system, allowing them

---

[130] Commission Decision of 11 January 2016 on the Excess Profit Exemption State Aid Scheme SA.37667 (2015/C) (ex-2015/NN) implemented by Belgium, C(2015) 9837 final (Brussels, 11 January 2016). The non-confidential version of this decision included an annex listing the companies that had entered into tax rulings with the Belgian authorities and the total amount of excess profit deduction allowed under these rulings.
[131] See para 149 but also from para 145 onwards.
[132] Commission Notice on the notion of state aid (2016), para 172.
[133] Ibid, para 150.
[134] See analysis in 8.5.3.
[135] Cases T-131/16 and T-263/16 Kingdom of Belgium and Magnetrol International v. European Commission, ECLI:EU:T:2019:91.
[136] Ibid, para 70.
[137] Ibid.

to influence the amount and the characteristics of the exemption and the conditions under which it was granted.[138] It was noted that the granting of the contested aid could not be done automatically through the legislation but required further implementing measures by the tax authorities, which precluded the existence of an aid scheme.[139] The Commission had approached the Belgian regime as a state aid scheme. Rather than assessing each of the individual rulings involved, the Commission had limited its review to only twenty-two out of the total sixty-six rulings. However, 'the Commission did not explain, in the contested decision, either the choice of that sample or why it had been considered to be representative of all of the advance rulings.'[140] As such, it was found that the Commission had erred as it failed to demonstrate why the selected sample was representative. A more detailed review was required.[141]

The Commission had now appealed the General Court's judgment,[142] arguing that it incorrectly classified the tax ruling practice as a scheme under Article 1(d) of Regulation 2015/1589 and misinterpreted its decision. Furthermore, in September 2019, the Commission opened separate in-depth investigations to assess whether the tax rulings granted by Belgium to thirty-nine multinational companies gave those companies an unfair advantage over their competitors, in breach of the state aid prohibition.[143]

Whatever the outcome of this case, as the General Court did not invalidate the Commission's substantive interpretation of the state aid rules, but rather challenged the methodology of assessment and the classification of the aid as a scheme, arguably, this ruling does not have an impact on other pending cases.

8.5.2 The Starbucks and Fiat Investigations

The Starbucks investigation[144] was over the tax ruling concluded in 2001 affecting a Dutch Starbucks entity – Starbucks Manufacturing BV (SMBV). Here, in the tax ruling, an arm's length remuneration was agreed for the activities performed in the Netherlands by SMBV, for the Starbucks group. The Commission argued that the ruling gave rise to state aid as it did not comply with the arm's length principle, on the basis of several factors. Firstly, the Commission had doubts that SMBV was a low-risk toll manufacturer. The arm's length remuneration accepted in the tax ruling depended on SMBV being considered a low-risk toll

---

[138] Ibid, para 113.
[139] Ibid, para 120.
[140] Ibid, para 127.
[141] For detailed commentary, see Dimitrios Kyriazis, 'The Belgian Excess Profits Case – A State Aid Anticlimax' (Kluwer Competition Law Blog, 5 March 2019), http://competitionlawblog.kluwercompetitionlaw.com/2019/03/05/the-belgian-excess-profits-case-a-state-aid-anticlimax.
[142] Case C-337/19P Commission v. Belgium and Magnetrol International.
[143] See press notice, https://ec.europa.eu/commission/presscorner/detail/en/ip_19_5578.
[144] SA.38374 State aid implemented by the Netherlands to Starbucks.

manufacturer. Secondly, the Commission questioned two adjustments made to the SMBV agreement in 2002 and 2004, specific elements of which were not in line with the OECD Transfer Pricing Guidelines. Thirdly, there were doubts as to the manner in which the amount of royalties paid by SMBV was calculated. The Commission presented a number of technical arguments and made references to the OECD Transfer Pricing Guidelines to support its claims.

The Fiat case[145] followed the same format. Here, the focus of the examination was the tax ruling given by Luxembourg to Fiat Finance and Trade Ltd (FFT). This was considered to be unlawful state aid on the basis of non-compliance with the arm's length principle. The transfer pricing report was found to be problematic, as it established a fixed tax base or a tax base that could vary only marginally, irrespective of any significant increase or decrease in the activities of FFT. As such, it was argued, the Luxembourg tax authorities permitted a fixed base while ignoring the actual performance of FFT. Furthermore, the Commission doubted the various methodologies used by Fiat to find the arm's length remuneration.

In its final decisions, the Commission used the same analytical tools as in the Belgian Excess Profits case and interpreted the arm's length principle as embedded in Art 107 TFEU.[146] The Commission concluded that SMBV and FFT had benefitted from unlawful state aid and ordered its recovery. While in the preliminary decisions the Commission appeared to resort to its own interpretation and application of the OECD Transfer Pricing Guidelines, which may not have been consistent with standard practices, and substituted its judgment for the business judgment of the undertakings, there was no need for this in the final decisions. Similar to the Belgian Excess Profits case, the Commission considered that the arm's length principle is neither the one derived from Article 9 of the OECD Model Tax Convention, nor the one under national transfer pricing provisions, but was a general principle under Article 107(1) TFEU that prevented distortion of competition.

Both final decisions were appealed, with mixed results. The General Court annulled the Commission decision in the Starbucks case[147] but upheld the Commission decision in the Fiat case.[148] In both cases, the General Court

---

[145] SA.38375 State aid which Luxembourg granted to Fiat.
[146] See the Starbucks final decision (Commission Decision (EU) 2017/502 of 21 October 2015 on state aid SA.38374 (2014/C ex-2014/NN) implemented by the Netherlands to Starbucks (notified under document C(2015) 7143), [2017] OJ L 83/38), para 264; the Fiat Finance final decision (Commission Decision (EU) 2016/2326 of 21 October 2015 on state aid SA.38375 (2014/C ex 2014/NN) which Luxembourg granted to Fiat (notified under document C(2015) 7152), [2016] OJ L 351/1), para 228. For commentary, see Ruth Bonnici, 'The European Commission's Arm's Length Standard: Relationship and Compatibility with the Arm's Length Principle under Transfer Pricing' (2019) 26(1) *International Transfer Pricing Journal* 1.
[147] Cases T-760/15 and T-636/16 Kingdom of the Netherlands and Others v. European Commission, ECLI:EU:T:2019:669.
[148] Cases T-755/15 and T-759/15 Fiat Chrysler Finance Europe v. Commission, ECLI:EU:T:2019:670.

confirmed that the Commission had the power to examine whether tax rulings by the Member States conferred state aid. However, it was emphasised that the Commission did not have, at this stage of the development of EU law, competence to allow it to define in an autonomous manner the 'normal' taxation of an integrated undertaking, by disregarding national tax rules. Although national tax rules defined 'normal' taxation and although the very existence of an advantage had to be established by reference to them, the fact remained that, if those national rules provided that stand-alone companies and integrated companies must be dealt with under the same conditions, Article 107(1) TFEU allowed the Commission to verify whether the pricing of intra-group transactions corresponded to the pricing of a transaction negotiated in market conditions.[149]

It was concluded that the Commission was entitled to use the arm's length principle as a 'tool' or 'benchmark' to investigate whether a tax ruling gave rise to a selective advantage under state aid rules.[150] The General Court emphasised that the Commission had the burden of proof to show that a tax ruling gave rise to an advantage. '[M]ere non-compliance with methodological requirements does not necessarily lead to a reduction of the tax burden.'[151] The Commission could not merely point at methodological deficiencies regarding the grant of the ruling but had to demonstrate that the alleged error by the Member State led to an outcome outside an arm's length range.[152] The Commission had failed this test in its Starbucks decision, which was annulled, while the Fiat decision was upheld.

The Commission has not appealed the judgment of the General Court in the Starbucks case. Luxembourg is, however, appealing the judgment in the Fiat case.

Overall, the General Court's confirmation that the arm's length principle can be used as a tool to investigate whether a tax ruling gave a selective advantage for the purposes of Article 107 TFEU appears to be a victory for the Commission. This is notwithstanding the fact that the General Court conceded that the Commission had no competence to define the normal taxation of an integrated undertaking. While the General Court did not explicitly say whether this arm's length principle (to be used as a tool) is to be interpreted in light of the OECD Transfer Pricing Guidelines – and affirmed the Commission's stance that it could not be formally bound by these Guidelines – a bias in favour of the OECD Transfer Pricing Guidelines was obvious. As the General Court noted, the OECD Transfer Pricing Guidelines were based on important work carried out by groups of renowned experts and reflected the international consensus achieved with regard to transfer pricing.[153]

---

[149] Cases T-760/15 and T-636/16 Starbucks, para 159; Cases T-755/15 and T-759/15 Fiat, paras 112–13.
[150] Cases T-760/15 and T-636/16 Starbucks, para 163; Cases T-755/15 and T-759/15 Fiat, para 159.
[151] Cases T-760/15 and T-636/16 Starbucks, para 201.
[152] Ibid.
[153] See Cases T-755/15 and T-759/15 Fiat, para 147; Cases T-760/15 and T-636/16 Starbucks, para 155.

8.5 Tax Rulings, Advance Pricing Agreements and State Aid

The fact that the General Court allowed some discretion as to what this arm's length principle is and how it should be interpreted (by not restricting it to the principles developed under the OECD Transfer Pricing Guidelines), might suggest that indeed what is at stake is an EU arm's length principle. This would go some way in buttressing the Commission's assertions in its final decisions. Arguably, these statements might also suggest that the arm's length principle in the state aid analysis does not depend on the challenged Member State's adoption of this method (or the OECD Transfer Pricing Guidelines) into its own domestic law.[154] If the Court of Justice follows such liberal interpretation of the reasoning, this is likely to bring about a momentous change in how the Member States interpret the arm's length principle.

On the other hand, aspects of the General Court's decision suggest that the decision might rest on narrower grounds and the arm's length principle was only used as a tool because the Member State's law mandated it (or a version of it).[155] Similarly, the fact that in Starbucks the Commission did not satisfy its burden of proof in showing an advantage because, according to the General Court, such an advantage can only be within the meaning of the state aid prohibition 'if the variation between the two comparables goes beyond the inaccuracies inherent in the methodology used to obtain that approximation'[156] – this could also point towards a narrower fact-based approach.

In the Apple case, the decision of the General Court arguably shows that the narrower approach has prevailed. Whether this approach is carried over to the judgment of the Court of Justice in Fiat remains to be seen.

8.5.3 The Apple Investigation

In the Apple investigation,[157] the Commission argued that the two tax rulings issued by Ireland to Apple had substantially and artificially lowered the tax paid by the company in Ireland since 1991. This was because the rulings endorsed a way to establish the taxable profits for two Irish incorporated companies of the Apple group (Apple Sales International (ASI) and Apple Operations Europe (AOE)) operating in Ireland through branches, which did not correspond to economic reality. Almost all sales profits recorded by the two companies were internally attributed to a head office and not the Irish branches. This head office was not based in any country and did not have any employees or own premises. It existed only on paper and could not have generated the attributed profits. As such, the profits allocated to the head office were

---

[154] Ruth Mason, 'Implications of the Rulings in Starbucks and Fiat for the Apple State Aid Case', *Tax Notes International* (07 October 2019) 15–22, 17.
[155] Cases T-755/15 and T-759/15 Fiat, para 145; Cases T-760/15 and T-636/16 Starbucks, para 146.
[156] Cases T-760/15 and T-636/16 Starbucks, para 152.
[157] State aid SA.38373 (2014/C) (ex-2014/NN) (ex-2014/CP) implemented by Ireland to Apple ([2017] OJ L 187/1). The summary of the Commission's final decision in this case was released on 30 August 2016. The non-confidential version of this final decision was subsequently published on 19 December 2016: C(2016) 5605 final.

not subject to tax in any country under specific provisions of the Irish tax law, which are no longer in force. Furthermore, the Commission argued that Ireland had granted to ASI and AOE an advantage as a result of not having allocated to their Irish branches certain intellectual property of the group and, consequently, all of ASI and AOE's profits deriving from Apple's sales outside Americas.

An important element of the Commission's decision was that:

> a tax measure which results in an integrated group company charging transfer prices that do not reflect those which would be charged in conditions of free competition, that is prices negotiated by independent undertakings negotiating under comparable circumstances at arm's length, confers a selective advantage on that company, in so far as it results in a reduction of its taxable base and thus its tax liability as determined under the ordinary rules of taxation of corporate profit.[158]

The same principle would apply to the internal dealings of different parts of the same integrated company, such as a branch that transacted with other parts of the company to which it belonged.[159] In other words, an endorsement of non-arm's length dealings was equated to a selective advantage.

The Commission found the existence of profit allocation methods endorsed by the Irish Revenue resulting in taxable profits for ASI and AOE that departed 'from a reliable approximation of a market-based outcome in line with the arm's length principle'[160] conferred a selective advantage, contrary to the state aid rules. According to the Commission, as a result of the allocation method endorsed in the tax rulings, Apple only paid an effective corporate tax rate that declined from 1 per cent in 2003 to 0.005 per cent in 2014 on the profits of ASI. The Commission ordered recovery of the illegal state aid for the ten years preceding the Commission's first request for information in 2013, which amounted to unpaid taxes of up to €13 billion, plus interest.

It was also noted that due to Apple's decision to record all sales in Ireland rather than in the countries where the Apple products were sold, this enabled Apple to avoid taxation on almost all profits generated by sales in the entire single market. It was conceded that this structure was outside the remit of state aid control. However, if other countries were to demand, under their domestic tax rules, from Apple to pay more tax on ASI and AOE profits over the same period, this would reduce the amount to be recovered by Ireland.[161]

The decision was appealed both by Apple and Ireland. In its appeal documents, Apple had argued that there was no legal requirement for profit allocation to be compliant with the arm's length principle. Apple and Ireland had also argued that the Commission fundamentally erred in failing to recognise that profit creating

---

[158] Apple final decision, para 251.
[159] Ibid, para 253.
[160] Ibid, para 258.
[161] Arguably, this opened the battlefield to more Member States to claim part of the taxable base from Apple. See the excellent analysis by Ruth Mason, 'Apple', 154 *Tax Notes* 735 (2017).

8.5 Tax Rulings, Advance Pricing Agreements and State Aid

activities, including the development of intellectual property, were attributable to the US, rather than Ireland.[162] The two branches simply could not be responsible for generating all of Apple's profits outside the US.

It is interesting to note that both the General Court and the Court of Justice turned down arguments that the US had the requisite interest needed in order to intervene in the proceedings.[163] The US had argued that tax revenues would be impacted by the recovery proceedings in Ireland, on the basis that foreign tax credits would be likely to offset US tax collected on future repatriation of profits. Both European courts found that the US could not prove that the company would repatriate profits, and thereby could not establish the necessary direct interest to be able to intervene in the proceedings.

Initially, Ireland failed to enforce the recovery decision, but later on, the full amount was recovered.[164] The hearing before the General Court took place in September 2019 and the judgment of the General Court came out on 15 July 2020.[165] This judgment followed the narrower, more conservative reading of the Fiat and Starbucks judgments discussed in 8.5.2, thus torpedoing what seemed to be the flagship case of the Commission.[166]

The General Court found that the Commission did not succeed in showing to the requisite legal standard that there was any unlawful state aid.

Firstly, the General Court agreed with the Commission that the reference framework, in this case, was the ordinary rules of taxation of corporate profit in Ireland, which included the provisions applicable to non-resident companies laid down in Section 25 of the Taxes Consolidation Act 1997.[167]

It was found that the allocation of profits to a branch of a company may lend itself to the application by analogy of the principles applicable to the prices of intra-group transactions within a group of undertakings if it were clear from national tax law that the profits derived from the activities of the branches of non-resident undertakings should be taxed as if they resulted from the economic activities of stand-alone undertakings operating under market conditions.[168] Where this was the case, the arm's length principle was an appropriate tool to determine whether the profits

---

[162] See the 14 pleas set out in Case T-892/16, available at https://eur-lex.europa.eu/legal-content/EN/TXT/?uri=CELEX:62016TN0892.

[163] See Order of the General Court of 15 December 2017, at ECLI:EU:T:2017:925. Also see Order of the Court of Justice of 17 May 2018, Case C-12/18 P(I) United States of America, ECLI:EU:C:2018:330.

[164] In October 2017, the Commission had referred Ireland to the Court of Justice for failing to enforce its recovery decision, but later on closed the infringement procedure, as Ireland recovered from Apple the amount due.

[165] Cases T-778/16 and T-892/16 Apple Sales International and Apple Operations Europe v. Commission, ECLI:EU:T:2020:338.

[166] Dimitrios Kyriazis, 'Apple: One Case to Rule Them All', at Kluwer Competition Law Blog, http://competitionlawblog.kluwercompetitionlaw.com/2020/07/16/apple-one-case-to-rule-them-all/?doing_wp_cron=1595268076.1229610443115234375000.

[167] Cases T-778/16 and T-892/16 Apple, paras 140–65.

[168] Ibid, paras 206–7.

allocated to such branches corresponded to the level that would have been obtained through carrying on that trade under market conditions.

Very importantly, the General Court emphasised that there is no freestanding obligation to apply the arm's length principle which arises from Article 107 TFEU, obliging Member States to apply that principle horizontally and in all areas of their national tax law.[169] The General Court reiterated that it fell within Member State competences to designate bases of assessment and spread the tax burden across the different factors of production and economic sectors in the absence of EU rules.[170] Although this did not mean that Article 107 TFEU would never apply in this context, 'the fact remains that, at the current stage of development of EU law, the Commission does not have the power independently to determine what constitutes the "normal" taxation of an integrated undertaking while disregarding the national rules of taxation'.[171]

In the present case, it was found that based on the national rules, the Commission had the competence to check whether the profits allocated to the Irish branches of ASI and AOE corresponded to the level of profits that would have been obtained if that activity had been carried on under market conditions.[172] Even though the Authorised OECD Approach (AOA) had not been incorporated into Irish tax law, due to the overlap between the application of the Irish legislation and the functional and factual analysis conducted as part of the first step of the analysis proposed by the AOA, the General Court found that the Commission could have relied on the AOA for the purposes of allocating profits to the Irish branches.[173]

It was concluded that the Commission was correct regarding the reference framework identified and the fact that the arm's length principle could be used to check the profit allocation to branches. The Commission was also correct in relying on the AOA approach.[174] However, crucially, the General Court found that the Commission made errors in applying both the arm's length principle and the AOA.[175]

On the Commission's primary line of argument (that all of the companies' income in question was attributable to Ireland), the Commission failed to demonstrate that the income related to activities carried out by the Irish branches. According to the General Court, the Commission should have shown that those profits represented the value of the activities carried out by the Irish branches, as established on the basis of a proper functional analysis. In particular, in determining whether the Apple group's intellectual property licences should have been allocated to the branches, the focus should have been on the actual activities and functions of

[169] Ibid, para 221.
[170] Ibid, para 222.
[171] Ibid, para 223.
[172] Ibid, para 224.
[173] Ibid, paras 239–40.
[174] Ibid, paras 246–8.
[175] Ibid, para 249.

the branches and the strategic decisions taken and implemented outside of those branches, rather than on the levels of activity (or perceived lack thereof) elsewhere in the companies (e.g. at the head office level).[176]

On the Commission's secondary line of argument (relating to methodological errors in allocating profits to Ireland), the General Court found that the Commission failed to show how these errors in the contested tax rulings would have led to a reduction in chargeable profits in Ireland and as such conferred an advantage to ASI and AOE. The Commission had challenged the choice of the tested party, the choice of operating costs as the profit level indicator for the Irish branches, and their remuneration in the contested tax rulings. However, in the view of the General Court, the Commission had not adequately demonstrated that there were more appropriate methodologies that would have given rise to higher taxable profits.[177] In particular, the Commission should have shown that the transfer pricing methodology endorsed in the tax rulings presented certain technical deficiencies, and that an advantage resulted from those deficiencies in the form of an actual reduction of the tax burden otherwise normally due in Ireland.[178] In that respect, the findings of the General Court on this point are very similar to the ones in the Starbucks case, discussed in 8.5.2.

As for the Commission's alternative line of argument (that the rulings were the result of discretion exercised by the Irish tax authorities), the Commission again did not succeed in showing that the Irish tax authorities exercised, through those tax rulings, a broad discretion that resulted in a selective advantage given to ASI and AOE as compared with other companies in comparable situations.[179]

The General Court's assertion that there is no freestanding obligation to apply the arm's length principle which arises from Article 107 TFEU[180] unequivocally goes contrary to the Commission's more liberal approach in several of its decisions. It also confirms the narrower reading of the Fiat and Starbucks judgments, suggesting an uphill struggle for the Commission in winning some of its pending investigations.

8.5.4 The McDonald's Investigation

This is the only investigation that the Commission did not fully pursue. It is useful to see the reasons why.

In its preliminary decision,[181] the Commission argued that tax rulings obtained by the McDonald's entities in Luxembourg constituted state aid. The rulings at stake

---

[176] Ibid, paras 255–311.
[177] Ibid, paras 315–481.
[178] Ibid, para 480.
[179] Ibid, paras 489–507.
[180] Ibid, para 221.
[181] State aid – Luxembourg – state aid SA.38945 (2015/C) (ex-2015/NN) – Alleged aid to McDonald's – Invitation to submit comments pursuant to Art 108(2) of the Treaty on the Functioning of the European Union (2016/C 258/03).

were an initial tax ruling and then a revised one, which confirmed the initial ruling. The rulings provided that McDonald's Europe (McD Europe) was exempt from tax because its royalty income was attributable to the United States despite the Luxembourg authorities knowing that the company was not taxed there.

The Commission argued that:

> the Luxembourg tax administration, by confirming in the revised tax ruling an erroneous interpretation of the Luxembourg-US DTT and the Luxembourg domestic law that transposes it, in full knowledge of the fact that the US Franchise Branch is not subject to taxation in the United States, confers a selective advantage to McD Europe for the purposes of Article 107(1) TFEU as compared to Luxembourg tax resident companies in a similar legal and factual situation that are taxed on all their accounting profits, since that erroneous interpretation results in the non-taxation of a sizeable portion of McD Europe's accounting profits.[182]

The Commission also argued that Luxembourg had not provided any possible justification for the selective treatment of McD Europe resulting from the revised tax ruling.[183] In any event, the Commission was unable to identify 'any possible ground for justifying the preferential treatment that could be said to derive directly from the intrinsic, basic or guiding principles of the reference system or that is the result of inherent mechanisms necessary for the functioning and effectiveness of that system.'[184]

Rather unexpectedly, the Commission closed this investigation,[185] as it concluded that there was no derogation from domestic law. The Commission conceded that it could not be established that the interpretation given by the second tax ruling to the Luxembourg-US income tax treaty was incorrect, even though it resulted in the double non-taxation of the royalties attributed to the US branch. As such, the Commission concluded that the Luxembourg authorities did not misapply the Luxembourg-US tax treaty and that the tax advantage conferred could not be considered state aid. The double non-taxation of profits arising in the case resulted from a mismatch between the legislation of the two countries and not by a misapplication of Luxembourg laws.

This development is very important. The McDonald's investigation was the Commission's poster case for the argument that double non-taxation arising from the favourable interpretation of a tax treaty provision endorsed by a tax ruling could amount to state aid. Arguably, by not pursuing this line of inquiry further, the Commission has also laid to rest the argument that disparities among tax systems and arbitrage resulting from the divergent interpretation of conflicting tax laws could

---

[182] Ibid, para 92.
[183] Ibid, para 93.
[184] Ibid, para 94.
[185] Commission Decision of 19 September 2018 on tax rulings SA.38945 (2015/C) (ex-2015/NN) (ex-2014/CP) granted by Luxembourg in favour of McDonald's Europe.

fall foul of the state aid rules. To an extent, this suggests that the Commission has imposed some limits to the scope of its own state aid tax investigations.

Notwithstanding the conclusion of the McDonald's investigation, fiscal state aid litigation is likely to continue with more investigations taking place.

8.5.5 *Other Investigations*

There are various other investigations at different stages of the process.

In the Amazon case,[186] the Commission investigated the tax ruling issued by Luxembourg in 2003 and extended in 2011, which lowered the tax paid by Amazon in Luxembourg. In particular, the tax ruling endorsed the payment of a royalty from Amazon EU to Amazon Europe Holding Technologies, which significantly reduced Amazon EU's taxable profits. The Commission argued that the level of the royalty payments, endorsed by the tax ruling, was inflated and did not reflect economic reality. On this basis, the Commission found that the tax ruling granted a selective economic advantage to Amazon by allowing the group to pay less tax than other companies subject to the same national tax rules. In fact, the ruling enabled Amazon to avoid taxation on three-quarters of the profits it made from all Amazon sales in the EU. It was concluded that Luxembourg granted undue tax benefits to Amazon of around €250 million (plus interest), contrary to the state aid prohibition. This decision has been appealed.[187]

In the GDF Suez investigation,[188] the Commission investigated several tax rulings given by Luxembourg concerning the tax treatment of financial transactions between four companies of the GDF Suez group, all based in Luxembourg. The tax rulings appeared to treat the same financial transaction between GDF Suez companies inconsistently, both as debt and equity, leading to double non-taxation.[189] The Commission found that the treatment endorsed in the tax rulings resulted in tax benefits in favour of GDF Suez, which were not available to other companies in Luxembourg subject to the same national taxation rules. This decision has now been appealed.[190]

Another interesting investigation relates to the group financing exemption of the UK CFC rules.[191] Between 2013 and 2018, the UK's CFC rules included a special

---

[186] Commission Decision of 04 October 2017 on state aid SA.38944 (2014/C) (ex-2014/NN) implemented by Luxembourg to Amazon (notified under document C(2017) 6740).

[187] See Case T-318/18 Amazon EU and Amazon.com v. Commission and T-816/17 Luxembourg v. Commission.

[188] Commission Decision of 20 June 2018 on state aid SA.44888 (2016/C) (ex-2016/NN) implemented by Luxembourg in favour of ENGIE, C(2018) 3839 final.

[189] From the perspective of the borrower companies, the transactions were treated as loans and as such interest was deductible. From the perspective of the lender companies, the income received was considered as equity remuneration and was not taxed.

[190] See Case T-525/18 ENGIE Global LNG Holding and Others v. Commission and Case T-516/18 Luxembourg v. Commission.

[191] Commission Decision (EU) 2019/1352 of 2 April 2019 on the state aid SA.44896 implemented by the United Kingdom concerning CFC Group Financing Exemption (notified under document C(2019) 2526).

rule for financing income – the group financing exemption. Under these rules, certain financing income (i.e. interest payments received from loans) of MNEs active in the UK was partially or fully exempt. More specifically, the UK rules exempted from reallocation to the UK (and, as such, UK taxation) financing income received by the offshore subsidiary from another foreign group company, even if this income was derived from UK activities or the capital used was connected with the UK. Therefore, an MNE active in the UK using this exemption was able to provide financing to a foreign group company using an offshore subsidiary, paying little or no tax on the profits from these transactions.

In its decision, the Commission found that the exemption was compliant with the state aid rules in cases where the financing income was derived from non-UK activities but not when the financing income was derived from UK activities. As such, the beneficiaries of the measure received an undue advantage over UK competitors who could not rely on such exemption. The UK government has appealed this decision to the Court of Justice.[192]

There are also pending investigations relating to IKEA,[193] Nike,[194] Huhtamäki[195] and others. Whether or not the Commission will succeed with its bold interpretation of the state aid prohibition very much depends on the outcome of the Fiat decision, which is under appeal. If the Court of Justice adopts an approach similar to that of the General Court in Apple, then many of these investigations might have to be closed down.

---

[192] Case T-363/19 UK v. Commission.
[193] State aid – Netherlands – state aid SA.46470 (2017/C) – Possible state aid in favour of Inter IKEA – Extension of the formal investigation – Invitation to submit comments pursuant to Art 108(2) of the Treaty on the Functioning of the European Union, C/2020/2597.
[194] State aid – Netherlands – state aid SA.51284 (2018/NN) – Possible state aid in favour of Nike Invitation to submit comments pursuant to Art 108(2) of the Treaty on the Functioning of the European Union.
[195] State aid – Luxembourg – state aid SA.50400 (2019/C) (ex 2019/NN-2) – Possible state aid in favour of Huhtamäki – Invitation to submit comments pursuant to Art 108(2) of the Treaty on the Functioning of the European Union.

9

EU Corporate Tax Law: More Interim Conclusions and Thoughts

This book aimed to provide an overview of the impact of EU law on Member State corporate tax systems.

In Chapter 1, the inherent limitations in the powers of the EU institutions to enact legislation in the field of direct taxes were discussed. The lack of Union competence in this area and the sensitivity of Member States to any attempts for harmonisation were identified as the main reasons for the scarce legislation. The use of 'proxy' legislative bases compounded the situation because for these bases unanimity was required – something very difficult to attain politically.

As a result of this legislative vacuum, it was noted that a number of tax obstacles continue to create serious impediments to the integration of the market. Many of these obstacles arise from the interaction of the taxation systems of Member States, especially when there is a different approach to the integration of shareholder and corporate taxes. This leads to economic double taxation, with taxes imposed on the same income even if the taxes are paid by different persons and affect domestic and foreign shareholders the same way. Obstacles could also arise as a result of juridical double taxation, when the same person is taxed twice by two different states over cross-border income. For some of these obstacles it was argued that the international tax community and the OECD Model Tax Convention do not offer solutions, or not very good ones. Especially as regards economic double taxation, the OECD Model Tax Convention largely defers to Member State discretion.

As mentioned in Chapter 1 and considered more fully throughout the book, EU law has had an impact on these and a number of other obstacles to cross-border movement, mainly as a result of an expansive interpretation of the fundamental freedoms. Contrary to established international tax practices and the OECD Model Tax Convention, under EU law it cannot be assumed that residents and non-residents are always in a non-comparable situation. When a Member State taxes residents and non-residents differently, then unless it is shown that they are not in a comparable situation, the taxation may be discriminatory. This has led to many developments in EU corporate tax law.

Chapter 1 also considered the historical background to some of the legislative proposals for the removal of tax obstacles in the cross-border movement of companies. In the various studies, reports or proposals initially produced, the suggestions varied from harmonisation of corporate taxes and imposition of a uniform rate on corporate profits (retained and distributed), to the establishment of minimum corporate tax rates and a minimum common tax base. Proposals for harmonisation were followed by proposals for coordination and ad hoc targeted measures. These led to piecemeal legislative solutions and soft law.

It was explained how with the advent of the BEPS project, the Commission was very active in producing various legislative proposals, most of which were very protective of Member State tax bases. The soft law initiatives also proved very important, as they laid the ground for the creation of a common external fiscal policy, even in the absence of a common internal fiscal policy. Furthermore, without the shackles of the formal legislative process, the Commission was very efficient in developing its own concepts of good tax governance and fair taxation. This has proved to be a springboard for further developments.

Chapter 2 examined the current instruments of positive integration that affect Member State corporate tax systems. It was shown that, notwithstanding the limitations of the Union's power to legislate in the direct tax field, there has been legislation in areas where it was deemed expedient for the proper functioning of the Internal Market. This legislation is, however, limited and targeted to specific situations. In all of the Directives examined, entitlement to benefits is restricted to companies listed in the Annexes of the Directives and subject to specific taxes also listed. Therefore, the benefits are not readily obtainable. In addition, from a purely practical point of view, the listing approach means that the Annexes have to be regularly updated to include new legal forms and sometimes new types of taxes created in Member States. While this is not the best method of legislative drafting, the Directives provide some (limited) solutions to problems identified in Chapter 1 and in subsequent chapters.

For instance, the Parent-Subsidiary Directive and the Interest and Royalties Directive try to address economic and juridical double taxation. However, their scope is not as extensive as that of the fundamental freedoms. They only deal with intra-group payments of dividends, interest and royalties, under very specific circumstances and subject to anti-abuse provisions. The shareholding requirement for entitlement to the Interest and Royalties Directive is still very high, despite suggestions to lower it and align it with the shareholding requirement of the Parent-Subsidiary Directive. Overall, due to the prescriptive nature of these Directives, it cannot really be said that they lead to the abolition of source taxation on passive income between group companies. Not only that, but recent case law in the context of these Directives, combined with the open-ended nature of the Parent-Subsidiary Directive's newly introduced general anti-abuse rule and the provision preventing hybrid arrangements suggest that the focus of both Directives now is not just the alleviation of double taxation, but also the prevention of double non-taxation and tax avoidance. The adoption of the Anti-Tax Avoidance Directive and the various amendments to the Directive on Administrative Cooperation, as well as the proposed directives to deal with digital taxation buttress this conclusion. Even the relaunched CCTB/CCCTB has morphed from a proposal to facilitate cross-border groupings and consolidation and simplify compliance, into an instrument which, inter alia, counters tax avoidance. In fact, the draft CCTB Directive contains provisions that are similar to those already adopted under the Anti-Tax Avoidance Directive.

These legislative developments are closely aligned with the current trends in the international tax community following from the OECD/G20's BEPS project. The Tax Dispute Resolution Mechanisms Directive is perhaps the only exception to this. This Directive broadens the scope of the EU rules on tax dispute resolution, which hitherto were limited to the Arbitration Convention and its focus on transfer pricing disputes. Although the Directive does not officially replace the Arbitration Convention, it provides an additional and, arguably, more efficient route for taxpayers to take in resolving their tax disputes with competent authorities.

The impact of negative integration was examined in the remainder of this book. It was shown that many important developments in the area of EU corporate tax law have been generated through judgments of the Court of Justice. What is truly admirable is that the Court of Justice has managed to overcome legislative inertia without formally reversing the important position that the EU lacks competence in direct tax matters. In fact, this is consistently reiterated in the case law, to be immediately qualified by the imposition of a duty on Member States to exercise the powers retained by them in accordance with EU law. As shown in Chapter 3, this duty has been interpreted to encompass compliance with general Treaty provisions such as the non-discrimination principle, the four fundamental freedoms and the state aid prohibition. To an extent, negative integration has helped the EU to (partly) address the legislative vacuum discussed in Chapter 1. Whether this legislative vacuum has been addressed in a satisfactory way is something questioned throughout the book. It is also questioned whether the principles developed in the Court's jurisprudence have been superseded by subsequently enacted legislative provisions, such as those of the Anti-Tax Avoidance Directive, especially if they are contradictory.

The general methodology of the Court of Justice in direct tax cases was considered in Chapter 3. The application of the various fundamental freedoms in the context of direct tax law were examined. Chapter 3 identified some trends and ad hoc principles that have developed in the Court's case law. The status of tax treaties and of the OECD Model Tax Convention in the Court's jurisprudence was also examined. It was made apparent that even though the OECD Model Tax Convention has not been used to interpret or modify EU law, the Court of Justice often deferred to its provisions to the extent that there was no major conflict with basic principles of EU law or that EU law required a different approach (e.g. the comparability of residents and non-residents point made above). Tax treaties also played an important role in assessing the actual tax burden on a cross-border activity or investment, when examining the compatibility of a national tax measure with EU law. It was shown that even though the Court of Justice is generally reluctant to consider the overall situation in which a national measure is applied and often ignores out-of-state benefits or burdens, tax treaties have been interpreted as forming part of the (domestic) legal context in which the measure arises.

The unsatisfactory nature of the litigation process was also discussed in Chapter 3. The arbitrary way in which cases get to the Court of Justice becomes even more apparent in later chapters. So do the difficulties of complying with what the author described as reverse subsidiarity – the idea that Member States, in exercising what is effectively their exclusive competence in a given area, have to take into account general principles of EU law including the voluminous case law of the Court of Justice and, as such, their competence is circumscribed.

In Chapter 4, the concept of corporate residence and its importance as a connecting factor for tax purposes was discussed. It was shown that while in international tax law this is a key concept for the attainment of certain benefits and the allocation of taxing rights, it is not as important – though not completely obsolete – under EU law, where the emphasis is on discrimination or restriction. Member States can determine whether a company falls under their tax jurisdiction and agree between them (or with a third country) on how to allocate this tax jurisdiction. EU law does not prescribe what connecting factors a Member State ought to have. A company incorporated in the home state cannot demand that the host state considers it tax resident if the host state adopts a different test of tax residence. However, to the extent that a company resident in the home state is in a comparable situation to a company resident in the host state, then any tax benefits conferred by the host state to a resident company may have to be extended to the non-resident (home state) company. Therefore, while the right to prescribe the requirements for a company to be tax resident remains within the discretion of Member States, the right to restrict the benefits attaching to such tax residence may not. Member States can still determine who is tax resident and who is not, but cannot deprive non-residents of benefits if they are in a comparable situation to residents. It was questioned whether, by requiring the extension of benefits to non-residents, this takes away the essence of residence as a connecting factor.

It was shown that the Court of Justice has been less willing to tamper with tax treaty residence. The restriction of treaty benefits to residents of contracting states to a tax treaty has not been found to be contrary to EU law. Benefits given to residents of either contracting state are considered an integral part of the tax treaty and cannot be extended to residents of non-contracting states. This is another example where the Court of Justice has chosen not to interfere with tax treaties. Arguably, it is a policy decision. Although a tax treaty benefit is technically different from a benefit conferred unilaterally by a Member State, a non-resident taxpayer denied this benefit is affected in the same way.

Following this analysis, some of the tax obstacles arising in the cross-border movement of companies were examined, the emphasis being firstly on direct investment. It was reiterated that EU law does not impose any immediate obligations on Member States on how to structure their corporate tax systems in terms of rates, taxable base, depreciation and so on. What EU law does is to prevent Member States from imposing rules that hinder a domestic company from carrying on its business in another Member State (home state obstacles), or rules that hinder a non-resident company from carrying on its business in a similar way to domestic companies (host state obstacles). Therefore, national tax rules affecting a single company cannot be subject to scrutiny under EU law, unless there is a cross-border element to these rules that falls within the scope of the fundamental freedoms.

In Chapter 4, the focus was on obstacles arising in the context of corporate groups and in relations between a head office and its permanent establishment. As far as the first category was concerned, it was shown that although the OECD Model Tax Convention and, in general, international tax law contained limited or no provisions to remove some of the obstacles discussed, there was extensive case law of the Court of Justice to that effect. The inability of a parent company to deduct expenses in foreign holdings or to absorb losses of a foreign subsidiary where expenses in domestic holdings could be deducted or losses from a domestic subsidiary could be offset against the parent company's profits were considered. In most of the cases examined, especially the earlier ones, the Court of Justice found freedom of establishment and/or the free movement of capital to be compromised and required the removal of the restrictions in situations where international tax law and the OECD Model Tax Convention were silent or deferred to the choices of the contracting states. In later times, however, the Court's judgments appear to be more nuanced and place greater weight on justifications such as the allocation of taxing powers between Member States and the prevention of tax avoidance. An overview of the case law on cross-border loss relief provided a good example of this development.

As for the second category of tax obstacles discussed in Chapter 4 – those arising in relations between a head office and its permanent establishment – here divergence with established international tax law and the OECD Model Tax Convention was noted. Whilst the norm under international tax law was for a host state to be able to treat permanent establishments differently from resident companies, certain limitations to this approach were identified under EU law. A Member State had discretion on how it defined branches or permanent establishments but not always on how it treated them for taxation purposes. There was no prima facie assumption that a permanent establishment of a non-resident company situated in the host state was not in a comparable situation to a resident company. What can be deduced from the case law is that when it comes to a non-resident company claiming equal tax treatment in the host state, the comparability criterion is usually satisfied when the permanent establishment – whether itself or on the basis of profits received – is taxed in a similar way to a resident company. Other regulatory or non-tax differences are not to be taken into account. It was questioned whether this was a satisfactory approach. In any case, it was shown how it has become more difficult for Member States to tax permanent establishments (of non-resident companies) in a more burdensome way than resident companies.

Chapter 5 focused on the taxation of portfolio investment in the EU, from a home state and a host state perspective. It was reiterated that the international tax community and the OECD Model Tax Convention sought to tackle juridical double taxation but economic double taxation was left to be addressed by Member States. This was reflected in the tax treatment of dividends, interest and royalties under the OECD Model Tax Convention. For example, under the OECD Model Tax Convention contracting states were not required to extend shareholder tax credits to either inbound or outbound dividends, but they could choose to do so anyway. An examination of the jurisprudence of the Court of Justice in this area showed that its approach was not always aligned with the OECD Model's approach.

For inbound dividends, the general principle is that shareholders (corporate or non-corporate) receiving foreign-sourced dividends should be treated the same way as shareholders receiving domestic dividends if they are in an objectively comparable situation, unless different treatment is justified. If the country of residence of the shareholder (the home state) chooses to provide reliefs for domestic dividends, then it must provide the same reliefs at least for EU-sourced dividends. The fact that economic double taxation is suffered because another state has imposed corporation tax on the underlying profits generating the dividends is not a relevant consideration. It is sufficient that economic double taxation has, in fact, been suffered by shareholders, whether they receive domestic or foreign-sourced dividends. However, it would seem from the Court's case law that not all types of reliefs have to be extended in this way – only reliefs for economic double taxation. It has been found that a home state is not obliged to give to shareholders a credit for foreign withholding taxes, irrespective of whether it gives such credit for domestic withholding taxes. Juridical double taxation in this context is considered to be the result of the parallel exercise of taxing powers by Member States and, as such, is outside the ambit of EU law. Recent cases were reviewed, some of which explored the equivalence of the credit and exemption methods in this context.

Case law on the taxation of outbound dividends starts from a similar premise to that on inbound dividends, but there are some subtle differences. The host state has to ensure equal tax treatment of resident and non-resident recipients of dividends, if they are in a comparable situation. From a host state perspective, resident and non-resident shareholders are in a comparable situation if they are both subject to host state taxes. In other words, a tax imposed by the host state only on outbound dividends, or a relief from economic double taxation only available to resident shareholders, could be discriminatory if the non-resident shareholder is also subject to tax on those dividends in the host state. As far as relief from juridical double taxation is concerned, contrary to the case law on inbound dividends, it was shown that the Court of Justice does not appear to be as insistent on this distinction when it comes to the obligations of the host state. It was questioned whether this was an intentional result or whether, due to the often complex legal framework, it was not always discernible to the Court of Justice that the cases dealt with juridical double taxation rather than economic double taxation. It is difficult to understand why the host state is required to prevent juridical double taxation on outbound dividends but the home state is not required to do so on inbound dividends. It was argued in Chapter 5 that case law on inbound and outbound dividends is not coherent on this point and the obligations of the home state and the host state are not symmetrical. Several of the more recent cases were discussed, most of which dealt with dividend payments to pension funds or other types of investment funds.

One issue that was confirmed from recent case law is that the same principles apply to payments of dividends and payments of interest. Although there have been no cases with royalty payments, there is no reason why these should be treated differently, especially since in non-portfolio relationships, the Parent-Subsidiary and the Interest and Royalties Directives show a clear convergence of approach for all these types of payments.

Aspects of corporate reorganisations were considered in Chapter 6. It was shown that although cross-border reorganisations such as mergers, divisions, transfers of assets and exchange of shares promote the Internal Market, many tax obstacles often exist. Unrealised capital gains and fiscal reserves may be taxed and previous year losses may not be carried over to the newly created or reorganised entity, especially if these are foreign losses. Financing costs may become non-deductible and thin capitalisation provisions could be triggered. These issues may increase the costs of the reorganisation, having an impact not only on the companies involved but also their shareholders. EU law provides targeted solutions to some of these problems but with many limitations.

The Merger Directive provides for tax deferral on qualifying assets and stock but only for specific types of transactions strictly defined, involving companies from two or more Member States and of a legal form set out in the Annex to the Directive. The Merger Directive is additionally restrictive as it only allows this tax deferral when there is a remaining permanent establishment of the acquiring company to take over the assets and liabilities of the transferring company. This is to ensure that upon future realisation of the deferred capital gains, these will form part of the tax base allocated to the Member State of the transferring company.

As shown in Chapter 6, much of the earlier case law on the Merger Directive centred on its anti-abuse provision. Later cases explored more technical issues pertaining to the Merger Directive, as well as the application of the fundamental freedoms in reorganisation scenarios and the interaction of the Directive with the exit tax case law.

As a result of the limitations of the Merger Directive, freedom of establishment and the free movement of capital have been used to ensure that a wider range of reorganisation operations are protected. Chapter 6 examined situations where a company migrates to another jurisdiction by transferring its seat and the exit tax implications of these. The early case law on exit taxes levied on emigrating individuals was briefly reviewed and contrasted with later case law which involved initially companies but subsequently also individuals and different types of transfers of assets. In this later case law, the Court of Justice mandated that Member States must give taxpayers the option to choose between immediate payment of the exit tax, or deferred payment with all its administrative difficulties, including (possibly) the payment of interest and the provision of a bank guarantee when there was a risk of non-recovery. In more recent cases, the Court of Justice found the phased deferral of exit taxes to be permissible and the payment of five yearly instalments proportional. The exit tax provision of the Anti-Tax Avoidance Directive has broadly codified these principles, whilst at the same time making it compulsory for Member States to have exit taxes in certain circumstances.

The concept of tax avoidance was examined in Chapter 7. It was shown that in harmonised and quasi-harmonised areas, the Court of Justice had already accepted a general principle of abuse of tax rights for the purposes of EU law. VAT cases and cases on the Merger Directive were discussed to illustrate the point. Up until recently, it was not clear whether there was a general principle of abuse of rights in the field of direct taxation, being a non-harmonised area. It was explained how this has changed following recent case law where it was unequivocally stated that there is a general legal principle that EU law cannot be relied upon for abusive or fraudulent ends. This conclusion was irrespective of whether the Member States implemented domestic or treaty-based or Directive-based anti-abuse provisions in their national tax systems.

This chapter also examined various types of anti-abuse rules and their compatibility with EU law. An attempt was made to assess the judgments of the Court of Justice in the area of controlled foreign companies, thin capitalisation and transfer pricing. The position following the introduction of the Anti-Tax Avoidance Directive was also assessed, whenever relevant. It was shown that there is some tension between established case law and the provisions of the Anti-Tax Avoidance Directive, most of which apply primarily in a mechanical way. What was also notable was the shift of emphasis from having the Court of Justice scrutinise national anti-abuse rules, to demanding from Member States to introduce de minimis anti-abuse rules based on this Directive. As regards transfer pricing rules, it was argued that the current judgments of the Court of Justice could give rise to variable interpretation of basic concepts of international tax law, due to the obscure relationship between the Court's commercial justification test and the OECD's arm's length principle.

It was questioned whether the adoption of uniform anti-abuse rules under the Anti-Tax Avoidance Directive was suitable, in the absence of a comprehensively harmonised corporate tax system. It was argued that these overall tensions and contradictions jeopardise legal certainty and undermine future efforts for a more streamlined EU corporate tax system.

The penultimate chapter to this book (Chapter 8) reviewed the increasing impact of the state aid prohibition on EU corporate tax law. This Chapter showed how this prohibition has affected the design of a country's tax system and certain aspects of its administration. The central role of the Commission and, to a lesser extent, national courts was explored. Relevant soft law and some important case law in this area were considered, before some of the high profile investigations focusing on tax rulings were analysed.

It was argued that although the Commission has been pushing for an EU interpretation of the arm's length principle encompassed within the state aid prohibition, recent judgments of the General Court have not really endorsed this approach. In these judgments, it was confirmed that there is no freestanding obligation arising under the state aid prohibition to apply the arm's length principle, because at this stage of the development of EU law, the Commission did not have competence to define in an autonomous manner the normal taxation of an integrated undertaking by disregarding national tax rules. The General Court ruled that the Commission could use the arm's length principle as a tool or benchmark to investigate whether a tax ruling gave rise to a selective advantage under state aid rules, but it had the burden of proof to show an advantage. The Commission could not merely point at methodological deficiencies regarding the grant of the ruling, but had to demonstrate that the error by the Member State led to an advantage for the purposes of the state aid prohibition. If the Court of Justice follows the spirit of the rulings of the General Court, then several of the Commission investigations will likely be affected. At the time of writing, the Court of Justice had not yet deliberated on any of these issues, though some of the decisions of the General Court were under appeal.

It is obvious from the above brief summary of each chapter that the developments as a result of the case law are far more significant than the advances of EU legislation. Whilst in the last few years there has been momentum to adopt certain legislative proposals pursuant to an anti-tax avoidance agenda, some of these new instruments are not fully aligned with earlier case law, generating confusion. Combined with the legal uncertainty sometimes caused by negative integration, this exacerbates the already problematic status quo.

As explained in the initial chapters to this book, the Court of Justice has no control as to what cases get to it and the questions referred. It was shown that there was an element of arbitrariness and randomness, inherent in a judicial process with multiple actors – the Commission, Member States, affected taxpayers and national courts. Effectively, the Court of Justice is asked to police the application of reverse subsidiarity by Member States: whether Member States comply with general EU law in exercising their exclusive powers.

The limitations of the judicial process become more apparent upon closer examination of some judgments of the Court of Justice. Certainly, the flexible use of the notion of precedent has enabled the Court of Justice to create pockets of case law that deal with specific themes, generating important developments in many areas where previous legislative attempts stagnated or were largely non-existent.

Especially in the early cases, the Court of Justice was more willing to break tradition with established principles of international tax law in order to protect the exercise of fundamental freedoms by EU nationals. This approach usually reached a high-water mark in certain cases, with the Court of Justice becoming more attuned to the possible repercussions from a clash with international tax law. Thereafter, the Court of Justice would place more emphasis on justifications, or on proportionality, or would give very broad guidance and leave the question for the national courts to decide.

It was conceded that the flexible use of precedent has in some areas led to fragmented principles and inconsistent results arising in analogous situations. This seemed to be the case as regards the jurisprudence in the area of cross-border loss relief rules. Compared with older (failed) initiatives for legislative action, the result was much more unsatisfactory in terms of legal certainty. Another area of case law was also perplexing: that on exit taxes. Here, the Court of Justice deviated from earlier judgments without much explanation. Not only that, but later case law was broadly codified by the adoption of a provision in the Anti-Tax Avoidance Directive making exit tax rules mandatory in certain circumstances.

The interaction of the principles set out in the case law of the Court of Justice with the provisions of the Anti-Tax Avoidance Directive was found to be problematic. The contradictions between established case law and some of these Directive provisions were baffling, especially when cases decided after the Directive was adopted mostly confirmed the earlier principles.

It seems that since the first edition of this book was published, some areas of law have become even less coherent and predictable. This makes it very difficult to monitor adherence to EU law by national courts, Member States and taxpayers. The phenomenon is likely to continue given the simultaneous (and uncoordinated) development of important legislative instruments and the Court's jurisprudence. The evolution of soft law initiatives which eventually become hard law (or have similar effects to hard law) exacerbates the situation. We are running the risk of having variable standards applicable in the same area; for example, a case law test for abuse of tax law, a general anti-avoidance rule in a Directive and the Commission's principle of fair taxation which is promoted in all its recent initiatives. This becomes even more challenging when the variable standards affect the interpretation of an entrenched concept under international tax law such as the arm's length principle. There is now case law of the Court of Justice on the basis of fundamental freedoms and different case law of the General Court on the basis of the state aid prohibition. There is also soft law as a result of older initiatives of the Joint Transfer Pricing Forum but also emerging soft law in the context of the Commission's initiatives on tax good governance. This uncoordinated and somehow erratic EU interference is not conducive to legal certainty and could affect the competitiveness of the EU. It erodes trust in the democratic processes underpinning the system and makes the development of a coherent body of EU corporate tax law even more challenging.

It is still to be questioned – as in the first edition to this book – whether the current situation is satisfactory or whether in some cases, notwithstanding Member States' exclusive competence, conceding to the Union the power to enact direct tax legislation may ensure a more harmonious coexistence of EU law and national legal systems. The author had argued in the first edition that the limitations of the EU judicial process in removing the many remaining tax obstacles to cross-border movement could be better addressed through legislation – be it comprehensive or targeted. With hindsight, it would seem that ad hoc targeted harmonising measures in areas where there is some pre-existing case law may be even more problematic unless these measures are closely aligned with the principles derived from this case law. Furthermore, ideally, any targeted legislative proposal should fit into a wider harmonising agenda which is endorsed by Member States. It is rather paradoxical to harmonise the exception to corporate tax rules (here, anti-abuse rules) when the underlying context – Member States' corporate tax systems – is broadly unharmonised and is likely to remain so, given the overall resistance towards the CCTB/CCCTB.

The Commission's soft law initiatives to tackle aggressive tax planning and to advance tax good governance seem to be circumventing some of this resistance. Using the momentum generated from the BEPS project and the overall international polemic against tax avoidance and aggressive tax planning, the Commission has managed to promote an expansionist agenda. Without a shred of competence to deal with these issues in the form of hard law (other than the measures introduced in the context of the Parent-Subsidiary Directive, the Anti-Tax Avoidance Directive and the Directive on Administrative Cooperation), the EU is now dictating the terms of when a third country is a cooperative tax jurisdiction - only for EU and Member State purposes so far. The EU has set the benchmarks for non-compliance with tax good governance, its institutions are given the task to police third-country tax systems on the basis of these benchmarks, and Member States are strongly encouraged to apply centrally developed sanctions. In other words, the Commission has remarkably managed to hijack the evolution of the concept of good tax governance, which had a very different meaning hitherto. What is further remarkable is that, technically, Member State tax systems are not bound by these EU standards – these are only relevant to third countries. There have been calls to internalise this process so that Member States will also be subject to the same scrutiny but this is unlikely to be agreed by Member States in the foreseeable future.

In Chapter 1, it was shown that the Commission is trying to erode the unanimity requirement to ensure more of its proposals are adopted. Whilst this is understandable given how difficult it has become for twenty-seven Member States with often competing interests to agree to any important tax proposals, the timing is not right.

Arguably, the unanimity requirement should be preserved, at least for the time being, due to the centrifugal tendencies in the EU, the prime example of which is

Brexit. At the time of writing, the UK had left the EU but the transition period had not yet ended. As explained in Chapter 1, no agreement has yet been reached with the EU and no extension to the transition period was sought by the British government. Whilst an agreement at the eleventh hour is always possible, the UK's departure is likely to be one of the most significant events in the history of the EU. A show of unity and respect amongst the remaining Member States is crucial for the preservation of the EU. Taking away a major power of Member States – the power to veto tax proposals – will severely undermine their tax sovereignty. Such move will further disenfranchise some Member States and increase euroscepticism.

Whilst at the early stages of Brexit it was thought that with the departure of the UK – one of the most recalcitrant Member States in terms of tax harmonisation – other similarly inclined Member States would be marginalised, the fiscal pressures brought by the Covid-19 pandemic would suggest otherwise. Currently, all Member States (and the international community as a whole) are reeling from the effects of the global pandemic. The European Council's agreement for a Recovery Plan has been welcomed by most Member States as a positive sign of EU leadership and solidarity. Tinkering with rules to take away some of the tax sovereignty of Member States at a time when Member States are relying heavily on their tax systems to help rescue their economies is ill-advised.

It is in any case doubtful that Member States will agree to give more powers to the EU in the area of taxation any time soon. The Commission's proposal to move to qualified majority voting in tax matters was premised on a legislative base (Art 48(7) TEU) which requires approval from all national Parliaments and the European Parliament in order to be adopted. This was unlikely to happen even in the absence of the pandemic.

Of course, scrapping Member States' veto powers might not be necessary after all. In the post-BEPS world, international consensus has been so strong as to de facto curtail Member State discretion in certain areas. Good examples of this are the rules on automatic exchange of information and administrative cooperation between countries, as well as the minimum standards that have emerged from the BEPS project. Therefore, with the change of dynamics in the international tax system, the fight against base erosion and profit shifting facilitated further tax integration in the EU. However, this was not the underlying objective of earlier harmonising initiatives considered in Chapter 1.

It is undeniable that the Commission has always striven for further tax harmonisation – even if the end result now is to strengthen domestic anti-abuse rules that might also detrimentally affect cross-border movement. What has also become obvious since the first edition to this book is that, notwithstanding the sometimes centrifugal tendencies in the European continent, the EU continues to move towards closer tax integration. This is still done in an unsystematic and often incoherent way due to the vagaries of the judicial process, the Commission's often controversial patchwork of soft law and hard law, as well as other political and quasi-political exigencies (e.g. Brexit, the BEPS project, the response to Covid-19, the OECD's proposed unified approach to taxing the digital economy etc).

It would seem that the EU's day of reckoning in the area of corporate tax law is not upon us just yet.

For EU product safety concerns, contact us at Calle de José Abascal, 56–1º,
28003 Madrid, Spain or eugpsr@cambridge.org.